FRAGILE BY DESIGN

THE PRINCETON ECONOMIC HISTORY OF THE WESTERN WORLD
Joel Mokyr, Series Editor

A list of titles in this series appears at the back of the book.

FRAGILE BY DESIGN

||||||||||||||||||||||||||||||||||||||||||||||||||||||||||||||||||||||||||||||||||

The Political Origins of
Banking Crises and Scarce Credit

CHARLES W. CALOMIRIS *and* STEPHEN H. HABER

PRINCETON UNIVERSITY PRESS
Princeton and Oxford

Published by Princeton University Press, 41 William Street, Princeton, New Jersey 08540
In the United Kingdom: Princeton University Press, 6 Oxford Street, Woodstock,
Oxfordshire OX20 1TW

press.princeton.edu

Jacket illustration: © Anne-Lise Boutin/Marlena Agency. Design by Jessica Massabrook.

Fifth printing and first paperback printing, 2015

Paperback ISBN: 978-0-691-16835-7

The Library of Congress has cataloged the cloth edition as follows:

Calomiris, Charles W.
Fragile by design : the political origins of banking crises and
scarce credit / Charles W. Calomiris and Stephen H. Haber.
pages   cm. — (The Princeton economic history
of the Western world)
Includes bibliographical references and index.
ISBN 978-0-691-15524-1 (hardcover : alk. paper)
1. Banks and banking—History. 2. Bank failures—History.
3. Credit—History. I. Haber, Stephen H., 1957– II. Title.
HG1561.C35   2014
332.109—dc23
2013033110

British Library Cataloging-in-Publication Data is available

This book has been composed in Sabon with Whitney display
by Princeton Editorial Associates Inc., Scottsdale Arizona.

Printed on acid-free paper. ∞

Printed in the United States of America

5 7 9 10 8 6

CONTENTS

SECTION THREE

Authoritarianism, Democratic Transitions, and the Game of Bank Bargains

SECTION FOUR

Going beyond Structural Narratives

PREFACE

Books are not written by chance. This one was written from 2010 to 2013, after the worst three decades of banking crises the world has ever seen, and in the immediate wake of the worst U.S. banking crisis since the Great Depression.

We have both spent much of our academic lives writing about banks and their politics and history and have been involved in advising governmental and regulatory agencies about the deficiencies of banking systems. Over the years, we have been struck by the disconnect between the way the public and the press experience and discuss banking crises and the way that we and our colleagues think about them as scholars.

Most popular narratives about banking problems focus on very short-term considerations (this quarter's lending growth, profits, or scandals) and on the personal details, including the moral failures, of the careers of bankers and regulators. While the public recognizes that banking problems are matters of intense political debate with serious consequences for the performance and stability of the economy, the media provide little discussion of the systematic role of politics in the determination of banking systems' performance. This deficiency leaves the public in a curious position: they know that they should be deeply concerned about banking regulation; they know that there are links between politics and banking; but they are unsure what those links are and even less sure what to do about them.

This book is an attempt both to bridge that gap and to offer a contribution to scholarship. We seek to explain the political roots of differences in banking-system performance across countries and over time. In order to do so, we integrate evidence and analytic tools from three distinct disciplines: history, political science, and economics.

We argue that banks' strengths and shortcomings are the predictable consequences of political bargains and that those bargains are structured by a society's fundamental political institutions. Citizens may be satisfied to blame the deficiencies of their country's banking system on the moral failings of bankers or regulators, or on "market failures" related to greed and fear, but when they do so, they miss the opportunity to see banks for what they really are, for better or worse: an institutional embodiment—a mirror of sorts—of the political system that is a product of a society's deep history.

This project grew out of our participation in the John and Jean De Nault Task Force on Property Rights at Stanford University's Hoover Institution. We had known one another for over two decades, and our paths had crossed at numerous conferences and workshops. It was within the De Nault task force, however, that the two of us first sat down together to explore three fundamental questions about banking that defined the starting point of this book: Why are some societies able to construct banking systems that avoid banking crises, while others are not? What makes some societies limit the right to charter a bank to a favored few, even though doing so limits the availability of credit to broad swaths of the population? Why do societies sometimes fail to protect the property rights of lenders, depositors, and bank stockholders in ways that undermine the ability of banks to raise funds or lend them?

Four years and many conversations and cross-country visits later, we completed this manuscript. Along the way, we accumulated more intellectual debts than we can ever repay. We are indebted to many colleagues at institutions around the world who offered comments on chapter drafts, or on the entire manuscript, including Daron Acemoglu, Terry Anderson, Michael Bordo, Michael Boskin, Florian Buck, Forrest Capie, Gerard Caprio, Matthew Carnes, Latika Chaudhary, Isaias Chávez, Gustavo del Angel-Mobarak, Darrell Duffie, Roy Elis, Richard Epstein, Nick Eubank, Adriane Fresh, Alex Galetovic, Richard Grossman, James Huffman, Scott Kieff, Dorothy Kronick, Sandra Kuntz Ficker, Ross Levine, Gary Libecap, Jonathan Macey, Noel Maurer, Allan Meltzer, Victor Menaldo, Joel Mokyr, Ian Morris, Aldo Musacchio, Larry Neal, Raquel Oliveira, Agustina Paglayan, Edward Pinto, Alex Pollock, Lucas Puente, Russ Roberts,

James Robinson, Jared Rubin, Thomas Sargent, Henry Smith, Paul Sniderman, William Summerhill, John Taylor, Larry Wall, Peter Wallison, and three anonymous referees. We also thank our students in classes at Columbia University and Stanford University, where we taught parts of the book in various courses; their reactions taught us a great deal about how to frame and organize the material. Our research assistants, Ishan Bhadkamkar, Ianni Drivas, and Patrick Kennedy, helped us find data and track references as well as providing cogent comments about chapters as they took shape.

We were fortunate to be able to present drafts of chapters at workshops and conferences and to receive valuable feedback. We thank the institutions that organized those workshops and conferences, including the Banco de México, the Center for Economic Studies of the Ludwig-Maximilians-Universität München, the Centro de Investigación y Docencia Económicas, Chapman University, the All-Chicago Friends of Economic History Dinner, the Federal Reserve Bank of Atlanta, Harvard Business School, the Hoover Institution's Working Group on Economic Policy, the International Monetary Fund, the London School of Economics, and the World Bank.

Research support does not grow on trees; we are therefore grateful to John Raisian and Richard Sousa, director and senior associate director of the Hoover Institution, respectively. Seth Ditchik, Beth Clevenger, and Terri O'Prey at Princeton University Press and Peter Strupp at Princeton Editorial Associates ably shepherded the manuscript through the production process. We owe special thanks to our series editor, Joel Mokyr, whose enthusiasm, humor, and constructive criticisms did much to improve the book and to facilitate its timely completion. Finally, we are deeply grateful to our wives, Nancy Calomiris and Marsy A. Haber, for their constant patience, support, and encouragement throughout the four years of our bicoastal collaboration.

We dedicate this book to our daughters. We hope that young people who read this book, including the three of them, will not misinterpret our discussions about political bargains as a call to cynicism about democratic politics. Our intent is rather to illustrate the value of learning history, thinking critically, and facing the hypocrisy of politicians with a sense of humor. They will need all three in a search for solutions to the deep problems that face democracies during the current global pandemic of banking crises.

SECTION ONE

||||||||||||||||||||||||||||||||||||||||

No Banks without States,
and No States without Banks

1

||||||||||||||||||||||

If Stable and Efficient Banks Are Such a Good Idea, Why Are They So Rare?

The majority of economists . . . tend to assume that financial institutions
will grow more or less spontaneously as the need for their services
arises—a case of demand creating its own supply. . . . Such an attitude
disposes of a complex matter far too summarily.

Rondo Cameron and Hugh Patrick,
Banking in the Early Stages of Industrialization (1967)

Everyone knows that life isn't fair, that "politics matters." We say it
when our favorite movie loses out at the Academy Awards. We say
it when the dolt in the cubicle down the hall, who plays golf with the
boss, gets the promotion we deserved. We say it when bridges to nowhere
are built because a powerful senator brings federal infrastructure dollars
to his home state. And we say it when well-connected entrepreneurs obtain billions in government subsidies to build factories that never stand a
chance of becoming competitive enterprises.

We recognize that politics is everywhere, but somehow we believe that
banking crises are apolitical, the result of unforeseen and extraordinary
circumstances, like earthquakes and hailstorms. We believe this because it
is the version of events told time and again by central bankers and treasury
officials, which is then repeated by business journalists and television talk-
ing heads. In that story, well-intentioned and highly skilled people do the
best they can to create effective financial institutions, allocate credit efficiently, and manage problems as they arise—but they are not omnipotent.
Unable to foresee every possible contingency, they are sometimes subjected
to strings of bad luck. "Economic shocks," which presumably could not
possibly have been anticipated, destabilize an otherwise smoothly running
system. Banking crises, according to this version of events, are much like
Tolstoy's unhappy families: they are all unhappy in their own ways.

This book takes exception with that view and suggests instead that the
politics that we see operating everywhere else around us also determines

3

whether societies suffer repeated banking crises (as in Argentina and the United States), or never suffer banking crises (as in Canada). By politics we do not mean temporary, idiosyncratic alliances among individuals of the type that get the dumbest guy in the company promoted to vice president for corporate strategy. We mean, instead, the way that the fundamental political institutions of a society structure the incentives of politicians, bankers, bank shareholders, depositors, debtors, and taxpayers to form coalitions in order to shape laws, policies, and regulations in their favor—often at the expense of everyone else. In this view, a country does not "choose" its banking system: rather it gets a banking system that is consistent with the institutions that govern its distribution of political power.

The Nonrandom Distribution of Banking Crises

Systemic bank insolvency crises like the U.S. subprime debacle of 2007–09 —a series of bank failures so catastrophic that the continued existence of the banking system itself is in doubt—do not happen without warning, like earthquakes or mountain lion attacks. Rather, they occur when banking systems are made vulnerable by construction, as the result of political choices. Banking systems are susceptible to collapse only when banks both expose themselves to high risk in making loans and other investments and have inadequate capital on their balance sheets to absorb the losses associated with those risky loans and investments. If a bank makes only solid loans to solid borrowers, there is little chance that its loan portfolio will suddenly become nonperforming. If a bank makes riskier loans to less solid borrowers but sets aside capital to cover the possibility that those loans will not be repaid, its shareholders will suffer a loss, but it will not become insolvent. These basic facts about banking crises are known to bankers or government regulators; they are as old as black thread.

By contrast, consider what occurs when bank capital is insufficient relative to bank risk. Bank losses can become so large that the negative net worth of banks totals a significant fraction of a country's gross domestic product (GDP). In this scenario, credit contracts, GDP falls, and the country sustains a recession driven by a banking crisis. Governments can prevent this outcome by propping up the banking system. They can make loans to the banks, purchase their nonperforming assets, buy their shares in order to provide them with adequate capital, or take them over entirely.

If such catastrophes were random events, all countries would suffer them with equal frequency. The fact is, however, that some countries have had many, whereas others have few or none. The United States, for example, is highly crisis prone. It had major banking crises in 1837, 1839, 1857, 1861, 1873, 1884, 1890, 1893, 1896, 1907, the 1920s, 1930–33, the 1980s, and 2007–09.[1] That is to say, the United States has had 14 banking crises over the past 180 years! Canada, which shares not only a 2,000-mile border with the United States but also a common culture and language, had only two brief and mild bank illiquidity crises during the same period, in 1837 and 1839, neither of which involved significant bank failures. Since that time, some Canadian banks have failed, but the country has experienced no systemic banking crises. The Canadian banking system has been extraordinarily stable—so stable, in fact, that there has been little need for government intervention in support of the banks since Canada became an independent country in 1867.

The nonrandom pattern of banking crises is also apparent in their distribution around the world since 1970. Some countries appear immune to the disease, while others are unusually susceptible. Consider the pattern that emerges when we look at data on the frequency of banking crises in

---

[1] Throughout this book we regard banking crises as either systemic insolvency crises or systemic illiquidity crises. Some crises, like the subprime lending crisis in the United States, and the other U.S. crises in 1837, 1839, 1857, 1861, the 1920s, 1930–33, and the 1980s, have involved extensive bank insolvency, not just moments of illiquidity when banks experience severe withdrawal pressures. Thresholds of insolvency sufficient to constitute a crisis are defined differently by different scholars, but roughly speaking, bank insolvency crises are usefully defined as events during which the negative net worth of banks, or the costs of government interventions to prevent those insolvencies, exceed some critical percentage of GDP. This approach underlies the databases on banking crises for the recent era derived by researchers at the World Bank and International Monetary Fund (e.g., Caprio and Klingebiel [2003]; Laeven and Valencia [2012]). A second class of banking crises is those that entail systemic illiquidity disruptions (e.g., widespread bank runs) but do not involve significant bank insolvencies or costly government interventions to prevent those insolvencies. Calomiris and Gorton (1991), for example, categorize the U.S. banking panics of 1873, 1884, 1890, 1893, 1896, and 1907 as systemic and important liquidity shocks even though they did not produce a high degree of bank insolvency. Both of these definitions of crises are more restrictive than those that are sometimes employed in the "financial crisis" literature (e.g., Reinhart and Rogoff [2009]), where negative events, such as the failure of a single large bank, are considered to be evidence of a crisis. By those less restrictive standards, the world's banking systems would appear to be even more crisis prone.

the 117 nations of the world that have populations in excess of 250,000, are not current or former communist countries, and have banking systems large enough to report data on private credit from commercial banks for at least 14 years between 1990 and 2010 in the World Bank's Financial Structure Database.[2] Only 34 of those 117 countries (29 percent) were crisis free from 1970 to 2010. Sixty-two countries had one crisis. Nineteen countries experienced two crises. One country underwent three crises, and another weathered no less than four. That is to say, countries that underwent banking crises outnumbered countries with stable banking systems by more than two to one, and 18 percent of the countries in the world appear to have been preternaturally crisis prone.

The country that experienced the most crises was Argentina, a nation so badly governed for so long that its political history is practically a synonym for mismanagement. The close runner-up (with three crises since 1970) was the Democratic Republic of the Congo, the nation whose brutal colonial experience served as the inspiration for Joseph Conrad's *Heart of Darkness,* which was governed after independence by one of the third world's longest-lived and most avaricious despots (Mobutu Sese Seko, who ruled from 1965 to 1997), and whose subsequent history is a template for tragedy.

The 19 countries that had two banking crises are also far from a random draw. The list includes Chad, the Central African Republic, Cameroon, Kenya, Nigeria, the Philippines, Thailand, Turkey, Bolivia, Ecuador, Brazil, Mexico, Colombia, Costa Rica, Chile, Uruguay, Spain, Sweden,

---

[2] We exclude former and current communist countries from this analysis because their state-run banking systems do not allocate credit but rather act as an accounting system for the state-controlled allocation of investment. The concept of a banking crisis has no real analytic meaning in such a system. Former communist countries have tended to be crisis prone. If we had included them in our data set, an even greater percentage of the countries of the world would be counted as crisis prone. We exclude countries that do not report at least 14 observations for the ratio of private credit by deposit money banks to GDP during the period 1990–2010. That is, in order to mitigate measurement error, we require observations for at least two-thirds of all possible observations for any country. We draw the credit data from the period 1990–2010 because the coverage of the World Bank Financial Structure Database tends to be less complete, especially for poorer countries, prior to 1990. We draw the data on banking crises from Laeven and Valencia (2012) and include both their "systemic" crises and their "borderline" crises in our definition of crises. We update their work by adding the case of Cyprus in 2013.

and . . . the United States. One of the striking features of this list is the paucity of high-income, well-governed countries on it. Of the 117 countries in our data set, roughly one-third are categorized by the World Bank as high-income nations. But only three of the 21 crisis-prone countries, 14 percent, are in this group. This suggests that, for the most part, being crisis prone is connected to other undesirable traits and outcomes. But that raises another troubling question. Why is the United States on this list?

The Nonrandom Distribution of Under-Banked Economies

There is, of course, more to having a good banking system than simply avoiding crises. Equally problematic are banking systems that provide too little credit relative to the size of the economy—a phenomenon known as under-banking. This outcome, too, appears not to be randomly distributed. Consider the striking contrast between Canada and Mexico, the United States' partners in the North American Free Trade Agreement (NAFTA). From 1990 to 2010, private bank lending to firms and households averaged 95 percent of GDP in Canada, but in Mexico the ratio was only 19 percent. The dramatic difference in those ratios means that Mexican families have a much more difficult time financing the purchase of homes, automobiles, and consumer goods, and Mexican business enterprises have much more difficulty in obtaining working capital, than their Canadian counterparts. The result is slower economic growth. Little wonder, then, that over 500,000 Mexicans—roughly half of all new entrants to the Mexican labor market—illegally cross the border to the United States each year.

As figure 1.1 shows, the stark difference between Canada and Mexico is part of a recurring pattern. In the world's poorest countries (those on the far left-hand side of the figure), including for example, the Democratic Republic of the Congo, the ratio of bank credit to GDP averages only 11 percent. In the richest countries (shown on the far right-hand side of the figure), the ratio of bank credit to GDP averages 87 percent.

Crucially, there is also substantial variance across countries within each of the four income groups, which suggests that the amount of credit extended within countries is not solely a function of demand for credit but also reflects constraints on the supply of credit. In other words, the fact that some countries in each income group extend much more credit than

Percentage of GDP

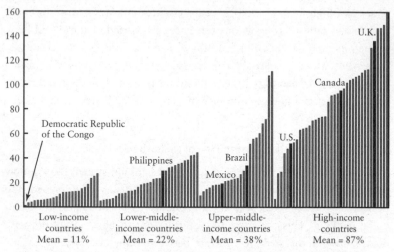

FIGURE 1.1 Average private credit from deposit money banks as a percentage of GDP, 1990–2010, by World Bank income classifications.

Source: World Bank (2012).

Note: For reasons of readability, only selected country names are shown on the *x* axis.

others in the same income group (or even the next-highest income group) suggests that many countries in all categories are under-banked. For example, Mexico appears to be under-banked relative to other countries in the same income group, and even has a lower ratio of credit to GDP than many countries in the next-lowest income group (e.g., the Philippines).

Being under-banked has huge social costs. A large and growing academic literature has shown that under-banked countries suffer lower economic growth than other countries. Economic historians have shown that Holland, Great Britain, and the United States experienced revolutions in financial intermediation and financial institutions *before* their rise to global economic hegemony in the eighteenth, nineteenth, and twentieth centuries, respectively. They also found that Russia, Germany, and Japan underwent similar financial revolutions before they narrowed the gap with the world's economic leaders in the late nineteenth and early twentieth centuries.[3] Financial economists using statistical methods to analyze the growth

[3] Gerschenkron (1962); Cameron et al. (1967); Sylla (1975; 2008); North and

of contemporary economies have reached similar conclusions. Whether they look at variance in outcomes across countries, across regions within countries, within countries over time, or across industries, their studies all demonstrate that higher levels of financial development produce faster rates of physical capital accumulation, faster economic growth, more rapid technological progress, faster job creation, and increased opportunities for social mobility.[4] Given the relationship between economic growth and the ability to project power internationally, under-banked countries are also at a disadvantage in defending their sovereignty and influencing events abroad. In short, being under-banked is a far more serious state of affairs than lacking capacity in the real sectors of the economy, such as textiles, sugar refining, or automobile manufacturing: finance facilitates the efficient operation of all other economic activities, including industrial sectors crucial to the defense of the state.

How Many Efficient and Stable Banking Systems Are There?

If very few countries have been free of banking crises since the 1970s, and if much of the world is under-banked, in how many countries is bank credit plentiful and the banking system stable? Answering this question requires us to draw a line between those economies where bank credit is abundant and those economies that are under-banked. If we define a country with abundant credit as one that has an average ratio of bank credit to GDP one standard deviation above the mean for the 117 countries in our data set (83 percent), which corresponds to the ratio in Australia, and

Weingast (1989); Neal (1990); de Vries and van der Woude (1997); Rousseau and Wachtel (1998); Rousseau (2003); Rousseau and Sylla (2003, 2004).

[4] King and Levine (1993), Levine and Zervos (1998), Taylor (1998), and Beck, Levine, and Loayza (2000) employed innovative statistical techniques to identify cross-country patterns. A later group of scholars—most notably Rajan and Zingales (1998), Wurgler (2000), Cetorelli and Gamberra (2001), Fisman and Love (2004), and Beck et al. (2008)—focused on the development of industries as well as countries, and they reached the same conclusion: finance leads growth. Research focusing on the growth of regions within countries by Jayaratne and Strahan (1996); Black and Strahan (2002); Guiso, Sapienza, and Zingales (2004); Cetorelli and Strahan (2006); Dehejia and Lleras-Muney (2007); and Correa (2008) produced broadly similar results. These studies built on the theoretical and narrative insights of Goldschmidt (1933); Gurley and Shaw (1960); Gurley, Patrick, and Shaw (1965); Goldsmith (1969); Shaw (1973); McKinnon (1973); and Fry (1988).

define a stable banking system as one that has been free of systemic crises since 1970, we arrive at a shocking answer: only six out of 117 countries— 5 percent—meet those criteria.[5]

The Puzzling Pervasiveness of Dysfunctional Banking

The puzzle of why societies tolerate unstable and scarce bank credit deepens when one considers the costs imposed by unstable and under-banked systems on those societies. In addition to the slower long-term growth produced by under-banking, unstable banking systems entail other costs. Banking crises magnify recessions, resulting in greater job losses, and taxpayers are forced to pay the price of rescuing bankers from the consequences of their own mistakes. Why do citizens tolerate this? Worldwide, that tab has been huge. Over the period 1970–2011, the median direct fiscal cost of banking crisis resolution was 6.8 percent of GDP, and the median increase in country indebtedness during a crisis was 12.1 percent of GDP. The cost of banking crises in terms of lost GDP (due to the effects of credit contractions, heightened sovereign-debt risk, and currency collapse on economic activity) also tends to be enormous: from 1970 through 2009, the median lost output during a banking crisis amounted to 23 percent of GDP.[6]

In thinking about this puzzle, one shouldn't assume that taxpayers have always been willing to pay for bank bailouts. Taxpayer-funded bailouts of banks are a recent phenomenon. Until the mid-twentieth century, the costs of failure tended to be borne by the bankers themselves, along with bank shareholders and depositors. Since then, however, the costs have been progressively shifted to taxpayers. How did bankers, regulators, and politicians come to impose these costs on taxpayers, and why do taxpayers put up with bearing those costs?

---

[5] One might think that making the standard for being credit-abundant conditional on a country's World Bank income group might reveal a larger number of credit-abundant, low-crisis countries. In fact, the opposite is the case. If we define a credit-abundant country as one in which the ratio of private credit to GDP is at least one standard deviation above the mean for that country's World Bank income group, and then ask how many of those countries have not had a banking crisis since 1970, the answer is three.

[6] Laeven and Valencia (2012), 17.

This shifting of losses onto taxpayers is especially puzzling because it tends to produce much larger losses and deeper recessions than a system in which shareholders and depositors bear the cost. A broad literature in financial economics has demonstrated that a system in which shareholders and depositors have money at risk imposes discipline on the behavior of bankers: at the first sign of trouble, stockholders start selling their shares, and depositors start moving their funds to more solvent banks.[7] As a result, some banks fail, some of the holders of bank liabilities (shareholders and depositors) are wiped out, credit contracts as bankers rush to reduce their exposure to risky classes of loans, and economic growth slows. The result is painful, but not tragic. Most important, bankers know the consequences of imprudent behavior and thus tend to maintain large buffers of capital and large portfolios of low-risk assets. As a consequence, systemic banking crises are rare. Contrast that outcome with the system that has come to be the norm since the mid-twentieth century. When losses are borne by taxpayers, the incentives of stockholders and depositors to discipline bankers are much weaker. Bankers are willing to take bigger risks, thereby increasing the probability of failure. As a result, after 1945 banks in the world's most developed economies became more highly leveraged and maintained smaller amounts of low-risk assets.[8]

---

[7] Calomiris and Powell (2001); Cull, Şenbet, and Sorge (2005); Demirgüç-Kunt and Detragiache (2002); Demirgüç-Kunt and Huizinga (2004); Demirguç-Kunt and Kane (2002); Calomiris and Wilson (2004); Barth, Caprio, and Levine (2006), chapter 4; Haber (2008a); Calomiris (2011a).

[8] Schularick and Taylor (2012). In theory, regulation can replace monitoring by shareholders and depositors, but the evidence is that regulators are subject to political pressures not to act (Brown and Dinc [2005]; Barth, Caprio, and Levine [2006], chapter 5). As a result, losses pile up as bankers throw good money after bad. Inevitably, the stock of unrecognized bad loans—known as "evergreened loans"—grows so large that the banking system is threatened with complete collapse, at which point the regulators are finally forced to step in. By then, however, the stock of bad loans is enormous. This means not only that the cost of cleaning up the failing banks is larger than it would be under a system in which shareholders and depositors disciplined bankers, but also that the recession that follows the banking crisis will be larger as well. It is not just that credit contracts; it contracts vertiginously. Moreover, the government has to find a way to reconcile the fiscal imbalance caused by the bank rescue, which means cutting spending, raising taxes, and increasing central bank interest rates in order to prevent a run on the currency. Not surprisingly, recessions associated with financial crises tend to be deeper than other recessions (Jordà, Schularick, and Taylor [2012]).

More puzzling still, costly crises and persistent under-banking occur even though banking systems are subject to close regulation and supervision by governments. In most countries, banks are regulated much like public utilities such as electricity generation: entry to the market is controlled by government agencies in order to assure that the firms providing the service remain profitable, and the government inspects their operations to make sure that they are providing efficient service to their customers while not taking imprudent risks. Why, then, do governments often look the other way when banks make loans to firms and households that have a high probability of default? In the same vein, why do some governments allow those same imprudent banks to deny service to customers who are good credit risks, to the point that in many countries, banks lend only to the enterprises controlled by their own board members?

Fragile by Design

If a stable banking system capable of providing stable access to credit to talented entrepreneurs and responsible households is such a good idea, then why are such systems so rare? How can it be that a sector of the economy that is highly regulated and closely supervised works so badly in so many countries? Our answer to this question is that the fragility of banks and the scarcity of bank credit reflect the structure of a country's fundamental political institutions. The crux of the problem is that all governments face inherent conflicts of interest when it comes to the operation of the banking system, but some types of government—particularly democracies whose political institutions limit the influence of populist coalitions—are better able to mitigate those conflicts of interest than others.

The next chapter examines these conflicts of interest more closely. For the moment let us simply say that they are of three basic types. First, governments simultaneously regulate banks and look to them as a source of finance. Second, governments enforce the credit contracts that discipline debtors on behalf of banks (and in the process assist in the seizing of debtor collateral), but they rely on those same debtors for political support. Third, governments allocate losses among creditors in the event of bank failures, but they may simultaneously look to the largest group of those creditors—bank depositors—for political support. The implication is inescapable: the property-rights system that structures banking is not a passive response to some efficiency criterion but rather the product of political deals that determine which laws are passed and which groups of people have licenses to contract with whom, for what, and on what terms. These deals are guided by the logic of politics, not the logic of the market.

The fact that the property-rights system underpinning banking systems is an outcome of political deal making means that there are no fully "private" banking systems; rather, modern banking is best thought of as a partnership between the government and a group of bankers, a partnership that is shaped by the institutions that govern the distribution of power in the political system. Government policies toward banks reflect the deals that gave rise to those partnerships, as well as the power of the interest groups whose consent is crucial to the ability of the political group in control of the government to sustain those deals. Banks are regulated and supervised according to technical criteria, and banking contracts are enforced according to abstruse laws, but those criteria and laws are not created and enforced by robots programmed to maximize social welfare; they are the outcomes of a political process—a game, as it were—whose stakes are wealth and power.

We call this process of deal making the Game of Bank Bargains.[9] The players are those with a stake in the performance of the banking system: the group in control of the government, bankers, minority shareholders, debtors, and depositors. The rules, which are set by the society's political institutions, determine which other groups must be included in the government-banker partnership and which can be left out in the cold because the rules of the political system make them powerless. Coalitions among the players form as the game is played, and those coalitions determine the rules governing bank entry (and hence the competitive structure and size of the banking sector), the flow of credit and its terms, the permissible activities of banks, and the allocation of losses when banks fail. What is at stake in the Game of Bank Bargains is, therefore, the distribution of the

---

[9] Our approach builds on the classic work of Olson (1965), Stigler (1971), Krueger (1974), and many others who conceive of government policies as reflecting conflicts among vested interests. A distinguishing feature of our work is the focus on the formation of partnerships of interests that control banking policy. These partnerships often straddle ideological and partisan boundaries.

benefits that come from a system of chartered banks. The group in control of the government always receives a share of those benefits, and the coalition that forges a partnership with the government splits the remainder.

Notice that our emphasis is not on the extent of regulation but rather on the goals that give rise to regulation and the way those goals are shaped by political bargains. In some countries, the institutions and coalitions are such that regulation improves market outcomes. In other countries, regulation is structured to achieve government objectives that also serve special interests, in spite of their disastrous consequences for society at large.

The struggle among political coalitions determines who gets to play what roles in the financial system; that is, who is granted what kind of banking charter, and which groups of borrowers get government-favored access to credit. A central aspect of the Game of Bank Bargains, therefore, is deciding the rules for entry into banking. It is rarely the case that government chooses a fully "open-access" chartering regime. Being selective about who gets to be a banker and deciding how much bankers are allowed to lend and to whom are crucial elements of the game.

Our goal in this book is to explain this game. We seek to understand the process by which different rules emerge in different countries and how the players operate within those differing sets of rules. We show how differences in fundamental political institutions across times and places produce differences in the rules of the game, and how those politically based rules sometimes result predictably in stable and plentiful bank credit, sometimes in unstable and scarce bank credit, and sometimes (as in the United States) in unstable and plentiful bank credit. Which players favor vertiginous increases in credit, and which players favor tight constraints on it? Under what circumstances can they forge durable political coalitions with other players that have an interest in the organization of the banking system? What are the terms of exchange among the members of these coalitions? Are there differences in the way the game is played under democratic and authoritarian political systems? Do those differences affect the durability of coalitions, the size and structure of banking systems, and the fragility of the banks?

In order to understand this inherently complex game, we trace the coevolution of politics and banking in detail for several countries, one country at a time, over long periods. We spell out how coalitions were formed, why some endured whereas others were undermined, how they brought about specific and important changes in the policies governing banking, how those policies determined which groups could access credit and which could not, and how some of those policies produced disastrous banking crises.

We are not the first to trace the historical evolution of banking systems in various countries or to note the importance of politics for shaping the evolution of banking systems; most obviously, we are building on the seminal contributions to economic history by Bray Hammond (1957), Alexander Gerschenkron (1962), Rondo Cameron (1967), and Richard Sylla (1975), and more recent historical scholarship by Eugene White (1983), Howard Bodenhorn (2003), and Richard Grossman (2010), among others. We also build on the growing literature on the political economy of finance, such as recent work by James Barth, Gerald Caprio, and Ross Levine (2006) and Raghuram Rajan (2010). Indeed, we could not have written this book had we not stood on the shoulders of several generations of financial economists and economic historians. We see our unique contribution as conceptualizing a general framework for understanding how political factors shape banking-system outcomes. We illustrate that framework with detailed narratives that span hundreds of years and integrate evidence and insights from a broad range of academic disciplines, including political history, economic history, financial economics, and political science.

What We Do in This Book, and Why We Do It

A necessary first step toward any kind of productive reform of banking systems is to understand why and how banking-system outcomes are produced by political bargains. In showing how the Game of Bank Bargains is played, we seek to show readers how the variants of the game that they have been drawn into (wittingly or not) in their respective countries may be imposing costs on them while benefiting others.

To accomplish that goal, we have to engage in two quite distinct enterprises. First we lay bare the logic of the Game of Bank Bargains; second, we show how the game has been played, and is currently played, in real-world settings. As much as we might have liked to, we did not pick these settings purely on the basis of which countries have the best beaches: we have chosen cases that allow us to demonstrate how variation in political institutions drives variation in the nature of government-banker partnerships and how variation in those partnerships then produces differences in the size, competitive structure, and stability of banking systems.

We begin by showing why there can be no banking systems without the police power of the state. In chapter 2 we focus, in particular, on the fundamental property-rights problems that societies have to solve in order to create a banking system. The idea that banking systems can exist outside a system of government regulation is simply a libertarian fairy tale.

Chapter 3 explains why governments need banks. We explore how and why the institution of the chartered bank emerged from the process by which Europe was reconfigured from a hodgepodge of duchies, principalities, city-states, and kingdoms into a set of modern nation-states beginning in the seventeenth century. We focus on the strong incentives for rulers to become aggressive proponents of many of the financial innovations that underpin all modern banking systems, such as chartered corporations, negotiable instruments, and sovereign-debt instruments. The rulers who encouraged innovation were able to create durable nation-states and global trading networks that dominated the rest of the globe. The rulers who failed to do so disappeared, and their territories were absorbed into those of some other sovereign. We then follow the evolution of government-banker partnerships, showing that as political systems became more complex in the nineteenth and twentieth centuries, those partnerships gave rise to a broad array of quasi-government, quasi-private entities, including central banks and special-purpose intermediaries (such as the mortgage repurchase giants Fannie Mae and Freddie Mac).

We then examine real countries over centuries of history to illustrate how the Game of Bank Bargains has been played in different political environments. We focus both on variation in political institutions across countries and, perhaps even more important, on variation in political institutions within countries over time.

We begin our case studies with England. In chapter 4 we show how and why the English government granted a monopoly charter to the country's first banking corporation, the Bank of England, after the Glorious Revolution of 1688—a political revolution that gave Parliament primacy over the crown. England no longer had an absolute monarch who could expropriate funds at will, but because it had an extremely limited electoral franchise, a group of wealthy financiers was able to form a durable coalition with the parties in control of Parliament, giving the Bank of England a set of unique privileges in exchange for a series of loans to the government. The result was a monopoly banking system that allocated credit narrowly and was inherently unstable.

In chapter 5 we explore how the Pax Britannica permitted both an expansion of the franchise and a relaxation of the government's need to finance expensive wars, thereby giving rise to political coalitions that favored a greater openness in bank chartering. The stable, efficient, and competitive banking system that Britain had forged by the dawn of the twentieth century was then repressed by the government once again in order to fight the "Thirty Years' War of the 20th Century"—the combination of World War I, rearmament, and World War II. After 1945, political coalitions that favored the creation of a welfare state and nationalized industries made the banking system mostly irrelevant. In short, the banking system operating today in London—which is not just the center of British banking but a hub of global finance—is actually a very recent phenomenon.

In chapter 6 we turn to the United States, covering the period from the Revolutionary War in the 1770s until the repeal of restrictions on interstate banking in the 1980s and 1990s. We include the case study of the United States for a variety of reasons, foremost among which is the illustrative power of U.S. banking history. If there are any readers who doubt our claim that banking regulation is and always has been all about politics, some familiarity with the first two centuries of U.S. banking history should change their minds.

Today, institutions like the Bank of America seem to have a branch or ATM on every corner. Until very recently, however, the Bank of America, like all the other large banks that currently dominate the U.S. market, was legally enjoined from having branches in more than one state: the Bank of America was a California bank. Perhaps more surprising still, until the 1970s, most U.S. states had laws that prevented banks from opening multiple branches even within the state. The result was that the U.S. banking system was composed of tens of thousands of "unit banks" (individual banks, with no branches) operating in thousands of quasi-segmented local markets. No other country had a banking system anything like this, and for good reason: a system composed of tens of thousands of unit banks is inherently unstable because banks can neither spread risks across regions nor move funds easily from one location to another to manage liquidity problems (like bank runs). Such a system is also operationally inefficient, because banks cannot take advantage of scale economies in administration. For all these reasons, Americans paid higher interest rates for loans (and received lower interest rates on their deposits) than they would have in a system of branching banks.

More surprising still, this was decidedly *not* the system that Alexander Hamilton had in mind when he crafted America's first banking institutions in the 1780s and 1790s. Hamilton's vision was undermined within a few decades by a very strange, and very determined, coalition of agrarian populists (who were opposed to corporations of any kind as well as to the elites who controlled them) and small bankers (who knew that they did not have a prayer of competing against big banks that could open branches as they pleased). One reason that this seemingly unlikely coalition was so successful was that it was able to exploit a fundamental institution of the American political system: federalism. Because banking legislation was largely the purview of states, not the central government, the populist-banker coalition could fight and win in the hallways of state capitols rather than face a national political debate. Successful state-level coalitions could then be used to influence the selection of locally elected congressmen to carry their cause to Washington. Every time a crisis wracked its inherently fragile system, this coalition managed to turn efforts at reform to its advantage—even outmaneuvering President Franklin Roosevelt in the writing of the Glass-Steagall Act. As we show in chapter 6, this coalition enjoyed a century and a half of dominance. Ultimately, it was undone by a combination of demographic, economic, and technological changes that undermined unit banks as a business model.

There is no escaping the Game of Bank Bargains: politics always intrudes into bank regulation. Chapter 7 drives that point home by examining how the U.S. banking system, freed of restrictions on branching and competition—a change that should have made the system more stable— became positioned during the 1990s for the spectacular banking crisis of 2007–09. The political coalition between unit bankers and small farmers was replaced by a new coalition between the rapidly growing megabanks and urban activist groups. Bankers had ambitious plans to merge and expand. Their plans were, however, subject to a political constraint: they needed to be judged as good citizens of the communities they served in order for the Federal Reserve Board to approve the mergers. Activist groups wanted to be able to direct credit to their memberships and constituencies, and the "good citizenship" criterion gave them a powerful lever with which to negotiate with merging banks. The bankers and the activists forged a coalition that consolidated the American banking industry into a set of megabanks that were too big to fail. That coalition was formed, among other things, by the contractual commitments of merging banks to channel more than $850 billion in credit through activist groups in exchange for the political support of those activist groups for bank mergers between 1992 and 2007.

In addition to these explicit agreements between banks and activist groups, banks committed an additional $3.6 trillion over the same years in order to rate as good citizens. Many steps were required to make these arrangements work, and we return to them in detail, but one of the most crucial was that the government-sponsored enterprises (GSEs) Fannie Mae and Freddie Mac, which repurchased and securitized mortgages, were pressured by the Clinton administration to lower their underwriting standards dramatically so that these loans could become part of Fannie and Freddie's portfolios. Once they consented to doing so, their progressively weaker underwriting standards applied to *everyone*. We cannot stress this point strongly enough: the politics of regulatory approval for bank mergers set in motion a process whose ultimate outcome was that large swaths of the American middle class were able to take advantage of mortgage-underwriting rules that, compared to those of any other country in the world and of earlier periods of America's own history, were inconceivably lax. The result was the rapid growth of mortgages with high probabilities of default for all classes of Americans. To provide just a glimpse of the data, a 2006 survey by the National Association of Realtors found that 46 percent of first-time homebuyers made no down payment at all, and the median down payment for first-time buyers was only 2 percent of the purchase price.[10] In short, the subprime crisis of 2007–09 was the outcome of a series of spectacular political deals that distorted the incentives of both bankers and debtors.

[10] Pinto (2011), 25.

As we have pointed out, severe bank-insolvency crises require a combination of imprudent lending and inadequate bank capital to back high-risk loans. In chapter 8 we focus on how, exactly, U.S. banks, like the GSEs, were allowed to back their portfolios of risky adjustable-rate mortgages, requiring low down payments and little or no documentation, with capital buffers that clearly were inadequate. Once again the devil is in the details, but one cannot escape the conclusion that the decisions made by regulatory agencies were driven by the logic of politics.

Our goal in examining this episode is not to blame either "Wall Street fat cats" or activist groups for America's 2007–09 banking crisis. Many books make those kinds of arguments—and, frankly, we think that they often miss the mark. The subprime lending crisis was simply the latest in a very long string of American banking crises. What must be explained is why the United States has a banking system that is so persistently crisis prone. What is it about American political institutions that generates incentives for bankers and populists to search one another out and forge such powerful coalitions?

Note, too, that our focus is on the institutions that shape the incentives of individuals and groups, not the individuals and groups per se. People everywhere (now and in the past) generally pursue their self-interest, and one of the ways they do that is by exercising their political rights. When political institutions encourage them to form coalitions, even with unlikely partners, in the pursuit of mutual advantage, they will do so. When political institutions offer only weak incentives for these parties to join forces, they will not do so. No individual or group of individuals is to blame for what happens. Indeed, placing blame is inherently unproductive because it distracts people from the important question: how could we change political institutions to reduce the incentives to form socially unproductive coalitions?

Chapter 9 highlights the crucial role played by politics in the organization of the U.S. banking system by contrasting it with that of Canada. Indeed, Canada presents something of a counterfactual experiment: it has a colonial and cultural heritage similar to that of the United States, but it does not have the particular set of political institutions and circumstances that created the United States' bizarre system of unit banking. Rather, Canada's political institutions were purposely constructed in such a way that almost all economic policies and regulations, including those pertaining to banking, had to be decided by a national, bicameral legislature, one of whose houses was appointed, not elected.

Although Canada, too, certainly had its share of populists and would-be unit bankers, they could not succeed in controlling the banking system, because they had to win their political struggles all at once at the national level, within a parliamentary structure that was designed not to be easily controlled by populist factions. The structure of the Canadian banking system was therefore strikingly different: from its beginnings, it was characterized by a small number of very large banks with extensive national networks of branches. The owners of those banks were never drawn into coalitions with Canadian populists to create and share rents at the expense of everyone else. The result has been not just lower costs of credit in Canada but also a much more stable banking system. Since the 1920s, the United States has suffered three systemic banking crises—the widespread bank failures of the Great Depression, the savings and loan crisis of the 1980s, and the subprime crisis of 2007–09—while Canada has suffered none.

Our examination of Mexico in chapters 10 and 11 allows us to explore the differences between banking systems in authoritarian and democratic political systems. Unlike Britain, the United States, and Canada, where elections have been part of the political system for centuries, and in which the right to vote was gradually expanded during the nineteenth and early twentieth centuries, Mexicans were denied the right to effective suffrage until the late 1990s. During most of its history, Mexico has been governed by one type of authoritarian system or another, and on several occasions those governments have engaged in either partial or total expropriations of the banking system. Thus the case of Mexico not only allows us to understand how authoritarian political leaders form coalitions with bank insiders and minority shareholders to create a banking system but also to understand the conditions under which autocrats break those coalitions by seizing the wealth of those same insiders and minority shareholders. The Mexican case also raises the question of how governments managed to coax bankers into forming new coalitions to create banking systems despite their history of periodic expropriation. The answer is that throughout Mexican history, the government tightly regulated bank entry in order to drive up rates of return high enough to compensate bank insiders and shareholders for the risk of expropriation. In Mexico, as elsewhere, banking was all about politics. Mexican political outcomes oscillated between periods of chaos (like civil wars, during which banking systems collapsed) and periods of relative calm, during which crony banking systems comprising a small number of banks allocated scarce credit among politically influential insiders. This pattern has only been broken since 1997, after Mexico began to democratize and the government opened up the banking system to foreign entry.

When fundamental political institutions change, the Game of Bank Bargains changes. There is perhaps no better case to test this proposition than Brazil, the subject of chapters 12 and 13. For most of its history as an independent country, Brazil has been governed by one form of autocracy or another. Indeed, it was not until 1989 that Brazil staged its first direct election for the presidency under rules of universal adult suffrage. Since that time, Brazil has been a stable democracy, but one in which strong populist currents dominate. Indeed, Brazil's political institutions combine features that tilt politics heavily in favor of populist constituencies: a strong president and a weak legislature; centralized tax collection, but decentralized government spending; centralized political parties; universal suffrage for persons over the age of 16; and a constitution that specifies a long list of "positive rights."

Can we then point to any discernible differences in how banks were regulated and operated under autocracy and democracy? The differences are not just discernible; they are dramatic. For most of Brazilian history, autocrats were able to use the Brazilian banking system as little more than a mechanism to levy an inflation tax. There was nothing subtle about this practice: at its peak in the late 1980s, inflation ran at nearly 2,500 percent per year, and the banks and the government split nearly 8 percent of GDP between them in inflation-tax revenues. There have been two exceptions to this pattern. The first was during the period 1831–89, when local oligarchies were able to constrain the Brazilian emperor, and there was barely any banking system at all. The second has been the years since Brazil democratized in 1989. Brazil's democratically elected governments quickly brought an end to inflation taxation; by the mid-1990s, inflation had fallen nearly to U.S. levels, a shift that forced banks to get into the business of actually lending money rather than just earning income off the float on checking accounts (the profit a bank makes by not paying interest to depositors while a check clears).

Populism creates its own set of demands on the banking system, however. Brazilian banks are no longer inflation-tax machines for the government, but some of them are now employment-generation machines. Two of the largest banks in Brazil are run by the government (although one of them has private shareholders). These banks allocate credit not according to market criteria but to help candidates win office by making sure that those candidates' business allies in politically contested districts have enough credit to maintain or increase levels of employment.

Chapter 14 summarizes the principal findings of the previous chapters and links the histories of our five case studies with the experiences of other countries to show that our approach has broad explanatory power.

In chapter 15 we consider what our findings have to say about the feasibility of libertarian policy advocacy, the limits of regulatory reform, the validity of various theoretical models of banking crises, and the durability of political institutions.

What We Don't Do in This Book, and Why

Some readers may wonder why we focus on banks rather than examining financial markets as well. We recognize, of course, that the history of financial markets and the institutions specific to them (for example, stock exchanges) also reflects important dimensions of financial-system development and can be the locus of financial instability (for example, sovereign-debt crises and stock-market crashes), and we explore some of those important connections in our historical narratives. We concentrate on banking systems, however, for a simple reason: financial markets have always been created and sustained by banks. No financial system has developed bond and stock markets without first developing a banking system. Brokers and dealers either are banks or rely on banks for the credit to manage their underwriting and trading activities, and the firms that access financial markets do so only after long periods in which they become seasoned prospects as the result of their interactions with banks. Conceptually, it is sometimes hard even to distinguish between bank-intermediation and financial-market instruments. Bills of exchange, for example, are bank IOUs, but they are also tradable financial instruments. Some early banks, such as the Bank of England, began as little more than sovereign-debt restructuring devices, and holding stock in those banks was akin to investing in sovereign debt. Throughout history and around the world, banking has been germinal and central to financial development of all kinds.

Furthermore, to the extent that financial markets can offer alternatives to banking finance, those alternatives tend to be constrained by the same factors that limit the supply of bank credit. In many countries the risk of expropriation by the government limits the ability of firms to use equity markets as a means of raising capital. This risk tends to be mitigated by managers' engaging in rent-seeking activities with members of the government itself, a practice that has the effect of reducing the amount of capital that can be mobilized by markets.[11] In short, securities markets also operate within a political context and do not allow an end run around the tight political constraints that limit the operation and performance of banks.

Other readers may wonder why we focus on chartered banks—the enterprises known as commercial banks, corporations that take deposits, make loans, and seem to place their ATMs just about anywhere they can rent six square feet of space—rather than private banks (also known as merchant banks or investment banks), such as the House of Rothschild or J. P. Morgan & Co. Private banks have existed since the invention of money in antiquity. The amount of capital that they could mobilize, however, was always constrained (see chapters 2 and 3). As chartered banks came into being, private banks deployed their skills and reputations to become coordinators of financial networks: they arranged lending syndicates, brokered international financial transactions, underwrote and distributed securities, and helped govern large nonfinancial corporations. The key credit suppliers of the modern era, however, have been chartered banks.

As we wrote this book, we were often asked by colleagues, referees, and students why we confined ourselves to a small number of case studies. Why five countries, instead of eight, ten, or twenty? As a practical matter,

---

[11] Haber, Razo, and Maurer (2003), chapters 2, 4, and 5, focus on the impact of rent seeking on the number of firms in any industry that can mobilize capital through securities markets. In their framework, rent seeking limits firm entry and exit. Stulz (2005) focuses on the impact of rent seeking on the amount of stock that any firm can offer to minority shareholders. In his framework, rent seeking requires a small number of powerful shareholders as a bulwark against government predation. These mechanisms are not mutually exclusive.

exploring how a country's institutions have changed over time is not an enterprise characterized by increasing returns to scale; there is an obvious tradeoff between the number of cases covered and the depth with which they can be discussed. Moreover, our purpose is not to provide an exhaustive history of the political economy of banking in every country around the globe; rather it is to develop and illustrate a general framework that we believe has wide explanatory power. We invite other researchers to test that framework against additional country cases as well as against large multicountry data sets.

Still other colleagues and students asked why we bothered with hundreds of years of history: why not just study the past couple of decades? For that matter, why not make things simpler yet and focus just on the last couple of decades in one country—a research strategy that has been employed to good effect by a number of scholars who have sought to unravel the causes of the U.S. subprime lending crisis?

Our answer is simple in principle, but the necessary methods are not simple in practice: when people want to understand the factors that shape complex systems and shift those systems from one equilibrium to another, they undertake multidimensional analyses—and one of the dimensions on which they focus intently is time. This is what a physician does, for example, when she is faced with a difficult diagnosis. She starts with fundamental, time-invariant factors, such as the patient's genetic predisposition toward particular diseases as deduced from a family medical history. She then looks at the patient's own medical history: what illnesses has the patient had in the past, what pathogens has she been exposed to, and what has been her health trajectory? She next gathers information on factors that affect health in the short run: diet, exercise, stress. The physician also gathers data from direct observation: tests of metabolic function, palpation of organs, and a review of symptoms. Finally, the physician compares the information from this patient to information from other patients she has treated and assesses all of it within a logical framework.

This approach allows her to rule out certain hypotheses because they are inconsistent with the timing of events (e.g., if A happened after B, then A could not have caused B); because they are inconsistent with comparative evidence (if A did not cause B in other cases, then A likely did not cause B in this case either, even if A preceded B in time); or because they are unlikely given the patient's underlying, time-invariant, characteristics (if no one in a patient's family has ever had disease X and there is a strong genetic component to that disease, then disease X is likely not the cause of the patient's symptoms). What is true of medicine also holds in the natural sciences that rely on observational methods (e.g., epidemiology, astronomy, and evolutionary biology) and in which accurate causal statements are important. It should be no less true in the social sciences.

Indeed, the medical diagnostic analogy is particularly apt for studying the world's banking systems, where good health has been the exception and an almost pathological combination of unstable and scarce credit has been the rule. As is frequently the case in medicine, the causes of good health are fundamental: stable banking systems that allocate credit broadly are an outcome of political systems characterized both by broad suffrage and constraining institutions that limit the incentives for bankers to form coalitions with populists. Understanding why this is the case requires a deep historical exploration into the origins and consequences of those political institutions. To that exploration we now turn.

2

‖‖‖‖‖‖‖‖‖‖‖‖‖‖‖‖‖‖

The Game of Bank Bargains

The great questions of the time are not decided by speeches and majority decisions—that was the error of 1848 and 1849—but by iron and blood.

Otto von Bismarck, September 20, 1862

Every reader of this book doubtless has at least one bank account. Most of us give little, if any, thought to the security of those accounts or the solvency of the banks where they are located. This complacency is an outcome of a rather complicated set of institutional practices that have been hammered out over the past four centuries. Without those practices —which are enforced by governments—there would be very good reasons to lie awake at night worrying about our money, because a bank is, by design, a potentially unstable enterprise.

This instability arises because the normal functioning of banks depends on three sets of property rights that only government can provide.[1] Banks need powerful governments. But power may not be wielded in the interest of bankers unless bankers can convince the group in control of the government to partner with them.

There is no avoiding the government-banker partnership. Thinking that one can do so is tantamount to a utopian dream—reminiscent of John Lennon's famous song "Imagine"—that human civilization can function without countries. Bankers who imagine that they can live in a world without countries will, despite Lennon's assurances, find it hard to do. They rely on the police power of the state. This power, however, is not under bankers' control: without some form of partnership, it may not be wielded in their interest. As Bismarck, Germany's "Iron Chancellor," might have said, for better or worse, successful bankers interested in solv-

---

[1] On this point, see also Haber, North, and Weingast (2008).

ing their fundamental property-rights problems must ally themselves with governments that have iron and blood at their disposal.

All governments are not, however, created the same. In some political systems, decision making is centralized in a single person with nearly absolute power and endless discretion. In others, decision making is diffused among the entire adult population through the franchise, and elected officials have strong limits on their authority and discretion. Still other systems fall between these two extremes. The nature of the government-banker partnership varies among these different types of political systems. Our goals in this chapter are therefore threefold: to show why it is not possible to create a banking system without a government-banker partnership; to explore the fundamental conflicts of interest inherent in such partnerships; and to show how differences in the institutions governing the political system mitigate some of those conflicts of interest while intensifying others.

It is extraordinarily difficult to mitigate simultaneously all of the conflicts of interest inherent in the partnership between banks and governments. Some political systems—namely democracies that blunt populist currents with strong, constraining institutions—can pull off the balancing act, but they are rare. As a result, the conflicts of interest inherent in government-banker partnerships make the banking systems of most countries fragile by design.

The Basics of Banking

To fully understand how potentially fragile banks are, and how extensively they depend on the state, it is useful to begin by stripping away all of the institutions that have been crafted by banks and governments (e.g., the legal system's enforcement of rights, limited liability for shareholders, and government supervisory and regulatory agencies) in order to lay bare the core property-rights problems inherent in the business of banking. We then explore how those problems are mitigated—but not solved—by the creation of laws, regulations, and government institutions. Our goal is not to encourage you to move your savings under your mattress but to provide an understanding of two crucial issues: why there are no banking systems without the active participation of governments, and why no government can be a completely neutral arbiter when it comes to the banking system. In short, our goal is to explore why banking is all about politics—and always has been.

Let us start with the basics: what outputs does a bank produce, and what inputs does it consume? The major outputs of a bank—its product —are debt contracts, primarily in the form of IOUs payable to the bank. The major inputs to the bank also are contracts, primarily in the form of IOUs payable to depositors. Though you may not realize it, when you deposit your paycheck in your bank, you are making a loan to the bank. The bank's basic business model is therefore unusual: its inputs and outputs are both loans.

Any enterprise whose inputs and outputs consist primarily of promises to repay debts is inherently unstable and risky. In the first place, bankers engage in a difficult balancing act: they borrow money from depositors and lend it to debtors, but they cannot predict with certainty that the debtor will repay the loan. Even the most honest borrower might default because of unforeseen circumstances, potentially causing the loss of the depositors' money.[2] In the second place, it is extraordinarily difficult, if not impossible, for bankers to exactly match the durations of their contracts with depositors and debtors. Bank deposits can typically be withdrawn on very short notice, but the loans financed by those deposits may extend for months, years, or even decades. In fact, bankers face the risk that, even if their banks are not insolvent, worried depositors might show up en masse to withdraw their money, and there might not be enough cash in the till to satisfy all those withdrawal demands.[3]

---

[2] The banker could attempt to solve this problem by offering the depositors very high interest rates to compensate them for the risk that debtors will renege, but that would only make the situation for the depositors riskier still: in order to honor the high-interest contracts with depositors, the banker would have to write contracts bearing even higher interest rates with debtors. The only debtors who would be attracted to such a contract would be those engaged in a venture promising a return even higher than the interest rate, which is to say one that is speculative and extremely risky.

[3] They may also fund their operations by borrowing from other creditors, including other banks. In developing countries, these sources of loanable funds tend to be of less quantitative importance than deposits. Moreover, the general problem—that banks are highly leveraged—persists regardless of the source of indebtedness. The leveraging of banks is a fundamental historical constant. Since ancient Greek times, banks have funded themselves with debt, not equity shares. There is an extensive literature in economic theory explaining banks' reliance on short-term debt financing; the essence of the argument is that sources of bank funding lack the information and control over

The obvious solution to both of these problems (which are referred to in the banking literature as *credit risk* and *liquidity risk*) is to create cushions in the balance sheet. The first type of cushion, called equity capital, is a block of money that is invested in the bank by stockholders. This gives the bank the ability to repay deposits in full even if some debtors fail to repay their loans. A second type of cushion is cash assets. Banks do not lend out every single penny they have; they hold some money in reserve.[4] The larger the bank—the greater its stock of deposit contracts and loan contracts—the larger the capital and cash cushions it requires in order to operate prudently.

The logic of banking, therefore, requires that banks raise deposits and equity capital to finance their operations and lend those resources to parties that are likely to repay the loans, while preserving some assets as cash. So long as depositors and suppliers of equity capital are willing to fund the bank, the banker maintains adequate capital and cash buffers, and the risk of loan default is not too great, the banker can operate a safe, sound, and profitable enterprise. But this is easier said than done.

Why would any investors want to provide this capital cushion? The risks are obvious. The banker—or more commonly a group of bank insiders (the founders, who are often its managers as well as its directors)—is asking equity investors to trust them. But what is to keep the bank insiders from losing the investors' money by taking wild bets or embezzling it?[5] The bank insiders may offer various means for outside investors

---

bank actions that would make equity financing feasible (D. Diamond [1984]; Calomiris and Kahn [1991]).

[4] The cash cushion allows banks both to reduce the overall riskiness of their assets and to reduce their liquidity risk (since cash can be used to finance depositor withdrawals). A higher proportion of cash assets makes it less likely that a decline in the value of risky loans will cause the bank to default on its deposit debts. For example, consider a bank whose assets consist of $80 in loans and $20 in cash, which are funded by $90 in deposits and $10 in equity capital, or net worth. An adverse shock that causes loans to decline in value by 11 percent will not cause this bank to become insolvent: the 11 percent decline in loan value leaves the bank with a net worth of $1.20. But if that bank held $100 in loans and no cash, an 11 percent adverse shock would result in bank insolvency: the net worth would be –$1.

[5] In technical terms, the bank insiders are offering minority shareholders (the outside equity investors) *cash-flow rights* (the right to be paid, as a function of income earned), but the bank insiders are maintaining most, if not all, of the *control rights* (a voice in running the firm).

to monitor their activities, but inevitably these will be imperfect.[6] Moreover, in a banking partnership, the bank insiders are asking investors to put their entire stock of wealth at risk: if the enterprise fails, each partner is singly liable for all of the debts of the firm.[7] Making matters worse, the bank is, by design, a very highly leveraged enterprise: it borrows money from one group of people and then lends most of it to another. The outside investors are therefore putting themselves at enormous risk. In short, the bank insiders need outsiders to invest their wealth in the bank in order to make the bank stable enough to attract depositors, but in doing so the insiders transfer the risk from depositors to equity investors!

How can banks induce outside investors to expose themselves to so much risk? There are several ways to solve this problem. Bank insiders can reassure outsiders about the security of the loan portfolio, at least in part, by pledging a large amount of their own wealth as equity capital. The legal system can also provide protections against embezzlement and fraud by insiders at the expense of outsiders. Finally, limiting the liability of stockholders can reduce their risk. Limited liability means that the equity investors are not jointly and severally liable for all the losses of the

---

[6] In the United States, bank insiders are separated into two groups: the managers and the board of directors. In theory, the managers report to the board, who are the agents of the minority shareholders. In practice, boards are often dominated by managers. There is a substantial corporate-governance literature examining conflicts of interest between stockholders and "entrenched" managers (who may engage in self-serving conduct in conflict with the interests of stockholders, including insufficient use of debt finance, insufficient risk taking, and a low supply of effort). In the United States and similar economies, where minority shareholders are protected from fraudulent behavior in the management of corporate assets (e.g., sales of corporate assets to firms controlled by management at below-market prices—typically referred to as "tunneling"), this is the main agency problem of corporate governance. In developing economies, where protections for minority shareholders are weak and laws against fraudulent transfers are less prevalent or less rigorously enforced, managers are typically the controlling shareholders of the firm: both the board and the management tend to be drawn from the families that initially founded the bank and continue to have a controlling interest. Here, corporate governance failures tend to take the form of tunneling and other fraudulent behavior: majority stockholders who are managers steal value from the firm, thereby transferring wealth from minority shareholders to themselves.

[7] This is why business partnerships with unlimited personal liability tend to limit the number of partners, why they create complicated covenants and conditions for partners, and why partners engage in costly monitoring of one another. One means of facilitating such monitoring is through social networks, which explains why some people attach so much value to membership in country clubs.

banking enterprise; their losses as minority shareholders are limited to some multiple of the amount of capital they actually invested in the bank.[8]

Without some combination of these protections for outside shareholders, it is very difficult to attract outside equity investors and thus very difficult to expand a bank much beyond the role of a medieval moneylender—an agent who could make loans and charge interest but not mobilize savings en masse. As it eventually developed, the limited liability bank broke the size barrier by bounding a shareholder's risk in proportion to the capital that he invests. Not surprisingly, the idea spread quickly and is now the basic organizational form of large-scale business enterprises around the planet. In fact, in the vast majority of countries, the first enterprises to seek charters granting their shareholders a limit on liability were banks: the special limited-liability acts for banks typically antedated general incorporation laws by decades.[9]

A bank cannot simply declare that its shareholders have limited liability or other legal protections. Only the government can offer these. It does so by granting privileges—through bank charters—and enforcing them in courts. A charter is not just a license; it is a contract between the bank and the government. That contract creates a set of obligations for banks, such as taxes on bank profits or capital, requirements for banks to maintain sufficient holdings of government fiat currency or government bonds, and requirements that banks submit to government supervision of their operations. It also confers a set of valuable privileges, such as the right to create money that serves as a legal tender for the payment of public and/

---

[8] In the simplest formulation, the stockholder's liability is limited to the amount of capital paid in to the bank. Under double or triple liability, the stockholder can be liable for two or three times the amount of capital paid in.

[9] This is not to say that limited liability is an absolute requirement for the existence of banks. If the risk faced by minority shareholders is sufficiently low, they may deploy their capital even without such protection. As a general rule, however, outside investors are reluctant to deploy their capital unless their liability is limited. Moreover, limited liability does not necessarily require that the shareholders' risk is limited to the value of their invested capital. Limits on liability have varied across countries and time. For example, some systems of double and triple liability held stockholders liable for capital calls equal to one to two times their paid-in capital. In other systems, the limits on a stockholder's liability increased the longer he or she owned the shares; and in others, similar to the current system in the United States, liability has been fully limited to the invested capital. In general, the equity structure of banks sets some limit on the liability of stockholders.

or private debts, the right to hold government deposits, and, of course, limited liability for its shareholders.

Not surprisingly, a government can get potential bankers to pay handsomely for a charter—especially if it limits the number of bank charters granted. Scarce charters not only make banks more profitable but also help fund banks at the time they are chartered. If charters are scarce, then potential shareholders will pay a premium in order to obtain a piece of a banking enterprise that they know will be able to earn monopoly profits. The premium that the minority shareholders are willing to pay for a share is a form of free financing for bank insiders, an extra buffer of value that reduces the amount of paid-in capital needed to attract depositors.

The Three Property-Rights Challenges of Banking

The granting of scarce bank charters helps to solve the problem of funding banks, but it exacerbates three fundamental property-rights problems. These come to the fore precisely because the government has defined banks as legal entities subject to its control.

First, the banks and the government have to create mechanisms that either prevent the government from expropriating the assets of the banks once they are created or compensate the banks' investors and depositors for accepting the risk that the banks' assets may be expropriated. Under the conditions of the charter, the bank cannot hide its wealth from the government: it has given the government the right to inspect, supervise, and regulate its operations.

Second, minority shareholders and depositors have to create mechanisms that either prevent the bank insiders from expropriating their capital through fraud or "tunneling" (the channeling of bank resources to firms owned by bank insiders) or that compensate minority shareholders and depositors for accepting the risk of expropriation. The charter from the government does not address this problem: it only limits the liability of shareholders toward depositors and other creditors.[10]

---

[10] Depositors and minority shareholders do not have to receive the same compensation for risk. Depositors are trapped: because they need the banks as a means of payment, they may be forced to accept negative real returns. In this case, they limit their exposure by limiting their deposits to the bare minimum necessary to meet current payments. We return to this issue later in this chapter.

Third, the bank has to create mechanisms that prevent bank borrowers from expropriating bank insiders, minority shareholders, and depositors by borrowing money from the bank and then reneging on the loan contract, or else it has to create mechanisms that compensate those groups for accepting the risk of expropriation by borrowers.

All three of these fundamental problems must be solved to make bankers willing to invest their own funds in the bank and to attract funds from depositors or outside stockholders. These problems are interdependent. Enforcing laws against fraud or tunneling by the bank insiders and enforcing loan contracts with debtors necessarily involve the police power of the government. But any government strong enough to carry out those functions is also strong enough to expropriate the bank. For a banking system to operate effectively, minority shareholders and depositors need the government to pass and enforce laws against tunneling, ensure that banks fulfill their contractual obligations, and create accounting standards and regulatory and supervisory agencies to facilitate evaluation of the bank by outsiders who are thinking of investing in bank stock or depositing their funds there. Similarly, the bank needs the courts and police to enforce loan and other counterparty contracts: without them, for example, collateral cannot be repossessed. Finally, depositors and shareholders may look to the government to reduce their risks by creating protections against loss through deposit insurance or bank bailouts. Can a government with the physical enforcement capacity to do all these things be trusted not to disenfranchise all the various contracting parties in its own selfish interest?

Conflicted Government

Further complicating the government's problem of credibly solving these three key property-rights challenges, the government is not a disinterested, independent party. In fact, the group in control of the government typically has multiple conflicts of interest when it comes to the banking system. The most obvious conflict of interest is that this group regulates banks—ostensibly to limit banks' exposures to risks—but also looks to banks as a source of public finance. That is, it simultaneously regulates the banks and borrows from, or taxes, them. It therefore has incentives to fashion a regulatory environment that favors government's (or government actors') access to finance at the expense of fashioning an environment conducive to a stable and efficient banking system.

Somewhat less obviously, the group in control of the government enforces credit contracts that discipline debtors on behalf of banks (and in the process assist in the seizing of debtor collateral), but it relies on those same debtors for political support. Nobody votes for the guy who just threw him out of his house and padlocked the door. This group therefore has incentives to refuse to enforce debt contracts or to help debtors forestall repayment, at the expense of both the stability of the banking system (in the short run) and the willingness of banks to extend credit (in the long run).

Finally, the group in control of the government allocates losses among creditors in the event of bank failures, but it may simultaneously look to the largest group of those creditors—bank depositors—for political support. It is hard to stay in power when you tell the electorate that the banks lost their life savings and you are not going to do anything about it. The group in control of the government may find it politically expedient to violate the contractual obligations of the banks to the senior creditors (holders of nondeposit liabilities, such as bonds). It may, for example, decide to force senior creditors to take a haircut (a write-down of the value of their claim against the bank) in order to keep the bank running and the deposit base intact. Doing so, however, creates a problem of moral hazard: in the case of insolvency, the owners of the bank's equity capital (the shareholders) should lose their entire investment, but by giving the senior creditors a haircut and keeping the bank running, the government has protected the shareholders from loss—and in so doing has also given them incentives to continue to take wild risks.

These conflicts of interest arise unavoidably. The business of banking is the creation and trading of contracts—between banks and governments, between banks and their creditors, between banks and their debtors, and between bank insiders (founders and majority shareholders) and bank minority shareholders. In the final instance, the group in control of the government must arbitrate all those contracts and allocate the losses when contracts cannot be fulfilled—and its members are not disinterested parties. In short, government officials may have tremendous incentives to behave opportunistically with respect to the property-rights system that underpins the banking system.[11]

---

[11] It is also important to recognize that the government is not a unitary actor. The actual work of government is done by bureaucrats whose interests rarely coincide with

Making matters worse still, the government has multiple opportunities to behave opportunistically. It can expropriate the banks outright to fund its needs; it can borrow from the banks and then renege on its debts; it can seize resources by printing fiat money that it uses to purchase goods and services; it can force banks to hold government bonds, currency, or deposits at the central bank as "reserves" that yield negative real interest rates; and it can force banks to make low-interest loans to government enterprises or other government-favored borrowers (who, in turn, find ways to reward the government for its favoritism). The government also has multiple opportunities to dispense largesse. It can grant favors to bank insiders, depositors, or debtors who are deemed crucial to maintaining its power. Examples of these actions by government include regulatory "forbearance" toward bank insiders (that is, deciding not to enforce regulations), insuring depositors beyond the statutory limits, and forcing banks to forgive debts.

Even worse, in response to reports of large losses at banks, the group in control of the government may decide that the path of least political resistance is to favor all of these groups—insiders, minority shareholders, depositors, and debtors—through rescues and bailouts funded by taxpayers. One means of doing so is to create a government safety net for credit-market participants, most often in the form of a deposit-insurance and bank-resolution system, which is typically designed to minimize the public visibility of the costs of bailouts and the allocation of the losses.

The existence of a system of deposit insurance, ironically, generates incentives for the parties in control of the government to use the banks to reward politically favored constituencies. In the absence of deposit insurance and government intervention into bank loss sharing, the combination of the first-come, first-served rule for depositors and the laws governing suspension of bank operations and receivership for failed banks, as

maximizing the wealth of the state, much less maximizing social welfare. In fact, the selfish objectives of bureaucrats may lead them to promulgate costly and ineffectual regulations in order to extract bribes from market participants to relax those same regulations (Barth, Caprio, and Levine [2006]). Although complex and ineffectual regulatory systems may accomplish little within the banking system and may be very costly to society, they may be chosen because they enable those who control impecunious or authoritarian governments to commit to providing ongoing resources to their allies within the bureaucracy. In particular, by establishing regulations, bureaucrats are empowered to extract payments that do not depend on centralized approval.

enforced by the courts, determines the allocation of losses associated with delinquent loans and failed banks. In other words, the savings of depositors are at risk. Depositors can therefore discipline bank insiders by withdrawing their funds when the insiders take imprudent risks—and it is this ability that gives depositors control rights over the bank. The seniority of deposits, depositors' rights to withdraw their deposits, and the transfer of control rights over banks in liquidation all have an essential social function, namely to encourage bankers to be prudent and honest in managing their risks.[12] The problem—if it may be called that—is that prudent lending practices may conflict with the desire of the parties in control of the government to channel credit to politically crucial groups. Deposit insurance paid for by taxpayer absorption of losses ex post facto "fixes" the problem: depositors no longer have an incentive to discipline the bank insiders because their funds are no longer at risk.[13] The bank insiders are now free to take riskier bets. This loss-allocation arrangement may have adverse consequences in encouraging excessive risk taking by banks, but it can also entail large gains to politicians and bankers.

The reason that taxpayers are often left holding the bag for bailing out insolvent banks is that the people who are arranging the rules that govern risk taking and loss sharing do not have to obtain taxpayers' active agreement. Because minority shareholders have to take the active step of buying bank shares, and depositors have to take the active step of placing their funds in a bank, both are interested parties to the deal. Taxpayers, however, have no such role. This does not mean that their preferences can be completely ignored. Imposing too great a loss on taxpayers can induce them to rise up against the group in control of the government. It does mean, however, that this group, bank insiders, minority shareholders, and depositors have plenty of leeway to fleece taxpayers.

Three factors generate that leeway. First, as Mancur Olson (1965) and George Stigler (1971) famously argued, it is difficult to coordinate opposition to any program that benefits few at the expense of many because of

---

[12] Calomiris and Kahn (1991).

[13] We are not claiming that deposit insurance necessarily increases bank risk or imposes losses on taxpayers. It is theoretically possible to design a deposit-insurance system that does not do either. For example, three antebellum U.S. states—Indiana, Ohio, and Iowa—operated deposit insurance systems that were self-funded and that actually increased bank stability. (See Calomiris [1990].)

the transactions costs of political activity. Second, taxpayers cannot easily identify the allocation of costs and benefits from bailouts, which is determined not by the courts but by a deposit-insurance resolution authority operating within the government under opaque circumstances and ad hoc arrangements. Third, because taxpayers are sometimes depositors, they may not be able to determine whether they are better or worse off as a result of the government's intervention.

This may all seem tremendously complicated—but that is exactly the point! Precisely because the group in control of the government is conducting various activities affecting a number of different constituencies—bank insiders, minority shareholders, debtors, taxpayer-depositors, and taxpayer-nondepositors—it is difficult, if not impossible, for many individuals to calculate the effects of these actions on their welfare. Most people cannot monitor every government decision that affects the value of their property rights. Both the intent of government financial policies and their actual economic consequences can be difficult to predict, especially if the government is simultaneously managing multiple regulatory and legal institutions, some of which potentially enhance the value of property rights and some of which reduce them.

The Politics of Financial Property Rights

The implication is inescapable: the property-rights system that structures banking has not evolved in response to some efficiency criterion in an anonymous "market" for institutions. Rather it is the product of deals arranged and enforced within an existing set of political institutions and hammered out by coalitions of market participants and the group in control of the government. These deals are intended to improve the welfare of the members of those coalitions and of the group in control of the government, not of society at large. Because the economic incentives of the bank insiders, minority shareholders, depositors, debtors, and taxpayers are not inherently aligned, the group in control of the government has ample reason to exploit those differences in incentives for its own political or economic ends. In particular, participants in the bargaining know that unanimity is not required for a deal to be made: the government simply has to cobble together a winning coalition. This situation implies that many parties may be excluded from beneficial deals.

The allocation of political power determines the composition of coalitions and the deals that they structure. The deals in turn determine which laws are passed, which judges are appointed, and which groups of people have which licenses to contract with whom, for what, and on what terms. They also determine the distribution of the burden of taxation, the allocation of public spending, the regulation of entry, the chartering of banks, the supervision of publicly traded companies, and the flow of credit and its terms. These bargains are exceptionally complex, involving explicit trades and implicit alliances, but at root they are about the creation and distribution of economic rents and the maintenance of political power. They are, in short, the outcome of a strategic interaction—a game, as it were: the Game of Bank Bargains.

Given the number of agents with cash-flow or control rights in banks, the heterogeneity of bank debtors, and the diversity of political systems, the set of potential coalitions and deals is quite large. Several characteristics of the Game of Bank Bargains are, however, clear as a matter of logic —and, as the following chapters show, as a matter of evidence too.

First, although the number of possible combinations of bank insiders, minority shareholders, taxpayer-depositors, taxpayer-nondepositors, debtors, and parties in control of the government is very large, not every combination can constitute a coalition. A coalition is a group of people who agree on an arrangement to allocate the rent created by the rules that govern an economic system and who are in a unique position to observe that allocation. That fact renders many possible combinations of parties nonviable: forming a coalition with one group may require those in control of the government simultaneously to behave opportunistically against other groups.

Second, authoritarian political systems are likely to generate different sets of coalitions from those in democracies. In an autocracy, the government cannot make a credible (time-consistent) commitment to the bank insiders, minority shareholders, and depositors that it will not expropriate them. In addition, in an autocracy, debtors (and individuals who wish to be debtors) cannot influence the group that controls the government through the ballot box. This makes it difficult for potential debtors— firms and households that seek credit but cannot obtain it—to force the government to liberalize the rules governing the allocation of bank charters in order to increase competition among banks, thereby making credit more freely available.

Third, precisely because creating a stable banking system that allocates credit broadly requires solutions to three distinct property-rights problems, transitions from autocracy to democracy, which ultimately reduce credit scarcity, do not result in an automatic and instantaneous reorganization of the banking system simply because debtors now have the right to vote. This point cannot be emphasized strongly enough: the property-rights problems endemic to all banking systems are mitigated by creating institutions; and, by definition, institutions (which act as repositories of rules and discretionary authority, created by previous rounds of political bargains) change slowly. This is particularly true of the institutions that permit banks to sanction debtors who attempt to expropriate the bank by failing to repay their loans. Efficient courts, honest police, and accurate property and commercial registers cannot be created with the stroke of a pen; they take considerable time and expense to develop. And, as we discuss below, there are good reasons why they tend not to develop under authoritarian political systems. Regime change may well bring about a reorganization of the banking system, but only after a considerable lag.

Fourth, given a range of possible coalitions within both democracies and autocracies, the results of these coalitions are not neutral with respect to the industrial organization of banking. That is, democracies can generate coalitions that undermine the stability of the banking system and its ability to provide credit: imagine, for example, a coalition between the group in control of the government and bank debtors, in which political support is exchanged for a moratorium on debt repayment. Autocracies can generate banking systems that are stable: imagine a coalition between an autocrat, bank insiders, and minority shareholders in which loans to the government are exchanged for binding limits on the issuance of new bank charters that raise rates of return of existing banks high enough to compensate the insiders and minority shareholders for the risk of expropriation. Thus there is not a bimodal distribution in the industrial structure of banking between democracies and autocracies. Rather, each generates different sets of possible coalitions such that, on average, democracies are more likely to give rise to stable banking systems characterized by relatively open entry and fewer restrictions on banks, while autocracies are more likely to give rise to unstable banking systems characterized by relatively limited entry and more restrictions on banks. Moreover, not all autocracies, and certainly not all democracies, play the game the same way. Nor can one take for granted that there will always be a government of any kind. Under chaos, banks cannot exist: it is hard to turn a profit when withdrawals are routinely made at gunpoint. We depict these differences in the Game of Bank Bargains in figure 2.1, a taxonomy of regimes and banking systems.

Autocratic Regimes

The branch of the figure labeled "Autocracy" refers to any political system —military junta, dictatorship, absolute monarchy, oligarchy—in which citizens do not shape policy outcomes through elections that are effective and politically significant.[14] Under autocracy, banks usually run a higher risk of government expropriation than under democracy; an autocrat typically has greater freedom of action than an elected official who faces the sanction of being removed in the next election.

Autocrats with Absolute Power

Under an autocrat with absolute power, the banking outcomes are the simplest. Absolute power creates a thorny problem for the autocrat: there may be nothing to stop him from expropriating anything that he chooses, but in that case, it will be virtually impossible to organize a banking system. Just about any highly visible enterprise is at risk of expropriation, but banks are particularly vulnerable. In the first place, a multitude of government policies can be used to expropriate, tax, or extort banks (such as outright nationalization, rules requiring directed loans, reserve requirements, transaction taxes, and the granting or revoking of valuable privileges). In the second place, the assets of banks tend to be highly liquid. This makes a bank a very different target of expropriation from, say, a farm, factory, or mine. If an autocrat confiscates one of those enterprises, it is valuable only because it can produce a stream of income, and that happens only if he can run it effectively. The autocrat has the option, of course, of selling the confiscated asset for immediate cash, but he has to

---

[14] As Riker ([1982], 5), makes clear: "Voting . . . is not equivalent to a democracy. Only voting that facilitates popular choice is democratic. This condition excludes voting both in oligarchic bodies and in plebiscites in communist and military tyrannies, where voting is no more than forced approbation. . . . To render them equivalent, voting must be surrounded with numerous institutions like political parties and free speech, which organize voting into genuine choice."

Regime	Government	Government-banker partnership	Banking system	Outcomes
Chaos	None	None	None	No state
Autocracy — Absolute power	None	None	Poverty trap
Autocracy — Centralized	Rent-creating and rent-sharing network	Narrow credit, locally stable	Strong state
Autocracy — Weakly centralized	Inflation-tax sharing between oligarchy and autocrat	Float banking	Mid-strength state
Autocracy — Local oligarchies	Little or no national chartering	Small, fragmented	Weak state
Democracy — Liberalism	Competitive banking with taxation	Broad credit, stable	Powerful state
Democracy — Populism	Welfare state reduces political pressure on banks	Limited role for banks	Powerful state
Democracy — Populism	Politically determined credit	Broad credit, unstable	Powerful state

FIGURE 2.1 Taxonomy of regimes and banking systems.

do so at a steep discount, because the buyer of the asset knows that there is little to prevent the autocrat from expropriating it again. The autocrat is therefore in the position of a thief selling his goods to a fence: he will receive only a small portion of the value of what he has taken because the buyer is bearing a serious expropriation risk. This problem does not loom large, however, when the assets being confiscated (or stolen) take the form of cash or other forms of liquid wealth: they are valued, without delay, at one hundred cents on the dollar.

The autocrat cannot solve this commitment problem by promising not to expropriate the banks: his wide authority and discretion mean that no promise he makes is credible, and thus private individuals are unlikely to found banks, buy bank stock, or deposit their wealth in banks. There may be banks owned and run by the government, which it uses to hold fiscal balances and which the public uses when it needs access to a payments system—such as the comically insolvent state-owned banks that Saddam Hussein ran in Iraq—but no sane person thinks of them as places to deposit wealth or apply for a loan.[15] The result is a poverty trap. The population understands that the government is rapacious; there is no banking system in any meaningful sense; the constraints on credit for firms and households cause the economy to grow slowly; the government has no source of private credit; and, thus, when its fiscal needs exceed tax revenues, it has strong incentives to expropriate private assets. This cycle can continue ad infinitum.

A Centralized, Autocratic Network

When an autocrat lacks absolute power but is still strong enough to hold sway, he has to build a network of alliances in order to hold onto power. Bankers are important nodes in such a network. Indeed, without them, the autocrat lacks the ability to finance expenditures in excess of tax revenues —expenditures that may be necessary to cement alliances with other politically or economically crucial groups.

The problem is that the autocrat has to induce bankers to deploy their capital in banks, but they have good reasons to believe that he will, under

---

[15] The risk of expropriation of depositor wealth under autocracy provides the intuition that underpins the concept of contract-intensive money, a measure of the quality of a country's property rights developed by Clague et al. (1999).

some circumstances, expropriate them. His wide authority means that no promise he makes not to do so is credible. The implication is that he has to compensate bankers for the probability that they will be expropriated, which is to say that he has to raise the rate of return on their capital above what they would obtain in a competitive market without expropriation risk by providing them with what economists call rents—a stream of income from a scarce privilege. Typically, the autocrat restricts the number of bank charters in order to minimize competition among banks, thereby allowing them to charge higher interest rates than would prevail under perfect competition. He may also confer additional privileges (e.g., the right to collect taxes as the government's agent) that raise rates of return. The bankers then share some of the resulting rents with the autocrat by providing loans to his government. They may also cement their alliance by extending credit to the business enterprises run by members of his family. In short, the autocrat and the bankers form a network of partnerships whose purpose is to create and share rents—a system that is sometimes called crony capitalism.

To take advantage of their banking charter, bank insiders must mobilize sufficient equity capital to serve as the footings on which asset and deposit growth are based. How can bank insiders get minority shareholders to buy stock in the bank? The insiders, of course, have every incentive to sell shares, because doing so reduces their exposure in the event that the autocrat decides to expropriate them or reduce their rents by reneging on the privileges he has granted. The problem is that the prospective minority shareholders also know this! Furthermore, they know that, to the degree that bank insiders have interests in nonfinancial enterprises, their incentive is to lend to those companies (typically on concessionary terms) rather than to their competitors. In addition, minority shareholders know that in an economic crisis, insider borrowers will not face harsh enforcement of loan contracts from their parent banks and thus will have strong incentives to default on their loans—a subject to which we return shortly. In short, the minority shareholders face a problem of expropriation from both the autocrat and the insiders, via concessionary insider lending and weak enforcement of insider delinquencies. Worse, they know that because the insiders are in a coalition with the autocrat, he may allow the insiders to expropriate the minority shareholders with impunity!

These problems are predictable, given the rules of the game, and minority shareholders will demand some form of *expected compensation* for the risk of double expropriation. That compensation must take the form of a high expected rate of return on their investment. For the bank to afford to pay that return to its stockholders, the special privileges awarded by the autocrat must be very lucrative indeed.

A competitively structured banking system will not emerge under these circumstances because it is not optimal from the standpoint of the autocrat or the bankers. In the presence of high expropriation risk, the high returns demanded by stockholders constrain entry and the growth of the system. A system that grants special licenses and privileges to favored bank insiders and restricts entry as part of a larger deal between bank insiders and the autocrat will generally arise. This deal provides a constant flow of a portion of the rents to the government, giving the autocrat a vested interest in the favored banks and thereby reducing the risk of expropriation. That reduced risk allows the banking system to be larger and less risky than it would be if the autocrat did not possess such a vested interest, and the gains of that improvement accrue as rents to the insiders and the autocrat.

The combination of constraints that characterizes the banking system of a centralized autocracy, therefore, produces a coalition of interests composed of three parties: the autocrat, the minority shareholders, and the bank insiders. The autocrat receives a steady source of public finance (directed credit, reserve requirements, bribes, and taxes) and a source of occasional emergency funding (various forms of expropriation in times of fiscal stress). The bank insiders earn rents, first as high-paid bank managers in a noncompetitive market and second through the above-normal returns they earn from owning nonfinancial enterprises that benefit from low interest charges on bank loans and special access to credit (advantages that also serve as barriers to competition from other firms). The minority shareholders earn compensation in the form of above-normal stock returns for the double-expropriation risk they face.

Within this arrangement, what is the function of the state as a regulator and supervisor of banking-system activities? Why, if there are just the three parties to the coalition and a few favored banks, does the autocrat bother with banking regulations? The answer is that a framework of banking laws and regulations saves the parties to the coalition from having to bargain continually over the distribution of rents. The regulations also serve as a means of signaling to potential bank competitors that they cannot compete with the favored insiders, because the laws are written in such a way as to make it nearly impossible to get a bank charter, and if they do get one, the regulators have ways of making them regret it!

The small and risky banking system that arises under centralized autocracy requires the participation of a third party: depositors. Bank depositors are in search of a low-risk, liquid means of saving. In a well-developed banking system, depositors tend to be highly selective, demanding a positive real return on their deposits and intolerant of any significant risk. In democracies, the competitive process generally results in positive returns and low risk of loss on bank deposits, although risks and returns vary across countries and time. But in a centralized autocratic banking system—where returns to equity holders must be high, loans to insider firms are subsidized, governments and bank insiders extract significant rents, and periodic fiscal crises result in expropriation—providing depositors with a positive real return on a low-risk deposit is much more challenging. How can depositors be induced to put their cash in the bank under these conditions?

One possibility is that government will try to protect depositors with taxpayer-financed deposit insurance. But the scale of that protection is inherently limited by the fiscal resources of the autocrat: governments that rely on banks as a primary means of fiscal support cannot simultaneously tax depositors and subsidize them! Thus deposit insurance cannot create a deep financial system within a centralized autocracy.

For the most part, therefore, depositors simply are not attracted to banks in a centralized autocratic banking system. Deposits in such systems often earn negative real returns and are subject to substantial risk of loss. In these systems, many depositors stay out of the formal financial system, holding foreign currency or commodities or other forms of wealth in lieu of bank deposits. But some deposit funds are still supplied to banks. After all, firms have to maintain bank balances to cover payrolls and accounts receivable, and some households must maintain minimal bank balances in order to execute certain payments. The transactions costs and legal constraints of avoiding the deposit market are prohibitively high for some purposes. A manufacturing firm in Zimbabwe, for example, cannot, as a practical matter, pay its workers with checks drawn on a bank in Ontario, Canada, and those workers cannot pay their phone bills with a check drawn on a bank in New York. In short, some depositors are trapped (in what economists describe as a situation of highly inelastic demand).

The implications of trapped depositors reinforce the tendency of the banks to allocate credit to the autocrat and the insiders. Precisely because they earn less than they would through alternative investments, depositors put no more of their liquid wealth into the banking system than they have to. Relative to the size of the economy, the deposit base is small. In consequence, the banks have little need to search for new lending opportunities beyond the credit already granted to the autocrat and the insiders. A small group of insiders controls all the bank credit in this society.

Now for the really bad news: this system of underdeveloped banks and scarce credit is self-reinforcing. Despite the lack of credit available to firms with highly profitable investment opportunities, the supply of credit tends not to improve. Even informal, nonbank moneylenders have a hard time supplementing the supply of credit in this repressed financial system because centralized autocratic banking systems also tend not to develop the legal foundations that would permit successful arm's-length lending to occur.

Whether institutions that ensure the enforcement of arm's-length loans can emerge depends on the preferences of the political coalition that runs the banking system. Banks and moneylenders develop costly systems of internal credit analysis only when they have to make loans to unrelated parties. Credit reporting services develop only when banks are willing to pay for them, which is to say when banks need to be able to sanction debtors with the threat of destroying their reputations in the case of default. Efficient property and commercial registers, which are necessary to credibly offer collateral that creditors would be able to repossess on borrowers' default, develop only when there is sufficient politically empowered demand for them. The same is true of honest police and judges. In short, the institutions that enforce contract rights are expensive to create and maintain. If banks do not need them because they do not need to make arm's-length loans, such institutions are not likely to emerge.

In centralized autocratic banking systems, not only are banks unwilling to incur costs to facilitate their participation in arm's-length lending, but they may actively oppose the creation of improved legal and informational institutions that would facilitate such financing by others. The reason is not hard to divine: any improvements in the institutions that permit arm's-length financing would erode the rents enjoyed by the banker's own nonfinancial firms by virtue of their privileged access to credit. In Mexico in 1995, for example, one of us was involved in an initiative to improve the registration of collateral interests in inventories and accounts receivable (which is routine under the United States Uniform Commercial Code registration procedures). That initiative, championed by the World Bank and other advisors, did not receive the support of Mexico's insider-lending banks. Not until those banks collapsed and were purchased by foreign banks were significant reforms of collateral registration adopted.

Not only does the autocratic, crony banking system allocate credit narrowly, it also tends to be unstable. One cause of instability is the lack of constraints on the autocrat's authority and discretion. During normal times he receives rents from the banking system from a variety of explicit or implicit taxes on banks, including forced lending to the government and nonremunerative reserves at the central bank. If, however, the autocrat requires finance in excess of what he can generate from taxation, he has an incentive to expropriate the banks. This is a desperate move, because the autocrat is forgoing loans tomorrow in exchange for a one-time infusion of cash today. The advantage of this move, however, is that it may allow the autocrat to live to see tomorrow.

A second cause of instability is the propensity of the bank insiders to lend to their own nonfinancial enterprises. During an economic crisis, the insiders may have incentives to loot their own banks to save those enterprises. The reason is simple, and the phenomenon has been extensively studied: the insiders have all of the control rights in the bank (because they run it), but they have only a portion of its cash-flow rights (because much of the money earned by the bank is paid to depositors and minority shareholders). To the extent that they have greater cash-flow rights in their other enterprises than they do in the bank—which is almost certainly the case because the bank, by design, minimizes the insiders' investment exposure—the insiders will be inclined to use the bank to rescue their other enterprises when times get hard. That is, they will make loans to their other enterprises and then default on those loans.[16] Not surpris-

---

[16] See Akerlof and Romer (1993); La Porta et al. (1997, 1998); Rajan and Zingales (1998); Johnson et al. (2000a); Johnson et al. (2000b); Laeven (2001); Bae, Kang, and Kim (2002); Mitton (2002); Habyarimana (2010); La Porta, López-de-Silanes, and Zamarripa (2003).

ingly, there is a strong empirical relationship connecting weak rule of law (which is to say countries governed by autocrats), insider lending, and slow credit growth.[17]

When stripped of all of the institutional complexities, the political deal that shapes bank risk-taking decisions and loss allocations under centralized autocracy can be seen as a rent-distribution system. The allocation of rents varies over time. At times when the autocrat's hold on power is tenuous and his very survival is at stake, his fiscal needs are so great that his best move is often to expropriate the banking system via some combination of high taxation, mandated loans to the state, high reserve requirements at the central bank, and nationalization of bank ownership. Expropriation makes all bank claimants—even politically powerful insiders —potential sources of government rent extraction. Minority shareholders and insiders must be compensated for this risk. They earn unusually high positive returns in normal times to compensate for the extremely negative returns from expropriation.

The large number of excluded debtors is a constant source of rent extraction. Through their exclusion from the credit system, as the result of the entry barriers that are necessary to provide high returns to bank shareholders during normal times, they suffer lost investment opportunities and competitive disadvantages.

Depositors are also a source of rent extraction for the other players in the banking game under centralized autocracy. In regimes both with and without deposit insurance, depositors are trapped and earn low or negative real returns. Depositors often are expropriated by fiscally strained governments despite de jure deposit insurance. This expropriation can take various forms, including inflating away the value of deposits by expanding the money supply or by "redenominating" deposits (see chapter 10).

Taxpayers are a source of rent extraction from the banking system only when there is deposit insurance or government bailouts of banks. During expropriations, taxpayers suffer substantial losses as the result of transfers to depositors and to the autocrat, with the exact proportions determined by the extent to which the autocrat expropriates the depositors.

[17] See Cull, Haber, and Imai (2011).

Thus the political institutions of autocracy generate a bank credit market far from any notion of allocative efficiency. Competition in the credit market is limited, as affiliates of bank insiders receive favored and subsidized access to finance. The market does not allocate credit broadly because the suppliers of credit do not benefit from its doing so. Talented entrepreneurs and hard-working families are starved for credit while a few cronies of the bank insiders are awash in funds. The system is small and inherently prone to crises: periodically, the insiders expropriate the minority shareholders and the depositors, and occasionally the autocrat expropriates everyone.

Those observing the realities of autocratic, crony banking systems for the first time may be outraged by their crony political bargains and their fragile, thin, and inefficient banks. These arrangements are likely to contradict readers' notions of fairness and incite them to decry their inherent inefficiencies and their disastrous implications for economic growth and social mobility. But these characteristics are not failures of the system. Rather, they are inherent in its design. Repressed banking systems are far from optimal, but they may be the best that the societies that create them can do under the political circumstances.

Weakly Centralized Autocratic Government and Inflation Machines

It takes a strong central government to run a national network of rent-sharing partnerships. Such partnerships imply that, if he wanted to, the autocrat could expropriate all of the banks. Often, however, autocrats do not have this kind of power. Indeed, many autocrats need the wealthy in their societies as much as, or more than, the wealthy need them. A banking system cannot exist, however, without legal institutions that make contracts enforceable, and the autocrat can certainly influence their creation and operation. In such cases, the autocrat may use his monopoly control over those institutions—particularly the currency system—to sustain his government by imposing an inflation tax.

Inflation taxation uses control of the means of payment (currency and deposits) to tax common citizens. The inflation tax is unique because, unlike direct taxes on income or wealth, it permits the government to levy a tax on people who own no significant property and earn almost nothing. We examine inflation taxes in considerable detail in chapters 11–13, but for now let us simply make clear how they generate income both for governments and banks.

Imagine that rather than taxing anyone, the government simply prints money as it needs it, so that over time increasing amounts of paper bills are chasing the same amount of goods and services. The result is inflation, and inflation automatically devalues assets held as cash. The government is, in essence, taxing the public, but it does so silently and automatically, by making the cash in their pockets (or stuffed into their mattresses) worth less with each passing day: yesterday, the dollar in my pocket bought a loaf a bread, but today that same dollar buys only half a loaf. Making the inflation tax more attractive still to an autocrat, the taxpayers may not even realize that they are being taxed. Indeed, the autocrat can pretend to be helping the poor the whole time that he is insidiously taxing them, by providing well-advertised government welfare programs financed through the inflation tax.

From the point of view of an oligarchy that shares power with an autocrat, the inflation tax is a rather neat trick. Rich people tend to hold much of their wealth in assets other than cash, and those assets tend to hold their value against inflation. Such assets include real estate, yachts, art collections, gold coins, foreign currencies, corporate securities, and the like. A very large proportion of the meager assets of the poor, in contrast, is in their pockets, in the form of cash. As a consequence, the burden of the inflation tax falls disproportionately on the poor.

Making the trick neater still, bankers and bank shareholders typically share in the revenues from the inflation tax. A society's medium of payment is actually held in two forms: currency (i.e., the money in people's pockets) and demand deposits (the money in checking accounts). The exact split of the inflation tax between the government and the banks is determined by several factors: the rate of inflation, whether the government or the banks issue the currency, the interest rate the central bank pays to banks on their reserves, the legally permissible interest rate on demand deposits, and the deposit-reserve ratio (the proportion of demand deposits that banks must place in the central bank). We return to these details in chapters 11–13 (discussing Mexico and Brazil), but for now, in the interest of fixing intuition, consider the simplest rent-sharing arrangement. Imagine that when the government needs to meet its expenses, it simply prints money. Assume that checking accounts pay zero interest (as is common around the world) and (unrealistically) that the government does not require that banks place any of their deposit base in the central bank.[18] Under these simplified assumptions, at each point in time the government earns inflation-tax revenues equal to the stock of cash multiplied by the rate of inflation, and the banks earn inflation-tax revenues equal to the balances of checking accounts multiplied by the rate of inflation.

When inflation is high, businesses and households try to keep their cash holdings and their deposit balances to the minimum needed as a means of paying for things. When inflation is very high, people transfer funds into checking accounts only for brief periods in order to write checks to make payments. Thus inflation erodes the value of checking-account balances only for the short period that the check is in transit (known as the period of float), and the inflation tax largely takes the form of a tax on the value of checks in the process of being collected (which we refer to in figure 2.1 as a tax on float banking). Nevertheless, if the rate of inflation is high enough, this practice can generate staggering amounts of revenue.

There must be a downside to this particular form of bank-government partnership, otherwise high inflation taxation would be ubiquitous. There are, in fact, several problems associated with inflation taxation. First, high inflation tends to hinder economic growth because it disrupts the ability of people to use markets: it is hard to write contracts or even to shop intelligently (which requires comparing prices and planning purchases) if prices are moving very fast. Second, high inflation induces the public to reduce their holdings of currency and deposits. This reduces the funds available for banks to lend to firms and households, which further reduces the economy's rate of growth. Third, when the government's fiscal needs jump, it has incentives to increase its share of the inflation tax by raising the deposit-reserve requirement to the point that it may completely com-

---

[18] The autocrat would not be able to collect a substantial inflation tax if he permitted private banks to offer unregulated deposits, which would allow the public an alternative means of storing wealth that did not suffer continuous loss. Therefore, a bank-government partnership based on inflation taxation requires that the government use its regulatory authority to control bank operations, particularly the interest rates offered on various kinds of deposits and the deposit reserves that must be held in the central bank.

mandeer banks' deposit bases, thereby causing bank credit to firms and households to shrink even more and pushing banks toward insolvency by appropriating an important source of their revenue.

Local Oligarchies

Autocrat-banker partnerships based on the administration of an inflation tax imply some degree of political centralization: the autocrat must be able to enforce his will on the institutions that govern banking, most particularly currency issues, interest rates on deposits, and the deposit-reserve ratio. What happens if the autocrat has not obtained even that modest level of political centralization? What if he is so weak that the state is really little more than congeries of local oligarchies? Those local oligarchies generally prefer to maintain control over banking (why share anything with the autocrat that you do not absolutely have to?) so that whatever banking system exists will serve their local needs. The result is a fragmented banking system reminiscent of medieval times; local oligarchs make use of their local banks, but no one from outside that oligarchy—the autocrat included—has access to credit.

Democracy

Democracy implies three very big differences from autocracy in the way that the Game of Bank Bargains is played. First, the risk of expropriation of bankers, minority shareholders, and depositors by the government is lower than under autocracy. By definition, an autocrat has greater freedom of action than an elected official who faces the sanction of being removed in the next election. Second, under democracy, potential debtors are no longer passive bystanders to the game; they can vote for politicians who promise to increase the amount of credit or to improve the terms on which credit is granted. They can be members of the political coalition that creates and divides rents in banking. Third, inflation taxes are a rare outcome. Voters are unwilling to bear all of the costs associated with inflation taxation when a much easier solution to the problem of government finance is at hand: voting for candidates who promise to tax the income and wealth of people richer than they are.

Not all democracies, as William Riker famously pointed out, are created alike: there are crucial philosophical and practical distinctions between democracies based on liberal conceptions of voting and those based on populist conceptions of voting. Those differences, in our view, have powerful implications for both the strategies of play and the outcomes in the Game of Bank Bargains. We depict those differences in the lower section of figure 2.1; but before we explore them, we must say a few words about liberalism and populism.

Liberals, many of whom trace their intellectual origins to Britain's Enlightenment, and whose influence can be found in the writings of people such as James Madison, believe that the function of voting is to control officials, and no more. Elections allow voters to replace corrupt or venal public officials and thereby constrain tyranny. There is nothing inherently good, wise, or just about the choices made through voting. They are merely decisions, with no special moral character. Precisely because there is nothing magical, or even necessarily competent, about decisions made through mass suffrage, liberals believe that democracy functions best in the presence of ancillary institutions (e.g., multicameral legislatures, unelected judges who serve without limits on their terms, and decentralized political parties) that provide additional constraints on tyranny, *including the tyranny that may be created by a democratic majority*. These ancillary institutions make it difficult for a majority to reduce the rights of a minority—whether that minority consists of the citizens who voted against the majority in the last election, a racial or ethnic group, the aged, believers in a particular religion, or shareholders in banks—by forcing legislation to pass through "veto gates" (decision points at which legislation can be blocked by small groups, such as a congressional subcommittee or an upper house of a legislature) in which the minority may have strength beyond its numbers.[19] In the liberal conception of democracy, unless there are institutions that allow minorities to veto majorities, mass suffrage can, paradoxically, undermine the very goal of democracy—the existence of a free and just society.[20]

Populists, whose philosophical origins date back to Jean-Jacques Rousseau, have a very different view: they believe that the function of voting is to allow society to divine the popular will and that satisfying the popular

[19] The operative word here is *difficult*, as distinct from *impossible*. Nothing in the liberal conception of democracy decrees that the rights of all minorities will necessarily be respected. If a minority cannot find a way to take advantage of a veto gate, then its rights can be reduced.

[20] Riker (1982), especially 9–11, 245, 248–50.

will is a moral imperative: it is inherently right and should be respected by government and embodied in social policy. By logical extension, voters elect officials to represent the popular will. As a further logical extension, neither elected officials nor the people voting as a corporate entity can be oppressors: the liberal preoccupation with the tyranny of the majority is a fiction that elites use to frighten the population into giving them power beyond their numbers. In the populist conception, democracy does not need veto gates but rather quite the opposite: it requires as few institutional constraints on public officials as possible, because those restraints prevent them from embodying the popular will in law and policy. Populists therefore have a very different conception of freedom from liberals. In the liberal conception, freedom is enjoyed by individuals and is defined by the absence of tyranny; in the populist conception, freedom means the ability to use government to implement the collective will of the people.[21]

All democratic political systems contain both liberal and populist elements. The U.S. Constitution, for example, includes a number of provisions intended as bulwarks against the tyranny of office holders (e.g., impeachment and regularly scheduled elections) and against the tyranny of majorities (e.g., indirect election for the president and, until 1913, senators, as well as an unelected federal judiciary, and a bicameral legislature). This decidedly liberal constitution has always contended against a strong populist countercurrent. Indeed, the impetus for scrapping the Articles of Confederation and replacing them with the Constitution was Daniel Shays's populist rebellion of 1786. Some of America's founding fathers, most famously Thomas Jefferson, were sympathetic to some precepts of populism. In the 1820s, with the election of Andrew Jackson, populism became more pronounced. (Jackson even ignored a ruling of the Supreme Court because it was inconsistent with the popular will to expropriate the lands of Native Americans.) Various political movements and politicians have since tapped into this broad populist current in order to advance diverse personal and ideological goals. Prominent examples include William Jennings Bryan's Populist Party, Franklin Roosevelt's New Deal, Richard Nixon's "silent majority," former House speaker (and failed presidential candidate) Newt Gingrich's calls for the arrest of "activist judges," and the speeches of Barack Obama denouncing "Wall Street fat

[21] Riker (1982), especially 11, 14, 238, 245, 247, 249.

cats." The policy goals of these politicians and their movements vary widely, but they all share a common populist core: they present the common people as disadvantaged by elites; they present the popular will of the common people as morally superior; and they present themselves as the vehicle through which elite roadblocks can be pushed aside and the popular will can become policy.

Democratic systems vary in the degree to which their political institutions favor liberal or populist conceptions of democracy. In the world's older democracies—those established in the eighteenth and nineteenth centuries—liberal elements tend to carry considerable weight, because those democracies were set up as replacements for monarchic systems that were almost synonymous with tyranny. In democracies of more recent vintage, populist elements tend to carry more weight, because they tend to have been forged out of societies characterized by vast inequalities in human capital, income, and wealth. Citizens whose life opportunities have been systematically constrained have strong incentives to oppose institutions that give elites power beyond their numbers.

Liberalism

Democracies in which liberal political institutions dominate populist currents tend to make it difficult for the parties in control of the government to expropriate property of any kind. Because the incentives to create a crony banking system are thereby weakened, bankers and shareholders do not have to be compensated for the risk of government expropriation. Second, because suffrage allows voters to remove venal or corrupt officials, it is difficult to sustain crony deals.[22] Indeed, the incentives run in the opposite direction: citizens can vote for candidates who promise to open up the banking system to greater levels of competition, thereby increasing the amount of credit and reducing its cost. The net result is a banking system that tends toward efficiency and stability. The positive effects of this system, as the lower section of figure 2.1 depicts, are considerable: abundant and stable credit tends to favor both economic growth and a strong state.

---

[22] This is not to say that crony capitalism never exists in liberal democracies, but voters can end crony deals by replacing the politicians who make them.

Populism

A democratic political system in which the populist current overwhelms liberal institutions gives rise to a very different game. What is to keep debtors from voting for representatives who promise to dramatically increase the supply of credit, improve the terms on which it is offered, and then forgive those debts when they prove difficult to repay? When populism dominates liberalism in shaping democratic institutions, the parties in control of the government may be unlikely to expropriate banks outright, but they may have strong incentives to help debtors do so.

Mitigating the threats posed by populism is difficult. Promises made by elected public officials to enforce the property rights of banks in relation to their debtors are not credible: inevitably there are occasions when politicians must make banks forgive debts, or get voted out of office. To make matters easier, public officials can avail themselves of all kinds of vaguely positive euphemisms, such as "mortgage relief act," and "debtor protection law." Whatever they choose to call the practice, the outcome is the same: in the short run, debtor relief often destabilizes the banking system by undermining creditors' property rights; and in the longer run banks simply extend less credit, because they know that they are vulnerable to expropriation by debtors in coalition with politicians.

We come back to the issue of populism's influence on banking systems as a matter of history in chapters 5–8 and 13, but here we note briefly that one frequently employed solution is for the parties in control of the government to construct a massive welfare state with nationalized housing, nationalized industries, and lifetime job security for workers. Under these circumstances, there is no need for the parties in control of the government to help debtors expropriate banks. This "solution" may come at a cost, of course, perhaps in the form of a lower overall level of productivity, but from the point of view of bankers it beats the alternative. At least they are no longer in the line of fire.[23]

When the welfare-state solution to the problem of populism is not feasible (because it is blocked either by low taxation capacity or by strongly federal political institutions that impede national policies of any type),

---

[23] If that productivity decline is sufficiently great, however, a popular backlash in favor of privatization and bank liberalization is a possibility. As we discuss in chapter 5, this occurred in Great Britain after the mid-1980s.

bankers have another, somewhat perverse option: they can join the populists in a coalition in favor of debtor relief! Doing so puts them in a position to ask for a government bailout in the short run and deposit insurance in the longer run. Both measures transfer the losses associated with debt forgiveness away from banks and onto taxpayers. In the even longer run, the bankers and populists can craft a deal to create and share rents. In that partnership, bankers share decision making about to whom they should lend, and on what terms, with politicians, who then make sure that their constituents get the credit they desire. In return, politicians compensate bankers by crafting regulations that increase their rate of return on capital. Examples include laws that constrain competition, allow banks to operate with high levels of leverage by substituting a government-run deposit insurance safety net for a shareholder-financed capital cushion, and provide taxpayer-financed subsidies or guarantees for risky loans to politically crucial constituencies. This partnership, of course, comes at a cost to everyone else in society, who must pay higher interest rates on loans, earn lower interest rates on deposits, and enjoy less access to credit than they would have otherwise. If you think that all this is just a theoretical abstraction, we encourage you to jump forward to the chapters on the United States.

From Static Comparisons to a Dynamic Conception of the State and Its Banks

In considering the central question of why banks need states, this chapter offers explanations, based in the logic of the property rights of banking and of political coalition formation, for some of the key puzzles about dysfunctional banking raised in chapter 1. Persistent credit scarcity and bank instability can be understood as equilibrium outcomes of the Game of Bank Bargains, resulting from particular sets of political institutions within which banking systems are constructed. Autocracies tend to produce scarce and unstable systems of bank credit. Democracies tend to produce banking systems with more abundant credit, but not necessarily stable ones.

These comparisons across regimes, of course, do not explain why and how autocratic modern states emerged, how they became democracies over time, or how banks helped propel that historical process forward.

Importantly, the political evolution that resulted first in autocratic and later in democratic versions of the modern state itself depended crucially on the existence of banks as tools of state building: banks were and are consciously employed by the group in control of the government to assist them in their competition with other states. That coevolution of banking and the structure of the modern state is the subject of chapter 3.

3

||||||||||||||||||||||||

Tools of Conquest and Survival
Why States Need Banks

A government that robs Peter to pay Paul
can always depend on the support of Paul.

George Bernard Shaw (1944)

Every nation-state has some form of government-chartered bank. Communist states have them. Democracies and autocracies have them. Even the sleaziest kleptocracies have them. The one exception proves the rule: Somalia, from 1990 to 2011, had no chartered banks. By then, however, it had ceased to be a functioning state; before its political collapse, it too had chartered banks.[1] Even states without armies—Costa Rica, for example—and those that do not tax the income, wealth, or consumption of their citizens—like Kuwait—still have chartered banks.[2]

Why are banks so essential to statehood that they are more ubiquitous than armies or taxes? Chartered banks and nation-states emerged as organizational forms at the same time, roughly the period since 1600. This was not a coincidence. Rather, the two institutions coevolved because banks helped to align the incentives of the three groups crucial to the cre-

---

[1] Tellingly, one of the first acts of Somalia's Transitional Federal Government was the creation of the Central Bank of Somalia in 2011; see Central Bank of Somalia (2011). On the continuing weakness of the government of Somalia, see McGroarty (2013).

[2] On Costa Rica, see Horvik and Aas (1981). Kuwait has no individual income tax, no inheritance or gift tax, no sales tax, and no value-added tax. It has a corporate profits tax, but this was put in place at the request of foreign oil companies who wished to receive tax credits in their home countries for the oil royalties they pay the Kuwaiti government. To the degree that Kuwaiti citizens pay any taxes, they do so via an excise on petroleum consumption and indirectly through a 4 percent tariff on imported goods, from which food products are exempt. These taxes typically account for less than 3 percent of total government revenue. Almost all revenue is derived from oil production. Baker (1986), 144–46.

ation of a viable state: rulers, merchants, and financiers. Merchants needed a powerful entity—a state—that could defend their expanding trading routes and enforce their increasingly complex contracts. Rulers needed merchants to build the commercial networks that glued their states together and sustained their overseas empires. Both merchants and rulers needed financiers: the merchants needed them to create and manage the financial instruments necessary to carry out trade at a distance, and the rulers needed them to provide the funds necessary to fight the seemingly endless wars involved in building viable states. The financiers, for their part, needed a state to enforce contracts with one another, with the merchants, and with foreign states. Aligning the incentives of these three groups was not an easy task. When the dust settled, however, a number of remarkable financial innovations had occurred. At their center stood the chartered bank: a joint-stock company owned by financiers that financed both trade and the state, in exchange for which the state provided the bank with a set of valuable privileges.

Once the modern chartered bank had been created, rulers learned how to use it to align the incentives of other groups that were essential to the maintenance of political order. During the nineteenth and twentieth centuries, they figured out how to deploy banks to direct credit to firms owned by their political allies, to channel finance to industries that employed key political constituencies, to smooth fluctuations in business cycles that created unemployment (and hence political discontent), and to subsidize a broad range of programs that aligned the incentives of citizens with the existing political order, such as credit for small businesses, student loans, and mortgage-guarantee programs that supported home ownership. In short, modern chartered banks evolved as states evolved: monarchs in seventeenth- and eighteenth-century Europe needed them to finance trade and war, and modern autocracies and democracies need them to help sustain the political order.

Origins of the "Modern World"

Historians define the "modern world" as the organizational structure of European society that arose to replace the medieval, feudal system that had governed European affairs from the ninth through the fifteenth centuries. Feudalism was a decentralized political structure overseeing primarily agrarian economies. Particular locations were linked politically and militarily through hierarchies of horse-riding, armor-clad nobles. Thousands of local European nobles held sway over small pieces of territory, which they defended from their castles and which produced sufficient surplus to finance the courts and military expenses of the feudal system.

By the sixteenth century, that decentralized organizational structure had begun to give way to a centralized structure of a few dominant European nation-states. Centralization began earlier in some countries than in others; Britain, France, Spain, Portugal, and the Dutch Republic became nations centuries before Germany and Italy, where the consolidation of political power continued until the latter half of the nineteenth century.

The demise of feudalism and the emergence of powerful nation-states reflected two parallel and mutually reinforcing developments: the military ability to conquer and defend territory and trade routes and the economic ability to construct and manage far-flung trading networks. States had to be able to exert centralized control over territory to a degree not seen since the demise of the Roman Empire while also being able to reach across oceans to conquer and trade with other continents, from which they received precious metals, sugar, coffee, tea, tobacco, and other valuable merchandise.

The emergence of nation-states with global reach was an extraordinarily competitive and violent process in which patience, neutrality, and passivity were not rewarded. War was endemic: budding nations had to conquer their neighbors or be conquered. Consider the Dutch Republic. From 1568 to 1648 it fought the Eighty Years' War against Spain for its political independence. It simultaneously fought in the pan-European Thirty Years' War from 1618 to 1648. The Treaty of Westphalia, which ended both wars, did not bring peace to the Dutch. No sooner did they obtain independence from Spain than they fought a series of wars against England for control of trade routes. Wars raged from 1652 to 1654, from 1665 to 1667, and then again from 1672 to 1674. Coincident with this third naval war against England, the Dutch had to face off against the French and a group of allied states, which included Sweden and Spain, in the Franco-Dutch war of 1672–78. The Dutch fought the French again from 1688 to 1697 in the War of the League of Augsburg. Soon thereafter they were drawn into the War of Spanish Succession, which stretched from 1701 to 1714, and in the 1740s they were drawn in to the protracted War of Austrian Succession. When you add it up, the Dutch Republic was at war on and off for nearly 150 years.[3]

Most of the competitors in Europe's intensely violent process of state building did not survive.[4] The earlier forms of political organization—the hundreds of duchies, principalities, and city-states—were obliterated, surviving to the present only as idiosyncratic legal conveniences (the Principality of Monaco, for example, seems to exist mainly in order to skirt French gaming laws) or as linguistic relics (e.g., the English word *county,* which initially referred to a jurisdiction under the sovereignty of a count but which now refers to various entities, including an administrative subdivision of a U.S. state). The Kingdom of France absorbed Burgundy and Brittany. The kingdoms of Castile and Aragon were joined in marriage and then absorbed adjoining regions, creating the country that we call Spain. England absorbed Cornwall, Wales, and Scotland and conquered Ireland, ultimately consolidating political control within a single parliament through the Act of Union in 1707. Modern Russia grew from a small territory, centered in Moscow, to include Ukraine, Kazakhstan, Azerbaijan, Georgia, and Siberia. Non-European societies that were governed by older and less efficient forms of political organization—dynastic empires, mini-kingdoms, or tribes, such as those found in Latin America, West Africa, and Central Asia—fell prey to the new global powerhouses.

What caused this dramatic political and economic transformation? A broad range of innovations in shipbuilding, navigation, and the tools of warfare came together beginning in the sixteenth century, transforming the capabilities of armies and navies and enabling conquest and trade on a global scale.[5] These breakthroughs included the compass, the astrolabe and quadrant (used to measure latitude), the "Great Invention" of the carrack—a three-masted ship that combined the advantages of lateen and

---

[3] For a perspective on the connections among Dutch war, finance, and political economy, including a skeptical view of the so-called Dutch tulip mania, see Garber (2000).

[4] Spruyt (1994).

[5] Of course, the modern world was not a mechanistic consequence of the development of military, shipbuilding, and navigation technologies. Advanced gunpowder, shipbuilding, and navigation technologies were developed centuries earlier in China, but China did not exploit them to build a global empire. Historians attribute China's decision not to pursue global conquest to its political structure and geography, which limited its external ambitions, in contrast to those of European sovereigns. See E. Jones (1981), Mokyr (1990), and Landes (1999).

square sails—the carvel construction technique for shipbuilding, the cannon, the harquebus, the musket, the telescope, various mathematical advances in navigation (especially trigonometry), and numerous incremental improvements in shipbuilding, geographical knowledge, and weaponry.[6] Europeans now had the capacity to trade on a scale that was previously unimaginable. They also had an unprecedented capacity to kill other people. Together, these capacities enabled European political entrepreneurs to centralize power, in the process creating an entity that we call the nation-state. They could then use the organizational capabilities of that state to project their power across the globe.

An ambitious ruler looking to build a state—and, beyond that, a trade-based empire—needed more than access to technology: he needed people and funds en masse. Not only did he need to finance a military force, but he also had to build a lasting network of occupation and trade. Thus, to succeed against his rivals he had to form alliances with multiple long-term partners—soldiers, sailors, settlers, merchants, and financiers—and do it faster than his competitors. Successful rulers quickly harnessed their ambitions to a set of effective and durable institutions that allowed them to forge lasting partnerships. Those who were slow to do so saw their militaries defeated, their trade networks diminished, and their proto-states turned into provinces of some more clever ruler's state. Especially slow learners might find their heads on pikes.[7]

Two factors appear to have been crucial in determining which states emerged as dominant: access to the Atlantic and the ability to forge durable partnerships with the social and economic groups that carried out trade and financed the state. The Atlantic was the gateway to the lucrative trade in slaves, precious metals, spices, silks, and other commodities that linked Europe, West Africa, the Americas, and Asia. A lack of access to the Atlantic probably explains why the city-states of Venice and Genoa, which

---

[6] For the detailed histories of these technological changes and others, see Jones (1981), Mokyr (1990), Landes (1999, 2000), and J. Diamond (1997).

[7] Some institutions were political (e.g., parliaments or courts), some were economic (e.g., chartered joint-stock companies), and some were social (e.g., religious affiliations, like the new Protestant groups that allied themselves closely with the state). In saying that these institutions were durable, we do not mean to suggest that they were perfectly reliable or set in stone; we mean that the institutions embodied advantages that made membership valuable and thus made alliances costly to reverse.

had been trading and financial powerhouses during the medieval period, failed to keep up with the state- and empire-building enterprises of Spain, Portugal, France, Britain, and the Dutch Republic.

The governments of some emerging nation-states, particularly England and the Dutch Republic, were able to pull further ahead of their rivals by establishing partnerships with merchants and financiers. These partnerships gave those groups considerable political power; particularly by creating parliaments that had to approve government spending and taxation.[8] They also gave merchants and financiers the ability to influence the nature of government debt contracts and the chartering of special corporations dedicated to the expansion of trade and empire, which explains in large part why the Dutch and the British, despite their late starts at empire building, were able to supplant Spain and Portugal as the world's dominant powers by the early eighteenth century.

A series of financial innovations came together in the late seventeenth century, producing the first chartered banks—privately owned joint-stock companies operating under special concession that financed long-distance trade and managed government debt. The chartered bank was not invented overnight: it was the outcome of a long series of institutional experiments, including the invention of new kinds of contracts, such as debt annuities and bills of exchange, and the creation of new forms of property ownership, such as the joint-stock company. Let us trace briefly the trajectory of each of these institutions and see how they were ultimately combined to create the chartered bank.

Innovations in Sovereign-Debt Contracts

Prior to the modern age, monarchs relied on loans from private bankers to fund their wars. When wars did not go well, rulers often defaulted on those loans, sometimes resulting in the failures of the lending bankers. As late as 1672, Britain's Charles II's "stop of the Exchequer" bankrupted many of London's private "goldsmith bankers" who had lent to the crown.

The increased scale and frequency of modern warfare made the fiscal situation more desperate still. Rulers had to find new ways to make their

---

[8] North and Weingast (1989); Barzel and Kiser (2002); Stasavage (2003). For a summary of the literature, see Acemoglu, Johnson, and Robinson (2005).

debts attractive to a broad range of holders. This was not easy, mainly because they were so powerful. How do you make the party in control of the guns and the law pay you back if he doesn't want to? Anticipating that problem, why lend to him in the first place? The problem becomes greater as the amount of debt grows and the strains on the tax system to fund debt increase. Given the importance to European rulers of financing war, creating a reliable means of paying sovereign debt was vital.

Among the first solutions to this problem was the creation of a new form of annuity debt, so called because rulers committed themselves to pay a perpetual annuity to the debt holder. Hapsburg Spain seems to have been the first nation to establish a permanent funded national debt in the sixteenth-century. That practice reflected its predecessor regimes' public-debt structures from late-medieval Catalonia (Aragon) and Castile. In 1489, the monarchs Ferdinand and Isabella sold a series of hereditary, perpetual, redeemable *juros de heredad* to finance the war that led to the federal union of Castile, Aragon, and Navarre in 1492.[9] Charles V relied heavily on this type of debt to raise money from creditors in the Hapsburg (southern) Netherlands in 1542, and it was soon copied by others. In order to make these annuity contracts credible to purchasers, as well as more liquid, they boasted five crucial features: they were perpetual; they were heritable; they came with regular coupon payments; they gave debt holders, even foreigners, stronger legal rights; and they came with fiscal reforms, such as dedicating the revenues from particular taxes to coupon payments, thereby making repayment more likely.[10]

There were also financial innovations that created new organizational forms on the buying side of the market, specifically the creation of networks of debt holders, who coordinated with one another in making bond purchases. By sharing information and punishing defaults collec-

---

[9] Drelichman (2013); Munro (2013).

[10] The Hapsburg innovation built upon the earlier demonstrated success of the debt-management practices of various Italian city-states. Venice had shown the benefits that sovereigns could gain from credible repayment, even to foreigners, when it extended such protections even to investors in Genoa (Pezzolo [2013]), and debt innovations also played a central role in the development of the Duchy of Milan (de Luca [2013]). Similarly, papal debt during the late medieval period was long-term and enjoyed a reputation for consistent servicing, nondiscrimination, and credible tax backing until the Napoleonic Wars destroyed the revenue base of the papacy (Caselli [2013]).

tively, they prevented rulers from strategically defaulting on them serially: a default on one debt holder would cause all the rest to refuse to purchase new debt offerings. Rulers would act in good faith because they were dealing with a united coalition of lenders. For example, Philip II of Spain had to rely on the services of Genoese bankers to pay his troops and naval forces, using their networks of correspondents throughout the Mediterranean and in northern Europe. When his revenues failed to cover his debt obligations, he became a serial defaulter, but the Genoese bankers, acting in concert, forced him to collateralize his short-term debts (called *asientos*) with longer-term and resalable *juros*, which were backed by specific taxes collected by the bankers or their agents. The Genoese also forced him to offer other contractual contingencies that limited their losses in the event of default. The debts were sold downstream by the Genoese to the many participants in their financial network, and the Genoese typically retained only fractions of the original debts. Ultimately, however, the accumulated expenses of the Thirty Years' War left Spain's central finances so damaged that even the ingenuity and cohesiveness of the Genoese bankers were not enough to protect creditors.[11]

The English and the Dutch were far more successful than the Spanish in stabilizing their public debt markets during the challenging seventeenth and eighteenth centuries. For the Dutch, successful debt management resulted largely from the effective collection of taxes.[12] In England, the Glorious Revolution of 1688 brought reforms that gave Parliament control over taxation and spending, decreasing the probability of sovereign default.[13] These changes reflected the fact that debt holders sat in Parliament and were able to form coalitions with other interest groups.[14] This was only part of the story, however. As we discuss in detail in chapter 4, the British hit upon another crucial innovation: the use of joint-stock companies as a form of public-private partnership for the management of government debts. They thereby brought together two financial innovations —annuities and joint-stock companies—creating a new type of institution,

---

[11] Drelichman and Voth (2008, 2010, 2011a,b) and Drelichman (2013).
[12] Gelderblom and Jonker (2013).
[13] North and Weingast (1989).
[14] Stasavage (2003).

a chartered bank designed to restructure sovereign debts and reduce their servicing costs.[15]

Joint-Stock Companies

Rulers had strong incentives to build trade-based empires: the bigger the empire, the more resources the ruler could command, and the more likely he could defeat rival rulers. Empire building, however, was itself an expensive undertaking. Europe's rulers therefore built empires by subcontracting much of the business of conquest, colonization, and trade to private companies. Indeed, the conquests of the Aztec and Inca empires had been carried out by private companies: the conquistadors were shareholders, most of whom had never swung a sword before.[16] These early companies were not perpetual in nature: they were liquidated as soon as the job of conquest was completed and the shareholders had divided up the spoils. Over time, however, rulers, merchants, and men with military skills for administering conquest refined these arrangements so that they would all, in the long run, be better off. The result was the creation of a joint-stock exploration and trading company with special monopoly rights over particular areas of the world.

A charter from the ruler not only helped stockholders and company managers maintain their monopoly, but the joint-stock form of their enterprise also made it easier to share profits, govern the firm, and trade shares. The first of these trading companies, the British East India Company (1600), was imitated quickly through the creation of other privileged joint-stock companies, such as the Dutch East and West India Companies (1602 and 1621), England's Hudson Bay Company (1670), and France's Mississippi Company (1684). Shares in these companies became the basis for the world's first stock markets. Over the next two centuries,

---

[15] The fiscal reforms emphasized by North and Weingast (1989) are probably best seen as a continuation of long-term improvements in domestic public finances (especially the excise tax of 1643 and other reforms during the period 1660–88, which eliminated tax farming and improved incentives and efficiency of collection). For more details, see Coffman (2013) and Coffman, Leonard, and Neal (2013). Murphy (2009) also shows that the creation of widely held lottery tickets and other sovereign debt encouraged public support for increased taxes to underwrite debt repayment during and after the 1690s.

[16] Lockhart (1972).

the joint-stock form of ownership gradually evolved into the structure that most large firms take today, the limited liability corporation.

Once rulers hit upon the idea of the chartered, joint-stock company as a way to finance the creation of an overseas empire, they realized that they could sell monopoly charters for a broad range of other activities of state. They could, in effect, carve the business of state into separate franchises, each of which was given particular, valuable privileges. Companies could be granted the rights to run a lottery, collect taxes (a practice known as tax farming), collect bridge or highway tolls, or—importantly for our purposes—operate a bank that served as the ruler's fiscal agent, holding the taxes collected in various parts of the country, paying his bills, and managing his debt issues.

Chartered Banks and Sovereign Debt

Much like the other financial innovations that underpinned the modern nation-state, the idea of a government-chartered bank, which would enjoy unique privileges in exchange for furthering the goals of the state, had deep roots. Rulers have been borrowing money from bankers for as long as rulers and money have existed. During the medieval era, when the scale of political entities—kingdoms, duchies, and city-states—was small, rulers borrowed from private bankers. As the scale of borrowing increased and the catastrophic implications of a sovereign default were magnified, however, these private banking houses gradually became less important in the business of state finance. Indeed, sovereign defaults wiped out many of the private banking houses of Europe. Private bankers, of course, persisted; some, such as the House of Rothschild, still exist today. To survive in the new environment of the modern world, however, these holdovers from the Renaissance model of private banking had to adapt: either they became shareholders in the new chartered banks, or they began to specialize in new types of financial intermediation (such as brokering mergers of nonfinancial firms) that relied more on their human capital as organizers of networks than on their financial capital, morphing over time into an entity that we call an investment bank.[17]

---

[17] See Flandreau (2003); Flandreau and Flores (2009); Flandreau et al. (2010, 2013); Ferguson (1998a,b); Strouse (1999); DeLong (1991); Ramirez (1995); Pak (2013).

The earliest example of a chartered bank's serving as a fiscal device of state was the Banco di San Giorgio of Genoa (1407). Although it was called a bank, it neither took deposits nor made loans to private parties. Neither did it serve as a clearinghouse for bills. Rather, it was a means of organizing and improving the finances of the city-state of Genoa. Specifically, it was "an organization endowed as a juridical body and assembled from a public organization, established to protect the rights of the creditors, and to reduce the risk of the Republic of Genoa refusing to pay its debts."[18] The bank was given substantial authority over tax collection, the structuring of debt issues, and disbursements to creditors. There were even long periods when the bank directly governed some of Genoa's overseas territories. In essence, the bank institutionalized a partnership that aligned the incentives of the political leaders of Genoa with those of its merchants and financiers. Its organizational structure reflected this careful alignment of interests. At the top of the organization stood eight administrators, the *protettori,* of whom seven represented the creditors and one the government. So intertwined was the operation of the bank with the functions of the state that Machiavelli called it "a state within a state."[19]

The use of a chartered joint-stock company as a mechanism for aligning the interests of the state and its debt holders through an institutionalized partnership became a central feature of English public finance in the late seventeenth and early eighteenth centuries. After the Glorious Revolution of 1688, the new King William III was struggling to finance his expensive war against Louis XIV of France. As we explore in more detail in chapter 4, the public financing scheme that emerged involved the creation of several chartered companies that provided credit to William and his successors as part of the deal for obtaining their charters. These companies included the Bank of England (1694), the Million Bank (1695), the rechartered British East India Company (1698), and the South Sea Company (1711).[20] The chartered companies were created and owned by powerful political leaders and served a mixture of commercial and government interests. Not only did they enjoy special business advantages, but their

---

[18] Marsilio (2013).

[19] Marsilio (2013).

[20] The British East India Company was originally chartered in 1600. Its rechartering in 1698 permitted foreign ownership, thereby expanding its access to funding.

political connections reduced their risk of exposure to sovereign default. Furthermore, their funding source—tradable equity—was a highly liquid financial instrument. They could, in effect, swap preexisting sovereign bonds held by individuals for shares in the chartered firm, thereby capitalizing the firm and consolidating the king's debts. By 1720, the proportion of public debt owned by the Bank of England, the South Sea Company, and the East India Company exceeded 70 percent.[21]

Other countries followed the British example of using chartered companies as a government financing vehicle. Indeed, as chapter 6 shows, U.S. state governments also used chartered companies for finance in the early nineteenth century. These efforts were not always successful. Perhaps the most egregious failure to align sovereign financial interests with a private joint-stock company was that of John Law's Mississippi Company in France. At the height of this scheme in 1720, the Mississippi Company (a conglomerate that combined tax farms, trading companies, and a bank), owned virtually all the tax rights of France, all its international trading rights, almost all its sovereign debt, and a monopoly on the right to print legal-tender currency. Indeed, to make the alignment of interests even clearer, Law himself served both as finance minister and head of the company! Unfortunately for France, John Law pushed things too far. Some aspects of his business plan amounted to financial alchemy, such as his attempt to peg the company's stock price at a very high level by using currency issued by his bank to purchase stock in the company that owned the bank. Nevertheless, the core idea of the Mississippi Company—the creation of a private-public partnership that aligned interests in order to reduce risk (e.g., simultaneously holding the public debt and owning the right to collect taxes to pay that debt) was fundamentally sound.[22] Indeed, the core idea of a single company's both owning sovereign debt and collecting the taxes to pay the debt served as the basis for the first chartered banks in many other countries.

Bills of Exchange, Global Trade and Capital Flows

Imagine how hard it would have been to create a global system of trade if gold or silver had to be transported by ship to pay for every item pur-

---

[21] Quinn (2008), figure 1.
[22] Neal (1990); Velde (2013).

chased in a foreign port. Imagine how much easier trade was made, therefore, by the invention of the bill of exchange, an IOU drawn on a bank to pay the bearer an amount of specie upon presentation. Imagine, further, how much easier things got once banks began to act as clearinghouses for bills of exchange: the bills of all associated banks could simply be reconciled with one another; opposing debts could be offset against one another, so that very little gold or silver had to change hands.

The bill of exchange was not only a substitute for gold or silver as a medium of exchange; it also provided a means of credit that allowed merchants to finance the purchase of goods to be sold elsewhere. For example, a merchant in Amsterdam could borrow from a bank there in the form of a paper bill endorsed by a banker, which could then be used to pay for goods in, say, the Dutch colony of Curaçao. A merchant in Curaçao was willing to accept that paper bill as payment because he had confidence in the promise of the Amsterdam banker whose name was on the bill. The Amsterdam-based merchant could then repay the banker who had endorsed the bill with the proceeds from the sale of the goods obtained in Curaçao. He might even repay that debt with a bill of exchange from the merchant who bought those goods.

The invention of bills of exchange required the legal enforcement of a new concept of debt, which became known as the negotiable instrument. This sort of instrument is familiar: a check is a negotiable instrument that can be transferred to another party by endorsing the check on the back, using the same "pay to the order of" instruction that appears on the front of the check. Prior to the development of negotiable instruments, debt was enforced as a personal obligation of one party to another. Under negotiable-instrument law, all endorsers of a bill were liable for its payment (according to the practice of "serial endorsement," which was perfected in Antwerp by the late sixteenth century). When a bill was used in payment for something, it was endorsed. A party who accepted the bill as payment simply had to have confidence in some (or even just one) of the signatures on it.

Negotiable bills of exchange allowed knowledge about parties within the global network to be conveyed credibly, because an endorsement represented a willingness to share liability: if party Z, who had a sterling reputation for probity and honesty, was willing to endorse a bill that had previously been endorsed by party Y, he was, in effect, expressing the utmost confidence in party Y, because if party Y defaulted, then party Z was on the hook. As bills were passed, their default risk therefore actually diminished: because each signature on a bill represented an individual from whom a creditor could collect, a larger number of signatures represented a greater probability of being able to collect.[23]

The willingness to enforce the new concept of indebtedness embodied in bills required the involvement of the state, which had to determine through its statutes and courts what sorts of contracts were enforceable under the law and on what terms. Modern rulers faced strong incentives to recognize and enforce the legitimacy of negotiable instruments: doing so not only facilitated trade within their empires but also encouraged financiers to set up shop in their major cities, thereby creating opportunities for rulers to finance their states.

Chartered Banks as the Centerpiece of Financial Innovation

Different forms of partnership emerged between modern states and chartered banks. The development of the chartered bank was driven by two essential needs: to finance trade over increasingly long distances, and to finance wars that were increasingly bloody and long. The relative strength of those two drivers determined whether the initial chartered banks were designed primarily to finance trade or to finance the state.

Some chartered banks focused primarily on trade, by promoting the interbank clearing of bills of exchange or other liabilities. The most important of these was the Wisselbank of Amsterdam (founded in 1609), a chartered bank that served as a global clearinghouse for bills of exchange, uniting thousands of account holders from all over Europe and economizing hugely on the amount of specie needed to redeem the bills that were cleared through its network.[24] Its design was informed by the example of a Venetian state-chartered bank established to facilitate the clearing of balances among the city's merchants, the Banco della Piazza di Rialto (1587). The Wisselbank served the interests of the government of Amster-

---

[23] Santarosa (2012).

[24] Because bills facilitated the movement of funds throughout the world, they became a vehicle for capital flows and speculation, not just for trade finance. By the eighteenth century, interest rates throughout most of Europe had converged to be nearly identical. See Neal (1990), 7; Jobst and Nogues-Marco (2013).

dam by promoting cost-effective international trade and capital flows. It did not, however, do much in the way of government lending.

At the other end of the continuum was the Bank of England (founded in 1694), which began as a mechanism to manage the debts of the British government and initially played no role as a central clearing facility for bills. London's goldsmith bankers saw the Bank of England, correctly, as a highly politicized entity. They therefore eschewed using it as a central clearinghouse, preferring to retain their bilateral system of interbank clearing long after the Bank of England had been created.[25]

Chartered banks in most countries typically came to act as financiers both of the state and of trade. Indeed, having a bank play both roles made it more attractive to the governments that issued the necessary charters: the government could award a group of financiers a monopoly charter for a bank, allowing it to earn income by discounting bills of exchange generated through trade, in exchange for which the financiers would share some of the resulting monopoly rents with the government by making loans to the government at attractive rates of interest. Alternatively, as in the case of state-chartered banks in the United States during the early nineteenth century, the financiers could share some of the rents with the government by giving it an equity (ownership) stake in the bank; they could finance the purchase of the government's equity stake by making it a loan, which would then be repaid out of the government's share of the bank's profits.

The creation of the chartered bank as a fundamental institution of the modern state soon gave rise to another fundamental innovation, one that is now so ubiquitous that there is almost certainly some of it in your wallet: fiat (paper) currency. Merchants in Amsterdam were plagued by the debasement of the gold and silver coins that constituted the measure of value and the unit of account. Some of these debasements were carried out by rulers, who periodically reduced the gold and silver content of their coins. The multiplicity of coins and mints in the Netherlands created an incentive for some mints to offer low-valued coins, which debtors would happily use to retire their debts. Counterfeiting—the creation of low-value imitations of full-value coins—was also a problem. Some individuals even clipped the edges of full-value coins and melted down the

---

[25] Quinn (1997); Neal and Quinn (2001).

clippings into valuable ingots. Gold and silver coins, in short, gave rise to price inflation and uncertainty about prices. This problem had existed ever since the invention of minted coins in ancient Athens, but as the volume of trade—and hence the volume of coinage—increased, it became particularly acute. Holland's Wisselbank solved this problem by creating a new measure of value based entirely on its paper liabilities. Because the merchants who ran the Wisselbank gained from establishing a stable measure of value, the new fiat unit of account proved more stable (less prone to inflation or price uncertainty) than coins.[26]

Anyone can issue an IOU and use it as a means of payment, but for an IOU—in particular, a banknote or any other paper money—to function as a legally accepted measure of value for settling debts, it had to be given legal-tender status under the law. A banknote that is "legal tender for debts public and private" can be used to pay both public debts (taxes) and private debts (bills of exchange or other debts). Not all chartered banks were given the right to issue legal tender from the beginning, although over time it became the rule. For example, the Bank of England's notes became legal tender in 1833.[27]

Financial innovations by chartered banks did not stop with the creation of fiat currency. Scotland's chartered banks of the mid-eighteenth century were particularly innovative, and over the next century their innovations were copied by chartered banks across the world. These included interest-bearing deposits, small-denomination banknotes that circulated as a medium of exchange, a jointly managed clearinghouse to exchange notes issued by different banks, lines of credit committed in advance and available for bank borrowers to use as needed, and branch banking. Although the Scots did not invent limited liability banking, they were the

---

[26] Quinn and Roberds (2009, 2010); Quinn (2013).

[27] The original use of legal-tender banknotes in Amsterdam as a way to control inflation is one of history's supreme ironies. Beginning with John Law's issuance of legal-tender notes to prop up the share prices of his Mississippi Company, Western governments soon figured out how to turn the ability to issue paper money (using both notes issued directly by the government or by government-chartered banks) into a new fiscal tool—known as the inflation tax—a means of forcing people to suffer erosion of the value of the wealth they held in the form of cash assets, to the benefit of the government or its chartered banks. The inflation tax became an important means of financing government in many countries during the nineteenth century and afterwards—a subject to which we return in chapters 11–13.

first to make extensive use of it. Limited liability was particularly advantageous because it removed a constraint that had discouraged investors from purchasing bank stock: they had been jointly and severally liable without limit for the debts of the bank.

Commercial Banking, Democracy, and Industrialization

The Darwinian struggles among states, and among business enterprises within states, did not end with the invention of the fully fledged chartered bank. Indeed, the pace of technological change only accelerated during the nineteenth and twentieth centuries, and as a result the two essential forces that gave rise to the nation-state and the chartered bank in the first place—trade and war—became ever more powerful. They created political pressures within states that no seventeenth- or eighteenth-century monarch could have imagined. They ultimately pushed nation-states to use chartered banks not just as vehicles to finance trade and war but also as mechanisms to finance a range of efforts to preserve political order, including the development of strategically important industries, the creation of inflationary currency issues, the pursuit of policies to stabilize employment, and the subsidization of home ownership. The ability to use banks to mobilize funds on a large scale to serve newly empowered domestic political interests was central to the statecraft of the new era. In short, the stakes in the Game of Bank Bargains had been raised.

In the late eighteenth century, as Ian Morris has pointed out, human beings made a crucial discovery. Until then, the ultimate source of all energy available had been the sun. Draft animals consumed plant matter synthesized from sunlight; water wheels were powered by a sun-driven water cycle; sails pushed boats across the ocean because variations in the intensity of solar radiation across the planet gave rise to predictable winds. At the end of the eighteenth century, however, human beings figured out how to capture the solar energy from eons past: coal, the product of forests that existed when dinosaurs walked the earth, could be burned to produce steam, providing reliable and seemingly endless amounts of power.[28]

The use of fossil fuels gave rise to a number of developments that changed the relationship between states and their populations. First, it

---

[28] Morris (2011), 100.

gave rise to a revolution in transportation and communications, particularly the steam-powered ship, the railroad, and the electrical telegraph. These changes enabled people and goods to be moved on a massive scale, accelerating and expanding trade. Tropical foods that until the nineteenth century had only been eaten by adventure seekers, such as bananas and pineapples, became staples on urban breakfast tables in the United States and Europe. Parts of the globe that previously had been isolated by distance could now tap into Europe's vast markets: steaks from Argentinian cattle could now be boiled into an unrecognizable gray mass in British kitchens. People who had been trapped by poverty in Sicily, Poland, Greece, or China could now move to more productive areas of the globe and thus improve their standard of living.

Second, industrial progress increased the efficiency with which human beings could kill each other and thus put states under even greater pressure to build powerful militaries or else be swallowed up by their rivals. By the latter half of the nineteenth century, fighting a successful war required railroads and steel mills. Without them a nation could neither build the efficient killing machines—breech-loading howitzers, machine guns, and steel-hulled battleships—that now decided military conflicts nor deploy those machines rapidly. Industrialization was not just about being able to drink more beer or wear mass-produced clothing; it was about survival as a state.

States needed more than weapons and battleships to win wars, however; they also needed to mobilize immense armies. The problem was not just the logistical one of putting enough men in the field with sufficient supplies, though that was difficult enough. It was a political problem as well: human beings tend to be unwilling to throw their bodies against killing machines unless they are strongly motivated to do so, and fear of being shot for cowardice by one's own officers provided only a limited incentive. European elites discovered something that the elites of Ancient Greece and the Roman Republic had figured out in the fifth century B.C.: enfranchised citizens with something to lose fight harder.[29] Those in power came under pressure to build redistributive welfare states.

This fundamental shift in bargaining power in favor of the masses meant that the rights of citizens to participate in elections expanded dra-

---

[29] For a discussion of the relationship between democracy and military conscription, see M. Levi (1997).

matically from the mid-nineteenth to the early twentieth centuries, and the right to vote brought with it the ability to demand policies designed to maintain full employment, provide a social safety net, and facilitate economic and social mobility.[30] As one leading scholar of the welfare state has put it in regard to Great Britain's experience: "Extending the voting share from 40 percent to 70 percent raised total social transfers, public pension spending, spending on primary-school teachers, and the income tax."[31]

States now had strong incentives to pursue much broader goals, and chartered banks provided a mechanism by which they could do so. Governments in democratic countries understood that the demand for economic and social mobility could be met, in part, by increasing access to credit. Indeed, as we show in later chapters, making bank credit more broadly available—not just to merchants but also to farmers and to homeowners—has been a constant theme of U.S. and Canadian history since the early nineteenth century.

The use of commercial banking systems to pursue the new goals of state was not confined to full-fledged democracies. The German chancellor Otto von Bismarck proved particularly adept at the new Game of Bank Bargains. Under his leadership, Germany created a banking system and securities markets that financed both the new German nation-state and new industrial firms.[32] The availability of finance allowed Germany to quickly catch up with and overtake Great Britain in the production of steel, chemicals, and electricity. Indeed, Germany's bankers did not just lend to industry; they helped to coordinate the creation of the powerful industrial cartels that characterized German manufacturing. And Germany's Iron Chancellor did not just build a powerful state that had world-class heavy industry and a disciplined army; he also led the world in the creation of national programs to provide old-age pensions, public medical care, and unemployment and industrial accident insurance. He did

---

[30] There is a large literature on the relationship between expansion of the franchise and the growth of the welfare state, including Lipset (1960), Moore (1966), Lindert (1994, 2004), and Acemoglu and Robinson (2000).

[31] Lindert (2004), 180.

[32] For discussions of the German case, see Riesser (1911), Gerschenkron (1962), R. Tilly (1967), Calomiris (1995), Guinnane (2002), Fohlin (2011), and chapter 14 of this book.

this not because he was a friend of the working man—quite the contrary —but because he understood that if he did not, the socialists would come to power and overturn the political order he was establishing.

Bank chartering was also part of a program of defensive moderniza-tion in other countries. Japan's Meiji Restoration of the late nineteenth and early twentieth centuries is the classic example: it was a conscious attempt to build a robust economy and military that could resist Russian and American moves into Asia. Central to that effort was the creation of a system of chartered banks.[33] In Russia and Mexico, political leaders con-sciously built banking systems as part of a more general project of rail-road building and industrial development intended to hold their avaricious neighbors (Germany and the United States, respectively) at bay.[34]

New Government-Chartered Entities: Central Banks and Special-Purpose Banks

The world in which the nation-state first emerged was overwhelmingly agrarian. Most people worked on farms, ate food that they grew them-selves, and slept in buildings that they constructed with their own hands. By the mid-nineteenth century, that world was fast disappearing. People increasingly worked in factories, ate food they bought with their wages, and slept in apartments owned by landlords who would not hesitate to throw them out onto the street if they failed to pay the rent. Rulers had to worry not only about keeping up with rivals in terms of military power and the control of trade routes but also about maintaining social peace. In an increasingly urbanized world, economic downturns did not mean peasants starving in isolated villages; they meant angry mobs rioting in the streets of the capital.

Governments therefore increasingly came to view their country's largest banks—in each country, typically the bank that had been managing their debt offerings for many years and that served as a central clearinghouse for bank bills—as a mechanism to maintain the stability of the financial system and hence the stability of the economy as a whole. The shifting

---

[33] See Patrick (1967).

[34] Mexico's banking system is the subject of chapters 10 and 11 of this book. Rus-sia's financial system is reviewed by Crisp (1967).

responsibilities of the Bank of England provide an example of this trend. The bank was initially founded to manage the government's fiscal affairs, and especially to help sustain the value of government debts during the country's seemingly interminable wars against France. In 1833, the bank's notes were given legal-tender status by Parliament, a move explicitly undertaken as a means to empower the bank to issue banknotes, as needed, to assist other banks during times of financial turmoil. By the late nineteenth century, the bank had become primarily a "banker's bank," with much of its business consisting in making loans to other banks and acting as a lender of last resort, a role that evolved over time (see chapter 5). By the end of the nineteenth century, the Bank of England had earned a reputation for effective prevention of financial crises.

By the late twentieth century, almost every country in the world had adopted the idea of establishing a central bank, although its specific forms varied. In addition to managing government finances and acting as lenders of last resort, in the twentieth century, central banks came to assume a new role as the managers of monetary policy. Under the gold standard, the ability of central banks to use their note-issuing or lending powers to influence the price level or domestic economic activity was sharply constrained by the commitment to convert their notes into a fixed amount of gold on demand. Having to maintain "external balance" in the market for foreign exchange under a fixed-exchange-rate regime prevented central banks from actively increasing or decreasing the amounts of money and credit in their national economies to target the "internal-balance" objectives of stable employment and income.

Central banks came to play much greater roles in economic stabilization after the collapse of the international gold standard during the Great Depression. With different nations' currencies no longer linked to a fixed gold value, fiat money, the supply of which was controlled by each government's central bank, became the unit of account and medium of exchange in each country. Until the 1970s, central banks tried, through the Bretton Woods system of fixed exchange rates, to maintain a quasi–gold standard by pegging exchange rates to the dollar and the dollar to gold, but this arrangement, too, fell apart.[35] Governments increasingly valued the ability

---

[35] The gold standard (a global standard of currency values) functioned roughly from 1821 to 1931, though there were interruptions, and worldwide adherence was never

to engage in activist monetary policy in order to promote employment and maintain social peace, rather than passively pursue the monetary policy consistent with maintaining a fixed international value of their currency. The growing political pressures on governments that underlay the increasing importance of countercyclical monetary policy have been so well articulated by Barry Eichengreen that we simply reproduce his analysis here:

> What was critical for the maintenance of pegged exchange rates . . . was protection for governments from pressure to trade exchange rate stability for other goals. Under the nineteenth-century gold standard the source of such protection was insulation from domestic politics. The pressure brought to bear on twentieth-century governments to subordinate currency stability to other objectives was not a feature of the nineteenth-century world. Because the right to vote was limited, the common laborers who suffered most from hard times were poorly positioned to object to increases in central bank interest rates adopted to defend the currency peg. Neither trade unions nor parliamentary labor parties had developed to the point where workers could insist that defense of the exchange rate be tempered by the pursuit of other objectives. . . . Come the twentieth century, these circumstances changed. . . . Universal male suffrage and the rise of trade unionism and parliamentary labor parties politicized monetary and fiscal policymaking. The rise of the welfare state and the post–World War II commitment to full employment sharpened the trade-off between internal and external balance. This shift . . . diminished the credibility of the authorities' resolve to defend the currency peg.[36]

The end of the gold standard meant that decisions about whether to favor stable exchange rates or promote full employment lay in the hands of a country's central bank, and neither the central bank nor the government could afford to neglect the short-term political costs of high unemployment.

---

complete. After World War II, the gold standard was replaced by the Bretton Woods system, a two-tiered system in which member countries' currencies were convertible into dollars and dollars were convertible into gold. That system fell apart in the early 1970s, as the value of the anchor currency—the dollar—became undermined by excessive U.S. issuance of dollars. Since the collapse of the Bretton Woods system, the world's main currencies have traded at varying exchange rates.

[36] Eichengreen (2008), 2.

The rise of democracy did more than create fiat money under activist central bank management; it also gave rise to new types of intermediaries that served specialized functions in the new welfare state. Special lending authorities, owned or financed by the government, were created to provide credit to targeted groups of recipients, sometimes identified only by sector (e.g., agriculture or housing) and sometimes by additional characteristics (e.g., small businesses, veterans, or middle-income homeowners). Such targeted lending facilities became powerful tools in the hands of politicians seeking to attract the support of particular constituencies.

Governments in every democracy have made ample use of such facilities. In the United States, housing and agriculture have traditionally been the most consistently targeted sectors for subsidized credit. Subsidies are particularly attractive if they can be delivered without having to recognize their costs within the government's budget, thus providing valuable benefits to supporters without their costs being apparent to taxpayers. In chapters 6–8, we trace the political process in the United States that gave rise to the growth of government-sponsored, special-purpose banks that subsidized first farm finance and later housing finance.

Modern autocracies also make use of both general commercial banks and specialized financial institutions that direct credit toward particular purposes. The formation of viable political coalitions in autocracies requires discouraging splinter groups. Autocrats design their deals to produce stable rent-sharing arrangements among powerful members of their coalition.[37] They grant valuable commercial bank charters to coalition members to institutionalize their rent-sharing arrangements. Additionally, autocrats may wish to charter specialized banks that provide credit for particular purposes, a practice that further institutionalizes long-term commitments to key members of the coalition, such as organized labor or farmers.

Partnership and Possibilities

Let us now circle back to the question we posed at the beginning of this chapter. Why are there no states without chartered banks? Our answer is

---

[37] Haber, Razo, and Maurer (2003) explore the logic of these kinds of relationships and then demonstrate empirically how those relationships worked in a canonical case. Acemoglu, Egorov, and Sonin (2012) provide a formal model of stable coalitions under autocracy.

that the evolution of the nation-state depended on a partnership among rulers, merchants, and financiers. Rulers needed merchants to build the commercial networks that glued their states together and ultimately supplied their tax revenues. Merchants needed increasingly capable rulers at the head of increasingly powerful states to defend their trade routes and enforce their increasingly complex contracts. Both the merchants and the rulers needed financiers: the merchants needed them to create and manage the financial instruments necessary to carry out trade at a distance, and the rulers needed them to provide the funds necessary to fight wars. The financiers, for their part, needed a state to enforce the contracts they wrote with one another, with merchants, and with foreign states. The various incentives of the three groups were aligned through a number of key financial innovations, all of which came together in the entity of the chartered bank. Thus we might emend Charles Tilly's famous phrase, "War made the state, and the state made war," to "States made banks, and banks made states."[38]

[38] C. Tilly (1975), 42.

4

Privileges with Burdens

*War, Empire, and the Monopoly
Structure of English Banking*

> We do not live, and I trust it will never be the fate of this country
> to live, under a democracy.
>
> Benjamin Disraeli, British prime minister (1867)

Visitors to contemporary London cannot fail to note its stature as a world financial capital. It is the home base for more than 500 banks, including a number of global giants such as NatWest, HSBC, and Barclays. It hosts one of the world's most active stock markets and some of its oldest and most important insurance companies, such as Lloyd's of London. Britain's imposing central bank, the Bank of England, has operated continuously in London since 1694. The British financial sector employs 4 out of every 100 British workers. It accounts for 10 percent of British national income, a contribution ten times greater than that of agriculture.

One might draw the conclusion that England has always had a large and sophisticated banking system. Indeed, one might hypothesize that England led the world into the Industrial Revolution in the late eighteenth century because bank credit was broadly available to its inventors and manufacturers. These inferences would be reasonable; but they would be wrong. The Bank of England was a monopoly set up to finance a government that spent more than it taxed and which was therefore willing to trade a set of lucrative privileges to a group of financiers in exchange for loans to the government. From 1694 to 1825, the Bank of England was the only bank in England that was allowed to take the form of a joint-stock company; all other banks had to be organized as partnerships and were limited in size. They were also subject to usury laws, which discouraged them from expanding their circle of borrowers: if a bank cannot charge a new client a higher interest rate to compensate for the fact it does not know much about him, it will not lend to that client at all. The government, which was not constrained by these usury laws, was therefore able to channel credit to itself rather than to the private sector. England industrialized not because manufacturers were awash in credit but rather in spite of the fact that the government had quite consciously constrained the growth of the banking system in order to favor itself and the Bank of England. The Industrial Revolution was financed out of the pockets of tinkerers and manufacturers, not through bank lending.

England's history of financial repression from the late seventeenth through the early nineteenth century was an outcome of its Game of Bank Bargains, and that game was driven by a military and imperial ambition that was disproportionate to the size of its population and geographic area. From 1689 until the defeat of Napoleon in 1815, England was almost constantly at war with France. The British financial system, including its bank chartering policy, was designed to maximize government access to war finance. In short, England exemplifies the idea that the chartered bank was an outcome of the need of a state to finance a Darwinian struggle against rival states.

These arrangements were durable because until the mid-nineteenth century, England limited the extent of the franchise. The deal that established the Bank of England as a monopoly in the late seventeenth century was possible because less than 10 percent of the population were eligible to vote according to criteria based on property ownership and gender. Britain was not a primitive autocracy: the Glorious Revolution of 1688 created powerful representative institutions that limited the authority and discretion of the crown, especially regarding taxation and the rights to property; but the nation was still far from a full-fledged democracy.

The Glorious Revolution and the Game of Bank Bargains

Before 1688, Britain's political and financial institutions were not much different from those found across much of Western Europe. Sovereign debt was a personal obligation of the monarch. The financial powers of government were divided and uncertain: the king depended on Parliament for access to some but not all revenues. Furthermore, the monarch could demand "forced loans" from individuals under threat of punishment without seeking approval from Parliament. In essence, the power to tax and issue public debt were divided between the crown and Parliament in a manner that made it likely that the crown would choose to issue debts that Parliament would choose not to repay. This was a highly unstable arrangement, so much so that in 1672 the government was unable to honor its debts, resulting in a moratorium on repayments and a partial repudiation of its obligations (the so-called stop of the Exchequer).

The origins of the Glorious Revolution of 1688 were more political and religious than financial, but it also had far-reaching consequences for finance. It toppled England's unpopular King James II and replaced him with his daughter, Mary, and her husband and cousin, William of Orange (who ruled alone after Mary's death in 1694). The reasons for James's unpopularity are not hard to divine: he was Catholic, an ally of France's corrupt and pompous Louis XIV, and a staunch believer in the divine right of kings.[1] Thus the Glorious Revolution should be understood as an assault on absolute sovereign power in its broadest sense. The origins of that assault go back at least as far as the beheading of Charles I (James II's father) in 1649, and they culminated in a civil war that then overthrew James II. The resulting constraints on absolute sovereign power were embodied in constitutional changes in 1689 with the writing of the English Bill of Rights, the Toleration Act, and the Mutiny Act, which committed the monarch to respect Parliament's laws. The Glorious Revolution also made the judiciary independent of the monarchy.

The process of driving James II into exile (into the court of his cousin, Louis XIV) and consolidating the power of Parliament over the king completely transformed the rules governing England's finances. Under the new regime, which was largely in place by 1697, the king could not tax or borrow without Parliament's consent.[2] Sovereign debt changed from being the monarch's personal debt to being the obligation of a nation. Moreover, the political system made debt default an unlikely Parliamentary choice, because many members of Parliament were holders of government debt obligations or had interests in enterprises that held government debt. Parliament also specified how taxes could be spent, diverting some funds from the sovereign's control and instituting audits of other spending.[3]

---

[1] For a detailed description of the Glorious Revolution and its consequences, see Pincus (2009).

[2] Dickson (1967), 48–73.

[3] The central argument has been advanced by North and Weingast (1989) and Weingast (1997). Elements of the story have been debated by Stasavage (2002, 2003,

The Glorious Revolution also had far-reaching consequences abroad. The crown's authority to tax and spend might have been constrained, but sovereign power survived in every other respect, and particularly in foreign affairs. England's ambitions and military alliances shifted dramatically. James II had been an enemy of the Dutch Republic and a close ally of France, largely for religious reasons—the Dutch, after all, were Protestants, and James II was a Catholic. The new king and queen, William and Mary, were Protestants. Moreover, William was Dutch. Thus, the Glorious Revolution ended hostilities between England and the Dutch Republic and led to a costly and enduring military conflict between England and France. This encompassed King William's War (1689–97), the Wars of Spanish Succession (1702–14), the War of Austrian Succession (1740–48), the Seven Years' War (which actually lasted nine years, from 1754 until 1763), the American Revolution (1775–83), the French Revolutionary Wars (1793–1802), and the Napoleonic Wars (1803–15).[4]

The primary challenge that England's new government faced was not a lack of popular support for waging war against Louis XIV, but rather the challenge of crafting a modern state that could both embody the new concept of a constitutional monarchy and provide the financial means to pay the enormous costs of defending that concept in modern Europe. Louis XIV was despised in England because he was the archetype of an absolute monarch (epitomized by his famous comment "L'état, c'est moi") who had clear ambitions to expand his reach into other European countries. In calling for war against Louis XIV, the House of Commons described him as a "disturber of the peace, and the common enemy of the Christian

---

2007); Pincus (2009), 366–99; Sussman and Yafeh (2006); Robinson (2006); and Murphy (2009), 53–65. Although there is some disagreement about how to measure the success of England's financial revolution, the political mechanism through which it occurred, and the precise timing of the improvements in market perceptions of sovereign credit worthiness, the consensus is that the changes that established England's reputation for sound public finances were largely completed by the 1720s. See also Plumb (1967).

[4] This shift was not just a reflection of the preferences of William and Mary. As one of the preeminent historians of the Glorious Revolution puts it: "By late 1688 it was clear that the majority of the political nation favored opposing the growing power of France by force of arms. William did not have to impose his foreign policy on an unwilling nation. Instead the English political nation had chosen to support the Prince of Orange in 1688 and 1689 precisely because he was likely to lead the country into the long-desired war against Louis XIV." Pincus (2009), 337.

world."[5] The issue that confronted the English government was how to pay for the war. Wars were no longer won by brave princes leading charges of mounted knights; they had become wars of attrition in which victory went to whichever side could mobilize more men and money.[6] The new war with France caused an immediate jump in public expenditures, which rose from about £4 million per year before 1688 to an average of about £6 million or more for the period 1688–1720.[7] Expenditures climbed with each new round of war. As one contemporary observed: "Never was there known before such vast debts owing for Excise and Customs, upon Bills and Bonds unsatisfied. All sorts of provisions grew to an extravagant price. . . . We had all the symptoms upon us of a Bankrupt State and an undone people."[8]

As William struggled to finance his expensive wars with Louis XIV, he had cause to be open to new ideas. He could, and did, raise taxes, but in the short run there is only so much additional tax revenue that any government can squeeze from the economy.[9] He also had a curious advantage that came from being a constitutional monarch rather than an absolute ruler: the fact that he could not default on his debts without the permission of Parliament gave his promises to repay greater credibility than they would have had otherwise. Nevertheless, he needed to innovate and experiment if he was going to borrow on the scale necessary to beat the French. He therefore tried a lottery as a means of raising funds. The Million Adventure Lottery of 1694 sold 100,000 lottery tickets for £10 each, promising all ticket holders £1 per year in interest income and awarding 2,500 lottery prizes. In contrast to private borrowing, in which interest rates were limited by usury laws to 6 percent, the lottery enabled the crown to pay higher returns to creditors. Even this move, however, was far from enough to solve William's financial problems. Not only did he need additional funds for new expenditures, but he also needed to stretch out the repayment period for his debts. That was a tough trick: he had to

[5] Pincus (2009), 340.
[6] C. Tilly (1990); Temin and Voth (2013).
[7] Temin and Voth (2013), 29. Expenditures continued to increase from 1720 to 1800, peaking at over £100 million a year during the Napoleonic Wars.
[8] The commentator is Haynes (1700), who is quoted in Cunningham (1907), 440 n. 3.
[9] The per capita tax burden in England quadrupled from 1688 to 1787. Temin and Voth (2013), chapter 2.

find a way to entice people to hold longer-term debt but not charge him very high interest rates for doing so.

The Bank of England as the Government's Monopoly Lender

The solution that William and Parliament hit upon was the founding of the Bank of England as a joint-stock, limited liability company in 1694. This was not the first time that the British government had created a chartered company. It had used them throughout the seventeenth century to subcontract the work of building an empire, allowing the operation of monopoly enterprises such as the East India Company (in 1600) in exchange for a payment to the government. It was, however, the first time that the government had granted a charter for an enterprise whose sole purpose was to lend money to the government: the bank's initial charter provided a £1.2 million loan to the government at 8 percent interest (compared with the 10 percent the government had paid in the Million Adventure Lottery that same year). The loan was redeemable after 1705; but if it was redeemed at that time, the Bank of England would be liquidated and its charter terminated. In essence, the government gave the bank the right to issue banknotes backed by the paid-in capital of its shareholders, and the bank then lent those notes to the government at interest. This meant that subscribers to Bank of England stock indirectly bought sovereign debt (the only initial asset of the bank) as well as the "option value" of the charter, which might allow the bank to undertake other profitable activities in the future if its charter were not terminated.

The organizers of the bank were prominent members of the Whig Party, and the Whigs shepherded the Bank of England charter through Parliament over objections from the Tory opposition. They were helped in no small part by the fact that the government's financial situation was desperate. As Winston Churchill observed of the period, "The English troops fighting on the Continent were being paid from day to day. The reserves of bullion were being rapidly depleted and English financial agents were obsessed by the fear of a complete breakdown."[10]

---

[10] Churchill (1998), 388. The founding of the Bank of England, however, was not inevitable. The goals of the two dominant political parties (the Whigs and the Tories) for the Glorious Revolution had never been identical, and after the fighting was over, their profound political differences reemerged. If the Tories had not lost power in 1693,

The government's success in garnering loan funds by creating the Bank of England encouraged it to engage in further experimentation. In 1695, Parliament granted a corporate charter to the Million Bank. This entity bought and pooled tickets from the 1694 Million Adventure Lottery, thereby making those tickets more liquid, lowering their default risk, and allowing investors to capture some benefits of diversification (by pooling the uncertainty related to winning the lottery's additional prizes). In 1696, the Tories in Parliament, who had resisted the charter for the Bank of England, succeeded in chartering a rival, the Land Bank, that would lend to the government at an interest rate of 7 percent. This enterprise never got off the ground to compete with the Bank of England, however, because its organizers failed to raise sufficient capital. In 1697, the government tried to raise yet more funds from a lottery—the so-called Malt Lottery—but that effort did not go well.[11] Its failure caused the government to go back to the Bank of England later that year for assistance to avoid defaulting on short-term government debts. The bank agreed to allow holders of the debts to convert them into Bank of England shares.

In exchange for this support, the government granted the bank the right to augment its capital and granted it a monopoly over chartered banking. The 1697 act was not subtle in granting this monopoly: "No other bank, or any corporation, society, fellowship, company or constitution in the nature of a bank shall be erected or established, permitted, suffered, countenanced or allowed by Act of Parliament." The act also made Bank of England stock personal, not real, property, thus exempting it from taxation.[12]

---

it is possible that they would have blocked the creation of the Bank of England (or some similar institution). See Pincus (2009).

[11]Various other banking schemes were contemplated in the 1690s, including some that envisioned a dramatic expansion of bank chartering in pursuit of expanding commerce throughout England. The most elaborate of these was Robert Murray's 1696 proposal, titled "A Proposal for a National Bank." Murray alone proposed multiple schemes for constructing banks. He admired the Dutch Wisselbank, which he described as "incomparably the best and greatest of the World." He envisioned the chartering of multiple banks throughout England to increase the supply of credit in support of the bills market. Many others constructed similar proposals to erect a commercially oriented and decentralized banking system throughout England. Although some of these ideas were pursued on a small scale with the establishment of private banks, the chartering proposals were rejected by Parliament. For a review of these proposals, see Richards (1958), 100–131.

[12]Broz and Grossman (2004), 48–72.

Subsequent attempts by nonbanking entities to engage in banking operations led to even stricter language in a 1708 act, which laid out the powers of the Bank of England in specific terms and prohibited any other corporation from engaging in them. Other banks could exist, but they had to be organized as partnerships, and those partnerships were limited to six members. These measures gave the Bank of England a definitive monopoly on joint-stock banking: any competing bank would have to operate on a very small scale. The 1708 act, which renewed the Bank of England's charter through 1732, was accompanied by a £400,000 interest-free loan to the government.[13]

The government and the Bank of England continued to sign such "loans for rents" contracts throughout the eighteenth and early nineteenth centuries. As J. Lawrence Broz and Richard Grossman have shown, the bank's charter was renewed nine times between 1694 and 1844, with each renewal typically accompanied by a low- or no-interest loan from the bank to the government. The 1764 charter renewal actually included a £110,000 gift to the government, on top of a loan with an interest rate of only 3 percent. The 1800 charter renewal, signed at the height of the French Revolutionary Wars, resulted in a £3 million interest free loan to the government. These special loans at the time of charter renewals were in addition to the bank's regular loans to the government.[14]

The founding of the Bank of England reduced the crown's financing costs for four reasons. First, the cost of borrowing was lower because the crown was unlikely to default on friends and key supporters in Parliament, who controlled the bank. Second, the government's debts to the Bank of England were structured as long-term obligations. Not only did this mean that the government avoided the uncertainty caused by continuously refinancing short-term debts through the longer term structure of the debt, but it also meant that the principal did not amortize: it had to be repaid only if the bank's charter was not renewed. Third, the Bank of England's special privileges were a form of intangible asset that added to its net worth, which lowered its cost of raising funds and allowed it to pass on some of those savings to the government. Fourth, unlike the prior hodgepodge of sovereign IOUs, Bank of England stock was a homo-

---

[13] Richards (1958), 146–47; Broz and Grossman (2004), 57.
[14] Broz and Grossman (2004), 52, 57.

geneous, perpetual, and tradable financial instrument. It was therefore much more liquid than the earlier nonhomogeneous, short-term debts issued by the crown, and that greater liquidity, by reducing the uncertainty of debt holders, reduced the rate of interest they charged.[15]

The government's financial needs were never-ending. In addition to the deals it made with the Bank of England, it also raised money by running lotteries and by exchanging other types of nonbank corporate charters for loans. For example, in 1698 it chartered a second company licensed to trade with the East Indies (in addition to the East India Company), the English Company Trading to the East Indies, which received its charter only after promising to lend £2 million to the government at 8 percent interest. Some of the corporate charters granted by Parliament were little more than veiled attempts to place government debt outside the Whig-dominated Bank of England. For example, in 1711, Parliament granted a charter to a group of financiers connected to the (then-dominant) Tory Party to found the South Sea Company. The charter granted a monopoly on trade with South America, in exchange for which the company bought up government debt: subscribers to the company could purchase shares with government debt issues. By 1720, the Bank of England, the South Sea Company, and the East India Company owned more than 70 percent of England's public debt.

There were limits to how far the government could go in squeezing debt-equity swaps or zero-interest loans out of chartered companies that were in business primarily to make money, not to subsidize the government. For example, after the War of Austrian Succession (1740–48), a government request for another debt-for-equity swap was refused by the East India Company and the South Sea Company. The Bank of England acquiesced under pressure. After three decades of meeting its interest payments on its debts, however, the government had come to be viewed by the public as a reliable borrower (a fact that was reflected in the interest rates it had to pay, which fell from 8 percent in the 1690s to roughly 5 percent in the 1720s). The government therefore began to place long-term debt issues with the public directly by issuing a new debt instrument, the

---

[15] When issuing an illiquid financial instrument, the issuer must pay more to holders than it would for a liquid instrument (because the liquid instrument offers an additional advantage to holders). See Quinn (2008).

callable consolidated perpetual annuity (consol). Consols paid a fixed percentage of their face value forever to their bearer but gave the government the option to purchase the debt at face value at any time (thus allowing it to refinance its debt if interest rates fell).[16] Even with the innovation of the consol, the Bank of England remained an important source of government finance, especially when the government's debt needs surged, as happened during the Napoleonic Wars.

To modern readers, these "loans for rents" arrangements may smack of corruption and cronyism. Indeed, Bank of England officials routinely paid bonuses to treasury officials to express their appreciation for their special business relationship. These arrangements did, however, have a clear bottom-line benefit to the state: England, unlike Holland and France, was able to avoid defaulting on its debts in the late seventeenth and eighteenth centuries. In consequence, the British government was able to borrow much more than its rivals, and at lower rates of interest, and therefore vanquish them on the seas and battlefields. When the dust settled at the end of the Napoleonic Wars in 1815, there was only one world power: Britain. France had been vanquished and would never threaten Britain again.

Financial "Repression" during the Industrial Revolution

It seems natural to posit a connection between the explosive growth of the Bank of England and other chartered companies and Britain's Industrial Revolution of the late eighteenth and early nineteenth centuries. Economic historians of England have, however, generally reached the opposite conclusion: the Industrial Revolution happened in spite of the revolution in public finance, not because of it. The Bank of England deployed its resources to serve government needs throughout the eighteenth and early nineteenth centuries. Those needs became acute during the Napoleonic Wars: ultimately, the government's heavy reliance on the bank pre-

---

[16] Although consols embody the issuer's implicit option to repay, and this option, holding all else constant, increases their market interest rate, the option to repay also has other consequences that could lower interest cost. In particular, by giving itself an option to prepay, the government created an incentive for itself to manage its finances well, because it stood to benefit from reductions in its default risk.

cipitated a lengthy suspension of convertibility of Bank of England notes into specie.[17]

The Bank of England's private business during the eighteenth century consisted of three principal activities. First, to fund its activities, in addition to offering stock, it issued paper money in the form of banknotes, which circulated as a means of payment. Those notes were not initially given the status of legal tender but rather were simply debts of the bank, convertible on demand into coin. Second, the bank accepted deposits from wealthy individuals and businesses. Third, in addition to purchasing government debt, the bank discounted bills of exchange for London merchants, meaning that it purchased bills at a discount to their face value (the promised amount to be paid under the terms of the bill). To a lesser degree, the bank also discounted promissory notes and made "advances" (loans), but the clientele for these services was quite narrow. Even as late as 1800–1815 (the earliest dates for which data are available), the number of private individuals entitled to discount at the Bank never exceeded 1,400;[18] for earlier periods the numbers were likely even smaller. The economic historian Rondo Cameron, in summing up the evidence about the activities of the Bank of England, put it succinctly, if grimly: "The Bank of England deserves priority of consideration [in the banking history of England] only by virtue of its political influence and legal status. Its creation resulted from the coupling of the government's urgent need for money with the bank promoters' desire for the profits of both speculation and monopoly. In this it set a pattern for the formation of national banks (later called central banks) in other countries, but its own contributions to industrial finance were negligible, if not negative."[19]

There were, of course, private banks operating in London and in England's secondary cities. Referred to as "goldsmith banks" (by virtue of their origins) in London and "country banks" in the rest of the country, these banks began to develop in the sixteenth century, as London became linked to the global markets in Antwerp and elsewhere in Europe.[20] They

---

[17] See Cannan (1925) and Hayek (1939).

[18] Cameron (1967a), 21.

[19] Cameron (1967a), 20. See also Bowen (1995).

[20] The jump from being a goldsmith to being a banker was not large. Goldsmiths quite naturally operated as money changers. Merchants, who tended to accumulate stocks of gold, used the goldsmith's vaults to store their reserves, which the goldsmiths

focused on discounting bills of exchange, though they also accepted deposits, made loans, and acted as brokers in securities markets. Although large numbers of goldsmith banks were driven out of business as the result of the stop of the Exchequer in 1672, many continued to operate during the eighteenth and nineteenth centuries, and some still survive today.

The laws that the government crafted in order to finance its own operations kept these banks very small and thus constrained the amount of credit that they could mobilize for industry. From 1697 to 1825, England's private banks were limited in several important ways. First, because the Bank of England was the only bank that could legally operate as a joint-stock company, no other chartered corporation (such as the East India Company or the South Sea Company) could act as a bank. This restriction also meant that a goldsmith bank or country bank could not raise equity capital in the public market: it had to be organized as a sole proprietorship or partnership. Second, the 1708 law that limited banking partnerships to no more than six partners severely limited the capital footings of those banks. Third, the Bank of England was given a monopoly over issuing notes in and around London, and it was allowed to squeeze even the non-London banks out of the note market through parliamentary acts that restricted their ability to issue small-denomination notes.[21] Banknotes are a source of bank funding that does not bear interest: thus the exclusive right to issue paper currency gave the Bank of England access to a low-cost means of funding that was unavailable to other banks, boosting its profits and putting its competitors at a significant disadvantage.[22]

---

could then lend at interest. The activities of the goldsmith bankers received a large boost after 1640, when Charles I seized the gold that merchants had deposited into the Royal Mint for safekeeping as a forced loan. Merchants avoided the Royal Mint thereafter, depositing their reserves instead with the goldsmiths. Richards (1958).

[21] In 1759, the minimum denomination permitted for Bank of England notes was reduced from £20 to £10. The minimum was further reduced to £5 in 1793. During the same period, the government squeezed the country banks: in 1775, a new policy set a £1 minimum for country banknotes, and in 1777 that limit was raised to £5.

[22] The fact that some country bankers did focus on industrial credit (see Pressnell [1956], 19–36; Brunt [2006]) indicates that the scarcity of industrial finance arose not from an unwillingness to supply credit but rather from constraints on the ability to do so. It is also important to note that despite the constraints noted here, many important infrastructure projects—toll roads, canals, waterworks, and ports—were successfully financed during the Industrial Revolution (Pressnell [1956], 372–400). For a review of

The government granted these privileges to the Bank of England in order to divert the supply of credit into government coffers and to ensure that the bank shared the benefits it received from regulation with the government. Another rule that favored the government's ability to attract funding, both from the Bank of England and from other creditors, was a usury law (a limit on the rate of interest on loans). Prior to 1714, interest rates on private debts could not exceed 6 percent. After 1714, the limit was lowered to 5 percent. That usury limit was not repealed until 1833.[23] Because government debts, including the perpetual debts the crown owed to the Bank of England, were not subject to these usury limits, all lenders had strong incentives to lend to the government rather than to private borrowers.[24] The 5 percent usury ceiling created a powerful disincentive for banks to lend to new, and hence risky, industrial enterprises. Scholars have inferred interest rates from the (low-risk) market in interbank bills of exchange and have found that those interest rates were typically within 2 percentage points of 5 percent and sometimes close to the 5 percent ceiling.[25] Thus usury limits typically would not have been a constraint on low-risk commercial finance, but they constituted an effective prohibition on "unseasoned credits" (credits to riskier industrial borrowers, which would have entailed higher default risk), unless those borrowers were able to evade the usury law.[26]

---

the legal underpinnings of corporate forms, which facilitated such projects, see Harris (2000).

[23] In 1833, short-term bills were exempted, an action that constituted the de facto repeal of usury laws. De jure repeal occurred in 1864 (Temin and Voth [2013]).

[24] According to Temin and Voth ([2013], 74), bonds were exempt from usury laws because "the government could always issue bonds at below par." While this is true, the necessary feature of bonds that exempted them from usury-law limits on interest was that the return of principal was either not contemplated or not a matter of certainty. Munro writes that "when we realize that in 1693, shortly after the Glorious Revolution, the crown was forced to borrow at 14 percent to finance William III's wars with France's Louis XIV, we can better appreciate the significance of annuities, which, of course, were always fully exempt from the usury laws." To be exempted from usury law, however, bonds did not have to be pure annuities, so long as the return of principal was not a contractual certainty. For a complete discussion of the legal history of English usury law during this period, see Campbell (1928).

[25] Flandreau et al. (2009); Jobst and Nogues-Marco (2013).

[26] Some scholars have questioned whether statutory usury limits actually constrained market behavior. Campbell (1928) points out that by structuring borrowing arrangements to give them some of the contractual features of annuities, borrowers could

The politicized nature of the Bank of England meant that in spite of its immense size, it did little to knit the hundreds of small goldsmith and country banks together into anything that resembled a network. This structure unnecessarily raised the costs of clearing transactions and the amount of idle cash balances that banks had to hold to do so.[27] The public certainly made use of its notes, and the bank financed commerce through the bills market. Private banks did not, however, clear their bills through the Bank of England but instead relied on a much more inefficient technology: they cleared their bills through bilateral exchanges until 1773, when they organized a clearinghouse that did not involve the Bank of England. Not until 1854 did interbank accounts at the Bank of England become the means of multilateral clearing of bank checks.[28]

It was not that the Bank of England avoided dealing with the private banks; rather, private bankers regarded the Bank of England as too politicized and too financially risky, because of its exposure to sovereign debt, to play the role of central clearing agent. Indeed, the relationship of the Bank of England to the crown was viewed by private bankers as smacking of cronyism: favors were openly traded between the two institutions and their agents. As one nineteenth-century commentator put it, "An insti-

---

exempt themselves from the usury law. Furthermore, the undesirable effects of those features could be avoided by combining a debt contract with annuity-like features and a life insurance contract. This form of what one might call "annuity arbitrage" was used, according to Campbell (1928), by many private borrowers to evade usury limits. It is also conceivable that market participants could have agreed to hide payments above the usury limit. Another means of evading the limit was "dry" exchange—a technique using two bills of exchange that convert a sum in pounds today into foreign currency in the future and convert foreign currency in the future back into pounds. The penalties for circumventing the law in this way, however, were quite severe. Borrowers could therefore use the threat of reporting such arrangements as a means of reducing interest payments to rates within the usury limit. Temin and Voth (2013) conclude that usury limits were obeyed by bankers; they note that during periods of rising interest rates, goldsmith bank lending was reduced, suggesting that the usury limits were binding on the supply of loans.

[27] Increased idle cash balances would be needed for two reasons. First, the lack of net clearing would mean that banks needed more cash to accomplish the physical bilateral clearings of their claims. Second, the absence of centralized clearing limited the ability of banks to assist each other by providing liquidity easily during crises (as they did in other countries—see chapter 6), which would have required banks to self-insure against liquidity risk with greater holdings of cash.

[28] Matthews (1921), 35–36.

tution so dependent on the Government of the day for the continuance of valuable rights was little able, as Mr. Ricardo observed, to withstand the cajoling of Ministers."[29] The bank's practice of paying bonuses to treasury officials did not end until 1797, when Prime Minister William Pitt put an end to it.

This situation kept the supply of bank credit for private purposes quite low throughout the eighteenth and early nineteenth centuries, precisely when it could have fostered the economic growth that industrialization made possible. The scarcity of credit helps to explain the puzzling disparity between the remarkable technological progress witnessed in England from 1750 to 1840 and the tepid overall economic growth of that period. Despite the high profitability of investment, the lack of credit meant that a manufacturing firm started by a tinkerer or inventor could grow only as fast as its owner could plow profits back into the firm.[30]

One might imagine that England's tinkerers, inventors, and manufacturers could have used stock offerings to circumvent the regulatory constraints on lending, but Parliament made sure that that gate too was closed and locked. The Bubble Act of 1720 was passed at the request of the South Sea Company as a means of preventing competing companies from issuing shares. The act chartered two new companies and then went on to prohibit all companies from issuing transferable shares or extending their businesses into areas not explicitly authorized in their charters without the explicit approval of Parliament or the crown. The Bubble Act was not repealed until 1825, the same year that Parliament finally began to undo the Bank of England's monopoly.[31]

The bottom line was that England's industrialists, as well as other risky private borrowers, were starved for funds. Savings were diverted from private to public purposes through a combination of banking and securities regulations. Peter Temin and Hans-Joachim Voth, in their detailed study of England's goldsmith bankers, sum it up as follows: "However useful finance is to economic growth in other contexts, our study reveals

---

[29]The commentator is G. Arbuthnot, in 1858, quoted by Schuster (1923), 10–11.

[30]Temin and Voth (2013).

[31]Although some scholars have argued that stock issuance was effectively constrained even before the Bubble Act, there is broad agreement that it came to a grinding halt in 1720, and that the repeal of the Bubble Act in 1825 brought an immediate boom in new incorporations and stock offerings.

that England's Financial Revolution in public borrowing enabled concurrent government activities to retard economic growth during the Industrial Revolution."[32]

Let Them Eat Inflation:
The Bank of England and the Napoleonic Wars

Protracted and costly war with France from 1793 to 1815 fundamentally changed the nature of the partnership between the Bank of England and the British government. Until the 1790s, the bank had basically held the rights to operate a monopoly in exchange for periodic loans to the government. Those loans came in the form of notes issued by the bank, backed by its capital, and convertible on demand by their users (the British public) into gold coin.[33] The French Revolutionary Wars and the Napoleonic Wars required a rethinking of the bank's role in public finance. These wars were like none the British had fought previously because of a crucial French innovation: the *levée en masse,* the forced mass conscription of the adult male population.[34]

Britain now had to fight on an unprecedented scale and therefore to mobilize greater financial resources than ever before. In addition to maintaining the largest navy in the world and mobilizing an army of some 220,000 men, the British government also funded the armies of many of its allies, an enterprise referred to as the Golden Cavalry of Saint George (named for the fact that Saint George, the patron saint of England, appeared on the British gold guinea coin).

---

[32] Temin and Voth (2013), 6.

[33] People were free to bring either gold or silver to the mint for coining, but given the established mint ratio, only gold bullion—the relatively overvalued metal, with a gold pound containing 123.25 grains of 22-carat gold—was supplied.

[34] Until the *levée* was introduced by the French in 1793, wars were fought by professional soldiers. Earlier mass conscriptions had occurred, but they were temporary, last-ditch efforts employed by desperate rulers who were about to be defeated. They had never been used to raise a mass army for offensive actions over a long period. Importantly, the *levée* was made possible by another innovation that the French revolutionaries adapted from the United States: the concept that society is composed of equal and free citizens, not royal subjects. In such a free society, citizens are supposed to believe that they have a collective responsibility to defend the state. They fight not for a king but for themselves.

The government also had to quell fears that the war, by causing trade to shrink, would make many of Britain's merchants insolvent and thereby set off a run on the banks. Thus, when the fiscally strapped government entered the war against France in 1793, it also had to commit to lending £5 million in Exchequer bills to British merchants. In the event, only half of that amount had to be issued, and the crisis receded. The strain on the public finances, however, did not evaporate quite so easily. As the government's fiscal problems worsened from 1794 to 1796, it increasingly turned to the Bank of England for loans—at a time when the bank was fighting to meet the same pressures of deposit withdrawals and note redemptions as other banks. Because of its special relationship with the government, the Bank of England could not, like other banks, contract its notes in circulation. As Friedrich Hayek observes, the "insistent and repeated demands from the government for loans not only made it impossible for the Bank to contract the note circulation, but actually led to a considerable expansion."[35]

There was a limit, of course, to the amount the Bank of England could lend to the government. The bills it printed and lent were convertible into gold; if it issued too many bills (beyond the amount demanded by the public to serve as a medium of exchange at prevailing gold prices for goods and services), then the public would bring the bills back for redemption. To solve this problem, in 1797 the Privy Council instructed the Bank of England to suspend convertibility of its liabilities into specie. The bank was now free to issue as many notes as it wanted, and thus the limit that the gold standard had implicitly imposed on government war borrowing was relaxed. In response to this move, all other banks in Britain suspended convertibility into specie as well (arguing that, effectively, they had no choice); their notes and deposits were now convertible into Bank of England notes. Thus, even though such notes were not yet an official legal tender, they functioned in place of gold as the effective monetary unit for the financial system. During the period of suspension, which lasted from 1797 to 1821, the pound had no fixed gold value. Its value was determined, roughly speaking, by the quantity of money that the Bank of England issued relative to the amount of economic activity in the national economy. Money growth was determined largely by government

[35] Hayek (1939), 39.

borrowing needs. In effect, the British government financed the Napoleonic Wars by using the Bank of England to levy an inflation tax.[36]

English Banking in the Scottish Mirror

From 1694 through 1825, while England's banking system consisted of the Bank of England and the country banks and goldsmith banks that operated on a small scale and under restrictive regulation, a completely different sort of banking system was evolving in neighboring Scotland. The Scottish system came to represent the very model of competition, innovation, accessibility to credit for the private sector, and stability—all the things the English banking system could have been but was not.[37]

The comparison was all the more galling to the English considering how relatively backward the Scots had been at the start of the eighteenth century. In 1705, John Law, who later played such an imaginative and destructive role in French finances, penned a monograph titled *Money and Trade Considered*. It laid out the case for chartering a Scottish land bank, a suggestion that was rejected by his countrymen. Law's main argument was that his plan offered a way for Scotland to overcome poverty and widespread financial distress and to assume its rightful role as the country "more capable of an extended Trade than any other Country of Europe."[38]

Law was right about Scotland's potential. Not only was Scotland at the heart of the British Enlightenment, but it also became central to the Atlantic trade between Britain and its colonies. Scottish manufacturing, husbandry, fisheries, and agriculture also thrived. Scotland's competitive

[36] The end of convertibility effectively replaced sovereign default risk with inflation risk, but the latter was of a more incremental nature than default. The unanticipated inflation of prices that accompanied suspension benefited all existing debtors (sovereign and private) by reducing the real values of their outstanding debts. The unanticipated nature of this inflation was key in this redistribution of wealth between creditors and debtors, because anticipated changes in prices are factored into interest rates. For further discussion of the effects of surprise inflations, see the discussion of the greenback suspension in the United States in 1862 in chapter 6 below and the discussions of deflationary and inflationary surprises during the Great Depression in Calomiris (1993b) and Kroszner (1999).

[37] Collins (2012), 17–18. Our discussion of the Scottish system also draws on Kerr (1884), Cameron (1967b), Checkland (1975), Munn (1981), and L. H. White (1984).

[38] Law (1705), 226.

system of banks, many of which operated networks of branches throughout the country, contributed to this success story by providing broad access to credit. The opening of branches was a major innovation: a bank branch can be opened in a remote location with much lower overhead cost than an entirely new bank because the branch can rely on headquarters to provide managerial, accounting, and operational services. All the branch needs is a clerk and till cash.

Unlike the Bank of England, which operated only from its Threadneedle Street headquarters, Scotland's branching banks often operated in areas that could not otherwise have supported a banking presence. Scottish banking innovations also included interest-bearing deposits, the interbank clearing of banknotes, and lines of credit (such as the "cash credit account" invented by the Royal Bank of Scotland in 1728) that permitted borrowers to arrange for credit in advance and draw on their accounts as needed. Scotland's system was also among the first banking systems to rely on small-denomination banknotes as a source of financing.[39]

At the heart of these innovations was the free chartering of banks. There were three specially chartered Scottish banks: the Bank of Scotland (1695), the Royal Bank of Scotland (1727), and the British Linen Company (1746). In addition, freely chartered provincial banks—that is, those chartered under common licensing rules rather than through the conferral of special privileges—also operated as of 1747, and freely chartered joint-stock banks were first established in 1810.

Competition among Scottish banks was fierce. In 1825, the three specially chartered banks operated an average of 15 branches each, while the freely chartered banks in the system averaged almost 3 branches per bank. At that time, English banks had virtually no branches. In 1802, bank assets per capita in Scotland were £7.5, in comparison to £6.0 in England. Scottish banks paid remarkably narrow spreads (roughly 1 percentage point) between rates of interest paid on loans and rates paid on deposits. The fact that they were able to do so while simultaneously earn-

---

[39] Not all Scottish banks operated with limited liability charters. Provincial, and later joint-stock, banks lacked limited liability but competed successfully with limited-liability chartered banks. Scottish banks also experimented with other ideas that were later abandoned, including the use of options clauses that established a contractual structure under which banks were allowed to suspend convertibility of their deposits. This rule was regarded as giving too much flexibility to banks and was eventually prohibited.

ing respectable rates of return for their shareholders implies a high level of efficiency.[40]

Just as remarkable, Scottish banks were much less likely to fail or to impose losses on their debt holders than were their English counterparts. Bank failure rates in England were almost five times those in Scotland from 1809 to 1830, and while losses to English debt holders were sometimes significant, there were virtually no losses on Scottish deposits or notes.[41] The lower failure risk of Scottish banks reflected their greater size, competitiveness, and portfolio diversification. Unlike English banks that were limited to six partners (a rule that kept them small and local), Scottish banks were typically large and diverse.

Why was Scotland's banking structure so different from England's? The question is made particularly salient by the fact that, since 1603, the sovereign of England and the sovereign of Scotland had been one and the same person. The answer is that the Scottish banking bargain was dramatically different from the bargain that had been struck in England. At the time that the Bank of England and the Bank of Scotland were created (in 1694 and 1695, respectively), England and Scotland had separate parliaments (and were separate kingdoms, though they shared a sovereign). When King William was hunting for a way to finance his war against France, Scotland was poor and remote. It was not clear what could be gained from creating a monopoly Scottish bank that would finance the crown. Moreover, the creation of such a bank would have required negotiating with the Scottish parliament, which, although it generally favored King William over the deposed James II, was not as committed to the idea of financing the king's imperial ambitions as the parliament of England was. In point of fact, the charter of the Bank of Scotland prohibited it from lending to the crown without an act of parliament—a fact that suggests that the Scottish parliament was conscious of the problems that could arise if the Bank of Scotland were turned into a vehicle of public finance. From the point of view of the crown, it was simply easier to adopt a policy of laissez-faire with respect to Scotland and to use the Bank of England (as well as other English joint-stock companies) to finance the crown's war efforts.

---

[40] According to L. H. White ([1984], 27), the Bank of Scotland paid average dividend returns to stockholders of 5 percent from 1729 to 1743.

[41] L. H. White (1984), 48.

The Bank of England proved sufficient to finance the crown's wars with France. Thus, even after the parliaments of England and Scotland were fused into a single parliament in 1707, there was no attempt by the crown to recraft the Scottish banking system to serve its war aims. For its part, Scotland committed itself not to become a separate base of political power that might withdraw from or otherwise act contrary to the interests of the British crown. Scotland responded to its favored status in banking by what might be described as an act of unilateral political disarmament. In 1707, in the Act of Union, Scotland disbanded its national parliament in a demonstration of allegiance to Britain.[42] Political union meant that the crown had little cause to worry about the economic consequences of its laissez-faire policy toward Scottish banks, trade, and industry. Despite political union, Scotland's banking system remained separate from those of England and Wales, and quite distinct from them, until liberalization led the other countries to imitate Scottish success—a subject to which we turn in the next chapter.

[42] See Keogh and Whelan (2001) and McKay (2008).

5

IIIIIIIIIIIIIIIIIIIIIIIII

Banks and Democracy

Britain in the Nineteenth and Twentieth Centuries

The time has come to deal with the House of Lords. The absolute veto of
a hereditary Chamber of titled persons over all legislation passed by the
elected representatives of the people in the House of Commons ought not
to continue. . . . As the years unfold, as civilisation expands, as the electors
become more numerous, more educated, more prosperous, they should
have more power, not less.

Winston Churchill (1909)

Britain's Game of Bank Bargains had been played in the eighteenth and
early nineteenth centuries by a very small sliver of the population, one
that was not particularly concerned about the effects of government policies on the ability of common people to obtain bank credit. After the end
of the Napoleonic Wars, however, that elite group gradually lost control
of the game.

Changes in the technology of warfare, beginning in the Napoleonic
Wars and accelerating in the decades leading up to World War I, induced
changes in Britain's narrowly defined suffrage rules, which dated from the
fifteenth century. A series of electoral reforms gradually expanded the
franchise. The 1832 "Great Reform" broke centuries of tradition by reducing the property qualifications for the franchise as well as reallocating
members of Parliament from lightly populated areas to more densely populated ones. An 1867 act further reduced property qualifications in urban
districts, so that roughly one-third of men, including some members of
the working class, had the right to vote. An 1884 act lowered the property requirement even more and extended the same voting qualifications
that applied in towns to the countryside, thereby giving the franchise to
roughly 60 percent of adult men. In 1918 the franchise was extended to
virtually all men and to married women over the age of 30, and in 1928
those last restrictions on the franchise were eliminated.

Along the way, the unelected and hereditary House of Lords gradually lost power to the elected House of Commons. Indeed, the 1832 Great Reform succeeded only because the king threatened that if the act failed to pass the House of Lords, he would create and award additional peerages to those who supported the broadening of the franchise. In 1911, the Parliament Act eliminated the right of the House of Lords to veto money bills and replaced a right to veto other bills with a right to delay those bills for a period not to exceed two years. This act, too, only succeeded because of royal pressure and the threat of creating additional peerages.

The fact that both the cost of waging war and the percentage of the population eligible to vote increased over time does not imply, of course, that changes in warfare directly caused the extension of the franchise. It is hard to imagine, however, that the Napoleonic Wars, which required the mobilization of human beings and treasure on a scale that was previously unimaginable, did not change the way that the British thought about themselves as a nation. By the beginning of the twentieth century, the connections between military and imperial demands and the empowerment of the majority were much clearer. One of the factors that drove the 1911 Parliament Act, which basically made the House of Lords irrelevant, was Britain's experience of mobilizing nearly 300,000 men to fight the Boer War. The 1918 reform, which gave the franchise to virtually all adult men as well as some women, drew the connection even more tightly: it was a recognition of the inequity of sending young men off to Europe's killing fields while denying them the right to vote.

How were the external challenges and internal changes in the allocation of political power reflected in the evolution of British banking? Its history after the Napoleonic Wars can be divided into four phases. The first phase, beginning in the early nineteenth century, saw the end of the Bank of England's monopoly over chartered banking with the establishment of competing chartered banks, operating on a branching basis and serving the domestic and international needs of private commerce and industry.[1] The transition from a monopoly banking system to a more open, competitive system did not immediately end systemic banking crises: they persisted for four decades, but by the 1870s, Britain had entered a second phase in which its banking system remained stable and allocated substan-

---

[1] See related discussions in Bowen (1995), 18, and Kynaston (1995).

tial credit to the private sector. Bank consolidation after the 1880s, however, eventually reduced the level of competition within the system.

A return to a focus on war needs and the transformation of British democracy in the first half of the twentieth century brought a third phase of banking history, characterized by government crowding out of credit (financial repression). From 1914 to 1945 Britain fought what is sometimes referred to as "the Second Thirty Years' War." The Labour Party, which had been inconsequential (controlling only 30 out of 670 seats in Parliament in 1906), grew in importance and became politically dominant after World War II.[2] After the war, Britain's electorate was free to vote for wealth redistribution, and they did so in overwhelming numbers.[3] The government took over management of much of the economy, nationalized many industries, and made the banking system largely irrelevant in the allocation of resources.

The adverse economic consequences of nationalization and government control—specifically, slow growth and increased inflation—set the stage for a fourth phase of British banking history, marked by the resurgence of the Conservative Party and the liberalization of banking laws. This phase began in 1970, but the changes were firmly established by Prime Minister Margaret Thatcher's "Big Bang" of 1986 and the rapid growth of the British financial services industry since that time. Thatcher's economic program of privatization, monetary discipline, and financial liberalization succeeded because she was able to convince the majority of British citizens that reduced taxes, privately owned industry and housing, and a commitment to low inflation would boost economic growth, jobs and wealth, and thereby serve the interests of the common people, not just the rich.

For more than a century, the British banking system had avoided banking crises.[4] The first significant problem since the 1860s was a wave of financial institution failures by shadow banks in the 1970s (the so-called secondary banking crisis), which was precipitated by dramatic swings in

---

[2] M. Gilbert (1997), 149.

[3] This is consistent with the predictions of Meltzer and Richard (1981), who show why the combination of an unequal income distribution and the creation of widespread suffrage and majority rule results in a growth in redistributive government.

[4] Even the disruptions associated with the collapse of international credit markets at the beginning of World War I were handled with little distress in the banking system.

interest rates caused by the government's unstable monetary policies. This banking crisis was, however, mild compared to the crises of the early to mid-nineteenth century. In contrast, the global banking crisis of 2007–09 brought the British banking system to its knees, precipitated major injections of public funds into the banking system, and raised new questions about the desirability of the government policies that had made London one of the great financial centers of the world. As of this writing, deep reforms of banking regulation are being contemplated, with uncertain success, and the longer-term political consequences of the crisis remain unknown.

The Challenges of the Pax Britannica

The victory of the Duke of Wellington at the Battle of Waterloo in June 1815 not only sent Napoleon into captivity in Saint Helena, a five-by-ten mile chunk of rock sitting in the middle of the South Atlantic; it also brought an end to nearly 130 years of war with France. The British government had accomplished its most important strategic goal: making sure that continental Europe remained politically divided and weak and thus unable to contest Britain's ability to build and maintain a world empire. Nearly a century later, Britain would face that challenge again, in the form of a fast-growing and highly militarized Germany—a subject to which we return later in this chapter. In 1815 there was, however, no Germany, just a group of separate German-speaking kingdoms. From the vantage point of 1815, Britain was finally at peace.

The Pax Britannica, the period of stability and hegemony that followed the defeat of Napoleon, came with two big challenges to the British state. The first was how to address the demands for political reform that had been percolating since the eighteenth century. Many of the ideals of republicanism that had fueled the American Revolution were British imports (though with plenty of colonial value added). Calls for reform could be set aside while Britain waged decades of war against France. Once Napoleon was defeated, however, it was difficult to ignore them. Indeed, the mobilization of a nation to fight against a revolutionary government that conceived of its population as citizens instead of subjects of the ruler must surely have encouraged a rethinking of what, exactly, it meant to be British. This rethinking did not all go in one direction: the murderous inclinations of France's Jacobins were so shocking that they provoked a reactionary impulse in Britain—a reaction perhaps best captured by the great orator and statesman Edmund Burke's *Reflections on the Revolution in France* (1790). Nevertheless, even antipopulist writings like this had to make an argument for a liberal conception of government and advocate gradual constitutional reform as a substitute for revolution. The fact that this rethinking of citizenship came on the heels of a long fight against another revolution—this one culturally closer to home, the American Revolution of 1775–83—could only have made it more profound.

From the eighteenth through the early nineteenth centuries, numerous unsuccessful attempts had been made by the Whigs to revise the voting rules for electing members of the House of Commons. The proposed reforms were intended to expand the franchise and shift voting power to urban centers, which had grown dramatically as a consequence of the Industrial Revolution and increased commerce. By 1832 reform could be resisted no longer. Violent demonstrations took place; governments were formed, failed, and re-formed; even King William IV interceded by threatening to create 80 new peerages (appointments to the House of Lords) that would be awarded to supporters of electoral reform.

The Representation of the People Act of 1832 (commonly known as the Reform Act or the Great Reform Act) increased the Parliamentary representation of the burgeoning industrial cities at the expense of locations with minuscule populations (the so-called rotten boroughs). It increased the number of eligible voters from about 400,000 to about 650,000 (approximately one-sixth of the adult male population) by relaxing the property-ownership requirement for voting.[5] By the standards of the twenty-first century, such a broadening of the electorate does not look terribly consequential, but by the standards of the early nineteenth century, the Great Reform was tremendously important.

Another challenge facing the British state after the defeat of Napoleon was how to reconfigure the relationship between the Bank of England and the British government now that the government no longer needed the bank for war finance. Calls to reconfigure that relationship went back

---

[5] Phillips and Wetherell ([1995], 411) show that the 1832 reform was a watershed event in British electoral politics. For further details on the political controversies leading up to the 1832 act and its consequences, see May (1896), Trevelyan (1922), Thorne (1986), Evans (1983), and Cragoe (2008).

at least as far as a 1780 speech in Parliament by Edmund Burke in which he laid out the case for reforming the accounting and disbursement practices of the government and, in particular, changing the rules for managing the accounts and cash flows that connected the Bank of England with the treasury.

The first step in reforming this relationship was to return to the gold standard. This change not only benefited the British public by eliminating the inflation tax; it also facilitated trade across the British empire by allowing merchants to operate in an environment of stable prices and fixed exchange rates. But the return to the gold standard and the convertibility of Bank of England notes was not painless, either economically or politically. In fact, the Bank of England resisted the necessary contraction in its balance sheet and went back to converting its notes to gold only in response to a parliamentary mandate in 1819, with the actual resumption of convertibility taking place in 1821—six years after hostilities with France had ended.[6]

The deflationary shock that accompanied the return to the gold standard depressed the economy and provoked vocal criticism of the Bank of England and the government.[7] The return to the gold standard required the bank to constrain the supply of its notes over the course of several years, so that the ratio of gold held by the bank relative to its notes would be sufficiently high to permit it to maintain a credible parity between its outstanding notes and its gold reserves.[8] In the years leading up to the resumption of convertibility, the supply of Bank of England notes fell from £27.2 million in 1815 to £20.3 million in 1821. The bank achieved this contraction largely by shedding private-sector loans and discounts, a policy that did not endear it to merchants and manufacturers.[9] Total private-

---

[6] Neal (1998), 55.

[7] See Acworth (1925).

[8] For a contemporary discussion of the relationship between the Bank's balance sheet and resumption, see Thornton (1802). A more recent commentary on this issue, which builds on Thornton, is found in Hayek (1978). See also the Bullion Report of 1810, reprinted, with commentary, as Cannan (1925).

[9] The increase in productivity related to the beginning of the Industrial Revolution in Britain offset somewhat the adjustment costs of returning to convertibility. Although the pound price of gold was restored to its prior value and the prices of tradable goods also fell to levels close to their presuspension values, wages and the prices of other nontradable goods remained elevated after the suspension (by some estimates, nominal wages were about 20 percent higher in 1821 than in 1793: see Gayer, Rostow, and Schwartz [1975], 1: 54, 167). This phenomenon—which is sometimes labeled the

sector assets held by the Bank of England fell from £20.7 million in 1815 to only £2.7 million in 1821. Holdings of government debt fell much less over the same period, from £24.2 million to £15.8 million.[10]

The popular discontent arising from these changes encouraged the second step in the reconfiguring of the Bank of England's relationship with the government: a string of reforms designed to end mutual back scratching. Some of these measures improved accounting (e.g., by requiring paper records of all transactions).[11] Others (such as the 1817 Act 57 George III, c. 48; and the 1819 Act 59 George III, c. 76) regulated the mode by which quarterly advances (loans) were made by the Bank of England to the treasury. These measures also precluded the bank from making advances to the government without the express approval of Parliament. As one contemporary noted: "These regulations . . . put it out of the power of the Government to obtain pecuniary accommodation from the Bank of an irregular character. . . . The relations between the Government and the Bank in regard to the management of the funds at the disposal of the latter body, must now be regulated by mutual consideration of the general interests of the community, and are so amenable to public control as to render irregular, or even questionable, proceedings practically impossible."[12]

Unwinding the Bank of England's Monopoly

The third and final step in the reconfiguration of the relationship between the Bank of England and the government was the ending of the bank's monopoly charter and its gradual conversion into a banker's bank and

---

Ricardo-Viner-Harrod-Balassa-Samuelson effect in honor of all the famous economists who espoused it—reflects the positive relative productivity growth in the British tradable goods sector (relative to other countries) that occurred during Britain's suspension of convertibility (that is, the productivity consequences of the British Industrial Revolution). According to this theory, if a country experiences relatively high productivity growth in its tradable goods sector, then the prices of nontradable goods in that country, including wages, must rise relative to those of other countries. This meant that wages and the prices of nontradables did not have to fall by as much during the resumption of convertibility of the pound.

[10] The decline in public securities holdings by the Bank of England reflected both the ability of the government to place its debts elsewhere and smaller government deficits. The improved fiscal position of the government was reflected in lower yields on government debt. See Neal (1998), 57.

[11] For a detailed chronological review, see Philippovich (1911), 183–210.

[12] Schuster (1923), 11, quoting Arbuthnot in 1858.

the lender of last resort in the financial system. This conversion was the outcome of numerous actions by Parliament over a long period to reduce the bank's privileges, which were met by determined, but ultimately unsuccessful, attempts by the bank to preserve those privileges. As part of those efforts, the Bank of England sought to preserve public support for its privileges, and lessen the demands for the chartering of competing banks, by accommodating demands for credit in the market for bills of exchange. The political exigencies of bill accommodation by the bank gave rise to a remarkably unstable banking system: there were major crises roughly every ten years between 1825 and 1866. Ultimately, however, as the privileges awarded to the Bank of England waned, so did its willingness to provide destabilizing accommodation. Over time, the nature of the Bank of England's assistance to the market became stabilizing as the bank was gradually transformed from a commercial bank that also financed the government into a lender of last resort charged with supporting a much broader banking system.

Manufacturers and merchants had long complained that the Bank of England's monopoly placed an unjust and costly constraint on the supply of private credit. London's merchants had organized protests to pressure the bank to broaden its discounting policies in 1793 and again in 1795. They issued a joint statement asserting that if the bank were unwilling to maintain sufficient discounting, "it will be requisite that some other Public Establishment should be created to supply the Deficiency; at the same time wishing that this assistance may be derived through the old and customary Channel, the Bank of England."[13] It was a direct threat to the bank: broaden access to credit, or we will push to charter a new bank that will meet our needs.

From the point of view of England's merchants and industrialists, the first best option would have been a competitive system of large banks with nationwide branch networks, of the sort that had developed in Scotland during the eighteenth century. The government's desire to preserve its control over the banking system through its special relationship with the Bank of England, however, had precluded that option. Thus at the end of the Napoleonic Wars, the English banking system consisted of the Bank of England, which did not branch beyond its headquarters on Threadneedle

[13] King (1936), 71–72.

Street, the goldsmith banks in London (which were still constrained by the six-partner rule), and several hundred small country banks that were also subject to the six-partner rule. Although the number of country banks had risen substantially, from about 100 in the 1780s to more than 300 in 1800 and more than 600 by 1810, their operations were inherently limited and local.[14]

In the nineteenth century, therefore, England's merchants and manufacturers had to make do with a second-best option: a market in London for discounting bills, whose most important participants were the Bank of England, the country banks, the goldsmith banks, and independent "bill brokers."[15] Although this system provided increased access to credit in remote areas, it was inherently unstable as well as inefficient when compared to a system of large, nationwide banks. Small banks could not easily diversify their risks across geographic regions or across different types of borrowers; neither could bankers easily shift funds within the system in order to head off runs. The system was inefficient at channeling financial resources from locations of surplus deposits (relative to lending opportunities) to locations of surplus loan opportunities relative to deposits; it relied on a series of bilateral exchanges to accomplish that goal. In addition, the small goldsmith banks and country banks could not exploit scale economies in administration and accounting.

Given the unique scale and location of the Bank of England, it played a leading role in making the bills market function—and the decisions it made in this regard therefore became the focus of controversy. Merchants and manufacturers viewed the bank's willingness to discount bills issued by country banks as the measure of its commitment to supporting the private sector, and critics often found that commitment wanting. The Bank of England, for its part, wanted to limit its exposure to low-quality paper and took the position that it could not serve as a central discounting facility for every bill issued by every country bank or bill broker. The struggle between the merchants and the bank was apparent in the bank's attempts

---

[14] Pressnell (1956) shows that the country banks were involved in a wide range of activities, including the finance of industrial working capital (19–36), wholesale trade (47–56, 357–65), agriculture (344–55), and canals, turnpikes, and other investment projects, through both the provision of credit and other facilitations of those projects (259–76, 372–400). On the limitations of the system, see Cameron (1967a), 24–25.

[15] King (1936), xii–xiii; Pressnell (1956), 75–104, 116–25.

to establish a classification system for bills and to price bills of different quality accordingly. Merchants opposed this system, and it was abandoned.[16] Eventually, the bank developed a policy of "accommodation" of the bills market (that is, it purchased bills held by other banks and bill brokers when they presented them to the bank). It did so even during times of systemic illiquidity. Even when this policy was not in the bank's economic interest, it served a political interest: the bank had to respond to public demands that it support the supply of credit during normal times and assist other banks during times of crisis.

Despite the Bank of England's desire to maintain its monopoly privileges, the rising tides of democracy and industrialization proved too much for it. The advocates of greater competition in bank chartering ultimately won the day because they could point to three powerful facts: England lacked sufficient sources of credit for the private sector; the English financial system had produced an unstable credit market that was unusually prone to commercial and bank failures; and there was ample evidence from outside England (especially in Scotland) that competitive chartering would produce greater access to credit with greater banking stability.

The timing of the reform of English bank chartering illustrates the power of specific historical events to precipitate long-contemplated changes. Political trends and logical arguments may favor reform, but major changes in the structure of financial systems often coincide with crises that galvanize the movement for reform.[17] In English banking, the galvanizing event was the banking crisis of 1825, arguably the first global banking crisis of the modern era and one with severe consequences for English merchants, manufacturers, artisans, and bankers.[18] Critics blamed the Bank of England

---

[16] King (1936), 53. Our examination of data on Bank of England discounting, however, shows that discount rates did vary across bills during the panics of 1857 and 1866, so clearly the bank subsequently was able to vary its discount rates according to perceived risks. We have not determined the starting date or the extent of such variation.

[17] For a discussion of the role of financial crises in precipitating major reforms, see Hoffman, Postel-Vinay, and Rosenthal (2007).

[18] As in all financial crises, it is difficult to allocate blame precisely, and in global crises like 1825 this applies all the more. One of the primary drivers, beginning in 1822, was a run-up in risky lending to newly independent Latin American countries, all of which went into default by 1825. The Bank of England played a major role in this lending boom. Once problems with these loans began to surface, the bank refused to

(and the banking structure that its privileges had produced) for the severity of the crisis. The lack of available liquidity outside London during the crisis produced commercial insolvencies and bank failures on a spectacular scale. Seventy-three out of 770 country banks failed. Bankruptcy filings in 1826 reached an unprecedented level. The inherent vulnerability of the country's small banks was clearly demonstrated, as were the costs to the private sector of the absence of liquidity providers (large banks) that could have supported the smaller banks operating outside London.[19]

The British public took away three lessons from the crisis of 1825. First, the Bank of England could not be relied on to manage the supply of money and credit in the economy. Second, its for-profit status meant that the bank was insufficiently committed to the public good. Third, the banking system that the bank's monopoly privileges had shaped was too centralized in London. Critics saw this centralization as contributing to destabilizing effects in other English towns and cities.[20] The chancellor of the Exchequer and the first lord of the treasury did not mince words when they wrote to the governor of the Bank of England: in the past, the Bank of England "may have been in Itself and by Itself fully equal to all the important Duties & Operations confided to it," but "the rise of country banks alone shows it is no longer up to the tasks required from the increased wealth and new wants of the Country."[21]

The policy response to this crisis was the Country Bankers' Act of 1826, which allowed (and strongly encouraged) the Bank of England to open branches outside London.[22] Over the ensuing years, it opened branches in numerous cities, and Manchester and Birmingham became particularly active branches.[23] Additionally, the act ended the bank's monopoly on char-

---

provide liquidity for participants in the London bills market, who were scrambling for cash. Neal (1998), 60–62, 70.

[19] Neal (1998), 65, 68–69.

[20] Other lessons were also learned, including the need to design more effective means of managing financial distress for nonbanks, the need to expand firms' access to securities markets, and the need to constrain the small-denomination note issues of country banks (small-denomination notes tend to be traded by less sophisticated parties, who may be less able to perceive and punish higher default risk).

[21] Neal (1998), 70–71.

[22] The crisis of 1825 also caused a rethinking of the strict rules governing the creation of limited liability companies. The Bubble Act of 1720 was therefore repealed in 1825.

[23] The Bank of England established branches in Manchester, Gloucester, Swansea, Birmingham, Liverpool, Bristol, and Leeds in 1828 and added branches in Exeter, New-

tered banking. Competing joint-stock banks could be chartered, although they would not be permitted to operate within a 65-mile radius of London, and their shareholders were not granted limited liability. These banks were not prohibited by law from issuing banknotes, but the Bank of England made it known that it would not deal with banks that entered that business, and this threat was sufficient to prevent the new joint-stock banks from issuing notes.[24] The Bank of England also made agreements with existing country banks: in exchange for the country banks' consenting not to issue banknotes, the Bank of England agreed to grant them more favorable discounting facilities at its new branches.[25] In essence, the act forced the Bank of England to increase credit by working with both the new joint-stock banks and the existing country banks. It was, however, able to craft arrangements that maintained its effective monopoly over note issues.

In 1833 the Bank of England's charter was up for renewal, and the government took this opportunity to erode the bank's monopoly further and to demand additional concessions. The government renewed the bank's charter through 1855, but the charter was revocable at the pleasure of Parliament after an initial grace period of 12 years. The 1833 Charter Act also removed the prohibition against joint-stock banks operating in London. The Bank of England now faced competition even in its home market, although that competition was somewhat attenuated by the fact that the act prohibited the new joint-stock banks of London from issuing banknotes.[26] In addition, the Act effectively eliminated the usury law lim-

---

castle, Hull, and Norwich in 1829. For a discussion of the related improvements in the efficiency of credit markets, see Ziegler (1990).

[24] Neal (1998), 73.

[25] Pressnell (1956), 179. The note issues of country banks fell, apparently at least in part as a consequence of this measure (Pressnell [1956], 158–65).

[26] The *Minutes of the Court of the Bank of England* makes it clear that the Bank did not give up its privileges without a fight. For example, the governor of the bank, with the advice of legal counsel, wrote numerous letters to the chancellor of the Exchequer, arguing that the admission of joint-stock banks into the London market would infringe on the bank's legal rights. In a letter dated August 6, 1833, he wrote: "We feel that we should act disingenuously by your Lordship if we did not state explicitly that it is their conviction as well as our own that Banks of Deposit cannot be permitted within the limit intended to be fixed as the local limit of the Bank's exclusive privilege within a positive infraction of the Agreement made between His Majesty's Government and the Bank of England and frequently recognized by your Lordship. The Directors therefore

iting loan interest to 5 percent, thereby broadening the pool of borrowers to whom the Bank of England and the new joint-stock banks could lend—in effect, making the credit market more competitive still.[27]

The 1833 act also made the Bank of England's notes a legal tender, meaning that they could be used in the payment of all legal debts. This was a bold move: it meant that Bank of England notes would have value on par with gold, regardless of the underlying financial condition of the bank, because those notes could be used to pay taxes. The parliamentary discussion of this provision made it clear that this new power was intended to encourage the Bank of England to provide liquidity to other banks (that is, lend money, by buying bills they were holding with Bank of England notes) during crises. The leading advocate in Parliament of making the bank's notes a legal tender, Lord Althorp, explicitly pointed to this advantage of freeing the bank from market discipline during crises.[28] In case Althorp's arguments were not hint enough about what Parliament wanted the bank to do, Parliament avoided any possibility of misunderstanding by reserving the right to revoke the bank's charter.

In 1844 Parliament made the Bank of England's position more difficult still: the Peel Act of that year gave the bank an airtight monopoly on new note issues but required it to maintain 100 percent specie reserves against those note issues. This requirement meant that the bank could not benefit financially from its monopoly on banknotes: both its notes and the 100 percent gold reserves held against its notes paid zero interest. The new requirement was instituted in order to discourage financial crises by constraining credit growth, but it had almost no effect, for the simple reason that it was founded on a flawed theory: the money supply consisted

---

rely upon the good faith of the Government to give them the full benefit of that agreement" (Bank of England [August 8, 1833]). The minutes also make it clear that these declarations were to no avail. The correspondence between the governor of the Bank of England and the chancellor of the Exchequer during 1833 indicates that parliamentary constraints on the chancellor would lead to major alterations to the bank's charter. This is explicitly stated, for example, in the chancellor's letter to the governor of July 3, 1833, apparently with regard to a proposed limited-liability provision that the two previously had agreed upon.

[27] The usury law was effectively repealed by exempting the Bank of England from usury limits in discounting bills of three months' or less duration. Andreades (1966), 262–64.

[28] Andreades (1966), 260.

not only of the stock of specie coins and banknotes but also the outstanding amount of bank deposits and bills of exchange, and these could expand independently of note issues by the Bank of England.[29] Thus the 1844 act did not effectively constrain credit growth, deposit growth, bill of exchange growth, or aggregate monetary growth.[30]

The 1844 Peel Act put the Bank of England in an untenable position: it had a political mandate to provide liquidity to other banks in times of crisis, but its capacity to issue notes to provide that liquidity was limited to its stock of gold reserves. How could the Bank inject cash into the market suddenly if its notes had to be backed 100 percent by gold? Furthermore, like any other bank, the Bank of England was a privately owned company, intended to make a profit, and constrained by the public's willingness to hold its notes and deposits, which excessive leveraging or risky lending could undermine. The answer to this problem was simple: the Peel Act was suspended during the 1847, 1857, and 1866 financial crises. Somewhat comically, each time, the Bank of England begged the government *not* to suspend the law.[31] The sight of a banker begging a regulator not to forbear in enforcing a regulation is rare, but in this case, the bank's motives were clear: so long as note creation was limited by regulation, the bank had an excuse to limit its purchases of bills issued by other banks. The government, of course, wanted the market to be "accommodated"—

---

[29] This 1844 reform came in response to a banking panic in 1836. Prior reforms had focused largely on chartering and on encouraging Bank of England liquidity provision. Under the Bank Act of 1844 (the brainchild of the so-called currency school), the focus of reform was to make the economy more stable by keeping aggregate money and credit adjustment flows from varying too much in response to changes in international trade and capital flows. A major problem with this theory, however, was that notes and specie did not account for the entire money supply; bank deposits were widely used, and bills of exchange were the principal means of payment used in business transactions. Thus the 1844 act did not effectively constrain the growth of credit, deposits, or bills of exchange, or aggregate monetary growth. For a more complete discussion, see King (1936), 32, and Hughes (1960), 250–58.

[30] Credit growth and specie flows moved in opposite directions in the 1850s, when specie was flowing out of London (mainly as a result of bimetallic arbitrage involving France) while credit was growing dramatically. From 1852 to 1857, currency outstanding fell from £34 million to £25 million, while the deposits of the five London joint-stock banks rose from £17.7 million to £40 million, and the average volume of bills of exchange in circulation (the asset intermediated in the London discount market) rose from £66 million to an estimated £180–200 million. Hughes (1960), 250–56, 258.

[31] Hughes (1960), 320–21; Bagehot (1962), 65–66.

that is, for the Bank of England to play the role of lender of last resort. It therefore always made sure that the regulation was suspended during crises, forcing the Bank of England to discount bills of exchange freely, including some that, from the bank's point of view, were of dubious value.

No Longer the Government's Monopoly Bank, but a Lender of Last Resort

The bank's accommodation of the discount market came to be relied upon by the rest of the banking industry and the British government to manage financial crises.[32] Consider, for example, this account of the actions of the bank during the 1857 crisis, which emphasizes the scale and scope of bank discounting activities: "The deposit runs on the London discount houses and their efforts to cover their deposits led to a surge of applications to the Bank for aid during the [1857] crisis. . . . From 10 to 12 November Overend & Gurney alone were given 1.8 million."[33] Needless to say, private market participants were aware of the bank's support of the bills market.[34] Indeed, many historians have argued that this aware-

---

[32] The bank was less generous in Scotland: two large Scottish banks failed in the 1857 crisis, although Hughes argues that the bank was right to deny credit due to the insolvency of these institutions (Hughes [1960], 311–31).

[33] The bank's discounts and advances were given to all sectors of the business community. Of the £79.4 million of accommodation given in 1857, £35.8 million was given in the last three months of the year. This figure represents for the most part the discounts of the panic period. Of this amount, half, or £17.8 million, was direct loans and discounts to merchants. Scottish banks received £1.3 million, country banks (including joint-stock banks in London and banks outside London) £7.1 million, and the discount houses £9.5 million. Of the country banks, those outside London received almost £6 million, while those inside the city received only about £1 million. The heaviest demand for accommodation came from the merchants, followed by the discount houses and the country bankers (Hughes [1960], 302–3, 305).

[34] The subsidization of risk by the bank did not follow from any attempt to undercut the market rate. In fact, the bank's rate was above market during the 1850s (Hughes [1960], 301). The essence of the bank's subsidy to the market was its willingness to accommodate demand, which meant that whatever rate the bank charged, the market could comfortably discount at below that rate. Describing the discounting of bills as a definitive put option is a bit of an overstatement. The bank could, and did, raise the rate of discount during panics, so the price of the option was a moving target. Indeed, Hughes ([1960], 371) remarks that the decision to raise the rate during the panic alarmed the market, a reaction that one could interpret as reflecting an adverse shock to market expectations. Also, the relaxation of the restrictive provisions of the

ness created perverse incentives for risk taking in the bills market, leading to undesirable tolerance for expanded leverage and low-quality credits during booms.[35] Of course, there was no explicit guarantee to convert bills to cash at the Bank of England, only an implicit one.[36]

In principle, the bank could have refused to accommodate bills both before and during banking crises. But that would have been difficult in practice for political reasons, because the Bank relied on the government, and on public opinion, to maintain its (dwindling) special privileges.[37] As one observer put it: "No special duty is, by law, imposed upon the Bank; yet that such duties exist through an unwritten law, that they have been recognized and are acted upon, is beyond doubt. They affect our commercial life so closely and are so indissolubly connected with the functions and duties which are properly those of the State that to look upon the Bank of England merely as a private trading institution, and not as virtually the State or Government bank, is an impossibility."[38]

1844 act, discussed below, was not a certainty, so the ability to exercise the put option was subject to doubt.

[35] See Hughes (1960), 264–65, citing Newmarch, arguing that market participants expected to be protected by the bank.

[36] Nevertheless, David Salomon, director of the London and Westminster Bank, recognized that the Bank of England's support for the bills market was central to the problem of credit-fueled bubbles. He was asked: "And do you think it is part of the functions of the Bank of England to discount a bill for anybody merely because the party holding the bill wishes to convert it to cash?" He responded: "As I said before, the Bank of England will have great difficulty in getting rid of that inconvenient idea which there is in the mind of the public, that the Bank of England is something more than an ordinary joint-stock bank" (Hughes [1960], 300).

[37] Writing in 1858 about the panic of 1857 and the supportive role played by the bank in resolving it, one contemporary wrote:

> There can be little doubt . . . of the advantage which accrues to commerce from the employment of these funds, either directly or indirectly, in the discount of bills. . . .
> [T]hey . . . find their way into the money market and are applied to the purposes of trade; but when the demands for money are great, and the rate of interest consequently high, great advantages are afforded by the resource the Bank of England affords under the system of management now pursued; such houses are assured that the funds at the disposal of the Bank will always be available for the legitimate objects of trade at the current rate of interest. Whence ensues that confidence which is derived from uniformity of system. The Bank of England has then come to be regarded as the centre and mainstay of mercantile credit.

Schuster (1923), 21–22, quoting Arbuthnot.

[38] Schuster (1923), 8.

The fact that the government looked to the Bank of England to act as a lender of last resort was especially apparent in the parliamentary inquiry into the bank's actions after the crisis of 1857. The questioning of the governor of the Bank of England by the parliamentary committee could not have been more telling. One historian of the bank summarized the results of the inquiry as follows:

> Witnesses were specially asked whether every house which applied, and deserved assistance, received it. From the evidence it appears that the Directors of the Bank of England went into the country to examine the accounts of banks in difficulties, in order to render assistance if they appeared to be sound. The Governor of the Bank of England was asked: "You did not refuse accommodation to any person, even up to the time when the Act was suspended, who brought you good securities." The answer was "No." "I think you have admitted that you did not act during that time upon purely banking considerations, but that you had public considerations in view?" "Yes." "You admit that the course which the relative position of the Bank took during that period is not one strictly in accordance with general banking rules?" "Yes."[39]

A "Tough Love" Lender of Last Resort

By 1857, it appeared that England's banking system had become one of the world's most unstable. (One of its main rivals for the title of most unstable was the United States, a subject to which we turn in chapter 6.) England had experienced severe banking crises, on average, about every 10 years—in 1825, 1836–37, 1847, and 1857—and they seemed to be getting worse over time.

A significant public debate ensued after the panic of 1857 about the political and economic weaknesses that had produced what today we would call the moral-hazard problem of central bank accommodation. When a central bank commits to providing liquidity to the market, such a commitment can encourage risk taking by bankers and bill brokers, who feel somewhat protected by their ability to sell paper to the central bank in a pinch. This can encourage carelessness in risk management and a ten-

[39] Schuster (1923), 22.

dency for those who feel protected to ride waves of optimism during booms. Parliamentary hearings in 1858 exposed some of the dangers of moral hazard and acknowledged that the existing accommodation policy, itself a creature of a political bargain rather than an explicit law, was not good public policy. *Bankers' Magazine* and the *Economist* also decried the destabilizing effects of the discounting policy of the bank.[40] These facts made it politically safer for the bank to change policy, and its court of directors passed the following resolution of March 11, 1858: "That habitual advances by Discount or Loan to Bill Brokers, Discount Companies and Money Dealers being calculated to lead them to rely on the assistance of the Bank of England for their security in time of pressure; Advances to Bill Brokers, Discount Companies and Money Dealers shall be confined to Loans made at the period of the Quarterly advances, or to Loans made under special and urgent circumstances which shall be communicated by the Governors at the earliest opportunity to the Court for its approval."[41]

Translated into plain English, the Bank of England announced that it was changing its discounting policies: in particular, the bank would be significantly less generous during lending booms and more discriminating during crises, although the court recognized that exceptional accommodation could still be made at its discretion during "special and urgent circumstances."

After this announced change, the bank ended its policy of accommodating bill brokers during normal times.[42] The test of its resolve to be more discriminating during crises came in the Overend & Gurney crisis of 1866. During that crisis, the bank acted as a lender of last resort, accommodating even the bill brokers that it viewed as fundamentally solvent but illiquid. It declined, however, to accommodate one of England's largest financial institutions, Overend & Gurney, which it viewed as not just illiquid, but insolvent, letting that bank fail.[43]

[40] King (1936), 202–3.
[41] Hughes (1960), 305.
[42] See Flandreau and Ugolini (2011).
[43] Because Overend & Gurney had been rescued in 1857 but was permitted to fail in 1866, the change in policy inspired the remark that "Overends broke the Bank in 1866 because it went, and in 1857 because it was not let go." The Bank of England provided liquidity to other banks and bill brokers that it considered to be solvent. As

It is difficult to isolate the effects of any single policy change on the long-run development of a financial system, but judging from the historical outcome, the Bank of England's new tough-love lending policy helped to stabilize the British banking system. The boom and bust cycles that had characterized British banking for four decades ended; no similarly severe banking crisis would recur in Britain until 2007–09. One interpretation of these facts is that in an environment in which imprudent banks do not get rescued, but prudent banks do, it pays to be a prudent bank.[44]

We would also stress, however, that the Bank of England's new policy regarding the bills market was made easier to implement by virtue of the fact that the bank was no longer the lender of last resort to a multitude of tiny (and inherently unstable) country banks and bill brokers. Rather, the series of legal changes instituted between 1826 (when joint-stock banks were first allowed to be formed outside London) and 1862 (when legislative changes finally permitted banks to operate as limited liability companies) produced a boom first in the number and later in the scale of chartered banks.[45] By 1836, just 11 years after the 1825 reform, there were 61 joint-stock banks operating 472 banking facilities (banks and branches) in England. By 1870, there were 111 joint-stock banks operating 1,127 banking facilities.[46] Not only were these joint-stock banks inherently more stable than the country banks and goldsmith banks that were now disappearing from the market, they were themselves becoming major sources of liquidity for the market. In addition, the growth of the joint-stock banks, as well as the growth in Bank of England branches, reduced demand for bill brokerage. In short, a system of large, nation-

---

best one can tell from comparing the amounts of credit provided by the Bank of England in 1857 and 1866, the bank behaved quite similarly in the amount granted, the rates charged, and the profiles of borrowers. That was not a violation of the rule it had established on March 11, 1858, which specifically called for relaxation during "special and urgent circumstances." The significant changes in policy were reflected in the decisions not to provide pro-cyclical accommodation to the bills brokers in the years leading up to the crisis and to allow Overend & Gurney to fail. See Flandreau and Ugolini (2011).

[44] Bagehot (1962); Andreades (1966); Hawtrey (1932, 1938); King (1936); Clapham (1944), vol. 2; Hughes (1960); Capie (2002, 2009).

[45] Collins (2012), 74–80.

[46] In all of Britain in 1870, 378 banks operated 2,738 banking facilities. Capie and Webber (1985), 576.

wide, branching banks had finally replaced an inherently unstable and inefficient system of country banks and bill brokers.[47]

Over the next four decades, the Bank of England fine-tuned its tools for stabilizing the British financial system. During periods when the economy was performing well, the bank varied the rate at which it discounted bills or made advances to banks in order to promote monetary and financial stability.[48] When the economy was performing less well, the bank undertook an innovative approach to assisting the financial system to return to stability. That approach was embodied in two mechanisms of central bank assistance.

First, the bank lent freely on good collateral during panics at a high rate of interest (a policy now known as Bagehot's rule). By lending against good collateral, the bank could provide liquidity to other banks but could suffer losses only to the extent that the borrowing institution failed *and* the collateral declined in value. By lending at high rates of interest, the bank discouraged free riding by borrowers who were not genuinely in need.

The second mechanism that the bank pioneered was to share risk with the other banks in the British financial system. An example was an innovative insurance arrangement between the Bank of England and the London clearing banks in the provision of credit guarantees to forestall the spread of the Barings crisis of 1890, which was caused by losses incurred by that bank in the Argentine bond market. The London banks created a guarantee fund to cover losses at Barings, and the Bank of England effectively underwrote the group's guarantee by offering additional significant funding. This insurance fund was sufficiently large to reassure depositors at the London banks that their money was not at risk because of Barings' financial difficulties.[49] The Bank of England's role was to provide a belt on

---

[47] Hughes (1960), 306. See also King (1936).

[48] Hawtrey (1932, 1938); Bagehot (1962); Andreades (1966); King (1936); Clapham (1944), vol. 2; Hughes (1960); Capie (2002, 2009).

[49] To say that the bank was innovative is not to say that it was uniquely innovative or that it was the first to use this sort of technique. E. White (2011) shows that the Banque de France used a similar two-tiered risk-sharing technique in its coordination of assistance (with French banks) for the Paris Bourse in 1882. In 1908, José Limantour, the finance minister of Mexico, used a somewhat different guarantee approach to assist Mexican banks to float debt backed by bank loans in the wake of the panic of 1907 (Conant [1910], and chapter 10 below).

top of the suspenders of mutual insurance by the other London banks, and it did so with little possibility of loss, particularly as the London clearing banks paid in an amount that exceeded the value of the immediately maturing obligations of Barings.[50] Both types of policies—Bagehot's rule and the mutual-guarantee fund—put the Bank of England in a senior position as a creditor, thereby minimizing the moral-hazard problems that can arise when central banks provide assistance to other participants in the banking system.

The Growth of Large-Scale Commercial Banks

The English banking system began as an insiders' game, primarily serving the fiscal interests of the State and the personal interests of a small group of well-connected private citizens. After the Napoleonic Wars, the political pressures that democratization and industrialization had put on the banking system, coupled with an end to the government's need for war finance, undid that monopoly arrangement. Moving from a system designed to finance government deficits to a system designed to finance the private sector was not a seamless process: Britain went through more than four decades of adjustment, which included banking crises in 1825, 1836–1837, 1847, 1857, and 1866.

By the end of the nineteenth century, however, the English banking system had finally achieved stability and broad credit provision. With the exception of an externally driven crisis that resulted from the beginning of World War I, Britain remained free of systemic banking crises for over a century after 1866.[51] At the same time, as figure 5.1 shows, the English banking system grew dramatically, in terms of both its deposit base relative to GDP and borrowers' access to banks or bank offices.[52]

British banks became increasingly large-scale enterprises. As figure 5.2 shows, the growth in the banking system during the last third of the nine-

---

[50] Clapham (1944), 2: 326–39; Andreades (1966), 366–67.

[51] For a detailed account of the crisis at the beginning of World War I, see Roberts, Reading, and Skene (2009).

[52] Some economic historians criticize British banks for being excessively conservative in their financing policies before World War I, and they attribute slower British growth in part to that timidity. Others regard the slowdown as reflecting the natural tendency of large economies to grow more slowly. For a review of this debate, see Collins (1995), especially chapter 4.

Banking offices per 10,000 population   Deposits as percentage of GDP

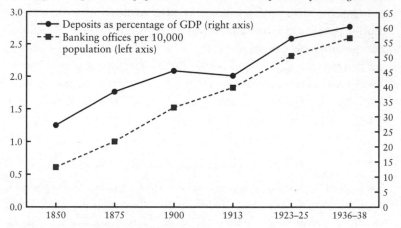

FIGURE 5.1 Size of the U.K. banking system, 1850–1938.

Source: Collins (2012), 46, 52, 53, 204, 206.

Note: Includes Ireland. Bank deposits in 1923–25 and 1936–38 are "net deposits," defined as total deposits less interbank deposits.

Number of banks   Number of bank offices

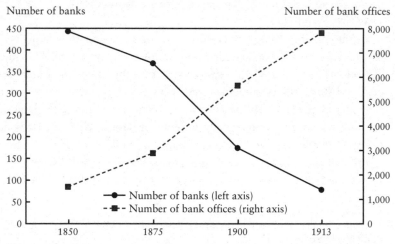

FIGURE 5.2 Number of banks and bank offices in the United Kingdom, 1850–1913.

Source: Collins (2012), 46, 52, 53, 204, 206.

Note: Does not include Ireland.

teenth century coincided with a rapid process of consolidation that gave rise to several dozen large banks with extensive branch networks.[53] By the beginning of the twentieth century, five large banks dominated the system —Barclays, Lloyds, Midland, National Provincial, and Westminster. By 1920, the "Big Five" accounted for about 80 percent of deposits and lending.[54] There is debate as to whether these five constituted a cartel, setting prices and rationing credit in order to earn rents. Some evidence points to cartel-like behavior, while other evidence suggests that the large banks competed against one another.[55] Regardless of whether one would judge the system as a cartel, by the early 1900s the continuing consolidation of the banking system was clearly having anticompetitive consequences. One study has examined the effects on bank stock returns around the timing of bank merger announcements from 1885 to 1925. During the early phase of bank consolidation, gains in stock prices for merging banks reflected efficiency gains from consolidations, and those consolidations occurred within a highly competitive environment. In the later years, however, much of the gains in banks' stock values at the time of merger announcements reflected the reductions in competition that attended the mergers. During this later period, the stock-price increases of the banks that were not participating in an announced merger rose on the announcement by an average of roughly 2 percent, providing evidence of gains from the reduced competition implied by the merger. The authors of that study also found that—consistent with increasing market power by banks in the loan market—the proportion of loans relative to assets declined over time.[56]

In the late nineteenth and early twentieth centuries, the British banking system also saw the expansion of new types of financial intermediaries that catered to particular niches of consumer banking. These included small savings and insurance institutions (friendly societies, building societies, trustee savings banks, and insurance companies), which were sometimes granted special tax exemptions. By 1873, there were about 1,500 building societies. The government also established a Post Office Savings Bank in 1861, which invested in public debt, performed prescribed func-

[53] For more details, see Sheppard (1971); Collins (2012).
[54] Billings and Capie (2007), 143–44.
[55] Capie and Billings (2004), 69–103.
[56] Braggion, Dwarkasing, and Moore (2012).

tions, paid a fixed interest rate, and limited the size of deposits. By 1904, there were over 15,000 branches of the Post Office Savings Bank and roughly 400 offices of trustee savings banks.[57] These new institutions reflected the rise of the middle class as both an economic reality and a political force seeking its own sources of financing.

War, Empire, and Expansion of the Franchise in the Twentieth Century

In the nineteenth and early twentieth centuries, the business of British banks, like that of the British economy, was largely focused on opportunities that connected Britain to the rest of the world. From 1870 to 1913, international financial investments—primarily in the form of bond issues —averaged roughly half of global GDP, a level unmatched until about 1990.[58] Great Britain, the wealthiest country with the most fully developed capital market, was the dominant supplier of international capital. British capital outflows grew dramatically, from £193 million between 1865 and 1869 to £920 million between 1900 and 1914.[59] In addition to making portfolio investments, many British firms established operations abroad and made substantial foreign direct investments: Britain was the world's largest foreign direct investor. For the period 1910–13, total net British foreign investment constituted more than 53 percent of Britain's domestic savings.[60]

British banks and financial markets played a central role in the expansion of Britain as a commercial empire in the late nineteenth and early twentieth centuries. A specialized group of British multinational banks

[57] Collins (2012), 58–59, 214–18.

[58] Obstfeld and Taylor (2004); Calomiris (2005), 36–41.

[59] Davis and Huttenback (1988), 48–49; Davis and Gallman (2001), 70; Calomiris (2005), 38.

[60] O'Rourke and Williamson (2000), 209. The data reported there are based on a data set constructed by Jones and Obstfeld (2001), reporting data on domestic capital formation and the capital account (net of gold flows). Under the assumption that total savings is equal to the sum of the capital account and domestic capital formation, the ratio of net foreign investment to domestic savings is equal to the ratio of the capital account (net of gold flows) divided by the sum of the capital account and domestic capital formation. The dataset on which this calculation is based is available at the website of the National Bureau of Economic Research (www.nber.org/databases/jones-obstfeld/).

operated substantial foreign branch networks and focused on the financing of international trade. In the 1830s these multinational banks began establishing branches in Australia, Canada, the West Indies, and the Mediterranean. By the outbreak of World War I, approximately 30 British banks owned more than 1,000 branches abroad, in the British Empire and elsewhere.[61]

Continuing Britain's global dominance into the twentieth century, however, was not simply a matter of maintaining the quality of the nation's financial and military institutions. Foreign competition was intensifying on both fronts. Germany's ambitions were growing rapidly. By the beginning of the twentieth century, Britain had been drawn into an arms race with Germany, and by 1914 it had once again entered a prolonged European conflict. In Asia, Japan was a rising power that would eventually challenge Britain for control of the Pacific. In the Americas, the United States was moving to consolidate its possessions and influence after its victory in the Spanish-American War. Technological changes in mass warfare meant that the wars of the future would involve unprecedented numbers of combatants and horrors on a massive scale. How could a small nation in the North Atlantic respond to these challenges?

Change for Britain was inevitable—including the eventual ceding of its dominant global economic role to its new competitors. Remaining at all influential in world economic and political affairs would require a disproportionate commitment to military service by Britain's relatively small population. This, in turn, implied the need to create a political partnership that would place equal weights on imperial ambition and the interest of the common man. That commitment to the popular interest implied a further expansion of the franchise—which took the form of suffrage for all adult men and some women—as well as the emasculation of the House of Lords.

The unsustainable combination of imperial power and elite control was a theme not only of political movements but also of fictional portrayals of pre–World War I Britain. For example, the popular Disney film adaptation of *Mary Poppins,* which is set in London in 1910, tells the story of a magical nanny who comes to live with an austere banker, his suffragette wife, and their two unhappy children. The tensions of the

[61] G. Jones (1993), 1, 7–12, 32–62.

moment are illustrated when the father's banking associates attempt to persuade his children that they can share in the grandeur of the empire by saving tuppence (two pennies), to finance imperial enterprise, rather than giving the money to a poor woman. This struggle over tuppence is an accurate reflection of the moment: Britain was at a turning point where the interests of the empire and the common man were in need of greater alignment.

Not surprisingly, at the same time that the Pax Britannica was coming under strain, so were the political institutions that gave the British upper class power beyond their numbers. A set of electoral reforms in 1867 and 1884 had broadened the franchise well beyond the Great Reform of 1832. The 1867 act reduced the property qualification to vote for residents in urban districts, so that roughly one-third of men, including some members of the working class, had the right to vote. The 1884 act reduced property qualifications even further and extended the new criteria to rural voters. With its ratification, roughly 60 percent of adult men, including a large swath of the working class, obtained the right to vote.

These two forces—the need to maintain military strength commensurate with the world's greatest empire and the expansion of the electoral franchise—had moved in parallel for much of Britain's modern history, occasionally crossing paths, one pushing the other forward. Now, at the dawn of the twentieth century, they converged much more tightly and would reinforce one another in a process that would turn the banking system into a mechanism of war finance, reinforce the cartelization of the system, and make it an inadequate provider of credit to the private economy for decades.

The first clear evidence of the political sea change that would transform Britain was the election of 1906, which produced a landslide for the Liberal Party and substantial gains for the Labour Party.[62] The Liberals succeeded by championing social reforms, such as legalizing strikes, limiting work hours, setting a minimum wage, enacting unemployment and health insurance, and reforming prisons. They also advocated fundamental political changes, including an end to the veto power of the House of Lords and the broadening of the franchise. The growing popular appeal

[62] M. Gilbert (1997), 149.

of these changes reflected the rapid growth of cities and the radicalization of industrial workers.[63]

Some sense of the social agenda of the Liberals, as well as their often firebrand tone, can be gleaned from this speech to the electors of Dundee in April 1908:

> I have accepted the unanimous invitation of your Executive to contest the city of Dundee at the impending by-election for the Liberal and Free Trade cause. . . . You will be asked to endorse the appeal of the Coal Miners for a little larger share of life and sunlight. . . . You will be urged to fortify the Government against the arbitrary and irresponsible partisanship of the House of Lords. . . . British democracy is now confronted by a vigorous Tory reaction. The social battle swings to and fro in uncertain decision. The fate of important legislation, conceived in the highest interests of the labouring classes of Britain, hangs in the balance. An electoral blow which should sweep the Liberals from power would fall . . . upon Labour representation in all its degrees. Let us be united. . . . The levers of social progression are still in the grasp of the Liberal party. . . . Shall we be given the strength? That is the question I come to ask Dundee.

---

[63] Britain was not the only country to enact ambitious social legislation in the years prior to World War I (Germany began to do so as far back as the 1880s); nor was it the only country to expand the franchise (Austria did so in 1907). The general political climate of the period was characterized by social unrest, mass political protests, riots, strikes, and an unprecedented number of political assassinations or attempted assassinations, many of them carried out by anarchists or socialists. The first Russian revolution of 1905 showed the vulnerability of autocratic empires. Targets of assassination attempts included the Italian king in 1900; the U.S. president in 1901; the king of Belgium, the Russian minister of education, the Russian minister of the interior and the Bulgarian minister of public instruction in 1902; the Serbian king, queen, prime minister, and minister of war in 1903; a Russian grand duke and the procurator of the Finnish senate in 1905; the Russian prime minister and a leading member of the Russian Duma in 1906; the prefect of St. Petersburg and the military procurator general of Russia in 1907; an Austro-Hungarian governor and numerous senior Ottoman officials in 1908; the chief of the Russian secret police, the aide-de-camp of the secretary of state for India, the public prosecutor for Bengal, and a Japanese prince and former prime minister in 1909; the Egyptian prime minister, the Russian prime minister, the Austrian minister of justice, and numerous British and Indian officials in 1910; two Spanish prime ministers in 1912; the king of Greece and the Turkish grand vizier in 1913; and the archduke of Austria-Hungary and his wife in 1914 (the event that ignited the conflict that became World War I). See M. Gilbert (1997), passim.

The agitator presenting this message was none other than Winston Churchill, who was to become the Tory prime minister of Great Britain and perhaps Britain's most famous defender of empire. The following year, Churchill gave the speech that provides the epigraph to this chapter, in which he called for stripping the House of Lords of its veto authority, thereby making it largely irrelevant. The tone of that speech is striking, as it reduces the House of Lords to the status of a political pest, standing in the way of progress for the whole nation.

Why was this staunch defender of empire so interested in empowering the working class? Although there is no doubt that Churchill had a personal passion for improving the lot of the poor (he was a sincere and energetic proponent of social policy and may have coined the phrase "the war on poverty"), it is also beyond doubt that Churchill's concern for the empire—especially the needs of military recruitment and mobilization—informed his early advocacy of social reforms and led him to ally himself with the Liberal Party.[64] The Liberals favored social and political reforms alongside a staunch advocacy of maintaining the strength of the British Empire. In his 1901 review of a book about poverty in England, Churchill noted all the moral arguments in favor of improving social policies toward the poor, but he also recognized that the most convincing argument for these policies to put before Parliament was that poverty "is a serious hindrance to recruiting [for the military]."[65] In Churchill's conception, success in war and preservation of empire were grounded in a willing partnership between the common man and the elite. Broad suffrage and social policies that protected the common man were useful for preserving the empire; their absence could be devastating.[66]

---

[64] It was the Liberal government of Herbert Henry Asquith (prime minister from 1908 to 1916) that led Great Britain into a naval arms race against Germany as well as into the Great War. As Asquith's first lord of the admiralty, Churchill spearheaded the conversion of the fleet to oil-fired, all-big-gun battleships (the so-called dreadnoughts) and directed naval operations until he was dismissed after the disastrous Battle of Gallipoli in 1915. After he was forced out of the government, Churchill obtained a commission as a lieutenant colonel in the British Army, leading the 6th Battalion of the Royal Scots Fusiliers on the Western Front.

[65] M. Gilbert (1991), 146. There was nothing starry-eyed about Churchill's advocacy of the empowerment of the common man, as his famous quip makes clear: "The best argument against democracy is a five-minute conversation with the average voter."

[66] In 1904 Churchill left the Tories to ally himself with Asquith, Lloyd George, and the other Liberal Party members, whose platform combined advocacy of imperial strength, free trade, and social policies to benefit the masses. Churchill's views were

While still a Conservative MP, Churchill had spoken about the threats associated with the new technology of warfare before the House of Commons in 1901: "I have frequently been astonished since I have been in this House to hear with what composure and how glibly Members, and even Ministers, talk of a European war. . . . There has been a great change," he went on, "which the House should not omit to notice." In former days, wars were fought by small armies of professional soldiers and "it was possible to limit the liabilities of the combatants," but now, "when mighty populations are impelled on each other, each individual severally embittered and inflamed, when the resources of science and civilization sweep away everything that might mitigate their fury, a European war can only end in the ruin of the vanquished and the scarcely less fatal commercial dislocation and exhaustion of the conquerors. Democracy is more vindictive than Cabinets. The wars of peoples will be more terrible than the wars of kings. We do not know what war is. We have had a glimpse of it in South Africa. Even in miniature it is hideous and appalling."[67]

Once the Liberals assumed control of the government, they began to put forward an ambitious agenda of reform measures, many of which were successfully opposed in the House of Lords. After narrowly surviving an election, in March 1910 the Liberals introduced legislation in the House of Commons to curb the power of the Lords. This legislation had the support of King Edward VII, who had the ability to appoint peers to the House of Lords to push through the bill. With that threat at hand, a compromise was reached whereby the House of Lords agreed on August 10, 1911, to be divested of the power to approve money bills in exchange for avoiding a massive infusion of Liberal peers. The Lords also lost the right to veto other bills: the most they could do was hold up approval for a period of two years.[68]

---

strongly shaped by spending time in South Africa during the Second Boer War, first as a war correspondent and then as an officer in the South African Light Horse. He returned from the war in 1900 to assume a Conservative seat in the House of Commons. This experience taught Churchill that the new technology of warfare (e.g., machine guns, barbed wire, and rapid-firing howitzers) required massive numbers of troops and brought unimagined horrors. At the beginning of the Boer War, the total British troop presence in South Africa was 12,000. It quickly increased to 280,000, of whom 22,000 died during the war. M. Gilbert (1997), 7–11, 57.

[67] M. Gilbert (1991), 143; M. Gilbert (1997), 51–52.
[68] M. Gilbert (1991), 230.

The effects of the 1911 evisceration of the House of Lords were soon magnified by the expansion of the franchise. The electoral reform of 1918 gave the right to vote to all men older than 21 and to women above the age of 30 with sufficient property. The property and higher age limits for women were removed in 1928.

The consequences of these changes for British democracy were far-reaching and permanent. The power to make and execute laws was now concentrated in the popularly elected House of Commons. We cannot overstress the importance of this change. As we discuss in chapter 2, all democracies contain populist currents as well as institutions that limit those currents to varying degrees in order to preclude a tyranny of the majority. What varies across democracies is the extent to which those decidedly liberal institutions—such as bicameral legislatures, indirect elections, and separation of powers—give minorities power beyond their numbers.

The British political system still retained some liberal bulwarks: the judiciary was independent of Parliament, and MPs were elected in single-member districts, a system that tends to produce victories for middle-of-the-road candidates. Nevertheless, by 1918 the constraints against policies designed to redistribute wealth in Britain were much weaker than they were in the contemporary United States. In the United States (the subject of the next chapter), the Senate and House had to concur on legislation, and the Senate's voting structure and cloture rule created the requirement for supermajorities (or complicated log rolls) in order to pass legislation. In addition, in the United States, there was an indirectly elected president with the power to veto legislation. Even with these institutions in place, U.S. bank-regulation policies were strongly influenced by a curious alliance between populists and bankers. In Britain, there was no need for such an alliance: as the result of electoral and institutional reforms, voters were able to elect candidates who promised to engage in massive wealth redistribution.

The "Second Thirty Years' War"

The period 1914–45 witnessed three devastating global shocks: World War I, the Great Depression, and World War II. Britain's banking system fared reasonably well through this period of upheaval, although there were unavoidable dislocations. For example, the market for international credit seized up with the outbreak of World War I, but Britain managed to avoid a full-fledged banking crisis.[69]

After World War I, Britain and other countries reestablished a fixed-exchange-rate system in which central banks exchanged each others' currencies at a price tied to gold (the so-called gold exchange standard). This system resulted in an overvaluation of the British pound, which reduced Britain's ability to compete in international markets against the United States. British exports suffered, declining from 24 percent of GDP in 1913 to 21 percent in 1929.[70] As Britain struggled to preserve its link to gold in reaction to capital outflows, the Bank of England raised the bank rate from 5.5 percent to 6.5 percent in September 1929. Unemployment was also rising, from an average of 9.1 percent in the 1920s to 12.8 percent in the 1930s. Under continuing deflationary pressure, in September 1931 Britain departed from the gold standard, which permitted an expansion of the money supply. The bank rate was reduced to 2 percent, the pound fell substantially against the dollar, and the British economy and banking system were spared the deflationary consequences that had been driving economic decline and a contraction in the supply of lending by banks.[71] The lending contraction reflected not only the shrinking supply of bank deposits, as the result of monetary contraction, but also banks' needs to reduce their asset risk during the recession, which encouraged them to accumulate cash and government securities.

The September 1931 devaluation spared the British economy and its banks from the worst consequences of the Great Depression, whose effects were global. Still, unemployment remained high, and many blamed Britain's banks, and their alleged lending cartel, for the slow improvement. Once Britain had left the gold standard, monetary policy was freed from having to maintain the fixed exchange rate. The money supply expanded, including bank deposits, but lending was slow to expand. This sluggishness reflected a combination of factors, including continuing concerns about portfolio risk and the difficulty of identifying desirable loan customers.[72] British banks managed their risks well, and Britain avoided

[69] Roberts, Reading, and Skene (2009); Collins (2012), 269–72.

[70] Moggridge (1972), 38; Park (2012), 5.

[71] Moggridge (1972), 163; Park (2012), 6.

[72] Grant (1937); Thomas (1978); Morton (1978); Winton (1982); Billings and Capie (2011); Park (2012).

the sorts of banking crises that swept many other countries.[73] Nonetheless, the scarcity of bank credit became a political issue. Politicians accused banks of purposely reducing lending to industry, despite the actions of the government and the Bank of England to encourage lending by lowering interest rates.[74]

Despite these criticisms, and despite the prior consolidation and increased market power of the Big Five, the British government did not challenge the concentrated structure of the banking system. One explanation was that the government saw a highly concentrated banking system as one with which it could more easily negotiate. Whether or not such an advantage was anticipated before Word War II, there is no doubt that it came to be important in the 1940s. According to two prominent scholars of British banking during this period, Forrest Capie and Mark Billings: "Political circumstances . . . in the 1940s effectively required the banks to sacrifice their returns to the war effort and resulted in controls which persisted for a long time afterwards. Government acceptance of the oligopoly in the postwar period could be considered as a *quid pro quo*."[75] Capie and Billings also find evidence for this new cooperation in the greater convergence of profit rates across banks during and after World War II. The extent to which a banking cartel had existed before World War II can be debated, but there is no doubt that the British banks coordinated their lending behavior during and after the war, both among themselves and with the active involvement of the government.

Two world wars had brought unprecedented government absorption of resources and government planning of production, displacing banks as the key allocators of financial resources in the economy and reducing the banking cartel to a private partner of the government planners. World War I alone was a lasting source of crowding out in the financial system; as late as 1925, holdings of government securities accounted for roughly 25 percent of all private wealth in Britain, compared to only 2.5 percent in 1914.[76] World War II added substantially to an already high level of government debt and did much more: it brought direct government management of the economy via rationing, licensing, price and rent controls,

---

[73] Billings and Capie (2011).
[74] Park (2012), 1.
[75] Capie and Billings (2001), 395.
[76] Collins (2012), 273.

foreign-exchange controls, requisitions, prohibitions, and conscription of labor.

These policies were intended to limit the cost to the government of waging war. By limiting competition from the private sector for labor and productive resources, the government could keep its expenditures low, and by limiting the private sector's ability to compete for bank credit, it could artificially depress interest rates on government debt.[77] For example, during World War II, the government maintained a Capital Issues Committee, which was empowered to vet all "applications" for new securities offerings; offerings required government approval, which was withheld unless the purpose was considered vital to the war effort (e.g., production of armaments). Bank lending was controlled through a process of "guidance," involving consultations between the treasury and the Bank of England to determine whether bank loans being proposed were in the national interest.[78] Under the new rationing regime, bank competition was limited, and bankers operated as members of a cartel that worked with the government to set prices, including the prices for government bonds at auction.

Constrained Banking, 1945–1970

After surviving the Nazi threat to its survival, Britain and its banks could finally return to a semblance of normalcy. Normalcy after 1945, however, looked nothing like the normalcy of pre-1914 Britain. The electoral reforms of 1918 and 1928, and the reduction in power of the House of Lords, now had real bite in a peacetime economy. The election of July 1945 gave the Labour Party a majority in Parliament for the first time in British history. Labour, led by Clement Attlee, argued that the retention and expansion of government wartime planning and controls was appropriate as a means of maintaining high employment after the war ended, and it embarked on a broad program of nationalizing industries.[79] The Labour government nationalized the Bank of England in 1945; the coal mines, civil aviation, and transport in 1946; electricity generation and dis-

[77] Collins (2012), 317–22.
[78] Collins (2012), 323.
[79] Chester (1975); Tiratsoo and Tomlinson (1998); Collins (2012), 327–28.

tribution in 1947; gas distribution in 1948; and the iron and steel industry in 1950.[80]

The new battle lines of British politics were now drawn: they concerned the extent of redistributive taxation, welfare transfers, and the nationalization of industry. The two major parties—Labour and the Conservatives —vied for public support by focusing on the tradeoffs between greater redistribution and faster economic growth from the perspective of the common man. In 1949, Churchill quoted Lloyd George's warning of twenty-five years earlier that "socialism means a community in bonds."[81] Even Churchill, however, knew how to find issues that resonated with the new electorate: his first speech as a Conservative candidate during the election campaign of 1951 (which returned him to lead the nation as prime minister) advocated an excess-profits tax on armaments manufacturers that had profited from the war. Between 1955 and 1975, the policy platforms of the two parties were in fact quite similar.

Britain's "new normal" had important implications for the banking system—but changes were implemented more through the government's role as regulator of the economy than via its ownership structure. The nationalization of the Bank of England was neither particularly surprising nor controversial as a matter of policy. Nor did it infringe on the private banks. It is generally believed by economists that a central bank that enjoys a monopoly over the creation of fiat currency, and is charged with varying its supply in pursuit of macroeconomic objectives, will fulfill those obligations better when it is not also charged as a private entity with the maximization of shareholder returns.[82] The private banks were left in private hands: unlike iron and steel, coal, electricity, and other crucial industries, they were not nationalized.[83]

The simplest explanation for the lack of bank nationalization is the lack of any need on the part of government to rely on the ownership of

---

[80] For more details on the history of British industrialization policy, see Chester (1975), Tomlinson (1994), and Tiratsoo and Tomlinson (1998).

[81] M. Gilbert (1991), 889.

[82] See Goodhart (1988), especially chapters 6–8.

[83] Some members of the Labour Party advocated nationalizing the banks, as well as creating a national investment bank. These calls for a nationalized banking system went as far back as 1932, when the party adopted a resolution to that effect. Interestingly, however, when Labour came to power, it did not nationalize the banks. Collins (2012), 212.

Percentage of GDP

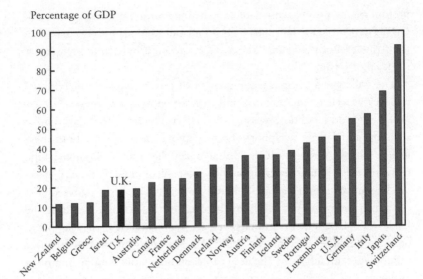

FIGURE 5.3 Private credit from deposit money banks as percentage of GDP, high-income OECD countries, average for 1960s.

Source: World Bank (2012).

banks to achieve redistributive objectives. The government could carry out redistribution directly through the nationalization of industry, taxation to finance welfare programs, and the provision of government-owned rental housing (council houses or council flats). In addition, the newly nationalized Bank of England was given the legal power to regulate the banking system in 1946. The credit controls and cartelization of banking that had been used in wartime as a means of facilitating the sale of treasury bills continued as part of the postwar management of deficit spending.[84] Given the nationalization of industry and the maintenance of bank credit and pricing controls, there was little point to nationalizing a banking system that had so little influence on the allocation of credit.

Just how unimportant the British banking system was to the British economy is depicted in figure 5.3, which compares the average level of private credit provided by depository banks during the decade 1960–69 across high-income OECD countries. The United Kingdom is close to the

---

[84] Collins (2012), 220, 317–48.

bottom of the group, with bank credit representing only 19 percent of GDP. That is roughly half the level of Finland, Iceland, and Sweden, one-third the level of the United States, Germany, and Italy, and one-quarter the level of Japan.

The willingness to repress the growth of private bank credit reflected two key aspects of the political and macroeconomic environment of the post-1945 world: political pressures to maintain high levels of government spending and deficits in support of job creation, and adherence to the new fixed exchange rate against the dollar under the Bretton Woods system. Government debt had reached roughly 300 percent of GDP in 1945, making Britain the world's greatest debtor nation.[85] The British government continued to borrow massively in the decades that followed, putting the Bank of England under continual pressure to expand the money supply in order to purchase government debt. The resulting growth in the money supply set off an inflation. The desire to contain inflation and maintain the exchange rate led the government to constrain private credit, using the credit controls it maintained over the cartelized banking system.

Ultimately, it was not possible for Britain to simultaneously maintain reasonably free capital markets, an expansionary monetary policy, and a fixed exchange rate against the dollar (an impossibility sometimes referred to in macroeconomics as the international monetary policy "trilemma"). Britain struggled for two decades to maintain both its external fixed exchange rate and its accommodating monetary policy, with varying limits on capital flows.[86] It faced continuing balance-of-payments deficits (reserve outflows), which resulted in periodic crises during which it would cobble together short-term solutions, sometimes with the help of the International Monetary Fund. In November 1967, Britain gave up the battle and devalued the pound.[87]

[85] Capie (2010), 139.

[86] Capital controls were loosened in the 1950s, then tightened in 1961 and again in 1965 and 1966. Capie (2010), 209–10, 295–300.

[87] For an overview of the British experience with money growth, inflation, trade, and balance of payments flows, see Capie (2010), 7–31; for a review of the ultimate collapse of the exchange rate, see pp. 138–251. Capie traces in great detail the economic policies undertaken, their consequences, and the ideological underpinnings of those policies. He shows that muddled thinking was a major contributor to the willingness to pursue the contradictory policy of monetary expansion and a fixed exchange rate. It was not until late in the 1960s that the prevailing economic mindset—which

During that long and ultimately unsuccessful fight to balance government borrowing needs and a fixed exchange rate, constraints on private credit were the primary policy tool used to limit inflationary pressures.[88] In the 1950s and 1960s, the Bank of England rarely employed interest-rate increases to combat inflation, although when it did so that tool was quite effective. Because raising interest rates harmed the government's ability to finance its own expenditures, however, the bank's primary instruments for controlling money and credit were its quantity controls over bank credit and banks' liquidity-ratio requirements (limits on the proportion of assets that banks could hold in loans). The concentrated structure of the British banking system, as during World War II, facilitated government control over bank credit.

Regulatory Arbitrage, Criticisms of Regulation, and the CCC Reform of 1971

One consequence of the new regime of cartelized banking and repressed private credit was the emergence of new markets and financial institutions to provide savings and funding opportunities for business enterprises and private individuals whose needs were not being met by the tightly regulated clearing banks (Britain's term for the regulated banks that cleared payments in the financial system). Savers wanted rates of interest above what the regulators were permitting the clearing banks to pay, and borrowers wanted more credit than those banks were willing to extend. Savers and borrowers therefore spurned the regulated clearing banks and created a parallel financial system (in today's language, a "shadow" financial system) that was outside the regulatory structure of the government.

The initial participants in this parallel system were merchant banks (acceptance houses) and foreign banks with offices in London. In 1960, there were 77 foreign banks operating in London; by 1970 there were 159.[89] Other homegrown intermediaries, including the so-called second-

---

insisted that the growth of the money supply was not relevant for inflation—was seriously challenged and eventually overturned. Capie's analysis of the report of the Radcliffe Committee in 1957 (pp. 77–137) provides a particularly telling window into the incoherent policy framework of the 1950s and 1960s.

[88] Capie (2010), 271–82.
[89] Capie (2010), 780.

ary banks (or fringe banks), operated under the radar of credit controls and raised wholesale deposits (large deposits made by institutional investors, large businesses, and other banks) in both sterling and in other currencies; the wholesale nature of their deposit bases made them exempt from cash-reserve requirements at the central bank. The first-tier clearing banks that were subject to credit controls also had ways of getting around them. For example, banks used offshore subsidiaries or associates in Dublin to make loans in what became known as the "Irish leakage."[90] The clearing banks, unlike the secondary banks, received requests from the government to restrain their lending (effectively forcing them to invest in lower-interest government securities), and they had to maintain unprofitable reserve requirements at the Bank of England and were subject to the interest rate limits on retail deposits, which limited their ability to attract funds.[91] Regulatory arbitrage favored intermediation by the secondary banks, whose market shares were growing.

The growing chorus of criticism of the government's tight controls over the banking system went beyond complaints from the clearing banks that they were losing market share. Critics had three main lines of argument. First, unnecessarily scarce credit for the private sector was depriving businesses of the ability to finance profitable projects. In 1971, a parliamentary Committee of Inquiry on Small Firms in Britain (whose conclusions were known informally as the Bolton Report) concluded that credit controls were disproportionately affecting the growth prospects of small firms.[92] Second, the cartelization of the banking system, which was a direct consequence of the credit control strategy, insulated the chartered clearing banks from competition and promoted a government-orchestrated monopoly of the banking system that was contrary to the public interest. The Parliamentary Monopolies Commission in 1968 criticized price fixing in banking as having "such a soporific effect on the banks that, so long as they exist, no bank system could greatly increase the degree of competition in it."[93] Third, credit controls had several deficiencies in comparison with traditional monetary policy (which works either through central bank purchases or sales of assets or by changing the interest rate

---

[90] Capie (2010), 434.
[91] Collins (2012), 365–80, 419–20, 439–40.
[92] Collins (2012), 446.
[93] Collins (2012), 415.

charged by the central bank) when it came to implementing counter-cyclical policies designed to smooth fluctuations in the business cycle. Credit controls were not transparent to the market and therefore could not foster learning and accountability on the part of monetary policy makers. Their use also did not conform to the views of many monetary economists that effective monetary policy requires the central bank to focus on measuring and controlling some combination of the money supply and interest rates.

The liberalization of credit markets would confer an additional benefit: London's banks would be better able to exploit the opportunities afforded by the city's status as a burgeoning international financial entrepôt. In the 1950s, what would eventually become known as the eurodollar market began to develop in London. Many depositors from continental Europe—especially Eastern Europe—wanted to hold dollar-denominated deposits in a country other than the United States. U.S. depositors, who were increasingly fleeing U.S. markets because of the regulatory limits on the interest banks could pay on deposits, also became important customers of London banks. Eurodollar deposits were still a small business in the early 1960s, but according to one estimate, they reached $130 billion in 1973.[94]

In response to the criticisms of government credit controls, from the perspectives of both improving monetary policy and the competitiveness of the banking system, the newly elected Conservative government, led by Prime Minister Edward Heath, moved to liberalize the banking system almost as soon as it came to power.[95] A new regime of competition and credit control (CCC) was adopted by the Bank of England in September 1971.[96] It removed quantitative constraints on bank lending, eliminated bank collusion in setting interest rates, and somewhat equalized the playing field between the clearing banks and the secondary banks by requiring

---

[94] Capie (2010), 186. It is important to note that balance-of-payments problems were unrelated to the development of the eurodollar markets. Because dollar deposits were not converted into pounds on entering Britain, they were not subject to exchange-rate risk and operated outside the British balance of payments (see Capie [2010], 184).

[95] Several people at the Bank of England and elsewhere led the call for a competitive banking system and an effective means of monetary control, including John Fforde, Andrew Crockett, and Charles Goodhart. See Capie (2010), 487–91, 702; Goodhart and Crockett (1970).

[96] Capie (2010), 427–523.

all banks to maintain reserve balances and by lowering the reserve requirements of the clearing banks. At the same time, the Bank of England proposed to shift to interest-rate targeting as the primary instrument of monetary policy, rather than imposing controls on credit through the clearing banks.[97] The result was an increase in lending by the clearing banks and a lasting improvement in their market share.[98]

The Troubled 1970s

Heath's policy changes marked the beginning of a rethinking of British banking regulation, but they did not engender an immediate golden age of economic or financial growth. In fact, the 1970s were the worst decade of the twentieth century for Britain with respect to monetary, financial, and macroeconomic performance.[99] Money, credit, and inflation grew sharply in the early 1970s, and the economy sagged, experiencing absolute declines in real GDP. The CCC was blamed for encouraging the growth in credit that had fueled the inflation, and Heath even considered reversing the banking reforms in 1973. While it was true that deregulation fueled the boom in credit supply, at its heart the problem was not the modest improvements in promoting competition in banking but rather the failure to adopt a monetary policy that could effectively control money and credit growth through appropriate tools (that is, open-market operations and changes in the bank rate).[100] It would take almost a decade after the CCC for the Bank of England and the government to recognize the importance of controlling aggregate money and to develop the ability to do so effectively. In the meantime, high and volatile inflation and slow economic growth plagued the economy. Voters responded by sending Heath packing in 1974, bringing the Labour Party back to power.

As figure 5.4 shows, the CCC had a modest effect on the ratio of private bank credit to GDP in the UK. The ratio of private credit from deposit

---

[97] The governor of the Bank of England described the 1971 policy shift as "a new approach to credit control designed to permit the price mechanism to function efficiently in the allocation of credit, and to free the banks from rigidities and restraints which have for far too long inhibited them from efficiently fulfilling their intermediary role in the financial system." Collins (2012), 489–90.

[98] Collins (2012), 381, 409, 416, 441.

[99] Capie (2010), 483.

[100] Capie (2010), 514–23, 644–706.

Percentage of GDP

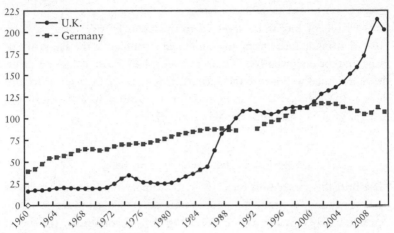

FIGURE 5.4 Private credit from deposit money banks as percentage of GDP, United Kingdom and Germany, 1960–2010.

Source: World Bank (2012).

money banks to GDP, which had averaged only 19 percent during the 1960s, crept up to 26 percent, on average, through the 1970s. This was an improvement, but not much of one: as figure 5.4 shows, at the end of the 1970s, British business enterprises and households were still credit starved compared to their German counterparts.

The volatility of inflation and interest rates during the 1970s created enormous challenges for banks. Banks with long-duration assets and short-duration liabilities suffered large losses as the result of an upward spike in inflation and interest rates in 1973. Inflation jumped from 2 percent in 1969 to 16 percent in 1970 and hit 27 percent in 1973. The bank rate rose in several installments from 7.5 percent in June 1973 to 13 percent by November 1973. Yields on long-term government securities rose from about 10 percent in June 1973 to about 16 percent by November.[101] The secondary banks were heavily invested in real-estate lending and had grown rapidly during the real-estate expansion of 1971–73, funding themselves with short-term wholesale debt. When inflation and interest rates rose, these banks suffered enormous losses and were unable to fund

[101] Capie (2010), 483, 512, 663.

their maturing liabilities. Thus was born the "secondary banking crisis" of 1973–75.[102]

The Bank of England responded to this crisis by organizing a "lifeboat" that made loans using the combined resources of the Bank of England and the major banks. This arrangement had much in common with the coordinated response to the Barings crisis of 1890. In an effort to stop the spread of the crisis, in 1974 additional measures were taken by the Bank of England, including outright bailouts.[103]

The Rise of Thatcher and the Big Bang

Most British voters almost certainly did not understand the intricacies of bank regulation, but they did understand that they lived in an economy that was barely growing. The reality of the British economy by the end of the 1970s was stark indeed: over the previous decade, inflation had averaged 13.7 percent, while real growth in GDP had averaged only 2.2 percent.[104] Government spending accounted for 46 percent of GDP in 1980.[105]

The task of convincing voters that they should bear the considerable pain of shifting policies, not just in banking but across the economy, fell to Margaret Thatcher, who assumed the post of prime minister after a Conservative electoral victory in 1979. Thatcher wasted little time in shifting the direction of the British economy. Her administration limited government spending, reduced spending on social services, and reduced income-tax rates. Thatcher privatized many of the industries that had been nationalized in the 1940s, and in that process she curbed the power of unions to strike. Her successful opposition to the demands of the coal miners' strike in 1984 set the stage for the eventual closure of unprofitable coal mines and the privatization of the remaining ones in 1994. The number of strikes fell from 1,221 in 1984 to 630 in 1990 and continued to fall thereafter.[106] Importantly for the banking industry, she permitted

---

[102] For a detailed account of the crisis, see Reid (1982) and Capie (2010), 524–86.

[103] Capie (2010), 556–86.

[104] Data are simple averages from the International Monetary Fund's World Economic Outlook Database for April 1999, available at www.imf.org/external/pubs/ft/weo/1999/01/data.

[105] Capie (2010), 12.

[106] Butler and Butler (1994), 375.

tenants to purchase government-provided council flats, which meant that banks gained new lending opportunities for home mortgage credit.

Another part of Thatcher's strategy for economic renewal was to revitalize the British financial sector—a process known as the Big Bang because of the suddenness of the sweeping changes that took place on October 27, 1986. Encouraging financial-sector growth was intended both to create jobs and to support the growth of the private economy; it was a companion measure to shutting down inefficient government-run firms. Some of the most widely publicized financial-reform measures focused on the London Stock Exchange: the abolition of fixed commission charges, the abolition of the distinction between stockjobbers and stockbrokers, and the change from open-outcry to electronic, screen-based trading.

The Thatcher government's policy stance toward the financial sector was actually much broader: it permitted and encouraged the growth of universal banks (those combining many services—such as commercial banking, investment banking, and foreign-exchange operations—within the same enterprise), thereby permitting British banks to become globally competitive. This required that the government eliminate distortions created by the regulatory system that had been in place since the 1940s, such as controls on deposit interest rates and on foreign-exchange transactions.[107]

The changes resulting from these policies were dramatic. As figure 5.4 shows, the Big Bang was associated with a significant rise in the proportion of bank lending relative to GDP: the ratio of private credit from deposit money banks rose from only 45 percent of GDP in 1985 to 100 percent by 1989 and then continued growing every year until 2010. In 1985, the ratio of private bank credit to GDP in Germany was roughly twice that of Great Britain; by 1989, British firms and households had more credit available to them than their German counterparts.

Because Thatcher's program delivered much of what it promised, namely higher growth and lower inflation, the Conservatives were able to remain in power and Thatcher to remain in office, until 1990. Remarkably, unemployment was quite high during the Thatcher years, but the electorate accepted it as the cost of reform. From 1981 to 1990, British

---

[107] Collins (2012), 423, 493, 507.

annual real GDP growth averaged 2.7 percent, and inflation fell to less than half its rate in the 1970s, to 6.2 percent.[108]

Thatcher's privatizations, labor reforms, and changes in monetary and financial policy were lasting. Thatcher's successors, including those from the Labour Party, built upon rather than reversed many of the policies that she had pushed through. The reason is not hard to divine: Thatcher's policies were not contrary to the interests of the median voter. This is not abstract theorizing. The leader of the Labour Party as of this writing, Edward Miliband, articulated it directly in 2011: "Some of what happened in the 1980s was right. It was right to let people buy their council houses. It was right to cut tax rates of 60, 70, 80 per cent. And it was right to change the rules on the closed shop, on strikes before ballots. These changes were right, and we were wrong to oppose it at the time."[109]

Perhaps the most important legacy of the Thatcher government was the proof it offered that a majority of citizens would support a reform program with front-loaded social costs and long-term social gains, one that reduced government spending and redistribution in the name of promoting growth. A famous quotation about democracy predicts that "the majority always votes for the candidates who promise the most benefits from the public treasury, with the result that every democracy will finally collapse due to its loose fiscal policy."[110] Margaret Thatcher proved that it ain't necessarily so.

The Banking Crisis of 2007–09 and the Future

If this chapter had been written in 2006, we would have been able to point to a remarkably stable century and a half in British banking since the Overend & Gurney crisis of 1866. During the early to mid-2000s a boom in the British housing market, combined with high bank leverage, left British banks vulnerable. Severe global financial shocks, primarily originating in the United States (see chapters 7 and 8), combined with the

---

[108] Simple averages from the International Monetary Fund's World Economic Outlook Database for April 1999.

[109] "Labour Party Conference" (2011).

[110] This famous quotation is sometimes attributed to Alexander Fraser Tytler, a Scottish judge and historian of the late eighteenth and early nineteenth centuries, but there is no credible evidence that he is the source.

vulnerable circumstances of British banks, precipitated a severe banking crisis. The banking collapse of 2007–09, which caused a number of Britain's largest banks to suffer among the worst distress of any banks in the world and produced massive government bailouts of British banks, has called into question the future of British banking.

It remains unclear whether the depth of the banking crisis in Britain should be regarded as an aberration or as an indication of a long-term weakening in the structure of the banking system and its regulation, which may be indicative of a new political bargain between the banks and the government—one in which banks expect to be protected and are thus able to undertake risk at the taxpayers' expense. The British government and regulatory authorities have responded to the crisis quite aggressively, but the implications of those regulatory responses remain subject to political uncertainties. For example, the slow growth of the British economy in the immediate aftermath of the 2007–09 crisis, combined with the tenuous hold on power of the Conservative-Liberal coalition, placed new pressures on the government to loosen credit standards and offer new credit subsidies to consumers. In March 2013 the government announced a program to partially guarantee mortgages with up to a 95 percent loan-to-value ratio for new home buyers. The first five years of the mortgage loan are interest-free. The government also announced a similar plan to subsidize mortgages for existing homes in 2014.[111] Critics denounced these credit subsidies as a potential cause of a new British housing bubble.

The large size of the British banking sector also has uncertain implications for the future. On the one hand, the large employment share of British banks may have given them special political power to extract ongoing subsidies from the government, which may portend further instability. On the other hand, the fact that Britain's financial sector is large relative to its economy pushes the politics in the opposite direction: the British simply cannot afford to devote massive taxpayer resources to repeatedly bail out their banks.

[111] Sherman (2013).

The Cost of Banker-Populist Alliances

The United States versus Canada

6

||||||||||||||||||||||||

Crippled by Populism
U.S. Banking from Colonial Times to 1990

The gentleman from Wisconsin has said he fears a Robespierre. My friend, in this land of the free you need fear no tyrant who will spring up from among the people. What we need is an Andrew Jackson to stand as Jackson stood, against the encroachments of aggregated wealth.

William Jennings Bryan, "Cross of Gold" speech (1896)

Understanding how outcomes vary in the Game of Bank Bargains is a central purpose of this book. Each country's rules of the game differ, as do the specific identities of the players and their stakes in the game. Governments always get their share of the benefits from playing the game, and the coalitions that forge a winning bargain with the government split the remainder.

The United States is no exception to this general principle. From the time of the Revolutionary War through the early nineteenth century, the dominant coalition was composed of political elites in both federal and state governments, many of whom were members of the Federalist Party, allied with a narrow group of financiers. This coalition of elites, perhaps best exemplified by its intellectual architect, Alexander Hamilton, was successful at financing a newly emerging nation as well as providing capital for the first stages of American commercial, agricultural, and industrial development. Because this coalition limited the number of banks that received charters, it tended not to provide credit to small farmers and artisans.[1]

A coalition composed of political and economic elites could not be sustained, however, in a political system characterized by federalism, populism, and an expanding franchise. It therefore gave way in a second era,

[1] As Bodenhorn ([2003], 137–44) shows, those farmers and artisans lost little time in chartering additional banks once the Federalists began to lose power.

which ran from the 1810s to roughly 1980, to a durable alliance between small "unit bankers" (operating banks with no branches) and agrarian populists (farmers who distrusted corporations of nearly every type, as well as the elites that controlled them). The government's share of the benefits shifted from direct taxation or ownership interests in banks to regulatory requirements that forced banks, and eventually a central bank, to lend to both state and national governments.

The economic organization of U.S. banking during this second era entailed significant costs: it was inherently unstable, noncompetitive, and inefficient in its allocation of credit. The banking system was composed of thousands of small banks that operated local monopolies, which meant that they were able to charge more for loans and pay less for deposits than they would have had they been obliged to compete with one another. The absence of branches meant that these banks could neither spread risk across regions nor easily move funds in order to head off bank runs.

Even the Great Depression was unable to break the coalition that supported this inefficient and unstable system. Rather, the agrarian populist–unit banker coalition used the depression to create a new set of institutions designed to prop up what was, fundamentally, a system that was fragile by design. These institutions included deposit insurance and a set of laws, including the notorious Regulation Q, that made it illegal for banks to pay interest on checking accounts and limited the interest rates they could pay on other types of accounts.

These institutions managed to stabilize the U.S. banking system for several decades, but they could work only if the government remained committed to conservative monetary and fiscal policies. Once the U.S. government began to depart from those policies in the 1960s, and inflation accelerated through the 1970s, the interest rates that could be legally offered by banks turned negative (inflation exceeded the interest rates offered on deposits), and the public began to pull their savings out of banks and place them with various bank competitors, such as money-market mutual funds. Technological innovations, such as the invention of the ATM in the 1970s, further undermined the system by allowing banks to skirt laws against branching. Thus by the 1980s, the conditions that had permitted a stable unit-bank system had crumbled. The result was the savings and loan crisis of the late 1980s, in which hundreds of small banks failed. Calls for reform produced regulatory changes at both the state and federal levels of government. In the 1990s, for the first time in U.S. history—and centuries after they appeared in other countries—large banks with nationwide branching networks were allowed to form.

The Colonial Origins of the Agrarian
Populist-Unit Banker Coalition

The fact that a coalition of farmers and small bankers was able to dismantle the banking institutions that had been set up by Alexander Hamilton, and that it was then able to establish an inefficient and unstable alternative that endured for more than 150 years, implies that something about this coalition was woven into the fabric of America's political institutions. In order to understand its influence, we therefore need to understand how it became part of the warp and weft of the American political system.

The 13 colonies that were to become the United States were a backwater surrounded by hostile neighbors. British colonists faced constant threats from the Spanish in Florida, the French in Quebec and the Ohio Valley, and the Indians, who often allied with the French, nearly everywhere else. In order to be viable, the 13 colonies had to be an armed camp. They had no obvious source of wealth, however, to pay for a large standing army. The colonies contained neither a Potosí that produced piles of silver coins nor a Pernambuco that yielded prodigious amounts of valuable sugar. Cotton would eventually offer enormous export earnings to the South, but only in the nineteenth century, after the cotton gin made it possible to process the short-staple varieties that could be grown in American soils. The one thing that the colonies did have, however, was seemingly endless expanses of farmland suitable for tobacco, maize, and wheat—provided that those lands could be cleared of Indians. Those crops share crucial characteristics that allow them to be grown efficiently on family farms: they are highly storable and exhibit modest scale economies in production.[2]

The combination of these factors—hostile neighbors, abundant land, and storable crops that could be grown on small production units—meant

---

[2] Binswanger and Rosenzweig (1986). The political implications of agricultural systems characterized by highly storable crops and modest economies of scale are analyzed by Haber (2012a).

that British America was a society of small, freeholding farmers who were armed to the teeth. Some colonies, such as Virginia, required every able-bodied male to own a firearm.[3] There were, of course, large landowners, British elites who were connected to the companies that had initially settled the 13 colonies on the franchise model (see chapter 3) or who had arrived later with the royal governors sent by the crown when the colonization companies failed. These elites looked down their noses at the small farmers, but they could not maintain a viable colony without them: what stood between the elites and the Spanish, French, and Indians were independent farmers who, as William Blathwayt, the auditor general of the colonies, observed in 1691, "all Learn to keep and use a gun with a Marvelous dexterity as soon as ever they have strength enough to lift it to their heads."[4]

America's common people were therefore able to achieve something that no group of small farmers had achieved since the Roman Republic: the right to vote. America's colonies might have had governors appointed by the king, but they also had colonial assemblies—houses of burgesses—that were popularly elected. In Virginia, the most prosperous and heavily populated of the 13 colonies, the first restrictions on suffrage were not imposed until 1670, and even these were far from onerous by the standards of the time.[5] Though the exact rules varied by colony and locality, adult male suffrage was widespread, with typically 40 to 50 percent of early eighteenth-century colonists (not including slaves) eligible to vote for colonial assemblies in the mid-Atlantic states, and 70 to 80 percent in New England and the South.[6] Large landowners initially dominated the elected assemblies, but by the mid-eighteenth century America's small farmers had begun to break away from the tradition of voting for their social betters.[7] As Alexander Spotswood, the colonial governor of Virginia from 1710 to 1723, put it: "The Mob of this Country, finding themselves able to carry whom they please, have generally chosen representatives of their own Clas, who as their principal Recommendation have declared their resolution to raise no Tax on the people, let the occasion be what it will."[8]

[3] Morgan (1975), 240; Wood (1991), 123.
[4] Morgan (1975), 240.
[5] Morgan (1975), 145.
[6] Keyssar (2000), 7.
[7] Wood (1991), 173.
[8] Morgan (1975), 360.

When America's colonial elites, the large landowners and merchants, decided to move for independence, they had to mobilize this class of armed, independent farmers against the British. That was no easy trick: they were essentially asking them to go toe to toe against the most disciplined and best-equipped army in the world. Motivating them to do so required appeals based on liberty, freedom, and equality. Once these inducements had been offered, there was no putting the genie back in the bottle. The process of revolution, as Gordon Wood has demonstrated, was a profoundly radicalizing experience. Thus, to the shock of America's elites, after independence the small farmers whom Washington had led across the Delaware would no longer doff their hats to their social betters or defer to them in matters of politics.[9] So profound was this transformation of American society that household employees now refused to use the terms *master* and *mistress* in addressing their employers, but adopted instead the word *boss* (derived from the Dutch word *baas*, which in New Amsterdam meant someone who was in charge but who was not a master, such as a sea captain).[10] Not surprisingly, within a few decades of independence, the successors of the group of gentlemen, one might almost say quasi-aristocrats, who had led the country in revolution—Washington, Madison, Hamilton, Adams, and Jefferson—were pushed out of the way with the election of Andrew Jackson. This transition was already in evidence by the presidential election of 1800, when Thomas Jefferson, who saw himself as the champion of the yeoman farmer, beat the Federalist John Adams. Foreshadowing Andrew Jackson's folksy appeal, Jefferson arrived at his inauguration ceremony plainly dressed, without escorts, and on his own horse, which he tied up himself before taking the oath of office.

The political figures associated with agrarian populism—Thomas Jefferson, Andrew Jackson, Abraham Lincoln, William Jennings Bryan, and Henry Steagall (namesake of the famous Glass-Steagall Act of 1933)—exercised a powerful influence over America's banking policies. These men were from different political parties. Thomas Jefferson was a Democratic Republican; Andrew Jackson was the founder of the Democratic Party; Abraham Lincoln was a Republican; and William Jennings Bryan

[9] Wood (1991), 175–212.
[10] Wood (1991), 184.

ran as a candidate of both the Populist and Democratic parties. What united them were strongly held views about the plight and moral superiority of the common man, who they believed deserved access to land and to credit. What united their agrarian populist followers was a deep suspicion of big-city businesses and businessmen, which they viewed as a threat to their way of life.

Because America's agrarian populists were united by what they were against, rather than what they were for, they never cohered into a single political movement. Instead, they joined coalitions with groups whose interests overlapped with theirs, such as the free-soil movement, which brought them together with abolitionists; the pro-inflation free-silver movement, which brought them together with Western miners; and, important for our purposes, the anti–branch banking movement, which brought them together with small bankers against big-city banks and bankers.

Why this coalition succeeded—and continued to hold sway long after most of the country's economy had ceased to be based in agriculture— can be traced to another fundamental feature of American politics: the United States' highly decentralized form of federalism. There was no single, monolithic American colony. The 13 colonies went to war against Great Britain as allied but separate entities, and when they won, they initially constituted themselves as 13 sovereign states joined in what was little more than a customs union. Drawing them together into a single nation, with a national government and constitution, required that the states retain considerable autonomy. Any power not specifically enumerated in the U.S. Constitution as the province of the national government was left to the states—and the Constitution was silent about the regulation of banking. This meant that agrarian populists and unit bankers did not have to win legislative fights at the national level until the twentieth century: they only had to win local contests, which was a far easier task.

Colonial Banks, Colonial Grievances

American history textbooks typically focus on taxation without representation as the grievance that drove colonial elites to opt for independence, but there were other elements of disharmony as well. Among these was the fact that American merchants and large landowners wanted to establish chartered banks but consistently met opposition from the British imperial government.

Even a colonial government needs access to credit in order to finance sudden increases in expenditures—to pay wartime military expenses, for example. It also has an interest in encouraging private investment in order to make the colony more economically viable. The 13 colonies that became the United States often played the role of banks themselves as a way to get around the restrictions on chartered banks imposed by the imperial government. These early banking initiatives took two forms: the issuance of paper bills of credit and the establishment of loan offices or land banks that issued bills that were backed by mortgages on land. A bill of credit was essentially an IOU printed by the colonial government that it used to pay its creditors and that it then accepted back in payment of taxes. The IOU had value because it was backed by the government's tax revenues. The first such bills of credit were issued by Massachusetts in 1690 in order to pay its soldiers fighting in King William's War. The practice was soon copied by other colonies and proved expedient in financing wars with the French and their Indian allies.

Land banks also were promoted by colonial governments. By allowing investors to receive credit, mortgage finance reduced the amount of liquid wealth needed to purchase land. Moreover, the land banks provided colonial governments with a source of finance: the banks printed bills backed by the mortgages they issued, thereby turning an illiquid, low-value asset (frontier real estate) into a liquid security that functioned as paper money and that could be used in payment of colonial taxes. One of the main exponents of the advantages of land banks was young Benjamin Franklin, who in 1729, at the age of 23, penned "A Modest Enquiry into the Nature and Necessities of a Paper Currency," in which he argued that providing credit for land development would attract immigrants to Pennsylvania and create a self-reinforcing virtuous cycle of credit growth, economic expansion, and land appreciation.

The British Empire did not smile on the banking experiments of its North American colonies. The crown wanted to protect the control it had allotted to the Bank of England and other British banks over the management of the markets for credit and international bills of exchange. In addition, British merchants claimed that the debts due them were being redefined and devalued by these colonial bills. Some colonies saw significant price inflation from the issuance of these bills. For example, parts of New England in the 1740s and 1750s experienced a doubling of prices as the result of the bills of credit that were not sufficiently backed by either taxes or land.[11] From the point of view of British merchants, the debts owed them in sterling were being repaid in devalued colonial bills.

The British government took the side of British merchants and acted to limit colonial governments' rights to issue legal-tender bills (bills accepted for all debts, both public and private). The restrictions initially applied only to New England (the source of the early inflationary bill issuance), but in 1764 they were applied to all colonies. The outcry in the colonies led to relaxations of the law in 1770 and 1773, which permitted the issuance of bills receivable for taxes but prohibited colonial governments from making those bills a legal tender for satisfaction of private debts.

National Beginnings

The American Revolution undermined the constraints that had prevented the chartering of banks. The nascent and fiscally strapped government desperately needed a chartered bank in order to finance its own survival. The revolution alone was enormously costly—the total financial cost was roughly equal to four or five times the income for all 13 colonies in 1774. This cost was financed mainly by borrowing; only about 13 percent of the cost of the war was financed by contemporaneous taxation. The remaining 87 percent was paid for by debt finance, both by the states and the national government. Most of that debt took the form of paper currency issues, which suffered great loss in value due to the heavy reliance on them and as the result of the decision not to redeem them in coin, as promised.[12]

---

[11] Wicker (1985); B. Smith (1985a,b).

[12] Perkins ([1994], 97–103) estimates the cost of the war at 165 million pounds sterling. Estimates of total income in 1774 range from $138 million to $173 million. At an exchange rate of $4.44 to the pound, this implies that the cost of the war was roughly four to five times annual income (Lindert and Williamson [forthcoming], 19, 26). This was a huge cost for the populace to bear, especially given the decline in income that occurred during the war. As Kulikoff writes ([forthcoming], 1): "War tore the country apart; refugees and soldiers wandered the countryside; armies stole cattle and crops; people starved. Trade atrophied; money lost its value; jobs disappeared, as employers —not knowing if they could sell what they made or hire workers—cut production."

The new American government's first chartered bank, the Bank of North America (BNA), grew out of war-financing needs. In 1781 the Continental Congress granted a special charter to a group of shareholders to create the BNA as a commercial bank that would also serve as the government's fiscal agent. Right from the beginning, however, the idea of a privately owned, national bank that had a special relationship with the central government ran into trouble. The fundamental problem was that the BNA competed with local banks that operated without charters. The wedge that these banks were able to drive between the BNA and its charter was that the Articles of Confederation were ambiguous as to whether the central government actually had the authority to charter a bank. The BNA therefore had to be rechartered by the state of Pennsylvania. No sooner was this charter granted, however, than, at the behest of local unchartered banks, the BNA came under attack in the Pennsylvania state legislature, which revoked the bank's charter in 1785. The legislature restored the charter two years later, following an agreement by the BNA to accept a series of restrictions on its activities that effectively meant that it could not serve as the banker to the central government.[13]

The Articles of Confederation were soon replaced by the Constitution of 1787, but the basic problem of state finance remained, as did opposition from some quarters to the chartering of banks by the national government. The new central government lost little time in chartering a bank to replace the BNA—the Bank of the United States (BUS), founded in 1791. This charter was unsuccessfully opposed by Thomas Jefferson, who argued that the national government did not possess the authority under the Constitution to charter a bank. Alexander Hamilton, however, successfully argued that bank chartering was part of the implied powers of the federal government. When the charter got to the floor of the House of Representatives, the split in the 39–19 vote reflected the populist inclinations of America's rural regions: the bank's victorious supporters were from the commercial classes, its opponents were mainly agrarians.[14]

For additional perspectives on the amount and pricing of currency emissions, see Bullock (1895); Ferguson (1961); Calomiris (1988a); Grubb (2008).

[13] Bodenhorn (2003), 128.

[14] Grossman (2010), 223.

The BUS was a commercial bank, owned and operated by wealthy Federalist financiers, fully capable of taking deposits and making loans to private parties. The federal government subscribed 20 percent of the BUS's capital, without paying for those shares: instead it received a loan from the bank and then repaid the loan out of the stream of dividends it received as a shareholder in the bank. In exchange, the BUS received a set of valuable privileges that were afforded no other bank: the right to limited liability for its shareholders; the right to hold federal government deposits; the right to charge the federal government interest on loans from the bank (notes issued by the bank to cover federal expenses); and the right to open branches throughout the country. In short, the BUS was the product of a deal: a select group of bankers financed the state, and the state gave those bankers a lucrative concession.[15]

Federalism and Early U.S. Chartering of Banks

Had America's political institutions granted the federal government the sole right to charter banks, the BUS might have completely dominated the financial system. The federal organization of the U.S. government prevented that from happening, however. Under the Constitution, the states lost both the right to tax imports and exports and the right to issue legal-tender paper money. In exchange, the federal government assumed the considerable debts that the states had amassed under the Articles of Confederation.

America's states might have shed their old debts, but they still needed ways to finance themselves. Ironically, one option derived from the Tenth Amendment to the Constitution, which stipulated that any power not explicitly delegated to the federal government, or explicitly denied to the states, resided with the states. The Constitution said that states did not

---

[15] Because Hamilton's victory took place in a democratic political system, it had to entail at least a few concessions to his Republican opponents. The BUS's charter specifically required a large number of directors, a fragmentation of ownership, and an even greater fragmentation of voting control. Some directors were Republicans, no shareholder could own more than 4 percent of the stock, and voting power of the shareholders diminished on a sliding scale as their percentage of the stock increased. Nevertheless, a select group, dominated by Federalists, controlled the bank and thereby obtained a tremendously lucrative concession.

have the right to issue legal-tender paper money, but it said nothing about the right of states to charter banks whose banknotes could circulate as currency (although they could not be made a legal tender). State-chartered banks, which often modeled their charters on that of the Bank of the United States, soon became a source of significant financing for state governments.[16] Governments received stock in their chartered banks, taxed their banks, and also passed laws requiring their banks to hold state government debts as backing for their note issues.

States, therefore, had strong fiscal incentives to create bank charters—and strong incentives to do whatever was necessary to maximize the value of those charters. States were often major owners of bank shares, especially prior to the 1830s, and they typically paid for those shares with a loan from the bank, which they then repaid out of the dividend stream. Because states received a larger stream of dividends when the banks earned monopoly rents, they constrained the number of banks within their borders. States might extract additional income from banks by threatening them with new entrants to the banking market: they therefore accepted "bonuses" from incumbent banks to deny the charter applications of potential competitors.[17] To further ensure that the interest of bankers remained aligned with the governments that chartered them, banks typically were not granted perpetual charters. When their charters expired, they had to pay a fee or "bonus" for a renewal.[18] Not surprisingly, circa 1810–30, bank dividends and bank taxes often accounted for as much as one third of total state revenues.[19]

Since states received no charter fees or other economic benefits from banks incorporated in other states, they had an interest in prohibiting interstate branching. Challenges to those prohibitions were rejected by the Supreme Court in the landmark case *Bank of Augusta v. Earle* (1839), in which the court affirmed that states could limit banking activities by out-of-state banks so long as those prohibited activities were specifically enumerated by statute.

Banking in the early republican United States was therefore characterized by segmented monopolies. The four largest cities in the United States

---

[16] Bodenhorn (2011).
[17] Bodenhorn (2003), 17, 244.
[18] Schwartz (1947), 427–40; Bodenhorn (2011), 163.
[19] Sylla, Legler, and Wallis (1987); Wallis, Sylla, and Legler (1994).

Number of banks or authorized bank capital

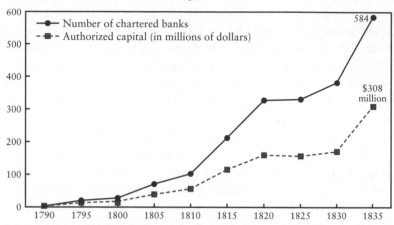

FIGURE 6.1 State-chartered banks in the United States, 1790–1835.

Source: Sylla (2008), 79.

in 1800—Boston, Philadelphia, New York, and Baltimore—had only two banks apiece. Smaller markets typically had only one bank, if they had a bank at all. As figure 6.1 shows, in 1800 there were only 28 banks (with total capital of only $17.4 million) in the entire country. Who was permitted to become a banker, and who would have access to credit from those banks, it should be emphasized, were determined on the basis of both economic and noneconomic criteria, such as political party affiliation.[20]

The Collapse of America's Insider Banking System

The system of a single national bank (the BUS) and segmented state monopolies was not sustainable in the long run under America's political institutions. At the center of the conflict over banking was the struggle over chartering authority between the central government and the states. Bankers with state charters had opposed the BUS from the time of its initial chartering in 1791. The reason for their opposition was straightforward: branches of the BUS—which were located in New York, Baltimore, Boston, Charleston (South Carolina), Norfolk, Savannah, New Orleans,

[20] Wallis, Sylla, and Legler (1994), 135–39; Bodenhorn (2003), 142; Majewski (2004).

Washington, DC, and Philadelphia—undermined local banking monopolies. State bankers therefore had incentives to form a coalition with the Jeffersonians, who were ideologically opposed to chartered corporations and "aristocratic" bankers, to eliminate the BUS. They initially tried to tax the banknotes of the BUS in order to give their own, state-chartered banks a competitive advantage. When that effort failed, they successfully lobbied state representatives not to renew the BUS charter. Indeed, the state legislatures of Massachusetts, Pennsylvania, and Maryland gave their senators explicit instructions to vote against the act. When the vote came, the rechartering of the BUS failed in both the House and the Senate.[21]

Parallel to the political fight over national chartering was the competition among the states resulting from the interaction of federalism, an expanding geographic frontier, and a broad suffrage, all of which helped to propel a growing demand for banks and an antipathy to the original practice of permitting only a few banking charters to the favored few. With strong incentives to compete against one another to attract a greater share of business enterprises and population, states pushed their legislatures to undertake steps that would connect them better to the emerging West.[22] In particular, state legislatures had incentives to construct canals and promote trade along water routes and roads that would funnel commerce from the expanding interior of the country through their states. The problem was how to pay for those improvements. Some states tried to finance them by issuing bonds to fund public-works projects, but this approach was discredited by a rash of unprofitable canal projects and debt defaults by eight states from 1841 to 1843.[23] Other states went a different route: they cut deals in which bankers gave the state a bonus to fund a public-works project in exchange for a bank charter. Such charter

[21] Lane (1997), 601–12; Wettereau (1942), 78 n. 97; Sylla (2000), 518–19; Rockoff (2000), 647; Grossman (2010), 225.

[22] Rothbard (2012), 81–147. Benmelech and Moskowitz (2010) show that competition among states influenced the relaxation of state usury laws during the nineteenth century. They argue that usury laws were passed at the behest of industrial incumbents who sought to limit the access to credit by new entrants. They find that the relaxation of usury laws in a neighboring state had a powerful influence on a state's tendency to relax its usury law. In other words, the power of incumbents to pursue anticompetitive practices was curtailed when the broader public interests suffered as the result of competition with other states.

[23] English (1996).

bonuses of course created an incentive for state legislatures to renege on the monopoly deals that they had already made with the incumbent banks.[24]

The same competitive and fiscal pressures also affected the distribution of political power within the states via changes in suffrage, and those changes in turn affected the politics of bank chartering. Legislatures of frontier states, eager to attract new residents, eliminated or reduced voting restrictions. Some of the original 13 states appear to have matched those more permissive voting laws to avoid losing population. By the mid-1820s, property qualifications for suffrage had been dropped or dramatically reduced in virtually all of the original states.[25] The extension of the suffrage distributed political power more broadly and thus allowed citizens who wanted broader access to credit to pressure legislatures to remove constraints on the chartering of banks.

Thus political competition within and among states undermined the incentives of state legislatures to constrain the numbers of charters they granted. Massachusetts began to increase the number of charters it granted as early as 1812, abandoning its strategy of holding bank stock as a source of state finance and instead levying taxes on bank capital. Pennsylvania followed with the Omnibus Banking Act of 1814. The act, passed over the objections of the state's governor, ended the cozy Philadelphia-based oligopoly that until then had dominated the state's banking industry.[26] Rhode Island also followed this lead: in 1826 it sold its bank shares, increased the numbers of charters it granted, and began to tax bank capital as a replacement for the income it had earned from dividends. It soon became, on a per capita basis, America's most heavily banked state.

Although the first third of the nineteenth century saw considerable expansion of access to credit, the reforms of this era did not allow all comers to charter banks or permit banks to open branches at will. Pennsylvania's Omnibus Banking Act of 1814, for example, divided the state into 27 banking districts and then allocated charters to 41 banks, with each district receiving at least one bank charter. For decades this law sharply constrained the establishment of new banks to compete with incumbents in locations of high demand. Another crucial aspect of the law

---

[24] Grinath, Wallis, and Sylla (1997); Bodenhorn (2003), 86, 148, 152, 228–34; Wallis, Sylla, and Grinath (2004).

[25] Engerman and Sokoloff (2012), 98–110; Keyssar (2000), chapter 2.

[26] Schwartz (1947); Bodenhorn (2003), 141–215.

was that banks were constrained from lending more than 20 percent of their capital to borrowers outside their districts, thereby further limiting the amount of competition within any particular banking district.[27] Furthermore, the prohibition of branching within the state (the common practice of Northern states) prevented unit banks from developing relationships with and gathering information about prospective borrowers elsewhere in the state, making bankers unwilling to lend to them. Indeed, research has shown that until the computer revolution, obtaining information about the quality of potential borrowers who were not located near a bank was prohibitively costly. As a result, until the 1990s most small business loans were made by banks located less than 51 miles away from the borrowers they served.[28]

The restrictions on competition in Pennsylvania's Omnibus Banking Law were part of a grand compromise among potential debtors, who sought increased access to credit; incumbent bankers, who sought rents by limiting competition; and the state government, which needed a source of income and a mechanism to fund public debt. The core feature of the deal was that banking monopolies would be allowed to persist: competition within local markets remained limited, albeit less so than before. Additional restrictions placed on the Pennsylvania banks showed that the chartering bill was designed not to exclude any category of local economic incumbents: 20 percent of banks' capital had to be lent to farmers, mechanics, and manufacturers; interest rates and bank indebtedness were capped by statute; and no more than 20 percent of capital could be invested in corporate or government securities. The rents earned by the local banking monopolies established by the 1814 statute were then shared with the state government. Banks had to pay a 6 percent tax on dividends, and banks were required by law to pay dividends or risk the revocation of their charter. In addition, the banks had to make loans to the state government, at the government's discretion, at an interest rate that could not exceed 5 percent.[29]

Pennsylvania was not alone in maintaining restrictions on bank charters. From 1830 to 1837 New York State received 535 petitions for char-

---

[27] Bodenhorn (2003), 142–43.
[28] Peterson and Rajan (2002).
[29] Bodenhorn (2003), 142–43.

ters but granted only 53. As we discuss below, those charters tended to be granted to insiders with ties to the political machine that ran the state government.[30]

This process of limited reform by states still allowed the U.S. banking system to grow at a rapid pace. As figure 6.1 shows, in 1820 there were 327 banks in operation with $160 million in capital—roughly three times as many banks and four times as much bank capital as in 1810. By 1835, there were 584 banks, with $308 million in capital—a nearly twofold increase in just 15 years. At this point, larger cities often had a dozen or more banks, while small towns had two or three.

As the number of banks increased, they were forced to search out new classes of borrowers. The result was that banks, particularly in the mid-Atlantic states, lent funds to an increasingly wide variety of merchants, artisans, and farmers.[31] Even in New England, where banks lent primarily to their own directors, the sheer number of banks and ease of new bank formation made access to credit less of a binding constraint on the growth of nonfinancial firms.[32]

The final blow to the insider era of bank chartering in the United States came in 1832, when Andrew Jackson successfully vetoed the rechartering of the Second Bank of the United States. That bank had been chartered in 1816, ironically by the very Republicans who had opposed the rechartering of the BUS in 1811. The War of 1812 demonstrated the importance to the government of a bank that could serve as its fiscal agent. The Second Bank of the United States was founded on the same principles as the first, and it faced opposition from the same local banker–agrarian populist coalition. The populist presidency of Andrew Jackson and the risky political gambling of the Second BUS's president, Nicholas Biddle, during the struggle over the rechartering of the bank resulted in its demise: Jackson vetoed the renewal of the bank's charter in 1832, forcing it to close in 1836.[33] From this point until roughly 1980, the coalition of small bankers and agrarian populists would dominate the politics of bank chartering and bank regulation in the United States.

[30] Bodenhorn (2006), 239–43.
[31] Wang (2006), 107.
[32] Lamoreaux (1994), 9, 13.
[33] For a more complete discussion, see Hammond (1947); Temin (1968); Engerman (1970); Rockoff (2000); Schweikart (1988); Rothbard (2012).

While there was considerable variation between states, the chartering of banks by special legislative acts tended to be replaced by so-called free-banking acts from the late 1830s onward. The severe panic of 1837, and the financial distress and economic depression that followed it, helped to accelerate that process. Substantial numbers of banks failed throughout the country. State monopoly banks that were closely involved in financing public works projects, especially in the South, collapsed most spectacularly, but the North also saw a very high failure rate.[34] The panic created a financial vacuum that needed to be filled and also exposed the weaknesses of the use of specially chartered banks to fund government-sponsored projects. The result of both reactions to the panic was the "free-banking era." Under free banking, bank charters no longer had to be approved by state legislatures. Rather, individuals could open banks provided that they registered with the state comptroller and deposited state or federal bonds with the comptroller as a guarantee of their note issues.

Readers may wonder how such a system of free entry could have been compatible with the fiscal needs of state governments. The answer lies in the fact that under free banking, all banknotes had to be 100 percent backed by high-grade securities—which, notably, included bonds issued by the state government—that were deposited with the state comptroller of the currency. Free banks were forced, in essence, to grant a loan to the state government in exchange for the right to operate.

New York was the first state to make the switch to free banking in 1838, and the reason for the switch was unambiguous: citizens who had been closed out of credit markets voted with a political party that promised to break the oligopoly that had controlled bank chartering. From the 1810s to the late 1830s, bank chartering in New York was controlled by the Albany Regency, a political machine run by Martin Van Buren. Also known as the Holy Alliance, this group was known for its sanctimonious and self-serving oratory against corruption. Nevertheless, its political philosophy was best expressed by one of its leading members, New York governor William Marcy, who coined the phrase "To the victors belong the spoils." Bank charters were granted only to friends of the Regency, in exchange for which the legislators received various bribes, such as the

[34] See Schweikart (1987), 48–90; McGrane (1924), 91–144.

ability to subscribe to initial public offerings of bank stock at par, even though the stock traded for a substantial premium.[35]

The Regency's hold on bank chartering came to an end when the state's voting laws were amended in 1826, allowing universal male suffrage. Within a decade, the Regency lost its control of the state legislature, and in 1838, in the wake of the panic, the dominant Whig Party enacted America's first free-banking law. By 1841, New Yorkers had established 43 free banks, with a total capital of $10.7 million. By 1849, the number of free banks had mushroomed to 111, with $16.8 million in paid-in capital. By 1859 there were 274 free banks with paid-in capital of $100.6 million.[36] Other states soon followed New York's lead. By the early 1860s, 21 states had adopted some variant of the New York law, and as they did so, they encouraged bank entry and increased competition.[37]

Economic interests as well as ideology contributed to the free-banking movement. Support for the passage of New York's free-banking law in 1838 was strongest in locations with a greater fraction of the labor force employed in commerce and manufacturing and those that lacked existing bank facilities.[38] Free banking was also a reaction to the popular dislike of the granting of special privileges, which were associated with favoritism, elitism, and corruption.

Free banking was not, however, a complete rethinking of the earlier system of segmented monopolies, and it did not result in a fully open-access system of banking within or across states. Most important, free banks were not permitted to branch. Given the high overhead costs of establishing a bank, this restriction effectively limited the entry of banks in sparsely populated areas. Because of regulatory costs and limited entry, the free-banking era was not associated with a dramatic increase in competition. Indeed, some research even suggests that the passage of free-banking statutes per se was not critical to the process of banking growth.[39]

---

[35] Bodenhorn (2003), 134, 186–88; Bodenhorn (2006); Gatell (1966), 26; Moss and Brennan (2004).

[36] Bodenhorn (2003), 186–92; Wallis, Sylla, and Legler (1994); Moss and Brennan (2004).

[37] Bodenhorn (1990), 682–86; Bodenhorn (1993), 531–35; Economopoulos and O'Neill (1995); Ng (1988); Rockoff (1974, 1985).

[38] Bodenhorn (2007), 23.

[39] Ng (1988).

Other research helps to explain why: despite the democratization of char-tering under free banking, the unit structure of New York's free-banking system significantly limited the expansion of bank credit in that state.[40] Because branching restrictions persisted, free banking simply expanded the number and reduced the size of local bank monopolies. It also re-moved the government from the position of awarding bank charters to its political allies. The results were twofold: some of the rents that had been earned by bankers were dissipated, and borrowers who had earlier been closed out of credit markets now had access to finance, though it came from banks that still had a great deal of local market power.

North-South Differences: Branching, Clearinghouses, and Liability Insurance

The banking experience of the South followed a different path from that of the North and Midwest after 1837. Unlike the North, where both free banks and specially chartered banks were prohibited from branching, most Southern states allowed banks to branch within the state.

Part of the explanation for this difference resides in North-South differ-ences in forms of wealth and the geographic mobility of the factors of pro-duction. In the North, the geographically segmented organization of the banking system was the outcome of a winning political coalition: bankers who wanted to create local monopolies allied with populists who disliked corporations of any type, but especially those associated with big-city "aristocrats." The populist support for unit banking reflected, in part, the advantages that some classes of local borrowers received from limiting bank entry through unit banking. Because unit banking tied local banks to the local economy, it made bankers more willing to continue to provide credit to their existing borrowers during lean times, unlike a branch bank that might move funds to other locations in pursuit of greener pastures. In central Illinois, for example, a fall in the price of corn reduced the income and property values of everyone in the local economy. Local bankers could reduce the supply of loans to their clients in response to that shock, but if they did, the only viable alternative investment was cash or securities, such as government bonds. Limited alternatives favored greater continuation of

[40] Bodenhorn (2008).

credit during lean times. This "credit-insurance" advantage can explain why states with relatively high agricultural wealth and a broad distribution of land tended to favor unit banking: large numbers of relatively prosperous farmers who were already on the client list of the local unit banker had a stake in preserving branching restrictions.[41]

In contrast to that of the North, wealth in the antebellum South consisted more of people than of land. The primary form of wealth was slaves, and slave labor was easily redeployable throughout the South.[42] Wealthy slave-owning Southerners had less to gain from the credit-risk insurance that locally bounded unit banking offered.

These fundamental differences in the distribution of productive assets between the North and South were reflected in North-South differences in the distribution of political power. In the South, political power was concentrated in the hands of large slave-owning planters, who tended to monopolize local and state offices. The relative political weakness of small white farmers (not to mention the complete disenfranchisement of the slave population) blunted populist demands for unit banks in the South. Thus the different structures of banking systems in the antebellum North and South can be understood as political outcomes that reflected different underlying economic interests.

Another reason for the relatively weak support of unit banking in the South is the fact that branching facilitated the development of an interbank "banker's acceptance" market to finance the movement of the cotton crop more cost-effectively. Fewer banks operating over greater distances made it easier for banks to accept each other's bills across regions, a major advantage in an export economy. Antebellum banks in the Southern branch-banking states of Tennessee and Kentucky had much higher holdings of trade acceptances than country banks in the unit-banking states of the North.[43]

The relative efficiency of a system of a few banks with a large number of branches arose in part from lower information costs. Suppose that a merchant wanted to export cotton from a rural area. To do so, he had to buy the cotton from farmers in that area, move it to a port in the East,

---

[41] Calomiris (2000), 64–67; Calomiris and Ramirez (2008).
[42] Wright (1986), 11, 17–50.
[43] Bodenhorn (1990), 37.

and ship it abroad for sale. That process took time and involved a substantial outlay of money. The existence of a system of banks, especially
banks with branches, made this process much easier. In the first place, the
merchant could finance the transaction by borrowing from his bank in
the East, and instead of the bank's advancing him cash, it could give him
a domestic bill, also known as a banker's acceptance. The bill was effectively an IOU. The merchant would then present that bill to a banker in
the cotton-growing area in exchange for cash, which the merchant could
use to purchase the cotton. The willingness of the second bank to accept
that bill depended on the rural banker's confidence in the creditworthiness of the bank on which it was drawn in the East. The key to making
this arrangement work was mutual knowledge within the banking system. Banks that accepted bills in exchange for cash had to be able to verify
the legitimacy of the bills and to judge the solvency of the bank standing
behind the bills. In a branching system where there were few banks,
mutual monitoring was considerably easier. In fact, for transactions between branches of the same bank, information costs were virtually zero.[44]

It was therefore not a coincidence that the U.S. South—where trade in
cotton was the dominant economic activity, the most important asset was
slaves, and political power was concentrated among the slave-owning
class—chose to organize its state-chartered banks on a branching basis:
export finance was the primary function of antebellum southern banks.

These fundamental differences made Northern banks much less stable
than those in the South.[45] The Northern banking system was composed of
a large number of geographically isolated unit banks that were subject to
substantial risk of loss on their loans as the result of severe local shocks

---

[44] Because branch banking was the exception rather than the rule in U.S. banking
history, bankers' acceptances and bills of exchange were rarely used in the United States
to finance crop movement, in contrast, for example, to the practice in Canada. As John
James has pointed out to us in private correspondence, national banks were also
barred by law from acting as guarantors, which meant that they could not participate
in the bills market. Of course, that prohibition did not apply to state-chartered banks.
Furthermore, the prohibition on national banks was lifted by the Federal Reserve Act,
but that change did not spur the development of the bills market. Thus unit banking,
not the legal prohibition on national bank participation in the bills market prior to
1913, was the primary cause of the lack of the development of a bills market in the
United States.

[45] Calomiris and Schweikart (1991).

(such as declines in crop prices). These smaller banks, operating in a more fragmented system, also found it more difficult to coordinate their responses to banking-system crises. They therefore faced a higher risk of failure. In the South, a small number of large and geographically overlapping branching banks were better diversified and better able to communicate and coordinate their responses during panics, making markets in each other's liabilities and agreeing to avoid disruptive withdrawals of cash from one another. The large numbers of banks in Northern banking systems also presented greater challenges for the interbank clearing of notes and deposits.

To compensate for their relatively low diversification, high coordination costs, and more complicated clearing networks, Northern states' unit-banking systems developed formal institutional mechanisms for sharing risk, managing their local responses to panics, and clearing notes and deposits. These took the form of bank clearinghouses and bank liability-insurance schemes, neither of which arose in the antebellum South.

Clearinghouses, which operated only locally in cities, performed the dual roles of managing the interbank transfers of notes and deposits during normal times and establishing rules for collective action during panics. Clearinghouse members made markets in each other's liabilities to limit each other's withdrawal risks during panics. In several extreme panics, the members of the New York City clearinghouse also issued clearinghouse notes, which were collective liabilities, for which they were mutually liable, which served to augment the supply of cash in the system. To prevent free riding on collective protection, clearinghouse members also passed and enforced regulatory requirements. Most importantly, New York City clearinghouse members were required to maintain a high level of cash assets (25 percent of their deposits), a practice that lowered both the credit risk and the liquidity risk of the banking system.

Six Northern states developed liability-insurance systems during the antebellum era. These followed two different models, and the choice of model had major implications for their success. One included a relatively large number of members with limited liability for each other's losses and with regulations on members established and enforced by the state government. The other limited membership to a small number of banks (typically around thirty banks statewide), required unlimited mutual liability of members for each other's losses, and gave the members responsibility for establishing and enforcing regulations. The incentive structures of the two models were therefore dramatically different. The first invited greater risk taking by member banks (the so-called moral-hazard problem), did not limit systemic risk during crises, and could not retain members once losses from failed members began to mount. The second system gave banks the incentive and the wherewithal to monitor one another in order to prevent free riding. The small number of members in these insured systems ensured that the benefits of members' monitoring one another were not diluted.

The three states that followed the first model (New York, Michigan, and Vermont) all saw their insured systems collapse with insurance claims outstanding. In the face of mounting losses from bank failures, surviving members exited the system by switching their charters to the free-banking alternative. In sharp contrast, the three states that followed the second model (Indiana, Ohio, and Iowa), enjoyed low risk and effective mutual protection. During banking panics, insured members in these states not only avoided failure but were also able to avoid significant deposit runs or suspensions of convertibility because they commanded the confidence of depositors.[46]

The Civil War and the Creation of the Dual National and State Chartering System

The challenges of financing the Civil War brought dramatic and lasting changes to the U.S. banking system. The Civil War led to the creation of the United States' first government-issued paper currency that had the status of legal tender for debts both public and private. It also brought the national government back into the business of chartering banks, something that it had not done since Jackson vetoed the charter for the Second Bank of the United States in 1832.

None of this happened seamlessly. The federal government had to take account of the agrarian populist–unit banker coalition that dominated the politics of banking. Indeed, the constitutionality of the issuance of a legal-tender currency was only affirmed by stacking the Supreme Court. The move to create a system of banks with national charters was met

[46] Golembe and Warburton (1958); Golembe (1960); Calomiris (1989, 1990).

with even more mixed success. When the dust settled, there were more state-chartered banks than nationally chartered banks, and national banks were national in name only; they were unit banks just like their state-chartered competitors.

When the Civil War broke out in April 1861, no one in the federal government expected it to drag on for four years and cost a fortune in treasure and lives. The early battles soon made clear, however, that the government was going to need big infusions of cash in order to beat the South into submission. It had various methods at its disposal: raising taxes, selling bonds to the public, placing bonds with banks, forcing banks to lend to it in exchange for the right to issue banknotes, taxing private banknotes, and printing fiat currency. It ultimately employed all of them, but as a first step it did what was politically easiest: it tried to sell bonds to the public. The public was not, however, receptive to these offerings. Secretary of the Treasury Salmon Chase therefore did the next easiest thing politically: he called upon the banks of New York, and those of other Eastern cities, to organize a syndicate to purchase government bonds at low rates of interest. They responded as Chase had hoped, evidently thinking that if the country's biggest banks were the government's creditors, then the government would be forced to behave prudently in its fiscal affairs.[47] After all, what government would want to bankrupt its own banking system?

Only a few months later, in December 1861, Secretary Chase did precisely that. In his annual report to Congress, Chase revealed the grim fiscal picture of a protracted civil war, and he proposed that further debt issues, rather than taxes, would be used to fund the expenditures to come. He was, in effect, telling the markets that the federal government was going to repay existing loans with new loans, and that those new loans would be repaid by a tax increase at some unspecified future date. The implication was that the government might continue this practice of continually rolling over existing debt while taking on new debt. The markets reacted accordingly: the value of government bonds fell dramatically. The banks, which had been stuffed full of government debt by the syndicated offering, were now caught in a difficult position: the value of one of their most important assets (the government bonds) had dropped in value,

[47] Calomiris (1991).

meaning that the value of their most important liabilities (the banknotes that they had issued and the deposits that they had taken) had to be reduced in value as well. As a consequence, the banks were forced to suspend convertibility: the public could not convert their deposits or notes drawn on these banks into gold or silver coin.

One lesson that may be drawn from this episode is that incompetent treasury secretaries are not just a recent phenomenon; but another, equally useful lesson is that a government can simultaneously bail out banks and finance itself by issuing a fiat paper currency. Until 1861, the dollar was defined only as a given amount of gold or silver, and the medium of exchange created by the national government was confined to gold and silver coins produced at the U.S. mint. Paper money was issued by private banks (and hence called banknotes), and thus did not have the status of legal tender. In February 1862, the federal government began to issue U.S. notes (also called legal-tender notes or greenbacks), a paper currency that had the status of legal tender. Importantly, greenbacks could not be converted into fixed amounts of gold or silver.

The primary purpose of creating this depreciated currency, and making it a legal tender for private and public debts, was to bail out the nation's banks.[48] Preexisting bank deposits or banknotes denominated in dollars that had previously been convertible into gold or silver could now be repaid in greenbacks, which were not convertible. The net worth of the banks was restored, while depositors and note holders were effectively expropriated. The greenback, of course, conferred an additional benefit on the federal government: it could pay for its expenditures by printing non-interest-bearing notes instead of issuing bonds on which it had to pay interest.[49]

The creation of the greenback was a bold move. The Constitutional Convention had left delegates deeply divided over the question of whether and how the federal government might issue paper currency.[50] As a compromise, the states were forbidden from issuing currency or establishing legal-tender laws, while the federal government was given the right to establish the value of the dollar and to coin money. The Constitution was,

---

[48] Hammond (1970).
[49] Mitchell (1903), 47.
[50] Hurst (1973), 3–27.

however, silent on whether the federal government could issue paper currency or declare it a legal tender. From 1791 to 1861, that silence was interpreted to mean that the federal government could set the dollar value of gold and silver brought to the mint (and of foreign coins used for payment in the United States, such as the Mexican peso, which circulated widely). It was also interpreted to mean that during time of war the government could issue paper currency that would be legal tender for public debts (i.e., the public could pay its taxes with this currency). The government had, in fact, done so during the War of 1812, and it did so again by issuing "demand notes" in 1861, which could be used to pay import tariffs on par with gold and silver coins.

The problem facing Secretary Chase—the potential collapse of a group of major East Coast banks—could not be solved, however, without undertaking bold new steps. He had to create a mechanism to bail out the banks that he himself had sunk, and thus, constitutional or not, the greenback was declared legal tender for debts both public and private. The banks could pay back their private debts to note holders and depositors in a fiat currency. Because of a bizarre twist of events, we know that Chase himself doubted the constitutionality of his act. The legal tender authority of the federal government was challenged in the courts, with the case ultimately coming before the Supreme Court in 1869—and Chase was now chief justice of the court. In *Hepburn v. Griswold,* Chase actually voted with the majority against the constitutionality of making greenbacks a legal tender for preexisting private contracts denominated in dollars! President Ulysses Grant appears not to have been amused. He added two additional Supreme Court justices—who he knew would vote favorably —to ensure that the legal tender authority of the federal government was affirmed. As a result, the 1869 decision was reversed in 1871 in *Parker v. Davis* and *Knox v. Lee.*[51]

Governments in need of war finance generally tinker on every margin they can, and thus Chase did not stop with the issuance of greenbacks. Indeed, the greenback was something of a stopgap measure for Chase. His larger goal was to simultaneously create a mechanism to finance the war and, reflecting his ideological orientation, to eliminate the confusion of a currency system comprising many different banks' notes that traded at

---

[51] Dunne (1960); Calomiris (1992a).

progressively steeper discounts the farther one moved away from a bank's office (where the notes could be redeemed). These discounts reflected both the costs of redemption imposed by physical distance and the perceived riskiness of a far-away issuer.[52]

The government's need to place a huge volume of new debts gave Chase a good reason to realize what he and others regarded as a desirable long-term change: to homogenize banknote issuance within newly created national banks chartered under the National Banking Act of 1863, and to require that banknotes be fully backed by government bonds. The federal government lacked the authority to abrogate the right of states to charter banks or to prevent state-chartered banks from issuing banknotes. It could, however, impose a 10 percent tax on notes issued by state-chartered banks while imposing only a 1 percent tax on those of national banks, thereby giving state banks strong incentives to obtain new federal charters. In order to capture some of the value of these new charters for the government's own uses, notes from national banks had to be backed at 111 percent of their value in holdings of U.S. treasury bonds, as well as additional holdings of U.S. notes. In short, the federal government was trading the right to issue banknotes for a loan! Banks took advantage of this opportunity, as one would expect, to different degrees: banks with relatively profitable loans issued fewer notes backed by government bonds and focused more on deposit-financed lending, while those with relatively unprofitable loans often took full advantage of the opportunity to issue notes backed by government bonds.[53]

Banks with national charters began to appear in 1863, and their notes soon drove the notes of state-chartered banks out of existence. They were, however, national banks only in the sense that their charter was granted by the federal government, not in the sense that they could operate nationwide branches. They continued to be subject to state laws that either made branching entirely illegal or limited the number of branches that could be operated. Thus the National Banking Act was essentially free banking on a national scale.

The creation of legal-tender notes and the chartering of national banks both illustrate a general truth: the government, as a partner in all political

[52] Gorton (1989); Calomiris and Kahn (1996).
[53] Calomiris (1988b, 1993a); Calomiris and Mason (2004).

coalitions that govern the rules of the game for bank chartering, implicitly reserves the right to extract resources from other partners during times of fiscal need. It was not a coincidence that a national government that had not attempted to charter a bank for three decades and had never declared its fiat money a legal tender chose to do both during the Civil War. It was also not a coincidence that the government then used those newly chartered banks as a captive market to place its growing debts.

The way that greenbacks and the national banks were rolled out by the federal government also illustrates another general truth: governments in representative democracies, especially those that also have strong institutions of federalism, cannot just do whatever they want. Chase could not, for example, finance the Civil War by destroying the banks (as his Mexican counterparts did when they fought their own civil war in 1914–17, during the Mexican Revolution; see chapter 10). Indeed, the creation of greenbacks was the result of the government's desire to limit the fallout that the banks would suffer from being partners with the government. Similarly, while the federal government did effectively expropriate state banks of their profits from note issuing, it did so in a way that allowed them to become partners with the government, by obtaining national bank charters in exchange for purchasing government debt. Moreover, the banking system that it created did not challenge the core policy of the populist–unit banker coalition: a system of segmented monopolies was preserved because even national banks had to conform to state laws regarding branching.

In fact, limits on the power and discretion of the parties in control of the Federal Government meant that they were not able to drive state-chartered banks out of existence. In the short run, the response of private banks was as the federal government expected. As figure 6.2 shows, the number of state-chartered banks declined from 1,579 in 1860 to 349 by 1865. The number of national banks grew dramatically during that same period, from zero to 1,294.

In the long run, however, the substitution of bank deposits for banknotes, and competition between the national and state chartering authorities, frustrated the federal government's goal of a single system of national banks and resulted instead in dual systems of state-chartered and nationally chartered banks. The federal government had effectively nationalized the right to issue banknotes by creating a 10 percent tax on the notes of

Number of banks   Percentage of assets in national banks

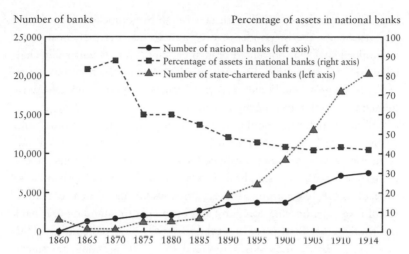

FIGURE 6.2 Number of U.S. banks by charter type, 1860–1914.

Sources: Lamoreaux (1991), 540; Davis and Gallman (2001), 268; Calomiris and White (1994), 151; U.S. Federal Reserve Board (1943), 24.

state-chartered banks in 1865. The law did not, however, say anything about checks drawn on accounts in state-chartered banks. State banks therefore aggressively pursued deposit banking, and checks drawn on those accounts became an increasingly common means of exchange in business transactions.[54] They appear to have been helped by state legislatures, which reduced the minimum capital requirements for state-chartered banks.[55] The result was that state-chartered banks actually outgrew federally chartered banks during the period 1865–1914. As figure 6.2 shows, in 1865 state banks accounted for only 21 percent of all banks and 13 percent of total bank assets. By 1890 there were more state banks than national banks, and state banks controlled the majority of assets. Circa 1914, 73 percent of all banks were state banks, and state banks controlled 58 percent of assets.

The result was a banking system with a most peculiar competitive and geographic structure. In 1914 there were 27,349 banks in the United States, 95 percent of which had no branches! The banks that did have

[54] Moss and Brennan (2004); Sylla (1975), 62–73; Davis and Gallman (2001), 272.
[55] Grossman (2010), 231, 236.

branches tended to be small, with fewer than five branches on average.[56] The reason for the preponderance of unit banks was that most states maintained laws that prevented branch banking, even by nationally chartered banks.[57] States that did not explicitly forbid branch banking typically had no provision in their laws for branches, and this lack effectively limited the creation of branching banks.

Unit bankers formed numerous local and state organizations to lobby against the relaxation of branch-banking restrictions. They even succeeded in getting the American Bankers Association to adopt resolutions in 1916 and 1924 opposing branch banking in any form.[58] Urban banks tried, of course, to get around these restrictions through the clever maneuver of forming a holding company and opening a freestanding unit bank in a rural market. State laws, however, effectively limited the utility of this maneuver, because those laws specified that a freestanding unit bank owned by a holding company had to be just that: freestanding. It could not share back-office operations with the urban bank and thus had to forgo the advantages of scale economies in administration. The high overhead costs implied by this business model meant that there were limited gains from creating a quasi–branch network. State laws thus served as effective and persistent barriers to entry.

Why did voters tolerate this arrangement? Why didn't they form a coalition with the urban bankers who wanted to open branches in their underserved markets? As we have already noted, unit banking was quite popular among borrowers in many states, perhaps because of the credit-insurance advantage it offered. For example, in 1924, Illinois held a referendum on whether to continue the unit-banking system, and unit banking won the support of voters.[59] Identifiable economic interests predict support for unit banking in the states where it was popular.[60] Apparently, landowning farmers in prosperous farming districts, who used unit banks to fund their operations and acquisitions, calculated that they had some-

---

[56] Calomiris and White (1994), 145–88; Davis and Gallman (2001), 272.

[57] Grossman (2010), 238.

[58] Abrams and Settle (1993), 689. Another banking association was more reliably opposed to branch banking; it was known as the United States Bankers Association Opposed to Branch Banking. See Abrams and Settle (1993), 702 n. 6.

[59] E. White (1984a).

[60] Abrams and Settle (1993); Calomiris (2000); Calomiris and Ramirez (2008).

thing to gain from unit banking. A local banker who was not part of a branch network had to lend to them or to no one. The higher interest rate they paid the unit banker for a loan was a premium for the insurance they received—the greater willingness of unit bankers to continue extending credit during adverse times.

A Uniquely Unstable System

Despite all of the changes in the organization of the U.S. banking system that occurred with the Civil War, its basic structure—a fragmented system composed of thousands of geographically isolated unit banks—did not change. As a result, the U.S. system remained remarkably unstable. From 1800 to 1861, there were five major banking crises: 1814–16, 1825, 1837–39, 1857, and 1861. From 1873 to 1907, there were six. Three of those crises (1873, 1893, 1907) saw widespread suspensions of the convertibility of bank deposits, which is to say depositors could write checks against their deposits but could not convert deposits into cash. In the other three crises (1884, 1890, 1896) suspension was avoided through collective actions by clearinghouses, which made markets in bank deposits and issued supplementary currency to add liquidity to the system. These post–Civil War crises were not, therefore, characterized by widespread bank failures, unlike the earlier crises. Nevertheless, they were highly disruptive to the U.S. financial system and the real economy.[61]

These periodic banking crises produced chaotic panics as depositors ran on the banks. They therefore exacerbated normal business-cycle fluctuations. In fact, U.S. banking crises were uniquely predictable events that happened at business-cycle peaks. Preceding World War I, every quarter in which the liabilities of failed businesses rose by more than 50 percent (seasonally adjusted) and the stock market fell by more than 8 percent, a panic happened in the following quarter. National panics never happened otherwise during this period.[62]

The U.S. was the only country in the world still suffering from these kinds of panics at the end of the nineteenth century.[63] The peculiar vulner-

---

[61] Because they required coordinated action by the clearinghouses, they met the definition of a banking crisis outlined in chapter 1.

[62] Calomiris and Gorton (1991).

[63] Bordo (1985).

ability of the U.S. system reflected three key weaknesses of unit banking—the lack of diversification of risk within banks (as was possible in branch-banking systems), the pyramiding of the banking system's reserves in New York City (which made the entire system vulnerable to securities-market-related shocks that affected New York's banks), and the difficulty of coordinating responses of banks to liquidity crises.

The Founding of the Federal Reserve

In the wake of the panic of 1907, bankers and government officials began a series of meetings and deliberations to address the persistent problem of banking panics in the United States. This group, convened as the National Monetary Commission, clearly understood that the unit-banking system was the core problem. The commission produced many volumes of material about banking throughout the world that is still a treasure trove to financial historians, including several volumes that discussed the sharp contrast between the stability of branch-banking systems (like those in neighboring Canada) and the crisis-prone unit-banking system of the United States.

Reforming the basic structure of the U.S. banking system was, however, politically infeasible. Instead, the commission proposed the next best thing: the creation of a central bank that would reduce liquidity risk in the banking system by making loans to banks that were under stress. It focused in particular on reducing seasonal liquidity risks related to the planting and harvesting cycle, which required substantial flows of funds from East Coast financial centers to the rest of the country.[64]

The decision not to alter the fragmented structure of the banking system was costly. First, because barriers to competition allowed less profitable banks to survive during normal times, they made bank failures more frequent during adverse times. Second, the barriers to entry implied by unit banking prevented productive competition among banks. Unit banks could face competition only from other unit banks, all of which faced high overhead costs that limited entry, especially in rural areas. Third, unit

---

[64] There is substantial evidence that the Federal Reserve System was effective in reducing seasonal and other liquidity risk in the banking system. Miron (1986); Richardson and Troost (2006); Bernstein, Hughson, and Weidenmier (2010).

banking inhibited financial integration across regions. Nationwide branching banks can easily move funds across regions to accommodate differences in demand and thereby equalize interest rates. In the absence of branching, large interest-rate differences across regions persisted well into the twentieth century. Finally, unit banking also promoted a growing mismatch between the size of banks and the needs of their prospective borrowers: small banks could not lend the sums needed by large industrial firms. The scale of industry grew substantially during the nineteenth century as steel and chemicals replaced textiles and shoes as the fastest-growing manufacturing sectors—but the scale of banks did not keep up. Thus, although banks had been important sources of funds for the industrial enterprises of the early nineteenth century, they played a much less important role in industrial finance by the end of the nineteenth century.[65]

Despite the enormous and obvious economic advantages from dispensing with unit banking, the National Monetary Commission focused on what was politically feasible, namely the creation of the Federal Reserve System. As envisioned by its founders, the Federal Reserve Banks would be a repository of excess reserves during times of low loan demand for their member banks and a source of additional reserves (via either lending to members or buying assets from them) during periods of high demand. To avoid fueling undesirable speculation in stock markets or real estate, the Federal Reserve banks would restrict their activities to purchasing or lending against "real bills," defined as commercial loans related to the financing of trade. At the Fed's founding, real bills were expected to be the key asset that would pass between member banks and their reserve banks. The goal of this system was to reduce liquidity risk by creating a decentralized system that was independent of the government.

The creation of the Fed required a set of compromises that reflected the power of particular constituencies rather than the economic intentions of the Fed founders. First, despite the recognition of the superiority

---

[65] Calomiris (1995); Giedeman (2005). It is important to emphasize that the alleged "money trust" operated by J. P. Morgan in the early twentieth century played virtually no role in providing bank loans, underwriting equity, or arranging the financing of new industrial enterprises. It, like other investment banks of the period, focused on bond underwriting, industrial reorganizations, and corporate governance of large firms. See Carosso (1970); DeLong (1991); Ramirez (1995); Calomiris (2000), chapters 4 and 5; and Pak (2012).

of a branch-banking system, the founding of the Fed did nothing to reform the peculiar market structure of America's unit-banking system. That was not an unintended consequence: the creation of the Fed required the support of unit bankers and their political allies.[66] Second, in the negotiations over the chartering of the Fed, rural interests were successful in pushing through a reform allowing national banks to lend against real estate—something that they had not been allowed to do previously because such loans were viewed as excessively risky by advocates of the real-bills doctrine, which included the founders of the Fed. To further placate rural interests' demands for credit backed by agricultural land, within three years of the founding of the Fed, a parallel system of twelve land banks was founded in 1916. These land banks were capitalized by the government, made loans with maturities of up to 40 years, and operated through a network of newly created national farm loan associations. By 1930, federal land banks owned about 12 percent of farm-mortgage indebtedness in the United States.[67]

Third, despite the founders' intentions that the Fed remain independent of the government, its creation ultimately provided the government with a mechanism that it could use to expand the money supply for its own fiscal ends—that is, to keep its funding costs low. The event that catalyzed this change should not be a surprise to readers of this book: the need to fund an expensive war brought significant rule changes that reduced the distance between the Fed and the treasury. Under the pressures of the war's financial challenges, in 1917 the Fed reduced reserve requirements for member banks, allowing credit to expand.[68] Collateral rules for Federal Reserve note issues were relaxed in 1917: the total amount of collateral was reduced, and more importantly, the Fed changed the rules in order to allow its member banks to use government bonds as collateral for loans they received from the Fed.[69] At the end of World War I, in the interest of boosting demand for outstanding treasury debts, the Fed also reduced its discount rate for loans collateralized by treasury securities. This set a precedent that was contrary to the intent of the Fed founders: discount-rate lending was supposed to include a premium to

[66] E. White (1983, 90–99; 1984b; 1985); Calomiris (2010b).
[67] Fishback and Wallis (2012), 30.
[68] Meltzer (2003), 79 n. 31.
[69] Meltzer (2003), 89.

discourage overuse of the discount window by member banks, but in the desire to accommodate the short-run needs of government finance, this policy principle was abandoned.[70]

The World War I precedent of making the Fed subservient to the interests of marketing treasury debt not only produced a short-term inflationary binge from 1917 to 1920;[71] it also set the stage for subsequent changes that eventually made the Federal Reserve a fiscal instrument of the U.S. treasury. Those changes included a 1932 reform—a temporary measure later made permanent—that permitted the use of treasury securities as collateral for Federal Reserve note issues.[72] In short, the Fed reflected the political compromises necessary to bring it into being and to sustain its existence. Those required the perpetuation of unit banking, the relaxation of limits on real-estate lending, and the eventual use of the Fed as a financing tool of the U.S. treasury.

State governments responded to the problem of bank instability with actions of their own. State legislatures basically had two options: stabilize existing unit banks by creating mandatory deposit insurance, or allow banks to consolidate by permitting them to open branches. These strategies are mutually exclusive. In a mixed system of unit banks and branch banks, the unit banks will find it difficult to survive unless there is deposit insurance, because depositors will move their funds to the inherently more stable banks with branch networks, which can spread risk across regions and transfer funds from one branch to another to head off runs.[73] A deposit-insurance system undermines these advantages of branch banks because it subsidizes the unit banks by providing them with access to deposits at low cost in spite of their higher underlying risks. As a result, in a mixed system that includes both unit banks and branch banks, the unit banks tend to favor state-run deposit insurance, because it allows them to compete with the branching banks, while banks with branch networks tend to oppose such insurance, because it undermines their competitive advantage over unit banks.

Between 1908 and 1917, eight states created mandatory deposit-insurance systems, and these demonstrate why the government-run deposit-

[70] Meltzer (2003), 73, 86.
[71] Meltzer (2003), 90–107.
[72] Meltzer (2003), 358, 417–18.
[73] Economides, Hubbard, and Palia (1996).

insurance option should have disappeared in favor of the branch-banking option. World War I was good for American agriculture, as worldwide food shortages pushed up prices. Those shortages, however, were short-lived. As world output grew, agricultural prices collapsed, and unit banks in rural areas of the United States began to fail. The wave of bank failures was the most severe in the agricultural states with state-run deposit-insurance systems. In fact, the evidence suggests that deposit insurance in those states destabilized the banking system by protecting bankers from the discipline of the deposit market: once depositors were insured, they were less concerned about the riskiness of the banks in which they placed their funds. That lack of concern created a tolerance for incompetence and risk taking, which resulted in imprudent lending during the World War I boom and unparalleled bank losses when agricultural prices fell after the war.[74]

The wave of bank failures during the 1920s was the largest since the 1830s. During the period 1873–1913, losses to depositors from banking crises in any particular year never exceeded 0.1 percent of GNP. In the years 1921–29, however, 5,712 banks failed, causing losses to depositors equal to 0.6 percent of average annual GNP.[75] All eight of the state deposit-insurance systems failed. Moreover, the losses were greatest in the three agricultural states with the longest-established deposit-insurance systems.[76]

As a result of these failures, popular support both for unit banking and deposit insurance began to crumble. By 1930, eight states, primarily in the West and South, permitted unrestricted, statewide branching. An additional 13 states permitted branching but tightly restricted the geographic extent of branch networks in order to protect unit bankers in rural areas from competition. From 1921 to 1930 the number of banks operating branches rose from 530 (with 1,281 branches) to 751 (with 3,522 branches). Banks also consolidated: the number of banks acquired in merger transactions ranged between 250 and 700 in each year.[77] As a result, as figure 6.3 shows, the total number of banks fell, but the number of branches increased.

---

[74] Calomiris (1990, 1992).

[75] Calomiris (2010b), 541.

[76] The ratio of "asset shortfalls" of failed banks (the difference between the deposit liabilities of the bank and the value of its assets) to the equity capital of surviving banks ranged between 0 and 0.57 for all but three agricultural states. In the three states with long-established, mandatory deposit insurance, however, the ratios were 0.94 (Nebraska), 2.26 (North Dakota), and 3.07 (South Dakota). Calomiris (1990), 292.

[77] Calomiris (2000), 46–58.

Number of banks, branches, or offices

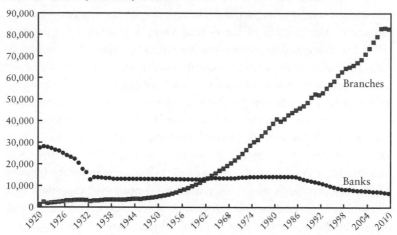

FIGURE 6.3 Number of U.S. banks and branches, 1920–2010.

Source: Computed from Federal Reserve (1943), 16, 297; Federal Deposit Insurance Corporation (n.d.).

The Great Depression, the Glass-Steagall Act, and Deposit Insurance

The wave of bank failures in the 1920s became a torrent during the Great Depression and threatened to completely undermine political support for unit banking. Between 1930 and 1933 more than 9,100 banks (38 percent of all banks) suspended operations (see figure 6.3). Depositors came to view unit banks (correctly) as more prone to failure. Moreover, the collapse of so many unit banks left thousands of agricultural communities, and even some suburbs of major cities, without any banks at all.[78] The widespread contraction of credit that was associated with so much bank distress magnified the severity of the Depression.[79] By 1933, to many observers, it seemed as if the days of unit banking were numbered. In response to the severe banking distress of the early 1930s, states further relaxed their branching laws. By the end of 1935, 13 of the 27 states that had prohibited branching entirely in 1930 had repealed the prohibition, and seven states passed legislation allowing statewide branching.[80]

---

[78] Abrams and Settle (1993), 691.

[79] Calomiris (1993b, 2003b).

[80] Abrams and Settle (1993), 687–88.

The regulatory reforms of the 1930s—particularly the creation of federal deposit insurance as part of the Glass-Steagall Act of 1933—reversed this trend. The creation of the Federal Deposit Insurance Corporation (FDIC) was designed to prop up unit banks and preserve their monopoly rents by insulating them from competition. Although the civics textbooks used by just about every American high school portray deposit insurance as a necessary step to save the banking system, all of the evidence indicates otherwise: it was the product of lobbying by unit bankers who wanted to stifle the growth of branch banking. First, the banking crisis of 1932–33 ended months before the establishment of FDIC insurance. Second, President Franklin Roosevelt, as well as his secretary of the treasury and his comptroller of the currency, *opposed* deposit insurance: they were all familiar with the disastrous experience of state-level experiments with deposit insurance during the early 1920s. Third, Senator Carter Glass and the Senate Banking Committee, who drafted the initial legislation, were also opposed to deposit insurance. They allowed it to be added to the Glass-Steagall Act only at the eleventh hour, in order to get the support of the populist chairman of the House Banking Committee, Representative Henry Steagall. In fact, that eleventh-hour deal limited coverage to small deposits; it was broadened to include larger deposits several years later, well after the banking crisis had ended. Fourth, even with this initial limitation of coverage, the American Bankers Association lobbied Roosevelt to veto the bill after it was log-rolled through Congress.[81]

Competition was further limited by other provisions of the 1933 act (under section 5144), which were designed to make it more difficult for "chains" or "groups" of unit banks to become organized within a holding company. Chains and groups were not fully integrated corporate entities and thus were imperfect substitutes for nationwide branch banking. They had evolved as a second-best means of bank consolidation. The 1933 act reined them in by requiring Federal Reserve Board approval for any voting of share interests in a bank by a bank holding company and by attaching costly burdens to that approval.

The 1933 act further discouraged bank consolidation by limiting bank involvement in securities underwriting. This was a new area of business

---

[81] Calomiris and White (1994); Economides, Hubbard, and Palia (1996); Calomiris (2010b).

for large U.S. banks in the 1920s. Shutting it down in 1933 removed a source of profitability for large banks located in money centers. The prohibition against paying interest on demand deposits—also known as Regulation Q—further hurt money-center banks by making it harder for them to attract deposits from country banks, which had been the norm during seasons of low demand for agricultural loans. Those interbank deposits sometimes served as the basis for lending to securities dealers in money centers. The intent of Regulation Q and limits on bank involvement in securities underwriting was to break the links between the commercial banking system and the securities markets, which Carter Glass believed had contributed to the Great Depression. The evidence, however, does not support that belief. As numerous scholars have shown, there was no evidence linking securities underwriting or lending by money-center banks to securities dealers with the Great Depression. Indeed, available evidence suggests that both banks and their clients benefited from linking securities underwriting and lending.[82]

The inclusion of deposit insurance in the 1933 act ended the long history of failed attempts by unit bankers and their allies to push through deposit-insurance legislation in Congress. Unit-bank supporters had tried on 150 separate occasions between the 1880s and the 1930s to create a federal deposit-insurance system. They succeeded this time not because the facts were on their side but because they had an able advocate in the person of Steagall, an Alabama populist who, as chairman of the House Banking Committee, held enough blocking power to force the addition of his legislative priority to the agenda of reforms.

Once the federal government guaranteed deposits by creating the FDIC, state legislatures faced reduced pressure from voters to allow branch bank-

---

[82] For a discussion of the evidence, see E. White (1986), Benston (1989), Kroszner and Rajan (1994), Ramirez (1995, 1999, 2002), and Neal and White (2012). E. White (1986) and Ramirez (2002) show that involvement in securities underwriting was a source of both profit and stability for banks prior to its prohibition. Kroszner and Rajan (1994) show that commercial bank affiliates' underwritings of debt performed at least as well as those of other underwriters. Benston (1989) argues that the prohibition on underwriting was done without any evidentiary basis. The 1933 prohibition on securities involvement applied to national banks and state banks that were members of the Fed. The prohibition was applied in 1935 to any deposit-taking entity. Ramirez (1995, 1999) shows that bank clients benefitted from permitting banks to be involved in securities markets.

ing. Only four states relaxed their branching laws between 1939 and 1979.[83] In fact, as late as the early 1970s, only 12 states allowed unrestricted intrastate branching, and no states allowed interstate branching.[84] The only incentives that depositors might have had to shift their funds out of unit banks and into branch banks were differences in deposit interest rates across the two bank types. That incentive had, however, also been undermined by another element of the Glass-Steagall Act: deposit interest rates were now regulated. In fact, interest payments on demand deposits (checking accounts) were legally prohibited.[85]

It is also interesting to note what the 1933 act did *not* do. Most of the banks that failed during the 1920s and 1930s were located in agricultural areas, and the evidence indicates that the primary contributor to bank distress during the 1920s and 1930s was declines in agricultural income and land values both in rural areas and in cities.[86] The most famous New York City bank failure during the 1930s was that of the Bank of United States (not to be confused with the Bank of the United States). That bank was speculating on New York City real estate and failed as the result of declines in real estate prices. Nevertheless, "Senator Glass was in favor of real estate lending by National Banks because it encouraged state banks as well to join the system!"[87] It was Carter Glass—the architect of the Federal Reserve Act of 1913—who had overseen the compromise permitting real estate lending by Federal Reserve member banks, instituted as a means of attracting support for the founding of the Fed. Once again, in the interest of maintaining Fed membership, the banking reforms of the 1930s turned a blind eye to the most important sources of bank instability. That is not surprising when one considers that agrarian interests would have strongly opposed any attempt to limit lending collateralized by real estate.

Not only did the reforms of the 1930s fail to limit real estate lending by banks, but new government initiatives designed to appeal to agrarian

---

[83] Calomiris (2000), 67.

[84] Some states did allow out-of-state bank holding companies to purchase banks within their borders, but the banks that did so could not share back-office operations with an out-of-state bank. Thus, in 1975, only 10 percent of the bank assets in the typical state were owned by a multistate bank holding company. Morgan, Rime, and Strahan (2004), 1555.

[85] Economides, Hubbard, and Palia (1996); Calomiris (2010b).

[86] See the review in Calomiris and Mason (2003a).

[87] Neal and White (2012), 109.

interests were established to provide government subsidies for real estate lending, both for housing and for farms. Farm real estate was already in distress in the 1920s, and the situation worsened substantially in the 1930s. Farm distress resulted in part from the rise in farm incomes during World War I, which encouraged the rapid expansion of farmland up to 1920. The 1920s and 1930s saw unprecedented declines in agricultural incomes and land values and rises in farm foreclosures. The Roosevelt government created a new Farm Credit Administration in 1933 to make emergency loans to farmers; it built on (and absorbed) the federal land banks that had been created in 1916. Farm mortgage lending quadrupled, and by the mid-1930s, national government lending accounted for more than half of farm mortgages. Additionally, in 1933 the Roosevelt government also created the Agricultural Adjustment Administration (AAA) and Commodity Credit Corporation (CCC). The AAA administered new programs that sought to limit farm production and reward farmers who agreed to remove land from production. The CCC lent money on a heavily subsidized basis to farmers, accepting payment in crops rather than dollars if crop prices were not sufficient for farm borrowers to repay in dollars.[88]

The housing market was also in distress. Housing prices nationwide fell by an average of 33 percent from 1930 to 1934. Mortgages at that time were mainly three- or five-year interest-only loans that "ballooned" at maturity, with typical loan-to-value ratios of about 50 percent; thus the declining incomes of homeowners and the fall in house prices put many people at risk of losing their homes. Between 1932 and 1933, 28 states passed foreclosure moratoriums to give borrowers more time to repay. In 1932, the Hoover administration and the Republican Congress set up a Federal Home Loan Board of 12 regional banks to make subsidized loans to lenders in support of viable mortgages. President Roosevelt added to this lending capacity by creating the Home Owners' Loan Corporation (HOLC) in 1933 to help distressed mortgage borrowers. The HOLC purchased over one million mortgage loans from lenders and restructured them using below-market interest rates and a long-term (15-year) amortization schedule. In addition, the Federal Housing Administration (FHA)

[88] For reviews of these programs and the history of agricultural finances and related banking distress during the 1920s and 1930s, see Nourse, Davis, and Black (1937); Halcrow (1953); Alston (1983, 1984); Alston, Grove, and Wheelock (1994); Calomiris (1992b); Libecap (1998); and Fishback and Wallis (2012).

was created in 1934 to provide mortgage guarantees. The Federal Savings and Loan Insurance Corporation was also created in 1934 to guarantee the deposits of savings and loan associations, which became the dominant lenders in the mortgage market. The Federal National Mortgage Association (Fannie Mae) was established in 1938 to purchase mortgages and thereby create a secondary market in mortgage credit.[89]

All of these steps—deposit insurance, Regulation Q, subsidized credit to farmers and homeowners—did in fact, produce a stable banking system, and that stability endured for decades. This strategy for stabilization could only work, however, if the government kept inflation in check by reining in deficits. Once the government began to run progressively larger deficits in the 1960s in order to simultaneously finance the war in Vietnam and President Lyndon Johnson's Great Society programs, inflation reared its ugly head, and Regulation Q drove depositors to move their funds out of the banking system, where they were effectively earning negative rates of return. Banks tried to hold onto their deposit base, but their efforts were pathetic compared to the problem they faced. Money-market mutual funds offered attractive rates of return. Unable to match those rates because of Regulation Q, banks offered nonmonetary "gifts" to clients opening new accounts—a steak knife for a small initial balance and toasters and clock radios for the big accounts.

The fact that banks in the wealthiest, most powerful country in the world competed on the basis of bizarre, almost laughable promotions and giveaways points to the amazing success of the populist–unit banker coalition. That coalition had succeeded in shutting down the Bank of the United States not once, but twice: in 1811 and again in 1832. It had survived the challenge posed by the Civil War. Indeed, it even managed to make sure that the Federal Government did not rock the boat when it passed the National Banking Act in order to finance the Civil War effort. National banks, like their state-chartered competitors, were unit banks.

The populist–unit banker coalition even turned the financial panics of the second half of the nineteenth century, the agricultural crises of the 1920s, and the Great Depression to its advantage. These shocks did not result in the disappearance of unit banking and the emergence of a more

---

[89] For a review of these and other New Deal relief programs, see Fishback and Wallis (2012) and Fishback, Rose and Snowden (2013).

efficient and stable system of large, regionally diversified banks with branch networks. Instead they resulted in the Federal Reserve, deposit insurance, and laws that capped bank interest rates. So successful was the populist–unit banker coalition that it even convinced the public that these institutions had been created to protect them from avaricious big city bankers, such as Mr. Potter in Frank Capra's film *It's a Wonderful Life*.

End of an Era: The Demise of the
Unit Banker–Agrarian Populist Coalition

Restrictions on both intrastate and interstate branch banking finally began to be undermined in the 1970s, but it took until the 1990s for the banking market to be completely opened up to competition. Five forces worked to undo the sway of the unit banker–agrarian populist coalition.

The first force was demographic: during the twentieth century, the United States was transformed from a predominantly rural to a predominantly urban country, which meant that voting power shifted away from rural areas toward America's cities. As of 1900, 45.8 million Americans lived in rural areas, compared to 30.2 million in cities and towns with more than 2,500 inhabitants. By 1920 rural and urban populations were roughly equal, and by 1940 the number living in cities or towns had grown to 74.4 million, compared to 57.2 million rural inhabitants. After World War II, the urban population share took off: by 1970, 133.4 million Americans lived in locations with more than 2,500 inhabitants, compared to 69.8 million living in rural areas.[90]

The second force was technological progress that eroded the ability of banks to extract rents from borrowers and depositors. Beginning in the 1970s, the computer revolution drove down the cost of information storage and retrieval, allowing prospective lenders anywhere in the country to assess a borrower's creditworthiness reasonably well without having to rely as much on "soft" information (knowledge of the borrower's "character," business relationships, and personal history) that could only be obtained locally. Technology also spurred much greater competition in deposit banking, especially with the introduction of automated teller machines

---

[90] These figures are derived from United States Bureau of the Census (1975), part. 1, 11, series A, 57–72.

linked via computer networks. After the networked ATM was patented in 1974, it took only two years before unit bankers started filing cases in both federal and state courts seeking to block their proliferation.[91] One of those cases, *Independent Bankers Association of New York State v. Marine Midland Bank,* reached the Supreme Court in 1985. The court ruled that an ATM was not a bank branch, thereby eviscerating state laws that set limits on banks with branch networks.

The third force was accelerating price inflation in the 1960s and 1970s, which spurred disintermediation from the regulated banking system and created the first of the post-1960 "shadow banking systems" of relatively unregulated finance companies and money-market mutual funds. Regulation Q had long limited the interest rate that could be paid on bank deposits. As inflation and nominal market rates of interest rose, the real interest rate payable on regulated deposits became increasingly negative, making it hard for banks to attract deposits. Instead, institutional depositors began to put their money into commercial paper (short-term IOUs issued by corporations and, increasingly, by finance companies) whose interest rates were set by markets rather than by legislation. Households soon followed suit, as money-market mutual funds began to allow customers to write checks against their portfolios of treasury bills and commercial paper. As figure 6.4 shows, the banking system's share of the financial system declined dramatically as the relative shares of other intermediaries—especially the new finance companies and money-market mutual funds—grew. Finance-company loans and commercial paper issues crowded out bank loans as sources of funding to industry, while commercial paper holdings by firms and money-market accounts crowded out bank deposits.

As technological change and inflation spurred the growth of alternatives to regulated banking and produced declines in the domestic core deposit and loan-market shares of regulated banks (shown in figure 6.4), a fourth worrying factor reared its head.[92] U.S. banks—which were relatively small and constrained in their geographic reach and product lines, compared

[91] The first such case, *Independent Bankers Association of America v. Smith,* 534 F.2d 921 (D.C. Cir. 1976), claimed that a "customer bank communications terminal" violated the McFadden Act of 1927. When efforts to block the technology failed, unit bankers filed suits claiming that ATMs not physically located in a bank building (e.g., an ATM in a supermarket) violated the McFadden Act.

[92] In figure 6.4, core deposits are defined to include all checking deposits and other small-time and savings deposits but not large deposits, which are generally viewed as not part of the "core" customer relationships of deposit taking and lending.

Percentage share

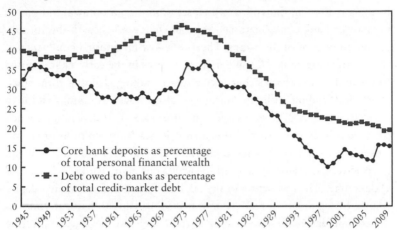

FIGURE 6.4 Declining importance of core deposits and bank credit, 1945–2010.
Source: Federal Reserve Board (n.d.).

with the banks of other developed countries—were losing global market share. Large foreign banks were even making inroads into U.S. markets by building relationships with large U.S. corporations. The Fed and many U.S. politicians became advocates of the deregulation of interest-rate ceilings, the removal of branching restrictions, and the elimination of limits on bank powers (especially the limits on corporate securities underwriting by banks) as a means of allowing U.S. banks to compete with their foreign counterparts. For example, the Fed chairman Alan Greenspan called for the expansion of bank powers: "The ability of banks to continue to hold their positions by operating on the margins of customer services is limited. Existing constraints, in conjunction with the continued undermining of the bank franchise by the new technology, are likely to limit the future profitability of banking. . . . If the aforementioned trends continue, banking will contract either relatively or absolutely." He later went on to argue: "In an environment of global competition, rapid financial innovation, and technological change, bankers understandably feel that the old portfolio and affiliate rules and the constraints on permissible activities of affiliates are no longer meaningful and likely to result in shrinking the banking system."[93]

[93] Greenspan (1988, 3–4; 1990, 5).

The fifth force driving the reform of banking regulation was a wave of banking distress in the 1980s, which set in motion a political movement in favor of bank consolidation—one that shared much with the consolidation movement of the 1920s. The 1980s saw an unusual confluence of shocks affecting banks. A spike in interest rates in the early 1980s caused banks and thrifts (banks that specialized in taking deposits from small savers and lending on home mortgages, also known as savings and loan associations, or S&Ls) with large exposures to real estate lending (which paid fixed interest rates) to suffer major losses.[94] Agricultural price collapses in the early 1980s caused many small rural banks to fail.[95] Oil and gas price collapses in the early 1980s wiped out many banks in Texas and Oklahoma.[96] The revocation of the tax laws governing accelerated depreciation for commercial real estate transactions caused major declines in the commercial real estate market in the Northeast, negatively affecting the banks that lent in that market. Evidence that banks had contributed to the size of their losses through aggressive risk taking and abuse of the protection afforded by deposit insurance and access to the Fed's discount window, sometimes after they were already deeply insolvent, further galvanized opposition to preserving the status quo.[97] In 1984, a government bailout of a bank deemed "too big to fail"—of Continental Illinois, a Chicago-based bank—was undertaken. As bank losses mounted, along with bank bailout costs, public sentiment began to shift.

The banking distress of the 1980s encouraged even many unit bankers, as well as bank borrowers and government officials, to favor the relaxation of branching restrictions. A unit banker facing the failure of his bank saw acquisition by a branching bank as a way to exit with some stock wealth and perhaps even a job in the new bank—an alternative preferable to losing everything. For borrowers at failing unit banks, the branching banks that were willing to buy weak banks represented a crucial source of

---

[94] See, for example, Barth, Bartholomew, and Labich (1989) and Wheelock (2006).

[95] See Calomiris, Hubbard, and Stock (1986).

[96] See Horvitz (1991).

[97] See Barth, Bartholomew, and Labich (1989); Brewer and Mondschean (1991, 1992); Brewer (1995); A. Gilbert (1991, 1994, 1995); Barth and Brumbaugh (1992); and Schwartz (1992). As Gilbert shows, lending behavior varied across Federal Reserve districts, and it is not obvious that Fed lending to insolvent banks contributed greatly to the size of losses.

funding. For the FDIC and federal government officials, the acquisition of small failing banks by larger banks reduced the costs of paying off the depositors of failed banks. For state governments, the new bank entrants were a welcome means of restoring local economic growth.

This period of banking distress is commonly known as the savings and loan crisis, but it is important to keep in mind that banking distress during the 1980s was not restricted to thrift institutions: it also involved a large number of commercial banks that were heavily exposed to a combination of shocks, including interest-rate volatility, declines in the values of residential and commercial real estate, energy price shocks that sank lenders that had funded oil and gas exploration, and agricultural price declines that were associated with severe farm distress. Nevertheless, the demise of S&Ls was the most dramatic and pervasive source of banking distress during the 1980s.

The business model of an S&L, to borrow short-term from depositors and then lend long-term on fixed-rate mortgages, was originally predicated on two conditions: a stable macroeconomic environment and discipline by depositors, enforced through the threat of deposit withdrawal in response to imprudent risk taking by bankers. The natural enemy of an S&L or bank with short-term deposits and fixed-rate mortgages is rising inflation, which causes interest rates in the economy to rise and hence the value of fixed-rate mortgages to fall. The losses associated with a moderate rise in interest rates, however, can generally be managed by prudent S&Ls, especially in the presence of depositor discipline. Depositor discipline encourages an S&L that experiences losses due to rising inflation to reduce its asset risks and increase its equity capital or else face severe withdrawal pressure. Hence the traditional business model of the S&L relied on low inflation volatility and low levels of protection of depositors: managers had to be able to match the term structures of their assets and liabilities, and depositors had to have incentives to move their funds if managers were gambling.[98]

By the 1980s, both of these conditions had changed markedly. The rapid growth in government spending, an expansionary monetary policy, and

---

[98] For discussions of the effectiveness of deposit-market discipline in limiting banking-system fragility, historically and today, see Calomiris and Wilson (2004) and Calomiris and Powell (2001).

the demise of the Bretton Woods foreign-exchange system during the 1970s produced a dramatic change in the economic environment: inflation, exchange rates, real estate and farm prices, oil prices, and GDP growth all became much more volatile. Indeed, inflation ran off the rails. In 1980, deposit insurance—per account, per bank—was raised to $100,000 in order to help banks hold onto their deposit bases in an era of high inflation and negative interest rates. The substantial expansion in government protection of banks and S&Ls insulated those financial institutions from the consequences of their own risk taking and thereby increased the incentives of weak institutions to magnify their risks. Things came to a head in 1979–82, after the Fed put in place a contractionary monetary policy designed to curb inflation. Interest rates skyrocketed. This caused problems for S&Ls because they had to pay dramatically higher interest rates on deposits, while the home mortgages that they held still earned only low fixed rates of return. This balance-sheet mismatch, along with the increases in loan defaults caused by the tightening of monetary policy, brought many S&Ls to the point of insolvency.[99]

If the losses related to interest-rate changes had been recognized and dealt with through S&L shrinkage, closures, or consolidations in the early 1980s, the S&L crisis would have been significant but not catastrophic. Instead, as losses began to mount, many weakened or insolvent S&Ls and commercial banks with S&L–style loan portfolios decided to throw "Hail Mary" passes by investing in junk bonds and speculative commercial real estate ventures—with the forbearance of the government supervisory agencies that were supposed to be monitoring them. Hail Mary passes rarely work in football, and, not surprisingly, they did not work for the S&Ls either. As losses mounted, the government supervisory agencies should have shut down insolvent banks or forced them to raise new capital to replace the capital they had lost. Instead, not only did they look the other way, but in 1982 they relaxed the limits on the types of assets that S&Ls could hold.[100] The change allowed the S&Ls to postpone the day of

---

[99] Note the similarity between the insolvency problems caused by high interest rates in the United States after 1979 and the secondary banking crisis in Britain in the 1970s, which we discuss in chapter 5.

[100] See Barth, Bartholomew, and Labich (1989); Barth (1991); Brewer and Mondschean (1991); Brewer (1995); Gilbert (1991, 1994, 1995); Schwartz (1992); L. J. White (1991).

reckoning, but in doing so it made the outcome much worse: between 1986 and 1995, 1,043 out of the country's 3,234 S&Ls had to be "resolved" by the federal government, which is to say that their losses had to be covered by taxpayers. The question of how to account for the true economic cost borne by taxpayers is a bit controversial: according to one FDIC study, the best estimate is $124 billion, but estimates by the U.S. General Accounting Office are higher, as the result of higher estimated direct costs and the inclusion of a variety of indirect costs. By any measure, however, the S&L crisis was a major shock to the financial system, the economy, and taxpayers.[101]

Bank Consolidation

Like the panic of 1907 and the Great Depression, the financial crisis of the 1980s exposed the inherent instability of financial institutions that could not diversify risk by pooling the risks of different regions or respond to difficulties by shifting resources across branches of an interconnected network.[102] Regulators and politicians saw an advantage in permitting large banks to acquire failing banks in exchange for limiting the cost of those failed banks to the FDIC. From 1979 to 1990, 15 states relaxed their branching restrictions.[103] Many states also permitted their banks to be acquired by large, out-of-state banks, many of which hailed from states like North Carolina, Ohio, and California, which had long permitted in-state branching.

A major blow to the state laws that prohibited interstate branching came in 1982, when Congress, in response to the savings and loan crisis, amended the Bank Holding Company Act of 1956 to allow failed banks to be acquired by any bank holding company, regardless of state laws.

---

[101] The $124 billion estimate is from Curry and Shibut (2000). See also U.S. General Accounting Office (1996). Economists generally view it as inappropriate to measure the costs of taxpayer protection using ex post cash lost, because this abstracts from the risks borne by taxpayers during the bailout, implying that true ex ante costs may be substantially higher. Furthermore, as we point out in chapter 1, crises also create economic costs beyond the costs of the bailouts. A study by the Congressional Budget Office ([1992], 35) concluded that cumulative losses in GDP resulting from the S&L crisis could exceed half a trillion 1990 dollars.

[102] Calomiris (2000), chapter 1. See also Kroszner and Strahan (1999).

[103] Calomiris (2000), 67.

This change induced many states to enter into regional or national reciprocal arrangements whereby their banks could be merged with banks
from another state (not just purchased by a holding company). Between
1984 and 1988, 38 states joined one of these reciprocal arrangements.[104]
Banks operating national branching networks accounted for only 10 percent of the U.S. banking system in the early 1980s. By the mid-1990s, they
accounted for more than 70 percent.[105] The final blow to the unit banks
came in 1994, when Congress codified the process that had been taking
place at the state level by passing the Riegle-Neal Interstate Banking and
Branching Efficiency Act. Banks could now branch both within states
and across state lines. This change was the death knell of the unit banker–
agrarian populist coalition that had shaped American banking institutions since the 1830s.

The demonstrable gains to the economy from the ability of banks to
branch within and across state lines were substantial. A large and continually growing literature demonstrates that the relaxation of branching
laws produced new access to credit for entrepreneurs, boosted investment
and income, and improved competition in banking. In so doing, it increased competition in the nonfinancial sectors of the economy, which
reduced unemployment and income inequality.[106] Finally, one might have
thought, the United States was making the obvious structural changes
needed to improve access to credit and ensure banking-system efficiency
and stability. As we show in chapters 7 and 8, however, such a judgment
would prove premature and incomplete.

[104] Kroszner and Strahan (1999).
[105] Calomiris (2010b).
[106] Jayaratne and Strahan (1996); Kroszner and Strahan (1999); Black and Strahan
(2001, 2002); Correa (2008); Beck, Levine, and Levkov (2010).

7

|||||||||||||||||||||||

The New U.S. Bank Bargain
Megabanks, Urban Activists,
and the Erosion of Mortgage Standards

The genius of you Americans is that you never make clear-cut stupid moves, only complicated stupid moves which make us wonder at the possibility that there may be something to them we are missing.

Gamal Abdel Nasser (1957)

The Riegle-Neal Interstate Banking and Branching Efficiency Act of 1994, by knocking down the last barriers to interstate banking, marked the demise of the unlikely coalition between unit banks and agrarian populists. The United States was now finally in a position to have a banking structure that was not fragile by design: instead of tens of thousands of unit banks that could not spread risk across regions, it could have a more stable system consisting mainly of larger banks, each with hundreds or thousands of branches. Within a few years of the passage of Riegle-Neal, those possibilities were realized in a rapid-fire series of mergers and acquisitions. JPMorgan Chase, for example, was created out of the merger of no less than 37 banks, creating a megabank with more than 220,000 employees and $2 trillion in assets as of 2011. The Bank of America, which was originally a California bank, merged with or acquired more than 50 other banks. As of 1998, when it merged with NationsBank, it really *was* the Bank of America.[1] Smaller regional banks continued to exist, as did some local banks that focused on niche markets. The landscape of American banking, however, had been fundamentally transformed.

How could it have been, then, that this more structurally sound system collapsed in the subprime crisis of 2007–09, only 13 years after the Riegle-Neal Act was passed? If the consolidation of the U.S. banking system put it on a more secure footing, why did some of the largest financial institu-

---

[1] Barth, Caprio, and Levine (2012), 63–64.

tions in the United States, including Citibank, AIG, Merrill Lynch, Bear Stearns, Lehman Brothers, Wachovia, Washington Mutual, and Countrywide Financial fail or have to be rescued by the government? Why did Fannie Mae and Freddie Mac, the two largest holders of American mortgage debt, collapse under a sea of bad loans, so that as of 2008 they effectively became government-owned banks? Why did the treasury have to spend $431 billion in 2008 to recapitalize the banking system through the Temporary Asset Repurchase Program (TARP), and why did Congress have to follow this up with a $787 billion emergency spending bill the following year to try to stimulate the economy and promote job creation?

The subprime crisis was notable not just for the spectacular magnitude of the economic collapse it caused but also for the unprecedented steps that the Federal Reserve and the U.S. government took to head off the economy's downward spiral.[2] The Fed cut its target federal funds rate and maintained it at a range of 0–0.25 percent for several years. It also instituted a series of liquidity-support programs designed to redirect short-term funds to primary dealers (firms that buy government securities directly from the treasury with the intention of reselling them to others) as well as to support the asset-backed commercial paper market, the mortgage-backed securities market, and money-market mutual funds. The Fed was so aggressive in these moves that its balance sheet tripled in size.[3] The Fed and the government also extended targeted guarantees to various categories of debts, including previously uninsured bank deposits, money-market mutual-fund shares, and mortgage-backed securities. When these steps proved inadequate to rekindle growth and the Fed could lower interest rates no more (because of the "zero bound" to nominal interest rates) it embarked on a policy of quantitative easing—essentially printing money in order to buy government debt. In addition, in the hope of changing the expectations of investors, the Fed undertook a new approach to monetary policy, known as policy guidance, announcing that it would maintain low interest rates and quantitative-easing policies for long periods into the future. It also committed to a program of purchasing hun-

---

[2] For two insiders' views, see Swagel (2009) and Bair (2012). For an outsider's account, based on interviews with insiders, see Sorkin (2009).

[3] For a review of the various policy interventions in response to the crisis, see Calomiris, Eisenbeis, and Litan (2012).

dreds of billions of dollars of mortgage-backed securities to support the housing market. Indeed, the combination of Fed mortgage-backed securities purchases, government ownership of Fannie Mae and Freddie Mac, and substantial growth in the market share of the Federal Housing Administration (FHA) essentially means that, as of this writing, the Fed and the treasury account for the vast majority of American mortgage funding.

We are far from the first to have asked how a system that should have been made more stable by consolidation became spectacularly less so. Various explanations have been advanced—more than we could possibly recount here. What everyone agrees on, however, is that the systemwide crash of 2007–09 was led by a crisis in housing finance, particularly in the market for "subprime" loans.[4] The bursting of the housing-finance bubble set off a collapse of markets that are usually regarded as nearly risk free. The volume of interbank deposits, asset-backed commercial paper, and "repos" (overnight collateralized loans between banks and other intermediaries) all contracted sharply.[5] As a result of the collapses of these markets for short-term debt, many banks were unable to access the markets that they depend on for funding, causing them to scramble to find the cash needed to fund their asset positions. Some market participants found themselves scrambling to sell massive amounts of noncash assets, which caused the value of those assets to decline at an alarming rate.

Banks also stopped extending new lines of credit to borrowers or reduced the amounts of the lines of credit that they were willing to renew. As bank lending dried up, business enterprises and households curtailed

---

[4] The word *subprime* has no agreed definition. It refers variously to mortgages for which borrowers have Fair, Isaac and Co. (FICO) credit scores of below 660; mortgages that are identified by originators or by holders as "subprime"; mortgages that are identified as "Alt-A" (another ill-defined category of mortgages, which generally captures the attributes of the mortgage contract, not just the borrower, such as a high loan-to-value ratio, or LTV); or mortgages with a default risk that is much greater (typically several times greater) than a traditional "prime" mortgage. We use the term in the last sense unless otherwise indicated.

[5] These normally nearly riskless short-term markets also experienced defaults, which had other ripple effects in the market. Lehman Brothers' default on its commercial paper obligations produced a "breaking of the buck" of a money-market mutual fund called the Reserve Primary Fund. (Breaking the buck is defined as a decline in the value of its shares to below $1.) This set in motion a run on money-market mutual funds and led to a temporary government guarantee of their share values.

spending, causing a self-reinforcing process of economic contraction.[6] Our colleagues Luc Laeven and Fabián Valencia of the International Monetary Fund estimate that from 2007 through 2011, the total cost of this contraction, in forgone growth, was a staggering 31 percent of GDP.[7]

The Heart of the Matter

While there is broad agreement about these basic facts, there is no consensus as to the fundamental causes of the subprime crisis. Fingers are pointed at changes in the internal culture of banks, the development of markets for mortgage-backed securities and other financial derivatives, Federal Reserve interest rates that were set too low, excessive risk taking by the leaders of Fannie Mae and Freddie Mac, Clinton-era redistributive policies, Bush-era free-market ideology, the repeal of the Glass-Steagall Act, vaguely defined steps toward deregulation, and malfeasance and incompetence on the part of individuals, among other factors. Some analysts have crafted narratives in which various combinations of these factors created a perfect storm that no one could have possibly foreseen.

Many of these accounts contain important elements of truth, but in our view they are incomplete. In particular, they often fail to provide a convincing explanation of why market participants allowed themselves to become so exposed to subprime mortgage risks.[8] Banking crises don't just happen. As we point out in chapter 1, banking systems are susceptible to

---

[6] For details on the propagation of the crisis and the role of collapsing market liquidity in increasing the duration and severity of financial crises more generally, see Calomiris (2009), Gorton (2010), Gorton and Metrick (2011), and Calomiris, Eisenbeis, and Litan (2012), as well as numerous references therein.

[7] Laeven and Valencia (2012), 26.

[8] One account, by McCarty, Poole, and Rosenthal (2013), traces the subprime crisis to political influences and points to some of the same contributors that we identify, including the influence of large banks, GSE mandates, and left-of-center political activism to promote affordable housing (pp. 17, 19, 44, 126–33). Their narrative points to a coincidental confluence of ideologies, interests, and constraints within the U.S. political process that prevented the interests of the majority from being realized (pp. 90–116). While we agree with some parts of their analysis, we believe that interests in the making of the subprime crisis converged not by coincidence but rather as the result of a partnership that was designed to transcend partisan and ideological differences in order to realize enormous economic gains for its partners. The merger movement and the preexisting Community Reinvestment Act were crucial catalysts for the formation of that partnership, which helped to align the partners' interests, drive legislative

collapse only when two conditions are met in combination: banks must take on sufficient risk in their loans and other investments, and they must have inadequate capital on their balance sheets to absorb the losses associated with those risky loans and investments. If a bank makes only solid loans to solid borrowers, there is little chance that its loan portfolio will all of a sudden become nonperforming. If a bank makes riskier loans to less solid borrowers but sets aside extra shareholder capital to cover the possibility that those loans will not be repaid, its shareholders will suffer a loss, but the bank will not become insolvent. Any coherent account of the subprime crisis must put this fundamental logic about banking crises at center stage and explain how it was that so many lenders ended up making so many risky loans while maintaining very little capital to protect themselves against insolvency.

Our goal in this chapter and the next is to construct an account of the subprime crisis that explains these two key features of the failure of risk management leading up to the crisis. By analyzing the forces that drove the increase in risky lending and the inadequacy of capital, we create a framework on which we can hang the other facts and insights that have emerged from the literature about the crisis, thereby creating a coherent narrative about what happened and why.

In this chapter we focus primarily on the first prerequisite for a banking crisis, examining the process by which bank loan portfolios became increasingly risky. How did it come to pass that in 1990 a mortgage applicant needed a 20 percent down payment, a good credit rating, and a stable, verifiable employment and income history in order to obtain a low-risk, 30-year fixed-rate mortgage, but by 2003 she could obtain a high-risk, negatively amortizing adjustable-rate mortgage by offering only a 3 percent down payment and simply stating her income and employment history, with no independent verification?

In chapter 8 we focus on the second prerequisite for a banking crisis: the process by which increased risk in bank assets was not matched by increased amounts of shareholder capital. Given the increasing laxity of underwriting standards, why did regulators not insist on additional capital buffers for banks and GSEs? In that chapter we show how the two key

---

reforms of the act and the GSEs, and resolve conflicts that otherwise would have arisen as the result of differences in ideology and interests.

factors of elevated mortgage risk and inadequate capital interacted to cause a catastrophe.

Politics All the Way Down

The acceptance of higher mortgage risk and low levels of bank and GSE capital were both essential aspects of a political bargain. At the core of this bargain was a coalition of two very unlikely partners: rapidly growing megabanks and activist groups that promoted the expansion of risky mortgage lending to poor and inner-city borrowers, such as the Association of Community Organizations for Reform Now (ACORN). Once branching limits were removed, bankers had ambitious plans for mergers. Their plans were, however, subject to a political constraint: they needed to be judged as good citizens of the communities they served in order to gain approval of the mergers from the Federal Reserve Board. Good citizenship came to be defined as being in compliance with the 1977 Community Reinvestment Act (CRA), a statute that originally sought to ensure that banks served their local communities. In theory, the CRA might have made sense in the context of the 1970s, when segmented banking markets gave lenders weak incentives to search for high-quality borrowers in low-income neighborhoods. As a practical matter, the CRA resulted in very few lending commitments by banks in the 1970s and 1980s. But this largely moribund piece of legislation became a very valuable chip in America's Game of Bank Bargains during the 1990s once the merger movement (which broke down segmented markets) got under way. For activist groups seeking to direct credit to their memberships and constituencies, the good-citizenship merger criterion was a powerful lever in negotiations with merging banks.

The bankers and the activists forged a coalition that consolidated the American banking industry into a set of megabanks that were too big to fail. As part of that merger process, they contractually committed more than $850 billion in credit to be channeled from the banks through the activist groups between 1992 and 2007. In addition to these explicit agreements, banks also committed an additional $3.6 trillion in CRA lending to underserved areas or low-income communities over the same years in order to obtain good-citizenship ratings.

Other partners had to be drawn into this coalition in order to make it stable. Banks would not make limitless commitments to their activist partners: CRA loans implied higher levels of risk for the bank than more traditional mortgage loans. Thus, under pressure from activist groups, Congress began to place regulatory mandates on the government sponsored enterprises (GSEs) that purchased and securitized mortgages, which included the Federal National Mortgage Association (FNMA, commonly known as Fannie Mae), and the Federal Home Loan Mortgage Corporation (FHLMC, commonly known as Freddie Mac), and the federal home loan banks (FHLBs). Fannie Mae and Freddie Mac, in particular, were required to repurchase mortgage loans made to targeted groups (i.e., individuals who had low incomes or lived in urban locations that were defined as underserved).

The government mandates on Fannie and Freddie were not vague statements of intent: they set specific targets that were continually raised across the 1990s and early 2000s. In order to meet these targets, Fannie and Freddie had to weaken their underwriting standards.[9] By the mid-1990s, Fannie and Freddie were agreeing to purchase mortgages with down payments of 3 percent (instead of the 20 percent that had been the industry standard). Soon afterward, they were buying mortgages with weak credit scores. By 2004, they were agreeing to purchase vast amounts of risky mortgage loans, including so called Alt-A loans with little or no documentation of income (which are also known as liar or low-doc loans). This change benefited both activist groups and megabanks: more credit could be directed to targeted constituencies at less cost to the banks because the banks were now able to resell some of their CRA-related mortgages to a GSE on favorable terms.

Fannie and Freddie were not sheep to be fleeced; they extracted several valuable concessions from Congress for agreeing to go along with these changes. Among the most important of these was that they were allowed

---

[9] The GSE targets were stated as portfolio proportions. Thus it was logically conceivable that Fannie and Freddie could have met the targets not by increasing their lending to targeted groups but by shrinking their lending to others. That choice would have meant, however, a steep decline in their profitability as well as a decline in their political support within the government, which was necessary to retain their government subsidies (in the form of protection of their debts).

to back their portfolios with paper-thin levels of capital that were much lower than those required of commercial banks. The GSEs, although reluctant at first, became enthusiastic partners of the megabank-activist coalition and served as an important element of the institutional glue that held the coalition together.[10]

Because the CRA was a crucial lever in the negotiations between merging banks and activist groups, much ink has been spilled by academics and activists in debating whether the CRA "caused" the subprime crisis. In our view, many of the participants in this debate miss two fundamental facts. The first is that the CRA would have been inconsequential had there not been a merger movement. Indeed, from 1977 to 1992, total CRA commitments represented only a trivial percentage of total American mortgage lending. From the point of view of merging banks, the rising costs of CRA compliance were simply part of the cost of doing business: there were enormous rents to be earned from growing big, and some of those rents had to be shared with groups that could otherwise block or slow the merging banks' expansion.[11]

Second, it is wrongheaded to pin all of the increased risk in bank loan portfolios on CRA loans. The evidence does indicate that banks perceived CRA loans to be riskier than their other loans, but that is not the whole

---

[10] Several books document the effects of Fannie Mae and Freddie Mac on the mortgage market leading up to the subprime crisis. Our discussion is necessarily compressed. For additional detail, see Rajan (2010), Morgenson and Rosner (2011), Acharya et al. (2011), Pinto (2011), and Wallison (2011).

[11] Brewer and Jagtiani (2013) examine stock-market effects of merger announcements from 1991 to 2004. They find that mergers that resulted in the combined institution's exceeding a certain size threshold resulted in unusually high value creation for the merging banks. Their results indicate that the market understood the special advantages of expansion. Whether those advantages consisted primarily of greater efficiency, greater market power, or greater protection from the government, the results clearly show that mergers that made banks very large brought special gains to stockholders. Other research, reviewed by Johnson and Kwak (2010), uses performance comparisons of banks to differentiate between fundamental economic advantages from greater bank size and political advantages (too-big-to-fail protection) and finds that fundamental advantages run out at small scale, implying that the size advantages of megabanks are political. Other, more recent studies reach different conclusions (Anderson and Joeveer [2012]; Wheelock and Wilson [2012]; Hughes and Mester [2013]). This area of research is complicated by the fact that performance comparisons between megabanks and small banks do not take into account differences in the clients being served, the products being produced, and the production processes used.

story. Mortgages to everyone—not just CRA borrowers—became much riskier. The requirement that Fannie and Freddie meet government-mandated targets for low-income and underserved area loans, so that they could purchase bank CRA loans, forced the GSEs to weaken their underwriting standards—and those weaker standards were applicable to *everyone* seeking a loan. Fannie and Freddie, by virtue of their size and their capacity to repurchase and securitize loans made by banks, set the standards for the entire industry. Thus large swaths of the American middle class—whether they realized it or not—were soon pulled into this megabank-urban activist-GSE coalition by jumping on the easy-credit bandwagon.

We cannot emphasize this fact strongly enough: when Fannie and Freddie agreed to purchase loans that required only a 3 percent down payment, no documentation of income or employment, and a far-from-perfect credit score, they changed the risk calculus of millions of American families, not just the urban poor. With the new underwriting standards, middle-class families could leverage up and buy a much bigger house in a nicer neighborhood. Given the small size of the ante, why not sit down at the table and play a few hands, especially when the potential jackpot—a suburban dream house—was sitting in front of you? The result was the rapid growth of mortgages with high probabilities of default for all classes of Americans. This is why damage from the subprime crisis was sustained both in low-income urban areas, such as Detroit, and in solidly middle-class communities, such as Hemet, California.[12]

One of the cruel ironies of America's post-1990 Game of Bank Bargains was that it was not a very efficient way to raise the living standards of the urban poor—at least not in the medium term. It is important to keep this

---

[12] As a matter of logic, it is conceivable that Fannie and Freddie could have selectively relaxed underwriting standards for targeted groups. As a practical matter, however, doing so would have been very difficult. First, selective relaxation of credit standards—effectively discriminating against most Americans by explicitly granting special arrangements to targeted groups—would have brought a political firestorm of criticism. Second, limiting the relaxed standards to a targeted few would have constituted an admission that higher leverage and a lack of documentation were very risky. That admission itself might have led to higher GSE capital requirements and would have fueled the concerns of GSE critics about their capital inadequacy. Fannie and Freddie appear to have found it more convenient to relax standards for everyone and pretend that doing so had little effect on the amount of risk that they were taking.

in mind at the outset: transferring income by distorting the incentives of bankers, the managers of GSEs, government agencies, and large swaths of the population through implicit housing subsidies contributed to a banking crisis of truly phenomenal proportions. That crisis likely undermined whatever short-run redistributive gains the subsidy programs achieved. A system of explicitly budgeted government tax-and-transfer programs to address inequality directly might have been politically more difficult to implement and therefore would probably have been of more modest scale, but it would have produced more lasting gains in addressing inequality.

There were of course potential losers in America's post-1990 Game of Bank Bargains: taxpayers who did not benefit from the weakening of underwriting standards and who would have to pay for a cleanup in the event of widespread mortgage defaults. Those individuals were effectively subsidizing everyone else, but most of them did not understand the game as it was being played, or even realize that the house had dealt them in. The subsidies they provided were not explicitly recognized in the government's budget: they were sets of implicit guarantees—hidden taxes—that would become visible only once the other players stood up from the gaming table and the house presented the taxpayers with a bill for charges that they had unwittingly agreed to pay.

There were public officials—congressmen, senators, bank supervisors, and regulators—who understood the game but who had good reason not to try to interrupt play or change the rules. Thus, if there is a lesson in this chapter about politics in democracies like that of the United States, this is it: the power of a political coalition is precisely the power to get a public official to go along with something that he knows is not in the long-run public interest because it is in his own short-term interest. From the point of view of the people who were in a position to understand America's post-1990 Game of Bank Bargains, the costs that society would bear were in the future, while the benefits of acquiescing were immediate. We come back to this theme more fully in the next chapter, but it bears mentioning more than once: public officials—particularly regulators, but some elected officials as well—knew how the game was likely to end, but they chose to sit on the sidelines with their hands folded neatly in their laps.[13]

---

[13] For a detailed analysis, see Barth, Caprio, and Levine (2012).

Lest we be misunderstood, our goal in this chapter and the next is not to blame large banks, the GSEs, the urban poor, activist groups, politicians, or regulators for the subprime crisis. People everywhere generally pursue their self-interest, and one of the ways they do that is by exercising their political rights. When they are able to form a political coalition in the pursuit of mutual advantage, they will do so. Politicians, no matter what their political party, similarly pursue their self-interest, which is to get reelected, and in order to do so, they seek out coalitions that will support them. No individual or group of individuals is to "blame" for what happens as a result of that coalition. Indeed, placing blame is an enterprise that is inherently unproductive because it trivializes the problem: it distracts us into thinking that our problems are caused by the moral flaws of other people rather than focusing on how our political institutions encourage socially costly coalitions.

Why Redistribute Income through the Banking System?

The rising power of a coalition between large banks and activist groups should be understood as an outcome of deeper social changes and America's rather unusual political institutions. In the decades after World War II, America became increasingly urban, and beginning in the mid-1970s, it started to become increasingly unequal in its distribution of income and wealth. A large number of low-income people were concentrated in cities, where it was easier for them to become organized, and where protest could quickly metastasize into widespread violence. American elites had seen this threat up close during the riots of the 1960s, and as inequality accelerated over the ensuing decades, policy makers grasped for ways to address inequality by directing credit to urban constituencies.

Similar shifts were occurring in Western Europe and elsewhere, but the United States was unusual in deciding to address inequality and urban poverty through a mix of bank and GSE regulation. In some Western European countries, the response to urbanization and inequality was to increase the scope of already-expansive welfare programs. The European solution was not, however, easy to achieve in the United States. In the first place, the institutions built into the U.S. Constitution militated against it. Indirect election of the president means that predominantly rural states, which would be less inclined to favor redistribution to urbanites, cannot

be ignored in presidential races; furthermore, a bicameral legislature, coupled to the cloture rule in the Senate, means that redistributive fiscal legislation requires supermajorities; and finally, a winner-take-all system for
electing congressmen and senators favors centrist candidates and parties,
unlike many European parliamentary systems, which encourage parties and
candidates on the ideological fringes.[14] In addition, the fact that the United
States had, by historical circumstance, been given the job of maintaining
international order meant that it had to expend a larger share of its tax
revenues on the military than the government of any other developed
Western nation.[15]

Demands for redistribution in the United States could not, therefore,
be met wholly through the fiscal system, as they were elsewhere. As politicians searched for off-budget methods of redistribution, they increasingly
turned to banking regulation as a policy tool. Political agreements in
Washington that used the regulation of the banking system as a means to
redistribute resources were easier to achieve because those agreements
were less visible to constituents who would pay the costs associated with
those choices. CRA requirements and GSE credit mandates were not part
of the government budget and were not widely reported or understood as
tax-and-transfer arrangements. Thus politicians representing predominantly rural states' interests could safely agree to those political deals in
exchange for other favors (a practice known as log rolling) without fear
of dire consequences from their constituents.

The political concessions made to the urban poor in the United States,
therefore—to use Raghuram Rajan's phrase—were to "let them eat credit."[16]
President Bill Clinton (in office from 1993 until 2001) explicitly champi-

[14] In a winner-take-all system such as the election of U.S. congressional representatives,
all seats are occupied by the individual winners of elections in their respective districts.
Most parliamentary systems, however, have some form of proportional representation, in
which seats in the legislature are apportioned to different political parties based on the
percentage of the votes obtained by each party. In such a system, voters do not "waste"
their vote by voting for a fringe party, as is the case in the United States. Indeed, if the
fringe party turns out to be the key to forming a coalition in the legislature, it may obtain
influence in policy well beyond the number of its members. Some parliamentary systems
include a mix of winner-take-all and proportional-representation electoral rules.

[15] McCarty, Poole, and Rosenthal (2006, 2013) analyze in detail the political polar-
ization that encouraged off-budget actions. See, in particular, McCarty, Poole, and
Rosenthal (2013), 105–6.

[16] Rajan (2010).

oned this unique U.S. approach to redistribution via banking regulation, which he advocated as part of his "third way" of creating opportunities for disadvantaged Americans. This approach became embraced by many politicians, of *both* political parties, as the most politically expedient way of addressing inequality and urban poverty.[17]

The Rise of the Megabanks

The catalyst for the formation of the activist–large bank coalition was the bank-merger wave that began in the 1980s with changes in state laws and accelerated in 1994 with the passage of the Riegle-Neal Act. The 1990s and early 2000s saw rapid consolidation of the banking industry and the formation of what have come to be known as megabanks.

The incentives to become a megabank were multiple. One obvious benefit was an increase in organizational efficiency. A bank with branches spread across the country could diversify risk across regions. It could also reap economies of scale by spreading its overhead costs for expensive information technology and high-salaried personnel across a larger asset base. Becoming bigger also enabled a bank to capture economies of scope, widening its income stream by providing a broader range of products and services. An additional advantage of becoming a megabank was the potential for obtaining market power. The ability to earn monopoly rents was not an inevitable consequence of increased size, but it was a possibility.

A final potential advantage to growing large was the implicit subsidy of too-big-to-fail protection. The prospect of receiving such protection increased during the 1980s. Most obviously, 1984 saw an important explicit federal government bailout of a failing U.S. bank. That bank, Continental Illinois, would be regarded today as a middle-sized bank. It was entwined with various other banks through its energy lending and interbank connections, but it operated only a few branches, all in Chicago. Fed Chairman Paul Volcker championed the Continental bailout, fearing that its collapse could spread financial contagion. Such concerns increased after the 1980s, as banks grew larger and spread into a greater number of markets and activities. Thus, by the 1990s, bankers had increasing reason

---

[17] Of course, not all politicians supported Clinton's "third way." Republicans representing rural constituencies often opposed it. See Schlesinger and Schroeder (1999).

to believe that large banks were likely to be saved from failure by a government bailout.

Too-big-to-fail protection, therefore, became an increasingly significant taxpayer subsidy enjoyed by large banks. This subsidy was not just hypothetical. By the 1990s, the ratings that big U.S. banks received from Moody's and other debt-rating organizations explicitly reflected the protection expected from the government: banks received a "stand-alone" rating measuring their financial strength without the subsidy and an overall rating that reflected the additional advantage of expected government protection.[18]

The Road to Hell Is Paved with Good Intentions

There was a crucial catch to the legal changes that permitted bank consolidation: even though large banks could now acquire smaller banks or merge, those acquisitions had to be approved by regulators. The Federal Reserve Board had the key decision-making authority, as the regulator of bank holding companies, but other bank regulators and the Justice Department also could weigh in to oppose mergers. The various regulators, especially the Fed, were susceptible to political pressures because Congress reviewed their actions and budgets. Moreover, Congress had the power to introduce legislation to amend the Federal Reserve Act, and members of Congress often threatened to do so. In short, if a well-organized group wanted to oppose a merger, it had political levers it could pull.

Several criteria could be used to block approval of a bank merger. First, an acquiring bank had to be financially strong. Second, the newly combined bank could not have excessive market power. This was not much of a constraint, because the Fed typically assessed this criterion by looking at a merged bank's deposit-market share rather than its ability to set prices in credit markets. The Fleet Financial–BankBoston merger of 1999 is a telling example: by combining the only two New England banks of significant size, it created a megabank that could set prices for business borrowers. Midsized businesses that were too big to borrow from the remaining small, local banks but too small to borrow in global markets were partic-

---

[18] For a thumbnail sketch of how these ratings are done, see Moody's Investors Service (2008).

Current dollars (billions)

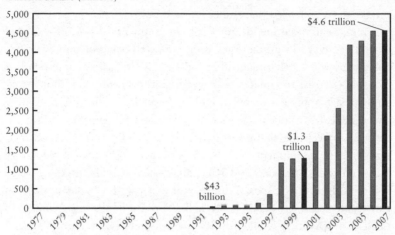

FIGURE 7.1 Cumulative CRA commitments, 1977–2007.
Source: National Community Reinvestment Coalition (2007b), 8.

ularly affected. They were not alone in objecting to the merger on these grounds: the mayor of Boston and the attorney general of Massachusetts did so as well. All to no avail: the Fed approved the merger, and interest spreads for business borrowers rose by a full percentage point.[19]

The third criterion for approval of a merger was good citizenship, and, unlike market power, this was indeed a binding constraint. In 1977, partly in response to claims that banks discriminated against borrowers in low-income, inner-city neighborhoods, the Community Reinvestment Act (CRA) was passed. The early years of the CRA do not appear to have produced much in the way of results: as figure 7.1 shows, from 1977 to 1992, only $43 billion in CRA commitments by banks was announced, and almost all of that lending occurred after 1989. By 1995, as the merger wave was intensifying, however, revisions to the CRA meant that banks faced adverse consequences for failing to comply with CRA requirements.[20] As President Clinton boasted in a July 1999 speech, "[CRA] was pretty well moribund until we took office. Over 95 percent of the commu-

---

[19] For a transcript of the meeting, see Federal Reserve Board (1999a).
[20] See, for example, Evanoff and Segal (1996, 1997).

nity investment . . . made in the 22 years of that law have been made in the six and a half years that I've been in office."[21]

Clinton embraced the idea of CRA commitments as part of his belief in a "third way" to promote the economic well-being of disadvantaged Americans without harming other individuals or business interests.[22] It stood in contrast to either a laissez-faire approach or a traditional tax-and-transfer approach to public policy. Implicit in Clinton's third way was the idea that policy makers really can cook free lunches. While it is certainly conceivable that smart policy choices might make everyone better off, CRA commitments were not a free lunch. Although the regulatory burden imposed on banks by CRA did not show up either in the government's budget or as a special category of expenses for banks in their income statements, CRA compliance had real costs: banks were required to make loans that they would not have made otherwise. As former Federal Home Loan Bank board member Lawrence White put it: "Either [CRA mandates are] redundant, because serving the local community is profitable anyway; or [they] require cross-subsidy, with above-normal profits from other services subsidizing the losses from the unprofitable service to the local community."[23] In short, the third-way policy approach, as embodied in CRA commitments, misrepresented invisible taxes and transfers as nonexistent ones.

Why did banks care about their CRA ratings? Banks could receive a range of CRA grades—outstanding, satisfactory, needs to improve, and substantial noncompliance—depending on the degree to which they were assessed as serving the needs of the communities where they operated. The main penalty for a weak rating was that it could scuttle a bank merger. A bank that was not pursuing an aggressive strategy of mergers and acquisitions did not, therefore, need to pay much attention to its CRA rating.[24] A bank with big ambitions to grow, however, needed a good rating.

This state of affairs meant that a bank seeking to expand through a strategy of mergers and acquisitions faced a strategic choice: it could either create its own CRA lending program or it could enlist activist groups as partners in creating a joint CRA lending program. The advantage of the

---

[21] Clinton (1999a).
[22] Schlesinger and Schroeder (1999).
[23] L. J. White (1992), 282.
[24] National Community Reinvestment Coalition (2007a), 26.

former approach was that the bank retained control of decision making about the allocation of the CRA loans. The advantage of the latter was that the bank could enlist the support of activist groups for its merger and acquisition activities, in exchange for which it effectively gave up control over the CRA portfolio. That is, the partnership aligned the incentives of activist groups with the bank, so that the activist groups would testify on behalf of a merging bank about its commitment to good citizenship.

From the point of view of an activist group, a formal partnership with a bank was unambiguously better than a CRA program run by the bank. A partnership gave the activist group control over the distribution of the bank's CRA portfolio; it also provided fee income and philanthropic funding from the bank. A bank-run program provided neither of these benefits and was viewed by activists as jumping the gun "in order to offset expected community group challenges to future expansion requests."[25] At least to judge from the merger of Fleet Financial and BankBoston, a bank-run CRA program was cause to actively oppose a merger. As the transcript of the Fed hearing for that merger makes clear, a coalition of Massachusetts activist groups testified against the merger because Fleet-BankBoston had committed $14.6 billion to CRA lending but refused to continue Fleet's CRA partnership with ACORN. Fleet-BankBoston, anticipating this opposition, actually paid the travel expenses of out-of-state activist groups to enable them to testify on the bank's behalf.[26]

There were therefore conditions under which it was in a bank's interest to enter into an explicit partnership with an activist group in advance of a Fed hearing, rather than running its own CRA credit program.[27] Some critics of the CRA described those deals as a form of legalized extortion.[28]

---

[25] Fishbein (1992), 300.

[26] Associated Press (1999). For a transcript of the meeting, see Federal Reserve Board (1999a). For the Fed's ruling, which pointed out that the CRA did not require banks to enter into explicit partnerships, see Federal Reserve Board (1999b).

[27] An inspection of the data on the two types of programs suggests that banks shifted away from partnerships with activists and toward bank-run CRA programs after 2000, perhaps because Senator Phil Gramm succeeded in passing legislation requiring such partnerships to be made public. National Community Reinvestment Coalition (2007a), 90–100.

[28] For example, see Husock (2000), where Senator Phil Gramm is quoted as referring to the CRA as a "vast extortion scheme." In *Washington Times* (2009), Representative Ed Royce is quoted referring to ACORN's actions under the CRA as "legalized extortion."

Regardless of the words used to describe them, the deals struck by banks and activist groups were a predictable outcome of the situation. Banks had every incentive to merge: they could capture scale economies in administration, diversify risk, obtain market power, and perhaps grow large enough to obtain too-big-to-fail protection. Activist groups had every incentive to threaten to show up at Fed hearings to complain that a bank involved in a merger was not a good citizen in order to obtain concessions from the merging banks: their organizations would prosper as the result of the CRA agreements that they negotiated, and their constituents would enjoy increased access to credit. Given the existence of the CRA, both sides had incentives to strike a deal to secure a bank merger, because if it were blocked, the bank would forgo the opportunity to increase its profits, and the activist group would forgo the opportunity to serve its members and increase the resources at its disposal. The politicians whose policies made these deals possible saw no reason to get in the way. As President Clinton proudly proclaimed in a 1999 speech, the banking-reform legislation of that year "establishes the principles that, as we expand the powers of banks, we will expand the reach of the [Community Reinvestment] Act."[29]

There was nothing subtle about the deals between merging banks and activist groups. In fact, an umbrella organization for activist groups, the National Community Reinvestment Coalition (NCRC), put together a 101-page guide on how to negotiate with banks that were in the process of merging. The NCRC guide did not shy away from encouraging activist organizations to take advantage of their leverage over a prospective bank merger: "When a lender desires to merge with another institution or open a branch, the lender must apply to the Federal Reserve Board and/or to its primary regulator for permission. If the lender has received low CRA rating [*sic*], the federal agency reviewing the lender's application has the authority to delay, deny, or condition the lender's application."[30] The guide goes on to say:

> Merger and acquisition activity presents significant opportunities for community groups to intervene in the approval process and raise CRA concerns and issues. Some banks are very desirous of Outstanding

---

[29] Clinton (1999b).
[30] National Community Reinvestment Coalition (2007a), 26.

ratings so that they can present a clean reinvestment record to regulators when they ask for permission to merge. . . . Activists should keep in mind that changes from Outstanding to Satisfactory ratings (and back again) is effective in leveraging reinvestment as well as changes from passing to failing ratings (and back again to passing). This is true regardless of whether the movement in ratings is the overall rating for the bank or a rating for particular geographical areas.[31]

The guide then explains how to affect a bank's grade: "Community organizations can offer written comments on a bank's CRA and fair lending performance when a bank has submitted an application to merge or acquire another bank or thrift. NCRC can assist community organizations in preparing comments on merger applications."[32] Finally, the guide makes clear that simply creating noise in a bank's CRA compliance file may allow a group to leverage resources, even if the bank has been CRA compliant: "Timely comments can influence a bank's CRA rating by directing examiners to particular areas of strength or weakness in a bank's lending, investments, or services in low- and moderate-income neighborhoods. . . . Even changing a rating from Outstanding to Satisfactory in one state or one part of the exam can motivate a bank to increase the number of loans, investments, and services to low- and moderate-income communities."[33]

There was also nothing subtle about the agreements struck between banks and activists. Activist groups entered into long-term contracts with banks in which they received specific commitments for housing and small business lending that would often be channeled through the activist groups themselves. Between 1977 and 2007 there were no fewer than 376 such agreements, involving scores of groups. These agreements included a $760 million commitment from the Bank of New York to ACORN, an $8 billion agreement between Wachovia Bank and New Jersey Citizen Action, and a $70 billion agreement between the Bank of America and the California Reinvestment Coalition.[34] In return, the activist groups agreed not to oppose those banks' pending mergers and acquisitions. Sometimes they even submitted documentation and testified in support of the merger. For example, when NationsBank merged with the Bank of America in 1998,

[31] National Community Reinvestment Coalition (2007a), 27.
[32] National Community Reinvestment Coalition (2007a), 8.
[33] National Community Reinvestment Coalition (2007a), 8.
[34] National Community Reinvestment Coalition (2007b), 11–17.

creating the largest bank in the United States, with $525 billion in assets, the president of ACORN Housing, George Butts, testified on behalf of the merging banks at the Fed hearing. His reasons for supporting the merger are best expressed in his own words:

> The ACORN Housing Corporation/NationsBank partnership alone has produced over $236 million in mortgages. Virtually all these loans were to lower income households, with small downpayments, with nontraditional credit, with cash on hand, and with older, urban housing stock. And these loans perform well with low delinquencies. Nations-Bank has been flexible. They were the first multistate lender to negotiate their mortgage underwriting standards with us. And their step forward did a lot to bring our kind of underwriting standards for low income people into the mainstream of the mortgage market. At the time these things were pretty radical, but today no one thinks twice about the appropriate use of low downpayments, nontraditional credit, food stamps as income, voluntary child support, cash on hand, or steady income rather than the same job for two years.[35]

ACORN was not the only activist group to testify on behalf of the merger: the executive director of the Neighborhood Assistance Corporation of America submitted testimony as well. His letter to the Fed noted that: "in addition to refinancing homeowners, the NationsBank/Bank of America reinvestment program [totaling $350 billion] will provide unbelievable home ownership opportunities for low and moderate income people and communities nationwide. The ability to purchase a home with no downpayment, no closing costs, no application fee, no perfect credit, at less than 7% interest is incredible. . . . They need to be applauded and supported. The regulators need to approve the application immediately."[36]

The Populist Harvest

The monetary commitments that activist organizations obtained from banks came in two forms. First, banks committed to supply mortgage and small business credit to borrowers identified by the activist organizations.

---

[35] Butts (1998). Also see Atlas (2010), 71.
[36] Marks (1998).

Dollars (billions)

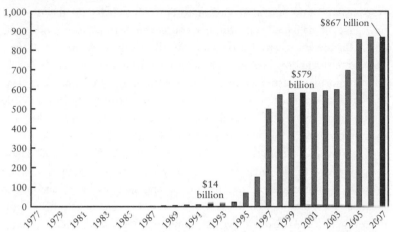

FIGURE 7.2 Cumulative value of CRA agreements between banks and activist groups, 1977–2007.

Source: National Community Reinvestment Coalition (2007b), 11–17.

As figure 7.2 shows, over the period 1977–2007, these directed credit commitments totaled $867 billion, with the overwhelming majority coming in the years after 1992. Banks also provided support to activist groups in the forms of fees for administering the directed-credit programs or direct contributions to those groups. Between 1993 and 2008, for example, ACORN received $13.5 million from the Bank of America, $9.5 million from JPMorgan Chase, $8.1 million from Citibank, $7.4 million from HSBC, and $1.4 million from Capital One.[37] As of 2000, the U.S. Senate Banking Committee estimated that the total of such fees and contributions to all activist groups came to $9.5 billion.[38] Given that new CRA agreements were made through 2007, the $9.5 billion figure almost certainly understates the extent of fees and contributions from banks.

How did activist groups intermediate the credit commitments that they received from banks? The Neighborhood Assistance Corporation of America (NACA) provides an example. As of 2012 it had obtained more than $13 billion in bank commitments for its own loan programs via partner-

[37] United States House of Representatives (2010), 42–43.
[38] Husock (2000).

ships with Bank of America, Fleet Financial, Citibank, First Union Bank, NationsBank, and others. According to NACA's website, the terms of the mortgages it delivered with these resources appeared "too good to be true." Borrowers received a one-size-fits-all mortgage with a fixed-rate, 30-year term, no down payment, no closing costs, no fees, no credit check, and no mortgage insurance premium. Additionally, NACA made it clear that it could provide financial assistance to borrowers having trouble making their payments.[39] But there was a catch: borrowers had to become members of NACA and were required to pledge to "participate in at least five actions and activities a year in support of NACA's mission." These actions and activities included "advocacy campaigns that may include protests, demonstrations, actions and/or engaging in litigation against persons or companies that discriminate against or victimize others," volunteering in a NACA office, participating in a "peer lending committee," or assisting "other Members with the home buying process."[40] NACA's terms attracted borrowers with very low credit ratings: 65 percent of NACA homeowners had a credit score of less than 620 (putting them in the high-risk borrower category), while nearly 50 percent scored less than 580 (very high risk).[41]

Considerable ink has been spilled by academics regarding the effects of CRA-directed credit arrangements on the amount and riskiness of bank lending. The evidence shows that had it not been for the CRA, banks would have made fewer and less risky loans. A 2012 study by Sumit Agarwal, Efraim Benmelech, and Amit Seru compares the portfolios of banks in the six quarters prior to a CRA evaluation relative to the portfolios of other banks not slated for evaluation. They find that an impending CRA examination caused banks to increase their lending by 5 percent and increased the default risk of those banks' mortgage loans by more than 15 percentage points.[42] This approach provides lower-bound estimates of

---

[39] NACA (n.d.).
[40] NACA (n.d.).
[41] Marks (n.d.).
[42] Agarwal et al. (2012) summarize their results as follows:

> We find that adherence to the act leads to riskier lending by banks: in the six quarters surrounding the CRA exams, lending is elevated on average by about 5 percent and these loans default about 15 percent more often. . . . We note that our estimates do not provide an assessment of the full impact of the CRA. This is because we are examining the effect of CRA evaluations relative to a baseline of banks not undergoing an exam. To the extent that there are adjustment costs in changing lending

both increased lending and increased levels of default risk resulting from the CRA.

Another approach to measuring the impact of CRA compliance is to focus on the increase in the level of CRA commitments over time. This is the approach taken by Edward Pinto, who assumes, conservatively, that the CRA had no binding effects on bank lending until the Clinton administration's CRA policy push. Under that assumption, Pinto concludes that by 2008, banks had undertaken $2.78 trillion dollars in CRA commitments that they would not have undertaken otherwise.[43] In short, however its effects are measured, banks' efforts to demonstrate CRA compliance had major effects on the amount and the riskiness of lending.

CRA agreements were crucial building blocks for many activist groups. Reflecting on the $220 million in bank mortgage money at his disposal, Tom Callahan, executive director of the Massachusetts Affordable Housing Alliance, said: "CRA is the backbone of everything we do."[44] CRA deals also had important consequences for the structure of the banking industry and its political alliance. They did more than prevent activists from blocking mergers: ironically, they turned activist groups into at least tacit *supporters* of a trend that one might have expected them to oppose, the emergence of megabanks that lessened competition. This point cannot be emphasized strongly enough: the provision of subsidized credit to activist groups to share with their constituents required a source of rent for banks. As we have pointed out before, there are no free lunches: directed credit arrangements between banks and activist groups necessarily involved cross-subsidization. Someone had to supply these rents, either via higher interest margins on loans or via implicit too-big-to-fail government protection for the banks.

In hindsight, the support by activist groups for mega-mergers is particularly ironic given what happened to many of the merged banks. Washington Mutual's 1999 merger with Home Savings of America provides an

---

behavior, this baseline level of lending behavior itself may be shifted toward catering to CRA compliance. Because our empirical strategy nets out the baseline effect, our estimates of CRA evaluations provide a lower bound to the actual impact of the Community Reinvestment Act. If adjustment costs in lending behavior are large and banks can't easily tilt their loan portfolio toward greater CRA compliance, the full impact of the CRA is potentially much greater than that estimated by the change in lending behavior around CRA exams.

[43] Pinto (2011), 15.
[44] Husock (2000).

example. This merger allowed WaMu to become the nation's largest thrift institution, sixth largest bank, and second largest seller of mortgages to Fannie Mae. The merger occasioned a $120 billion CRA agreement with the Greenlining Institute, the California Reinvestment Coalition, and the Washington Reinvestment Alliance. In a November 2003 presentation to the Florida Minority Community Reinvestment Coalition, a Greenlining Institute activist described Washington Mutual's agreement with these groups as illustrating "best practices."[45] The terms included a pledge by WaMu to provide $120 billion over ten years in various lending and community development programs, including loans to targeted low-income borrowers with low down payments. In addition, WaMu pledged to provide philanthropy equal to at least 2 percent of its pretax earnings. The "best practices" label is especially ironic in the case of WaMu because it became one of America's worst-run banks and among the largest and earliest banks to fail in the 2007–09 subprime crisis. Its practice of finding a way to grant a mortgage to almost anyone who walked in the door earned it the scrutiny of the United States Senate Permanent Subcommittee on Investigations, whose 2011 report on how WaMu conducted its business employed adjectives such as "shoddy," "fraudulent," and "problem plagued."[46]

No Free Lunch: The Rise of the GSEs

The unlikely coalition between megabanks and activist groups soon drew in more partners: the managers and stockholders of Fannie Mae and Freddie Mac. The resulting coalition proved to be quite durable, as it came to include powerful politicians from both the Republican and Democratic

---

[45] Florida Minority Community Reinvestment Coalition (2003).

[46] The subcommittee's detailed investigation of WaMu is perhaps best summed up in its opening pages (United States Senate [2011], 2–3):

> This case study focuses on how one bank's search for increased growth and profit led to the origination and securitization of hundreds of billions of dollars in high risk, poor quality mortgages that ultimately plummeted in value, hurting investors, the bank, and the U.S. financial system. WaMu had held itself out as a prudent lender, but in reality the bank turned increasingly to high risk loans. Over a four-year period, those high risk loans grew from 19% of WaMu's loan originations in 2003, to 55% in 2006, while its lower risk, fixed rate loans fell from 64% to 25% of its originations.

parties. It also succeeded in creating a process by which the underwriting standards at Fannie and Freddie, and hence of the entire mortgage industry, were weakened, so that trillions of dollars in mortgage credit was extended to borrowers with high probabilities of defaulting.

When Congress first set up the agencies that became the housing GSEs, it did not set out to create a system of highly privileged, extremely lucrative, taxpayer-subsidized private firms that had strong political incentives to reduce underwriting standards in the home mortgage market. Indeed, the first government-owned special-purpose banks were not even set up to provide home mortgage credit: they were part of the earlier bank bargain, and their subsidies were targeted instead at agrarian populists. In 1916, Congress created a system of 12 federal land banks whose purpose was to make mortgage loans to farmers. Congress left the market for home mortgages to commercial banks, thrifts, and insurance companies. These lenders tended to follow extremely conservative lending standards designed to minimize the probability of default: mortgages typically had five-year terms, had loan-to-value (LTV) ratios in the area of 50 percent, carried adjustable rates, and had a balloon payment due at maturity.[47] Even these prudent standards were not enough, however, to prevent widespread defaults during the Great Depression.

As a result, the Roosevelt administration stepped in to support the market for home mortgages, building on the experience of the federal land banks to set up an alphabet soup of credit cooperatives and government-owned special purpose banks. These institutions were also successors to the efforts of the Hoover administration in 1932, which set up federal home loan banks, government-organized credit cooperatives that were capitalized by their member banks (commercial banks, thrifts, and credit unions). FHLBs borrowed from the market at terms that reflected their special status and made "advances" to their own member institutions in order to fund their home-mortgage portfolios. In 1933, the FDR government established the Home Owners' Loan Corporation (HOLC), a government-owned, special-purpose bank that bought up home mortgages in default. The HOLC was intended to be short-lived, and it was: by 1935 it had ceased buying distressed mortgages and began to sell those

---

[47] Rajan (2010), 32. For more details on the history of the U.S. mortgage market, see Fishback, Snowden, and White (forthcoming) and Rose and Snowden (2012).

that it had purchased. In 1934, the government chartered the Federal Housing Administration (FHA), a government entity that guaranteed the repayment of mortgages in exchange for a low fee. This was a far-reaching move: banks now had incentives to make mortgages at longer terms, lower interest rates, and higher LTV ratios because the risk of default was borne by the government.[48] In 1938, the FDR government chartered Fannie Mae, which was designed to repurchase FHA-guaranteed mortgage loans from banks and thrifts, thereby increasing the supply of mortgage credit. As World War II drew to a close, the GI Bill of 1944 turned the Veterans Administration into a special-purpose bank: a VA loan program was created, as a temporary postwar readjustment program, to help returning soldiers purchase homes. It soon became a permanent housing subsidy for former military personnel.[49]

These special-purpose government banks were created to serve worthy goals, but there are no free lunches. Targeting certain classes of loans for favored treatment inevitably taxes businesses and households in one way or another. If a government-owned bank makes a loan that a private lender will not make, or if it agrees to repurchase a loan made by a private lender, that implies a subsidy received by the borrower: taxpayers are covering the difference between what the borrower would pay for that loan on the open market and what the borrower is paying for that loan from the government. The government-owned bank, after all, still has to borrow the money to make the loan, and taxpayers are responsible for those

[48] Although government housing-policy interventions did much to encourage the establishment of long-term, amortizing mortgages in the United States, such mortgages had been invented by building and loan associations many decades earlier and grew in popularity in the 1910s and 1920s. Indeed, Rose and Snowden (2012) show that the shocks of the Depression, not just the housing policy interventions of the New Deal, were instrumental in promoting the use of long-term, amortizing mortgages.

[49] Federal tax policy also provides housing subsidies for homeowners and low-income renters. First, the low-income housing tax credit (LIHTC) provides tax credits for low-income households for new or rehabilitated rental housing, with rents limited relative to tenant income. Second, there are exemptions from federal taxation for some states that issue debt to finance housing projects. Third, interest payments on mortgages, on principal up to a maximum amount, and property taxes are tax deductible. For broad reviews of all federal interventions into housing, see Jaffee and Quigley (2009, 2011). Jaffee and Quigley (2007, 2009) estimate that the LIHTC represented only $5.8 billion in forgone revenues in 2007 and that tax-exempt bonds cost about $1.9 billion in federal revenue. In contrast, the deduction for homeowners' mortgage payments and property taxes cost $117.4 billion.

debts. If a government-owned bank guarantees a loan made by a private bank, that implies a subsidy to the bank and the borrower: taxpayers will cover the cost of bailing out the bank if the borrower is unable or unwilling to repay the loan, and the bank can charge the borrower a lower interest rate because the government guarantee reduces the default risk to zero.

The lunch might not have looked entirely free, but because taxpayers were picking up part of the tab, borrowers had an incentive to supersize their meals. The size of the interest-rate subsidy received by the borrower was a function of the size of the loan: the more a household was allowed to borrow at a favorable interest rate, the larger the subsidy it received. Thus borrowers seeking to expand the size of the implicit subsidy they received from the government faced strong incentives to maximize loan-to-value ratios and loan-to-income ratios.[50] The result was that special-purpose government banks did not just create subsidies: they encouraged borrowers to become more highly leveraged than they would have been otherwise.[51]

By the 1960s, the liabilities of government-owned, special-purpose banks had grown sizable, and the cost of their implicit subsidies began to impinge on other government goals, particularly the simultaneous prosecution of the Vietnam War and the War on Poverty. The government therefore decided to spin off part of Fannie Mae, allowing it to issue shares and become a privately owned GSE, a corporation with private shareholders and managers that operated with huge implicit public subsidies—in particular, an implicit government guarantee of its debts. Fannie was also exempted from state and local income taxes and the federal bankruptcy code, and it had a line of credit with the U.S. Treasury. From the point of view of a private investor, therefore, Fannie was implicitly backed

[50] For example, if a prospective mortgage borrower without government policy interventions would have had to pay, say, an 8 percent interest rate on a mortgage with a 97 percent loan-to-value ratio, but could borrow that amount at a 5 percent interest rate in the presence of government subsidies, then the implied subsidy would be nearly 3 percent of the value of the borrower's home per year.

[51] There are other ways to encourage home ownership that are less distortionary. For example, in Australia, first-time home buyers receive a government subsidy toward their down payments. The Australian housing subsidy program therefore helps first-time buyers to qualify for loans by reducing their loan-to-value ratios (LTVs)—the opposite of the U.S. system.

by the full faith and credit of the U.S. government—and thus could borrow at roughly the same rate of interest as the government. In addition, Fannie's securities did not have to be registered with the Securities and Exchange Commission: they were considered government securities under the Securities and Exchange Act of 1934 and could therefore be pledged as collateral for debts owed to the federal government. These features gave Fannie insuperable advantages over fully private firms that might choose to enter the market against it. In exchange for those benefits, Fannie Mae had to support the government's politically determined housing goals. In effect, turning Fannie into a GSE moved the cost of its subsidies off the government's balance sheet. Nevertheless, an implicit subsidy—and a contingent liability—remained.

When Fannie Mae was privatized in 1968, it was split in two. One of the new entities, which remained a government agency called the Government National Mortgage Association (GNMA, or Ginnie Mae), securitized mortgages that had guarantees from government entities such as the FHA or VA; the other (which retained the name Fannie Mae) was turned into a GSE and was charged with repurchasing and securitizing loans without the benefit of (explicit) government guarantees. In 1971, the government created an additional housing-finance GSE, the Federal Home Loan Mortgage Corporation (FHLMC, known as Freddie Mac) that was designed to compete with Fannie Mae. Initially, the shares of Freddie Mac were owned by the FHLBs and their member banks, but in 1989, Freddie Mac was converted into a publicly owned GSE like Fannie Mae and with the same special privileges.

Creating Fannie Mae and Freddie Mac as private companies with public responsibilities made sense from the point of view of Washington politicians who wanted to keep subsidizing housing finance while disguising its cost, but the unusual structure of these two GSEs created perverse incentives for their managers. They were supposed to maximize returns to their shareholders, and to that end they could repurchase and securitize a loan made by any private lender, *whether or not that loan carried an FHA or VA guarantee,* so long as the value of the loan did not exceed thresholds set by the government. At the same time, however, their tax exemptions and the implicit government guarantees of their liabilities gave the government the right to influence the GSEs' business practices. Thus Fannie and Freddie had to go along with the lending goals Congress set for them—and those goals, it would turn out, were to increase substantially the rate of home ownership by making housing affordable for constituencies that would not otherwise qualify for mortgage credit.

Be Careful What You Wish For

The political importance of the housing GSEs—Fannie Mae, Freddie Mac, and the FHLBs—increased substantially with the collapse of the savings and loan industry in the 1980s. Favorable chartering and regulation of thrifts had been one of the primary tools of government subsidization of mortgage finance until the late 1980s. After many years during which regulatory accounting for thrifts helped to disguise losses in order to avoid dealing with massive insolvencies, President George H. W. Bush's administration pressed to recognize the losses of insolvent and undercapitalized thrifts. That decision precipitated the closure of much of the industry under the new requirements of the Financial Institutions Reform, Recovery, and Enforcement Act (FIRREA) of 1989. Michael Boskin, who served as the chairman of Bush's Council of Economic Advisers, wanted to go further and suggested reforming the housing GSEs at the same time. But that reform was not politically feasible, especially given the impending closure of so many thrift institutions; Fannie and Freddie were more important than ever as a means of subsidizing mortgage credit. As Boskin puts it:

> In the course of negotiating FIRREA, we had several meetings with the leadership of both parties in both the House and Senate. At one meeting in the Cabinet Room, I suggested we expand our efforts from the Savings and Loans to other analogous situations where the government, i.e. taxpayers, were on the hook for losses whereas private investors got the gains, e.g. the GSEs, with their (implicit) government backing, which allowed them to borrow at subsidized rates. It was soon made clear to me that any attempt to limit the GSEs would derail the S&L cleanup, the more immediately pressing issue. Worse yet, Congress was soon back expanding the remit of the GSEs.[52]

Not coincidentally, 1989 also saw the beginning of government mandates requiring another group of government-chartered housing GSEs—the

[52] Michael J. Boskin, personal communication, June 21, 2012.

twelve FHLBs—to begin a special program of support for low-income housing. Beginning in 1989, FHLBs were required to set aside 10 percent of their net earnings in support of low- and moderate-income housing programs.

Although Fannie and Freddie and the FHLBs expanded in response to the collapse of the thrift industry in the late 1980s, they continued to target their mortgage subsidies toward prime mortgages for middle-income homeowners. In fact, according to studies by HUD and by the Federal Reserve Board, Fannie Mae and Freddie Mac avoided bearing the higher default risk associated with high-risk borrowers by requiring them either to make higher down payments or to obtain private mortgage insurance.[53] Thus, analysts expressing concern about Fannie and Freddie in the mid-1990s were primarily worried about the risk of loss associated with possible *prepayments* of mortgages by homeowners seeking to refinance at lower interest rates.[54]

Many economists complained that Fannie and Freddie were using substantial taxpayer resources (flowing from the implicit guarantee of their debts by the government) without providing any commensurate public good. Why, critics wondered, given the existence of FHA, VA, and GNMA programs—all of which were part of the federal budget and targeted at subsidizing mortgages—did it make sense to have additional off-budget mortgage subsidies that were not fully subject to government control and accountability? After all, critics argued, banks too could purchase and securitize mortgages. But banks were being crowded out from holding or securitizing mortgages by these two privileged giants because of the advantages that the government had bestowed on them. The same critics went on to point out that the unusual structures of Fannie and Freddie encouraged excessive risk taking at the public's expense: the government's

---

[53] See Canner, Passmore, and Surette (1996) and Bunce and Sheessele (1996). The political pressures on Fannie and Freddie to do more for risky borrowers had a long history. In 1978, HUD Secretary Patricia Roberts Harris tried to impose mandates on the GSEs to lend to low- and moderate-income households, but she was rebuffed by the "ensuing political brouhaha" (Weicher [2001], 125).

[54] Canner, Passmore, and Surette (1996); Calomiris (2001). Prepayment risk refers to the possibility that a mortgage may be paid off (either due to refinancing or sale of the home) at a time of falling interest rates. Such an outcome could lead to problems for GSEs who had promised a high coupon on their debts but lost high-interest mortgages with which to service those debts.

implicit guarantee of their debts, without much in the way of regulatory or supervisory oversight, meant that their managers had strong incentives to lend with borrowed money and little equity capital. Congress did not get around to creating a regulatory agency to set capital standards and other rules for Fannie Mae and Freddie Mac until 1992, and even then, that agency had very limited enforcement powers. Fannie and Freddie had become tremendously profitable, government-protected, highly leveraged, and lightly regulated enterprises that were rapidly coming to dominate the mortgage market. In 1990, the two organizations accounted for roughly a quarter of all single-family home mortgages; by 2003, their share had risen to half.[55]

The chorus of opposition to the privileges enjoyed by Fannie and Freddie grew particularly loud by the early 1990s. Among the many calls for reform were proposals to increase GSEs' minimum required equity-capital ratios, to limit their growth, to remove their connections to the government, and to abolish them altogether.[56]

There is an old saying that you should be careful what you wish for, and the response of Congress to the attacks on Fannie and Freddie proves its wisdom. Congressmen are not in the business of supporting the public interest: they're in the business of getting reelected, and those with large urban constituencies were aware of the importance of their low-income constituents in achieving that goal. Thus, at just about the same time that large banks and activist organizations were crafting their own special arrangements, the activist organizations were using their growing clout in Congress to put pressure on Fannie and Freddie. Their reasoning was that unless Fannie and Freddie led the way to lower underwriting standards, the amount of credit that could be mobilized from the banks via CRA agreements would be marginal. Thus, in 1991, when Senator Alan Dixon of Illinois convened a Senate subcommittee hearing and invited representatives from ACORN and other activist groups to testify, they went after the underwriting standards of Fannie and Freddie with hammer and tongs.[57] In his testimony before the subcommittee, the director of ACORN Housing explicitly drew a link between the ability of banks to sell their

---

[55] Jaffee (2010), 1; Pinto (2011), 56.

[56] Wallison (2001).

[57] Pinto (2011), 40; Fishbein (2003), 112–13. The transcript of the hearing can be found at United States Senate (1991).

loans to the GSEs and the willingness of those banks to participate in CRA partnerships with ACORN: "Many of the lenders we work with who now hold multimillion dollar CRA portfolios have told us that they may soon be unable to originate more of these loans if they remain unable to sell them to Fannie Mae or Freddie Mac."[58] He also noted that "it is ACORN's observation that the underwriting criteria employed by Fannie Mae and Freddie Mac have been developed not for the general mortgage market, which includes low and moderate income homeowners, but for a middle income and substantially suburban mortgage market. As a result, it is our firm belief that the underwriting standards dictated by the secondary mortgage market are, at a minimum, income discriminatory and may, by extension, be racially discriminatory."[59]

The result was exactly the opposite of what Fannie and Freddie's critics had hoped for: rather than eliminate the implicit guarantee of Fannie and Freddie's debts, Congress reasoned that their taxpayer-financed subsidies should be shared with low-income Americans. Congress therefore enacted significant changes in the rules governing Fannie and Freddie, giving them substantial new responsibilities to promote home ownership by low-income and inner-city Americans. These changes were embodied in the Federal Housing Enterprise Safety and Soundness Act (usually called the GSE Act), which was signed into law by President Bush just prior to the 1992 elections. The GSE Act, among other things, required the Department of Housing and Urban Development (HUD) to develop affordable housing goals for Fannie and Freddie. In 1993, HUD required the GSEs, as an interim measure, to devote 30 percent of their loans to "low and moderate income" borrowers. HUD also established a category of "low and very low income" borrowers, setting the interim level for these "special affordable" loans at 1 percent of Fannie and Freddie loan acquisitions. As figure 7.3 shows, both interim limits were soon raised quite substantially.[60]

The sponsors of the GSE Act understood that the purpose of the mandates was to force Fannie and Freddie to lower their underwriting requirements and thereby lead private banks into originating loans to low-income

---

[58] United States Senate (1991), 95.
[59] United States Senate (1991), 93–94.
[60] Pinto (2011), 54.

Percentage of loans purchased

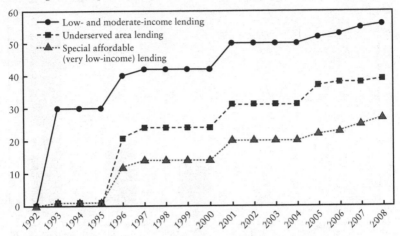

FIGURE 7.3 HUD loan repurchase mandates for Fannie and Freddie, 1992–2008.

Source: Pinto (2011), 76, 87, 104, 105.

Note: Fannie and Freddie actual loan purchases met these goals.

urban constituents. This strategy was made clear in a 1991 HUD report: "The market influence of Fannie Mae and Freddie Mac extends well beyond the number of loans they buy or securitize; their underwriting standards for primary loans are widely adopted and amount to national underwriting standards for a substantial fraction of all mortgage loans."[61]

Congress therefore mandated that Fannie and Freddie consider repurchasing mortgages with down payments of 5 percent or less and approving borrowers with histories of delinquent credit. Importantly, it also directed Fannie and Freddie to "affirmatively assist banks in meeting their CRA obligations."[62] As Edward Pinto has pointed out, when Congress told Fannie and Freddie to purchase mortgages with down payments of percent, it was taking a huge step: in 1992, a conventional mortgage loan with a 5 percent down payment did not even exist outside FHA or VA guaranteed programs.[63] In effect, because Fannie and Freddie repurchased

[61] Advisory Commission on Regulatory Barriers to Affordable Housing (1991), chapter 5, p. 3.

[62] As quoted in Pinto (2011), 55.

[63] Pinto (2011), 55.

Percentage

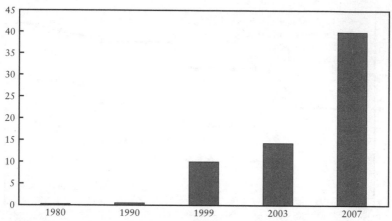

1980   1990   1999   2003   2007

FIGURE 7.4 Percentage of home purchases in the United States with a down payment of 3 percent or less, 1980–2007.

Source: Pinto (2011), 24–25.

roughly one of every four mortgages originated, they were being asked to lead private banks into a segment of the market that they had historically avoided precisely because it was so risky.

Pushing Fannie and Freddie to purchase highly leveraged, risky mortgages targeted toward particular borrowers had huge effects on the mortgage market. Beginning in 1994, Fannie and Freddie started buying loans with down payments of only 3 percent. Low underwriting standards are not an excludable good: everyone, including big swaths of the American middle class, could take advantage of these permissive lending rules—and many duly did so. As a result, the number of such loans mushroomed: as figure 7.4 shows, circa 1990, only 1 in 200 mortgages had such a high LTV ratio; by 1999, 1 in 10 did; by 2007, 2 out of every 5 mortgages had an LTV of 3 percent or less.[64]

The managers and shareholders of Fannie and Freddie were being asked to bear new burdens, but they were not powerless, passive observers. They could see that in the negotiations over the 1992 GSE Act, they were being outflanked by activist groups and their congressional allies. Thus they made the best move they could: they got on the bandwagon in

[64] Pinto (2011), 25.

order to shape the legislation to their liking. As described by Raghuram Rajan, Fannie and Freddie used the passage of the GSE Act to ensure that they would be "allowed to hold less capital than other regulated financial institutions and that their new regulator, an office within HUD—which had no experience in financial-services regulation—was subject to appropriation. This meant that if the regulator actually started constraining the agencies [Fannie and Freddie], the GSEs' friends in Congress could cut the budget."[65] Fannie and Freddie spent more than $200 million lobbying Congress to avoid tighter oversight.[66] In short, they agreed to go along with the congressional mandates provided that they could borrow the money—with taxpayers providing an implicit guarantee of their debts—to fund the risky loans they were being required to make. Fannie's and Freddie's managers and shareholders profited handsomely from the new deal, at least in the short run. For example, in 2003 alone, Franklin Raines, the CEO of Fannie Mae, received $20 million in compensation.

Clinton and the Third Way, Redux

The victory of Bill Clinton over George Bush in the 1992 presidential election solidified the coalition of large banks, activist groups, Fannie and Freddie, and powerful allied politicians. Under the Clinton Administration, HUD mandates for low-income lending by Fannie and Freddie increased steadily, as shown in figure 7.3. As of 1995 (applicable to 1996), the HUD goal applied to the GSEs for low- and moderate-income loans was raised from 30 to 40 percent. The goal for "special affordable" (very-low-income) loans was raised from 1 to 12 percent. At the same time, HUD introduced yet another category of mandated lending, "underserved," which had to equal 21 percent of all loan acquisitions. These were overlapping categories, but taken as a group they suggest that, as of 1996, more than half of Fannie and Freddie loan repurchases likely were in the mandated categories. The Clinton administration subsequently increased all of these mandates. On the eve of leaving office, Clinton's secretary of HUD pushed the mandate for low- and moderate-income lending up to 50 percent of all Fannie and Freddie loans, for special affordable lending to 20 percent, and for underserved to 31 percent. Again, these were overlapping categories, but taken as a group they suggest that, as of

---

[65] Rajan (2010), 35. Also see Hagerty (2012), 85–95.
[66] Acharya et al. (2011), 32.

2001, two out of every three loans purchased by Fannie and Freddie likely were in the mandated categories.[67]

In setting these quotas, the Clinton administration was quite conscious of the fact that Fannie and Freddie were going to have to apply much less prudent underwriting requirements. As HUD director Henry Cisneros put it in describing the 1994 National Homeownership Strategy, "For many potential homebuyers, the lack of cash available to accumulate the required down payment and closing costs is a serious impediment to purchasing a home. Other households do not have sufficient available income to make the monthly payments on mortgages financed at market interest rates for standard term loans. Financing strategies, fueled by the creativity and resources of the private and public sectors, should address both of these barriers to homeownership."[68] In plain English, he was saying that HUD was going to weaken underwriting standards.

Andrew Cuomo replaced Henry Cisneros as secretary of HUD in 1997, where he remained until the presidency of George W. Bush and continued Cisneros's advocacy of weak underwriting standards.[69] As a recent review of HUD policies over the past 30 years put it:

> Like Cisneros, Cuomo's main policy legacy was promoting subsidies for increasing the home ownership rate and weakening safeguards against excessive mortgage market risks. For example, Cuomo successfully advocated that Congress raise the ceiling on FHA-insured mortgages while lowering down-payment requirements. . . . Cuomo also supported efforts to have home sellers funnel money to nonprofit groups to help pay for buyers' down payments and closing costs. . . . Cuomo portrayed his efforts as helping to increase homeownership rates for minorities, but he also had an interest in pleasing mortgage industry officials who would later help finance his gubernatorial campaign. . . . Cuomo's HUD pressured Fannie and Freddie to purchase greater volumes of high-risk loans offered to less credit-worthy borrowers. . . . Cuomo applied pressure by having HUD publicly "investigate" whether Fannie and

---

[67] Pinto (2011), 76, 87, 104, 105; Hagerty (2012), 112.

[68] As quoted in Rajan (2010), 36. See also DeHaven (2009).

[69] Cisneros was forced to resign amid a Justice Department investigation into misstatements that he made to the FBI regarding payments he had made to a former mistress. In 2001, he joined the board of Fannie Mae's biggest client and the most aggressive originator of subprime mortgages, Countrywide Financial.

Freddie were sufficiently in compliance with government fair-lending standards designed to prevent discrimination.[70]

Although Fannie and Freddie were always able to meet those HUD targets, the task became increasingly difficult: the amount of money that the GSEs were required to direct to low-income borrowers was rising, but the number of creditworthy low-income borrowers was relatively constant.[71] According to a 2005 staff report of the House Financial Services Committee, Fannie and Freddie engaged in a wide variety of ploys to hit their targets, such as "double counting" loans, a stratagem by which they bought a loan in one year, sold it back to the lender the next, and then repurchased it again the year after, each time counting it as a new purchase. Banks went along with these and other dubious transactions, earning "tens, and sometimes hundreds of millions of dollars in fees as inducements."[72] In fact, knowing that Fannie and Freddie were under pressure, banks were able to earn premiums by having Fannie and Freddie bid against one another at the end of each year for mortgages that met HUD target criteria.[73]

Filling the growing gap between HUD targets and the pool of qualified borrowers required Fannie and Freddie to undermine their underwriting standards. One crucial step in that process was their decision to purchase mortgages with high loan-to-value ratios (low down payments). Pinpointing the exact number of high-LTV mortgages they purchased is difficult, because, as found in the 2012 legal settlement between them and the Securities and Exchange Commission, the GSEs systematically misstated their exposure to high-risk mortgage lending. (The settlement was the resolution of a lawsuit by the SEC, which alleged that Fannie and Freddie had misled investors.)[74]

---

[70] DeHaven (2009), 8.

[71] As with all binding regulatory requirements, actual levels of lending to targeted groups are the sum of the required amounts and a small additional "buffer" (to ensure compliance, actual levels must be targeted at slightly above the minimum), and therefore, actual amounts of lending to targeted groups remained slightly higher than the mandated amounts shown in figure 7.3.

[72] As quoted in Hagerty (2012), 155.

[73] Hagerty (2012), 156.

[74] The SEC alleges, for example, that, Freddie Mac told investors that its exposure through its single-family subprime loans during the 18-month period from early 2007

The increasing tolerance for low down payments was not enough, however, to sustain the growth in Fannie and Freddie loan repurchases necessary to meet their HUD mandates. Fannie and Freddie also had to buy increasing numbers of loans with low FICO scores. Indeed, the GSEs accounted for roughly one-half of all such lending by the late 1990s. They also aggressively moved into the markets for adjustable-rate mortgage loans (ARMs) and interest-only loans. In fact, by 2006, 15.2 percent of Fannie's portfolio was interest-only loans.[75]

Even these steps were not sufficient to allow the GSEs to meet their HUD mandates. Thus in 2004, Fannie and Freddie removed the limits that they had earlier placed on their purchases of so-called no-docs loans (which are generally included within the category of Alt-A mortgage loans). No-docs mortgages are those for which the borrower does not have to document income by providing pay stubs, W-2 forms, and the like. As a result, commercial banks and other mortgage lenders increasingly tolerated poor credit histories, and were willing to accept less and less documentation, because they knew that they could sell risky loans to Fannie or Freddie. Even if they could not sell them, they could bundle them into a mortgage-backed security guaranteed by Fannie or Freddie (bought for only 45 cents for every $100 in loans) and then hold those insured securities in their own portfolios or sell them to third parties—a subject we examine at length in the next chapter.

When Freddie Mac decided to make its aggressive move into no-docs loans, its own risk managers pointed out that it was a grave error—in a series of e-mails to Freddie's senior managers. On April 1, 2004, Freddie Mac risk manager David Andrukonis wrote to Tracy Mooney, a vice president, that "while you, Don [Bisenius, a senior vice president] and I will make the case for sound credit, it's not the theme coming from the top of the company and inevitably people down the line play follow the leader." In another e-mail that same day, Don Bisenius wrote to Michael May (senior vice president of operations), "We did no-doc lending before, took inordinate losses and generated significant fraud cases. I'm not sure what makes us think we're so much smarter this time around." A few days later,

---

to August 2008 was only $2 billion to $6 billion, when the actual number was $141 billion at the end of 2006 and about $244 billion by mid-2008.

[75] Acharya et al. (2011), 38, 39.

Andrukonis wrote yet another e-mail expressing concerns about no-docs loans, this one to chief operating officer Paul Peterson: "In 1990 we called this product 'dangerous' and eliminated it from the marketplace." He went on to say: "We are less likely to get the house price appreciation we've had in the past 10 years to bail this program out if there's a hole in it."[76]

These warnings appear to have fallen on deaf ears, because politics was driving decision making. A July 14, 2004 e-mail from senior vice president Robert Tsien to Dick Syron, chair and CEO of Freddie Mac, suggests as much: "Tipping the scale in favor of no cap [on no-doc lending] at this time was the pragmatic consideration that, under the current circumstances, a cap would be interpreted by external critics as additional proof we are not really committed to affordable lending."

Freddie Mac's risk managers appear not to have given up their concerns about high-risk lending easily. On September 7, 2004, Donna Cogswell, a colleague of Andrukonis in risk management, e-mailed Syron warning that Freddie's decisions to debase underwriting standards would have widespread consequences for the mortgage market. She specifically described the ramifications of Freddie Mac's continued participation in no-docs loans as effectively "mak[ing] a market" in these types of mortgages. She also tried to sway management by appealing to their sense of decency: "What better way to highlight our sense of mission than to walk away from profitable business because it hurts the borrowers we are trying to serve?" The next day, Andrukonis wrote an e-mail that one can interpret as drawing a line in the sand. He wrote to May: "At last week's risk management meeting I mentioned that I had reached my own conclusion on this product [no-docs loans] from a reputation risk perspective. I said that I thought you and or Bob Tsien had the responsibility to bring the business recommendation to Dick [Syron], who was going to make

[76] These internal Freddie Mac e-mails were provided to Charles Calomiris by the staff of the Committee on Oversight and Government Reform of the U.S. House of Representatives. They were included in Calomiris's testimony to that committee. They also served as the basis for a *Wall Street Journal* op ed article by Calomiris. See Calomiris (2008, 2011b). Charles Duhigg of the *New York Times* interviewed current and former high-ranking executives of Freddie Mac, including David Andrukonis, along with regulators, analysts, and shareholders. Those interviews indicated that "the chief executive of the mortgage giant Freddie Mac rejected internal warnings that could have protected the company from some of the financial crises now engulfing it" (Duhigg [2008]).

the decision. . . . What I want Dick to know is that he can approve of us doing these loans, but it will be against my recommendation." Andruko-nis was forced out of Freddie Mac the following year.

Representative Henry Waxman, who chaired the Committee on Over-sight and Government Reform in which these e-mails came to light, summed up the situation in his opening statement to the hearings:

> The documents [reviewed by the committee] make clear that Fannie Mae and Freddie Mac knew what they were doing. Their own risk managers raised warning after warning about the dangers of investing heavily in the subprime and alternative mortgage market, but these warnings were ignored. In 2004, Freddie Mac's chief risk officer sent an e-mail to CEO [Richard] Syron urging Freddie Mac to stop pur-chasing loans with no income or asset requirements as soon as practica-ble. The risk officer warned that mortgage lenders were targeting bor-rowers who would have trouble qualifying for a mortgage if their financial position were adequately disclosed and that the "potential for the perception and the reality of predatory lending with this product is great." But, Mr. Syron did not accept the chief risk officer's recommen-dation. Instead, the company fired him.[77]

The worries of Freddie's risk managers about the effects of no-docs loans were confirmed in a painstaking analysis of the sources of increased mortgage risk by the financial economists Uday Rajan, Amit Seru, and Vikrant Vig. Their paper, which seeks to explain the failure of models of mortgage risk to accurately predict the risk of default, shows that more than half of the mortgage losses that occurred in excess of those antici-pated by lenders can be attributed to low-doc and no-doc lending. If the mortgage-underwriting standards in effect at Fannie and Freddie circa 2003 had remained in place, nothing on the magnitude of the subprime crisis would have occurred.[78]

---

[77] United States House of Representatives (2008), 2.

[78] A recent study by Hernandez-Murillo, Ghent, and Owyang (2012), using dis-continuity regression analysis, finds no evidence that the GSEs' losses on risky mort-gages were greater for HUD-mandate-related borrowers than for other borrowers. This is interesting, but it is also fully consistent with the narrative provided by the Freddie Mac risk managers and the results of Rajan, Seru, and Vig (2010). The Freddie Mac risk managers claimed that the caps on *all* no-docs and low-docs mortgages were

A study by Christopher Mayer, Karen Pence, and Shane Sherlund also traces the subprime crisis to a combination of deteriorating underwriting standards, "manifested most dramatically by lenders allowing borrowers to forgo down payments entirely," and falling house prices. They also explore and reject an alternative narrative about the subprime collapse—that it was the result of the use of innovative and complicated mortgage structures that confused consumers. They show that the tsunami of mortgage defaults that became the subprime crisis reflected first and foremost the willingness of lenders to make much riskier mortgages than they had made before.[79]

Despite the varying definitions of *subprime* and problems in the accounting practices of Fannie and Freddie, which gave rise in 2011 to an SEC lawsuit against their senior managers, the available data allow researchers to make a reasonable estimate of the extent of Fannie's and Freddie's high-risk mortgage lending. The approach taken by Edward Pinto (Fannie Mae chief credit officer from 1987 to 1989) and Peter Wallison (a former member of the government's Financial Crisis Inquiry Commission) is to focus on the characteristics of the mortgages rather than on how Fannie and Freddie labeled them. Using data from the SEC's nonprosecution agreements with Fannie and Freddie, they find that at the height of the mortgage bubble, Fannie and Freddie were exposed to more than 13 million subprime or Alt-A loans with a total value of $2 trillion.[80] Ironically, *Alt-A* is an abbreviation for "alternative to agency," meaning (prior to the relaxation of mortgage standards) a mortgage that a bank could not sell to Fannie or Freddie because it did not meet the GSEs' underwriting standards. Times certainly had changed.

Viral Acharya, Matthew Richardson, Stijn van Nieuwerburgh, and Lawrence White take a different approach, based only on the data that were available prior to the SEC settlement (which therefore likely underestimate GSE exposures to high-risk lending). They categorize new mort-

---

removed in 2004 in order to meet HUD mandates, not that the caps were removed *only* for loans that met HUD-mandate-related criteria. Thus, the discontinuity analysis finding is not surprising and does not contradict the view that the HUD mandates drove the GSEs' expansion into risky lending.

[79] Mayer, Pence, and Sherlund (2009).

[80] Pinto and Wallison (2011). Their early estimates of subprime losses were lower than the $2 trillion found by the SEC, but the estimates grew over time.

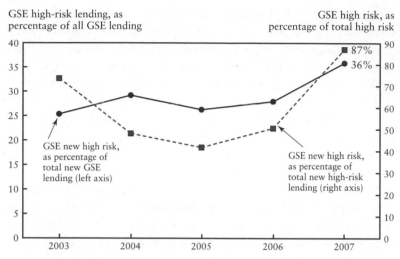

GSE high-risk lending, as
percentage of all GSE lending

GSE high risk, as
percentage of total high risk

FIGURE 7.5 GSE high-risk mortgages, as percentages of new GSE lending and of all new lending, 2003–07.

Source: Acharya et al. (2011), 59.

Note: High risk is defined as an LTV ratio greater than 80 or a FICO score below 660.

gages with LTVs greater than 80 percent and/or FICO scores below 660 as "high-risk." The sum of all new high-risk loans acquired by the GSEs over the period 2003–07 was $1.5 trillion. The researchers use the same method to estimate the new high-risk mortgages held outside the GSEs and then compute two ratios: the percentage of mortgages held by GSEs that were high risk, and the percentage of all new mortgages held both by the GSEs and by private entities that were high risk. Their estimates, presented in figure 7.5, indicate that high-risk lending accounted for 25 percent of new GSE mortgages in 2003, a figure that grew to 36 percent by 2007: the average for the period 2003–07 was 28 percent. Their data also indicate that the GSEs ended up acquiring most of America's exposure to new high-risk mortgages. Over the period 2003–07, the GSEs acquired 60 percent of all new high-risk mortgages. By 2007, they were acquiring nearly all of it. No matter how one looks at the data, there is no doubt that Fannie and Freddie were stuffed full of mortgages with high probabilities of default.[81]

[81] Acharya et al. (2011).

The Clinton administration went beyond reforms to Fannie and Freddie in supporting redistribution via affordable housing. The FHA helped subsidize home purchases for low-income citizens by insuring their mortgages, thereby making those mortgages acceptable to banks and other lenders. It had operated with fairly traditional underwriting standards prior to the 1990s. Indeed, FHA was originally conceived of as facilitating "economically sound" self-amortizing mortgages, with terms of up to 20 years and down payments of 20 percent.[82] In 2000, under pressure from the Clinton administration, the FHA changed its credit standards. It reduced minimum down-payment requirements to only 3 percent while simultaneously increasing the maximum size of the mortgage that it would guarantee and halving the premium it charged borrowers for the guarantee.[83] As a result, the rate of defaults on FHA-guaranteed mortgages jumped markedly. In the 1950s, foreclosure starts (the first step in the foreclosure process, in which the lender legally notifies the borrower that she is in default) for FHA-guaranteed mortgages in any year never exceeded 0.37 percent of all mortgages; for conventional mortgages, the figure was 0.15 percent. Foreclosure starts for both FHA mortgages and non-FHA (prime) mortgages rose after the 1950s, but from 1960 to 1990, the gap between FHA and non-FHA foreclosure starts remained small. Beginning in the 1990s, foreclosure rates for both types of mortgages increased. For the period 2002–07, average foreclosure starts for FHA mortgages rose to 3.51 percent per year, compared to 0.85 percent for conventional prime mortgages. By 2012, FHA foreclosure starts had reached 5 percent.[84] Generous lending by FHLBs also fueled the decline in underwriting standards. Just as GSE purchases and guarantees reduced the costs that banks bore from originating risky mortgages, FHLB advances made risky mortgage lending cheaper for banks.

---

[82] Jaffee and Quigley (2009).

[83] Rajan (2010), 37.

[84] Authors' calculations. These shifts in the foreclosure rates on FHA mortgages understate the dimensions of the change, because as of 2002 the FHA required banks and other mortgage originators to follow more forgiving guidelines in the renegotiation of delinquent mortgages. Prior to the rule change, the probability that a mortgage that was 90 days delinquent would be foreclosed was 75 percent. After the rule change, the probability fell to 25 percent. Data prior to 1998 are from Elmer and Seelig (1998). Data after 1997 are from the Mortgage Bankers Association and were generously provided to us by Edward Pinto.

Between 1989 and 2005, FHLB total assets grew from about $175 billion to $1 trillion.[85]

Why No Push-Back?

Readers may wonder why the Republican Party did not push back against these policy changes. The Republicans, after all, had obtained a congressional majority in the 1994 midterm elections. There were some Republican members of Congress, particularly Representative Richard Baker (Louisiana), Representative Jim Leach (Iowa), and Senator Richard Shelby (Alabama) who vocally objected to what was taking place and who thought that the ambit of Fannie and Freddie should be reduced, if not eliminated entirely. These three members of Congress, not coincidentally, were all from rural states: they did not represent low-income, urban constituencies but instead represented elements of the losing coalition in the Game of Bank Bargains in the 1990s. They were not calling the shots.

Federal Reserve Chairman Alan Greenspan also weighed in against Fannie and Freddie. In spring 2000, he wrote an open letter to Congressman Richard Baker, urging Congress to consider the potentially destabilizing role of the subsidization of mortgage finance.[86] In subsequent Congressional testimony in 2005, Greenspan argued against the notion that Fannie and Freddie were necessary to promote stability or liquidity in the market. "We have been unable to find any purpose for the huge balance sheets of the GSEs other than profit creation through the exploitation of the market-granted subsidy."[87]

In his testimony, Greenspan referred to Fed research indicating that Fannie's and Freddie's purchases of their own or each other's mortgage-backed securities with their market-subsidized debt did not contribute use-

---

[85] A detailed analysis of the history, structure, governance, and operation of the FHLBs can be found in Flannery and Frame (2006). Advances to members by FHLBs could be quite large and were particularly relied on by major high-risk mortgage lenders that failed during the subprime crisis. For example, Countrywide turned to the Atlanta Federal Home Loan Bank for a total of $51.5 billion in loans during the crisis to keep itself afloat as credit dried up elsewhere. In 2007, the San Francisco FHLB was particularly active, accounting for roughly a third of the whole system's advances. It lent IndyMac $10 billion in advances and Washington Mutual $31 billion.

[86] Greenspan (2000).

[87] Greenspan (2005).

fully to mortgage market liquidity, to the enhancement of capital markets in the United States, or to the lowering of mortgage rates for homeowners.

Greenspan also emphasized that the risks inherent in Fannie and Freddie's implicit government guarantees made it impossible for market discipline to limit their growth, which potentially made the housing market less stable. He worried about the systemic risk being created by the GSEs and called for the establishment of new regulatory authority to limit the growth and risks of the GSEs:

> As I concluded last year, the GSEs need a regulator with authority on a par with banking regulators, with a free hand to set appropriate capital standards, and with a clear and credible process sanctioned by the Congress for placing a GSE in receivership, where the conditions under which debt holders take losses are made clear. However, if legislation takes only these actions and does not limit GSE portfolios, we run the risk of solidifying investors' perceptions that the GSEs are instruments of the government and that their debt is equivalent to government debt. The GSEs will have increased facility to continue to grow faster than the overall home-mortgage market; indeed since their portfolios are not constrained, by law, to exclusively home mortgages, GSEs can grow virtually without limit. Without restrictions on the size of GSE balance sheets, we put at risk our ability to preserve safe and sound financial markets in the United States, a key ingredient of support for homeownership.[88]

Richard Carnell, assistant secretary of the treasury for financial institutions in the Clinton administration, also argued for reining in Fannie and Freddie. In 2001, he pointed out that "the perceived implicit backing" enjoyed by Fannie and Freddie "tends to impart a greater net subsidy [from taxpayers] than explicit federal deposit insurance." He went on to note that the "perceived implicit backing of GSEs has no limits"; that "no credible, workable receivership mechanism exists [to wind down] Fannie and Freddie"; and that the GSEs "reap the benefits of special company-specific laws and avoid the discipline of generic law."[89]

Robert Seiler, a government economist who analyzed the implied subsidies of Fannie and Freddie at the Congressional Budget Office and par-

[88] Greenspan (2005).
[89] Carnell (2001), 62–71.

ticipated in their regulation at the Office of Federal Housing Enterprise Oversight, questioned whether taxpayers were deriving significant benefits from subsidizing the GSEs, especially given that Fannie Mae and Freddie Mac were "tacitly colluding" in the market for securitizing conforming fixed-rate mortgages. Seiler concluded that much of the government's subsidy to Fannie and Freddie was passed to their own stockholders rather than to homeowners in the form of lower mortgage interest rates.[90]

There were also attacks on Fannie and Freddie from the left of the political spectrum. One of the most damning (and prescient) of these came from Ralph Nader, whom we quote at length:

> These enterprises have swiftly and skillfully managed to pick up the roughshod tactics of the private corporate world and at the same time cling tightly to one of the federal government's deepest and most lucrative welfare troughs. The combination has produced two government-sponsored enterprises that are not only too big to be allowed to fail but perhaps too influential and too publicly connected to be regulated or shaped effectively in the public interest. Any suggestion that their power be limited or that subsidies be reduced triggers an immediate no-holds-barred counterattack from Fannie and Freddie. As John Buckley, Fannie Mae's vice president for communications, bluntly told the *Wall Street Journal,* "We're not casual about managing our political risk." . . . Fannie and Freddie are extremely skilled at playing the heart strings to the fullest about America's love affair with home-ownership. Rarely does a Fannie Mae newspaper advertisement appear . . . without emphasis on . . . "helping families achieve the American Dream." . . . Letting any industry—exalted missions notwithstanding—climb on a self-constructed pedestal and remain exempt from serious independent inquiry is foreign to a market economy and a democratic system of government. Such exemptions from normal checks and balances can also be quite expensive for taxpayers.[91]

Friends in High Places

One reason that these critiques fell on deaf ears was that Fannie and Freddie made a huge effort to attract powerful allies within the Republican

[90] Seiler (2001), 25.
[91] Nader (2001), 110.

Party. One was House Speaker Newt Gingrich, who ultimately received more than $1.6 million in consulting fees from Freddie Mac after leaving Congress in 1999. As a *New York Times* article by Eric Lichtblau describes, Gingrich "aligned himself with Freddie and Fannie on a number of key issues—defending them in Congress against political attacks, joining with them on housing projects, and seeing top aides go work for them. While Mr. Gingrich has minimized his past connections to the two closely related companies on the [2012] campaign trail, his Congressional record shows that his political and financial ties to the firms run deeper and farther back than he has acknowledged publicly and, in fact, set the stage for the lucrative consulting work that followed."[92] Indeed, Lichtblau's article points out that it was not just Gingrich who went to work for Freddie Mac after he left Congress: Fannie Mae hired Arne L. Christenson, Gingrich's chief of staff, as a top executive and lobbyist in 1999.

The efforts of Fannie and Freddie to "manage political risk" went well beyond their relationship with Gingrich. Between 1998 and 2008, Fannie spent $79.5 million and Freddie spent $94.9 million on lobbying Congress, making them the twentieth and thirteenth biggest spenders on lobbying during that period. Fannie Mae also established 55 "partnership offices" in the districts and states of important lawmakers. As a 2005 *Fortune* magazine article explained, these offices were "frequently staffed by ex-politicos (Bob Simpson, who heads the South Dakota office, was an aide

---

[92] Lichtblau (2012) goes on to point out that

in a showdown critical to the companies' fortunes, Mr. Gingrich played an important behind-the-scenes role in helping block a proposal in 1995 that would have forced Fannie and Freddie—rather than taxpayers—to pay potentially billions of dollars in increased fees, according to interviews and press accounts at the time. At the time, Representative Jim Leach, a senior Republican from Iowa who led the House banking committee and was a fierce critic of Fannie and Freddie, wanted the companies to pay the bulk of about $4.8 billion to finance a reserve for ailing savings and loan institutions. . . . "Newt was quite a pragmatist," said a Republican official who was involved in the fee increase debate and spoke on the condition of anonymity to avoid becoming embroiled in the current Republican race. In coming to the defense of Freddie and Fannie, Mr. Gingrich "was going with the consensus of his party—of both parties, really," the official said. [Gingrich's] visit to a Belfast neighborhood in 1998 to start building a home for a low-income family was part of a foreign extension of an American program called "The House that Congress Built." The Belfast project was sponsored principally by Fannie and Freddie, along with Habitat for Humanity and the National Association of Realtors. The Realtors' association called the housing project "a truly unique partnership" between lawmakers and the housing industry.

to Democratic Senate leader Tom Daschle, for instance)." The opening of a partnership office was often accompanied "by an announcement that Fannie's American Communities Fund [ACF] will make an investment in a high-impact local project."[93] A HUD investigation into these offices found that "the activities of the partnership offices were not confined to affordable housing initiatives. . . . Rather, a central purpose of the Partnership Offices was to engage in activities that were primarily designed to obtain access to or influence members of Congress." ACF projects were disproportionately located in the home districts of House and Senate lawmakers who sat on the banking committees that oversaw Fannie or the subcommittees that funded its federal regulator.[94]

Fannie and Freddie also worked directly with politicians, making sure that they could trumpet high-visibility community development projects in their districts or states. For example, one of the GSEs' most ardent supporters in Congress, Senator Charles Schumer of New York, put out a press release dated November 20, 2006, and headlined: "Schumer Announces up to $100 Million Freddie Mac Commitment to Address Fort Drum and Watertown Housing Crunch." The heading continues: "Schumer Unveils New Freddie Mac Plan with HSBC That Includes Low-Interest Low-Downpayment Loans. In June, Schumer Urged Freddie Mac and Fannie Mae Step Up to the Plate and Deliver Concrete Plans—Today Freddie Mac Is Following Through."[95]

Fannie and Freddie were also not shy about assisting their allies with political campaign donations and grants for academic research that supported their business model. For the 2000–2008 election cycles, Fannie, Freddie, and their employees contributed more than $14.6 million to the campaign funds of dozens of senators and representatives, especially those who held key positions on congressional committees charged with overseeing them.[96] Some of the top recipients of contributions included Senator Christopher Dodd, Representative Barney Frank, Senator Barack Obama, Senator Joseph Biden, and Senator Charles Schumer. Fannie and Freddie also fought back against academic critics who sounded the alarm about their political deals and the economic risks that those deals entailed. In fact, in his role as a senior vice president for Fannie, Arne Christenson

[93] McLean (2005).
[94] Associated Press (2005). See also Common Cause (2008).
[95] Common Cause (2008).
[96] Wallison and Calomiris (2009).

launched a series called the "Fannie Mae Papers," paying for studies by eminent scholars that supported the view that the probability of default by Fannie or Freddie was extremely small.[97]

Countrywide and Friends

Fannie and Freddie had one additional source of support: mortgage originators who saw the GSE mandates as a business opportunity. The three largest of these were Countrywide Financial, Wells Fargo, and Washington Mutual.[98] Their basic business model was to originate mortgages under the new underwriting standards, sell or securitize them, and earn fee income on the transactions. Mortgage originators pursuing this strategy were swallowing up their smaller competitors and originating vast quantities of mortgages, many of which they sold to Fannie and Freddie. The growth in the GSEs' high-risk mortgage lending was achieved mainly by partnering with a very small number of very large banks: 93 percent of the $4.5 trillion in post-1995 CRA commitments reported by the National Community Reinvestment Coalition came from just four banks—Bank of America, Citibank, JPMorgan Chase, and Wells Fargo—and the various banks with whom they had merged, which included the origination giants Countrywide and Washington Mutual.[99]

Once the Game of Bank Bargains had created a huge mortgage industry to intermediate government-subsidized risk in the mortgage market, that industry began to play an active role in the political coalition supporting government subsidization of mortgage risk. Mortgage-industry firms increased their campaign contributions to Congress sharply around 2000. One study found that campaign contributions had an increasingly powerful influence on congressional representatives' voting behavior on housing-finance legislation. Campaign contributions had a significant effect on roughly 20 percent of the mortgage-finance-related votes in 2003–04; in contrast, only 3 percent of mortgage-finance-related votes seem to have been affected by contributions in 1995–96.[100]

---

[97] Hagerty (2012), 113.
[98] Acharya et al. (2011), 73.
[99] Pinto (2011), 173.
[100] Mian, Sufi, and Trebbi (2010a). Related studies that find similar evidence of the political power of mortgage-related lobbying include Igan, Mishra, and Tressel (2009);

Given the growing strength of the coalition in favor of subsidizing risky mortgage lending, it should not come as a surprise that when Republican president George W. Bush came into office in 2000, he did not change course on housing-finance subsidies. Indeed, he embraced the Clinton policies, and, as figure 7.3 shows, actually increased the affordable-housing mandates that Clinton had imposed on Fannie and Freddie: low- and moderate-income loans grew to account for 56 percent of all Fannie and Freddie lending, special affordable loans 27 percent, and underserved 39 percent. While, again, these were overlapping categories, taken as a group they suggest that by 2008, something on the order of 80 percent of Fannie or Freddie mortgage purchases in the secondary market were likely in one of the mandated categories.[101]

Underlying this decision was pure politics, as revealed by a June 2002 trip that Bush made to Atlanta to unveil his "blueprint for the American Dream" in a predominantly African American church. At that meeting he announced the goal of raising the number of minority homeowners by 5.5 million by 2010.[102] Later, in explaining how he would achieve this goal, the Republican president made his strategy clear: "I am proud to report that Fannie Mae has heard the call, and, as I understand, it's about $440 billion over a period of time. They've used their influence to create that much capital available for the type of homeowner we're talking about here. It's in their charter; it now needs to be implemented. Freddie Mac is interested in helping. I appreciate both of those agencies providing the underpinnings of good capital."[103]

The State of the Housing Finance Market
Just before the Bubble Burst

What then was the state of the American housing finance market as of 2006–07? A few salient facts paint a picture of a very fragile system. In figure 7.6 we provide estimates of the size of America's high-risk mortgage market. Following Acharya and colleagues, we define *high-risk* as includ-

---

Mian, Sufi, and Trebbi (2010b); Epstein, O'Halloran, and McAllister (2010); and Romer and Weingast (1991).

[101] Pinto (2011), 87.

[102] McLean and Nocera (2010), 168.

[103] Quoted in Rajan (2010), 35–36.

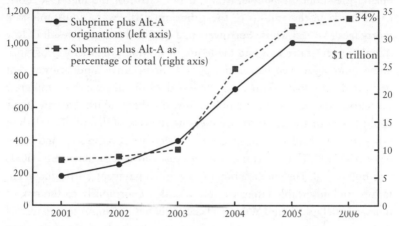

Subprime plus Alt-A mortgage originations (billions of dollars)

Subprime plus Alt-A mortgage originations, as percentage of all mortgage lending

FIGURE 7.6 High-risk mortgage originations, U.S. market, 2001–06.

Source: Acharya et al. (2011), 46.

Note: High-risk mortgages are defined as subprime plus Alt-A mortgages.

ing both subprime and Alt-A mortgages.[104] These high-risk loan categories were virtually nonexistent until the late 1990s.[105] In 2001, new high-risk mortgages totaled $180 billion and accounted for 8 percent of total new mortgage lending. Three years later, new high-risk mortgages totaled $715 billion and accounted for 24 percent of new mortgage lending. By 2006, new high-risk mortgages equaled $1 trillion and accounted for 36 percent of all new mortgage lending. If we take the sum of these new high-risk mortgages over the period 2001–06, the result is a shocking $3.5 trillion. Pinto and Wallison, using a different method, find that by June 2008 there were approximately 28 million subprime and Alt-A loans outstanding, with a total value of approximately $4.8 trillion. That is to say, roughly half of all mortgages outstanding in mid-2008 were high risk. However it is measured, the subprime bubble was immense.[106]

[104] Acharya et al. (2011) also include home-equity lines of credit as high-risk mortgage loans. In order to produce lower-bound estimates, we do not include these. Had we done so, the percentage of high-risk loans would be even higher than those in figure 7.6.

[105] Acharya et al. (2011), 45.

[106] Pinto and Wallison (2011).

There was a further dimension to the riskiness of mortgage origination during the subprime bubble. Many, if not most, of the high-risk mortgages made in the run-up to the subprime crisis were adjustable-rate mortgages (ARMs) whose borrowers had qualified only as a result of low initial "teaser" rates and had made use of no-docs, high-LTV programs. Some mortgages even had initial periods of negative amortization that permitted early loan payments to be less than the interest due. If interest rates rose, the debt-servicing obligations on these adjustable-rate loans could rise dramatically, further increasing the risk of default. Nearly half (48 percent) of all the mortgages originated in 2004, 2005, and 2006 were ARMs.[107] The percentage of high-risk mortgages that were ARMs was higher still. The combination of low down payments, little documentation, and adjustable interest rates all added enormously to the risk of mortgage default. James Wilcox has constructed a composite measure of these various changes in underwriting standards from 1996 through 2008. Of course, underwriting standards had begun to fall even before 1996, because Fannie and Freddie began to purchase mortgages with only 3 percent down payments in 1994. Even with this downward bias in Wilcox's estimates, he finds that underwriting standards declined steadily from 2002 through 2006. He also finds that the decline had large and statistically significant effects on the volume of mortgages and the run-up in house prices during those years.[108]

Household mortgage debt ballooned as increasing numbers of families took advantage of financing programs that really were too good to be true. In 1996, the ratio of household mortgage debt to GDP was 54 percent. By 2006, it had swelled to 89 percent. That jump of 35 percentage points over a single decade was larger than the entire increase in the ratio of household debt to GDP between 1951 and 1996.[109]

In sum, by the early 2000s weak underwriting standards had become an entitlement available to all mortgage borrowers. What had begun as a step in 1992 to get banks to increase their CRA lending commitments had over time became a set of amazingly lax lending standards that anyone could take advantage of. The result was that millions of American middle-

---

[107] Acharya et al. (2011), 46.
[108] Wilcox (2009).
[109] Acharya et al. (2011), 48.

class families became very highly leveraged. It would not take much to push them into default: they were already teetering on the edge when they bought their homes. All that would have to happen to start a major crisis was for housing prices to stall, for a recession to reduce employment for overindebted new homeowners, or for interest rates to go up a bit. Indeed, many mortgages' interest rates were slated to rise even without action by the Fed; once the adjustable-rate loans made in 2004, 2005, and 2006 began to reset beyond their initial teaser rates, many ARM borrowers were likely to fall behind in their payments.

Conclusion

The transformation and growth of the housing GSEs during the 1990s and 2000s, like the consolidation and transformation of nationwide banks, were the embodiment of a new bargain intermediated by influential politicians. The bargain was struck through the creation of special privileges and responsibilities—CRA agreements and GSE mandates.

The new U.S. banking bargain combined new and unlikely partners. The power of the winning coalition grew over time as powerful actors were added to its core. The coalition began as a rent-sharing game between activist groups and regional banks intent on being granted the right to merge and become national megabanks. Then the GSEs, which initially were reluctant partners, joined the coalition. The participation of the GSEs in subsidizing risky mortgages, and doing so with a highly leveraged financing structure, substantially magnified the stakes of the game. Large swaths of the American middle class were now drawn in, because Fannie and Freddie's low underwriting standards were not an excludable good. Finally, as the efforts of the coalition transformed the nature of mortgage origination, a new interest group of low-quality mortgage originators sought to perpetuate and expand its fee-earning potential from mortgage origination and servicing. Like a hurricane strengthening itself over the open sea, the winning coalition grew in force. It would make landfall in the crisis of 2007–09.

8

||||||||||||||||||||||||

Leverage, Regulatory Failure,
and the Subprime Crisis

If stupidity got us into this mess, why can't it get us out?
Will Rogers

In the previous chapter we explore how an unlikely coalition of megabanks and urban activist groups took shape over roughly two decades
prior to 2007, and we show how that coalition came to control American
housing-finance policies. One secret of its success was its ability to draw
in other unlikely partners, such as the managers and shareholders of Fannie Mae and Freddie Mac, a number of large mortgage originators such
as Countrywide Financial, and influential politicians on both sides of the
aisle.

One of the principal accomplishments of that coalition was to bring
about a dramatic decline in the underwriting standards of Fannie Mae and
Freddie Mac; and those standards, once lowered, *applied to everyone.* As
we discuss in the previous chapter, by 2007, 2 out of every 5 new mortgages granted had a down payment of 3 percent or less. Amazingly, a 2006
survey done by the National Association of Realtors found that 46 percent
of first-time home buyers put down no money at all, and the median first-
time buyer put down only 2 percent of the purchase price.[1] Large parts of
the American middle class were able to take advantage of mortgage underwriting rules that, compared to those of any other country in the world or
to America's own history, were inconceivably lax. The result was the rapid
growth of mortgages with high probabilities of default.

The subprime crisis was not caused solely by weak mortgage underwriting standards. Those standards certainly played a powerful role: they

---

[1] Pinto (2011), 25.

provided fuel for the fire by increasing the riskiness of mortgages. Regulators could have prevented this fuel from igniting into a banking crisis, however, had they required banks and the GSEs to maintain higher capital ratios in their balance sheets, thus avoiding the solvency problems that precipitated the crisis. That is, if prudential regulation had ensured the institutions' safety and soundness, then government housing-finance subsidies would have caused losses to banks and GSEs but not the collapse of financial intermediaries that made the crisis so severe. To continue the firestorm metaphor, if housing-finance policies were the fuel for the subprime crisis, then weak prudential regulation was a hot, dry wind that made that fuel extraordinarily flammable.

It is tempting to think of these two factors—subsidies for mortgage risk and lax prudential regulation—as being completely independent of one another. That view allows the subprime crisis to be seen as the outcome of two disconnected forces that just happened to converge, implying that the probability of recurrence is low. Unfortunately, that would be a misreading of events. Both factors reflected the same underlying political deal that required a tolerance for risk. As we explain below, regulators could have imposed higher capital ratios on banks and GSEs, but doing so would have raised the cost of taking on increased mortgage risk, making lenders less willing to supply risky mortgages. Obviously, then, strong prudential regulation would have subverted the goal of expanding home ownership, which was a central part of the bargain to which big banks, activist groups, GSEs, and politicians were all parties. Simply put, Fannie, Freddie, Citibank, Washington Mutual, and others were not going to continue to buy or securitize trillions of dollars in low-quality mortgages if too much of the capital at stake belonged to their shareholders. They would play only if they could borrow the money, and their creditors lent them the funds only because they believed (correctly) that the debts would be guaranteed by American taxpayers. In particular, the capital standards that were applied to securitizations allowed banks and GSEs to back their mortgage portfolios with especially low proportions of equity capital— roughly two cents on the dollar. Given an environment in which risk-taking with borrowed money was considered normal, it is easy to understand why some bankers, particularly those who were having trouble competing against more efficient rivals, decided that the right strategy was to throw caution to the wind.

We cannot stress this point about the underlying institutional environment strongly enough. Neither the aggressive subsidization of mortgage risk that resulted from federal housing-finance policies and programs nor the costly failure of prudential regulation would have been tolerated by the political system if those two policy choices had not been made *together*, as part of America's peculiar Game of Bank Bargains. This is the central causal claim of this chapter, and it provides an answer to the question posed by Will Rogers at the head of this chapter: it is hard for a society to learn, and thereby overcome the "stupidity" that gives rise to destructive banking crises, if the stupidity is the logical outcome of the self-interested behavior of a powerful coalition.

Regulatory Failure

In order to understand how the failure of prudential regulation contributed to the subprime crisis, we need to consider the logic of bank capital cushions. In post-1990 America, banks and GSEs enjoyed the protection of government safety nets that guaranteed or otherwise reduced the default risk of their debts. Those safety nets took the form of deposit insurance, access to Fed and FHLB lending, implicit guarantees of GSE debts, and implicit too-big-to-fail guarantees of bank debts that were not covered by deposit insurance. These safety nets should be thought of as subsidies: they allowed banks and GSEs to hold less capital and pay lower interest rates on their debts than they would have had to otherwise, because they reduced the risk of default on their debts and weakened the incentives of their creditors to monitor them and demand increases in equity capital.

The value of the subsidies provided by these government safety nets varied according to two criteria, producing some rather perverse incentives. First, the larger the bank or GSE, the larger the value of the safety net, and hence the larger the value of the subsidy. A small bank, one that was not too big to fail, received protection only from the deposit-insurance system. Indeed, in the case of insolvency, it could be taken over by the FDIC, which would guarantee its deposits and then arrange the sale of the bank to a competitor, thereby wiping out the shareholders and perhaps the bank's uninsured creditors.

Second, the more debt that a bank or GSE took on relative to its equity capital, the larger the value of the safety net, and hence the larger the subsidy. A metaphor from the circus perhaps makes the intuition clear: a safety net is not of much value to a high-wire performer if the wire is three feet above the ground. The higher the wire, the higher the value of the net. For a bank or GSE, the higher the leverage, the higher the default risk being borne by the government from protecting the debts. As the value of the safety-net subsidy rose with leverage, so did the share price of the bank or GSE that enjoyed that subsidy: the share price reflected the ability of the bank or GSE to borrow at an artificially low rate compared to the amount it would have had to pay on its debts without the government's backing.[2] Shareholders of banks and GSEs therefore were rewarded by the government safety net for having as little skin in the game as possible. In such a situation, shareholders may choose to maximize their leverage, pay a low rate of interest to their creditors, and then pocket the profits. This is a risky strategy because it is possible that shareholders will end up with nothing (if the value of the bank's assets declines sufficiently), but on average, higher leverage increases the rate of return to shareholders.

Bank and GSE managers that build their business strategy around maximizing the value of their safety-net protection, therefore, do two things: they seek to grow as large as possible, and they do not voluntarily maintain large amounts of equity capital to fund their operations. In short, they look for ways to grow large with borrowed money.

Given the safety nets afforded to big banks and GSEs, their creditors had very weak incentives to demand that shareholders put up more equity capital than the government required. After all, the government was implicitly guaranteeing that debt holders would be repaid, regardless of what happened to the lending institution. The too-big-to-fail protection enjoyed by both the GSEs and the megabanks was even recognized in the bond ratings that their debts received from ratings agencies such as Moody's and Standard and Poor's. If creditors were not going to be the source of discipline for these enterprises, where would it come from?

The only entities that could force the shareholders of banks and GSEs to deploy adequate capital were government regulators. Unfortunately, the government had already set the precedent for low shareholder equity

---

[2] For a theoretical explanation, see Merton (1977). For empirical evidence, related to thrift behavior in the 1980s, see Brewer (1995).

for the GSEs back in 1992, when Fannie and Freddie were first being subjected to regulation as part of the GSE Act. That act not only brought in HUD's low-income lending mandates, it also allowed the GSEs to fund those mandates with a huge proportion of borrowed money. In order to draw reluctant managers and shareholders into the low-income mortgage market, the GSE Act of 1992 specified that Fannie and Freddie had to hold only $2.50 of capital for every $100 of mortgages in their portfolio. They could borrow the other $97.50 at a very low rate of interest, given the generous implicit government guarantee of their debts. At the time, commercial banks were required to hold $4.00 in capital against every $100 in their mortgage portfolios.[3]

Buying mortgages from commercial banks and thrifts was only a part of Fannie's and Freddie's business. They could also purchase mortgages and turn them into mortgage-backed securities (MBSs), and they could then sell these MBSs in the secondary market as being virtually riskless because Fannie and Freddie guaranteed them against default risk on the underlying mortgages. To do so they only needed to set aside 45 cents for every $100 in mortgages as a protection against default risk (a capital buffer to cover possible losses) on these MBSs.[4] In addition to their implicit backing from the U.S. Treasury, Fannie and Freddie also enjoyed huge economies of scale, which gave them the ability to diversify across groups of guaranteed mortgages. The appeal of MBS intermediation is straightforward: it increases the amount of mortgage credit available to potential homeowners. Fannie and Freddie could buy the mortgages made by banks and thrifts, and investors could, in effect, buy those mortgages from Fannie and Freddie (with a guarantee of repayment), thereby allowing Fannie and Freddie to buy more mortgages from banks and thrifts, who could then provide more credit to home buyers.

This structure of housing finance created an opportunity for what economists call regulatory arbitrage. If a commercial bank made a mortgage and held it in its portfolio, it had to hold $4.00 in capital per $100 lent as a capital cushion. But if a bank bought a highly rated mortgage-backed security (produced either by one of the GSEs or by a bank that had securitized the mortgages in an off-balance sheet entity, run by its own origi-

---

[3] For more details, see Acharya et al. (2011), 24–25.
[4] Acharya et al. (2011), 24.

nation department), regulators required it to maintain only $1.60 in capital for every $100 invested.[5] The logic for requiring less capital against AAA-rated mortgage-backed securities than against mortgages themselves was simple: the security enjoyed a guarantee from Fannie, Freddie, or some bank originator, and the value of the guarantee, in turn, reflected the combination of their equity capital and the government guarantees that those intermediaries enjoyed. This meant that, for example, if a bank sold a mortgage to Fannie or Freddie, and then bought the same amount back as a mortgage-backed security, the amount of capital that the entire financial system (banks plus GSEs) had to hold against that mortgage was really only $2.05 for every $100 lent ($1.60 from the bank and the 45 cents for the guarantee of the mortgage from Fannie or Freddie when they created the security).

Regulatory arbitrage did not stop with the purchase of the mortgage-backed security by the bank that originated the mortgage. Mortgages are not all created alike; some borrowers have better credit ratings, higher ratios of income to debt, and larger down payments than others. Securitizing banks could bundle together mortgages of different qualities, creating different classes of mortgage-backed securities (with AAA rated the highest and BBB the lowest). A business soon developed in creating collateralized debt obligations (CDOs). These were entities that acted as conduits, repackaging mortgage-backed securities and debts from other sorts of securitizations, often with low ratings. Mortgage-backed securities became the most important part of the assets of these CDO conduits. The purchases of CDO assets were financed primarily by debt issues. These CDO debts were essentially derivatives of mortgage-backed securities (that is, the value of the CDO debt issues was derived from the value of the mortgage-backed securities they held as assets). CDOs were particularly useful for banks that issued mortgage-backed securities because they allowed them to package less attractive mortgage-backed securities into a "diversified" bundle. The volume of CDOs issued increased dramatically in the early 2000s, rising from $100–150 billion a year in 1998–2004 to $250 billion in 2005 and $500 billion in 2006.[6]

---

[5] For the details on the capital requirements for bank-originated MBSs, see Calomiris (2009).

[6] Calomiris (2009).

Investors in or originators of mortgage-backed securities and CDO debts could also purchase a form of insurance through a vehicle called a credit default swap (CDS)—an innovation pioneered by J. P. Morgan in 1994. This was basically a promise by a bank or insurance company to buy a security at its face value from a counterparty if that security had a "credit-related event," such as a missed interest payment. A CDS insurance contract was judged by regulators to have the same degree of risk as the securities issued by the investment bank or insurance company that had issued the CDS. Thus, if a bank created a CDO conduit that held subprime or Alt-A mortgage-backed securities as its assets but arranged to have a CDS contract with a AAA-rated insurance company to guarantee its CDO debts, *then those CDO debts were treated as having a AAA rating for capital regulatory purposes.*[7]

It is commonly asserted that this alphabet soup of securities—MBSs, CDOs, and CDSs—was created by banks, investment banks, and GSEs in order to take advantage of unsuspecting investors. The banks, it is alleged, were originating junk mortgages and either securitizing the mortgages themselves or shoveling them out the door to GSEs to be held by the GSEs or securitized and resold. There is only one problem with this story: Fannie and Freddie, as well as commercial banks, such as Citibank, Bank of America, and Wells Fargo, and investment banks, such as Goldman Sachs and Lehman Brothers, had portfolios full of mortgage-backed securities as well as derivatives of those securities (CDOs and CDSs).[8] They were creating them not just to sell to neophytes but so that they could hold mortgage risk with lower regulatory capital requirements, thereby raising their rates of return on capital. This is why, when the subprime crisis hit, many large commercial banks and investment banks, as well as Fannie and Freddie, became insolvent: they were stuffed full of their own securities, whose values fell like stones once the underlying mortgages started to default.

Let us be clear: we are not claiming that securitization, per se, caused the subprime crisis. Securities backed by credit-card loans, for example, have operated reasonably well for three decades. Credit-card-based securities continued to be issued until September 2008, when all financial trans-

---

[7] Our discussion of CDOs and CDSs draws from Barth, Caprio, and Levine (2012), 72–73, 91–93.

[8] Acharya et al. (2011), 49.

actions shrank dramatically, but those securities have since recovered. Likewise, securities backed by prime mortgages did not evidence anything like the losses that showed up in the securities backed by subprime mortgage loans. Nor are we saying that the ability of banks to create and trade derivatives of securities, such as CDOs, were responsible for the subprime crisis. Derivatives are essential tools that allow banks and investors, as well as nonfinancial companies, to hedge risk.

We *are* saying, however, that in order for this system of MBSs, CDOs, and CDSs to work, either of two conditions had to hold. Either the underlying asset—the mortgages themselves—really had to be sufficiently low in risk that a small amount of capital was sufficient protection against loss, or someone in the securitization food chain had to be putting up a level of capital appropriate to cover the potential losses. Otherwise defaults on the underlying mortgages would knock the system over like a house of cards: the firms holding those securities would see their (modest) shareholder capital wiped out in order to cover the losses on the securities and derivatives. As it turned out, neither condition held: the underlying mortgage assets were very high risk, and no one in the food chain was putting up sufficient levels of capital to cover the potential losses. For that reason, when the bill came due, it was paid by taxpayers.

Asleep at the Wheel

Why did government regulators—the Fed, the FDIC, the SEC, and the Office of Federal Housing Enterprise Oversight (OFHEO)—allow the institutions that participated in the market for mortgage-backed securities and their derivatives to put up inadequate capital cushions? Why did they not require the participants to put more of their shareholders' capital at risk rather than taxpayers' wealth?

The reasons for the inadequate capital ratios of the GSEs (the lowest of any regulated financial institutions) are explained in chapter 7: they were the outcome of political bargaining. In essence, the GSEs accepted new mandates to subsidize mortgages for the urban poor in exchange for larger government safety-net subsidies that resulted from low capital requirements and weak regulatory oversight.[9]

---

[9] OFHEO was established in 1992 by the Federal Housing Enterprises Financial Safety and Soundness Act of 1992. OFHEO's regulatory powers were much more lim-

What about the banks? It is often asserted that the lack of prudential oversight on the part of the Fed, the FDIC, and the SEC was caused by "deregulation." Let us clear up that misconception. The U.S. banking market certainly did undergo a process of deregulation that stretched from the late 1970s to the late 1990s, as state governments and the federal government gradually knocked down the barriers that had prevented banks from opening branches either within states or across state lines. The interest-rate caps that prevented banks from competing against one another for deposits, and which had therefore chased deposits out of the banking system during the high-inflation 1970s, were also phased out. Finally, the federal government removed the restrictions that had separated commercial banking from investment banking since the Great Depression.

None of these steps, however, weakened *prudential* regulation—the role played by regulators and supervisors in ensuring the safe operation of the banking system and securities markets. In fact, the reforms that allowed banks to branch both within and across state lines actually made the banking system more stable by permitting banks to spread risk across regions. In a similar vein, the 1999 reform that allowed commercial bank holding companies to maintain investment-banking subsidiaries mitigated the cost of the subprime crisis once it hit. It allowed the orderly acquisitions of Merrill Lynch and Bear Stearns by Bank of America and JPMorgan Chase, respectively, once those investment banks became insolvent. It also permitted Goldman Sachs and Morgan Stanley to convert into commercial bank holding companies in 2008, giving them greater access to the government safety net.[10]

---

ited than those of the Fed or the FDIC. For a discussion of the politics of OFHEO's weak powers, see Hagerty (2012), 85–95, and Rajan (2010), 35.

[10] Investment banks actually experienced *increased* regulation in the years prior to the subprime crisis. In response to pressures from European regulators, U.S. regulators agreed in 2002 that investment banks would abide by Basel standards, and it subjected them for the first time to that system of risk-based capital regulation. Furthermore, many new prudential regulations, particularly with respect to securitization, were promulgated in the 2000s. Some academics mistakenly claim that the subprime crisis was caused by an SEC rule change that allowed the investment banks to increase their leverage ratios in 2004, but this is not correct. The leverage ratios of large investment banks were actually higher before the rule change than after it, so the rule change could not have caused an increase in leverage (see McLean [2012]).

The problem was not a lack of regulation, just piles and piles of ineffectual regulation. The capital levels for commercial banks were initially set at $4 for every $100 in mortgage loans, in accordance with the international Basel capital standards that were set in 1988.[11] The capital levels for Fannie and Freddie—$2.50 for every $100 in mortgage loans held, and $0.45 for mortgage guarantees—were established in 1992. All of these capital requirements were established in the context of a housing-finance market with 20 percent down payments and fixed rate, 30-year mortgages that were held by banks in their own portfolios. No one imagined a world of no-money-down, no-docs, negatively amortizing ARMs. They also could not have imagined a world in which Fannie and Freddie accounted for half the mortgage market, and 80 percent of mortgages were securitized (which reduced their effective capital adequacy ratios by half, to $2.05 for every $100). They might already have understood that some banks had too-big-to-fail protection, but from the vantage point of 1988 or 1992, observers certainly could not have imagined the explosive growth of a small group of megabanks with trillions of dollars in assets. To give some sense of proportion, as of this writing, the Bank of America operates more than 5,000 branches across all 50 states and is among the five largest corporations (measured by total revenue) in the United States (only Walmart, General Electric, and a few oil companies are larger). But in 1988, when commercial-bank capital-adequacy ratios for home mortgages were established, the Bank of America was a California-only operation and had actually been shedding branches and subsidiaries over the previous several years.

Did the Fed, the FDIC, and the SEC (which had prudential regulatory authority over investment banks as of 2002) fail to see these immense changes in the housing-finance market and the risks they implied? Or did they see these changes and risks but lack the power to do anything about them? The answer to both questions is a solid no. Our colleagues James Barth, Gerard Caprio, and Ross Levine have looked into this question in considerable detail and have concluded that these "financial guardians" failed to perform the essential task of controlling risk by protected banks

---

[11] As the Basel standards evolved, and as U.S. regulations changed, the amount of capital required against mortgages or MBSs changed. For large banks, it was increasingly determined by the banks' own modeling of the risks attendant to these assets. See Calomiris (2009), especially 45 n. 19.

despite ample warning signs of problems that were building in the banking system and despite ample power to intervene. Prudential regulators had the authority to increase banks' capital requirements and to limit their investments in risky assets. In fact, over time, with the adoption of the revised Basel II system of risk measurement, large banks and investment banks enjoyed the benefit of rule changes that allowed them effectively to decide for themselves the appropriate level of their capital cushion, based on their own mathematical models.[12] Regulators, of course, retained the power to reject banks' measures of their own risks or to impose higher minimum capital ratio requirements for a given level of risk, but they did not do so.

Making a Bad Situation Worse

Did policy makers and regulators do *anything?* Actually, they did; they made a bad situation worse. First, they effectively subcontracted the work of regulation to private firms—the ratings agencies, such as Moody's, Fitch, and Standard and Poor's, who were in the business of evaluating corporate debt securities. Second, they took steps to undermine whatever weak incentives those agencies had to provide accurate ratings. Third, Fed monetary policy shifted the incentives of home buyers in the direction of taking even greater risks. By themselves, these steps were not enough to have created the firestorm that was the subprime crisis, but in the context of America's housing-finance policies and weak prudential regulation, they amounted to three more logs thrown on the fire.

Subcontracting Regulation to the Ratings Agencies

In order for a bank to purchase a mortgage-backed security or a CDO and treat it as a AAA-rated asset that required limited amounts of capital as a cushion, it needed a ratings agency to certify that it was a AAA security. To do so, the agency had to be designated by the SEC as a Nationally Recognized Statistical Rating Organization (NRSRO), a category created by the SEC in 1975. An oligopoly quickly developed: Moody's, Fitch, and Standard and Poor's soon controlled about 90 percent of the world market for securities ratings.

---

[12] Barth, Caprio, and Levine (2012), chapter 4.

The NRSRO business model had a conflict of interest baked into it. Issuers of mortgage-backed securities and CDOs cared about the ratings those securities received because the buyers of the securities were all regulated intermediaries, such as banks, insurance companies, pensions, and mutual funds. All of those buyers stood to gain from ratings that underestimated risk, because better ratings meant lower capital requirements for the banks and insurance companies that held those debts and more favorable treatment (with respect to suitability regulations, which limit the amounts of various types of investments that may be held by a pension fund). Issuers would ask all three NRSROs to inform them in advance how their securities would be rated (a process known as ratings shopping) and would drop the NRSROs that offered the least favorable rating.[13]

In order to produce inflated ratings of subprime-related securities, the ratings agencies employed risk models that were deeply and observably flawed.[14] They were based on two key assumptions that are almost laughable: that an absence of income or employment documentation was not associated with higher levels of mortgage default risk, and that house prices could *never* fall. The models employed housing-price stress tests based on the experience of the previous ten years. This meant that as late as 2007, modelers relied on trends in housing prices during only a single recession (the 2001 downturn) in order to estimate the potential fall in house prices during any future economic downturn. The 2001 recession was unique, however, with respect to housing prices: it was the only recession in U.S. history in which housing-price growth was sharply positive.[15]

---

[13] It is sometimes argued that the fact that securitizers paid for the ratings inherently made the ratings too favorable. That is not correct: if buyers of securities had wanted accurate ratings, they would have penalized ratings shopping rather than rewarding it (Calomiris [2009]). Just as it is irrelevant for the price of a good whether the consumer or the shopkeeper "pays" the sales tax to the government, it is irrelevant who pays the ratings fee. What is relevant is that the ultimate demand for debased ratings, which came from the regulatory treatment of the buy side of the market, drove ratings shopping. For early evidence on ratings inflation and its connection to regulation, see Cantor and Packer (1994).

[14] For more details, see Mason and Rosner (2007a,b).

[15] In point of fact, even a significant probability of a flattening of house prices posed great risks for subprime mortgages, because the assumption of low default risk for risky loans was dependent on continued house appreciation to prevent losses on foreclosure. The ratings agencies did notice the problem, but they did not react to it very

In short, the models worked from the assumption that any future recession would not cause a fall in housing prices, even though the long-term history of American housing prices—not to mention an immense body of economic theory—strongly indicated otherwise.

Institutional investors and regulators were well aware of the deficiencies of these models. For example, as of December 2005, data published by Moody's on Baa-rated CDOs (lower quality than top-rated securities, but still "investment grade") showed that that these debts had a 20 percent rate of default, on average, over the five years from the date of origination. Moody's also published data on Baa-rated corporate securities, which experienced only a 2 percent probability of default, on average, over the five years from origination. Any first-year business-school student could understand what that meant: despite the claimed uniformity of the rating scales, a CDO was 10 times as risky as a similarly rated corporate debt.[16] Barth, Caprio, and Levine sum up the accuracy of the ratings as follows: "Any financial professional protesting that they purchased AAA-rated mortgage securities because they were convinced they were safe instruments either was disingenuous or not paying attention, arguably because they were blinded by the high pay they received in exchange for not questioning the ratings."[17]

An action by the U.S. government in 2006 made this situation even worse than it already was. The concern, unbelievably, was that some of the ratings agencies were being too conservative in their ratings of mortgage-backed securities. Under pressure from the ratings agency that was providing the most inflated ratings on mortgage-backed securities, and other vested interests, legislation was passed that prodded the SEC to propose "anti-notching" regulations that made it easier for sponsors to avoid the

---

much. In December 2006 Fitch correctly predicted that "the sensitivity of sub-prime performance to the rate of HPA [home price appreciation] and the large number of borrowers facing scheduled payment increases in 2007 should continue to put negative pressure on the sector. Fitch expects delinquencies to rise by at least an additional 50% from current levels throughout the next year and for the general ratings environment to be negative, as the number of downgrades is expected to outnumber the number of upgrades." Nevertheless, it was not until the middle of 2007 that these serious problems were reflected in significant (albeit still inadequate) changes in modeling assumptions by the ratings agencies. Calomiris (2009), 14.

[16] Calomiris (2009), 17.

[17] Barth, Caprio, and Levine (2012), 69.

opinions of uncooperative ratings agencies.[18] Because a CDO was a derivative of a pool of other securities that had already been rated, ratings agencies evaluating the debts of a CDO were implicitly being asked to re-rate the MBSs and other securities that were the assets of a CDO conduit. When asked to rate a CDO that contained subprime MBSs, Moody's, say, would offer either to rate the underlying MBSs from scratch or to "notch" (adjust by ratings downgrades) the ratings that had been given by, say, Fitch. The anti-notching rules that were passed in 2006, if they had been implemented, would essentially have forced each agency rating CDOs to accept the ratings of the assets of the CDO that had been provided by other agencies, without adjustment.

Although the anti-notching requirement was not implemented—because the implementing regulations were still being drafted as the subprime crisis erupted—it was important for two reasons. First, it shows how far the Congress and the Bush administration were willing to go to encourage risk taking in the mortgage market. Second, because it signaled policy makers' preferences, it probably had an immediate effect on the behavior of the ratings agencies in 2006. It constituted an attack on any remaining conservatism within the ratings industry: trying to swim against the tide of ratings inflation would put a ratings agency at risk of running afoul of the SEC. In effect, Congress was forcing the more conservative ratings agencies to adopt the opinions of the least conservative.

The Fed and Its Monetary Policy

The Fed does more than regulate banks. It also sets America's monetary policy, and it does so largely by adjusting the federal funds rate, the rate of interest paid by banks on overnight loans to one another. The Fed raises and lowers its target fed funds rate in order to manage "aggregate demand," which in turn is related to the level of employment and the rate of inflation. Stanford economist John Taylor famously invented a formula—appropriately named the Taylor Rule—that estimates the monetary policy "reaction function" of the Fed—that is, how the Fed has set the federal funds rate in reaction to the condition of the economy.

Taylor and other economists have pointed out that, compared to its previous behavior, from 2002 to 2005 the Fed ran an extraordinarily loose

---

[18] Calomiris (2009), 19.

monetary policy.[19] According to the Taylor Rule, if the Fed had been behaving the way it did in the prior two decades, the federal funds rate should have been, on average, about 2 percentage points higher in the years 2002–05.[20] Fed officials have offered many explanations for the looseness of monetary policy during these years, and it is beyond our scope to evaluate whether the organization was justified in this aggressive, discretionary departure from the Taylor Rule.

One thing seems clear: the Fed should have anticipated and taken into account one of the main predictable consequences of the hyper-loose monetary policy of 2002–05, namely the lower pricing of risk. Financial historians have documented across many countries and many years the tendency for risk "spreads" (the amount of interest charged in excess of the risk-free rate of interest to compensate for bearing risk) to decline when central banks loosen monetary policy.[21] Financial economists have shown that the phenomenon of declining risk spreads applies to a wide variety of financial instruments, including stocks, bonds, and bank loans. When the real federal funds rate falls, the spreads demanded by equity investors, bondholders, and banks all predictably fall as well.[22] In the mortgage market, a loose monetary policy makes banks more likely to fund risky mortgages and consumers more likely to borrow funds to buy houses that they cannot really afford. Taylor and other economists have therefore argued that loose monetary policy played an important role in the subprime crisis: if risk seems cheap, then people and banks will take on a lot more of it.[23]

---

[19] See J. Taylor (2009). Simpler gauges of monetary policy also imply loose monetary policy. The "real" fed funds rate—the nominal federal funds rate less expected inflation, as gauged by market surveys—measures how low interest rates are after adjusting for changes in purchasing power. Higher expected inflation reduces the real rate because borrowers expect to pay back their loans with cheaper future dollars. From 2002 to 2005, the real fed funds rate was persistently negative, implying an interbank cost of funds that let borrowers profit from borrowing, even if they only invested the borrowed funds in a bundle of commodities and stored them for subsequent sale! The only other time that the real fed funds rate was negative for four consecutive years was 1975–78, the high-water mark of the "great inflation" of the 1960s and 1970s.

[20] See Calomiris (2009).

[21] Bordo (2007); Bordo and Wheelock (2007, 2009).

[22] See Dell'Ariccia, Igan, and Laeven (2012); Jiménez et al. (2007); Altunbas et al. (2009); and Bekaert, Hoerova, and Lo Duca (2010).

[23] See Taylor (2009).

It seems likely that loose monetary policy contributed to the fire-storm that had already been ignited by housing-finance policies and weak prudential regulation. But monetary policy alone could not have caused the crisis. First of all, loose monetary policy did not begin until 2002; the initial growth of mortgage risk and the decline in prudential regulatory standards predated it. Loose monetary policy would not have been quite so dangerous for the housing-finance market had there not already been a deterioration in underwriting standards that began in 1994. (In this regard, we note that the effects of loose monetary policy should affect all risky assets, but the crisis of 2007–09 originated in the mortgage market, not in other forms of securitized consumer debt, such as credit cards, which did not see a deterioration in their underwriting standards.) Second, the danger posed by loose monetary policy for the mortgage market could have been contained had the Fed realized its effects and forced banks to maintain higher levels of capital—something that, as we have already discussed, it did not do. Finally, when one looks at historical and international banking crises, loose monetary policy generally is not a sufficient condition for producing a banking crisis of the severity of the subprime crisis. Monetary policy can lead to the over-pricing of risky assets, which can promote bubbles and crashes in stock and real estate markets, but banking crises require more: namely, a decision by banks to invest in those risky assets and to back them with insufficient capital. The United States saw a residential real-estate price boom and bust in the 1920s, but it did not result in a banking crisis for the simple reason that mortgages had high down payments and banks had high capital ratios.[24]

Hear No Evil, See No Evil

Regulatory policy failures were not confined to inaction prior to the crisis; as events unfolded, regulators were also slow to take action that would have limited the systemic consequences of the mortgage losses. The subprime crisis unfolded over a long period, from the spring of 2007 through the fall of 2008, at which point the debt markets on which the banking system depended ceased to function normally, and the government finally intervened aggressively to prevent systemwide failures.

[24] E. White (forthcoming).

Market participants certainly saw a growing risk of a systemic crisis: over the two years prior to the September 2008 collapse, at the large U.S. financial institutions that required intervention in the fall of 2008, the ratio of the market value to the book value of their equity declined persistently.[25] There was ample opportunity for banks to issue new shares in order to recapitalize themselves and for regulators to require them to do so. Indeed, the equity market was wide open; global banks had raised nearly $450 billion in capital from September 2007 to September 2008.[26] Merrill Lynch, Citibank, Lehman, AIG, and other big U.S. banks chose, however, not to replace their lost equity through new offerings. They apparently hoped that equity prices would rise, allowing them to become recapitalized with less dilution of existing stockholders. They also appear to have believed (correctly, with the significant exception of Lehman) that they had too-big-to-fail protection. Why go to the markets to raise new capital when you are confident that the government is going to bail you out?

Once the losses from the big banks' mortgage investments started to become obvious, regulators and supervisors could have intervened. They could have forced the banks to recognize losses sooner and go to the market to acquire more capital.[27] Once again, however, they effectively sat on the sidelines, watching the crisis unfold before their eyes.

Delayed action by regulators and supervisors in response to bank losses has been quite common worldwide over the past three decades. In government-protected banking systems, not only are regulators very forgiving about regulatory enforcement prior to crises (for the politically motivated reasons we have already reviewed), but they are also very slow to force banks to deal with their loan losses when crises arise. Forcing banks to recapitalize themselves tends to further contract the supply of credit in the short term. This may reduce the probability of a financial meltdown, but short-term credit contractions also have economic and political costs, especially when an election is near.[28]

---

[25] Calomiris and Herring (2012).

[26] Calomiris (2009).

[27] Calomiris and Herring (2012).

[28] For more on U.S. forbearance during the subprime crisis, see Barth, Caprio, and Levine (2012); Calomiris and Herring (2012); and McCarty, Poole, and Rosenthal (2013), 10–11, 22. For cross-country evidence, see Calomiris, Klingebiel, and Laeven (2005) and Brown and Dinc (2005).

In the case of the subprime crisis, it is easy to see why regulators were willing to forbear and hope for the best: any action to force banks and GSEs to raise capital in 2007 and early 2008 would not only have created a short-term credit crunch, it would also have had far-reaching consequences for the entire supply chain of mortgage credit and the powerful political coalition that had constructed it. America's post-1990 Game of Bank Bargains led to low capital requirements in mortgage finance as a result of the deals that had to be made at the time of the GSE Act of 1992. Once those bargains were struck, allowing Fannie and Freddie to back mortgages that they acquired with lower levels of capital than those that prevailed in the commercial banking industry and allowing them to guarantee mortgages with even lower levels of capital, the die was cast. Regulatory arbitrage and the various avant-garde financial innovations soon followed. It would have taken a brave regulator, indeed, to try to force the unraveling of this Gordian knot.

If there had been a serious effort by the Fed, the FDIC, or the SEC to increase the levels of prudential capital or the degree of regulatory oversight of ratings agencies, what would have been the likely response? Commercial banks, investment banks, GSEs, and ratings agencies would have fought tooth and nail to retain the low capital requirements that afforded them high rates of return. The battle over prudential capital regulation would have been public and ugly. And before any of us becomes too self-righteous about regulatory failure, ask yourself this: if you had been a prospective homeowner, how would you have reacted to the prospect of mortgage rates rising in 2006 or 2007 as a consequence of aggressive actions by regulators? Regulators are aware of the political environment in which they operate.

From the point of view of regulators before the summer of 2008, it was easier to look the other way rather than get dragged into a bloody fight. Indeed, all the instances in which they had already looked the other way—gone along to get along—would be marshaled by the commercial banks, the investment banks, the GSEs, and the ratings agencies as evidence that demands for increased prudential capital *now* were capricious and hypocritical: if what we did before was okay, and you said it was okay, then how can you say that it is not okay now? The choice before regulators, in this light, was easy: they could get into a fight that they might well lose, or they could tolerate what was taking place and then let taxpayers pay for the cleanup.

The incentives of the Fed to look the other way may have been particularly strong. As political scientists often point out, delegation of power to regulators can be used intentionally as a way to make the enforcement of rules more prone to political influence, if the regulators are subject to the pressure of interest groups.[29] Why would the Fed be perceived as more willing than other bank regulators to avoid upsetting the applecart of political bargains? As critics have noted, the Fed regards monetary-policy independence as its primary concern and is always worried about potential encroachment by Congress or the administration that could threaten that independence. According to this view, the Fed seeks to expand its regulatory power to enhance its monetary independence, and Congress grants the Fed regulatory powers because it knows that the Fed will not jeopardize its monetary independence by fighting with key members of Congress or the president over regulatory policy.[30]

The history of the expansion of the Fed's purview is consistent with this analysis. The Federal Reserve Board's role as regulator of bank consolidation began in the 1930s, when it was charged with regulating bank "groups and chains," which later evolved into the entities known as bank holding companies. In the 1930s, the Fed was the obvious choice for the task because it was the only actor capable of assembling the information necessary to enforce the new rules arising from Glass-Steagall and other acts.[31] Fed regulation of bank holding companies then grew over time. During the merger wave of the 1990s, the Fed (rather than the Justice Department, which is charged with enforcing antitrust laws) was assigned the central role in approving bank acquisitions and mergers. The Fed was also named the dominant prudential regulator, instead of the Office of the Comptroller of the Currency, the FDIC, or some newly created regulator, and this role grew over time.[32] In 1999, under the Gramm-Leach-Bliley Act, the Fed became the "umbrella regulator" with special overarching regulatory authority.

[29] McCarty, Poole, and Rosenthal (2013), 10–11, 22; O'Halloran and McAllister (2012).

[30] Hawke (1988); Calomiris (2006, 2010a).

[31] Calomiris (2013).

[32] As Calomiris (2006) shows, in the last decades of the twentieth century, many countries moved away from allowing their monetary authorities to also act as the main regulators of their banking systems.

Why Didn't All Banks Take the Plunge?

Just because it was possible for a bank to ride the housing finance bubble by taking huge risks with insufficient capital does not mean that it had to do so. Bankers faced a choice: they could try to make money the old-fashioned way, by seeking out high-quality lending and other financial opportunities and then matching the level of risk they were taking to an appropriate capital cushion; or they could take wild risks by exploiting a weak regulatory environment and a generous government safety net. In fact, not all banks took the wild risks that the GSEs, Washington Mutual, Citibank, Bear Stearns, and others chose.[33] What led other banks to sit out the subprime lending binge?

To put this question in the context of the housing-finance market, consider two hypothetical bankers, Banker A and Banker B. Both bankers had to make at least some risky mortgage originations because of government housing-finance mandates, but Banker A, being prudent, minimized that activity, by choosing to sell those mortgages to Fannie or Freddie, and then redeploying the funds to sounder investments. Banker B, on the other hand, chose to originate lots of subprime mortgages, securitized them through Fannie, Freddie, or an investment bank, and then held those same mortgages as MBSs, meaning that they could now be backed with much less capital than the original mortgages.

As with many choices in life, Banker B might have been encouraged to make the high-risk choice by having a set of strategic options inferior to those of Banker A. In order to make a profit following Banker A's example, Banker B would need to match Banker A in terms of the quality of his management personnel and operational efficiency. In the jargon of financial economics, his bank would need to have the same "franchise value" as Banker A's. In the absence of a high franchise value, the real choice facing Banker B was shrinking his business (because he would lose in a head-to-head competition with Banker A) or adopting a strategy that would

---

[33] It is important to emphasize that the banks focusing on these risks knew that they were doing so. As Ellul and Yerramilli (2010) show, banks with higher losses were also perceived as riskier by the market before the crisis and maintained lower investments in risk management. Igan, Mishra, and Tressel (2012) show that the banks that built their businesses around risky mortgage lending also spent more on lobbying for lax regulation of mortgages.

allow him to earn a high rate of return by taking greater risks and relying on government safety net subsidies to bolster his inferior franchise. By exploiting the value of the safety-net subsidy, Banker B could create as much stock value and earnings as Banker A. Of course, stock in Bank B would be a much riskier investment, but that might be the best Banker B could do for his shareholders, given a lower franchise value. Even if this was not the best arrangement for the stockholders, the high earnings and high stock price of Bank B would likely permit Banker B to earn a handsome executive bonus. If the market crashed (as, of course, it did) he would be forced out as CEO, but in the meantime, Banker B could make a very decent living![34]

There is some evidence that variations in the franchise value of banks—the ability of their management teams to develop strong client lists that provided them with solid and profitable investment opportunities—played a role in the subprime crisis. It did not directly cause the crisis—housing-finance policies that eroded underwriting standards and weak prudential regulation did that. Such variations may, however, have determined which banks were worst affected by the crisis and aggravated its overall severity.

Experiences of U.S. banks during the subprime crisis were strikingly different. Managers at Fannie, Freddie, Bear Stearns, Lehman Brothers, Citibank, UBS, Wachovia, Washington Mutual, Countrywide, AIG, and Merrill Lynch took on enormous mortgage-related risks from 2000 to 2006, while managers at Deutsche Bank, JPMorgan Chase, Goldman Sachs, Bank of America, Met Life, Credit Suisse, HSBC, Standard Chartered, and many others chose not to do so.

What evidence is there that differences in risk taking prior to the crisis reflected differences in franchise value? The evidence is not conclusive, but it is highly suggestive. Casual empiricism suggests that the banks with the highest franchise values tended to be more conservative prior to the crisis. Because they had strong risk-management systems and took on lower risk relative to their capital during the boom years, they did not require bailouts during the crisis. That list includes Goldman Sachs, JPMorgan Chase, and Deutsche Bank. The banks that suffered most dur-

---

[34] For a discussion of the role of compensation in promoting incentive problems of bankers during the subprime boom, see Calomiris (2009) and Barth, Caprio, and Levine (2012), 74–79.

ing the crisis were considered by financial professionals to have weaker franchises and were more tolerant of risk taking: Bear Stearns, Lehman Brothers, and Citibank. At Citibank, poor internal organization and a history of risks gone bad had plagued the bank for three decades. A systematic study of this issue by Rüdiger Fahlenbrach, Robert Prilmeier, and René Stulz found that the banks that experienced the biggest losses during the subprime crisis tended to be the same ones that had invested in, or advanced credit to, Long-Term Capital Management, a massive hedge fund whose aggressive investment model caused the firm to collapse and nearly set off a systemic financial crisis in 1998.[35]

Additional evidence for the view that banks differed in their taste for risk comes from a study by Andrew Ellul and Vijay Yerramilli showing that differences in risk taking among bank holding companies were predictable on the basis of the relative strength of their institutional commitment to risk management.[36] Some banks appear to have purposely not invested in risk management, precisely because strong risk-management units would have prevented the senior management from taking value-destroying risks! As a proxy for the commitment to risk management, Ellul and Yerramilli employ the ratio of the compensation paid to the chief risk officer to that of the chief executive officer. They find that banks with a high ratio (i.e., well-compensated risk managers) took on less risk in 2006 and suffered lower losses during the subprime bust.

Looking at the available evidence, we are of the view that a complete explanation of the subprime crisis must take account not only of the central influences of government housing-finance policies that weakened mortgage lending standards and prudential regulatory failures—both of which reflect the deeper political bargain that sustained them—but also of differences among banks, including differences in their competitive abilities, which may have encouraged some managers to purposely take on exceptionally high risks.

Dodd-Frank to the Rescue?

The subprime crisis revealed deep flaws in U.S. housing-finance policy and prudential regulation. Just as the Great Depression and the savings

---

[35] Fahlenbrach, Prilmeier, and Stulz (2012).
[36] Ellul and Yerramilli (2010).

and loan crisis led to regulatory reform (see chapter 6), as of this writing there has been a significant regulatory response to the subprime crisis. The Dodd-Frank Act of 2010 is producing many regulatory changes. The prior waves of reform did little to improve the banking system, a problem we attribute to political constraints on reform. Will the Dodd-Frank reforms work better?

Academics generally agree that there are three sets of key problems to resolve. First, banks must be required to manage their risks more prudently, hold more capital, and recognize losses in a more timely manner. Second, government mortgage policies must be reformed to end the destabilizing subsidization of risky mortgage lending through Fannie, Freddie, and the FHA. Third, large financial institutions must be prevented from free riding on too-big-to-fail protection.

Unfortunately, most academics would also agree that Dodd-Frank does not offer much hope for solving these problems. A full review of the Dodd-Frank Act is beyond our scope.[37] We confine ourselves to a few observations. Despite its unprecedented length and complexity, Yogi Berra might have said of the Dodd-Frank Act of 2010, "It's déjà vu all over again!" As in the regulatory response to the 1930s and 1980s crises, politicians have promulgated many prudential reforms. Like the earlier reforms, so far Dodd-Frank does very little to address the root causes of the crisis that inspired it. It does little to change the way regulators measure bank risk exposures or bank losses, it does not even begin to address the need for the reform of housing finance subsidies, and the too-big-to-fail problem persists: indeed, it has now been codified.

Under Title II of Dodd-Frank, when a too-big-to-fail financial institution becomes distressed, various parties in the government acting together must decide whether to offer it assistance or to simply liquidate it without assistance. If assistance is offered, and if government losses result from that assistance, then a special tax is levied on surviving institutions to pay for those losses. While its stated intent is to avoid future bailouts, this new authority establishes explicit procedures for bailing out too-big-to-fail institutions and for levying fees to fund those bailouts. The likely path

---

[37] See Calomiris, Eisenbeis, and Litan (2012) for an overview. For an example of pessimism about Dodd-Frank's effectiveness, see McCarty, Poole, and Rosenthal (2013), 254–61.

of least political resistance if a large bank becomes insolvent will be another bailout, rubber-stamped by whichever politicians, judges, and bureaucrats are authorized to approve it. Financial institutions in trouble will argue that anything less will bring the world to an end, and few politicians, bureaucrats, or judges will want to bear the personal risks of standing in the way.

In an eerie reminder of Carter Glass's role in financial reform in 1933, the former Fed chairman Paul Volcker—who, as an unofficial advisor to President Obama, was given a pedestal from which to shape the financial-reform agenda—made securities trading the central focus of his proposed reforms. In 1933, despite the fact that the banking collapse was unrelated to securities-market entanglements of banks, Glass used the reform opportunity to pursue his own pet project—the separation of commercial and investment banking. Like Glass in 1933, rather than focusing his reform advice on the real-estate markets that had crippled the financial system, Volcker waged a campaign against one of his longstanding pet peeves—proprietary trading. He even succeeded in convincing Congress to add the "Volcker Rule"—which prohibits proprietary trading by banks—to the Dodd-Frank Act, even though there is not much evidence to suggest that proprietary trading contributed to the subprime crisis.[38]

Dodd-Frank also enhanced the Fed's regulatory and supervisory power by making it the key prudential regulator of "systemically important" nonbank financial institutions, as well as bank holding companies. The Fed's supervisory and regulatory powers were expanded in spite of its failure to supervise and regulate effectively in the years leading up to the 2007–09 crisis. Ironically, had it not been for the crisis, the Fed might have lost much of this authority. Just prior to the crisis, Treasury Secretary Henry Paulson had initiated an examination of optimal financial regulatory and supervisory structure, and the special task force that he assembled had concluded that the Fed should be stripped of most of these

---

[38] Proprietary trading is defined as trading by a bank in stocks, bonds, currencies, commodities, their derivatives, or other financial instruments with the firm's own money rather than its customers' money, so as to make a profit for itself. This activity, which is prohibited under the new Volcker Rule, is difficult to distinguish from market making, where banks take positions in the market on their own account to facilitate an orderly market for trading.

functions and a new regulator established to undertake them.[39] The task force's report, "Blueprint for a Modernized Financial Regulatory Structure," also suggested that the Federal Trade Commission and the Justice Department should become the primary antitrust regulators in banking and that the Fed's role in these areas should be sharply diminished.[40] The crisis, however, led to the abandonment of these reform proposals. In the postcrisis environment leading up to the passage of Dodd-Frank, the Fed was able to convince Congress and the administration to expand, rather than contract, its supervisory and regulatory role.

Conclusion

The subprime crisis is likely not the last such crisis that American readers of this book will experience. Understanding how and why it unfolded, we hope, should provide a guide not just to understanding the causes of future crises but perhaps also to how the United States, and other countries, might avoid them.

The subprime crisis was, first and foremost, the outcome of a political bargain. Since the 1980s, and accelerating through the 1990s and 2000s, banks, along with GSEs, were allowed to grow into enormous enterprises. This expansion afforded them increased economies of scale, economies of scope, potential for market power, and levels of too-big-to-fail protection. In exchange, they had to share some of the resulting rents with activist groups—a move that policy makers saw as a politically easy way to address the serious social and economic problems that affected America's urban poor. This situation created an opportunity for activist groups to leverage the rules so that they could garner a share of the rents being earned by banks for themselves and their members.

Banks would not engage in this kind of rent sharing without limit, however. They knew that they would be able to do more at lower cost to themselves if they could either sell the resulting high-risk mortgages to

[39] United States Department of the Treasury (2008), 144: "In terms of its recast regulatory role, the Federal Reserve should have specific authority regarding: gathering appropriate information, disclosing information, collaborating with the other regulators on rulemaking, and taking corrective actions when necessary in the interest of overall financial market stability."

[40] United States Department of the Treasury (2008), 145–46.

Fannie or Freddie or support them with low levels of prudential capital, which meant securitizing them. Thus activists used their influence in Congress in the banks' favor to impose HUD mandates on Fannie and Freddie mortgage purchases and to force Fannie and Freddie to loosen their underwriting standards. Fannie and Freddie went along, but only on condition that they were granted the right to finance their mortgages and mortgage-backed securities with money that they borrowed, with an implicit guarantee of their debts coming from taxpayers.

Once the basic rules of this game were laid down in the early 1990s, the game unfolded in a predictable manner. Fannie and Freddie were forced to reduce their underwriting standards to accommodate increasing lending mandates to targeted groups. Importantly, those weaker standards were applied to all borrowers: to have done otherwise would have been a tacit admission that a portion of their portfolio was, in fact, high risk, which would have alarmed their shareholders. Many commercial banks, knowing that they could either sell high-risk loans to Fannie and Freddie or convert them into mortgage-backed securities guaranteed by Fannie and Freddie, jumped into the subprime securitization market. Indeed, much of the business of America's largest banks, especially the ones with weaker management teams, consisted of originating risky loans that could be securitized and then held as a high-quality asset that could be backed with paper-thin levels of capital.

Policy makers and regulators fully understood what was happening. They could have stopped the subprime mortgage risk machine by changing the rules about HUD mandates or prudential capital requirements, but they chose not to do so. Instead, regulators stood by and watched: in essence, they subcontracted the regulation of banking to private firms that sold ratings and whose incentives were therefore aligned with those of issuers and purchasers of securities, who wanted those products to have inflated ratings. Politicians and regulators from both sides of the political aisle were involved in actively supporting this game and in passively permitting it to unfold. This was not a partisan issue: it is perhaps better described as an urban versus rural issue, since the Republican opposition to it was largely from rural constituencies.

If there is therefore a lesson to be learned from this chapter, it is that readers should not expect politicians or regulators to do much to prevent the next banking crisis. Consumers might think more about their own behavior in financial markets. Although the subprime risk binge arose initially as a result of the dominance of a particular political coalition, participation soon became quite widespread. By the time the bubble burst, roughly half of all mortgage borrowers were playing. Many of them wound up worse off as a result.

9

||||||||||||||||||||||

Durable Partners
Politics and Banking in Canada

Ah, three hours next to the dullest man in Canada—
and that's a pretty competitive category.
The Girl in the Café (2005)

Citizens of the United States, much like the British character Ruth in the movie *The Girl in the Café*, often make fun of our purportedly dull neighbors to the north. Canadians don't seem to mind too much. After all, dullness can be a blessing. During the 2007–09 financial crisis, hundreds of banks failed in the United States, and the Federal Reserve and treasury had to marshal massive quantities of taxpayer dollars in loans, guarantees, and bailouts to prevent the collapse of still more—including some of the very largest. Canada's banks, however, never came under severe pressure and never required a taxpayer-financed bailout.

The extraordinary stability of the Canadian banking system has been one of its most visible and oft-noted characteristics for nearly two centuries. Since 1840 the United States has had 12 major banking crises, while Canada has had none—not even during the Great Depression.[1] In fact, the last Canadian banking crisis occurred in 1839, and that was the result of contagion from the United States.[2] Even that crisis, which forced Canada's banks to suspend convertibility of their notes and deposits, produced no bank failures—while hundreds of U.S. banks failed. This Canadian achievement is especially remarkable in light of the fact that Canada is a staples-based economy, heavily reliant on exports, and thus largely at the mercy of international variations in its terms of trade. Canada therefore has tended to have dramatic fluctuations in its business cycles, but these have not translated into banking crises.

[1] Haubrich (1990).
[2] Johnson (1910).

More remarkable still, the stability of Canada's banks was accomplished with little government intervention to protect bank liabilities or shore up failing banks. Indeed, Canada did not found a central bank until 1935, and that was done primarily because farmers in the Canadian West—displaying the understandable inflationist advocacy of commodity-producing debtors—demanded that the government pursue an activist monetary policy during the Great Depression. Unlike central banks in many other countries, the Bank of Canada was not created to effect institutional changes in banking regulation: Canadian banks in the 1930s, as before, had few problems in need of curing. Even more remarkably, at the same time that the Canadian banking system was achieving its record of consistent stability, it was also outperforming U.S. banks with respect to many other criteria, including greater access to banking services in remote areas and more competitive pricing of loan and deposit interest rates.

How did Canada do it? Part of the answer is that the Canadian banking system has a very different structure from that of the United States; it is composed of a small number of very large banks with nationwide branches. This structure has not only allowed Canadian banks to diversify their loan portfolios across regions, it has also allowed them to transfer funds in order to shore up banks in regions affected by an adverse economic shock. Nationwide branch banking has also allowed Canada's banks to capture scale economies in administration while competing among themselves for business in local markets. Canadian banks, historically, have charged lower interest-rate spreads (the difference between loan interest rates and deposit interest rates) than U.S. banks.

One potential shortcoming of a concentrated system such as Canada's is that it could undermine competition among banks, resulting in less credit at higher prices for households and business enterprises. Canada's democratic political institutions—particularly its popularly elected lower house—have, however, limited the extent to which the banks can earn monopoly profits. The threat of political backlash against the banks is institutionalized in a rather peculiar practice: for over a century and a half, the Canadian parliament has carried out periodic legislative reviews and rechartering of its banks. Until 1992, this occurred every ten years; since 1992, it has occurred every five years. The practice of revising the Bank Act and rechartering the banks is not solely a stick with which to threaten bankers; it is also a carrot that rewards sound business practices by giving the bankers themselves a voice in the crafting of the new legislation. In short, widespread suffrage in Canada has given Canadian bankers strong reasons to follow the dictum "Pigs get fat, hogs get slaughtered."

These structural and regulatory differences, however, raise a more fundamental question: what political factors have produced a Canadian banking system able to perform so much better than that of the United States? Why did two former British colonies that shared a common culture, a common knowledge of British and European banking history, and a porous border diverge so sharply when it came to banking? This puzzle is even more striking in light of the fact that when Canadian policy makers looked for models on which to base their system, they looked across the border to the United States. The earliest banks in Canada (beginning with the Bank of Montreal in 1817) were modeled closely and explicitly on the nationally chartered, multibranch Bank of the United States (founded in 1791).

Why did Canadians retain that basic structure for the next two centuries, whereas Americans rejected it? America's rejection of branch banks during the nineteenth century was not, as we discuss in chapter 6, the result of ignorance. Rather, it was the result of politics, and specifically of a particular set of political coalitions that existed in the United States and the strongly decentralized federal political structure within which they bargained over banking. Understanding why Canada retained a system based on a small number of banks with the power to branch across provincial lines therefore requires us to understand the factors that shaped political coalitions and political structures in Canada.

While we do not want to short-change the specifics—indeed, we address them in detail below—a single, overarching factor shaped Canada's political economy: Britain's determination to hold onto Canada as a colony. Following the American Revolution, this goal appeared difficult because the vast majority of the Canadian population in the late eighteenth century was of French origin. Nevertheless, Britain succeeded. Canada had no American-style revolution, in which a commercial elite made common cause with farmers against British rule. Rather, it remained part of the British Empire. In fact, it was not until 1982 that Canada obtained full parliamentary independence from Britain; and to this day Canada remains a constitutional monarchy with Britain's Queen Elizabeth II as sovereign.

Holding Canada in the empire required British policy makers to engage in a series of institutional experiments beginning in the 1790s that were designed to simultaneously cede increased self-government to their Canadian subjects while limiting the political power of the large French population. They did so not simply out of chauvinism but to sustain Canada as an economically viable colony. The solution that they eventually hit upon was a federal system that gave the central government a monopoly over economic policy making. Canada's 1867 constitution even allowed the national government to nullify laws that had been passed by individual provinces (e.g., French-speaking Quebec). Systematic malapportionment in the upper house of the Canadian parliament ensured that the French would always hold a minority of the seats. In short, the need to solve a difficult problem of empire—crafting colonial political institutions so that the French population of Quebec could not hold up the economic development of the Canadian interior—gave rise to a regulatory system in which the central government held a monopoly on the right to charter banks. Provincial governments could not create local, territorially demarcated banks that could serve as the nucleus of an anti–national bank coalition, as happened in the United States.

The Political Origins of the Canadian Banking System

Two major divisions characterized Canadian society in the late eighteenth century. The first was linguistic and cultural. Britain and France had battled over Canada since 1689. In 1763, at the end of the Seven Years' War, the French, having lost the cities of Montreal and Quebec, finally ceded their claims. Yet when they withdrew, the overwhelming majority of the 161,000 inhabitants of the British colony of Canada—at the time simply called Quebec, and extending into modern-day Ohio—were French.[3]

The second major division was economic and occupational. Canadian society in the late eighteenth century was roughly divided into three groups. First, there was a group one might call the British overlords: wealthy landowners and merchants who were intensely loyal to the crown. This group would later come to be pejoratively known in Quebec as the Château

---

[3] The far northern reaches of Canada, above Quebec, which at the time were called Rupert's Land, remained under the direct control of the Hudson Bay Company. Nova Scotia, which at the time also included the present-day province of New Brunswick, was treated as a separate British colony, from which the French were forcibly expelled in 1755.

Clique and in Ontario as the Family Compact, epithets that captured its status as an entrenched oligarchy. A second group comprised merchants who were not part of this oligarchy. Like the U.S. Founding Fathers, Canada's merchants were entrepreneurial men whose wealth was of recent vintage and who lobbied for policies that would promote economic growth and a more open political and economic system (that is, one not controlled by the British overlords). Unlike the Founding Fathers, however, Canada's merchants were not clamoring for a revolution to overthrow British rule. The reason for their loyalty is not hard to divine: there was a third group that was a threat to both the merchants and the overlords that was populist, agrarian, and overwhelmingly French.

Crafting a viable colony was made even more difficult by several features of Canada's geography. These were its east-west geographic breadth; the fact that much of its natural-resource wealth, including its best farmland, was located deep in the interior; and the fact that that interior was geographically contiguous with the United States. These geographic factors mattered multiplicatively, not just additively; that is, each factor magnified the importance of the others and made the managing of a large French-origin population even more problematic.

In order to visualize the problem facing the British population of Canada, and by extension the British government, it is helpful to compare it to the situation of the original 13 colonies of the United States. Because all of them had direct access to the Atlantic Ocean, all 13 had largely independent opportunities for trade. The situation changed, of course, once the U.S. population spread beyond the Appalachians and inland commerce via turnpikes, canals, and railroads created important interdependencies across states; but initially, the actions of any one of the 13 colonies had little effect on the others' ability to trade with the rest of the world.

In Canada, by contrast, access to external markets for producers in Canada's vast interior depended on the transport of goods across other provinces. Specifically, it required the ability to navigate the Saint Lawrence River, which connects the Great Lakes to the Atlantic Ocean. There are two choke points along the Saint Lawrence: the Lachine Rapids, which had to be portaged until a canal was built around them; and a band of cliffs at a narrowing of the river, just before it empties into the Gulf of Saint Lawrence. The portage at the Lachine Rapids became the city of

Montreal. The cliffs near the Gulf of Saint Lawrence were the locus of a massive French citadel whose guns dominated the river; that citadel became the city of Quebec. The famous British victory over the French at the Battle of Quebec in 1759 was decisive because the citadel was the key to controlling the entire water transportation system, from the shores of the Great Lakes to the Atlantic.

The British military victory over the French had no effect, however, on the constraint imposed by the Lachine Rapids. Overcoming that constraint required the construction of a canal, and that meant obtaining the cooperation of the population of Montreal and its hinterland, which is to say the Quebecois. Making matters more difficult still, as shipping technology changed, the canal had to be periodically deepened and widened. The central role of Montreal meant that, if economic decisions about the province of Quebec were made irrespective of (or perhaps even purposely contrary to) the interests of other parts in Canada, the economic prospects of those other provinces could be seriously reduced.

The fact that those other provinces were geographically contiguous with the United States made the British policy problem even more serious. What would prevent recently arrived, English-speaking agricultural and commercial groups from the areas west of Montreal, frustrated by decisions made by French-dominated Quebec, from choosing to become part of the United States or supporting a U.S. invasion of Canada? In the late eighteenth century this question would have been a theoretical abstraction. Most of the crown's English-speaking Canadian subjects in the late eighteenth century were, in fact, loyalists who had fled the United States after 1783. They were completely dominant in the region that now comprises the province of Ontario and were in many senses more British than the British. During the nineteenth century, however, the threat of an amalgamation of the English-speaking regions of the Canadian interior with the United States became increasingly real. During the War of 1812, the United States had invaded Canada but was repulsed. Canadian merchants made veiled threats in the 1830s that they would seek political union with the United States. U.S. presidential candidate James Polk made his threatened war over the contested border of the Oregon Territory a central part of his 1844 bid for the presidency, immortalized by the battle cry "Fifty-Four Forty or Fight." For several years after the end of the U.S. Civil War, as many as 25,000 U.S. veterans of Irish descent, known variously as the

Fenian Brotherhood, the Irish Republican Brotherhood, and the Irish Republican Army, plotted the invasion of Canada as a first step toward an Irish revolution against Britain. Although their various attempts at invasion failed, the U.S. government sometimes gave comfort and support to this group and encouraged their efforts. Ultimately, however, the United States decided to disarm them and prevent the launching of what otherwise would have been a serious military campaign against Canada.

Thus, the province of Quebec was not just economically important to Great Britain in its own right: it was essential to Canada's future as a British colony. Unless British control over Quebec could be assured, the French would be able to block crucial commercial progress for all of Canada, a feat that would also have encouraged U.S. opportunism.

The Search for a Durable Bargain

The first attempt at creating a governable equilibrium was the Canada Act of 1791, promulgated by the British prime minister William Pitt. The 1791 act split Quebec in two, creating an English-dominated province, Upper Canada (modern-day Ontario), populated largely by loyalists who had emigrated from the United States; and a French-dominated province, Lower Canada (modern-day Quebec). Both provinces had their own legislatures, the lower houses of which were popularly elected. Pitt preserved British control over both provinces in three ways: via British parliamentary oversight of provincial laws, the power to name the provincial governors, and the creation of an appointed upper house in the provincial legislature called the Legislative Council. A subset of the Legislative Council, called the Executive Council, served as a cabinet for the appointed British governors. In short, Pitt's 1791 Canada Act was designed to placate the French by creating a separate French enclave under beneficent British control while simultaneously creating conditions that would attract British colonists.

Pitt was not far-sighted enough to see that there was no disconnecting the economic future of Lower Canada from the rest of British North America; nor could he have imagined the tide of British and American immigration into Canada after 1790. As of 1790 there were only 161,000 inhabitants in all of Canada, virtually all of them in Lower Canada. Four decades later, the population had grown almost fivefold, to 780,000, and nearly one-third of this population were English-speaking residents of Upper Canada. Pitt's solution to the "French problem" now backfired. The assembly of Lower Canada gave the French a vehicle to express their frustrated aspirations and to create unpleasant consequences for the British in Upper Canada in the hope of buying themselves even more autonomy.

The response of the British was not as the French had anticipated. In the 1830s Canada's merchants started organizing "constitutional associations" to articulate and promote their agenda, one of whose key planks was ending French obstruction of policies promoting the economic development of the interior. There was nothing subtle about their complaints. As the Constitutional Association of Quebec put it in November 1834: "Injury cannot be inflicted on us, without affecting them; and the French party may yet be taught, that the majority upon which they count for success, will, in the hour of trial, prove a weak defense against the awakened energies of an insulted and oppressed people."[4] They specifically argued that the negative effects of Lower Canada's policies on the other provinces justified a consolidation of economic authority that would permit policies that favored national commercial expansion.

The Constitutional Association of Montreal was even less subtle. In 1836 its membership objected vehemently to Lower Canada's opposition to a proposed canal project at the Lachine Rapids and made clear the cost to the British government of not addressing their concerns: "Upper Canada, repulsed in her endeavors to open a direct channel of communication to the sea, has been driven to cultivate commercial relations with the United States, whose policy is more congenial with her own. Nova Scotia and New Brunswick will learn, with indignant surprise, that the destruction of their most important interests is countenanced and supported by the Assembly of [Lower Canada]."[5] They also made specific reference to the geographic reality that was at the heart of the problem:

> Connected as are the Provinces of British America by a chain of Rivers and Lakes, affording the means of creating an uninterrupted water communication between their extremities, at a small expense; possess-

---

[4] Christie (1866), 41.
[5] Christie (1866), 264.

ing within themselves the elements of all extensive trade by the interchange of those products which are peculiar to each, and forming parts of the same Empire, they have the undoubted right to require that these advantages shall not be sacrificed by the inertness or mistaken policy of any one state; more especially when, as in the case of Lower Canada, that state, from geographical position, exercises a prepondering influence on the prosperity of all. . . . The St. Lawrence canal, at this moment in active progress, will complete an uninterrupted navigation for vessels of considerable burden from the upper Lakes to the line dividing that Province from Lower Canada; but at that point, the spirit of English enterprise encounters the influence of French domination; the vast designs of rendering the remotest of the inland seas accessible to vessels from the ocean is there frustrated by the anti-commercial policy of the French leaders; we look in vain to their proceedings for any manifestation of a desire to co-operate in the great work of public improvement.[6]

Canada's regional economic-policy conflict was not just a matter of development externalities: a deep cultural divide and animosity encouraged uncooperativeness between regions. From the standpoint of many Canadians of British origin, it was simply intolerable that Canada's most important province and city were controlled, in effect, by foreigners. The French were Catholic, while the British were Protestant; the French were "feudal" in their laws and institutional heritage, while the British merchants fought for fee-simple titling of land and the creation of land registries to improve liquidity and encourage timber development; the French were agricultural in occupation, while the British were mercantile; and, crucially, the French were local in their aspirations, while the British dreamed of ambitious public works and a national future to rival that of the United States. This problem of how to deal with the foreigners within was clearly expressed by the members of the Constitutional Association of Montreal:

For half a century [we] have been subjected to the domination of a party [in the Assembly], whose policy has been to retain the distinguishing attributes of a foreign race, and to crush in others that spirit

[6] Christie (1866), 265–66.

of enterprise which they are unable or unwilling to emulate. . . . Upper Canada and the United States bear ample testimony of the floodtide of prosperity, the result of unresisted enterprise and of equitable laws, which has rewarded their efforts. Lower Canada, where another race predominates, presents a solitary exception to this general march of improvement. . . . It were incredible to suppose that a [British] minority, constituting nearly one-third of the entire population, imbued with the same ardour for improvement that honorably distinguishes their race throughout the North American continent, and possessing the undisputed control of all the great interests of the colony, would resign themselves to the benumbing sway of a majority differing from them so essentially on all important points, whilst any mode of deliverance was open to their choice.[7]

These sentiments found a welcome reception in Upper Canada. In 1836, Upper Canada's lieutenant governor, Sir John Colborne, made this clear: "The peculiar position of Lower Canada, and the similar constitution under which the institutions of both colonies are secured, do not allow the dissensions in that Province to be regarded by you with indifference, nor indeed without deep regret, anxiety and apprehension; the injurious effects of these influences have already been experienced; they have tended apparently to discourage emigration, and the transfer of capital to this country."[8] So strong were these views that, in 1837, the Assembly of Upper Canada voted to express its willingness to annex the "City and Island of Montreal."[9]

Pitt's Canada Act of 1791 had a second fatal flaw: it allowed the British overlords, who dominated the legislative and executive councils in both Upper and Lower Canada, to run roughshod over the merchants and farmers. In the late eighteenth century, when almost no one lived in Upper Canada, and Lower Canada was overwhelmingly French, this did not present a huge problem. But, as immigration swelled the English-speaking population, demands by both merchants and farmers for greater political power increased. Thus a second plank of the constitutional associations was the demand for greater voice in the selection of the upper houses of the legislature. They sought a government that was centralized

[7] Christie (1866), 263.
[8] Christie (1866), 155–56.
[9] Christie (1866), 347.

but not corrupt or exclusionary. The Constitutional Association of Montreal, in November 1834, was outspoken in its call for reform of the Legislative Council:

> Although the Legislative Council, as at present constituted, commands our respect as possessing a majority of independent members, we consider that it yet contains too many persons holding dependent situations under the Crown and liable to be acted upon by undue influence. The accumulation of offices in the family and connection of a leading member of the Legislative Council, deserves to be held up to public reprehension. The irresponsible manner in which the Land Granting Department is conducted, the salary disproportioned to the duties performed, which is attached to the office, and other abuses connected with the Woods and Forests, demand revision.[10]

The British government initially attempted to quell the complaints of the constitutional associations by signaling Canada's merchants that its interests were aligned with theirs and not with the numerically dominant French. In 1835, the newly appointed governor general, Lord Gosford, stated publicly: "Of the British, and especially of the commercial classes, I would ask, is it possible you should suppose that there can be any design to sacrifice your interests, when it is clear to all the world that commerce is one of the main supports to the British system of finance?"[11]

Gosford's attempt to head off rebellion failed. In 1837, frustration with the Château Clique and the Family Compact, particularly their control of the legislative councils and their abuse of that control for their own economic ends, boiled over into violent, if short-lived and unsuccessful, populist insurrections in both Upper and Lower Canada. The rebellion in Upper Canada was easily dealt with, but that in Lower Canada, much to the concern of both Canadian merchants and the British government, proved more difficult to put down.

The 1837 rebellions presented British policy makers with a difficult problem. On the one hand, they had to find a way to appease demands for greater political representation by both English- and French-speaking Canadians, and at the same time they had to make sure that the French-origin population would not be empowered to block the development of

[10] Christie (1866), 40–41.
[11] Christie (1866), 126.

the colony. The solution they chose, in the 1840 Act of Union, was a variant on one of the key demands of the merchant-backed constitutional associations: it unified Upper and Lower Canada into a single province called the United Province of Canada, with a single legislature. The Act of Union gave each of the former provinces the same number of seats in the new legislature, regardless of the fact that Lower Canada had a much larger population than Upper Canada. The act therefore ensured that the French could not muster a majority in the lower assembly in order to block English proposals. In addition, the British parliament retained rights of review and approval over a range of matters and appointed governors and members of the Legislative Council. The Act of Union did, however, grant some local voice in the selection of the members of that upper house. Taken as a whole, the Act of Union was a victory for Canada's merchants.

The Act of Union also proved not to be a durable bargain. Canada's merchants had gained most of what they had demanded, but there was no getting around the fact that the crown's interests were not perfectly aligned with theirs. As with British policy toward the original American colonies, British policy toward Canada often gave greater weight to British domestic interests than to colonial ones. This problem was exacerbated by the growth of the English-speaking population of Upper Canada, swelled by a tide of immigrants from Ireland, Scotland, and England into the Canadian interior after 1840. As the French lost their numerical majority, the growing British population demanded greater political representation.

The arrangement that eventually emerged in order to satisfy these demands, the British North American Act of 1867 (also known as the Constitution Act), became the basis for the modern nation of Canada. The act conceded greater political autonomy to Canadians—so much so that Canada effectively became a sovereign nation—while simultaneously limiting the power of the French. The United Province of Canada was again split in two: what had been Upper Canada was renamed Ontario, and Lower Canada was renamed Quebec. At the same time, two maritime provinces, New Brunswick and Nova Scotia, which had been separately governed by Britain since the eighteenth century, were folded into the new country, creating a confederation of four provinces named the Dominion of Canada. The French were now outnumbered, both as a proportion of the population and as a proportion of the provinces. Within a few years, the British drove the last nails into the French coffin by adding three more (virtually unpopulated) provinces: Manitoba (1870), British Columbia (1871), and Prince Edward Island (1873). Quebec was now just one of seven provinces.

The Canadian confederation created a political system in which the population of French origin, which constituted roughly one-third of the Canadian population in the early 1870s, could not drive national or even local policies.[12] French Canadians could exercise the power of their numbers in the lower house of the legislature, which was elected by local districts based on population, but they could not gain a parliamentary majority. Moreover, as in the United States, elections for the lower house were to be decided by first-past-the-post contests. Such systems favor the election of centrist candidates because voters know that candidates from fringe parties, even if they more closely represent those voters' preferences, cannot win: voting for a fringe candidate means "wasting" your vote. The result is that such electoral systems favor the emergence of two dominant political parties that fight over the median voter—a pattern so well known in political science that it is called Duverger's Law. In Canada, the two parties that emerged had national, not regional, bases. Even if the French Canadians came to control one of these parties and took control of the lower house, any laws they passed could be overturned by the Senate, whose members were appointed for life by a British governor general. Making matters even worse from the point of view of the French, Senate seats were allocated not based on population but on a per-province basis. In the mid-1870s, that allocation gave Quebec just 24 of the 96 seats, even though it contained 32 percent of the total population.[13] Moreover, the power of the French population in Quebec was lessened by a rule stipulating that in Quebec only, senators would represent local districts. This provision ensured that there would be a number of English senators among the province's 24-member delegation, because Montreal had a sizable English-speaking population.[14]

[12] Statistics Canada (1983), Series A125–163.
[13] Statistics Canada (1983), Series A2–14.
[14] The British appear to have been conscious of the need for the unelected Senate to be viewed as legitimate. The governor general therefore was mindful of the need to appoint senators who represented their local communities, but at the same time he needed to have a means by which to constrain the size of any French-Canadian bloc in the Senate.

Furthermore, the membership of Canada's Senate under the constitution of 1867 ensured that merchant and banker interests, and the interests of property owners in general, would be protected against populist attacks. All legislation had to be approved by the Senate, which was designed to be a body of "second sober thought" to check the excesses of the House of Commons. To ensure sufficient sobriety of thought, membership in the Senate was subject to a wealth test: senators had to possess $4,000 in land wealth—a threshold that was significant in the nineteenth century, though it has ceased to be a binding constraint. The selection mechanism for senators, however, continues to be binding: senators are appointed by provincial governors, subject to the approval of the monarch of Great Britain (although in practice, the Canadian prime minister has a great deal of say in who is appointed to the Senate). Until 1965, senators were appointed for life; since then, they may not sit after age 75. Just in case the Senate loses its way as a protector of conservative principles, additional senators (as many as eight) can be appointed with the approval of the British monarch. (This provision has been employed only once, in 1990, when it gave Prime Minister Brian Mulroney the majority he needed to pass a pro-business tax reform.)

In order to further limit the power of the French in Quebec, the British North America Act of 1867 centralized authority in the national government. Any power not specifically delegated to the provinces was left to the national government: this arrangement was the polar opposite of the U.S. system, in which nonenumerated rights are reserved for the states. Second, the act specifically granted authority over commercial, economic, and banking policy to the national government. Third, it effectively gave the national government the right to nullify any action by a provincial government provided that such nullification was "declared by the Parliament of Canada to be for the general advantage of Canada or for the advantage of two or more of the provinces."[15]

Centralized Banking in a Centralized Federation

These characteristics of the Canadian political system had far-reaching implications for banking legislation. In the United States, bank chartering

[15] McInnis (1959), 294.

was dominated by fragmented state-level decisions until the 1980s, allowing local coalitions in favor of unit banking to shape policies. Those coalitions, as we discuss in chapter 6, quickly undermined any effort to establish large banks with multiple branches. In Canada, authority over banking was centralized from the very beginning. Because any political bargaining among coalitions had to take place at the national level, the initial system of large banks with multiple branches was never seriously threatened.

How did the centralization of political power in Canada entrench a system of branch banking? Political bargaining at the state or provincial level is more likely to result in a unit-banking law than bargaining at the national level. First, at the national level, all vested interests are aggregated, with weights that depend on various determinants of their relative political power. A policy (like unit banking) that may be a local political winner in particular locations (e.g., Illinois or Kansas, where the combination of incumbent unit bankers and "populist" supporters of unit banking might dominate) will have a much harder time winning backing at the national level, where a majority of the political weight (including national coalitions of commercial and industrial interests) favors branching. Second, bargaining at the state or provincial level effectively precludes a system of banks with national branches. A state government's decision about branching affects that state only. Even if, say, Kansas passes a law allowing branching, that law does not allow the establishment of a nationwide branching network unless the Kansas legislature can coordinate simultaneous actions by the other state legislatures (a far-fetched idea).

In Canada, the political fights over banking were national from the beginning. The national aggregation of vested interests took into account the benefits of bank-chartering rules for nationally organized constituencies, and the outcomes of those political battles applied to the nation as a whole. Regional factions and coordination problems that plagued U.S. banking policy for two centuries were absent by construction in Canada.

The geography of Canada meant, in addition, that one of the most important constituencies—merchants—became a strong lobby in favor of a system dominated by a small number of large banks with the ability to branch as they pleased. Canada's natural resources—its wheat lands, forests, and mineral deposits—were located in isolated regions, separated by vast areas that were for the merchants' intents and purposes effectively uninhabited. The primary task facing Canadian merchants was not to move food from hinterlands to cities and manufactures from one city to another, as was the case in the northern United States: it was to move raw materials across Canada and then across the North Atlantic to Great Britain. Canadian merchants therefore saw it as in their interest to promote a system of nationwide banks that could transact in international bills of exchange and domestic bank bills over long distances. As one scholar put it, it was advantageous for them to devise a system whereby "the bank practically has title to all agricultural products which are being moved by means of its funds."[16] In this sense, Canadian merchants were somewhat similar to merchants in the U.S. South, who favored a branch banking system because it facilitated the export of cotton. Canadian merchants, however, were able to exert influence on national banking policy, while the best that merchants in the U.S. South could do was influence the banking policies of individual states.

The Long Reach of Initial Conditions

Canada's particular set of institutions and coalitions shaped a banking system that remained remarkably stable over two centuries. One of the most striking things about the divergent banking histories of the United States and Canada is that both began as alliances of merchant-financiers and political elites. In the United States, that narrow coalition was quickly undermined by populist farmers who made common cause with small bankers. In Canada, political institutions may have kept populist currents in check—and therefore kept a unit banker–agrarian populist coalition from controlling the politics of bank chartering—but they still forced political elites to cede their monopoly control over banking and gradually expand the number of charters to the point that all markets became contestable.

Like their American counterparts, Canadians in the late eighteenth century complained about the lack of money and credit and sought to create banks that could provide both.[17] They were strongly influenced by the example of the Bank of the United States. Indeed, almost as soon as the first legislature was set up in Lower Canada in 1792, British merchants

---

[16] Johnson (1910), 48.
[17] See Redish (1984).

in Montreal began to lobby for a chartered bank. Unsurprisingly, the charter was opposed by the French and defeated twice. Frustrated, the boosters of the Bank of Montreal decided to go ahead without a charter, and thus the bank began operating as a "limited co-partnership" in November 1817 (that is, as a joint-stock company without limited liability). The following year, the legislature finally approved the charter. This was not, however, the only hurdle: it took an additional four years to obtain the crown's approval. The bank was finally chartered in 1822.

The charter of the Bank of Montreal emulated Hamilton's 1791 charter for the Bank of the United States, although it was not identical in all respects. Shareholders' liability initially was limited to the value of their shares. The bank was permitted to open branches throughout the country, that is, in both Lower Canada and Upper Canada. It was required to issue an annual report to shareholders specifying its profits, its quantity of bad debts, and its outstanding banknotes. It was prohibited from investing in or lending against real estate. The total amount of its debts was limited to three times its paid-in capital, and its currency issues were limited to the sum of its paid-in capital plus its specie reserves. The government could require statements from the directors in response to its inquiries at any time. Unlike Hamilton's bank, the government did not own shares in the Bank of Montreal: its initial shareholders were all politically influential merchants.[18] Importantly, the bank was granted a charter for only ten years. This charter was continually renewed (unlike that of Hamilton's Bank of the United States), and it set an important norm for all subsequent bank chartering in Canada.

The Bank of Montreal and the specific features of its charter became a model for other banks. These features included a limited charter duration, the right to issue notes against the general assets of the bank, the right to open branches nationwide, and the requirement to disclose accounting information to the government. Several new banks, which also tended to be owned by politically influential merchants, were established on the heels of the chartering of the Bank of Montreal. The Quebec Bank and the Bank of Canada in Montreal opened their doors in 1818, and, like the Bank of Montreal, were granted ten-year charters by the crown in 1822.[19]

---

[18] McIvor (1958), 30.
[19] The Bank of Canada in Montreal was absorbed by the Bank of Montreal in 1831. In

While political influence was crucial to obtaining early bank charters in Lower Canada, the partnership between the government and the banks was even more apparent in Upper Canada. A petition for the Bank of Upper Canada was favorably received by its legislature in January 1817, but it failed to gain royal approval within the two-year period stipulated by the legislature, so its charter lapsed. Apparently, although its sponsors were connected, they were not connected well enough. A second bank, the Chartered Bank of Upper Canada, was approved by the legislature in 1819 and received a charter from the crown in 1821. Why the promoters of this bank succeeded in obtaining a charter where others had failed is not hard to discern given who owned the Chartered Bank of Upper Canada. Nine of its 15 directors were members of either the Executive or the Legislative Council, and most of the others were associated in one way or another with the government.[20] The Chartered Bank of Upper Canada might just as well have been named the "Bank of the Family Compact." The political ties of the founding group conferred additional benefits that increased the value of their bank. Its charter included a provision permitting the government to subscribe to its stock, which is to say that it received a capital subsidy from the government. Not only was this subsidy valuable in and of itself, but it also gave the government a direct financial interest in the success of the bank. Not surprisingly, the bank's powerful political patrons exerted "determined opposition" against new charter proposals from other groups of would-be bankers.[21]

Upper Canada might have been run by a clique of powerful British overlords, but it was not a banana republic. As it filled with new immigrants who pushed out the frontier and expanded the timber industry, the demand for banking services increased.[22] Those new immigrants, moreover, had the power to elect members of the Legislative Assembly (the lower house) who could represent their interests. When the Chartered Bank of Upper Canada therefore requested a new charter to expand its capital, the Legislative Assembly refused to grant it unless the Legislative Council (the upper house, which was dominated by the Family Compact) agreed

---

1833, the City Bank of Montreal was chartered, but it operated as a local institution of limited means.

[20] McIvor (1958), 34.
[21] McIvor (1958), 36.
[22] McIvor (1958), 36.

to a charter for a competing bank organized by Kingston merchants. The deal was sealed in 1832, and both legislative houses approved both bills, expanding the capital of the Chartered Bank of Upper Canada and simultaneously chartering the Commercial Bank of the Midland District. Only one other bank managed to obtain a charter in Upper Canada in the 1830s: the Gore Bank, which was chartered in 1836, with the economizing innovation (later imitated by other Canadian bank charters) of double liability: that is, its shareholders were held liable for twice their subscribed capital.[23] In 1836–37, nine other bank charters were submitted, but they were "returned for further consideration" by the crown; after the commercial depression of 1837–39, they were withdrawn. As one might imagine would be the case in a rapidly growing frontier area, small, private (unchartered) banks sporadically sprang up to compete with the chartered banks, but most of these operated only briefly.

Almost all of these initial banks had their charters renewed for a second ten-year period in the early 1830s, so that by the time of the union of Upper and Lower Canada in 1841, the basic contours of the modern Canadian banking system had already been laid down. Canadian banking was virtually synonymous with a small number of large banks with branch networks. When union occurred, there were only one unchartered and three chartered banks in Lower Canada, and two unchartered and three chartered banks in Upper Canada. In addition, one British-based bank—the Bank of British North America—had its charter extended to permit it to operate in Canada beginning in 1836.

Challenges and Responses

The special charters granted to Canadian branching banks were decried by populist interests from the beginning, and that opposition grew over time.[24] A serious challenge was mounted in 1850, when an agrarian popu-

---

[23] Double liability, which became the rule in both Canada and the United States, was a means of economizing on paid-in capital and thus reducing the need for prospective bank stockholders to liquidate their wealth in order to invest in bank stock. The non-paid-in wealth of stockholders, therefore, could serve a dual purpose, providing financial strength to the bank (through extended liability) while continuing to serve its economic functions in the forms of land, property, equipment, inventories, and other assets.

[24] McIvor (1958), 30.

list movement that favored unit banking pushed for legislation to create a free-banking system modeled on that of New York State. One benefit, from the point of view of the Canadian government, was that this proposal would create a mechanism for state finance: the free banks would have to back their currency issues with high-grade securities, which is to say with government bond issues. That is, like free banks in the United States, the banks would receive a charter in exchange for a loan to the government. The law allowing the founding of free banks was passed. In addition, banks that did not join the new unit free-banking system were required to pay a 1 percent tax on their note issues. Crucially, however, there was not sufficient support in the legislature to abolish the original branch-banking system. Moreover, despite the tax on their notes, branching banks did not convert to the new system. The result was that very few banks were actually founded under the free-bank system, and only two managed to survive for more than a brief period. The provisions of the free-banking act pertaining to note issues were therefore repealed in 1866, and the act as a whole was repealed in 1880.[25]

The 1850s populist banking challenge was an object lesson in the need to centralize economic policy making when the architects of the Canadian constitution of 1867 sat down to craft the division of power between national and provincial authorities. National authority over banking (and over economic matters as a whole) was consciously designed to preserve the existing nationwide branching system and to promote other related policies that would encourage markets to develop across provinces, as well as internationally—including policies actively supporting the construction of transportation infrastructure, particularly a national railroad system. Not surprisingly, at the very first session of the Canadian parliament, pending the promulgation of a more comprehensive set of statutes regarding banks, an interim "Act Respecting Banks" was passed, which provided that any banks chartered anywhere in Canada could operate branches throughout Canada. These included not only the 19 banks that had been founded in Ontario and Quebec but also the eight chartered banks already operating in New Brunswick and Nova Scotia, the provinces that were added to Canada as part of the 1867 Constitution Act.

[25] McIvor (1958), 50.

One of the major themes of this book is that chartered banks represent a partnership between the parties in control of the government and the founders and shareholders of the banks. Bank chartering in the Dominion of Canada was no exception. In fact, the new government lost no time in trying to craft a bargain with the Bank of Montreal to create a privileged position for the bank in exchange for its providing finance for the government. In 1868, Sir John Rose, Canada's first minister of finance, recommended that the country completely recast its banking system along the lines of the U.S. National Banking Act, which is to say that all note issues would be 100 percent backed by government securities, and unit banks with small minimum capitalizations would be created in every county. The implications of Rose's proposal were far-reaching: the right to issue banknotes would now require a loan to the government, and extant banks, which operated branch networks, might be forced to become unit banks at the time of their next charter renewal—with the notable exception of the Bank of Montreal, whose role as the government's fiscal agent would almost certainly require that it be allowed to maintain its branches. Rose's proposal was therefore an attempt to go back to the cronyism of the Château Clique, but with an interesting twist. It gave the farmers of the Canadian West something that their U.S. counterparts had already obtained: unit banks that would have no choice but to lend to them because of the high costs of obtaining information about distant borrowers. The extant banks, allied with the country's merchants, pushed back hard—so hard, in fact, that the resulting floor fight in the lower house forced Rose to withdraw his proposal and resign as finance minister.[26] Rose was thrown under the bus, and the free-banking movement with him.

The deal crafted by Rose's successor benefited all of the incumbent banks but forced them to share some of their rents with the government. The Dominion Notes Act of 1870 and the Bank Act of 1871 prohibited banks from issuing notes in denominations of less than $5, leaving the lower-denomination niche to government-issued Dominion notes. Banks were then required to maintain a portion—between one-third and one-half—of their cash reserves against *their* outstanding note issues in the

---

[26] See Curtis (1947), 116; Bordo, Redish, and Rockoff (2011), 10; McIvor (1958), 65–66.

form of Dominion notes. That is, in order to issue notes, they had to stuff their vaults with the government's notes, in essence providing the government with a zero-interest loan. In order to keep this system from generating a wild inflation, the acts created several firewalls: the government was not allowed to print more than $9 million in Dominion notes; those notes were convertible to gold; the government was required to maintain a 20 percent hard-currency reserve against its notes; and banks' note issues were limited to their paid-in capital. Nevertheless, the government obtained a considerable benefit from the seignorage between its note issues and the 20 percent reserve requirement. From 1872 until 1913, Dominion notes constituted about one-fifth of outstanding paper currency.[27]

Other provisions of the 1870 and 1871 bank acts codified various aspects of the extant Canadian banking system while also improving on that system on the margin. The acts created a uniform system of bank chartering with the following features: double liability, a minimum capital of $500,000, ten-year bank charters, and the submission of monthly bank financial statements to the government. The acts also regulated what constituted acceptable collateral for bills of exchange and other loans. Importantly, in a blow to agrarian interests, lending against land was prohibited. That is, Canadian banking legislation hewed closely to the "real bills" doctrine; mortgage credit was seen as overly risky. From 1867 to 1874, the paid-in capital of Canadian chartered banks doubled, banknote circulation tripled, and deposits grew more than fourfold.[28]

In a banking system with no restrictions on branching and no deposit insurance, there is a strong impetus toward consolidation. Depositors tend to favor the banks that they view as the most solvent, which also tend to be the most widely diversified and largest banks. Single-office or less prudently run banks tend either to be acquired or to fail. This process had been short-circuited in the United States by state laws that enjoined banks from opening branches; the resulting system of unstable unit banks was then propped up by the creation of the Federal Reserve in 1913, and unit banks were further insulated from competition by deposit insurance and Regulation Q in the 1930s. In Canada, these forces did not come into play. In 1890, the Canadian banking system was composed of 38 char-

---

[27] McIvor (1958), 66–67.
[28] McIvor (1958), 71.

tered banks.[29] By 1922, there were only 17 banks, by 1944 there were ten, and by 1966 there were only eight.[30]

How did the surviving banks and the government respond to the bank failures that were an inevitable part of this process of consolidation? When a bank fails, it potentially endangers all other banks, because depositors may believe that other banks may also be insolvent. Such concerns can motivate deposit withdrawals and even lead to bank runs, and those runs can become a self-fulfilling prophecy if banks cannot liquidate their assets fast enough to satisfy their depositors. The Canadian banking system dealt with this problem through a largely market-based system. When a bank became insolvent, the Bank of Montreal played the role of coordinator in chief to prevent an isolated problem from becoming a systemic one.[31] The Bank of Montreal, however, did not always step in: it allowed smaller banks to fail.[32] This was an important attribute of the system: unless depositors knew that they could suffer losses, they would have no incentive to monitor the behavior of the bankers. When a bank that was large enough to threaten the entire system failed, however, the Bank of Montreal stepped in to coordinate a response by the other banks. This happened in 1906, when the Bank of Ontario failed, and again in 1908, when the Sovereign Bank of Canada failed. In these cases, the Bank of Montreal orchestrated takeovers of the insolvent banks. In the case of the Bank of Ontario, the process was so seamless that the failed banks' depositors were not even aware that there was anything to be concerned about.

On the evening of October 12 [1906] the bankers in Toronto and Montreal heard with surprise that the Bank of Ontario had got beyond its depth and would not open its doors the next morning. Its

---

[29] E. Walker (1923), 146.

[30] Legislative barriers do not appear to explain consolidation. From 1890 to 1929, 25 new bank charters were issued, but only 11 appear to have been utilized, while from 1920 to 1966 5 new bank charters were issued, but only 2 were utilized. The binding constraint appears to have been not the charter but the ability to raise sufficient capital to capture scale economies. Carr, Mathewson, and Quigley (1995), 1138.

[31] Note holders were protected by a Circulation Redemption Fund, established in 1890, to which each bank contributed 5 percent of its circulation, in effect making the banks mutual guarantors of each other's note issues.

[32] For a list of liquidated banks, see Vreeland (1910), 219; see also Johnson (1910), 127, and Breckenridge (1910), 166–74.

capital was \$1,500,000 and its deposits \$1,200,000. The leading bankers in the dominion dreaded the effect which the failure of such a bank might have. The Bank of Montreal agreed to take over the assets and pay all the liabilities, provided a number of other banks would agree to share with it any losses. Its offer was accepted and a representative of the Bank of Montreal took the night train for Toronto. . . . [T]he bank opened for business the next day with the following notice over its door: "This is the Bank of Montreal."[33]

The contrast between this method of dealing with bank failures and that of the United States could not be more striking. In the United States, the ability of banks to coordinate their responses to crises was confined to the collective action of particular cities' clearinghouses, branching banks in the South, or other localized bank networks.[34] When shocks associated with recessions raised significant liquidity problems for U.S. banks, nationwide banking panics resulted (in 1857, 1873, 1884, 1890, 1893, 1896, and 1907), even though (with the exception of the panic of 1857) these were not times of severe loss to banks or widespread bank failure.[35] Four of those recessionary shocks (1857, 1873, 1893, and 1907) resulted in widespread suspensions of convertibility: that is, banks refused to redeem their own deposits.

American bankers tried to face these moments of systemic risk with collective action, but their efforts failed. For example, during the panic of 1907, the New York clearinghouse and the private banker J. P. Morgan tried to coordinate interbank assistance, but Morgan relied primarily on moral suasion, since his bank accounted for only a small part of the system. Indeed, the fragmented structure of the U.S. banking system meant that New York banks as a whole were too small to meet the banking system's liquidity needs. In Canada, in contrast, the Bank of Montreal was a huge institution that commanded a significant share of the country's credit. Its partners in coordinating assistance to troubled institutions were also large. Together they accounted for virtually the entire credit and deposit system.

Canadian bankers were conscious of the differences in performance and stability between the Canadian and U.S. banking systems. They attributed those differences to the fundamental structural difference between the

[33] Johnson (1910), 124–25.
[34] Calomiris (1989, 1990).
[35] Calomiris and Gorton (1991).

Canadian branching system and the U.S. unit bank system. As the Canadian banker E.L. Stewart Patterson wrote in 1917: "Practically every country in the world except the United States has recognized the utility, if not the absolute necessity, of the branch system of banking in handling commodities as liquid as money or credit. A bank system without branches is on par with a city without waterworks or a country without a railroad so far as an equable distribution of credit is concerned."[36]

The Canadian government occasionally provided additional support to the banking system. Canada's economy was largely agricultural, and thus substantial seasonal swings in the demand for credit had always been a source of stress for the banking system. These stresses became particularly pronounced in 1907 as a result of the worldwide 1907–08 financial crisis. It was this crisis, in fact, that took down three relatively small Canadian banks, more than had failed in any previous (or subsequent) year. In response, the Canadian government introduced some changes to the rules governing Dominion notes that were designed to provide a source of emergency liquidity. First, in 1907, the government issued additional Dominion notes, which it lent to the banking system. Second, in 1908, it increased the limit on banknote issues from 100 percent to 115 percent of a bank's paid-in capital plus its other capital accounts during the crop-moving season.[37] These changes were later codified in the general revision of Canada's banking act in 1913. Again, the contrast with the United States is striking. In response to the crisis of 1907, the United States created the Federal Reserve in order to help prop up its unit banks. Canada simply changed the rules governing note issues during the harvest season.[38]

Persistent Consolidation

Why was there no political pressure to reverse the course of bank consolidation? How could it have been that a society composed largely of small

[36] Patterson (1917), 60.

[37] McIvor (1958), 84.

[38] In the agricultural economies of the United States and Canada, seasonal fluctuations in the demand for credit were pronounced. In a diversified branch banking system like Canada's, seasonal swings in credit tend to result in milder seasonal variation in interest rates because the elasticity of loan supply is greater (Calomiris [2011a]), but nevertheless seasonal swings in banking-system loan demand can still produce severe shocks to liquidity.

farmers tolerated a banking system in which they could not put up farm-land as collateral, in which depositors could lose their savings, and in which a small group of bankers in eastern Canada controlled the flow of credit and its terms? Farmers in the Canadian West were, in fact, of the view that the banks charged usurious rates of interest on loans, paid paltry interest on deposits, earned excessive profits, and sought to control the businesses to which they advanced credit.[39] Indeed, some critics held that Canada's banks formed "a huge 'money trust'" that worked "together for the exploitation of the country."[40]

One factor mitigating populist demands was that Canada's rural areas had a high level of access to banking services, thanks to the inherent efficiency of a system in which banks could capture scale economies by centralizing administration and operations. Circa 1911, the provinces of Western Canada (Alberta, British Columbia, Manitoba, and Saskatchewan) had 21 banks operating roughly 900 branches. The average incorporated town had only 900 inhabitants but, amazingly, had two competing banks. The average incorporated village had only 230 inhabitants (which is to say about 40–50 families) and yet typically had a bank branch.[41] While they did not lend against real estate, these branches did provide credit to farmers—so much so that by the 1920s the hundreds of small, private (unincorporated) banking houses that had dotted the Canadian countryside during the late nineteenth century had disappeared.[42]

More fundamentally, the political institutions of Canada made it difficult to enact legislation that would have changed the basic rules of the game of Canadian banking. Reforms to banking law had to be worked out in the House of Commons, where it was much harder to create and sustain a winning agrarian coalition than it would have been at the provincial level. Any reform that got through the House of Commons then had to be approved by the Senate, whose members were appointed by the governor general. Groups favoring the status quo in banking law were therefore able to delay reforms, propose watered-down compromises, or block change entirely.

---

[39] Swanson (1914), 305–6, 310.
[40] Swanson (1914), 313.
[41] Eckardt (1913), 159–63.
[42] Neufeld (2001), 327.

A particularly telling example is provided by the decennial revision of the Bank Act, which was scheduled to take place in 1911. A coalition of populists and conservatives was loaded for bear: four banks had failed from 1906–08, and then in 1910 the Farmer's Bank went under, losing every last cent of its depositors' savings.[43] Depositors in the bank made common cause with its shareholders, who were subject to additional assessments of capital because Canadian banks were chartered with double liability. They demanded that the government compensate them, alleging that the minister of finance had been negligent in granting the bank the Treasury Board certificate it needed to activate its charter in 1906. The issue emerged as a hot-button topic in the 1911 elections: Conservative Party candidates even promised compensation for depositors if they were elected.[44] The coalition of conservatives and populists also demanded sweeping changes to the Bank Act, including requiring parliamentary approval for any further bank mergers or acquisitions, instituting government supervision of the banks, and empowering banks to lend on real estate.

Opponents of these reforms saw them for what they were: the outcome of a coalition of special interests. Indeed, no one could reasonably argue that allowing banks to lend on real estate would increase bank stability, given the association in other countries between real-estate lending and the greater risk of bank failure. Opponents of reform engaged in parliamentary tactics to continually delay the revision of the Bank Act. That strategy apparently worked: when the revision to the Bank Act was finally passed in 1913, all of the demands for reform had been eviscerated. Instead of government supervision of the banks, there would be compulsory annual audits of the banks' financial statements by their own shareholders. Instead of being able to lend on real estate, banks would be allowed to lend on farm stock and grain in storage. And bank mergers and acquisitions would not require legislative approval but only the consent of the minister of finance.[45] As for the idea that depositors in the Farmer's Bank deserved compensation for their losses, it died a slow death. A royal commission in 1913 determined that the loss to depositors was

---

[43] Carr, Mathewson, and Quigley (1995), 1140.
[44] Carr, Mathewson, and Quigley (1995), 1139.
[45] Swanson (1914), 314; Weaver (1913), 136–42.

the fault of the bank's managers, not of the Treasury Board. A subsequent attempt by a Conservative minister of finance to pass a bill compensating depositors failed when the Senate tabled the motion for six months—and never revived it.[46]

A similar example of the power of Canada's political institutions to blunt populist demands can be seen in the case of the Home Bank failure in 1923. Here again, depositors claimed that their losses (equal to roughly 75 percent of their deposits) should be fully compensated by the government because the minister of finance had failed to look into allegations of fraud at the bank going back to 1916. A royal commission found that the depositors had a "moral claim in equity," implying that although there was no legal requirement for compensation, the minister of finance had not been sufficiently attentive to the evidence of malfeasance by the bank's managers and directors. A subsequent government investigation found, however, that most of the bank's losses had been sustained before 1916, and thus any moral obligation of the government was limited to the amount lost since then, which the investigators estimated at 35 percent of deposits. The House of Commons voted in 1925 to honor that 35 percent liability, but the Senate was unwilling to go along. Its members argued that the government had no legal obligation to depositors, and thus payments should be made only in cases of genuine hardship. The final version of the act therefore provided 35 percent compensation to depositors only if their deposits were less than $500 or if they could demonstrate special need. As a result, the government provided compensation equal to 22 percent of the deposit base.[47]

Broader demands for deposit insurance went unheeded. The House of Commons conducted hearings in 1913 and 1924—in the wake of the failures of the Farmer's Bank and the Home Bank, respectively—and both times rejected the idea. At both hearings they were swayed by evidence about the adverse effects of state-run deposit-insurance systems in the

---

[46] Carr, Mathewson, and Quigley (1995), 1140–41.

[47] Carr, Mathewson, and Quigley (1995), 1142–43, 1152. The failure of the Home Bank also led to the creation of an inspector general of banks, responsible for monitoring bank solvency. This did not imply, however, that the government accepted responsibility for bank failures. The revision to the Bank Act in 1927 made clear that the government was not responsible for losses to depositors, shareholders, or creditors of banks.

United States. The conclusion of the Canadian Department of Finance was unambiguous in this regard: "[The mutual guarantee of bank deposits] has proved unworkable in the United States and is basically unsound as it means that the conservative and properly operated bank would be called upon to bear the losses through mismanagement, fraud, and otherwise incurred by competitors over whom it has no control. The final outcome would only be a disaster as the public would not be called upon to discriminate between sound institutions, with whom their funds would be safe, and the others." [48]

Amending the Durable Bargain:
The Great Depression and Beyond

The political institutions that underpinned the Canadian banking system —and hence the basic organization of the banking system itself—also proved to be remarkably resilient to the Great Depression. Canada was a primary product producer, and as the demand for timber, minerals, and cereals collapsed, the economy contracted sharply. No Canadian banks actually failed during the Depression.[49] Nevertheless, Canadian populists blamed the country's orthodox monetary and banking policies for the state of the economy.[50] Nowhere were these sentiments stronger than in the West, where populists had long resented the Eastern "money trust" that they claimed ran the country. In Alberta, a fringe political party espousing a crank economic theory, the Social Credit Party, took over the legislature in a landslide victory in 1935. The federal government used its constitutional powers to nullify much of the subsequent legislation passed by the Alberta legislature—which included the payment of "social dividends" to all adult citizens and the establishment of price controls based on the notion of "just prices"—but it was clear that mainstream national parties needed to do more than just block confused, if well-intentioned, economic reforms.

[48] Quoted in Carr, Mathewson, and Quigley (1995), 1151–52.

[49] Kryzanowski and Roberts (1993) argue that the Canadian government supported the banks through implicit deposit insurance. Carr, Mathewson, and Quigley (1995) make a convincing case against the implicit-insurance hypothesis. See also Carr, Mathewson, and Quigley (1994).

[50] McIvor (1958), 159.

The Canadian government therefore organized a commission, chaired by an English central banker who was a well-known advocate of central banks, to gather information and come up with recommendations. Unsurprisingly, the commission concluded that what Canada needed was a central bank. In an equally unsurprising response, the government embraced that recommendation, establishing the Bank of Canada in 1935. As an economic matter, the creation of the Bank of Canada had little effect on the commercial banking system: there simply wasn't much broken that needed fixing. Indeed, scholars of Canadian banking history have concluded that within the confines of a fixed-exchange-rate system, the Bank of Canada had little to add to the financial system.[51] Its establishment did, however, give the government the ability to meet inflationist demands from Western farmers to expand the money supply by creating a central bank with the power to issue fiat money. Subsequent reforms, again driven by populist demands, made the Bank of Canada a government-owned entity (as of 1938), and gave it a monopoly on note issue (as of 1944).[52] When all was said and done, the Canadian banks came through the Great Depression more or less the way they went into it. They had lost a valuable privilege—the right to print money—but the basic structure of the banking industry remained intact.

Canada's distinctive set of institutions governing banking also proved to be robust to demands for increased access to credit and the rise of new nonbank intermediaries following World War II. The Canadian banking system had been designed to facilitate lending in support of long-distance trade, and Canada's commercial banks were legally prohibited from making loans collateralized by real estate.[53] A usury law placed a 7 percent cap on the amount of interest that was legally recoverable. These restrictions limited the riskiness of bank loans and also created a somewhat uneasy relationship between bankers and farmers, who tended to view

---

[51] Bordo and Redish (1987); Bordo, Redish, and Rockoff (2011), 19.

[52] The commercial banks did not formally lose the right to issue notes until the 1944 revision to the Bank Act. In recognition of the lower risk this implied, bank shares as of 1944 no longer carried double liability: stockholders were liable only for the face value of their shares. See Curtis (1947), 120.

[53] Redish (2003) shows that mortgage credit constituted roughly half of total financial-system credit in Upper Canada in the first half of the nineteenth century. These loans were provided by local, private lenders, not chartered banks.

themselves as starved for credit. As Canada became increasingly indus-trial and increasingly urban, other groups, such as small manufacturers, who needed credit for fixed and working capital, and urbanites, who wished to buy homes, also began to resent the constraints imposed by a banking system that was not designed to fulfill their needs for credit.[54]

The demands of these groups became particularly salient during and after World War II. During the war, Canadian manufacturers dramatically ramped up production: in fact, they produced much of the war material for the British armed forces. This expansion fueled the growth of an urban working class. From 1939 to 1944, the number of manufacturing workers nearly tripled: by the end of the war, they accounted for nearly half of the civilian labor force.[55] After the war, the return of hundreds of thousands of Canadian soldiers, sailors, and airmen drove the process of urbanization—and the demand for urban housing—still harder.[56] The government took a number of steps to provide housing credit to this obvi-ously crucial urban constituency. Importantly, it did not do so through the banks, which remained unable to make loans against real estate—and which did not lobby for the right to do so.[57] In fact, the 1944 revision to the Bank Act made it even less likely that banks would be able to service the growing urban loan market because it reduced the amount of interest that they could legally recover from 7 percent to 6 percent, thereby reduc-ing incentives for risky lending. Rather, the government attempted to sat-isfy demands for real-estate lending with its rewriting of the National Housing Act in 1944 and the establishment of the Central Mortgage and Housing Corporation the following year. The CMHC was a crown corpo-ration, financed by the sale of bonds to the treasury. Its purpose was to

---

[54] Since the closing days of World War I, there had been a series of modestly funded government programs designed to facilitate mortgage credit through "near banks" (typically finance companies operated by insurance corporations), but these efforts produced trivial outcomes. For example, the Dominion Housing Act of 1935 managed to fund the construction of only 4,899 housing units from 1935 through 1938. See Canadamortgage.com (n.d.); Curtis (1947), 120.

[55] By 1944, manufacturing employment had reached just over 2 million, while the total civilian labor force was just over 4.5 million. Statistics Canada (1983), Series D124–133 and R1–22.

[56] In 1944, there were nearly 800,000 soldiers, sailors, and airmen in the Canadian armed forces. Statistics Canada (1983), Series D124–133.

[57] Neufeld (2001), 328.

provide supplementary financing, as well as explicit government guarantees, to finance companies (which were usually owned by insurance companies) in order to encourage them to make mortgage loans to homeowners, builders, and developers. As of 1947, the CMHC was also authorized to make direct loans to homeowners or builders in certain areas.[58] In short, Canadian taxpayers subsidized insurance companies to get into the mortgage business, and when the market looked unattractive to those companies (even with government guarantees), taxpayers directly subsidized home builders.[59]

The banks did not fight terribly hard against these reforms in the 1940s. Canadian bankers apparently did not view their particular form of the Game of Bank Bargains as a winner-take-all contest. Why not allow a few crumbs to be thrown to the losers (aspiring homeowners) in order to keep them from forming a coalition with farmers that might upset the entire game?

By the 1950s, however, these crumbs were starting to look like whole slices, and by the 1960s it looked as if the nonbank intermediaries were going to be allowed to open their own bakeries. In 1955, finance companies, savings institutions, and trust companies—referred to collectively in Canada as *near banks*—controlled 24 percent of financial institution assets. By 1962 they controlled 32 percent and, by 1967, 36 percent.[60] The banks therefore began to move against the near banks by pushing for reforms that would eliminate their advantages in the 1954 and 1967 revisions to the Bank Act.[61] In the 1954 revision, the CMHC got out of the business of joint lending with near banks: instead it provided mortgage insurance for National Housing Act loans as well as direct subsidies for housing construction. In addition, the 1954 revision allowed the

---

[58] Canadamortgage.com (n.d.); Curtis (1947), 120.

[59] Twenty-six percent of all housing construction between 1944 and 1953—just over 200,000 homes—was financed through the National Housing Act, with the CMHC providing 36 percent of the funds (and the rest coming from finance companies). Starting in 1944, the government also provided credit to small and medium-sized manufacturers by creating the Industrial Development Bank, a wholly owned subsidiary of the Bank of Canada. This bank was capitalized at $25 million and could make loans for periods of up to 15 years. See Curtis (1947), 120; Canadamortgage.com (n.d.).

[60] Leach (1969), 135.

[61] Leach (1969), 134–35; Neufeld (2001), 329.

banks to enter the mortgage market by participating in the CMHC-insured programs.[62]

The 1967 revision to the Bank Act drove a spike into the heart of the near banks by lifting many of the restrictions on the chartered banks. The act eliminated interest-rate caps on bank lending. It also allowed banks to enter the conventional (uninsured) mortgage market. Finally, it changed bank-deposit reserve ratios from 8 percent on all accounts to 4 percent on time deposits and 12 percent on demand deposits.[63] The best the near banks appear to have been able to do in the legislative tug-of-war was to get the government to place a ceiling equal to 10 percent of deposits on banks' holdings in conventional (uninsured) mortgages and to introduce deposit insurance for accounts up to $20,000, thereby protecting their deposit base against encroachment by the banks. It is not known whether the banks fought very hard against either of these limits: the 10 percent ceiling was not binding at the time,[64] and from the point of view of the banks, the limited extent of deposit insurance may not have offered a very large subsidy to their near-bank competitors. That is, they may have thought that they could crush the finance and trust companies and end up with a government subsidy too.[65]

The 1980, 1987, and 1992 revisions to the Bank Act effectively removed any threat posed by the near banks. As of 1980, banks were allowed to operate subsidiary mortgage-finance companies, thereby getting around the limits that had been set on their conventional mortgage holdings. The 1987 revision removed restrictions on banks' owning securities brokerages. Within a year, the five largest banks entered the market either by buying one of the country's major brokerages or by starting their own.[66] In 1992, all remaining restrictions were knocked down: banks were allowed to own insurance companies, mortgage loan companies, and trust companies; and their own mortgage lending was no longer limited by

---

[62] See Canadamortgage.com (n.d.); Freedman (1998), 7, 22.

[63] Leach (1969), 134.

[64] Freedman (1998), 8.

[65] Deposit insurance did, however, result in an increase in the risk of failure of banks that relied on it (Carr, Mathewson, and Quigley [1994], 58–64). No banks or trust and mortgage-loan companies failed in Canada from 1949 to 1966. From 1968 to 1985, 22 institutions failed.

[66] Bordo, Redish, and Rockoff (2011), 23.

statute. In addition, the 1992 revision to the Bank Act eliminated deposit reserve requirements. The net result was that Canada's banks were able to buy up the near banks that had struggled to compete with them and emerge as tremendous financial conglomerates.[67] As of the late 1990s, they accounted for two-thirds of nonmortgage consumer lending (e.g., automobile loans and credit-card lending) and 55 percent of residential mortgage lending. Canada's banks also became major providers of industrial finance. In 1998, for example, credit from banks equaled the amount raised by business from the sale of equities, was triple the amount raised by the sale of bonded debt, and dwarfed the commercial paper market by an order of magnitude. Banks also owned the major securities dealers.[68]

The Canadian banking system also proved robust to the threat posed by U.S. banks, which began to enter the Canadian market after 1980. Until that time, foreign banks had been barred from opening subsidiaries or purchasing controlling interests in Canadian banks.[69] A series of legal revisions (in 1980 and 1985) allowed foreign banks to open separately capitalized subsidiaries, although these operations were subject to size limitations.[70] These limits were subsequently removed by the 1989 Canada–United States Free Trade Agreement. The 1997 revision to the Bank Act went further: it allowed foreign banks to open branches in Canada without establishing a separately capitalized subsidiary.[71]

Canada's banks were, however, able to insulate themselves from foreign competition through legislative and regulatory mechanisms. Canadian banks are divided into three groups: schedule I banks (domestically owned banks chartered in Canada); schedule II banks (foreign-owned banks chartered in Canada); and schedule III banks (branches owned by foreign banks operating without a Canadian charter). Schedule I banks of significant size cannot be acquired by a foreign bank because they are required to be "widely held." Foreign branches are not able to accept deposits smaller than $150,000 or to participate in the deposit insurance system, and they

[67] Freedman (1998), 8–15.

[68] Freedman (1998), 22–28.

[69] The 1967 revision to the Bank Act made it illegal for any shareholder to own more than 10 percent of a bank's shares; foreign shareholders as a group could not own more than 25 percent of shares. Freedman (1998), 8.

[70] Initially, the holdings of foreign bank subsidiaries were not allowed to exceed 8 percent of the total domestic assets of Canadian banks. The limit was raised to 16 percent in 1985. Freedman (1998), 8–9.

[71] Freedman (1998), 8–9.

are disadvantaged by various other restrictions on their operations and their legal status as creditors.[72] Schedule II banks (foreign subsidiaries) face three kinds of barriers: first, they must overcome numerous one-time hurdles to obtain a charter; second, and more importantly, once they have obtained a charter, their ability to grow could be constrained by discretionary regulation of their capital ratio requirements, their liquidity ratio requirements, and discretionary limits placed on the amounts of various types of assets they are allowed to hold.[73] Even if those limits were not immediately applied, the knowledge that they could be applied, if the foreign bank grew to be a significant challenge to domestic banks, discourages growth. Third, possessing a branching network is a key to successful competition, but the "widely held" limit makes it virtually impossible for a foreign entrant to establish a large branching network through acquisition. The only alternative is building a network of "de novo" branches, which is time consuming and expensive. These limits make it much more costly for foreign subsidiaries to compete in Canadian loan and deposit markets. As a result of these various legislative and regulatory limits, Canadian banking remains largely that—Canadian. At the end of 2011, more than two decades after the Canada–U.S. Free Trade Agreement, foreign banks accounted for only 7.1 percent of banking-system assets.[74]

Was There a Dark Side?

Compared to the U.S. banking system, the Canadian system has been remarkably stable. Stability can, however, come at the expense of efficiency. Imagine, for example, a banking system composed of a single monopolist that pays nothing for deposits and lends only to borrowers with AAA

---

[72] Freedman (1998); Gouvin (2001); Davies Ward Phillips & Vineberg LLP (n.d.). Schedule I and schedule II banks can hold and enforce a "Bank Act security," a legal construct that can be useful as a protection against loan loss. Foreign branches rely solely on provincial security rights, which, in some cases, can be inferior. See Uniform Law Conference of Canada (n.d.).

[73] According to Davies Ward Phillips & Vineberg LLP (n.d.), Canadian bank regulators have the right to establish whatever limitations or conditions "the Superintendent deems necessary," and these include "limitations on the assets that a bank can have on its balance sheet; higher minimum capital requirements; liquidity deposits from shareholders; and limitations on the growth of a bank's business in specific sectors or with respect to certain business activities."

[74] Canadian Bankers Association (2012).

credit ratings who are personally known to the directors of the bank. Such a system would be extremely stable, but stability would come at the cost of slower economic growth and lower rates of social mobility. Entrepreneurs with good ideas, but no track records or personal connections, would be starved for credit; small businesses would not be able to borrow their way through short-run downturns in the business cycle; and households would not be able to finance lumpy investments, such as home purchases or college educations.

Let us then sift through the evidence in order to see whether the stability of the Canadian banking system was achieved at these kinds of costs, keeping in mind a view long held in both academic and popular circles that Canadian banks are a comfortable oligopoly that constrains credit in order to drive up interest-rate spreads and earn supernormal profits.[75]

Reality always pales in comparison to utopia, and thus any reasoned answer to the question of whether Canada sacrificed efficiency for stability requires us to first answer the question, "Efficient compared to what?" There are basically two ways to answer this question. One is to compare the performance of the Canadian banking system to that of another real-world economy, such as the United States. A second is to look for evidence that the Canadian banking system operated as if it had a perfectly competitive market structure. The (implicit) comparison in this exercise is to a hypothetical banking system composed of profit-maximizing firms that compete ferociously on the basis of price and cost.

In comparing the performance of the Canadian and U.S. banking systems, the simplest way to start is to ask about the price of credit: has it historically been higher or lower in Canada than in the United States? The answer, from several studies that have looked at data from the entire twentieth century, is that, on average, interest rates charged on loans were the same in the two countries. The interest rates paid on deposits, however, were *higher* in Canada![76] Canadian banks actually charged *smaller* interest-rate spreads than U.S. banks. These facts suggest that the Canadian system, consisting of a few very large banks with branch networks, gave rise to greater price competition than the U.S. system, composed of thousands of small banks operating in restricted local markets.

---

[75] Bordo, Rockoff, and Redish (1994), 326.
[76] Bordo, Rockoff, and Redish (1994), 325–41; Nichols and Hendrickson (1997), 681.

The evidence on the price of credit also suggests that regional interest-rate differentials were overcome much earlier in Canada than in the United States. In the U.S. antebellum period, when the country was smaller and the South was linked by a network of branching banks (and occasionally by the First and Second Banks of the United States), interest-rate differences across regions were small.[77] As the United States expanded, and as it increasingly came to rely on segmented unit banks to provide credit, interregional interest-rate differentials became huge. During the 1890s, interest rates on the highest-quality loans (known as first-class two-name paper, in reference to the fact that the paper was the joint obligation of two parties with good credit) in western U.S. cities were typically between 4 percent and 8 percent higher than interest rates in eastern cities, and those large differences were still visible in the 1920s.[78] Not so in Canada, where during the last two decades of the nineteenth century, interest rates in the West never exceeded 1 or 2 percent of the rates charged in Montreal or Toronto for loans of similar risk characteristics.[79] In the 1920s, Canadian interest-rate differences across regions remained small. As one contemporary observed, "So perfectly is this distribution of capital made, that as between the highest class of borrower in Montreal or Toronto, and the ordinary merchant in the Northwest, the difference in interest paid is not more than one or two percent."[80]

If Canadian banks historically operated in a more competitive environment than U.S. banks, how did Canadian banks manage to make more money than U.S. banks? Although this fact underpins the view that Canadian banks operated as a cozy oligopoly, the real answer is that Canada's generally less-restrictive regulatory environment—which crucially includes the ability to operate national branch networks—allowed Canadian banks to capture scale economies in back-office operations, operate with less capital than U.S. banks, and deploy that capital more efficiently.[81] In 1920,

---

[77] Bodenhorn (2000), 128–64.

[78] Breckenridge (1899a); Riefler (1930), 79–95; Calomiris (2000), 30–33; Breckenridge (1899b), 5, 55.

[79] H. White (1902), 53–54.

[80] Willit (1930), 185.

[81] How was this risk-management hat trick possible? There were two influences at work. First, interbank coordination orchestrated by the Bank of Montreal limited systemic risk. Second, branch banking promotes superior loan diversification. If a bank operates branches nationwide, it can pool lending risks from different regions specializing in different products. Thus, a nationwide bank's loan portfolio is less risky than

Credit as percentage of GDP

FIGURE 9.1 Ratio of commercial bank private credit to GDP, Canada and the United States, 1910–2010.

Source: Statistics Canada (1983); *Bank of Canada Statistical Review* (various dates); *Bank of Canada Review* (various dates); Federal Reserve Board (1943, 1971); United States Bureau of Economic Analysis (various dates); Federal Deposit Insurance Corporation (n.d.).

Note: Canada series excludes foreign lending.

for example, Canadian banks maintained a capital-to-asset ratio of 8.6 percent, compared to 11.5 percent in the United States. In that same year, Canadian banks lent out 72.7 percent of their assets, compared to only 53.1 percent in the United States. Those differences remained remarkably stable over the rest of the twentieth century. Moreover, those differences in balance-sheet composition, along with comparable differences in administrative costs, account for nearly all of the difference in profitability between Canadian and U.S. banks.[82]

What about the quantity of credit supplied? Figure 9.1 compares chartered commercial bank lending to the private sector as a percentage of GDP in Canada and the United States from 1910 to 2010. This figure illustrates three facts, each of which indicates that the supply of credit in

---

that of a bank making loans in only one locale. Lower loan risk allows the nationwide bank to hold a higher proportion of loans relative to assets without undertaking more risk per dollar of assets.

[82] Bordo, Rockoff, and Redish (1987), 336; Nichols and Hendrickson (1997), 681.

Canada was not hampered by its concentrated banking system. First, on average over time, the Canadian credit to GDP ratio is equal to or greater than that of the United States. This is remarkable given Canada's lower population density. Second, the increasing concentration of the Canadian banking system over time was associated with an increase in the supply of credit, both over time and in comparison with the contemporary United States. Third, a large contributor to the Canadian banks' growth in credit was the acquisition of near banks and the expansion of chartered banks into new activities over time, which was made possible by the process of regularly updating Canadian banking regulations. These periodic reviews allowed banks to lobby regulators, so that they were not pushed aside by nonbank intermediaries associated with financial innovations. In contrast, as we show in chapter 6, U.S. banks lost market share to the shadow banking system, especially after the 1960s, as thrifts, finance companies, credit unions, insurance companies, mutual funds, investment banks, and hedge funds grew at the expense of commercial banks.

What about the distribution of that credit—in particular, the availability of credit in rural areas? Again, the question is "Compared to what?" When comparison is with the United States, three observable indicators suggest that the Canadian branching system served rural customers more effectively than the U.S. unit-bank system. First, as we noted previously, rural areas in Canada, unlike those of the United States, enjoyed costs of credit that were close to those of urban areas.

Second, lower information costs associated with branching in Canada facilitated the transacting in bankers' acceptances and bills of exchange over long distances, a process that is extremely useful for financing the movement of rural produce. As we have noted before, Canadian branch banking allowed a single bank to manage the movement and export of crops and retain legal title to the goods in transit as collateral throughout the process, which economized on the cost of credit.[83] This capacity was not available in the United States, which is why bankers' acceptances or bills-of-exchange lending in support of crop movements was relatively rare.

Third, rural areas in Canada were much better supplied with banking facilities than those in the United States. As a general rule, countries with low population densities, such as Canada, tend to have a hard time supplying credit to farmers because sparse rural populations do not generate enough activity to justify the establishment of local banking offices. Data about the number of bank offices (headquarters or branches) per capita suggest that Canada had a higher ratio than the United States. Circa 1912, there was one bank office for every 2,847 inhabitants in Canada, compared to one for every 3,407 inhabitants in the more densely populated United States.[84] By 1940 those differences in bank access had widened: there was one bank per 3,410 inhabitants per banking office in Canada, compared to one per 7,325 inhabitants in the United States.[85] The principal reason for the wider availability of banking in Canada was its branch system. Because Canadian banks could consolidate administration in a single back office, the marginal cost of opening a branch office in a town of only 200 souls out on the prairie was trivial.

It is one thing to show that the Canadian banking system was no more monopolistic than the U.S. banking system, but it is another to show that it was highly competitive. The U.S. system, after all, was composed of segmented monopolies for much of the twentieth century. Judging Canada's system as "better" at providing credit than the U.S. system might be akin to saying that the New York mobster John Gotti was a good citizen because he was the best-behaved prisoner in solitary confinement. In order to make the argument that Canada's system produced sufficient competition, one has to draw a hypothetical comparison to a system in which markets are highly contestable. Two pioneering empirical studies have used econometric methods to assess the degree of competitiveness among Canadian banks.[86] Despite the high concentration of Canada's banking system, which is inherent to a system based on nationwide branching, both studies reject the view that Canadian banks enjoy monopolies by virtue of their large size. One of those studies goes further. For the period 1969–85, it estimates the slope of banks' marginal revenue functions (which economists use to measure the market power of firms) to gauge the extent to which banks act as competitive price takers. The author finds that marginal-revenue curves are flat and concludes that "the estimates are consistent with perfect competition."[87]

Canadian banks have historically also been much more efficient in managing risk than U.S. banks. In particular, they have been able to achieve lower risk of default on their debts. These differences emerged early.

---

[84] Patterson (1917), 62.
[85] Chapman and Westerfield (1942), 342–43.
[86] Nathan and Neave (1989); Shaffer (1993).
[87] Shaffer (1993), 57. Subsequent research agrees; see Allen and Engert (2007).

Percentage in arrears

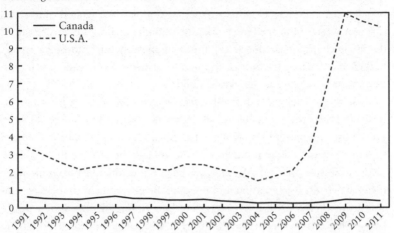

FIGURE 9.2 U.S. and Canadian mortgages in arrears, 1991–2011.

Source: Federal Reserve Board (n.d.); Canadian Bankers Association (2012).

Note: In the U.S., mortgages are in arrears if payment is overdue by 30 days; in Canada the period is 90 days. Thus the most meaningful comparison is the ratio of the two countries' data over time.

Holders of Canadian banks' notes were protected after 1890 by a system of mutual insurance among banks, but that system did not apply to deposits. Nevertheless, depositors, on average, bore little risk of loss. Between 1867 and 1889, 13 Canadian banks failed, and data on losses are available for 11 of these cases. In eight of them, depositor losses were essentially zero.[88] From 1890 to 1966 only 12 banks failed, and depositor losses were zero in six of them. The other six were such small institutions that the losses they imposed on depositors were trivial: on average, the losses of these six banks averaged 0.2 percent of total bank deposits.[89] Looking back over all of Canadian banking history and comparing the average loss rates to depositors in the U.S. and Canada, losses to depositors in Canada were 30 percent lower than in the United States.[90]

The superior ability of Canadian banks to manage risk has persisted. Figure 9.2 demonstrates the striking difference between risk management

[88] Vreeland (1910), 219.

[89] Carr, Mathewson, and Quigley (1995), 1139.

[90] Williamson (1989). The ratio is computed as the losses on deposits of failed banks divided by the total deposits in the system.

in Canada and the United States in recent years. Canada's banking system avoided the 2007–09 banking crisis that crippled the United States and much of Western Europe. The relaxation of underwriting standards that we discuss in chapter 7 produced a quintupling of residential mortgage arrears in the United States. In contrast, Canadian residential mortgage arrears displayed characteristic, and enviable, dullness.[91]

Despite the exemplary historic performance of Canadian banking, the growing concentration of control of the financial system by five banks since 1990 raises deep concerns. When a handful of banks control the financial system, there is a risk that banks will, individually or as a group, be able to secure excessive political influence, which could enable them to undermine the effectiveness of regulation and pressure the government to tolerate anti-competitive behavior. In 2003, a report by Bain & Co. assembled some troubling evidence that was at least consistent with, if not proof of, declining competition in Canadian banking since 1990. Two thousand branches were closed nationwide from 1990 to 2003. The interest margins of Canadian banks did not fall as much as those of banks operating in other countries.[92]

Canada's political system has proved resilient against pressures from banks in the interest of preserving competition. In 1998, the minister of finance rejected two proposed merger deals, much to the consternation of Canadian bankers. In explaining that decision, the minister made it clear that, in the government's view, no further consolidation of the industry would be in the public interest, for three reasons. First, it could lead to an undesirable reduction in competition. Second, it would expose the economy to the risk of a credit crunch if one bank's problems forced it to limit its supply of credit. Third, in response to these first two risks, Canada might have to lower its barriers to foreign-controlled banks, resulting in "a substantial reduction of Canadian ownership and control" in the banking system. In other words, the government drew a line in the sand in 1998, telling the Canadian banks that further consolidation would not be allowed.[93]

----

[91] Kiff (2009); Ratnovski and Huang (2009).

[92] The 2003 Bain & Co. study is included in Canada Department of Finance (2003). Of course, one could object that the declining spreads witnessed in other countries' banking systems in the 2000s reflected problems of underpriced risk rather than competitive advantages and that those problems subsequently showed themselves in the crisis of 2007–09, which Canada avoided.

[93] The finance minister's 1998 explanation (Canada Department of Finance [2003]) was clear:

We are not suggesting that Canada's banking system is perfectly competitive today. Indeed, like many critics, we worry that the Canadian banking system has become too concentrated. Nevertheless, the bulk of the empirical evidence on Canadian banking and politics suggests that Canada's durable bargain continues to deliver a remarkably successful combination of stable banking, abundant credit, and a commitment to preserving competition in financial services.

Conclusion

Canada and the United States have a great deal in common. Both were North American colonies of Great Britain. Both had strong populist movements, which vied for control of their financial systems. In the United States, the result was a roller coaster of structural change in the banking system that reflected the shifting political coalitions influencing banking regulation. Canada's unusual political institutions, which were an outcome of its geography and colonial history, ensured the durability of the partnership between bankers, merchants, and the parties in control of the government.

By any standard, Canada already has one of the most concentrated banking systems in the world. Allowing the mergers would mean leaving decisions on credit allocation —which are so crucial to the efficient functioning of the economy—in the hands of even fewer, larger institutions, thereby raising serious concerns that go well beyond the issue of competition. . . . Concentrating so much credit decision-making in the hands of so few institutions also has implications from the standpoint of how well we manage the overall economy. No single large institution should be so large as to have a major influence on the overall availability of credit in the country. If circumstances were to lead to a large dominant institution having to restrain lending, the resulting withdrawal could lead to a "credit crunch" with adverse consequences on the economy as a whole.

The minister explicitly pointed to the potential unintended consequences for foreign entry of permitting further domestic consolidation:

Historically, in Canada, when a financial institution has faced difficulties, one possibility has always been to sell its operations to other stronger Canadian competitors. However, after such a merger, a sale to a domestic firm could seriously reduce the level of competition within the Canadian sector. If this were not acceptable, we could be faced with a situation where the only other option would be a sale to a foreign institution. But given the size of the banks that would result from these proposed mergers [RBC/BMO, CIBC/TD], such a sale of assets to a foreign institution would result in a substantial reduction of Canadian ownership and control. Therefore, faced with a firm in financial difficulty, and with fewer domestic institutions, we could find ourselves in a situation where we might have to put other fundamental policy objectives, such as the need for competition or Canadian control, into question in order to preserve our ability to address potential problems. In other words, the sheer size of the institutions that would result from these mergers would constrain the alternatives available to regulators and to government.

Many observers of the Canadian banking system credit its superior performance to its regulatory structure. In this view, Canadian banks' conservative risk management reflects the diligent oversight of regulators as well as the threat that failure to abide by the letter and the spirit of regulation will cause the loss of valuable privileges. As we have emphasized, Canada developed the practice of enacting a new banking law on a regular schedule that coincides with the rechartering of its banks. This continual remaking of all bank charters, according to a number of scholars, has an obvious impact on bank behavior: banks want to avoid getting on the wrong side of the government.[94] One particularly powerful weapon in the government's quiver is the dismantling of the laws that give Canadian banks preferred positions relative to foreign entrants—for example, the $150,000 minimum on foreign branches' deposits, or the various barriers faced by schedule II banks. There is clearly some merit to this view. When a country has a deposit-insurance safety net, it is subject to potential problems of moral hazard, and thus prudential regulators become an important bulwark against excessive risk taking by bankers.

Effective regulation and supervision cannot, however, entirely account for the stability of the Canadian banking system. In the first place, for most of Canada's history there was neither a safety net nor much government regulation of risk. Second, Canada's practice of periodically revising the Bank Act and rechartering the banks is not solely a stick with which to discipline wayward bankers: it is also a carrot with which to reward good risk management by ensuring the preservation of banks' franchise values.[95] When someone knows that his business has a future, he has strong incentives to preserve his business for that future. In Canada, the periodic revision of regulation allows the government to make sure that the banks are not left behind by financial innovations, thus enabling them to preserve both the asset and liability sides of their customer relationships. On the asset side, for example, when Canada's banks realized that they were becoming marginalized by their exclusion from the mortgage market in the 1950s and 1960s, the government was induced to rewrite

[94] Vittas, Frazer, and Metaxas-Vittas (1988); Bordo, Redish, and Rockoff (2011).

[95] In contrast, as we note in chapter 8, banks with low franchise values may choose not to manage risk properly, preferring to undertake value-destroying risks. See also our related discussion of the relationship between bank concentration and stability in chapter 15.

the laws permitting them to enter that market. As a result, the commercial banks crushed and absorbed the near banks. On the liabilities side, banks have been able to retain their core deposits. Unlike banks in the United States, which fund much of their lending with money they borrow in whole-sale markets, Canadian banks have held onto traditional depositors. Doing so has allowed them to provide loans at lower cost to borrowers and to avoid the risks that arise when banks rely on more volatile wholesale money markets.[96]

More fundamentally, these advantageous features of the Canadian regulatory system should not be seen as independent causes of the success of Canadian banking. Rather, Canada's regulatory system—limited-duration charters, nationwide branching, and conservative regulation—are all outcomes of Canada's Game of Bank Bargains. If smart regulation alone accounted for Canada's success, it would be easily emulated. Unfortunately for the rest of the world, that is not the case.

[96] Ratnovski and Huang (2009), 17–18.

Authoritarianism, Democratic Transitions,
and the Game of Bank Bargains

10

Mexico
Chaos Makes Cronyism Look Good

The weak, the unprepared, those who lack the tools in order to emerge victorious against evolution must perish and leave the struggle to the more powerful.

José Limantour, Mexican treasury minister, 1901

Our theoretical framework for understanding the structure and performance of banking systems within autocratic political systems incorporates a number of principles. First, there can be no banking system without a stable government. Second, centralizing authoritarian governments can expropriate their banking systems with ease, which tends to make their banking systems smaller than those of democracies. Third, authoritarian governments and bankers can align their incentives by forming a rent-generating partnership. The experience of Mexico illustrates every one of these principles. Since 1997, Mexico's transition from a centralized authoritarian state to a fledgling democracy has had a dramatic impact on the political bargain that underpins the banking system and thus on the structure of the banking system itself.

Indeed, Mexican history is a natural laboratory for studying the relationship between political institutions and banking systems. From independence in 1821 until 1876, the Mexican political system was characterized by chaos. There were attempts to create stable, republican governments, but these were all stillborn, the victims of foreign invasions, internal coups, or civil wars. Needless to say, Mexico had nothing that even began to approximate a banking system during this period. What rational investor would deploy his wealth to provide the capital footings for a bank in an environment in which governments, and factions that aspired to be governments, had every incentive to expropriate that wealth in order to hold onto power, or seize it?

Warlordism ended when a tremendously able political entrepreneur, General Porfirio Díaz, figured out that there were rents to be earned from foreign trade and investment and that those rents could be used to align the incentives of rival politicians in order to create a stable authoritarian system. One key part of Díaz's "Pax Porfiriana," which endured from 1877 to 1911, was the creation of a banking system that extended credit to his government, thereby providing him the financial wherewithal to consolidate power. Díaz and Mexico's financiers crafted a set of institutions designed to coax capital into the banking system by systematically limiting competition. The rents generated by this system of segmented monopolies were then split between the bankers (who, in addition to earning dividends and directors' fees, used the banks to fund their nonfinancial enterprises), bank minority shareholders (who earned healthy dividends), the government (which obtained access to low-interest loans), and the individuals in control of the government (who obtained board seats for themselves and their family members, as well as loans that were forgiven by the banks). Everyone outside this coalition—which is to say the vast majority of the Mexican population—was left out in the cold, with no political voice, no credit, and limited opportunities for economic mobility.

The lack of opportunity—both among the common people and among the elites outside the governing coalition—fueled a rebellion against Díaz in 1910 and sent him into exile in France in 1911. The victors of that revolution, however, soon fell to fighting among themselves. From 1911 to 1928, Mexico was torn apart by civil wars, rebellions, military coups, and political assassinations. The banking system quickly disintegrated, because every side in the revolution, regardless of its stated ideology, preyed on the banks in order to finance its military campaigns.

Political stability was eventually reestablished in 1929, when the warlords who had managed to survive the Mexican Revolution and its bloody aftermath sat down to create a political party to broker differences among themselves. The organization that they created, initially called the Partido Nacional Revolucionario (the National Revolutionary Party—PNR) was not a political party in the usual sense of the word: it did not run slates of candidates embracing any particular policy platform. Rather, it was a forum in which conflicts among warlords, political bosses, and corrupt labor leaders were brokered. Those leaders then decided who would run for which office and what the vote counts would be. In time, this model of a political party as a forum to "predetermine" elections became institutionalized, giving rise to the Partido Revolucionario Institucional (PRI), which effectively monopolized power until the late 1990s.

The PRI murdered, jailed, and tortured its opponents. It controlled the flow of information by using its leverage over the mass media. It financed its candidates' electoral campaigns directly out of the federal treasury. It administered Mexico's elections, and it counted the votes. Not surprisingly, it won every presidential election from 1929 to 2000, when it was finally forced to admit that its candidate had been defeated by the candidate of an opposition party. It also dominated both houses of Mexico's congress, as well as every state house, until the late 1990s. The PRI used its control of every branch of government to shape Mexico's regulatory and legal systems: PRI politicians named state and federal judges, the federal bureaucracy, and the directors of government-owned firms.

So complete was the PRI's hegemony that it was difficult to induce investors to provide the capital for a banking system. Indeed, investors were so nervous about being expropriated by the government that the commercial banking system from the 1920s to the 1970s was minuscule, even by the standards of Porfirian Mexico. The PRI, however, needed a banking system in order to sustain its rule: it relied on the political support of urban, unionized workers whose labor federations were official elements of the party, and generating secure jobs for those workers required a sufficiently large industrial sector and a banking system that could finance it. The government therefore created a complex system of development banks that served as second-tier lenders, repurchasing loans made by commercial banks through special programs designed to channel credit to sectors that the PRI deemed crucial.

The Mexican banking system was sustained by implicit government guarantees. Bankers, shareholders, and depositors in commercial banks did not bear the risk of loans gone bad: rather, the risk was borne by taxpayers, who not only financed the development banks but also wound up owning more than 1,000 inefficient enterprises. These were the product of a system in which reckless bets could be covered by government-owned banks set up to ensure that the unionized workers who supported the PRI would have jobs for life.

The Lost Nineteenth Century

If Mexican society over the long run could be characterized in a single word, it would be *inequality*. The pyramids of Tenochtitlán, the great city-state at the heart of the Aztec Empire, were built by extracting tribute from hundreds of smaller, less powerful city-states spread across central Mexico. The military-political elites of those subject city-states, in turn, extracted tribute, in labor and in kind, from millions of small farmers. The Spaniards, when they conquered Tenochtitlán in 1521, simply installed themselves at the top of this hierarchy—and then refined it by requiring the indigenous population to pay their taxes in coin rather than labor and maize.

The path to Mexican independence, especially when contrasted with that of the United States, gives a sense of just how unevenly political power, wealth, and human capital were distributed. In the United States, a colonial elite of self-made men mobilized and led a literate, property-owning citizen army against British rule. In Mexico, a European colonial elite, fearing what would happen to them if the mass of illiterate and impoverished Indians and mestizos gained power, joined with the Spanish viceroy and his army to put down a popular independence movement that sprang to life in 1810. Those elites were so afraid that independence might spark revolution from below that they put the heads of the executed leaders of the 1810 Hidalgo Rebellion on public display for 11 years —until the same elites decided to declare independence in 1821.

It was not that Mexico's elites had a change of heart. Rather, they declared independence because they concluded that the Spanish army—the same organization that launched Francisco Franco a century later—was *too liberal*. The event that pushed them into rebellion was the acceptance of the Spanish constitution of 1812 by King Ferdinand VII, who had been forced to accept it by a revolt of midlevel army officers in 1820. Mexico's colonial elites deemed this constitution, which embraced universal male suffrage and constitutional monarchy, as dangerous, and thus declared independence from Spain. The notions of equality and liberty that fueled the American Revolution were nowhere to be found in Mexico's reactionary, antirepublican independence movement, a contrast highlighted by the form of each country's first federal executive: in the United States, George Washington, the military leader of the revolution against Great Britain, became the first president; in Mexico, Agustín de Iturbide, a royalist general who had fought against the independence movement of 1810, had himself named emperor.

Iturbide lasted only eight months in power, but even after he was removed, political power remained concentrated among the country's narrow elite. One subgroup of that elite, the Conservatives, sought to retain all of the political and economic institutions of the colonial era, including the centralization of political power and exemptions from trial in civil courts for the army and clergy. A second subgroup, the Liberals, wanted a federal republic in which states would be granted considerable autonomy and in which the political economy of the country would be guided by laissez-faire principles. Both sides agreed on one issue: suffrage should be restricted, and Europeanized elites should run the country. The right to vote in early nineteenth-century Mexico was therefore constrained both by wealth and literacy requirements, effectively limiting the suffrage to a tiny sliver of the population.[1]

Mexico's conservatives and liberals agreed on the disenfranchisement of the mass of the population, but they could not agree on much else. Their conflicts precipitated a seemingly endless series of coups and civil wars from independence to 1876. From 1821 to 1876, Mexico had 75 presidents. For every constitutional president, there were four irregular, interim, or provisional presidents. One political-military strongman, Antonio López de Santa Ana, occupied the presidency on 11 different occasions.[2] All sides in this endless jockeying for power preyed on the property rights of their opponents. Every government that came to power also inherited a depleted treasury and no ready source of income. To meet their need for a source of public finance, Mexico's nineteenth-century governments borrowed from the country's wealthy merchant-financiers, who operated private banks. Many of these loans were little more than forced extortions. When governments changed, or when sitting governments faced sufficient threats, they reneged on those debts, often destroying the fortunes of the merchant-financiers in the process.[3]

Amid this background of political instability and bankruptcy, the Mexican state fell apart and remained weak, divided, and troubled. Provinces

[1] Engerman et al. (2012), 24.
[2] Stevens (1991), 11; Haber, Razo, and Maurer (2003), 42.
[3] Meyer Cosío (1985); Tenenbaum (1986); Walker (1987), chapters 5, 7, 8.

seceded almost at will: first the states of Central America in 1822–23, then Texas in 1836, and then (temporarily) the Yucatán in 1841. The remaining provinces were run as independent fiefdoms by their governors, some of whom were more warlords than politicians. Foreign powers invaded Mexico: the United States took half the national territory by force in 1846–48, and France invaded in 1862–63 and imposed a puppet government headed by the emperor Maximilian, who ruled until he was overthrown in 1867.

Breaking out of this equilibrium proved difficult. Soldiers, police, and bureaucrats had to be paid. Transportation barriers, which fueled the independence of provincial warlords, had to be overcome with the construction of a national railroad network (Mexico is a mountainous country with almost no navigable rivers). All of this was costly, but the central government had no ready source of revenue. Taxes could not be raised because they were collected by the states, not the central government. In fact, the strongmen who ruled the provinces had every incentive to derail any attempt by the federal government to reform the tax system, because their de facto fiefdoms would have been eroded by centralized tax collection.[4] Obtaining foreign credit was not an option: Mexico, as a serial defaulter, was effectively locked out of international capital markets.[5] The country's private bankers had already been expropriated via debt defaults on various occasions in the decades since independence.

The severity of the problem is made evident by one of the Mexican government's most desperate moves. Precisely because credit was so scarce, in 1830 the country's manufacturers pressured the government into founding an industrial development bank, the Banco de Avío, which was financed by a surtax on import tariffs. In 1842, desperate for cash, the government sold off its assets, which is to say that it expropriated its own bank.[6]

Mexico had no banking system to speak of during this period. Deploying capital in a chartered bank would have required investors to make a public declaration of the bank's assets, which would have created a target for expropriation. To the degree that there was any financial intermediation at all, it was through the private banking houses of the merchant-

---

[4] Carmagnani (1994), 268–69; Haber, Razo, and Maurer (2003), 84.
[5] Marichal (2002), 95–100; Maurer and Gomberg (2004), 1090.
[6] Potash (1983), 118–19.

financiers. These, however, lacked the advantages of the chartered banks that operated in other countries: they could not mobilize capital by selling equity to outside investors protected by limited liability; they did not have primacy as a creditor in the event of borrower bankruptcy; they were not subject to credible government supervision that might support their reputation as sound institutions; and their notes had neither the status of legal tender nor even the protection of the government against counterfeiters. Mexico's private banking houses were thus necessarily limited in scale.[7]

When Mexico finally issued its first bank charter in 1863, it was to a foreign entity (the Bank of London, Mexico, and South America), and the charter was granted by the puppet emperor Maximilian. That bank, and a small American-owned bank chartered by the government of the northern border state of Chihuahua, were the only two banking corporations in the entire country until the late 1870s.[8]

Creating a Crony Banking System under a Stable Dictatorship

In the last decades of the nineteenth century, Porfirio Díaz finally brought political stability to Mexico. Like many presidents before him, Díaz came to power through a military insurrection. Unlike his predecessors, however, Díaz managed to hang on to power for 35 years, from 1876 to 1911.

Though the PRI regime that came after Díaz worked hard to portray him as an absolute dictator, the Díaz regime was really a very careful balancing act between Díaz and other powerful political-military figures and economic elites. Initially, Díaz was careful not to antagonize these other interests. For example, from 1880 to 1884 he stepped down from the presidency in favor of one of his political allies, General Manuel Gónzalez (who still allowed Díaz to pull the strings). Díaz then "won" the presidential election of 1884, a victory that was assured when the army arrested and murdered the one politician who had the temerity to suggest that he would also stand as a candidate. There were, however, limits on the degree to which Díaz could rely on naked displays of force: the state governors often commanded militias that outnumbered the federal army.

---

[7] Meyer Cosío (1985); Cerutti (1985); Walker (1986), chapter 5.
[8] Maurer (2002), 18.

Díaz therefore focused more on gradually undermining or coopting his political rivals than on openly attacking them. He gradually replaced recalcitrant state governors with loyalists when the former died or stepped aside. He also created the post of *jefe político* (literally, political boss), a federal appointee assigned to every major city in each state, whose job was to exert federal control at the municipal level, thereby undermining the power of governors. These steps allowed Díaz to circulate lists of preferred congressional candidates to loyal state governors so that they could assure the "correct" electoral outcomes. Politically crucial governors, senators, congressmen, and cabinet members were then rewarded with board seats and other perquisites from the economic elites allied with the Díaz regime.

By the 1890s, Mexico's congress and senate had become largely irrelevant to the substance of policy making; the vast majority of senate roll-call votes were unanimous. Indeed, in 1890 the legislature rewrote the constitution to allow Díaz's continual reelection. Other reforms in the 1890s centralized taxation authority in the central government, further reducing the independence of state governors. As a result, Díaz increasingly negotiated over policy directly with powerful economic elites rather than with governors, senators, or congressmen. He thereby accomplished what no president before him had been able to do: he created political order and encouraged investment in an economy that had been moribund since independence. He did so, however, by institutionalizing corruption and fomenting a gerontocracy.[9]

Díaz had an advantage in this program of political centralization that was not available to any previous Mexican president: the ability to integrate with the U.S. economy. In the mid-nineteenth century, the U.S. economy, from Mexico's perspective, was a distant theoretical abstraction. By the time Díaz seized power, however, the U.S. economic center of gravity, and its railroad system, had moved westward. What adjoined Mexico on its northern frontier was no longer a desert but one of the largest economies in the world. It was now possible for Mexico to trade with the United States in ways that had been previously unimaginable. The possibility of trade, in turn, meant that there were positive returns to be earned

[9] Knight (1986), 15–30; Haber, Razo, and Maurer (2003), 42–51; Luna Argudín (2006), 267–22, 505–51; Razo (2008), 65–77.

by investing in sectors that produced tradable goods, particularly mining and ranching. Despite the aphorism "Poor Mexico, so far from God, so close to the United States!," proximity to the United States was an advantage that the Díaz regime exploited quite successfully.

What Díaz needed most was a source of finance that could jump-start the quasi-virtuous cycle of political order, centralization, private investment, and tax revenues. Simply promising not to behave like his predecessors would not have been credible: Mexico's political institutions could not impose binding limits on Díaz's authority. In fact, during the early years of his rule, Díaz himself had reneged on debts to some of the banks that had been founded in Mexico City.[10] Not surprisingly, during that period the banking system remained minuscule: as late as 1884 there were still only eight banks in the entire country, five of which were small operations in Chihuahua.[11]

The solution that Díaz and his financiers hit on was similar to the one that had been used by England in 1694: create a semiofficial superbank whose investors would be compensated for the risk of expropriation by the offer of extremely high rates of return and whose monopoly on public finance would prevent the government from defaulting selectively on some lenders while obtaining fresh credits from others. This superbank was created through the merger of two banks in Mexico City, which became the Banco Nacional de México (Banamex).

The charter that created Banamex, along with the accompanying legislation that protected its monopoly (the Commercial Code of 1884), resembled in some respects the deal that had created the Bank of England. The merged bank was allowed to increase its uncalled capital by 8 million pesos, the government received a credit line from the bank in the exact same amount (at a below-market interest rate of 6 percent), and the bank was then granted a set of extremely lucrative privileges. Those included the rights to issue banknotes to the value of three times the amount of its reserves, to act as the treasury's fiscal agent, to monopolize government lending, to tax-farm customs receipts, and to run the mint. In addition, the government established a 5 percent tax on all banknotes and then exempted Banamex notes from the tax. Crucially, the Commercial Code of

---

[10] Maurer and Gomberg (2004), 1096.
[11] Haber, Razo, and Maurer (2003), 84.

1884 removed the authority of state governments to issue bank charters, meaning that Banamex's monopoly could not be undone by a state government. In fact, not only did Mexico's treasury minister control the chartering of new banks, but his consent was necessary if a bank sought to increase its capital.[12]

There was a fundamental problem, however, with this arrangement: some politically powerful groups stood to lose a great deal from it. One of those groups was the financiers that owned the few already extant banks, particularly stockholders in the Bank of London, Mexico, and South America (known in Mexico as the Banco de Londres y México—BLM), which had been chartered in 1863. Another was a group of strongmen turned state governors, who had an interest in awarding bank charters to their cronies in exchange for loans to them and their governments. The BLM, therefore, filed suit in federal court and obtained an injunction against the Commercial Code of 1884 on the grounds that it violated the antimonopoly clause of Mexico's constitution of 1857.

Díaz therefore had to find a way to satisfy, or neutralize, all of the various parties to the dispute. In the short run, the solution was that the treasury minister granted charters to state banks on an ad hoc basis while Banamex acted as the treasury's sole financial agent. In the long run, Díaz's treasury minister, José Limantour, brokered a deal that satisfied all the parties to the conflict. This deal, codified in the General Banking Act of 1897, was remarkable for the way in which it divided the market into segmented monopolies. Indeed, Limantour acknowledged this when he wrote: "In following this plan the new law will no doubt give birth, at least in the early years of its operation, to a sort of banking oligarchy."[13]

The General Banking Act of 1897

The Banking Act of 1897 divided the banking system into three sectors: banks of issue, which emitted banknotes, discounted bills, and made commercial loans; mortgage banks, which lent long term on agricultural and urban properties; and industrial banks (*bancos refaccionarios*), which

---

[12] Batíz V. (1985), 286, 287, 293; Ludlow (1985), 334–36; Haber (1991), 568; Maurer (2002), 23–24; Haber, Razo, and Maurer (2003), 84–86; Maurer and Gomberg (2004), 1097–1110.

[13] Quoted in Maurer (2002), 34.

were supposed to make long-term loans to agricultural, mining, and industrial enterprises. But only one of those sectors, the banks of issue, actually prospered under the new regime. Limitations on the number of charters the government was willing to grant to mortgage banks, along with difficulties in enforcing contract rights on real property, meant that there were never more than three mortgage banks in the entire country.[14] From 1897 to 1911, total mortgage-bank assets averaged only 6 percent of total banking system assets.[15]

The industrial banks also faltered. They were at a distinct disadvantage against banks of issue because they could not issue banknotes. They had to compete, however, in the same markets as banks of issue, because the latter were able to skirt the laws that restricted the term of their loans (to six months) by continually renewing credits as they expired.[16] As a consequence, there were never more than six chartered industrial banks, and their combined assets, on average, accounted for only 10 percent of the banking system. Moreover, the largest bank of this type (the Banco Central Mexicano) did not actually make any loans. Instead, it operated a banknote clearinghouse that competed with Banamex; the industrial bank charter was just a ruse allowing it to open its doors legally.[17]

Mexico's actual banking system—as opposed to the one that existed on paper—was concentrated in the banks of issue, which accounted for 84 percent of all banking assets and was divided into segmented, territorial oligopolies. Foremost among the banks of issue was Banamex, which retained the tax exemptions and special privileges it had been granted in 1884. Banamex had to share the Mexico City market, as well as the right to open branches nationally, with the BLM. The BLM was also granted the same 3:1 note-reserve ratio as Banamex (all other banks of issue were allowed only a 2:1 ratio). Banamex retained its position as the federal government's fiscal agent, although it agreed to reduce the fees it charged and to open an additional million-peso credit line to the government. That is to say, Banamex once again extended a loan to the Díaz government and received a set of lucrative privileges in exchange.[18]

[14] Riguzzi (2002).
[15] Haber (2008a), 222.
[16] Maurer (2002), 95.
[17] Haber (2008a), 222–23.
[18] Maurer (2002), 40–44; Haber, Razo, and Maurer (2003), 86–87.

The 1897 law satisfied state governors by allowing the treasury minister to grant charters to banks of issue whose activities were confined to particular concession territories, which were usually contiguous with state lines. This essentially meant that the governor of each state could arrange a charter for a group of his cronies, who then extended credit to the state government in return. In some cases, the governor sat on the board of directors of the bank. Somewhat more rarely, banks extended loans to the state governor and then forgave the loans.[19]

A series of regulatory barriers to entry ensured that only one territorial bank of issue could operate in any particular concession territory. First, banks without a federal charter were prohibited from issuing notes, meaning that they could not effectively compete against chartered banks. Second, because banks with territorial charters were not allowed to branch outside their concession territories, banks chartered in one state could not challenge the monopoly of a bank in an adjoining state. Third, the government established a minimum capital requirement for a bank of issue equivalent to 250,000 dollars—five times the minimum amount needed to found a national bank in the United States. Fourth, the government levied a 2 percent tax on bank capital and a 5 percent tax on banknotes—but exempted the first bank of issue in each state from those taxes. Finally, because state governments were not allowed to grant bank charters, these barriers to entry could not be eroded through regulatory competition; all bank charters, as well as additions to bank capital, had to be approved by the treasury minister. In effect, the only threat to the monopoly of a state bank could come from a branch of Banamex or the BLM.[20]

To reduce the risk that the banks of issue might be expropriated by the central government, the economic interests of Mexico's bankers were aligned with the interests of the power brokers of the Díaz dictatorship, who received seats on the boards of the major banks and thus were entitled to directors' fees and stock distributions. The board of directors of Banamex, for example, included the president of Congress, the undersecretary of the treasury, the senator for the Federal District, the president's

[19] Haber, Razo, and Maurer (2003), 89–90; Cerutti (2003), 187, 192–219; Gamboa Ojeda (2003), 105, 122–213; Rodríguez López (2003), 255, 269–324; Romero Ibarra (2003), 218–19, 223–26.
[20] Marichal (1985), 257–325; Haber (1991), 567–658 ; Maurer (2002), 23–33; Haber, Razo, and Maurer (2003), 84–87.

chief of staff, and the brother of the secretary of the treasury. The chairman of the board of the BLM was none other than the war minister. Joining him on the board was a powerful federal senator. Banks with limited territorial concessions were similarly populated with powerful politicians, the only difference being that state governors rather than cabinet ministers sat on their boards. From the point of view of the bank insiders, these appointments served as a sort of crude insurance policy. Díaz would be less likely to restructure their lucrative deals if a share of the rents from those deals flowed directly into the hands of the power brokers in his administration.[21]

These banks were not the independent credit intermediaries posited by economic theory, taking deposits and making arm's-length loans to a wide variety of firms and households. In the first place, they had very small deposit bases: in 1897, deposits (exclusive of those securing credit lines) accounted for only 2 percent of total bank liabilities. As late as 1910, they accounted for only 16 percent.[22] Rather, most bank liabilities were composed of note issues. It was those notes, backed by fractional shareholder capital, that were lent out by the banks. In the second place, the biggest private debtors of the banks were their own board members, who were also Mexico's most important industrialists. From 1886 to 1901, 100 percent of all non-government or non-government-guaranteed lending by Banamex went to insiders. Estimates for other banks show that anywhere from 29 to 86 percent of their non-government loan portfolios went to their own directors or their family members. At the Banco de Coahuila, an astounding 72 percent of loans in 1908 went to a single firm owned by family members of a director.[23]

Being a bank stockholder clearly was good for bank insiders, who received special banking concessions from the government, established networks for rent sharing with influential government officials, and operated their banks largely to fund their own industrial enterprises. But what was in it for the minority stockholders who contributed to their banks' capital? The bank insiders had a license to print money—in the form of note issues—and then lent those notes mostly to themselves. Moreover, they

---

[21] Haber, Razo, and Maurer (2003), 88–90; Razo (2008), chapters 5 and 6.
[22] Haber (2008a), 224.
[23] Maurer and Haber (2007), 562–653.

were insiders not simply in the sense that they were the banks' founders and majority shareholders but also in the sense that they had ties to the power brokers of the Díaz dictatorship. What would keep the controlling shareholders from expropriating the minority shareholders through tunneling and fraud while the Díaz government looked the other way?

The answers to this question were threefold. First, the partnership between the Díaz government and the bankers generated a stream of earnings and dividends that were shared with minority shareholders. The average annual return on the book value of equity in the banks of issue from 1901 to 1912 was 12 percent. Moreover, there was no year in which the average rate of return was negative and only one year (1908) in which it was zero. Mexican banks paid out high and regular dividends. In fact, an investor who purchased an index of banking stock weighted by market capitalization would have earned an average real return of 9 percent per year—more than double the return from investing in the Dow Jones Industrials. As a result, investors looked on bank stocks favorably: bank shares traded at an average premium of 33 percent over their book value.[24]

Second, bank directors had capital at risk. Mexico's commercial code required the founding group (who became the directors) to subscribe to the first tranche of the bank's capital.

Third, minority shareholders were not an anonymous public; they tended to be other bankers, and they insisted on the appointment of independent directors.[25] This meant that there was a dense network of interlocking directorates that produced cross-monitoring.[26] Moreover, the directors—both the insiders and the independents—had strong incentives to monitor each other closely; a good deal of the money they were playing with was their own. The deposit bases of these banks were quite small (never exceeding 16 percent of assets), and thus their capital ratios were high by modern standards—typically on the order of 25 to 30 percent— and much of that capital was owned by the directors themselves.[27] As a result, the directors of the banks watched each other like hawks; the loans made to insiders tended to be granted on fairly conservative terms and

[24] Maurer and Haber (2007), 565–658.
[25] Maurer and Haber (2007), 561.
[26] Razo (2008), chapter 6; Musacchio (2009a).
[27] Haber (2008a), 224.

were usually made to directors as individuals, rather than to their enterprises. In addition, they were typically secured by liquid assets, such as cash, government securities, or corporate securities, which were physically held by the bank. If the loan went into default, the bank could simply keep the securities.[28]

The evidence suggests that Mexican banks lent primarily to their own directors because those loans were deemed safest. Safety resulted from a system in which the incentives of borrowers and lenders were aligned by their participation in powerful networks. The Mexican insider lending network reflected not only the dominance of a preexisting powerful elite but also the unique informational advantages that accompany insider lending, which have been noted in other countries as well.[29] Experience had taught Mexico's bankers that they lacked good mechanisms to assess the quality of arm's-length borrowers. Unable to tell good credit risks from bad, they responded by placing onerous requirements on arm's-length borrowers, but these gave rise to "adverse selection": that is, the requirements were acceptable only to relatively desperate, low-quality borrowers.[30]

Minutes of board meetings make it clear that boards of directors viewed insider loans as less risky than arm's-length loans. In one particularly informative debate among the board members of Banamex, some members objected to a loan being made to another bank—until it was pointed out that the recipient bank was a good credit risk because it lent only to its own board members![31] In fact, insider loans were viewed as of such high quality that when the government organized a rescue of the country's smaller banks in 1908 (because of the transmission of the U.S. crisis of 1907 to Mexico), by chartering a bank (the Caja de Préstamos) whose purpose was to repurchase high-quality bank loans and bank-issued mortgage bonds in order to inject liquidity into the banking system, that bank repurchased insider loans.[32]

That rescue operation was arguably the first loan securitization in history, which is also testimony to the sophistication and innovativeness of

---

[28] Maurer and Haber (2007), 563.
[29] Lamoreaux (1994); Cull, Haber, and Imai (2011).
[30] Maurer (2002), 97–98; Maurer and Haber (2007), 561–652.
[31] Maurer (2002), 98.
[32] Oñate (1998), 191–99; Maurer (2002), 97; Maurer and Haber (2007), 564–655.

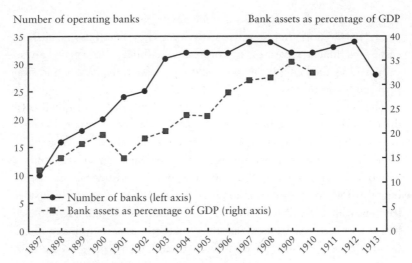

FIGURE 10.1 Size of the Mexican banking system, 1897–1913.

Source: Maurer and Haber (2007), 559.

the Mexican banking system circa 1900. Lest readers express skepticism about the quality of those loans and conclude that the bankers were passing their bad loans off to the government, it is worth noting that the shareholders of the Caja de Préstamos were Mexico's largest banks, and the Caja de Préstamos was one of the few banking rescues in history that actually made money, generating real returns to the claimants on its assets that exceeded the returns available to an investor who instead put his money in a portfolio of the Dow Jones Industrials.[33]

The resilience of the Mexican banking system in 1907–08, in the wake of the financial shocks imported from the crisis that erupted in the United States, reflected its inherent stability. The Díaz-era banking system was, in fact, extraordinarily stable—at least while Díaz remained in power. As figure 10.1 shows, the number of reporting banks and total bank assets increased steadily. In 1897, when Díaz's regulatory system was finally in place, the entire banking system, including mortgage banks, investment banks, and banks of issue, comprised just ten banks with total assets equal to only 12 percent of GDP. By 1910 (Díaz's last full year in office before

[33] Maurer and Haber (2007), 566, 569.

he was overthrown), there were 32 banks with total assets equal to 32 percent of GDP. Over this 13-year period there was only one downturn, in 1908–09, when seven small banks of issue failed; two were later rechartered as investment banks, and the others were purchased by larger, more solvent banks.[34]

The markets for banknotes and bank deposits appear to have been competitive during the Porfiriato, and both classes of bank debt holders seem to have exerted market discipline on Mexican banks. One study finds that measures of bank fundamentals during the period 1900–1910 are useful in predicting the changes in outstanding amounts of deposits and notes. In other words, banks that demonstrated financial strength to note holders and depositors were able to increase their leverage in the forms of notes and deposits. In 1904, under the auspices of the Banco Central Mexicano (the clearinghouse that had been established by smaller banks to get around the Banamex monopoly on note clearing), a limited mutual-protection system was established among the banks to provide liquidity assistance. The number of participating banks was small, and each was quite well informed about the others. For those two reasons, the system appears to have functioned reasonably well. Unlike many experiments with mutual protection in the United States, but much like the successful U.S. antebellum mutual-protection systems of Ohio and Indiana, which shared those two key features (see chapter 6), the Mexican mutual-protection system enabled its member banks to survive the fallout of 1907–08 and avoided undermining market discipline.[35]

No Bed of Roses

The Díaz-era banking system was a vast improvement over what had existed before. For the first time, Mexico had a stable banking system capable of providing credit in support of industrialization. Because the banking system also provided the government with a source of public finance, Díaz did not have to prey on property rights in order to maintain his hold on power. This security encouraged investment and productivity growth. With the help of Banamex's directors, who earned commissions and fees

---

[34] Maurer and Haber (2007), 565.
[35] Huybens, Jordan, and Pratap (2005), 763.

from the transaction, Díaz was also able to renegotiate Mexico's foreign debt—which had been in default for several decades—allowing Mexico to once again access international capital markets.[36]

In short, Díaz's strategy of creating a banking system by the extension of lucrative privileges and the creation of barriers to entry worked: the banking partnership between the government and the elite gave him the financial breathing room he needed to slowly recraft the tax codes governing mining, petroleum, and interstate commerce and gradually increase government tax revenues to the point that he ran balanced budgets.[37] State governors obtained a similar advantage from their share of the banking bargains: the banks within their borders were a steady source of loans to state governments.[38]

There were, however, several downsides to this system when compared to a system with a more competitive structure. As Noel Maurer has shown, the concentrated nature of the system meant that the two largest banks (Banamex and the BLM), which controlled more than half of all assets, could use their market power to ration credit in order to drive up their rates of return. They did so by maintaining excess liquidity, which is to say that they held more of their assets in cash than was actually necessary. As a result, their stockholders earned substantial rents: the ratios of the market value of their shares to the book value of their assets were substantially higher than those for other banks.[39]

Even if Banamex and the BLM had not pushed to limit credit, bank capital, and therefore bank lending, was limited by weak incentives to compete. Plainly put, in a system in which there were typically no more than three banks in any market, banks had little incentive to seek out new borrowers. From the point of view of the directors, why go to all the trouble and expense of establishing the private and public institutions that would allow them to administer arm's-length loans (e.g., credit bureaus, effective registration of collateral interests, and credible enforcement of creditors' rights in courts) when they could just lend to their own commer-

---

[36] Marichal (2002).

[37] Carmagnani (1994); Haber, Razo, and Maurer (2003), 192–98, 237–46.

[38] Aguilar (2003), 66–67; Ludlow (2003), 143, 158; Romero Ibarra (2003), 225; Olveda (2003), 305; Rodríguez López (2003), 266–67.

[39] Maurer (2002), chapter 4.

cial, manufacturing, and mining companies? Here the Mexican experience reflected a more general tendency of autocratic regimes preceding World War II, which is documented in other countries: autocracy tends to result in lower banking-system depth relative to GDP than democracies.[40]

These insider-lending policies were no secret to the minority shareholders. Indeed, they bought bank shares fully expecting the directors to lend to their nonfinancial firms. Porfirian banks essentially acted like investment clubs: wealthy people bought bank shares, which backed banknote issues (at a ratio of 1:2 or 1:3, depending on the bank), and then banks lent those notes to a portfolio of enterprises owned by the bank directors and their families. This system of governance and lending was little different from that of nineteenth-century New England, in which banks owned by industrialists acted as the treasury arms of the region's major industrial and commercial groups.[41]

There was, however, a major difference between Mexico and New England: Mexico had a few dozen banks, while New England had hundreds. Indeed, in Mexico, the vast majority of markets had only three banks: a branch of Banamex, a branch of the BLM, and the bank that held that state's territorial concession. The logical consequences of a small number of banks and a high level of insider lending were scarce credit and an unusually high concentration of finance-dependent, downstream industries. These phenomena are reflected in the structure of Mexico's cotton-textile industry—an industry that in most countries, because of its relatively small minimum efficient scale of production, is typically considered as a textbook case of perfect competition. Not so in Porfirian Mexico! Not only did Mexico's cotton-textile industry exhibit indices of concentration roughly double those of other major textile-producing countries, but concentration actually increased as the industry grew. That is not the result that one would anticipate from an industry characterized by constant-returns-to-scale technology, but it is a predictable consequence of the existence of very few banks, whose directors are also the owners of the country's major manufacturing companies.[42]

---

[40] Bordo and Rousseau (2012).
[41] Lamoreaux (1994).
[42] Haber (1991, 1997); Haber, Razo, and Maurer (2003), 131–32; Maurer and Haber (2007), 573–74.

When Things Fall Apart: The Mexican Revolution

The Porfiriato contained the seeds of its own collapse. The Díaz regime had created a successful partnership with a select group of large landowners, bankers, industrialists, and miners. In doing so, however, the regime alienated other elite groups who, although they benefited from economic growth generally, were effectively excluded from the lucrative arrangements that underpinned the government-elite partnership. In a country that was overwhelmingly agrarian, most farmers and ranchers— even large ones—had no access to credit. The commercial banks were largely focused on financing the manufacturing and mining enterprises of their own directors. Mexico also had a large and fast-growing mining sector, but miners paid much higher prices for dynamite than they would have otherwise because there was a national dynamite monopoly run by a group of influential industrialists and regime insiders. As one contemporary observer stated about this firm: "This is a country where it is claimed that the Government will not allow a monopoly; but it is different when the government is interested, and when the head officials are shareholders."[43]

In 1910, these disaffected elites organized themselves and mobilized two groups that had been marginalized by the Díaz regime: small farmers who had lost their lands to an elite land grab sanctioned by the regime, and a growing class of miners, railwaymen, and factory workers whose efforts at unionization had been met with bullets and hangings. This unlikely coalition formed around Francisco Madero, a scion of a wealthy mining and ranching family from the north of the country, who announced his candidacy for the 1910 presidential race—and was jailed for not understanding that no one was supposed to run against Díaz. Madero soon escaped from confinement, and his coalition of supporters took up armed force against Díaz. Once they forced Díaz into exile in France in 1911, however, the coalition members soon fell to fighting among themselves. What followed was a ten-year period of coups, rebellions, and civil wars that are collectively referred to as the Mexican Revolution.

All sides in this conflict preyed on the banking system in order to sustain their military campaigns. Indeed, the logic of conflict required that they do so: the banks were a source of ready cash, and any faction that

[43] Quoted in Haber, Razo, and Maurer (2003), 137.

did not grab that cash would be defeated by a faction with fewer scruples. One of the ironies of the Mexican Revolution was that the two figures most closely identified with business interests—Victoriano Huerta, a Díaz-era army general who tried to reinstall the ancien régime, and Venustiano Carranza, a wealthy landowner who led the coalition first against Huerta and then against the more radical elements of the revolution who wanted to redistribute property and wealth—were the most aggressive predators on the banks. By the time they were done, Mexico's banking system was in tatters: virtually all of the Díaz-era banks had been dissolved, save Banamex and the BLM, and those banks had been stripped of most of their assets.

Large-scale predation against the banks started in 1913 under the counterrevolutionary government of Huerta, who was locked in a vicious struggle against the forces of Emiliano Zapata, Pancho Villa, and Carranza. After exhausting the government's credit lines at Banamex, Huerta turned to extortion by threatening taxes on bank deposits unless the banks would grant him loans. When extortion failed to produce sufficient revenues, Huerta began to seize bank specie reserves. When those were exhausted, he declared that banknotes were legal tender in order to increase their value (accepting them had been voluntary until that point) and then forced the banks into lending ever-increasing amounts to the government —financed, of course, by note issues.[44] The consequence was high inflation—a government's taxation source of last resort and an artifact of the creation of legal tender currency. In the last years of the Díaz regime (1901–10), inflation had averaged less than 4 percent; from 1910 to 1921, the price level doubled.[45]

The opposition to Huerta used much the same tactics, though on a smaller scale. In 1913, Villa's troops sacked Banamex's Torreón offices in the northern state of Coahuila, seized its specie reserves, and drew up drafts for 30,000 dollars on New York, 30,000 francs on Paris, and 2,000 pounds on London. Carranza was no better. In 1914 he confiscated banks and bank branches in Sonora, liquidating their assets to finance his military efforts, while armed movements affiliated with him seized over half a million pesos from the Durango branch of the BLM.[46]

[44] Haber, Razo, and Maurer (2003), 93–97.
[45] Inflation is defined using the wholesale price index reported in Mexico, INEGI (n.d.), table 19.7.
[46] Haber, Razo, and Maurer (2003), 93–97.

The coup de grâce for the banking system was delivered once Huerta had been defeated and Carranza faced off against Zapata and Villa. Ironically, it came from the probusiness movement of Carranza, not the more radical Zapata and Villa. Carranza seems to have been constrained by ideology only in that his predatory actions were covered by a cynical veneer of legality. Once he gained control of Mexico City in 1915, Carranza reinstated the provisions of the General Banking Act of 1897 and then declared that the government would liquidate banks that had issued more banknotes than were permitted under that act—knowing full well that the banks had been forced by Huerta to do so. Three weeks later, Carranza sent commissions to find out which banks had complied with the law. Those that had not succeeded in accomplishing this near-impossible task were given only 45 days to comply or else be declared bankrupt by the government—which would give the government the right to seize their specie reserves and liquidate their other assets. When the bankers protested, the government arrested their managers. Of the 27 banks that were in operation when Carranza seized Mexico City, only 9 remained.[47]

The following year, still in need of funds to prosecute his war against Villa and Zapata, Carranza went after the specie reserves of the remaining banks. On September 15, 1916, the Carrancistas assumed control of the banks and appointed intervention boards to supervise their operations. To preserve a semblance of legality, Carranza did not simply have the intervention boards sack the banks' vaults. Rather, he amended the General Banking Act to increase the legally required ratio of specie reserves to banknotes from 50 percent to 100 percent for banks with limited territorial charters. He then declared them bankrupt because their note issues exceeded the new reserve requirements, giving the intervention boards the authority to liquidate the banks' assets and seize their specie reserves.

Carranza also went after Banamex, first demanding loans under threat of seizure if the bank refused and then confiscating its gold and silver reserves by having the intervention boards withdraw the Banamex deposits owned by the territorial banks under their control. By 1917, Banamex teetered on the edge of bankruptcy. Not satisfied, however, that he had

---

[47] Haber, Razo, and Maurer (2003), 96–97, 108.

extracted every last centavo from Banamex, in 1919 Carranza told Banamex's directors that if they guaranteed the payment of a money order for the importation of 4,000 tons of wheat from the United States, he would repeal the decree placing Mexico's banks under the supervision of the intervention boards. Once they agreed, and guaranteed the note, Carranza reneged both on the removal of the intervention boards and the payment of the money order.[48]

In light of the history of the Díaz regime's partnership with bankers in Mexico, why did Carranza choose to expropriate the banks rather than form a new partnership with them for mutual gain? Amid the military chaos of the Mexican Revolution, the formation of a stable coalition simply was not feasible. For an autocrat fighting to survive, neither the credibility gain from fulfilling promises nor the availability of bank credit to fund domestic production was a primary concern.

Just how much damage Huerta and Carranza did is captured by a simple statistic: the ratio of total bank assets to GDP, a rough proxy for the size of the banking system. In 1910, that ratio was 32 percent. By 1921 it was only 5 percent. To put this in perspective, in 1910 Mexico's banking system was about the same size (relative to GDP) as it is today, whereas in 1921 it was roughly the same size as the current banking system of Chad.[49]

All the King's Horses, and All the King's Men . . .

The lack of a functioning banking system jeopardized the survival of Mexico's post-1920 governments. In fact, calling them governments implies a good deal more stability and institutionalization than actually existed. The Mexican political system in the 1920s was little more than a fragile coalition of warlords, allied with corrupt labor leaders and headed by two political-military strongmen who had been part of the Carrancista movement, Alvaro Obregón and Plutarco Elias Calles. Obregón, in fact,

---

[48] Haber, Razo, and Maurer (2003), 97.

[49] We know, on the basis of detailed data on banking system assets and liabilities, that most of this damage occurred under the Huerta and Carranza presidencies, because as late as December 1913, banking-system assets, deposits, and reserves were still at their prerevolutionary levels. See Mexico, Secretaria del Estado y del Despacho de Hacienda y Credito Publico y Comercio (1913), 272–73.

came to power in 1920 by staging a coup against Carranza and assassinating him. Obregón ruled until 1924, stepping aside to allow Calles to win a rigged election; Calles, in return, rigged the election of 1928 for Obregón. They probably would have traded the presidency back and forth for some time if Obregón had not been shot dead by a religious fanatic the day after "winning" the 1928 election.

The Obregón-Calles regime faced several threats to its survival, including two attempted military coups, an armed rebellion led by the treasury minister, and a church-state civil war, known as the Cristero Rebellion, that dragged on inconclusively for three years. Obregón and Calles tried to obtain the revenues they needed to fight those movements by increasing taxation on mining and petroleum but failed at both.[50] This meant that they had strong incentives to create a banking system from which they could borrow. At the same time, the private sector—most importantly the country's manufacturers—was clamoring for the creation of a banking system that could finance its operations. Given the fact that Obregón and Calles were trying to hold together a fragile coalition and that a crucial part of that coalition—which even provided paramilitary support—was the country's newly unionized industrial workers, keeping the factories operating was as important as finding a source of public finance.

The Obregón government initially tried to revive the banking system by reintroducing the Díaz-era system. In 1921, in a gesture intended to restore confidence, it returned to their owners twelve banks that had been seized during the revolution. Unfortunately, only five were healthy enough to reopen, and several of those were so weak that they failed over the next twelve months.

Obregón then tried to solve his problems by creating a state-owned bank. He revived the Caja de Préstamos (the Díaz-era enterprise that had been created to engineer the 1908 banking-system rescue), which, although inactive, still existed as a legal entity. He issued bonds to purchase the shares that were still held by private banks. The announced plan was to service the bonds from the bank's revenues. The problem was, however, that Obregón needed every centavo he could lay his hands on to retain his precarious hold on power, and so he never made any of the promised interest payments to the bondholders.

[50] Haber, Razo, and Maurer (2003), 208–12; 262–66.

The volatile political situation also meant that the bank's assets were allocated in a manner that was equally unviable: loans were distributed to politically crucial clients for far more than the value of the collateral presented in guarantee, and they were never repaid. A sense of the situation can be summed up by this reply by General Arnulfo González to a repayment request: "As you see, my debts have a political origin. When the general management [financed me], it did so under a personal agreement with the President of the Republic, from whom I had directly requested the loan in order to finance a political campaign. . . . In my opinion it is only the most natural thing in the world that since this institution is a direct dependency of the government, it would serve the government's political interests and extend its benefits . . . with the equity and justice of which I consider myself a provider."[51] Not surprisingly, the Caja de Préstamos collapsed within a year of its founding.

Obregón and Calles, therefore, went back to the drawing board to come up with a plan to coax the country's private financiers into deploying their capital in a banking system from which the government could borrow. To do so, they took a page from the Díaz regime's book: they gave the bankers themselves considerable say in the system's design so that they would expect to earn above-normal returns compensating them for the risk of expropriation. In late 1924, treasury minister Alberto Pani called a special convention of government officials and bankers, some of whom had been major figures in the prerevolutionary banking system.

The Convention of 1924–25

The laws crafted at the 1924–25 convention were designed to give the bankers incentives to deploy their capital by raising rates of return through the creation of barriers to entry. First, all preexisting banks were grandfathered in. Second, the incumbent bankers were appointed to a newly created national banking commission, which gave them considerable influence to block the entry of new banks as well as to influence other aspects of banking and credit policy. Third, in order to make it difficult for other banks to enter the market, the minimum capital requirement was set at 500,000 pesos (roughly 250,000 1924 dollars). For banks

[51] Haber, Razo, and Maurer (2003), 100.

that wished to operate a branch or office in Mexico City, the minimum capital was set at one million pesos. Fourth, obtaining a bank charter required the specific approval of the treasury minister and the president. Fifth—and this was a new twist—the convention established a new commercial bank, the Banco de México (Banxico), whose shares were owned both by private banks and by the government. The purpose of Banxico was threefold: to serve as the treasury's fiscal agent, to rediscount notes from shareholder banks, and to advance credit to business enterprises.

Banxico embodied a complicated commitment device that grew out of a political bargain among Mexico's leading bankers and politicians. Because the bankers worried about expropriation via forced lending or selective defaults, Banxico was granted a monopoly on government lending so that it could not default on loans to some bankers while borrowing more from others. If the government abrogated one bank's property rights, it would abrogate all banks' property rights, because they all held stock in Banxico. Collective risk meant lower individual risk.

The bankers also worried that the government might abrogate this arrangement in order to satisfy its international obligations. To forestall that concern, Calles defaulted on Mexico's international debt. To make the arrangement more binding still, the government used Banxico's rediscount facilities to put up a hostage to guarantee its good behavior. When private banks borrowed from Banxico they received gold, which they moved out of the country. This gold would be lost if the government seized the banks' domestic assets. In fact, from 1926 to 1929, 7.5 percent of all Mexican commercial bank assets were deposited abroad.[52] Any predatory government would have to weigh the gains from predation against the almost certain loss of some of Banxico's capital.

There was, of course, another constituency whose incentives had to be aligned with the new institutional framework—the warlords turned politicians who ran the government. Unless they had something to lose by reneging, there was no reason for anyone to believe that they would abide by the deal. The advantage they would put at risk was loans—big ones, in fact—from Banxico to their private business enterprises. The list of Banxico's debtors reads like a Who's Who of the Calles administration, including foreign minister Aaron Sáenz, education minister Moisés Sáenz

[52] Maurer (2002), 177.

Percentage of GDP

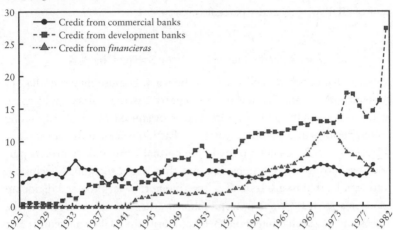

FIGURE 10.2 Sources of credit in Mexico, 1925–82.

Source: Mexico, INEGI (2009).

(Aaron's brother), industry, commerce, and labor minister Luis M. Morones (who also happened to head the labor federation that represented organized workers), treasury minister Alberto J. Pani (who had organized the 1924–25 banking convention), ex–treasury minister Luis Cabrera, ex-President Álvaro Obregón, and President Calles himself, along with several of his family members.[53]

Although this deal was far from ironclad, it did coax some capital back into the banking system. The ratio of bank assets to GDP had actually fallen from 5 percent in 1921 to 4 percent by 1925, but it then jumped to 8 percent in 1926 and to 12 percent in 1929. Nevertheless, these numbers were not impressive. In the first place, even at 12 percent of GDP, this banking system was still only one-third the size of the banking system that had existed at the end of the Díaz period. In the second place, much of this growth appears to have taken place within Banxico, most of whose shares were owned by the government, rather than at the privately owned commercial banks. Figure 10.2 shows commercial bank lending excluding loans from Banxico, and the results are not impressive: commercial

[53] Haber, Razo, and Maurer (2003), 106–7.

bank lending (of which Banxico's loans were a part) equaled only 4 percent of GDP in 1925 and 5 percent in 1929.

Banking under the Perfect Dictatorship of the PRI

Mexico's bankers had good reason to be wary, because they soon had to contend with yet another new regime, a party-based dictatorship. In 1929, in the wake of Obregón's murder, Calles organized Mexico's remaining military leaders into a political party, the Partido Nacional Revolucionario (PNR). The PNR was not a party in the normal sense of the word: its purpose was not to win elections, because that was a foregone conclusion. Rather, it existed to arbitrate disputes among the warlords and divide up spoils in a predictable and peaceful manner. After a series of reforms in the 1930s and 1940s that integrated Mexico's organized labor movement and peasant confederation into its organizational structure, this party became the Partido Revolucionario Institucional (PRI).

The PRI held a complete monopoly on political power. It financed its campaigns out of the federal treasury, decided which parties could run against it, monitored the elections, counted the votes, and certified the results. Not surprisingly, it "won" every gubernatorial and senatorial election from the late 1920s to the 1980s and every presidential election until 2000. To maintain a facade of democracy, it crafted a complex set of electoral rules that allowed other parties, some of which were actually subsidized by the government, to win seats in the federal Chamber of Deputies (Mexico's lower house of congress)—but the PRI dominated that chamber by an overwhelming majority until the late 1990s.

The PRI as a Centralizing Authoritarian Network

The PRI's ability to win elections by overwhelming margins depended on the distribution of patronage to two large groups: small farmers and unionized urban workers.[54] The PRI invented complex mechanisms for controlling these groups, thereby creating one of the most powerful, centralized, and enduring authoritarian governments of the twentieth century. Part of its genius was that it wrapped all of this control in the mantle of social justice while actually giving the population almost no political voice.

[54] This section draws heavily on Haber et al. (2008), chapter 2.

The system of patronage that linked millions of small farmers with the PRI was rooted in the peculiar nature of Mexico's postrevolutionary agrarian reform. Under pressure from agrarian radicals, Carranza had agreed to Article 27 of the Constitution of 1917, which created a legal basis for a land reform. Until the 1930s, however, Mexico's presidents largely ignored this article of the constitution.[55] This situation changed dramatically once President Lázaro Cárdenas (in office 1934–40) decided to turn the PNR into a party of the masses organized by occupation. In the process, Cárdenas redistributed 45.4 million acres—almost 10 percent of Mexico's total land area—benefiting some 723,000 families. The land reform did not end with Cárdenas: his successors distributed an additional 78.1 million acres between 1940 and 1970.[56]

To maintain centralized control over rural constituents, Mexico's land reform did not give individual farmers title to the land they cultivated. Instead, it gave rise to the *ejido,* a collective form of ownership in which neither the *ejido* as a corporate entity nor *ejidatarios* as individuals could legally sell or rent their land. The inalienability of ejidal land meant that nobody wanted to lend against it. *Ejidatarios* were, therefore, almost completely dependent on government development banks to finance the purchase of seeds, tools, and fertilizer.[57]

The *ejido* was an amazingly inefficient way to grow food but an amazingly effective way to get votes for the PRI. *Ejidos* were production units, but they were members of a National Peasants' Confederation, which itself was a formal part of the PRI. The *ejido* was like a roach motel: you could check in, but you couldn't check out. Precisely because *ejidos* were not private property, efficient *ejidatarios* could not expand their operations by purchasing neighboring parcels or borrow from commercial banks to raise their productivity. At the same time, inefficient *ejidatarios* could not leave the land without losing their right to cultivate it. The PRI was able to use the *ejido* as a mechanism to mobilize millions of votes—through

---

[55] Carranza, Obregón, and Calles collectively redistributed only approximately 4 percent of Mexico's agricultural land, and much of this land fell under the control of powerful revolutionary generals or politicians—Obregón and Calles among them. In 1930, Calles, who at the time ruled through a puppet president, declared the agrarian reform a failure and called for an end to land redistribution. Markiewicz (1993), 55, 59.

[56] Haber et al. (2008), 30–31.

[57] Haber et al. (2008), 31.

collective and nonsecret balloting arrangements—in exchange for govern-ment-bestowed benefits to the *ejido* such as credit, territorial expansion, infrastructure projects, public services, and subsidized purchases of *ejido* output. These purchases were especially valuable to *ejidatarios* because the government maintained artificially low food prices in the cities in order to secure the support of its urban constituents. All of these benefits could be withdrawn if *ejidatarios* failed to vote for the PRI.[58]

One of the supreme ironies of the PRI's relationship to Mexico's small farmers was its appropriation of the images of agrarian revolutionaries, such as Emiliano Zapata and Pancho Villa. The truth of the matter was quite different. Zapata and Villa had nothing to do with the origins of the PRI. In point of fact, the victors of the revolution who ultimately gave rise to the PRI, Obregón and Calles, had ordered the assassinations of Zapata in 1919 and Villa in 1923. Moreover, the same patronage machine through which the PRI maintained control over rural voters ensured low agricul-tural productivity and incomes.[59]

Urban voters were also controlled through patronage networks. Because urban society was more socially heterogeneous and mobile, voters were less easily manipulated. Urban demonstrations were also easier to organize and harder to suppress. The PRI did not, however, need the support of all urban voters, or even a majority of them: it needed only a critical mass of urban-ites that could be mobilized as activist supporters for the party. Unionized workers fit the bill perfectly, because unions had monopoly rights to orga-nize and were a formal part of the PRI. In return for their loyalty to the PRI, these unionized workers, who were a minority even in the urban cen-ters, received a host of benefits not available to other members of society.

Among the politically most important of such arrangements were those protecting the position of union leaders and rank-and-file members. "Offi-cial" labor leaders kept the peace in industrial relations and reliably deliv-ered union members' votes to the PRI. In fact, Mexico's unions were part of a national federation, the Confederation of Mexican Workers (CTM), which was a formal wing of the PRI. The unions produced benefits for rank-and-file workers. Foremost among these was job security: it was

[58] Haber et al. (2008), 30–33.
[59] Haber et al. (2008), 32.

nearly impossible to dismiss a unionized worker. Job security was further enhanced by competition-limiting contract laws: a federal labor code established industry-wide wage scales and work rules, thereby setting essentially the same labor costs for all enterprises they regulated.[60]

Unionized workers, and their families, also had preferential access to government social-welfare programs, including retirement pensions and government-subsidized health care. Workers in the formal sector, where the unionized population was concentrated, were covered by the Mexican Social Security Institute (IMSS), which as of 1950 covered only 16 percent of the country's labor force. Unionized workers also benefited from government housing programs. In 1972, the government created the National Worker Housing Institute (INFONAVIT), a federal agency that collected a 5 percent levy from employers on most formal-sector workers' wages and used those revenues to construct subsidized housing. The benefits of this program were targeted, in practice, to unions that were affiliated with the CTM.[61]

To protect both unionized workers and the industrialist allies of the PRI, the Mexican government maintained high barriers to foreign trade. In 1947, the PRI introduced a system of import permits. In time, this system covered everything imported into the country. For preserving job security within a tightly controlled network, this permit system was nearly ideal. Businesses could not apply for a permit until the imported goods had already arrived in customs, at which point the government could deny the permit. No sane person—not even a postmodern English professor at an American university—would even think about importing goods under this system unless he was already a member of the PRI's network. Access to import permits therefore not only served to block foreign competition; it also blocked domestic competition by limiting access to foreign-produced capital and intermediate goods.[62]

This complex system of patronage enabled the PRI to maintain electoral dominance for decades on end. It thereby controlled Mexico's regulatory and legal systems: PRI leaders named state and federal judges and

---

[60] Haber et al. (2008), 33–34.
[61] Haber et al. (2008), 35.
[62] Reynolds (1970), 221–22; Haber et al. (2008), 41–44.

the directors of government-owned firms and determined appointments in the federal bureaucracy. It was, in the words of the Peruvian novelist Mario Vargas Llosa, "a perfect dictatorship."

The PRI and the Banks

As soon as this party-based dictatorship started to take shape in the 1930s, the government began to claw back some of the policy-making authority that the Obregón-Calles regime had delegated to private bankers. In 1932, the government converted Banxico into a central bank. A further reform in 1936 required commercial banks to maintain cash reserves in Banxico, which is to say that banks had to lend part of their deposit base to the government. That same law also transferred many bank supervisory functions from the banker-influenced National Banking Commission to Banxico. In a further set of reforms enacted in 1941, the government forced commercial banks to divest their investment-banking operations into separate corporations, called *financieras*.[63]

Once the government began to renegotiate the deal that had been forged in 1924–25, Mexico's financiers began to pull back. As figure 10.2 shows, the banking system, minuscule as it already was, actually began to shrink; credit from commercial banks fell from 7 percent of GDP in 1933 to 3 percent by 1939, even though the Mexican economy grew at a brisk pace during the late 1930s.[64] Bank credit remained at those depressed levels for the next 40 years. This pattern holds even if we include credit from the separate investment-banking operations, which bumped up the amount of total private credit from privately owned banks by only a trivial amount until the 1960s. In fact, at its peak, *combined* commercial and investment bank lending was only 17 percent of GDP, and that level was not reached until 1972. That is to say, during the period 1925–78, the amount of credit issued by private banks relative to GDP likely never exceeded its 1910 levels.[65]

[63] Del Angel-Mobarak (2002), chapter 3.
[64] Cárdenas (2000), 195–211.
[65] We assume that the Díaz-era banks had fairly standard loan-to-asset ratios of roughly 50 percent, an assumption that squares with what we know about the composition of their balance sheets. Thus, their ratio of assets to GDP of 32 percent in 1910 would translate into a loans-to-GDP ratio of 16 percent.

The pervasive distrust of the government by Mexico's leading financiers and industrialists presented the PRI with a problem: to sustain its hold on power, the party needed an alternative to private banks as a means to support a growing industrial sector and thereby retain its loyal faction of industrial workers. The PRI's electoral strategy had given rise to a privileged class of unionized, urban service and industrial workers who not only voted for the party in large numbers but could be mobilized for rallies and demonstrations designed to show the rest of the urban population that protest against the PRI was futile. The fact that the owners of Mexico's industrial enterprises also tended to be the owners of its banks further complicated the PRI's problem. If it did not find a way to sustain the banking system, it could not finance a growing industrial base, and without that industrial base it could not monopolize power.[66]

To solve this problem, the PRI created a broad array of government-owned development banks. The first of these had been founded in the 1920s to provide credit to agriculture—as well as to provide loans to revolutionary generals turned landowners—but in the 1930s and 1940s, government-owned banks mushroomed, and they were increasingly used to provide long-term finance for Mexico's growing manufacturing sector. As figure 10.2 shows, by the 1950s, credit from development banks exceeded credit from commercial banks and investment banks combined. Indeed, by the 1970s, credit from the government-owned development banks so dwarfed credit from commercial banks and investment banks that the government allowed these privately owned banks to merge, creating enterprises called multibanks.

In theory, government development banks were supposed to provide credit to small and medium-sized enterprises in order to level the playing field against the large industrial conglomerates that mobilized credit from the commercial banks and investment banks. Mexico's industrial conglomerates typically owned both a commercial bank and an investment bank, and the portfolios of those banks tended to be composed of shares held in the enterprises that were part of the conglomerates.[67] The commercial and investment banks were, in essence, the treasury divisions of

[66] For a more complete discussion of the sources of electoral support of the PRI, see Haber et al. (2008) 27–37; Magaloni (2006).

[67] Del Angel-Mobarak (2002), chapters 4, 5; Del Angel-Mobarak (2005), 44.

the conglomerates. As a practical matter, however, the government-owned development banks tended to allocate most of their credit to the very same industrial conglomerates that received financing from private banks. The political pressure to lend to large firms, which tended to have large, unionized, and politically influential labor forces, simply outweighed whatever original mandate the development banks may have had. This meant that industrial and commercial conglomerates could fund risky enterprises through the development banks rather than from the private banks that were under their control.[68]

The commercial banks, investment banks, and development banks therefore all worked together to finance Mexico's largest industrial and commercial enterprises. The development banks tended to serve as second-tier lenders, repurchasing loans made by commercial banks through special programs designed to channel credit to sectors that the government deemed crucial. In fact, as of 1942, the government actually required private banks to allocate 60 percent of their loans to such directed credit programs.[69] These programs represented a government guarantee to private banks because all of the default risk was borne by the development bank. Not surprisingly, Mexico's banking system became stable and profitable.

For all its stability, however, the development banks gave rise to a system that encouraged reckless behavior. Because shareholders and depositors in commercial and investment banks did not bear the risk of loans gone bad, the risk was borne by the taxpayers who ultimately subsidized the development banks. Development banks also made direct loans to private manufacturers, further subsidizing large industrial firms as well as the private banks that were affiliated with them, while putting taxpayer funds at risk. The largest development bank, Nacional Financiera (NAFIN), founded in 1934, obtained its capital by selling government-guaranteed bonds and then made long-term loans to manufacturers that were collateralized by blocks of shares issued by those firms. NAFIN was supposed to provide credit to small and mid-sized manufacturing companies, which were often unable to obtain financing from commercial and investment banks. As a practical matter, however, NAFIN allocated most of its credit to the same industrial conglomerates that received financing from private

---

[68] Cárdenas (2000), 190, 195.
[69] Del Angel-Mobarak (2002), 299.

banks.[70] Worse, because of the political importance of their workforces, the government came to use NAFIN as a mechanism to bail out manufacturers that were not economically viable. Even worse, the policy of bailouts encouraged moral hazard: knowing that they would be bailed out, manufacturers undertook high-risk activities of doubtful expected profitability.[71]

The end result was that the Mexican government, which is to say Mexican taxpayers, came to own a wide range of commercial and industrial enterprises of dubious value, including sugar refiners, steel mills, airlines, and hotels. By the early 1980s there were 1,155 such state-owned firms, most of which were perennial money losers.[72] As the next chapter shows, this was not a sustainable equilibrium.

[70] Cárdenas (2000), 190.
[71] Cárdenas (2000), 195.
[72] Haber et al. (2008), 53.

11

|||||||||||||||||||||||

When Autocracy Fails

Banking and Politics in Mexico since 1982

We are neither of the left, nor of the right, but entirely the opposite.

Cantinflas (a famous Mexican comedian), making
fun of Luis Echeverría Alvarez, president of Mexico

Mexico's bankers had always been wary of the Partido Revoluciona-rio Institucional (PRI). They knew that the bargain that they had struck with the party was little more than an alliance of convenience. That wariness proved to be well founded. In 1982, President José López Portillo expropriated the banking system with the stroke of a pen. For the next nine years, the banking system basically existed to finance federal government deficits, to channel credit to state-owned firms, and to provide finance for politically crucial producer and consumer groups based on criteria other than economic viability. The economy went into a tailspin. The economic stagnation of the 1980s—Mexico's so-called lost decade—had considerable political consequences: the Mexican population increasingly lost confidence in the PRI, while opposition parties gained traction in municipal, state, and federal elections.

The response by President Carlos Salinas de Gortari (in office 1988–94) was to privatize most of the country's state-owned firms, particularly the banks. But who would buy a bank from a government that had seized it just nine years before—especially when the government was making it clear that it wanted top dollar? The answer was someone who was not actually going to put up much of his own capital, because he could get the government to allow him to pay for the bank with money that he was borrowing from the bank itself, with the collateral being shares in the bank! We examine the details of this rather strange set of transactions below, but suffice it to say here that the newly privatized banking system collapsed after just three years, the resulting bailout cost Mexican taxpayers 15 percent of

GDP, the economy contracted sharply, and voters shifted their allegiance to opposition parties. In 1997, the PRI, for the first time in its history, lost control of the lower house of congress. In 2000, it lost the presidency.

Mexico has been building a democracy since 1997, and that process has necessarily been slow: democratic institutions that simultaneously enfranchise citizens and constrain the authority and discretion of elected (and unelected) officials can take generations to develop. One of the first things that happened in Mexico's slow process of democratization was that the government unilaterally broke the partnership that had existed with bankers throughout the twentieth century. As of 1997, foreign banks were allowed to purchase majority control in Mexican financial institutions. Foreign banks were quick to take advantage of the opportunity: within a few years all of Mexico's large banks were foreign owned. Later reforms changed bankruptcy laws in order to allow banks to repossess collateral more easily. More recently, the government has further opened up the banking system to increased competition.

These changes have not eliminated all of the shortcomings of the Mexican banking system overnight: Mexico continues to have a highly concentrated banking system that allocates less credit than banks in other upper-middle-income countries. Nevertheless, the changes in Mexican banking system regulation over the past decade would have been unimaginable during the heyday of the PRI.

A Fragile Bargain

The alliance of convenience between Mexico's bankers and the PRI dictatorship was always fragile. The main thing that held it together was the PRI's need to reward organized labor for its political support. Organized workers were employed by industrial conglomerates, and those industrial conglomerates tended to also own banks, which acted as their treasury arm. The close connections between banks and industrial conglomerates provided bankers a modicum of protection, because it was not possible for the PRI to pit the manufacturers and bankers against one another; but there was no clear mechanism by which the bankers could retaliate politically if the government decided to expropriate them. It was not as if industrial workers would declare a general strike if the government raised the reserve-to-deposit ratio on banks. The PRI's relationship with the bankers existed as an analytic abstraction, not a day-to-day working partnership. If the political calculus of the PRI leadership changed, the bankers could do little to protect themselves.

Such a change began in the 1970s, as government expenditures outstripped revenues by a wide margin, and it eventually resulted in the unwinding of the partnership between the PRI and the bankers. Before that happened, however, the government first tried to solve its fiscal problems by levying an inflation tax. During the 1950s, the Mexican government had run balanced budgets; the fiscal deficit was typically on the order of 0.1 percent of GDP. In the 1960s, however, it began to spend at a rate that outpaced growth in its revenues: deficits escalated, averaging 1.9 percent of GDP across the decade. The situation worsened during the 1970s: the fiscal deficit averaged 6.6 percent of GDP. By 1981, it had swelled to 18 percent of GDP.[1]

The PRI could have solved its fiscal problem by increasing taxes, but it chose not to antagonize the bankers and industrialists who—even though they distrusted the PRI—were its implicit partners. As a result, the Mexican government collected tax revenues at approximately the same ratio to GDP as Latin America's poorest countries, such as Honduras. Government revenues were low mainly because capital was, in effect, not taxed. The lack of capital taxation was not an accident: in 1961, the government convened a distinguished group of economists to advise it on how to increase revenues, and they recommended that the government create a stock and bond registry so that it could tax corporate dividends and interest payments, require banks and bond-issuing entities to withhold tax on interest they paid to individuals, and revise the tax laws so that wealthy individuals had to file a consolidated income-tax return (rather than being allowed to fragment their income into separate categories that had lower tax rates). Those recommendations were ignored. The treasury minister even stated publicly that taxes on the wealthy could not be increased without their acquiescence. In the 1970s, the government revived the recommendations, but they were scuttled after a series of private consultations between the treasury minister and leading industrialists.[2]

---

[1] Haber et al. (2008), 58; Bazdresch and Levy (1991), 252.
[2] Izquierdo (1995), 69–81; Elizondo Mayer-Serra (2001), 116–17, 131–38; P. Smith (1991), 358, 368; Haber et al. (2008), 38–39.

Unwilling to bear the political costs of raising taxes or cutting expenditures, the government directed the central bank to expand the money supply, which had the predictable effect of raising the annual rate of inflation from less than 3 percent during the 1960s to double digits in the mid-1970s. By 1981, inflation was 28 percent, and the Mexican government was financing a significant fraction of its deficits through an inflation tax.

As we discuss in chapter 2, inflation-tax revenues can be shared with commercial banks. In Mexico, however, presidents Luis Echeverría and José López Portillo dramatically raised bank reserve requirements to make sure that their governments would capture virtually all the revenues. Reserve ratios climbed from just 3 percent of deposits in 1959 to 46 percent by 1979.[3] The central bank paid interest on those reserves, but that interest rate was below the rate of inflation. In addition, the government established interest-rate ceilings.[4] This meant that the Banco de México held a large proportion of private banks' deposits, on which banks earned lower income than they could have done in the open market. At the same time, the deposits that were left at the banks' disposal were subject to interest-rate caps. The banks were thus forced to offer interest rates on deposits that were lower than the prevailing rate of inflation. Depositors responded in a predictable manner: they withdrew their money from the banking system. The ratio of bank deposits to GDP had been climbing, growing from 17 percent in 1960 to 29 percent by 1969. The inflation tax caused disintermediation: by 1979, the ratio of deposits to GDP had fallen back to 24 percent.[5]

The combination of falling deposits and forced lending to the government via increasing deposit-reserve requirements had a predictable effect. The supply of bank credit for private purposes declined dramatically. As figure 10.2 shows, the ratio of credit from commercial banks and *financieras* relative to GDP had reached 17 percent in 1970. By 1977, it had fallen to 11 percent. At this point, Mexico's bankers began to express concern that they were going to be expropriated.[6]

The situation facing bankers turned worse in the early 1980s. In addition to printing money to fund escalating deficits, President López Portillo

---

[3] International Monetary Fund (n.d.).
[4] Del Angel-Mobarak (2002), 285.
[5] World Bank (2012).
[6] Del Angel-Mobarak and Martinelli Montoya (2009), 21.

borrowed heavily abroad, believing that a combination of rising petroleum prices and discoveries of new reserves in the Gulf of Mexico would
allow him to service the growing debt. When the price of oil collapsed in
early 1982, López Portillo had to scramble to avoid a foreign-debt default.
He converted U.S. dollar–denominated savings accounts into pesos at the
official rate of exchange (which was approximately one-third less than
the rate on the parallel exchange market), thereby expropriating the assets
of individuals and firms holding dollar accounts. When these measures
proved insufficient, he declared that the government was temporarily sus-
pending payments on Mexico's foreign debt, a step that only accelerated
the run on the peso.

Citizens and business enterprises responded by converting their peso
assets into dollars, which they then moved out of the country, partly with
the assistance of commercial banks. López Portillo responded by blaming
the bankers for the collapse of the exchange rate and expropriated the
banks on September 1, 1982, with the stroke of a pen. The expropriation, which required a constitutional amendment, was ratified by the PRI-
controlled Mexican congress with virtually no debate. The bankers received compensation in the form of government bonds, but these were of
dubious value: after all, the government had already stopped payment on
its foreign debt, and the country was entering a time of very high inflation.

For the next seven years, Mexico's banks were administered to satisfy
a simple, politically determined calculus. Banks continued to take deposits and clear checks, but they directed more than half of their lending to
the government in order to fund its deficits. As a consequence, firms and
households were starved for credit. As figure 11.1 shows, by 1987 the
ratio of private-sector loans to GDP was only 9 percent—roughly 60 percent of its level just five years before. Worse, much of that private credit
was directed to politically crucial producer and consumer groups based
on criteria other than their capacity to repay loans. Politically favored
borrowers tend to be riskier borrowers, and Mexico's were no exception;
by the late 1980s the ratio of nonperforming loans to total loans began to
climb markedly. The government may have owned the banks, but those
banks were becoming increasingly unprofitable.[7]

---

[7] Gunther, Moore, and Short (1996).

Credit as percentage of GDP

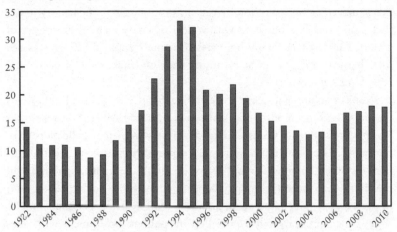

FIGURE 11.1 Private credit from deposit money banks as percent of GDP, Mexico, 1982–2010.

Source: World Bank (2012).

How Do You Sell Banks that You Just Stole?

The Mexican economy limped along through the rest of the 1980s, with the government simultaneously trying to control high and rising inflation, address skyrocketing unemployment, and restore public confidence in the PRI. In the 1970s, the population had been led to believe that Mexico was on its way to becoming a high-income country; now they were watching that vision evaporate as incomes and living standards collapsed. López Portillo's successor, Miguel de la Madrid Hurtado (in office 1982–88), did what he could, but he was limited by a fundamental fact: the Mexican government had been spending beyond its means for close to two decades. President de la Madrid could neither raise taxes effectively nor borrow abroad to finance these deficits. He therefore focused on cutting spending and opening up the economy to foreign trade.[8]

When President Carlos Salinas came to office in 1988, he faced a daunting task. He inherited a stagnant economy that was weighed down by a massive public-sector debt and thousands of poorly performing state-

---

[8] Haber et al. (2008), 68–77, provides a brief history of the steps by which Mexico liberalized foreign trade.

owned enterprises. He also headed a party that was rapidly losing legitimacy. Indeed, he won election by the smallest margin in the history of the PRI (and even that outcome was widely asserted to be the product of fraud). This last fact cannot be stressed strongly enough. Salinas was not just charged with getting the economy back on track: the fate of the PRI rested in his hands.

Salinas's solution to these overlapping fiscal and political challenges was to sell off much of the vast collection of state-owned enterprises that his predecessors had amassed. The crown jewels of that collection were the banks. Their sale not only provided the government with extraordinary revenues that it used to pay down the public debt, but it also reduced the drain that those (perennially unprofitable) firms put on the annual budget, thereby helping to bring inflation under control. The sale of many state-owned enterprises also provided the Salinas government with one-time revenues that could be used as partial funding for the social programs that were a crucial part of the PRI's strategy to win the 1994 presidential elections and reestablish its political dominance.[9]

In retrospect, the government's approach toward selling the banks might be regarded as myopic, but there were good reasons for myopia. Political and fiscal considerations gave Salinas strong incentives to sell the banks as fast as possible and maximize the revenues from that sale. The result was that bank privatization was accomplished in just 18 months. The government raised $12.4 billion dollars from the sale—three times the book value of the banks.

Why, one might ask, would investors pay such a high price for banks that the government had seized only nine years before? Why wouldn't they have offered a low price to compensate them for the risk that the government might just expropriate them all over again? An additional risk, as the bankers well knew, was that the government did not have to engage in de jure expropriation to reduce their property rights. It could carry out a de facto expropriation through a combination of increasing deposit-reserve requirements, increasing the money supply (to increase the inflation rate), and imposing interest-rate ceilings. They knew this because the government had engaged in precisely that combination of moves in the 1970s.[10]

[9] Magaloni (2006).
[10] Haber (2005), 2329.

The bankers were nevertheless willing to pay three times the banks' book value because they were able to craft a deal in which they did not actually have to put up much of their own money for the purchases; they borrowed those funds, sometimes from the banks they were buying. As we shall see, this step sealed the future of the banking system by precipitating a series of government decisions that almost guaranteed that the banks would be run in an imprudent, if not reckless, manner.[11] Because the bankers had very little capital at risk, they had little incentive to lend money in a prudent manner. Minority shareholders also had very little capital at risk and so had weak incentives to monitor or discipline the insiders. Depositors were insured against loss by the government without limit, giving them every incentive to put their funds in the bank that paid the highest interest rates, regardless of the riskiness of its loan portfolio. The government designed a set of accounting rules that inflated the value of bank assets; that made it difficult for anyone, including its own supervisors, to know what was actually taking place inside the banks. The only group that had serious money at risk was the one group that was not represented in the negotiations: Mexico's taxpayers, who would have to fund the deposit-insurance system when it collapsed. Indeed, one way of thinking about this transaction is that the Mexican government and Mexico's bank insiders jointly expropriated Mexican taxpayers. The taxpayers retaliated by voting out the PRI, precisely because it had forged a government-banker partnership that was guaranteed to fail.

Limited competition was a key feature of the grand bargain of bank privatization in the 1990s. To induce investors to offer high prices for the banks despite the possible risks they faced, the Salinas administration signaled potential bidders that they would not have to operate in a competitive environment. When privatized in 1991, the Mexican banking industry was composed of 18 banks, four of which controlled approximately 70 percent of total bank assets. The government did not break up these banks; instead, it sold them as is. In addition, the government made it clear that it would use its regulatory authority to control entry into the banking industry (obtaining a bank charter required the permission of the treasury minister).[12] The government also signaled potential bidders that they would

---

[11] This section draws heavily on Haber (2005).
[12] Haber (2005), 2329.

not have to compete against foreign banks, which, as before, were not allowed to participate in the 1991–92 bank auctions.[13] Foreign banks continued to be effectively excluded from the Mexican market during the negotiations over NAFTA.[14] The government was, in effect, selling the rights to operate an oligopoly.[15]

Having reduced banking system competition, thereby raising banks' likely rate of return on capital, the Salinas administration then structured the bank auction process to maximize prices. The rules of the auction specified that bids would be sealed and that the managerial expertise of the bidding groups would be taken into account.[16] The latter condition, however, applied only if the second-highest bid was within 3 percent of the highest offer made.[17]

---

[13] Foreign ownership of Mexican banks had always been restricted. In 1966 this situation was codified by President Gustavo Díaz Ordaz, who required that the banking industry be domestically owned. This was part of a more general initiative to force foreign investors in a broad range of enterprises to sell majority stakes to Mexican owners. See Izquierdo (1995), 112, 119.

[14] The provisions governing banking in the 1994 NAFTA agreement severely limited the participation of foreign banks in Mexico. NAFTA stipulated that U.S. and Canadian banks could own no more than 30 percent of a Mexican bank's capital. It also stipulated that U.S. and Canadian banks could not purchase a controlling interest in any Mexican bank whose market share exceeded 1.5 percent and that the total market share under their control could not exceed 8 percent. This restriction meant that foreign banks were effectively excluded from the market, because there were only two banks with market shares of 1.5 percent or less. Over a six-year transitional period, U.S. and Canadian banks could gradually hold larger market shares, up to a maximum of 15 percent by the year 2000. Even after this transitional period, however, NAFTA granted the Mexican government the right to freeze the purchases of Mexican banks by U.S. and Canadian concerns for a three-year period if foreign banks as a group controlled more than 25 percent of the market. Foreign banks were also still subject to the rule that they could own no more than 30 percent of a Mexican bank's stock. See Murillo (2005).

[15] It is debated whether Salinas insisted on excluding foreign banks from the market, both during the bank privatization and during the NAFTA negotiations, because he sought to signal that he was selling a secure oligopoly (see, e.g., Haber [2005]) or because he had sound economic reasons for believing that the payments system must be in the hands of Mexican bankers (see, e.g., Suárez Dávila [2010]). Regardless of Salinas's intentions, from the point of view of Mexico's bankers, the exclusion of foreign banks from the market should have caused them to bid more aggressively: they knew that foreign entrants could not reduce their market power.

[16] Unal and Navarro (1999).

[17] Haber (2005), 2329.

The government also maximized the price it received by following accounting practices that were not in line with generally accepted accounting standards. One of the most lenient of Mexico's bank accounting rules, dating from the period of government ownership, was that when a loan was past due, only the interest in arrears was counted as nonperforming. The principal of such a loan could be rolled over and counted as a performing asset. Moreover, the past-due interest could be rolled into the principal, and the capitalized interest could then be recorded as income. Modifying this rule, as well as others that inflated bank capital and assets, would have lowered the banks' book value of capital by increasing the ratio of nonperforming to total loans, lowering banks' reported rates of return, and decreasing the book value of assets.[18] By inflating bank capital, the accounting rules allowed the banks to satisfy regulatory capital requirements without having to raise additional capital. How much lower the bank valuations would have been without these accounting gimmicks is difficult to know. It is known, however, that the Salinas administration contracted outside consulting firms to provide a realistic valuation of the banks—but it did not make the results of those studies public.[19] Instead, it told the bankers that they could receive reimbursements for nonperforming bank assets once they had taken possession of the banks.

This point merits emphasis: the bankers were not able to conduct a detailed analysis of the quality of the assets prior to the auction. They were promised, instead, that after they purchased the banks they could receive reimbursements from the government for assets that were not properly valued. One prominent banker from the pre-1982 era went so far as to say that the auction process amounted to being asked to bid on a house by looking at it from the outside with the doors and windows shut tight. What kind of banker would participate in such a deal? The answer is either a banker who is not gambling with his own money or a banker who does not know what he is doing. To make matters worse, the evidence indicates that the government subsequently failed to honor its promise to repurchase incorrectly valued assets.[20]

---

[18] A summary of these laws, as well as information about their reform after 1997, can be found in Del Angel-Mobarak, Haber, and Musacchio (2006).

[19] Unal and Navarro (1999).

[20] Espinosa Rugarcía and Cárdenas Sánchez (2011), 3: 55, 73.

Rather than conducting a single round of sealed bids, the Salinas administration sold the banks in six rounds of bidding between June 1991 and July 1992. This arrangement increased competition in the bidding for the banks sold in the later rounds, thus creating a cascade effect. The most important determinant of the bid-to-book-value ratio for a bank (that is, the amount bid as a proportion of the bank's nominal value) was the bidding round in which it was purchased. All other things being equal (in terms of the size of the bank, its profitability, and the number of bidders), each additional round of bidding pushed up the bid-to-book-value ratio by 30 percentage points.[21]

This set of arrangements produced an income of 12.4 billion dollars for the Mexican government, with a weighted average bid-to-book-value ratio of 3.04. A ratio of that magnitude suggests that bankers paid a substantial premium. In bank mergers in the United States during the 1980s, for example, the average bid-to-book-value ratio was 1.89.[22] The Mexican ratio is especially high in light of the fact that the banks up for auction were not healthy enterprises: they already had mounting portfolios of past-due loans.[23] An analysis of the market value of traded shares around the time of the bank auctions is consistent with this view: the prices paid at auction were 45 percent above the value of that equity as priced by the Mexican stock market.[24]

The government knew that, given the risk of expropriation and the low and uncertain quality of the loan portfolio, it would be hard to inspire aggressive bidding for its banks. But, knowing that bidders are always more generous when bidding with other people's money, it made sure that the bidders were able to borrow on favorable terms. The ideal lenders for such a purpose were the banks themselves, and neither the fiscally strapped government nor the bidders had a reason to object to letting the banks assist in funding their own acquisition.[25]

The original payment plan devised by the government called for a 30 percent payment within three days after the announcement of the auction winner, with the remaining 70 percent due within 30 days. The bank-

[21] Haber (2005), 2330.
[22] Unal and Navarro (1999).
[23] Gunther, Moore, and Short (1996).
[24] Unal and Navarro (1999).
[25] Mackey (1999), 55, 61, 141, 216.

ers, however, convinced the Salinas administration to give them more time to finance their purchases with outside sources of funds. Under the new rules, the first payment was reduced to 20 percent, a second payment of 20 percent was due 30 days later, and the remaining 60 percent was to be paid within four months after that. The bankers used the five-month period between the auction and the final payment date to raise the necessary funds from outside investors.[26] These funds came from small Mexican investors, bonds floated on the stock market, foreign banks, other Mexican banks, and, in some cases, the bank that had been purchased. That is, some shareholders were able to finance or refinance their share purchases with a loan from the bank they were purchasing, with the collateral for the loan being the shares that were being purchased. In the case of Bancomer, the largest bank in the system, 20 percent of the *first payment* made to the government by the winning bidders was actually financed by a loan to the bidders from the bank—a fact that its pre-1982 owner characterized as "monstrous."[27] In another case, a group of purchasers financed 75 percent of the total cost of acquiring a bank through a loan from the same bank.[28]

The government's policy in this regard was disastrous, because it meant that bank insiders and minority shareholders actually had very little of their own capital at risk. This was, in short, exactly the opposite set of incentives that bankers and minority shareholders faced under the Díaz-era system, in which banks were highly capitalized with insiders' resources, and the incentives to monitor lending were extremely strong.

This set of arrangements implied that to avoid a high risk of bank failures, Mexico's regulators would have to be vigilant monitors of the banks and effective enforcers of constraints on them. That was, however, not possible: Mexico's regulators were inexperienced, and the tools they had at their disposal were blunt in the extreme. Indeed, the government itself

[26] Unal and Navarro (1999).

[27] Espinosa Rugarcía and Cárdenas Sánchez (2011), 3: 11–12.

[28] Mackey (1999), 55, 61, 141, 216. In the case of Banca Serfin (Mexico's third largest) an additional departure from the usual procedures might also have reduced the director's capital at risk. Departing from its practice in all the other bank auctions, the government held back 16 percent of the stock from the bidding process. The group that bought the bank had the option to purchase this remaining share after the auction process closed. Unal and Navarro (1999).

had designed Mexico's extremely permissive bank accounting standards to accomplish its political purposes. Regulators had bosses, and those bosses would never have supported any attempt to force banks to recognize their losses and raise adequate capital. In fact, prior to 1995, the National Banking Commission did not have the technological means to gather information from the banks in a timely manner. It also lacked the legal authority and autonomy to properly supervise the banks.[29]

The lack of effective monitoring by bank supervisors and regulators, and by bank directors, meant that Mexico's depositors could not rely on the net worth of the banks to provide a buffer against losses on deposits. Thus, the risky logic of the privatization required that depositors be protected by something else. As a technical matter, bank deposits in Mexico were only insured up to the available resources in FOBAPROA (the Fondo Bancario de Protección al Ahorro, or Banking Fund for the Protection of Savings, Mexico's government-run deposit insurance system). As a practical matter, however, FOBAPROA had the ability to borrow from the central bank.[30] The Banco de México's guarantee, moreover, was not just implicit, as a consequence of its fiduciary relationship to FOBAPROA: it was an explicit promise. The Banco de México was supposed to publish, in December of each year, the maximum amount of bank obligations that would be protected by FOBAPROA during the following year. Its 1993, 1994, and 1995 statements did not, however, actually list amounts. Instead, the Banco de México stated that FOBAPROA would provide a blanket guarantee of virtually all bank liabilities (deposits, loans, and credits, including those from other banks).[31] Some classes of bank liabilities were excluded, but as a practical matter, deposit insurance was unlimited—and even covered some loans made by banks to one another.[32] Making matters worse, there were no general guidelines regarding limitations and restrictions on FOBAPROA programs. Rather, participation was to be determined on a case-by-case basis.[33] In short, the government signed a blank check in case catastrophe struck.

Precisely because there was unlimited deposit insurance, bank depositors did not police banks by withdrawing funds from banks with risky

[29] Mackey (1999), 97.
[30] Mackey (1999), 44.
[31] The text of the Banco de México's statement can be found in Mackey (1999), 53.
[32] Mackey (1999), 55.
[33] Mackey (1999), 52.

loan portfolios. Not surprisingly, in contrast to the evidence that market discipline operated in the deposit market during the Porfiriato, changes in the growth of time deposits and their interest rates in Mexico from 1991 to 1996 were unrelated to various measures of banks' riskiness.[34] In short, Mexico's bank insiders had been given a license to engage in a "heads I win, tails you lose" gamble. If their bets paid off, they would earn handsome profits. If their bets failed, the losses would be passed on to Mexico's taxpayers, who would have to fund the liabilities of the deposit insurance system.

Bank credit grew at a breakneck pace, doubling from 1991 to 1994 (see figure 11.1). Housing loans grew at an even faster rate: from December 1991 to December 1994, real lending for housing and real estate nearly tripled. Moreover, this is a lower-bound estimate of the growth of housing lending because it includes only performing loans. Much of the housing portfolio was nonperforming, and the principal value and past-due interest of those loans were continually rolled over into an accounting category called "rediscounts." The value of these rediscounts was nearly equal to the total value of housing loans in December 1994, which implies that housing lending might have grown as much as sixfold in just three years.[35] The rapid growth in lending was not matched by the growth in deposits. From 1992 through 1994, loans outstripped deposits by roughly 20 percent; the difference was funded through interbank lending, predominantly from foreign banks in foreign currency.[36]

Fast run-ups in bank credit typically imply perfunctory loan reviews, and Mexico was a textbook case of the phenomenon. Credit analysis at Mexico's banks was virtually nonexistent.[37] Because these banks had historically been the treasury arms of industrial and commercial conglomerates, they had had little need to invest in credit-reporting systems. When the government owned and ran the banks, the biggest bank debtor was the government itself, and any other lending was channeled to politically crucial firms and interest groups. Banks could not rely on information gathered by other creditors as a substitute, because Mexico did not have

---

[34] Martinez Peria and Schmukler (2001); Huybens, Jordan, and Pratap (2005).
[35] Haber (2005), 2336–38.
[36] Mackey (1999), 60, 98.
[37] Mackey (1999), 56.

a system of private credit reporting.[38] The country's first private credit bureaus were not founded until July 1993, and it was not until February 1995 that rules were established governing their operation.[39]

As a consequence, even more rapid than the growth in lending was the growth of nonperforming loans. Generally accepted accounting standards treat both the principal and interest of a loan in arrears as nonperforming once a specified period of time has passed, typically 90 days in the United States. As we have already noted, Mexico's idiosyncratic accounting rules, designed by the government to conceal the true state of the banks at the time of privatization, did not follow these standards. Rather, banks were allowed to separate out principal in arrears from interest in arrears, with only the latter being treated as nonperforming. The past-due principal could be rediscounted or renewed, which is to say endlessly rolled over, or "evergreened." In December 1991, the declared nonperforming loan ratio was 3.6 percent; by December 1994 it had climbed to 6.1 percent. This would have been bad enough, but if one adds the rediscounts to the declared nonperforming loans, then the default rate was 13.5 percent in December 1991 and 17.1 percent in December 1994.[40]

The practice of rediscounting loans began to be phased out in 1995. Instead, banks began to renew or restructure unpaid principal and treated these rollovers as performing. An accounting that treats these rollovers as past-due loans produces striking changes in the measure of nonperforming loans: the figure for December 1996 rises from 5.7 to 32.5 percent. Even this figure is likely an underestimate of loan default risk, because beginning in February 1995, banks were allowed to swap many of their loans for promissory notes from Mexico's deposit-insurance system as part of a bailout (a subject we discuss in detail below). If we add the value of those deposit-insurance promissory notes to the value of declared nonperforming loans, rediscounts, and restructured or renewed loans, the percentage of loans that were nonperforming actually exceeds the percentage of loans in good standing: for December 1996, the nonperformance ratio would have been 52.6 percent.[41]

---

[38] Negrin (2000).
[39] Mackey (1999), 25.
[40] Haber (2005), 2338.
[41] Haber (2005), 2338.

As if Mexico's poor accounting standards were not enough of a burden on taxpayers, the banking system was also heavily exposed to exchange-rate risk. Mexico's bank insiders had funded their loan books by borrowing funds in dollars and then making loans in dollars to Mexican firms that did not have dollar sources of income. In fact, foreign-currency loans represented roughly one-third of total loans made by Mexican banks.[42] This is, of course, another mistake that would be made only by a banker who either did not know what he was doing or who was gambling with someone else's money. This gamble succeeded as long as the government was able to maintain a stable, pegged exchange rate of the peso to the dollar, but by late 1994 investors had come to understand the Salinas government's crawling-peg exchange-rate system for what it was: a charade designed to hold down inflation temporarily and make foreign-produced goods look inexpensive to Mexican voters by grossly over-valuing the peso. This situation was not sustainable. Once the peso started to slide in December 1994, the government of newly elected President Ernesto Zedillo tried in desperation to prevent a devaluation by raising central-bank interest rates in order to attract investors to Mexican government securities. Mortgage interest rates, which tended to be adjustable, jumped to 74 percent by March 1995, from 22 percent just five months before.[43] Worse, the peso collapsed anyway, falling to nearly half its value against the dollar in the space of a few days.

The business enterprises that had borrowed from the banks in dollars, but which did not have dollar sources of income to service those loans, saw the value of their loan principal double almost overnight. The combination of rapidly rising interest rates and increases in the peso value of dollar-denominated loans pushed risky but still-performing loans into default. The banks became deeply insolvent.

The government responded with a bailout of the banking system, which ultimately cost Mexican taxpayers roughly 15 percent of GDP.[44] The National Banking and Securities Commission (known by its Spanish acronym, CNBV) seized control of 12 banks in serious financial distress and suspended shareholder rights. Another three banks went through de facto

---

[42] Krueger and Tornell (1999).

[43] Gruben and McComb (1997).

[44] For a more complete description of the various programs used to bail out the banks, see Haber (2005), 2339–43.

interventions (meaning that their shareholders retained control of the bank). Thus, of Mexico's 18 banks, 15 were sufficiently distressed to require intervention.

One of the most striking features of this bailout was a loan repurchase program run by FOBAPROA. In exchange for their nonperforming assets, banks received a nontradable, zero-coupon, ten-year FOBAPROA promissory note that carried an interest rate slightly below the government treasury bond rate. Banks were charged with collecting the principal and interest on the loans transferred to FOBAPROA. As a practical matter, however, they did not do so.[45] In short, Mexican taxpayers bought the banks' bad loans.

Mexico's bankers likely anticipated the intervention and bailout and took advantage of it to save their nonfinancial firms. One study has shown that 20 percent of all large loans from 1995 to 1998 went to bank directors. These insider loans carried lower rates of interest than arm's-length loans (by 4 percentage points), had a 33 percent higher probability of default, and had a 30 percent lower collateral recovery rate.[46]

The looting of the banks to save the nonfinancial enterprises of their directors was made possible by a revision of the rules governing the FOBAPROA loan-repurchase program. When the program was first instituted in 1995, the government declared that past-due loans, loans held by companies in bankruptcy, loans discounted with development banks, loans denominated in UDIS (a unit of account created to protect debtors from exchange-rate risk during the early stages of the bailout), and loans to related parties (directors, their families, or their firms) were ineligible for repurchase. As the situation of the banking system deteriorated, the government dropped these restrictions.[47] Making matters even worse, there were no established limitations and restrictions on FOBAPROA programs: all decisions were made on a case-by-case basis.[48] Not surprisingly, the FOBAPROA bailout was not (as originally anticipated in early 1995) a one-time event. Rather, it became an open-ended mechanism, with loans being transferred from the banks to FOBAPROA through 1999. Thus the percentage of bank loan portfolios composed of FOBAPROA bonds grew

---

[45] Krueger and Tornell (1999); Murillo (2002).
[46] La Porta, López-de-Silanes, and Zamarripa (2003).
[47] Mackey (1999), 70.
[48] Mackey (1999), 52.

from 9 percent in 1995 to 20 percent in 1996, and 29 percent in 1997 and 1998, finally topping out at 35 percent in 1999. For the same reason, bank interventions were not a one-time event but were spread out from 1994 to 2001.[49] As of June 1999, the total cost of the bailout programs was 692 billion pesos (65 billion dollars), roughly 15 percent of Mexican GNP.[50]

The 1995–96 Banking Crisis:
A Death Blow to the PRI's Monopoly on Power

The fact that the banking-system bailout involved an implicit transfer from taxpayers to bank stockholders, who included some of Mexico's wealthiest men, produced a political firestorm in Mexico. It fueled the expansion of a national debtors' protest movement, the most prominent manifestation of which was an organization known as El Barzón (named for the yoke ring to which an ox-drawn plow is attached). Perhaps most crucially, it contributed to the growth of opposition political parties, which were able to channel the anger of millions of middle-class families and small business owners who had been pushed into bankruptcy by the surge in interest rates and the dramatic shrinkage in credit. In 1997, in the run-up to the midterm elections for Mexico's lower house of congress, opposition party representatives insisted on an investigation into the bank bailout before they would approve any further funds. This maneuver held up approval of the 1999 federal budget for nine months.

As a result of the growing power of opposition parties in congress, the government disbanded FOBAPROA and replaced it with a new, more autonomous, deposit-guarantee agency, the Bank Savings Protection Institute (known by its Mexican acronym, IPAB). Most (although not all) FOBAPROA bonds were swapped for IPAB bonds, and IPAB was given the task of recouping and liquidating the assets backed by those bonds. This was a de facto admission that the loans that had been swapped for FOBAPROA promissory notes were unrecoverable. Congress also agreed that the annual cost of the banking rescue would be paid for by the government out of each year's budget.[51] This was an admission that the new IPAB

---

[49] Haber (2005), 2342.
[50] Murillo (2002), 24, 27.
[51] McQuerry (1999).

bonds had the status of sovereign debt—and that Mexico's taxpayers were on the hook.

Democratization and the Forging of a New Banker-Government Partnership

By 1997, not only was the Mexican banking system in ruins, but so was the PRI. Almost all of Mexico's banks were insolvent and had basically been renationalized through government intervention. The PRI had lost the support of the industrialists and bankers in 1982, when López Portillo expropriated the banking system. It had lost the support of organized industrial workers, who had long been its most faithful followers, when, in a calculated gamble to rekindle growth, it abandoned its longstanding policies of trade protection and joined the General Agreement on Tariffs and Trade in 1986 and NAFTA in 1994.[52] The collapse of the banking system, and the widespread personal and business bankruptcies that followed, undermined whatever support the PRI had left.

Electoral reforms, pushed by opposition parties all through the 1980s and 1990s, could now bear fruit. The 1997 midterm elections denied the PRI a majority in the Chamber of Deputies (the lower house of congress) for the first time in the party's history. Within two years, the PRI would lose control of nearly half of Mexico's governorships, and in 2000 it would lose the presidency to a candidate from an opposition probusiness party. Mexico was undergoing a rapid transition to democracy.[53]

The Mexican president, Ernesto Zedillo, was therefore in a difficult situation circa 1997. If the PRI was to survive as a party, he had to find a way to get the economy moving again, which meant that he had to find a way to craft a new government-banker partnership.[54] By now, however, bankers (and potential bankers) had good reason not to trust the PRI: they had been expropriated in 1982 and then corralled into a privatization program that made them into national villains. Zedillo and his team,

---

[52] For an analysis of the decision of the Mexican government to abandon protectionism and embrace free trade, see Haber et al. (2008), chapter 4.

[53] For an analysis of the process by which opposition parties challenged the PRI and forced reforms to electoral rules, see Haber et al. (2008), chapter 5.

[54] This section draws heavily on Haber and Musacchio (2013).

for their part, had good reasons not to trust the bankers: the 1991–92 bank privatization process was carried out with capital that in many cases was fictitious, and once the privatization started to fall apart, the bankers tunneled into their own banks to assist their own industrial enterprises, leaving taxpayers to foot the bill and the PRI to take the blame.

The Zedillo government therefore did something that no Mexican government had done since the dictatorship of Porfirio Díaz: it allowed foreigners to own Mexican banks. Foreign banks had always operated a few small representation offices in Mexico, but commercial banking had been reserved for domestic owners all through the twentieth century. In February 1995, at the start of the 1995–96 banking crisis, foreign banks were permitted to purchase Mexican banks with market shares of 6 percent or less. This restriction kept the largest Mexican banks off the table. In 1996, all restrictions were removed on foreign bank ownership (with the new regulations going into effect in 1997). In December 1996, foreign banks controlled only 7 percent of total bank assets in Mexico. By December 1999, that figure had risen to 20 percent, and as of December 2003 it stood at 82 percent, a level that has held more or less constant since that time (see figure 11.2).[55] Mexico's banking system therefore came to be controlled not by firms named Banamex, Bancomer, and Serfin, but by big international banks such as Citibank, HSBC, and BBV.

From the point of view of the Zedillo government, foreign bank ownership had several advantages. First, foreign-owned banks could be counted on to recapitalize the banking system with real, not fictitious, capital. They would not request the kind of forbearance that their Mexican counterparts had asked for in 1991, when they were allowed to buy the banks with loans from the same banks. Second, foreign bankers had weak incentives to tunnel into their own banks during an economic downturn, because, unlike their Mexican counterparts, they did not own nonfinancial companies. Third, global universal banks operating in Mexico could not reasonably expect to be bailed out by Mexican taxpayers in the event of insolvency. What Mexican taxpayer would consent to rescuing Citibank? Fourth, foreign bankers would be accountable not just to Mexican regulators but also to regulators and shareholders in their home

---

[55] Haber and Musacchio (2013).

Loan market share (percent)

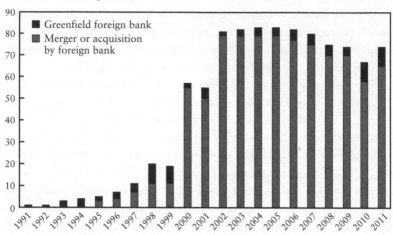

FIGURE 11.2 Market share of foreign banks in Mexico, 1991–2011.

Source: Haber and Musacchio (2013).

Note: Greenfield operations refers to newly established bank branches rather than acquired ones.

countries. In short, foreign bankers would have a lot to lose, and little to gain, from being opportunistic partners.[56]

From the point of view of foreign bankers, investing in the Mexican banking system by buying up existing banks made sense. In the first place, they saw Mexico as a large, untapped market. In the second place, unlike their Mexican counterparts, they could not be easily expropriated. Foreign bankers in Mexico, especially those from the United States and Canada, could access protection against the Mexican government from their home governments as well as from international tribunals under NAFTA.[57]

[56] Haber and Musacchio (2013).

[57] Article 1110(1) of NAFTA is quite explicit on this point: "No Party may directly or indirectly nationalize or expropriate an investment of another Party . . . or take a measure tantamount to nationalization or expropriation . . . except: (a) for a public purpose; (b) on a nondiscriminatory basis; (c) in accordance with due process of law . . . and (d) in payment of compensation." Article 1139 extends this guarantee against expropriation to all "property, tangible or intangible, acquired in the expectation or used for the purpose of economic benefit or other business purpose." NAFTA also creates international institutions with the authority to sanction signatory governments that violate its terms. Investors who believe that the Mexican government has violated the terms of NAFTA may demand compensation and have the case judged by a NAFTA

These assurances gained additional force after 2000, once Mexico had gone even further down the path of democratization and, importantly, of divided government.

Forging a partnership with foreign bankers put the Zedillo government in a much stronger position to craft a set of regulatory and accounting rules that would help prevent a rerun of the disaster of 1991–95. These rules were adopted at the time of the announcement that foreign bankers would be allowed to enter the market. First, the government made insider lending more difficult. Banks were required to publish consolidated accounts that included the operations of their subsidiaries. Banks were also precluded from making loans to bank officers and employees that were not part of their employee benefits programs. Related-party loans were allowed, but they could not exceed the net capital of the bank. Second, banks were required to diversify risk. As of June 1998, bank loans to any individual could not exceed 10 percent of the bank's net capital or 0.5 percent of the total net capital of all banks. The same law enjoined banks from granting loans to companies that exceeded 30 percent of the bank's net capital or 6 percent of the total net capital of all banks. Third, the government increased capital requirements and established reserve minimums in accordance with the riskiness of a bank's portfolio. In particular, banks were required to access the credit records of borrowers (by using a credit bureau). Loans for which the credit records were not checked (or in which they were checked but the borrowers' records were poor) had to be provisioned at 100 percent.[58] Fourth, new accounting standards, which more closely approximate generally accepted accounting standards, went into effect.[59] Finally, the rules governing deposit insurance were reformed. Unlike its predecessor (FOBAPROA), IPAB did not provide unlimited insurance. As of January 1, 2005, insurance has been limited to 400,000 UDIS (roughly 100,000 dollars at the current

---

tribunal. Moreover, they can go before a NAFTA tribunal to appeal judicial decisions made in Mexico that they consider to be against national or international law. The decisions of NAFTA tribunals can be appealed to national courts, but only in the country where the case is brought. This means that Mexico cannot use its court system to summarily overturn the decisions of a NAFTA tribunal. If it did so, thereby violating the provisions of NAFTA, the other signatory governments could impose trade sanctions. Condon and Sinha (2003), 127–29.

[58] Mackey (1999), 117.

[59] Del Angel-Mobarak, Haber, and Musacchio (2006).

rate of exchange) and covers bank deposits only, instead of a broad range of bank liabilities.

The foreign purchases of Mexican banks took place over almost six years. This transition period allows us an opportunity to test the hypothesis that the government actively favored foreign bankers over domestic ones. In 2000, Banamex, Mexico's second largest bank, which was then still in Mexican hands, announced a surprise bid to take over Bancomer (Mexico's largest bank, which was already under contract to be acquired by the Spanish bank BBV). Government officials at Mexico's Banking Commission rejected Banamex's bid. Within a year of that failed attempt, Banamex—which saw itself as no match for the deep pockets of foreign lenders—sold itself to Citibank.

Much ink has been spilled regarding the welfare effects of this new partnership between a democratic Mexican government and a group of large foreign banks. One recent study concludes that Mexico's banks are much better capitalized and much more profitable today than they have been at least since the 1970s, and the Mexican banking system as a whole is much more stable today than at any point since 1910. That study also finds no evidence of a downside to foreign entry: foreign banks do not appear to charge larger interest-rate spreads or provide less credit than either Mexican banks today or the same banks prior to being sold to foreign concerns. The one big difference that the study detects is that foreign-owned banks are much more cautious when it comes to screening borrowers: all else being equal, the purchase of a Mexican bank by a foreign bank caused the ratio of nonperforming loans to fall by 6.5 percentage points.[60]

None of this is to say that the new partnership between foreign bankers and a democratic Mexican government has provided Mexican businesses and households with abundant credit. Far from it: Mexico continues to be woefully under-banked, as figures 1.1 and 11.1 indicate. Credit from commercial banks as a percentage of GDP has climbed rapidly since 2004, when the process of foreign acquisition and mergers was completed. But even with that growth, the amount of credit available to Mexican business enterprises and households in 2010 was little higher than when the banks were initially privatized in 1991. For that matter, in 2010 it was at roughly the same level (as a percentage of GDP) as in 1910.

[60] Haber and Musacchio (2013).

Fixing the under-banking problem will require far more than a change in ownership: it will require building institutions that allow debtors to offer property as collateral and that will allow banks to repossess it at low cost. Those institutions are not, however, created at the stroke of a pen. They require considerable public and private investments in efficient courts, honest police, and accurate property and commercial registers. As of this writing, these institutions are all works in progress.

12

‖‖‖‖‖‖‖‖‖‖‖‖‖‖‖‖‖

Inflation Machines

Banking and State Finance in Imperial Brazil

Never promise a poor person, and never owe a rich one.
Brazilian proverb

Every country has a claim to fame. Large, diverse countries like Brazil have more than one. Soccer, coffee, and samba come to mind. So does inflation. Over the past two centuries, Brazil's average rate of inflation has been among the highest of any country in the world. At its peak, in 1993, it hit a staggering 2,477 percent per year.

Brazil's inflation rate has waxed and waned over time. As figures 12.1 and 12.2 show, inflation was significant throughout the 1820s, in the early 1890s, and from the mid-1950s to the mid-1990s. It was relatively weak from 1830 to 1889 and in the years since 1994. What drove the episodes of high inflation, and why were some periods apparently immune from the inflationary disease?

The answer is to be found in a close study of Brazil's Game of Bank Bargains. In every country we have examined, fiscal affairs have fundamentally shaped the Game of Bank Bargains, but in Brazil, they practically defined the entire game. In England, the need to wage war on Louis XIV drove the founding of the Bank of England. In the United States, the creation of national banks during the Civil War allowed the government to share in the profits that banks earned from printing zero-interest-paying banknotes. In Canada, the government required its banks to hold Dominion notes, which forced banks to share the profits from their banknote issues. In Mexico, when the government was finally strong enough during the Díaz dictatorship, it cut a deal with bankers to share the rents that came from building a crony network of banks and industrialists.

Inflation (percent)

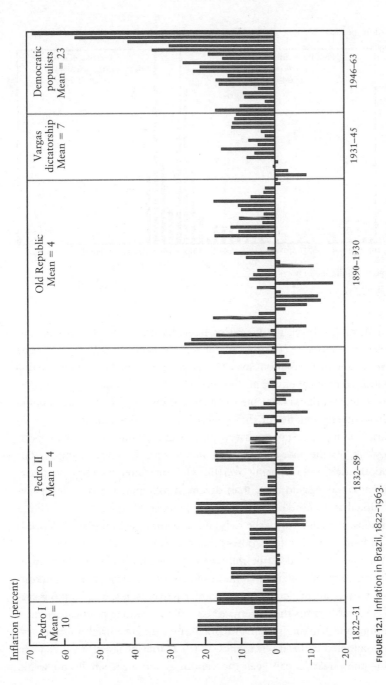

FIGURE 12.1 Inflation in Brazil, 1822–1963.

Source: 1822 to 1870 data are three-year averages, based on: Lobo (1978); Catão (1992); Lees, Botts, and Cysne (1990); Brazil, Ministerio do Trabalho, Industria e Comércio (1946). All of these series were retrieved from IPEA (n.d.).

Inflation (percent)

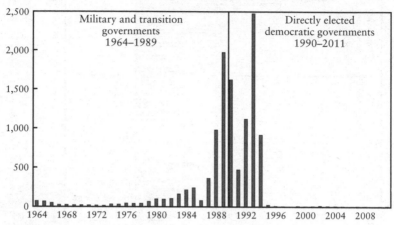

FIGURE 12.2 Inflation in Brazil, 1964–2011.

Source: IPEA (n.d.).

In Brazil, however, the Game of Bank Bargains and the struggles to finance the state were consistently one and the same. Brazil's high average inflation, and its fluctuations over time, reflected dramatic shifts in the distribution of political power in a society whose distribution of human capital is so uneven that a tiny elite owns practically everything worth taxing. That inequality has meant that every Brazilian government has had to choose among three unattractive options: tax no one, and remain poor and weak; tax the poor via inflation, and become dangerously unpopular; or tax the rich, and risk being overthrown immediately. No Brazilian government could ever do more than dream of following the Brazilian proverb quoted at the head of this chapter: in practice, to rule they had to build coalitions, sometimes with the rich and sometimes with the poor, depending on fundamental shifts in power that occurred over time.

It is one thing to describe that reality; it is another to understand it. What drove the changing outcomes in Brazil's banking game? Our taxonomy of governments, government-banker partnerships, and banking systems in figure 2.1 fits the patterns of covariation among political regimes, inflation, and banking systems in Brazil. In a decentralized political system dominated by local oligarchies—such as that of Brazil from 1831 to 1889—the oligarchs can keep the central government small and weak.

They resist either having to pay taxes in support of a more ambitious central government or permitting the central government to levy an economically debilitating inflation tax.

Weak autocrats, who find it difficult to enforce the collection of taxes from producers and consumers, have far greater success collecting the inflation tax through bank chartering for a simple reason: banks cannot operate without the active assistance of the government. As we describe in chapter 2, banks depend on the government to grant them legal rights and to enforce their contracts; thus banks are dependent even on weak governments in ways that nonbank enterprises are not. That essential difference explains why inflation taxation is so appealing to weak autocrats and therefore why bank chartering authority is their primary fiscal tool.

In a political system where the autocrat is weak, but still strong enough to insist on sharing bank chartering power with his oligarchic allies—as in the regimes that have held sway for most of Brazilian history—inflation taxation is typically the path of least resistance for funding the government. In a democracy—such as the government that has prevailed in Brazil since 1989—the people who pay the inflation tax can vote, and consequently inflation taxation becomes less feasible. Citizens will vote instead to tax the wealthy. Of course, there are limits to this source of taxation, too: the reduced investment and slower economic growth that result from high taxation of the wealthy may temper such populist preferences, and the wealthy can push back by threatening to exit the country with their assets.

In this chapter we focus on the period of the Brazilian monarchy, which stretched from 1808 to 1889. This period began with a twenty-year experiment in inflation taxation, which was used to fund the government of a series of absolutist monarchs. Brazil's domestically born elite of sugar planters and merchants viewed the second of these absolutists and his inflation tax with hostility. They forced him first to accept a constitution that provided for representation of the elite in 1824 and later, in 1831, to abdicate in favor of his infant son. From 1831 to 1889, the Brazilian central government was weak in the extreme: real authority and power rested with the local oligarchs and merchants, who used their control of parliament to make sure that the government could not use the banking system to levy an inflation tax—or do much else. During these periods, banks could not provide much in the way of credit to the private sector.

The Long Reach of Initial Conditions

To understand the nature of play in Brazil's Game of Bank Bargains, we begin with two overarching initial conditions that shaped Brazil's economic and political institutions. First, Brazil is an immense country whose geographic features militated against the creation of vibrant interregional markets or the centralization of political power. Indeed, for most of its colonial and postcolonial history, Brazil was not so much a country as it was a number of independent pockets of settlement exploiting local natural-resource bases. These pockets of settlement, strung out along thousands of miles of coastline, were isolated from one another by the Brazil Current, which made northerly coastal travel extraordinarily difficult until the advent of steam-powered ships in the late nineteenth century. Nor did Brazil's rivers serve to link markets and people: they either flowed in the wrong direction (the Paraná, for example, flows from the interior of the state of São Paulo toward Paraguay before debouching into the Atlantic at Buenos Aires) or flowed through scenically beautiful but economically marginal destinations (e.g., the Amazon Basin). Development of the interior, therefore, did not begin until the very end of the nineteenth century, when railroads were finally built.[1] Even then, the railroad network linked the interiors of three states only: São Paulo, Minas Gerais, and Rio de Janeiro. In short, by virtue of its geography, until well into the twentieth century Brazil was predisposed to be a series of local economies and local political entities. As one historian put it: "There was no great sense of national identity in Brazil. The centre-south, the northeast, and the north were to a large extent different worlds . . . separated by huge distances and poor communications."[2]

Brazil's geography had another important aspect: its location made it irrelevant to geopolitical conflicts. It did not figure in the long struggle between England and France in the eighteenth century, unlike the United States and Canada, which directly participated in the Seven Years' War (known in U.S. history as the French and Indian War). It was far from the front lines of the military struggles that defined the twentieth century. Its

---

[1] Summerhill (2003) provides an analysis of transportation systems in Brazil before and after the construction of railroads and demonstrates the positive impact of railroads on Brazilian economic growth.

[2] Bethell (1989), 41.

participation in World War I and World War II was therefore minimal. Because the Brazilian population never had to be mobilized en masse to fight in defense of the state, a significant pressure that favored the expansion of the franchise in other countries was absent in Brazil. In the United States, by contrast, the existence of a heavily armed yeomanry was essential to the survival of the colonies in the seventeenth and eighteenth centuries, and thus even before independence American farmers had wrested the right to vote for colonial assemblies from the English government, many decades before English citizens obtained similar rights (see chapter 6). In Britain, the expansion of the franchise in the twentieth century, as well as the reduction in the power of the House of Lords, reflected its status as a small country with a vast empire that had to fight large-scale wars against much more populous countries (see chapter 5). Brazil's geography made these pressures virtually nonexistent.

The second overarching initial condition was that Brazil's soils and climate were ideal for sugar cultivation, and thus from the sixteenth century onward it was one of the world's major sugar producers. Sugar has a number of features that predisposed it to being grown on immense plantations with slave labor. If cut sugar cane is left unprocessed for more than 12 hours, the crop is lost to fermentation. Additionally, there are tremendous economies of scale in the milling of cane and the processing of the resulting cane juice into sugar: grinding mills and boilers left idle represent money lost. As a result, there has to be very careful coordination of the harvesting and processing of sugar. The most efficient organization of production is for the processors to own the plantations where the cane is grown, so that cane can be cut and delivered to the mill at a pace dictated by the machines. That organization of production presents something of a problem from the point of view of managing a labor force: cutting cane with a machete in the tropical sun at a pace determined by immense grinding machines is not just backbreaking, it is soul destroying. The grim solution was to use slaves, organized into gangs, so that the pace of work could be maintained regardless of what happened to backs or souls.[3]

---

[3] Binswanger and Rosenzweig (1986); Dye (1998). That is not to say that slaveowners placed no value on their slave property. Although slaveowners did bear financial loss from exhausting, injuring, or shortening the lives of slaves, they did not have to worry about the suffering of slave laborers to the same extent that they would have had they employed free labor, which would have demanded a compensating dif-

Black population as percentage of total

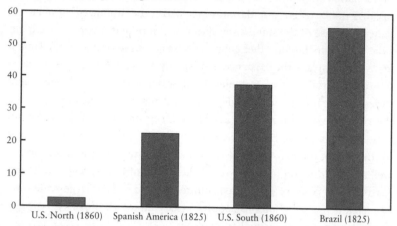

FIGURE 12.3 Black population as percentage of total population, New World societies, circa 1825–60.

Source: Engerman and Sokoloff (1997), 267.

Brazil was, as a consequence, the quintessential slave society of the New World. More African slaves were transported to Brazil than to any other New World destination, and Brazil was the last New World society to outlaw slavery, in 1888.[4] Some sense of the extent of slavery in Brazil can be gleaned from figure 12.3, which provides estimates of the percentage of the population described as black in the U.S. North, the U.S. South, Spanish America, and Brazil in the mid-nineteenth century. Brazil was the only one of these societies in which blacks made up more than half of the population.[5]

---

ferential for such unpleasant work. Furthermore, in contrast to the United States (where the prohibition on the importation of slaves caused their economic value to soar after 1807), in Brazil the importation of slaves continued until 1850.

[4] According to the estimates in Engerman and Sokoloff ([1997], 264), from 1500 to 1760, 1.2 million slaves were brought to Brazil. Slightly more (1.3 million) were brought to all of British America, but that figure includes slaves destined for both the United States and the Caribbean. Klein and Vinson ([2007], 273) put the Brazilian slave population at 1 million in the late eighteenth century, compared with 476,000 in the British Caribbean and 575,000 in the United States.

[5] These ratios likely understate the differences between Brazil and the U.S. South, because the Brazilian data are from 1825 and the U.S. data are from 1860. Because the

By the standards of Brazil, the nineteenth-century U.S. South was practically an egalitarian utopia: in the United States, slaves never exceeded one-third of the Southern population, and the modal Southerner was not a slave-owning planter but rather a small farmer who relied on the labor of his family to till the fields and harvest the crops. Not so in Brazil, where slaves performed almost every task, from cutting cane to picking coffee, from sweeping urban streets to manning sailing ships. So deeply ingrained was slavery in almost every facet of Brazilian society that in the early nineteenth century, nearly half of the population of the capital city of Rio de Janeiro was enslaved.[6]

Slavery left indelible marks on Brazilian society. Indeed, as we discuss in considerable detail below, Brazil's plantation owners fought tooth and nail to make sure that Brazil remained a society of a few haves and many have-nots, even after it was eclipsed as the world's leading producer of sugar, and even after the plantation owners were forced to replace slaves with (paid) immigrant labor. Some sense of their success can be gleaned from figure 12.4, which presents data on the distribution of income around the world in 1970 (the first year for which there are sufficient cross-country data to provide a meaningful comparison). The only country in this sample with greater income inequality than Brazil was Kenya. Even South Africa, the country that invented apartheid, had a more equal distribution of income than Brazil. Brazil's highly unequal distribution of income mirrored other inequalities, most particularly tremendous disparities in educational attainment across social classes. Some sense of this can be captured in the shocking fact that, as of 1950, two-thirds of Brazil's population over the age of 25 had never been to school at all, and the average level of educational attainment was only 1.4 years. Even the Philippines, home of "booty capitalism,"[7] could boast higher levels of investment in human capital than Brazil.[8] In short, if one were looking for the most extreme example of an unequal society whose roots are located in plantation slavery, Brazil is it.

---

slave trade continued to bring Africans to Brazil for another 25 years, the ratio of blacks in the total population would have been even higher by 1860.

[6] Barman (1988), 49.

[7] Hutchroft (1998).

[8] Barro and Lee (2010).

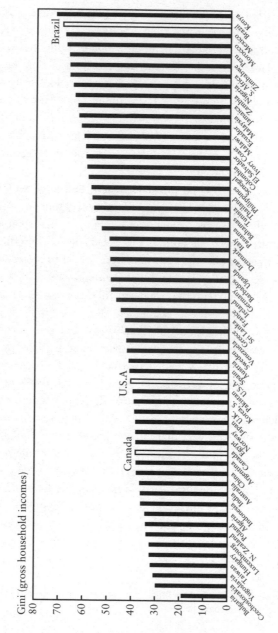

FIGURE 12.4 Distribution of income, by country, 1970.

Source: Solt (2009).

Inflation Taxation at the Outset

Colonial Brazil was not a proto-nation as the United States was prior to its independence. Rather, it was a set of quasi-independent local economies that were run as fiefdoms by plantation owners. In terms of its political and administrative structure, it had more in common with other Portuguese entrepôt economies, such as Angola, than it did with the 13 colonies that were to become the United States, or even with the more important Spanish colonies of the New World, such as Mexico. In Mexico, for example, silver from mining towns in the north had to pass through Mexico City, where it was minted and taxed, before continuing to the port city of Veracruz. In Brazil, planters bought slaves and loaded sugar at local ports. They were more concerned with the sugar refineries of Amsterdam than the tiny coterie of bureaucrats in the colonial capital (Salvador until 1763, Rio de Janeiro thereafter). The focus on sugar production for export both reflected and reinforced the lack of transportation and communication links among the Brazilian provinces. As one history of Brazil points out, "Before steam navigation it took less time to travel from Maranhão [in Brazil's North] to Lisbon than to Rio de Janeiro."[9]

Brazil's political affairs changed abruptly in 1807, when Napoleon, in alliance with the king of Spain, invaded Portugal. Lisbon fell without resistance, and Prince Regent João, along with his entire court, numbering in the thousands, fled Lisbon for Rio de Janeiro, escorted by a squadron of British warships. Upon his arrival, Dom João (the Dom connoting his exalted status) elevated Brazil from a colony to a kingdom and then declared that he would run what was left of the Portuguese Empire from Rio de Janeiro. Unfortunately, Brazil possessed almost nothing in the way of a national administrative apparatus: everything, including ministries, courts, and an army, had to be constructed from scratch.

Dom João could not finance the construction of a state by taxing the local elites. Not only were they spread out across an immense coastline, but they were resistant to the idea of paying for an expensive royal court. The situation was so desperate that in 1809 Dom João had to borrow £600,000 from the British government simply to keep the basic machin-

[9] Bethell and Carvalho (1989), 48.

ery of government running.[10] The British did not, of course, make this loan simply out of the goodness of their hearts: the following year, the British government extracted a series of treaties from Dom João designed to give British merchants preferential rights. Among their demands was a 15 percent cap on the import tariff on British goods.[11] Desperate to keep his government afloat, Dom João agreed to the terms, even though tariffs were among his potentially largest and most easily collected sources of taxation.[12]

To alleviate his fiscal problems, Dom João adopted a solution that had already been pioneered by European kings as they played the deadly game of nation building: in 1808 he granted a charter to a group of financiers to found a monopoly bank, the Banco do Brasil, that would have the power to issue legal-tender paper money. Dom João then used the Banco do Brasil to finance his government by having the bank buy government bonds with money that it printed. As the quantity of banknotes increased, so did inflation. In essence, the Banco do Brasil was the government's agent in creating an inflation tax. The bank and its shareholders shared in the proceeds of that inflation tax by virtue of the fact that the bank held the government's deposits without paying any interest on them. The newly formed Banco do Brasil was also, at least in theory, useful to Brazil's planters and merchants in processing payments for long-distance trade.

There was, however, a problem with this scheme: the Banco do Brasil's shareholders had no good reason to believe that Dom João would repay the loans advanced to him. He therefore had to coax investors into buying Banco do Brasil shares by granting the bank a continually expanding set of lucrative privileges, including monopolies on the issuance of paper money, the export of luxury goods, and the handling of government financial operations; the right to have debts to the bank treated as having the same legal standing as debts owed to the royal treasury; and the right to collect new taxes that he imposed—and to hold onto those taxes as

---

[10] Barman (1988), 45–46.

[11] Barman (1988), 48.

[12] This cap on import tariffs was subsequently extended in an 1827 commercial treaty with Great Britain that remained in effect until 1844. Remarkably, Great Britain offered no reciprocity, charging 180 percent on Brazilian sugar and 300 percent on Brazilian coffee imported into England. In 1828, the low tariffs on British goods were extended to all of Brazil's trading partners. Haber and Klein (1997), 245–46.

interest-free deposits for a period of ten years. Even all these promised privileges proved insufficient to convince investors that Banco do Brasil stock was a good bet. It took an entire year for the bank to sell the 100 shares necessary for it to begin operations; in addition, Dom João was obliged to confer the title of gentleman (*comenda de cavelheiro*) on all principal shareholders. Even with these inducements, it would take an additional eight years for the bank to achieve its original capitalization goals.[13]

The government of Dom João increasingly came to rely on the inflation tax to finance its operations—so much so that between 1814 and 1820, the stock of banknotes in circulation increased eightfold.[14] The nominal rate of return on owner's equity in the Banco do Brasil from 1810 to 1820 averaged 10 percent per year, which, as near as can be known, probably did not exceed the rate of inflation by a wide margin. The shareholders responded by paying out virtually all of the available returns to themselves as dividends; they appear to have reinvested in the bank only to the minimum degree required by its articles of incorporation.[15]

There was no end in sight to Dom João's fiscal problems. The British had driven the last French troops from Portuguese soil by 1812, but Dom João evinced no interest in returning to Lisbon. Portugal was effectively governed by the British officer Lord Beresford, who commanded its army. By 1820, Beresford had become so concerned about the possibility of a constitutionalist revolution, much like the one that had recently taken place in Spain, that he sailed for Rio de Janeiro in order to rouse Dom João out of inactivity. He succeeded in getting Dom João to agree to pay the Brazilian army out of the treasury in Rio de Janeiro (rather than the treasury in Lisbon), and Beresford returned to Lisbon with the funds needed to meet the back pay of the Portuguese army. Meeting those expenses meant, however, that Dom João had to renege on the arrangement by which the Banco do Brasil held the proceeds from new taxes. At the stroke of a pen he stripped the bank's shareholders of much of their share in the proceeds of the inflation tax.

To rescue the bank from the consequences of his own actions, Dom João granted the bank the monopoly that he had held on the mining of all

---

[13] Peláez and Suzigan (1976), 40; Peláez (1975), 460–61; Marchant (1965), 116.
[14] Barman (1988), 56.
[15] Haber (2012b), 286.

precious metals. In addition, he deposited his stock of diamonds, as well as virtually all objects of value owned by him and his court (literally the crown jewels), into the bank as backing for its note issues. But he soon reneged on these promises, too, when he had to face a republican uprising in Portugal that required his speedy return, and his wealth. He and his court withdrew all of the wealth that they had deposited in the bank and returned to Lisbon.[16] The Banco do Brasil was forced to suspend convertibility of its notes as a result.

A New World Monarchy:
Inflation Taxation under Dom Pedro I

To Dom João, there was no Brazilian or Portuguese nation in the modern sense of the word: there was the royal house of Braganza, and what mattered was its continuation. When Dom João returned to Lisbon in 1821, he therefore left his son, Dom Pedro, behind in Brazil, with instructions to declare independence should that step prove politically expedient for the Braganza dynasty. In 1822, at the urging of local elites who feared that they would be reduced to second-class status now that Dom João was ruling from Lisbon, Dom Pedro declared Brazil independent and established himself as emperor.

Dom Pedro faced the same problem as his father: the only ready source of tax revenues was a planter-merchant oligarchy that had weak incentives to support an expensive royal court. Dom Pedro could not increase import tariffs to solve this problem; his government was still bound by the treaty limiting duties on imports from Britain to 15 percent ad valorum —a treaty that Britain would soon force Dom Pedro to extend until 1844. Thus, Dom Pedro continued to use the Banco do Brasil much as his father had done, as a vehicle for administering an inflation tax through note issues.[17]

Brazil's elites understood that an emperor who could borrow as he pleased from a bank that he controlled was a recipe for their ruin. What would prevent him from issuing government debt with reckless abandon, and then, when the Banco do Brasil was stuffed full of those debts, default-

---

[16] Peláez and Suzigan (1976), 43; Marchant (1965), 116.
[17] Peláez (1975).

ing on them? What would be the value of the fiat money issued by the Banco do Brasil once that happened? To the degree that they personally held Banco do Brasil notes and shares, as well as treasury bonds issued by Dom Pedro's government, their wealth was at risk. Furthermore, how would they maintain social order when the agents of the state—particularly the army—were paid in paper money that might become worthless as a result of a government default?

The threat posed by Dom Pedro's financial policies was a symptom of a broader problem: he was an absolutist. He had signaled as much at his coronation as emperor in 1822. The ritual had closely followed the coronation ceremony of the Holy Roman Emperors. As one historian of the period eloquently put it, Dom Pedro "was not only crowned but anointed: he was thus chosen and consecrated by God."[18]

The result of this basic conflict—between a metropolitan monarch whose frame of reference appears to have been the Middle Ages and a planter-merchant elite that wanted a figurehead king through whom they could rule—was a drawn-out political battle that ultimately led to Dom Pedro's being deposed. He was obligated to call a constituent assembly to draft a constitution, but, to his dismay, that assembly produced a document that gave the preponderance of power to an elected lower house that he could neither dissolve nor effectively override. He responded by dissolving the constituent assembly and dispersing its members at bayonet point. His Council of State, a set of trusted Portuguese-born advisors, then rewrote the constitution, toning down its more republican features. Though Dom Pedro had promised elections for a second constituent assembly to ratify the constitution, a revolt against his high-handedness by the elite of the northern province of Pernambuco caused him to rethink that idea. Instead he asked Brazil's town councils to ratify the constitution.[19]

The 1824 constitution was a compromise. Dom Pedro could not establish an absolutist state, but neither could the planter-merchant oligarchy reduce him to a figurehead. Importantly, the new constitution insulated both groups from the political demands of the great mass of the population. First, the franchise was restricted on the basis of income and civil standing: those with incomes less than 100 milreis (the equivalent of US$98

[18] Barman (1988), 101.
[19] Barman (1988), 118–23.

in 1824) were excluded, as were women, slaves, servants, and men under the age of 25 (21 if married). Second, elections for the Chamber of Deputies were indirect: voters cast ballots for electors, who in turn voted for deputies; and electors had to meet a minimum-income threshold twice that of voters. Third, the Chamber of Deputies voted on legislation as part of a larger body, the General Assembly, which included the 102 indirectly elected deputies plus 50 senators who had life tenure and were named by the emperor. Fourth, each senator was picked by the emperor from a list of three candidates nominated by the electors. Fifth, the emperor was granted a "regulating power" that gave him the authority to dissolve the Chamber of Deputies, dismiss his ministers freely, suspend judges and magistrates, and grant pardons. In case there was any ambiguity surrounding this authority, Article 99 of the constitution stated that "the person of the Emperor is inviolable and sacred; he is not subject to any accountability." Finally, all laws and decrees had to be signed by the emperor. He could effectively veto any legislation.[20]

Three features of the constitution of 1824 limited the emperor's authority and discretion. First, the constitution gave the parliament, and not the emperor, the right to make, amend, and suspend laws. Second, the parliament had the responsibility to tax, spend, borrow, and regulate payment of the national debt.[21] The emperor could, of course, dismiss a parliament that refused to grant him the right to take on additional debt or raise taxes, but doing so meant that there would be a new election for deputies, who might be even more reluctant to grant his requests. Third, the constitution institutionalized the Council of State that Pedro had hurriedly created in 1823. The 13-member council had to be consulted "in all serious matters and general points of public administration, . . . as on all occasions when the Emperor wishes to exercise any of the functions given to the regulating power."[22] Importantly, the members of the Council of State were "accountable for the counsels they give which are opposed to the laws and patently harmful to the interest of the State," with judgments about possible derelictions of duty left to the Senate.[23] The emperor chose

---

[20] Barman (1988), 123–25.
[21] Barman (1988), 123–25, 132; Summerhill (2008).
[22] Barman (1988), 126.
[23] Barman (1988), 126.

the Council of State, but the expectation was that he would choose among the country's notables, who included some of Brazil's wealthiest men.[24]

The constitution of 1824, as William Summerhill has shown, therefore, gave the planter-merchant oligarchy the ability to constrain the emperor.[25] One visible way in which they did so was closing the Banco do Brasil when its initial charter ran out in 1829, putting an end to a bank that had been little more than a mechanism to levy an inflation tax.[26] Dissolving the bank would reduce inflationary money creation and pressure the government to limit its deficit spending. In 1828, government expenditures were roughly twice the level of its tax revenues, with the rest financed by foreign borrowing or Banco do Brasil note issues.[27] The resulting deficit was financed largely by money creation, which produced an inflation that ran at an average of 10 percent per year from 1822 to 1831. Worldwide, median inflation rates in the nineteenth century were only 0.7 percent. In fact, Brazil's inflation under Dom Pedro was high even by the standards of the twentieth century, when worldwide inflation averaged 5 percent.[28] As figure 12.1 shows, the closing of the Banco do Brasil in 1829 brought a substantial decline in Brazil's high rate of inflation.

The second way in which parliament pushed back against the emperor was to openly challenge his authority, ultimately forcing him to abdicate in favor of his five-year-old son. The continual fiscal crisis of the government emboldened the more liberal elements of the Brazilian oligarchy, who by the 1828 election for deputies began to cast themselves as an organized opposition. Once seated, in 1830, those opposition deputies slashed the government's budget, forced the resignation of army officers born outside Brazil, and redefined treason to make it virtually impossible to prove. Given the volatile political mood of the capital, Dom Pedro succumbed to pressure and signed these laws. He was down but not out: within months he dismissed the cabinet, replacing opposition ministers

[24] Summerhill (forthcoming).

[25] Summerhill (2008).

[26] Marchant (1965), 116. When parliament closed the bank in 1829, it recognized that its note issues would have to be redeemed. Given that the government could not actually redeem them in specie, it gave the treasury the authority to issue sufficient notes to redeem the now-defunct Banco do Brasil issues.

[27] Barman (1988), 155.

[28] Worldwide inflation figures for 1800 to 1913 are from Reinhart and Rogoff (2011), 1678. Data for Brazil are from figure 12.1, based on Lobo (1978).

with nobility from his inner circle. The population, at the urging of the opposition leadership, took to the streets, and the army refused to come to the emperor's aid. On April 7, 1831, Dom Pedro abdicated and returned to Portugal, leaving his five-year-old son as regent. Parliament lost little time in making sure that the three-person regency that governed until Dom Pedro II came of age had little monarchical authority: the regents, named by the General Assembly, were expressly denied the right to veto legislation, declare war, grant titles and honors, or dissolve the Chamber of Deputies.[29]

A Minimalist State

Brazil's planter-merchant oligarchy was now free to run the country as it saw fit, and what it saw fit to do was very little. The elite's approach to governance was minimalist in the extreme: given the choice between taxing itself, running an inflation tax through a government bank, or having a small and weak state, the elite chose the weak-state option.[30]

Indeed, the central government held sway over Rio de Janeiro and its environs and not much else—a fact that was codified in the 1834 Ato Adicional (an amendment to the constitution of 1824), which created legislatures in each of the provinces. As a practical matter, even after Dom Pedro II came of age and assumed the throne in 1842, the oligarchs that dominated the provinces held all the real power. They owned the land; they decided who worked and under what conditions; they ran the elections and decided who "won"; they controlled the local governments and judiciaries; and they commanded the provincial units of the National Guard. From the point of view of the average Brazilian citizen, the oligarchy was the state.

Despite their preference for weak government, Brazil's local oligarchs were resolute in one respect: they made sure that the changes taking place in the world around them did not force them to share power with a growing class of free laborers. There were two forces in favor of free labor, both of which were external: demands from the British that Brazil abolish

---

[29] Barman (1988), 152, 158–59, 163.
[30] It is striking that in a country where slaves and land constituted the most important stocks of wealth, the government chose not to tax property. Hanley (2005), 25.

slavery, and the arrival of the coffee plant, a nonnative species. These, along with Brazil's 1824 electoral laws, constituted a serious threat to the sugar-planter elite. Coffee can be grown efficiently on small farms. Given the choice, most people prefer to work their own farms rather than have someone else's boot on their necks. Brazil's suffrage laws also provided another incentive for independent farming: property owners had the right to vote.

To hold off the threat of having to share power with an emergent class of independent small farmers, the Brazilian elite dragged its feet on ending slavery, prolonging its existence for six decades after the British had begun to pressure them. As early as 1826, the British forced the Brazilian government to sign a treaty ending the slave trade, but Brazil's planters and merchants simply ignored the law, continuing to import 40,000 to 50,000 slaves per year. In 1850 the British government decided that it was no longer going to tolerate hollow promises: it blockaded Brazil's ports, boarded inbound ships, and freed their human cargoes. Two decades later, after slavery had ended almost everywhere else (including Portugal's African colonies), the Brazilian parliament finally passed a "free womb" law, specifying that all children henceforth born of slave parents would be free. Under increased pressure from abolitionists, in 1885, the Brazilian parliament passed a law freeing all slaves over the age of 60—a move that can be viewed as the height of cynicism, inasmuch as the cost of maintaining aged slaves probably exceeded their marginal product. Only in 1888 was slavery abolished.

Throughout the nineteenth century, Brazil's planter-merchant elite also fought a successful rearguard action against the spread of small farms, and hence small farmers. The new opportunities created by coffee production and the decline of slavery ultimately proved too much for the planters' efforts, but they did succeed in delaying the transition to a competitive labor market and limiting the extent of small-scale landowners for more than half a century. Beginning in the 1850s, Brazilian coffee production began to take off.[31] By the early 1880s, Brazil was producing 60 percent of the world's coffee, a figure that grew to 75 percent by the first decade of the twentieth century.[32] As the proportion of the population in bondage

---

[31] The classic work on the expansion of coffee cultivation in Brazil is Stein (1958).
[32] Holloway (1980), 175–76.

declined, the Brazilian elite worked hard to make sure that former slaves, as well as the Southern European immigrants who were replacing them in the fields, did not envision any option but to work on a plantation. In 1850, the parliament passed a law precluding free access to land. The law specified that if a landowner could not provide documentation showing that his land was acquired through inheritance or grant, the land was forfeited and returned to the government for future sale. In a society in which most people could neither read nor write, common people could not produce this kind of documentation. For good measure, the 1850 law also specified that vacant frontier land purchased from the government had to be paid for immediately in cash—in contrast to the homesteading laws of the United States and Canada, which allowed small farmers to pay for their land over time, out of the income they earned from their farms.[33]

The planters' battle against the encroachment of small farms populated by free laborers was quite successful for many years. Even though coffee could have been grown on small farms, for the most part, it was not. In Rio de Janeiro's highly productive Parahyba Valley, for example, an 1890 survey revealed that 70 percent of the land—57,000 acres—was owned by just 41 individuals.[34] As late as the 1920s, immigrant farmers controlled only a tiny portion of Brazil's coffee lands and trees.[35]

The Brazilian plantocracy also made sure that if some pitiful immigrant or former slave clawed a small farm out of the frontier lands against all odds, he still would not have the right to vote. The constitution of 1824 restricted the franchise on the basis of income, but it set a threshold that could be met by a farmer of even modest means—for the obvious reason that there were few farmers of modest means in 1824. In 1881, once it became clear that such a class of voters might come into existence, the parliament restricted the franchise still further by substituting a literacy test

---

[33] Some historians have pointed out that very few squatters were ever forced off their lands by these laws, but that critique misses the point. It takes three to six years for a coffee tree to reach maturity, and thus a coffee farmer could not even think about going into business without access to credit; but he could not obtain a mortgage if he did not hold legal title to the land. Mortgage lending was governed by Law 1237 of 1864, by the Bank Reform Bill of November 1888, and by Law 169A of 1890. Hanley (2005), 53, 123, 125, 136. Data in Stein ([1958], 245) indicate that bank mortgages were extended only to a small number of large plantations.

[34] Stein (1958), 225.

[35] Holloway (1980), 138–66.

for the property and income requirement. In a country with no public education system, the literacy test was an effective constraint on suffrage.

Minimal Government, Minimal Banks

The Brazilian elites' minimalist approach to national governance is underlined by the fact that until the creation of Brazil's first commercial code in 1850, the nation had no rules governing the enforcement of contracts, the procedures for bankruptcies, or the acceptance and transferability of bills of exchange.[36] This legal void placed in doubt the viability of the small, private banks that sprang up in Brazil's port cities in order to discount the IOUs that merchants and planters wrote each other after the closure of the Banco do Brasil. It was unclear whether their currency issues (in the form of short-term debt instruments of three to five days' duration, called *vales*) or the debt contracts they wrote were even legally enforceable. It is, therefore, not surprising that the seven banks created during this period that ultimately succeeded in obtaining charters tended to be owned by members of parliament: their political connections gave unique credibility to the contracts they wrote.[37]

This medieval banking system could provide neither the financial underpinnings for a state nor the working capital needed by the growing coffee economy. The Brazilian parliament and Dom Pedro II therefore crafted a commercial code in 1850 that made it possible to create limited liability, joint-stock banks. They revised this code in 1860 and 1882; each time, they made sure it would permit nothing that even remotely resembled free banking. Rather, as William Summerhill has shown, the Brazilian government tightly constrained the number of banks so as to minimize competition. This raised rates of return on bank stock, and those rents were shared with the politicians who sat on the boards of the privileged banks.[38]

Under the commercial code of 1850, each company charter had to be separately approved either by the emperor's cabinet (for firms in Rio de Janeiro) or by a provincial president (for firms outside Rio de Janeiro). Importantly, the provincial presidents (equivalent to state governors) were

---

[36] Hanley (2005), 31; Summerhill (forthcoming).
[37] Summerhill (forthcoming).
[38] Summerhill (forthcoming).

appointed by the cabinet and hence were responsible to it. In short, the right to grant charters was centralized. If a firm was granted a special concession or privilege, its charter also had to be approved by parliament.[39] In 1860 the formation of joint-stock, limited-liability banks was made more difficult still: charters now also had to be approved by the emperor's Council of State as well as the cabinet and parliament. The rate at which chartered companies of any type were formed, already low in the 1850s, slowed to a crawl after this revision.[40] The 1860 law was eventually liberalized in an 1882 general-incorporation law, but that law still required financial firms that engaged in mortgage lending or issued notes to obtain special approval, which is to say that general incorporation did not apply to banks.[41]

Almost as soon as the ink dried on the 1850 commercial code, the government engineered the merger of two banks into a government-run superbank. In 1851, an entrepreneurial merchant and industrialist, Irineu Evangelista de Sousa (later the Baron and Viscount of Mauá, the name by which he is most commonly known), obtained a charter to found the Banco de Comércio e Indústria do Brasil (commonly known as the second Banco do Brasil). Two years later, when the emperor's cabinet sought to create a new (third) Banco do Brasil in order to obtain an interest-free loan for the government, it forced Mauá to merge his bank with one of the banks that had been allowed to form under special license in the 1830s, the Banco Commercial.[42] In exchange, the third Banco do Brasil agreed to purchase and retire 10 million milreis in old treasury notes, using notes that it issued. This "agreement" required that Mauá be replaced as president of the bank by a member of parliament, a move that the government made somewhat palatable to Mauá and other shareholders by conferring a set of lucrative privileges on the bank. These included a monopoly on note issues, the ability to issue notes against its reserves at a ratio of two to one, and the right to redeem its notes either in gold or treasury bills, at the bank's choosing.

---

[39] Hanley (2005), 30–33; Summerhill (forthcoming).
[40] Summerhill (forthcoming).
[41] Hanley (2005), 66; Musacchio (2009b), 33.
[42] The government's ability to force this merger came from the fact that in granting a corporate charter, it typically reserved the right to dissolve the corporation by decree without prior consultation of the shareholders. Barman (1981), 251; Marchant (1965), 120–22.

We cannot stress the value of this privilege strongly enough. A bank that can issue notes up to twice the value of its paid-in capital can earn income from its capital three times over: once from the interest it earns on the government bonds that it must purchase in order to back its notes, and then twice more by lending those notes at interest.

Even these arrangements did not fully satisfy Mauá: in 1854, in opposition to the government, he created another bank, organized not as a corporation but as a limited partnership with transferable shares. He did so precisely because he wished the new bank, Mauá, MacGregor and Company, to be "exempt from government tutelage."[43] Mauá was no naïf, however: he shared his plan in advance with the prime minister (president of the Council of State), the Marquis of Paraná, and made sure that six of the minister's relatives were shareholders—to no avail. Mauá's new bank set off a firestorm inside the government, meeting opposition from the minister of justice and the Council of State. The government moved against the new bank, decreeing that although limited partnerships could exist, they could not be formed through the creation of transferable shares. Mauá had to draw a new partnership deed. The government had made itself clear: if you wish to own stock in a limited-liability joint-stock bank, or anything approximating one, you will own stock in our bank or in no bank at all.[44]

In case anyone failed to get the message, the Viscount of Itaborahy, who preceded the Marquis of Paraná as prime minister, was named president of the third Banco do Brasil. The government then forced four banks in the north of the country to give up their charters and become branches of the third Banco do Brasil. At almost the same time, it allowed the Banco do Brasil to increase its note issues from twice to three times the value of its net paid-in capital.[45]

Other banks were founded during this period, but in an environment in which the cabinet (and later the Council of State) had to approve every charter and could commandeer a bank's capital through the stroke of a pen, they were, unsurprisingly, few in number. Expropriation was not merely an imagined risk. In 1857, in order to encourage the formation

[43] Barman (1981), 250.
[44] Schulz (2008), 36; Barman (1981), 239–64; Marchant (1965), 112–13.
[45] Marchant (1965), 119; Schulz (2008), 30, 41.

of other banks, the cabinet undermined the Banco do Brasil's monopoly of note issue. It then undid the rights of the newly privileged note-issuing banks in 1862, once again giving this valuable monopoly to the Banco do Brasil. Four years later, to finance the war with Paraguay, it rescinded that monopoly so that the treasury could print notes, and it also appropriated all of the gold held by the Banco do Brasil.[46]

As late as 1875, there were only 12 banks in operation in the entire country, including the Banco do Brasil and three small foreign banks. Of the remaining eight, six were located in Rio de Janeiro, which meant that outside the capital city a Brazilian citizen would find only two tiny, single-office banks in operation: one in the port city of Santos and the other in the port city of Recife. This banking system was stunningly small—and the Banco do Brasil accounted for roughly one-third of it. Even according to the most generous assumptions, the total value of lending from these banks to the private sector likely did not exceed 20 percent of GDP and was likely much closer to 15 percent.[47] Moreover, even this lending appears to have been limited to a small group of insiders. A study of the São Paulo affiliate of the Banco do Brasil sums it up this way: "When the directors would meet, one would say to another: 'You, Baron Such-and-So, do you need any money?' And Baron Such-and-So would always respond, 'No.' The directors would close the meeting without deciding anything further, because they did not lend money to outsiders."[48]

The uncertainty over property rights made it crucial to have a group of political insiders on the bank's board. By statute, during the period when the Banco do Brasil had the right to issue legal-tender notes, its president was appointed by the government. During this period, 13 out of the

[46] Summerhill (forthcoming); Schulz (2008), 36.

[47] We estimate the ratio of private credit to GDP by the following method. We obtain the nominal capital and reserves of the banks from data published in the *Jornal do commercio* (various dates) to calculate total equity. To convert owner's equity to private-sector loans, we calculate the ratio of these variables from data on mortgage loans and discounts in the Banco do Brasil (1875). We then apply that conversion factor to the equity data on all other banks. We take GDP from Goldsmith (1986), 23. Under the assumption that the ratio of owner's equity to lending was the same for other banks as for the Banco do Brasil, the ratio of private-sector credit to GDP would have been 20 percent. The size of the Banco do Brasil may, however, have given it greater leverage than its competitors. If we assume that those banks were one-third less leveraged than the Banco do Brasil, the ratio of credit to GDP would have been 15 percent.

[48] Quoted in Levi (1987), 69.

bank's 61 directors ultimately served in the Chamber of Deputies, the Senate, the cabinet, or the Council of State. More telling still, even after the bank lost the right to issue notes in 1866, its shareholders continued to choose a political insider as president: its first elected president was Francisco de Sales Torres-Homem, a four-term federal deputy, senator, and former finance minister. Its later presidents had similar pedigrees.

What was true of the Banco do Brasil was true of the other banks as well: their boards were basically a Who's Who of the Brazilian political elite. Seven of Brazil's prime ministers from this period later served as bank presidents or directors. These insiders appear not only to have protected banks' property rights but also to have lobbied to make sure that few charters would be granted for competing banks. Their intervention may also have been crucial in obtaining government support during an 1875 banking crisis (the result of the spread of the panic of 1873 from the developed world to Brazil), when the government extended 15 loans to three banks over a period of four months in order to keep them afloat.[49]

During this period of limited and insider-controlled private credit provision, for the most part, the banking system was not used by the government to run an inflation tax. In fact, with the exception of the period 1853–66, the right to issue legal tender was awarded only to the treasury —and the treasury could not print notes at will because the right to issue debt obligations was held by parliament. Nor does the evidence suggest that the government forced banks to hold treasury bonds. The one exception was the Banco do Brasil: in 1871, treasury bonds accounted for 22 percent of its assets.[50] This was still, however, a small proportion of the total government debt. The vast majority of Brazil's public debt was held by individual Brazilian citizens or foreigners, who looked at it as a safe investment. Unlike other Latin American governments, the imperial Brazilian government always met the payments on its bond debt.[51]

There were two big downsides to Brazil's minimalist approach to banking: limited credit meant that the Brazilian economy grew more slowly than it would have otherwise, and Brazil's central government remained poor and weak. Dom Pedro II did not have much in the way of a tax base.

---

[49] Summerhill (forthcoming); Schulz (2008), 44.
[50] Summerhill (forthcoming).
[51] Summerhill (2008).

He could not tax the income, wealth, or consumption of the Brazilian oligarchy because they controlled parliament, and parliament had to approve all taxes.[52] He could borrow by selling bonds in the London and Rio de Janeiro markets, but the extent of such borrowing was necessarily limited by the market's perception of the extent of his tax revenues.[53]

The government could and did tax the export of Brazilian coffee, but coffee exports were quite modest in the mid-nineteenth century because of the high cost of shipping coffee from the interior to the coast on the backs of mules. When it rained, the cost increased further because the mules sank knee-deep into the mud. Railroads would have alleviated the problem, but, as in most countries, the construction of long-distance railroads required public subsidies. Dom Pedro II was in a catch-22: he needed railroads so that the country could export more coffee, which would give him a more robust tax base; but he could not build railroads because he did not have enough tax revenues. He could not borrow his way out of the problem because the extent of that borrowing was limited by his tax capacity. Railroad growth in Brazil thus could not get under way in earnest until the 1880s, when it was financed by British foreign investors operating with profit guarantees from the government.[54]

Brazil's situation, as well as that of Dom Pedro II's government, is perhaps best summed up not in statistics but in the pathetic performance of the Brazilian army in the war against tiny and backward Paraguay in the 1860s—a war that Dom Pedro II fought only because Paraguay declared war on Brazil. The entire population of Paraguay numbered only some 400,000 people, who subsisted largely by exporting yerba mate (a tea) to the equally poor interior provinces of Argentina. The Paraguayan army mostly used antiquated, smooth-bore muskets, and its navy had only one genuine gunboat. Nevertheless, it took Brazil six years to achieve victory. While his army floundered, Dom Pedro II continued to do the only things that his depleted treasury had permitted him to do since becoming emperor: he studied the flora and fauna of Brazil, and mastered esoteric languages (including Sanskrit, Arabic, Greek, Hebrew, Chinese, Occitan, and Tupi, the language spoken by Brazil's Indians).

[52] Leff (1997), 50–57.
[53] Summerhill (2008).
[54] Summerhill (2003), chapters 2 and 3.

13

||||||||||||||||||||||

The Democratic Consequences
of Inflation-Tax Banking in Brazil

I assumed my government during an inflationary spiral that was destroying the rewards of work. . . . I was a slave of the people and today I am
freeing myself for eternal life. But this people, whose slave I was, will no
longer be slave to anyone. My sacrifice will remain forever in your souls
and my blood will be the price of your ransom. . . . Serenely, I take my first
step on the road to eternity and I leave life to enter history.

Brazilian president Getúlio Vargas, from his suicide note (1954)

An overarching theme of this book is that political circumstances define
the nature of the Game of Bank Bargains, which in turn, defines the
types of banks that can arise in a society. Chapter 12 shows that the persistently weak, autocratic government of colonial and imperial Brazil gave
it a small and unstable banking system. To the extent that nationally chartered banks existed, their main function was state finance, which they
performed primarily by levying an inflation tax.

In this chapter, we review the downfall of Brazil's royalty and the rise
of democracy. The transition was not smooth. The Old Republic, which
succeeded the monarchy, was not particularly democratic. It was followed
by a series of long-lived autocratic and short-lived quasi-democratic governments. Inflation taxation in the interest of state finance became, once
again, the primary function of Brazilian banks. Over time, Brazilians figured out ways to evade the inflation tax (by holding continually lower
levels of cash and traditional bank deposits), and thus the government responded by driving up the rate of inflation even more to try to produce
the same revenue from a declining tax base. Beginning in the late 1980s,
inflation became so high, and so unpopular, that it helped to undermine
Brazil's military government and encourage the rise of democracy.

For most of Brazil's history, democracy was a dream. Until the late
1980s, the institutions that governed the political system were designed to
make sure that the vast majority of the population had almost no say in

government policy making. The reasons for the persistence of authoritarian political institutions are not hard to identify: from its colonial origins to the present, Brazil has been one of the most unequal societies on the planet. Elites rationally feared that if the poor had political power, they would vote for wealth redistribution. Accordingly, elites used their wealth and military power to shape the country's political rules to perpetuate their control of the economy, the banking system, the electoral process, the courts, and access to education. Skewed distributions of political power and of economic opportunity reinforced one another, allowing both to persist for centuries.

When stable democracy with broad suffrage finally arose in Brazil in the late 1980s, strong liberal political institutions were not on the menu. Like those of other recently founded democracies, Brazil's 1988 constitution provides weak checks against populist currents. It creates a directly elected, powerful federal executive whose actions are difficult for the legislature to block. In addition to regular voting, it establishes other forms of direct participation in law making, such as plebiscites, referenda, and the possibility for ordinary citizens—everyone age 16 or above—to propose laws. Finally, the constitution specifies a long list of "positive rights" for citizens—which explains why it runs to 425 pages. It includes detailed rules governing such matters as unemployment insurance, wages, bonuses, rates of overtime pay, profit sharing, parental leave, paid vacations, healthcare, and union exclusivity. By elevating these policies to rights guaranteed by the constitution, the architects of the constitution ensured that elected governments could not diminish them by statute. These rights can be changed only by amending the constitution, which requires supermajority voting on two occasions in both legislative chambers of government.

Constitutions such as Brazil's do not arise by accident. They are forged out of societies characterized by vast inequalities in human capital, income, and wealth. Citizens whose life opportunities have been systematically constrained have strong incentives to favor political institutions that level the playing field or even tilt it in their favor.

The vast differences in Brazil's political institutions before and after 1989 gave rise to dramatic changes in the banking system. Prior to 1989, the Game of Bank Bargains in Brazil produced either the tiniest, most rudimentary banking system imaginable or a banking system designed to extract an inflation tax whose revenues were divided between the government and the banks. There was nothing subtle about the Brazilian inflation tax: at its peak, the annual transfer from the holders of cash and checking account balances to the government and the banks was an amazing 8 percent of GDP. To the degree that banks existed for any other purposes, they served either as a mechanism for state governments to circumvent the limits placed on their fiscal spending or as a means of mobilizing capital to fund the privileged commercial and industrial enterprises owned by bankers.

After 1989, the Game of Bank Bargains in Brazil revolved around the creation of employment opportunities for politically crucial voters. Brazil's democratically elected governments sought to end the country's notoriously unpopular hyperinflation, the burden of which had fallen mainly on the great mass of the poor. Under democracy, voters favored candidates who not only promised to end inflation but actually did so. Similar electoral pressures explain why Brazil's democratically elected presidents pushed state governors to privatize the state banks that they controlled: denying state governments a bank from which they could finance deficits was essential to ending hyperinflation, because the need to continually bail out those banks imposed a fiscal burden on the federal government that in turn drove the need to raise revenues through an inflation tax.

The median Brazilian voter wanted more than an end to inflation, however: she also sought the redistribution of income and opportunities. Brazil's post-1989 democratic governments have had to walk a populist tightrope: while increasing taxation on the wealthy to finance a welfare state, they have had to limit the extent of fiscal redistribution in order to keep the interests of elites aligned with democracy and prevent them from taking their wealth elsewhere. Thus a significant amount of redistribution takes place through government-owned banks that allocate credit on the basis of the employment opportunities that their lending creates for voters. In fact, three of the largest banks in Brazil, which jointly control more than 40 percent of total bank assets, are government owned. Thus, even though post-1989 governments have sought to revive the privately owned banking system in order to create profit opportunities for bankers and credit for entrepreneurs and households, the government's redistributive goals limit those efforts. Much of the country's savings are targeted at supporting politically visible job-creation programs, not investments of ambitious firms or the consumption of households.

Goodbye Slavery, Hello Easy Credit

The Brazil that Dom Pedro II "governed" in the 1880s was a very different Brazil from the nation that existed when he assumed the throne in 1842. The growth of the coffee economy and the end of the slave trade meant that from 1850 onward, Brazil was filling with immigrants, and the demand generated by those immigrant workers encouraged the growth of modern factories producing beer, cotton cloth, cigarettes, and other consumer goods. The growth of manufacturing gave rise to industrialists and industrial workers, who were not content to let a narrow elite of plantation owners run the country for their own benefit.[1] The embarrassing performance of the armed forces in the war with Paraguay showed the need for a more professional army, and the younger officers of that army could not help but notice that Brazil's political and economic institutions put the country at a huge disadvantage compared to the societies to whom they looked for inspiration, particularly republican France. The south-central regions of the country, such as São Paulo and Minas Gerais, were eclipsing Rio de Janeiro and the northeast in economic importance, and their elites were demanding the right to elect their own provincial presidents. By the 1880s, Dom Pedro II was aged and sick, and active republican and abolitionist movements were challenging his imperial authority.

One pillar of support for the monarchy remained: Brazil's slave owners, who for most of the country's history had been the source of all real power. They had run local governments and commanded state militias. They had run the elections and decided who "won." They had owned the land as well as most of the people, and they had decided who worked and under what conditions. By the late 1880s, however, the world had changed. Slave owners no longer controlled everything. They no longer dominated the parliament, and they did not hold sway over the emperor's daughter, the Princess Isabela. When Dom Pedro II was out of the country for medical treatment in 1888, Princess Isabela conspired with a group of liberals who controlled parliament to free the last of the slaves. She probably did not realize it, but she had removed the one bulwark that stood

---

[1] For a comparison of the growth of industry in Brazil and in other Latin American countries during this period, see Haber (2006a).

between her and a boat that would shortly take her and her father into exile.

Dom Pedro II, along with the Viscount of Ouro Preto, who served both as the emperor's prime minister and minister of finance, however, fully understood the implications of her act. When the emperor returned from Europe, he and Ouro Preto, scrambling to find a way to placate the planters, offered them something that they had been lobbying for since the 1870s: easy credit. Ouro Preto signed agreements between the government, the Banco do Brasil, and the Banco do Bahia to make long-term, low-interest loans to planters, with half of the money coming from the government and the other half from the banks. The banks took the government's money and lent it out but provided none of their own. When these measures proved inadequate, Ouro Preto signed similar contracts with 17 other banks. Those banks happily lent out the funds allocated to them, interest-free, by the government but then reneged on lending out their own funds. Instead, they asked Ouro Preto for more government money, which he provided. In fact, the monarchy was anxious to make deals with individual banks to pump credit into the countryside in order to sustain its rule. For example, the Banco de Crédito Real received 5 million milreis from the federal treasury just months before the empire's collapse, which allowed the bank to triple the amount of credit it granted in long-term, low-interest agricultural mortgages to São Paulo plantation owners.[2]

To fuel this lending boom, Ouro Preto also allowed some banks to print their own banknotes, which was a dramatic departure from earlier practice. Importantly, banks were not required to redeem their notes for currency: notes were redeemable 20 percent in currency and 80 percent in treasury bonds that the banks had been required to buy in order to back their note issues. Moreover, the government did not accept these banknotes as payment for import tariffs, which were its single biggest source of revenue.[3]

Banks sprang up overnight to take advantage of these subsidies, and existing banks grew their capital bases by issuing more equity so that they could qualify for even more interest-free government money. There is some evidence that the banks did not always use these funds to pro-

---

[2] Hanley (2005), 122–23; Schulz (2008), 74–77.
[3] Hanley (2005), 122.

vide fresh credit to planters: rather they sometimes converted the past-due, short-term loans to planters into long-term mortgages and then lent the government-subsidized funds to others—including individuals who then used them to purchase bank shares.[4]

These operations gave rise to a boom in the market for bank shares and the establishment of many new banks. Unfortunately for Pedro II, however, credit subsidies did not buy him the preservation of his monarchy. On November 15, 1889, the army rose against the government; the emperor went into exile the following day.

Goodbye Monarchy, Hello Financial Swindles

The interim military government that came to power after the fall of the monarchy needed not only to curry favor with the planters but also to find ways to finance itself. Thus its finance minister, Rui Barbosa, not only continued Ouro Preto's lending program to agriculture; he also engaged in an experiment in financial engineering that was, to put it mildly, completely reckless. It was, however, reckless by necessity, a tool used by a desperate government to hold together a fragile political coalition. The core of Barbosa's plan was to simultaneously obtain a loan for his government and expand the money supply to make credit easily available to planters, merchants, and industrialists.[5]

Within two months of coming to power, Barbosa pushed through a banking reform that not only made it easier to establish a commercial bank but also encouraged the formation of German-style universal banks whose portfolios would include significant amounts of long-term mortgage credit. Barbosa authorized three of these banks to issue up to 450,000 contos (a conto is a thousand milreis) in notes backed by government bonds—a sum that soon had to be reduced to 250,000 contos under protest from his colleagues, because Barbosa had essentially authorized the banks to more than double the money supply. In effect, Barbosa had exchanged a loan to the government for the right to print notes that could be lent at interest. The terms of that loan were quite remarkable: the inter-

---

[4] Schulz (2008), 74–77.

[5] For even greater detail on the financial swindles of this bank-driven stock-market boom, known as the *Encilhamento*, see Schulz (2008).

est rate on the government bonds that the banks agreed to purchase in order to back their note issues was reduced from 5 percent to 2 percent. In exchange, the bankers extracted a number of concessions from the government: free land; preference in obtaining contracts for railroads and other public works projects, such as canals; preference in obtaining mining contracts; and the right to expropriate land in order to carry out those projects. They were also granted tax exemptions on companies they founded, which included relief from import tariffs on inputs needed for "railways, river development, mines, or other sources of production."[6] By permitting the bankers to invest in commercial and industrial enterprises, Barbosa had not simply given them the right to issue currency: he had implicitly given them a license to print money that they could lend to their own industrial and commercial firms, with the collateral for those loans consisting of the stock in those same firms. In short, he traded a loan to the government for the right to build a house of cards.[7]

On the same day that Barbosa made this deal, he reformed the general-incorporation law to make it easier for corporate insiders to take advantage of minority shareholders.[8] Until 1890, Brazil had operated with a form of reserve liability similar to that which existed in Great Britain, which made a stockholder who had not yet paid in the full value of his shares liable for their full face value. The shareholder's personal "reserve liability" persisted even if he traded away his partially paid-in shares, with the period of liability extending for five years. This feature of the law was intended to reduce the incentives for unscrupulous promoters to create fly-by-night corporations designed to swindle investors. Barbosa's new incorporation law conspicuously dropped these provisions: stockholders who had not paid in the face value of their shares were fully liable for that value only until the annual meeting of shareholders approved the company's accounts.[9]

---

[6] Quoted in Hanley (2005), 124.

[7] Hanley (2005), 124–25; Schulz (2008), 80–81.

[8] General incorporation did not apply to banks or firms that had government concessions. As in all previous iterations of Brazilian corporate law, banks required specific government authorizations to operate. Musacchio (2009b), 33.

[9] Initially, shareholders only had to pay in 10 percent of the capital in order for the firm to start operations and only 20 percent to begin trading their shares. These ratios were increased to 30 percent and 40 percent, respectively, in 1891, in order to curtail fly-by-night swindles. That same reform also required joint-stock companies to publish

Not all economic historians of Brazil condemn Barbosa's general-incorporation law. Some point out that many of Brazil's largest manufacturing companies were created in a series of IPOs during this period, and thus they credit Barbosa with reforms that advanced industrial development.[10] Others point out that, however positive the contributions of manufacturing companies to Brazilian economic development, the founding of new banks of issue, coupled to these changes in corporate law, created a perfect setup for fraud. As John Schulz has illustrated, until the laws were revised in 1891 to curtail swindles, a banker could establish a manufacturing, real estate, or commercial company through general incorporation, obtain a special concession from the government that gave the firm the appearance of value, pay in 10 percent of the capital with money he printed, and then sell the shares to investors, who would purchase them because (a) the banker had a prior reputation for making money, and (b) shareholders had to pay in only 10 percent of the share's face value. The banker could then use the proceeds of that sale to (a) pay himself a handsome director's fee, (b) buy (overpriced) inputs for the new firm from other firms that he controlled, (c) purchase shares of his own company on the market in order to bump up its stock price, and (d) pay the shareholders a dividend. Having convinced the shareholders that all was proceeding smoothly—they had, after all, received a healthy dividend, and the stock price had increased— he could call up an additional 10 percent of the subscribed capital and repeat the process, thereby gradually transferring the wealth of the shareholders to his own pockets. By the time shareholders figured out that they had been fleeced, the banker would have long ago sold his shares.[11]

In 1890, Barbosa went even further: in addition to the authorizations that he had already granted to three banks to issue notes against government bonds, he now allowed two additional banks (the Banco do Brasil and the Banco Nacional) to issue notes equal to twice their capital, up to 50,000 contos each, "backed" by gold but not convertible into gold. In

---

in a major newspaper a full stockholder list, the statutes of the company, and information about the deal with the broker or bank that underwrote the IPO. The government also gave itself an incentive to enforce the laws, because corporate dividends were now taxed at 5 percent. Haber (2003), 265; Hanley (2005), 86–88, 93–98; Schulz (2008), 81–82; Musacchio (2009b), 33–34, 43–44.

[10] Stein (1957), 87–88; Haber (1998); Hanley (2005), 167–68.
[11] Schulz (2008), 85–86.

other words, the notes were not really backed by anything. As if this was not bad enough, one of the banks that had received authorization in 1889 to issue 50,000 contos in notes against government bonds, the Banco de Crédito Real (owned by the financier Francisco Mayrink), appears not to have actually bought any bonds at all: it just printed money. Later in 1890, Barbosa extended the right to issue interest-bearing, "nonconvertible, gold-backed notes" to five additional banks, one of which, the Banco dos Estados Unidos do Brasil, was also owned by Mayrink. When all was said and done, Barbosa's authorizations meant that the Brazilian money supply doubled from 1890 to 1891. Much of that monetary growth had been turned into loans to fictitious or quasi-fictitious enterprises, including scores of new banks that had taken advantage of Barbosa's reforms to the general-incorporation law.[12]

This situation was made even more tenuous by the fact that many of the agricultural mortgage contracts that banks were entering into were of dubious value. Brazilian law prohibited the breakup of estates in order to settle a debt. Banks could not, therefore, repossess any part of an estate, including its buildings or machinery, to settle a loan in default if doing so reduced the productive capacity of the estate.[13] Some banks reacted prudently, by not advancing credit to planters at all. Others responded by granting mortgages largely by issuing notes that were not really backed by anything. The Banco de Crédito Real, for example, became the largest mortgage lender in the state of São Paulo. It eventually collapsed under a sea of uncollectable mortgage loans in 1905. The liquidation administrators stated that many of its agricultural loans were made with a "lack of care in assessing the proposals for mortgage loans; [and] the lack of scruples in the respective valuations, which were generally exaggerated."[14] They estimated that the portfolio was overstated by at least 60 percent and that many of the bank's assets were worthless. The implication was that the notes that the bank had issued to the planters, and which now circulated in the economy as money, were also worth considerably less than their face value.[15]

---

[12] Schulz (2008), 84.
[13] Hanley (2005), 147.
[14] Quoted in Hanley (2005), 140.
[15] During the 1890s these notes generally traded at 60 to 70 percent of their face value. Hanley (2005), 140, 148.

The More Things Change, the More They
Stay the Same: The Old Republic

The election of a constituent assembly in November 1890 to write a constitution for a Brazilian "republic" did little to change the autocratic state of affairs. All of the ministers of the interim military government, except one, were elected to the constituent assembly. The government that came to power in the following year was republican in name only: it was full of generals who had staged the 1889 coup. The rules governing the franchise under this republic were even more tightly constrained than they had been under the monarchy—roughly 5 percent of the population had the right to vote—and its political rules gave the president greater latitude in policy making than the emperor had enjoyed. Although power shifted somewhat to include new, progressive industrial and commercial elements, particularly from the rapidly growing state of São Paulo, the republic was still dominated by a narrowly defined, wealthy elite. The one major change was that the constitution recognized Brazil's fundamental political fragmentation by creating a federal system that gave considerable autonomy to the states. Nevertheless, elections in this system were predetermined: the elites of the two largest states—São Paulo and Minas Gerais—simply alternated the presidency between them.

The writing of a constitution for the republic created yet another opportunity for financial legerdemain. In December 1890, Barbosa allowed several of the country's largest banks to merge, creating a monstrously large bank of issue that was stuffed full of loans of dubious quality. The Banco dos Estados Unidos do Brasil merged with the Banco Nacional to create the Banco da República, which was allowed to retain all of the privileges of its predecessor banks. In addition, the Banco da República purchased the note-issuing privileges of the Banco do Brasil. The resulting megabank was allowed to issue notes up to three times the value of the combined capital of the Banco dos Estados Unidos do Brasil, the Banco Nacional, and the Banco do Brasil. Those notes were to be convertible into gold, but only if the value of the milreis exceeded 27 British pence for an entire year—an occurrence that was extremely unlikely, because the rapid growth in the money supply meant that the Brazilian milreis traded at only 20 pence at the time the Banco da República deal was made. Within a year, it would be trading at 12 pence.[16]

---

[16] Schulz (2008), 87, 93.

Why Barbosa took the country down a path that could only lead to a financial meltdown is a question that has long interested historians of Brazil. One explanation is incompetence, though it is hard to imagine someone making so many bad decisions in so short a time out of pure ignorance or stupidity. Another explanation is that Barbosa was desperate: he needed to obtain the political support of the planters, who wanted easy credit, and he also needed to finance a fledgling government. Allowing banks to print currency wildly certainly made it easy for planters to obtain credit. Moreover, the fact that the banks used some of the notes they issued to purchase government bonds was, in effect, a way to levy an inflation tax on the population. This latter explanation fits a crucial fact: Brazil's 1891 constitution denied the central government access to a crucial source of tax income, revenues from export taxes, which were now collected directly by states.

A third potential explanation, which is not inconsistent with the first or second, is that Barbosa received a share of the rent from the deals that he helped to craft. In August 1890, while Barbosa was still minister of the treasury, Francisco Mayrink—the principal shareholder of the Banco de Crédito Real do Brasil and the Banco dos Estados Unidos do Brasil (soon to become the Banco da República), as well as a major promoter of numerous other corporations—bought Barbosa a mansion as a gift. The English-language *Rio News,* commenting on this transaction, noted that "in this selfish, wicked world, men do not give away $100,000 to a public official through patriotism or personal admiration."[17] After leaving office, Barbosa was appointed a director of several of Mayrink's companies.[18]

Regardless of his motivations, Barbosa's moves produced a speculative bubble. Banks used the money that they printed to purchase shares of corporations that were owned by their own directors, and the resultant run-up in prices convinced everyone else to jump into the market. Hundreds of IPOs were floated for new companies within a matter of months, and their shares were subscribed within days, if not hours.[19] The nominal capital of corporations listed on the Rio de Janeiro and São Paulo exchanges, which had stood in May 1888 at 410,000 contos (roughly US$136 million in 1888), doubled to 963,965 contos by December 1889 and then

[17] Quoted in Schulz (2008), 84.
[18] Schulz (2008), 84.
[19] Musacchio (2009b), 42.

Number of banks   Capitalization (millions of 1900 milreis)

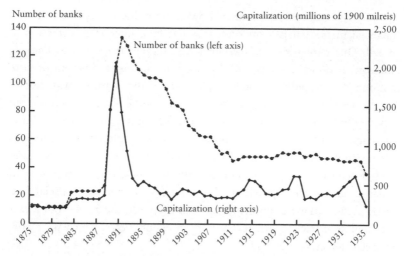

FIGURE 13.1 Size of the Brazilian banking system, 1875–1935.

Source: Estimated from stock-market data in *Jornal do commercio,* various issues.

doubled again by December 1890. By December 1891, it had reached 3,778,695 contos, a fourfold increase in just three years. The market capitalization of Brazilian corporations grew from 15 percent of GDP in the late 1880s to 40 percent by 1891.[20] The growth of the banking system was similarly spectacular. In 1888 there were only 27 banks in the entire country. In 1891, as figure 13.1 indicates, there were 133. Their total real capitalization (in 1900 milreis) was four times that of the 1888 banks.

When the bubble began to deflate at the end of 1891, the new republican government, now headed by General Manuel Deodoro da Fonseca, asked congress to authorize the Banco da República to issue an additional 600,000 contos in notes with no real backing. Deodoro was, in effect, trying to support stock prices through an expansion of the money supply. When congress demurred, Deodoro closed it down. Deodoro's stockmarket coup, as it is known, did not last long. The elites of São Paulo rebelled, and the navy and parts of the army supported their cause. Deodoro was forced to resign in favor of the vice president, another military leader.[21]

---

[20] Haber (1998), 286; Musacchio (2009b), 43.
[21] Schulz (2008), 92–93.

No financial manipulation could stave off the inevitable: the bubble created by Ouro Preto, Barbosa, and Barbosa's successor, Henrique Pereira de Lucena, burst at the end of 1891, bringing down most of Brazil's banks. As figure 13.1 shows, the number of functioning banks fell dramatically from 1891 onward. In an attempt to restore stability, President Floriano Peixoto asked congress to pass a banking-reform bill. When congress refused to go along, he simply imposed the new law by decree while congress was out of session. In December 1892 he merged the Banco da República and the (third) Banco do Brasil, creating the Banco da República do Brasil, to which he gave a monopoly over all new note issues. The government appointed three of the nine directors of the bank, including its president and vice president.[22]

Inflation Taxation Again: The (Fourth) Banco do Brasil

Brazil's banks continued to fail throughout the 1890s; the unrecoverable loans that they had made during the boom years of 1888–91 could only be papered over for so long. Nor could the government continue to paper over its own insolvency. In 1898 it had to sign a debt-consolidation loan with the House of Rothschild, which required that the government reduce the money supply as a condition of refinancing its debt. This step ended the slide in the value of the milreis, but the real appreciation of the exchange rate set off a two-year recession, one result of which was a bank run that took down many of the remaining banks.[23]

Even Peixoto's creation, the Banco da República do Brasil, which controlled roughly one third of all banking system assets and served as the government's bank, became increasingly insolvent. Given its size and the fact that it acted as the treasury's agent, however, it had implicit too-big-to-fail insurance, which the bank appears to have taken advantage of throughout the 1890s: it required continual loans and other support from the treasury to stay afloat.[24] Nevertheless, it too failed in the 1900 banking crisis, with the treasury taking over the administrative control of the bank and disbanding its commercial operations.[25] In 1906, the republican

---

[22] Triner (2000), 46; Schulz (2008), 107–8.
[23] Hanley (2005), 149–51, 171–78; Musacchio (2009b), 50.
[24] Schulz (2008), 114, 119.
[25] Triner (2000), 72–73.

government recognized that the credits it had extended to the bank were unrecoverable. It therefore nationalized the bank and turned it into a fourth incarnation of the Banco do Brasil. Shareholders received new Banco do Brasil shares, the government converted the debts owed by the bank to the treasury into equity, and additional equity was sold to new investors.

Like its predecessors, the fourth Banco do Brasil was a commercial bank fully capable of taking deposits and making private loans. It also acted as the treasury's fiscal agent, holding government balances and making loans to it. It was not allowed to act as a universal bank: it could not invest in the securities of other corporations, nor could it extend loans with terms greater than six months. As with the third Banco do Brasil, the president of Brazil named the president of the bank and one of its four directors. This bank differed from its predecessors, however, in that the central government was its most important stockholder, owning almost one-third of its shares. With a brief exception from 1923 to 1926, it was not allowed to issue currency: that privilege was reserved for the treasury. In short, the fourth Banco do Brasil was set up as a commercial bank that, because of its ownership structure, would be inclined to invest in treasury notes and bills.[26]

For the rest of the Old Republic—indeed for the rest of the twentieth century—the Brazilian banking system was dominated by the fourth Banco do Brasil. The source of that dominance is not hard to divine: in addition to holding the government's balances, the Banco do Brasil was the only bank in the country that was legally allowed to establish an interstate branching network. All other banks could only branch within their states of initial incorporation.[27] In 1923, the federal government increased its control over the bank by increasing its capital, from 70,000 to 100,000 contos, with the treasury subscribing all of the additional notes. That is to say, it became for all intents and purposes a state-owned central bank whose purpose was to channel deposits from its branches throughout the country into loans to the treasury. In 1925, just after the government increased its control over the bank through an additional capital subscription, loans from the bank to the treasury accounted for 25 percent of

---

[26] Topik (1987), 39.
[27] Triner (2000), 152.

its entire asset base. Issuing notes for rediscount by the Banco do Brasil became a mechanism by which the treasury funded deficits that were between one-third and one-half of government revenues.[28] The fact that the Banco do Brasil was highly profitable, with a rate of return on equity about twice that of all other banks, meant that it was able to provide the treasury, its major shareholder, with a steady stream of dividend income.[29]

Aldo Musacchio's estimates of the ratio of bank credit to GDP indicate that this Banco do Brasil–dominated banking system extended very little credit for private purposes. From the Banco do Brasil's founding in 1906 to the overthrow of the republic in 1930, bank credit to individuals, farms, and business enterprises averaged only 13 percent of GDP. Once the treasury became the dominant shareholder in 1923, that ratio was even lower, only 6 percent of GDP.[30]

Out with the Old, In with the Old

The Old Republic was in many respects a continuation of the Brazilian monarchy. The rules governing the franchise prevented most people from having any political voice at all, and the president was indirectly elected by congress. The central government remained poor and weak. States had the right to impose export taxes, contract foreign loans, and organize their own militias. Regional elites continued to run their states as quasi-fiefs. What held the system together was that the two most economically important states, São Paulo and Minas Gerais, used their control of the legislature to trade the presidency between themselves.[31] Being elected governor of one of these states was typically understood as a step toward the presidency. Legislators from São Paulo and Minas Gerais then made sure that the economic policies of the central government favored their states with trade protection for manufacturing and price supports for coffee through government purchases of excess stocks.

The Great Depression seriously challenged the deals that sustained this coalition of Paulista and Mineiro elites. The price of coffee completely

---

[28] Topik (1987), 45–52; Triner (2000), 54.

[29] Berg and Haber (2009).

[30] Musacchio (2009b), 64. The only countries in the contemporary world that have private credit ratios this low are disaster areas, such as Haiti, Yemen, and Sierra Leone.

[31] Triner (2000), 18–19.

collapsed. Manufacturing output fell. Unemployment was widespread. The governor of the southern state of Rio Grande do Sul, Getúlio Vargas, put together a coalition called the Liberal Alliance that promised to restore Brazilian economic growth and provide a higher degree of inclusion for the workers who populated Brazil's rapidly growing industrial cities of São Paulo, Belo Horizonte, and Rio de Janeiro. When the election was subsequently stolen, elements of the army carried out a bloodless coup to install Vargas in power.

Vargas was from a wealthy family and was very much a political insider. Indeed, he had served as minister of finance from 1926 to 1928. Nevertheless, he understood that Brazilian society had become more urban, industrial, and working class since the founding of the republic in 1891, and he capitalized on support from urban constituencies to create a Latin version of authoritarian populism, which had much in common with the fascist and national socialist movements that were sweeping much of Europe at the time. He used his peculiar blend of populism, anticommunism, anti-Semitism, and fascism to create a dictatorship that lasted from 1930 until 1945. Like other dictators of that era, such as Benito Mussolini, Vargas presented himself as the embodiment of the will of the people, as the epigraph of this chapter shows. He ultimately banned political parties and seized control of labor unions. When one embodies the will of the people, such middlemen are unnecessary.

Banking Policy under Authoritarian Populism

Vargas inherited a banking system in which the most important bank was state owned and was essentially used to channel deposits into loans to the government or to politically crucial constituencies. Vargas, who wanted to build a welfare state and support the growth of the manufacturing industries that employed his base of support, saw little need to rethink Brazil's banking system. Prior to the revolution of 1930, the Banco do Brasil had been used to funnel money to coffee planters; now it could be used to funnel money to politically favored industrialists and to buy government bonds to finance a growing welfare state.[32]

---

[32] For an examination of the accomplishments and limitations of Vargas's welfare state, see Fischer (2008).

Vargas was also responsible for promoting and expanding a largely moribund, government-owned savings bank, the Caixa Econômica Federal (CEF), using it much the same way he used the Banco do Brasil: as a means to build a lasting political coalition. In emulation of a long Western European tradition of government savings banks that encouraged the poor to save, the Brazilian banking legislation of 1860 created a popular savings institution called the Caixa Econômica e Monte de Socorro, which was as much a pawn shop as it was a savings and loan association. During the Old Republic, this institution's name was changed to the CEF, it was allowed to accept slightly larger deposits (the size of individual weekly deposits and the balance of any account were capped by law), and it was allowed to invest its deposit base in government securities. Nevertheless, the CEF was of quite modest scale; no one appears to have given it much thought.

Vargas, however, understood that expanding a government-run, popular savings bank could allow him to capture yet more savings to fund government deficits while simultaneously portraying himself as the "father of the poor." In 1934, the CEF and other *caixas* (savings banks) were granted exemptions from the taxes levied on commercial bank transactions, and they were allowed to grant mortgage loans and to make loans to state and municipal governments. Furthermore, commercial banks were allowed to deposit part of their portfolios in the *caixas*. By the mid-1930s, 30 percent of the deposit base of the commercial banks was located in the *caixas*.[33]

Brazil had a fleeting experiment with democracy when Vargas was pushed out by the military in 1945, but in a country characterized by extreme inequality of wealth and opportunity, it is difficult, if not impossible, to keep the populist genie in the bottle. It should not come as a surprise, therefore, that the Brazilian public elected Vargas as president in 1951. Within three years his populist excesses caused him once again to run afoul of the Brazilian military. Vargas fought to retain power and was implicated in an attempted assassination of an opposition leader. Rather than get tossed out in a coup, Vargas shot himself in the chest with his .38 Colt revolver.

The elected governments that followed Vargas's suicide differed in style but not in substance. Indeed, the presidents during the period 1954–64

[33]Von Mettenheim (2006), 45.

tended to be Vargas disciples: they were populists who sought to spur industrial development and expand a welfare state in order to reward their core urban, working-class constituencies. Like Vargas, they funded these initiatives not by increasing taxes but through an inflation tax whose incidence, ironically, fell on their constituents. Although this detracted from their popularity, they had little choice: despite their populist rhetoric, their hold on power was tenuous. If they tried to finance their ambitions by taxing the rich, they feared the rich might exit the country or overthrow them (a risk that, as we shall see, was not far-fetched).

The financing model of Vargas and the populist governments that followed him was simple: the treasury issued notes in order to cover government expenditures in excess of tax receipts, thereby setting off an inflation. The holders of cash and of bank deposits that earned either no interest or a rate of interest lower than the rate of inflation essentially paid a tax that was a function of the inflation rate. The government collected 100 percent of the inflation tax on cash. It split the inflation tax on bank deposits with the banks and *caixas,* with the exact split determined by the ratio of bank deposits to cash in the economy, the interest rate paid on deposits by the banks, and the required reserve-to-deposit ratio set by the government (the percentage of a bank's deposit base that had to be held in non-interest-bearing cash reserves at the central bank, which until 1965 was the government-owned Banco do Brasil).

In figure 13.2 we present estimates of the magnitude of the Brazilian inflation tax, as it is generally defined, from 1947 to 1986.[34] During Vargas's term in power from 1951 to 1954, inflation began to accelerate as he increased spending in order to satisfy his constituents without a concomitant increase in taxation. The inflation rate during these four years averaged 17 percent (compared to 7 percent for the four previous years), which generated an inflation tax that averaged 3.3 percent of GDP. Seventy-five

---

[34] We follow the general practice in the literature of defining the inflation tax as the product of the inflation rate and the sum of cash held by the public and cash reserves held by banks at the central bank. This measure, however, neglects an additional profit the government earns from inflation when that inflation is not anticipated by the market. Anticipated inflation raises the interest rate paid on debts, including government bonds. But if actual inflation exceeds anticipated inflation, then the government (like all debtors of fixed-income obligations that are not indexed to inflation) enjoys a capital gain equal to the capital loss suffered by creditors when unanticipated inflation raises interest rates.

Percentage of GDP

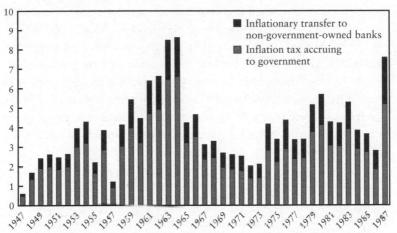

FIGURE 13.2 Brazilian inflation tax as a percentage of GDP, 1947–87.

Source: Calculated from data in Lees, Botts, and Cysne (1990), 38. 39, 127.

Note: We adjust their data to account for the fact that 40.6 percent of the deposit base was held by government-owned banks.

percent of this tax (2.5 percent of GDP) accrued to the government, while the remaining 25 percent (0.8 percent of GDP) was captured by non-government-owned banks.[35]

Inflation taxes work only if the government practices financial repression. It has to prevent the population from evading the tax by turning their cash into bank accounts that earn an interest rate that exceeds the inflation rate. Capping interest rates, however, drives deposits out of the banking system, which reduces the amount of credit available for private-sector lending, which in turn reduces the rate of growth of private-sector employment. Vargas was the first, but not the last, to face this dilemma. He bought political support with social-welfare and employment-generation programs that benefited urban industrial workers; but by paying for those programs with an inflation tax, he discouraged the growth of employment

[35] Data from Lees, Botts, and Cysne (1990), 38–39. We adjust their data to account for the fact that 40.6 percent of the deposit base was held in government-owned banks. Thus the government earned 40.6 percent of the inflationary transfer to the banking system.

opportunities for those same workers. Vargas came up with a profoundly ironic solution: he created a government-owned development bank, the Banco Nacional de Desenvolvimento Econômico e Social (BNDES), financed by the treasury, to fund enterprises that employed large numbers of workers. That is to say, because the printing of money discouraged privately owned banks from lending, Vargas printed yet more money to create a government-owned bank that would lend to firms chosen by the government. These tended to be government-owned enterprises engaged in the labor-intensive job of building infrastructure, such as roads, bridges, and port facilities.[36]

The Vicious Cycle of Inflation Tax Evasion

The problem with "solutions" such as BNDES is that printing currency to lend to employers generates yet more inflation; and as the inflation rate rises, the population flees the banking system even more rapidly than before, because the value of their cash assets is now declining even faster. But a population that avoids holding cash or bank deposits is evading the inflation tax! In response to a shrinking demand for cash and bank deposits, to meet a given amount of government financing needs, the government has to print yet more money. But the resulting increase in inflation causes further declines in the inflation tax base. Furthermore, it constrains investment, in part because of the shrinkage of the banking system but also because it is difficult for private-sector producers to make decisions about production and investment when they cannot predict the price level—which means that the real (nonfinancial) economy produces less growth and fewer jobs than otherwise. The government has to respond by expanding state-run enterprises, but it must also fund an even larger proportion of the government budget from the inflation tax. The net result is a rate of inflation that spirals upward, a banking system that spirals downward, and an economy that becomes increasingly dominated by state-owned enterprises whose raison d'être is not to be economically competitive but to generate employment.

Economic theory and empirical evidence from many countries suggest that, initially, as inflation rises, the total government revenue from the

[36] Lees, Botts, and Cysne (1990), 336–37.

inflation tax rises, too. But over time, if the inflation rate rises sufficiently, the reduction in the inflation tax base (the decline in the demand for cash and demand deposits) more than offsets the rising rate of inflation, and the total revenue earned from the inflation tax (in units of real purchasing power) eventually declines.

A glance at figures 12.1, 13.2, and 13.3 shows this process of accelerating inflation, decelerating inflation tax revenues, and falling private sector investment in action. From 1951 to 1964 the annual rate of inflation steadily accelerated, rising dramatically from an already high 15 percent to a staggering 73 percent. During the same period, government revenues from the inflation tax initially grew in real terms, from 1.9 percent of GDP to 6.6 percent of GDP. The proportion of investment by the private sector shrank, and eventually the majority of new investment had to come from government firms. The government's share of gross fixed capital formation grew from 16 percent in 1947 to 28 percent in 1954, and then to 50 percent by 1960. By 1969, the government's share in new capital formation hit 60 percent. Some sense of what this meant may be summarized in the following statistic: in 1972, 56 percent of the assets of Brazil's 50 largest nonfinancial corporations were owned by government-owned

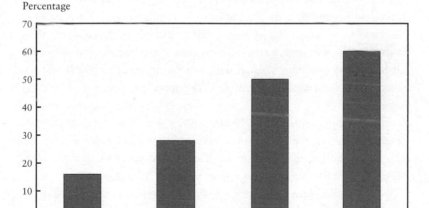

FIGURE 13.3 Public-sector share of gross fixed-capital formation, Brazil, 1947–69.
Source: Graham (1982), 42.

firms.[37] As figure 13.2 shows, the acceleration of inflation during the 1970s and 1980s was not associated with an increase in the ratio of inflation tax revenue to GDP. It appears that, as the economy adapted to rising inflation by reducing the demand for cash, the shrinking tax base of the inflation tax more than offset the effect of a higher inflation rate.

The government soon found that an extreme reliance on inflation taxation could have negative political as well as economic consequences. By 1964, the Brazilian military realized that not only had the populist genie escaped from the bottle, but he was asking the poor to make three wishes. Inflation was out of control. A Vargas disciple, João Goulart, was president. An attempt by Brazilian elites to limit his power, by recrafting the constitution so that power would reside with a prime minister rather than a president, failed when the population refused to approve the constitutional change in a plebiscite. The military therefore engineered a coup and imposed a dictatorship that endured from 1964 to 1985.

Banking and Inflation under the Military Dictatorship

The military government's main accomplishment, other than institutionalizing corruption and torture, was to push Brazil's inflation rate through the roof. They did not set out to do so, but they faced the same unpalatable choice that had confronted every Brazilian government since 1808: they could tax the rich, they could have a small and weak state, or they could run an unpopular inflation tax. Given their dependence on the Brazilian elite, the first option was off the table. The second option was also out of the question: they wanted Brazil to flex its muscles, not become a banana republic. That left the inflation-tax option, and despite all of their anti-inflation rhetoric and currency-reform plans, the evidence is that they jumped on it with alacrity. During the 21 years that the military governed the country, the inflation rate averaged 69 percent per year, more than twice the inflation rate in the decade that preceded the coup; in 1985, the military's final year in power, inflation hit 242 percent.

As figure 13.2 shows, despite the huge acceleration in the rate of inflation in the 1970s and 1980s, the total revenue the government extracted through inflation taxation for the most part was lower under the military

[37] Graham (1982), 32.

dictatorship than it had been in the early 1960s. As the cost of holding cash rose, people increasingly found ways to avoid doing so. In the 1970s, Brazil's financial system, like that of the United States (which was reacting to its own era of rising inflation taxation) became highly innovative as it sought ways to assist customers to dodge the inflation tax. Like their predecessors, the generals responded to reductions in the inflation tax base by boosting the inflation rate ever higher.

This vicious cycle of an ever-declining inflation tax base and an ever-rising inflation rate eventually backfired on the generals. Not only did their reliance on inflation taxation produce astonishingly high rates of inflation, but the burden of the inflation tax became increasingly concentrated on the declining number of people who were unable to evade it, especially the poor. As we have already discussed, the public had a strong incentive to dodge the inflation tax by exchanging the cash that was depreciating in their pockets, or in their zero-interest checking accounts, into other financial or real assets that earned a market rate of return (which was relatively insulated from the effects of inflation). Inflation dodges took a variety of forms, including treasury bills, interest-paying deposit accounts at *financieras* (finance companies), treasury bonds imperfectly indexed to inflation, and repurchase agreements between commercial banks and their depositors. Repurchase agreements (repos) allowed depositors to transfer deposits into treasury bills at the end of each day to avoid having their deposits counted for purposes of the reserve requirement at the central bank. Thus they allowed depositors to have the liquidity of a deposit with the interest payment of a treasury bill.

These dodges allowed the total demand for cash plus bank deposits, in real terms, to fall by half during the 1970s. As inflation rose, there was a clearly observable relationship between the increasing volume of the repo market and the decline in money demand. Similarly, as inflation rose, the relative shares of government treasury bill and bond holdings and finance-company deposits rose as a fraction of total financial assets.[38]

Dodging the inflation tax was not possible for everyone. Poorer people who relied exclusively on cash for transacting business had no escape. Similarly, bank depositors who could not maintain account balances sufficient to qualify for the daily repo trades could not avoid the inflation

---

[38] Calomiris and Domowitz (1989).

tax on their deposits. And only the very rich could afford to engage in direct purchases of large-denomination treasury bills and bonds.[39] Even the various dodges available to the rich and to business owners were imperfect. No rational person would willingly keep money in a non-interest-bearing checking account when inflation averaged 69 percent per year, but even business enterprises and the wealthy had to hold some deposits to make payments by check. No one was completely immune from inflation taxation.

The fact that business enterprises and households had to use their checking accounts as a means of payment meant that Brazilian banks primarily made their profits not from the spread between the interest rates they paid on deposits and the interest rates they received on loans—because inflation had chased the deposit base out of the banks—but rather from the "float" on checks during the two to three days that it took for checks to be debited to the account of the payer and credited to the account of the payee. During that period of float, the payer must maintain a sufficient balance in his checking account to cover the payment, and that balance will depreciate as the result of inflation. The military government did not allow the banks to keep the entirety of this float revenue; it required them to place a significant portion of their checking-account balances into a deposit reserve held in the central bank, essentially commandeering a large part of the float income for the government.

The inflation tax might have generated revenue for the government, but it left banks unable to extend much credit to business enterprises or households, choking off economic growth. Banks simply could not raise significant deposit resources to lend.[40] They therefore shrank their lending departments and focused instead on expanding their branching networks so that they could compete for deposits by offering greater convenience. Bankers' main role in the financial system was to assist depositors in investing in government securities, particularly via repos.

---

[39] One inflation dodge that was available to everyone was currency exchange. A gray market for trading in dollars operated throughout the high-inflation period. Nonetheless, banks could not offer deposits denominated in dollars, and many cash transactions could be executed only in local currency.

[40] Additionally, banks had to meet various lending mandates, which limited what they could earn on their loans.

Why did the military government permit inflation dodges? After all, it knew how to use its regulatory authority to force banks to pay zero interest on demand deposits and to require banks to hold large proportions of deposits on reserve at the central bank. It could have prohibited repo trading, too, but it chose not to do so. In addition, the government indexed the principal of government bonds to inflation to limit the inflation risk borne by its bondholders.

Brazil's generals were willing to ameliorate the adverse effects of the inflation tax on some classes of assets for two reasons. First, by permitting the financial system to create some substitutes for bank deposits—treasury-bill repurchase agreements, inflation-indexed government bonds, and intermediation by finance companies—the government limited the transfer of wealth out of the country. Second, the permissible inflation dodges pushed savings into purchasing government bills and bonds, which gave the government a captive domestic market for savings from which to draw at very low (often negative) real (inflation-adjusted) rates of interest.

Nevertheless, permitting inflation dodges also meant that the inflation tax base (checking accounts) would shrink, forcing the government to raise the rate of inflation sky-high by the 1980s. Moreover, there was no guarantee that accelerating inflation would continue to deliver a sufficient amount of inflation-tax revenue: at sufficiently high rates of inflation, inflation-tax revenue will decline even while inflation continues to increase. By the later years of military rule, inflation spiraled out of control, exceeding 200 percent per year by 1984; and, as shown in figure 13.2, inflation-tax revenue relative to GDP began to shrink. Furthermore, the population became increasingly discontented with the economic costs of high inflation. The generals increasingly came to look like incompetent buffoons. Demands for democracy became stronger, and support for the generals withered even among Brazilian elites.

The generals tried to placate the population with various schemes for government-directed credit to favored sectors or segments of the population, but this was like trying to bail water out of a sinking ship with a spoon. For the inflation tax to work as a revenue-generating device, it inevitably produced financial repression and regressive taxation. There was no avoiding those facts or their political consequences. The military dictatorship's days were numbered.

The Return of Democracy and the
End of Inflation-Tax Banking

The mismanagement of the Brazilian economy by the generals forced the military back into the barracks in 1985 and initiated a process of democratization that culminated in a new constitution in 1988 and the country's first direct elections for president under universal suffrage in 1989. Since that time, Brazilian mass politics has reflected the country's strong populist current. It is difficult to characterize the ideological orientation of the first president elected under the 1988 constitution, Fernando Collor, because he was impeached on corruption charges only two years into his term, but his successors have been from either the left wing of the Social Democratic Party or from the pragmatic wing of the Workers' Party.

One of the top priorities of Brazil's democratic governments since 1990 has been to redistribute income. One crucial step was to end the inflation tax, because its incidence falls disproportionately on the poor. As a result, in 1993 and 1994 the government of Itamar Franco instituted the Real Plan, which was an attempt to curb inflation by simultaneously promising to cut spending, raising interest rates, and creating an overvalued currency. This was no easy task. Reductions in government spending (even when they are in the interest of the general population) are almost never a cause célèbre of mass demonstrations. There was little option, however, because the mobility of the elite, and of their assets, limited the ability of the government to raise tax rates on the wealthy.

This constraint on the government's ability to increase taxes on the elite is nicely illustrated by a joke that made the rounds during the 1990s. Luiz Inácio Lula da Silva (known as Lula, a left-of-center political leader who became president in 2002) is giving a speech to a youth rally. In the front, he notices a large group of well-heeled young Brazilians. With every promise he makes to tax the rich, they explode in applause and cheers. After the speech, he approaches them to ask why these obviously rich young people are so supportive of his ideas. One of them responds: "Because my parents tell me that if you are elected, we will be moving to Paris."

Given the challenges it faced, it was far from obvious that the Real Plan would succeed. The announcement of the plan did little to commit the government to any immediate, concrete reforms, nor did it make any explicit long-term commitment to peg the real to the dollar. The government's greatest asset in its battle to end inflation was its large stock of foreign-currency reserves (worth roughly $38 billion), which could be employed to defend the new currency against depreciation. But those reserves would be of little use if deficit spending did not end.

Ultimately, the success of the Real Plan is a testament to the prevailing logic of the Game of Bank Bargains. A democratic government will not survive for long if it cannot end a regressive tax. As figure 12.2 shows, inflation came to a grinding halt, falling from 2,477 percent in 1993 to 917 percent in 1994, 22 percent in 1995, 10 percent in 1996, and 5 percent in 1997—a level that has held more or less constant.

The positive consequences for the banking system of reducing government deficits and inflation were immediate, dramatic, and far-reaching. For Brazil's private banks, the announcement of the Real Plan put them in a difficult position. There was no way to play it safe. Banks had to position themselves based on their best guess of whether the plan would be a success or a failure (like the many attempted currency reforms that had preceded it).

If the Real Plan worked, banks would have to move out of the float business and into the business of making profits from lending. That would require dramatic changes in their branching networks and staffs—in particular, they would need far fewer tellers and many more loan officers. Bankers that did nothing to position themselves for this tectonic shift in the banking environment would fail to acquire good customers and lose out to the competition.

If the Real Plan failed, however, a bank that had bet on its success by building a loan portfolio would have to scramble to reestablish its float business. For example, Banco Itaú, which was one of the large Brazilian banks grappling with this strategic challenge in 1994, had already been burned by its bet in favor of a previous inflation reform (the Cruzado Plan of 1986) and had suffered large losses when it proved unsuccessful.[41] In the end, Banco Itaú bet in favor of the Real Plan and was rewarded by being able to play a major role in the expansion of the Brazilian banking industry.

---

[41] Beim (2001).

State-Owned Bank Privatizations

The dramatic decline in inflation required a government commitment to reducing deficits, and this was no easy matter. A central problem was that the national government's fiscal spending was not entirely under its own direct control. Part of the process of fiscal reform, therefore, entailed the reform of state government operations that had implications for national deficits: in particular, privatization of the banks owned by Brazil's states.

Brazilian state governments had all taken a page out of the federal government's playbook and created state-owned banks. Initially conceived as sources of credit subsidies for local economic interests, such as coffee planters, these banks became mechanisms by which states financed their budget deficits. The oldest of the state-owned banks went back to the 1920s, when the governments of both Minas Gerais and São Paulo became the dominant shareholders of struggling private banks.[42] By the 1970s, virtually every one of Brazil's 19 states owned a commercial bank, and some owned savings banks as well. During the 1980s, those banks controlled 13 percent of the banking system's deposit base.[43]

The fiscal trickery of the state-owned bank relied on the fact that the Brazilian central government would not allow a state bank to fail. Thus, a state bank would lend recklessly, both to politically crucial constituents and to the state government itself, and then seek a rescue from the Banco Central do Brasil (established in 1965 as a central bank), which would have to fund the rescue by issuing currency or by borrowing from the treasury. After the rescue, the state bank could go right back to making the same types of bad loans. Massive waves of state-bank failures and government bailouts occurred in 1989, 1993, and 1997.[44] The costs of the last bailout were aggravated by the contractionary effects of the Real Plan. To defend the anti-inflationary policy, the government raised interest rates, which produced a substantial economic slowdown, which in turn resulted in a wave of defaults and bankruptcies that raised loan losses at all banks.[45]

---

[42] Triner (2000), 168, 171.

[43] Lees, Botts, and Cysne (1990), 125–27.

[44] For discussions of the histories of these bailouts, the political bargains that they entailed, and the history of reforms that brought them to an end, see Baer and Nazmi (2000); Ness (2000); Sola, Garman, and Marques (2001); Bevilaqua (2002); Rodden (2008); and Feler (2011), 4–7.

[45] Baer and Nazmi (2000).

Once the federal government became serious about constraining fiscal deficits, it also had to become serious about shutting down state-owned banks and finding other means of credibly limiting its exposure to the fiscal costs of bailing out state governments. As early as 1993, the federal government amended the constitution to forbid states to issue new debts prior to December 1999, except in payment of judicial claims in existence at the time of the 1988 constitution.[46] Then it pushed the states to privatize their state-owned banks, an operation that was largely complete by 2000.[47] Finally, it enacted legislation in 2000 that prohibited central bank or national government bailouts of insolvent banks without specific legislative action and subjected officials that violated that law to criminal penalties. The 2000 reforms also required the president to set yearly debt limits for all segments of the public sector and set penalties for subnational governments that violated those limits. Illegal efforts to issue bonds were subject to prison sentences.[48]

These measures transformed the Brazilian banking system. As several researchers have shown, privatized state-owned banks ceased to be a fiscal albatross and functioned more efficiently, especially in comparison with state-owned banks that were restructured rather than privatized.[49] There is also evidence that privatization enhanced productivity in the real economy. A study by Leo Feler finds that after bank privatization, lending, employment, and wages decreased in Brazil's least wealthy localities but increased in more wealthy areas. The implication is that privatization led to a reallocation of credit to those areas that were more likely to employ it efficiently.[50]

There's Always a *Jeitinho*

The 2000 reforms reduced the willingness of the central bank to provide assistance to failing banks. This became clear during the global banking crisis of 2008–09, when the central bank demurred from providing even

---

[46] Bevilaqua (2002), 15.

[47] Beck, Crivelli, and Summerhill (2005).

[48] These took the form of the Fiscal Responsibility Law (Supplementary Law 101, approved May 2000), and the Penal Law for Fiscal Crimes (approved October 2000). See Rodden (2006), chapter 8.

[49] Beck, Crivelli, and Summerhill (2005); Nakane and Weintraub (2005).

[50] Feler (2011), 25–26.

short-term liquidity assistance.[51] Instead, the central bank coaxed the private deposit-insurance agency (the Fundo Garantidor de Créditos, or FGC) to increase its insurance limits and convinced large banks to lend to smaller ones. In a sense, the central bank used its regulatory powers of coercion as a substitute for providing direct assistance.

Although the national government made it extremely difficult for the state governments or the central bank to bail out an insolvent bank without approval of the national legislature, it retained the option of engineering discretionary bailouts. That is, the national government gave itself what Brazilians call a *jeitinho*—a way to circumvent the rules. Even though the central bank was unable to play a direct role in the resolution process, that did not mean that insolvent banks were necessarily liquidated (or that they will be in future Brazilian banking crises). Liquidation did happen in at least one case—that of Cruzeiro do Sul in 2012—but another option was for state-owned banks to absorb insolvent banks' losses via acquisition. Although state-owned banks, like the government, had been forbidden from buying distressed banks prior to 2008, in the midst of the 2008 crisis the government passed a bill (Provisional Act 443 of 2008, which then became Law 11908 of 2009) to permit state-owned banks to purchase other banks or assets.[52] The Banco do Brasil's acquisition of a large stake in Banco Votorantim was an important example.[53] The government also used its regulatory powers to enlist private banks' assistance in the public interest. In one case, the central bank allegedly used regulatory pressure to push a privately owned bank, BTG Pactual, to acquire PanAmericano after PanAmericano was found to have engaged in an accounting fraud that rendered it insolvent.[54] Furthermore, as troubled banks shrank or disappeared, the government softened the short-term

[51] International Monetary Fund (2012a), 31.

[52] As Valadao and Gico ([2009], 22) explain: "The Constitution allows the President to issue law-like decrees in cases of urgency and relevance that are immediately legally enforceable. These decrees, called provisional measures, must be submitted hitherto to Congress for referral. The measures mentioned above were largely regulated by Medida Provisória no. 443, October 21, 2008 (Brazil). This provisional measure was transformed into law by the National Congress: Law no. 11,908 of March 3, 2009, available at www.jusbrasil.com.br/legislacao/4332/lei-2004-53." See also International Monetary Fund (2012a), 31.

[53] BancoVotorantim (2013).

[54] See "Brazil: Failure Demonstrates Pressure on Small Banks" (2012).

blow to the economy by having its state-owned banks increase their lending and cut their loan rates.[55]

Using government-owned banks to support the private banking system during a crisis illustrates one of the most curious features of Brazil's post-1990 democratic governments. Although the national government basically forced state governments to privatize their banks and limit their spending and debt issuance, it chose not to privatize the banks that it owned—the Banco do Brasil, BNDES, and the CEF. As of this writing, these three banks account for 41 percent of all assets in the Brazilian banking system.

The logic of politics explains this choice. There are basically three ways that a government can redistribute income. It can shift the tax burden; it can increase spending on the poor; or it can use the banking system to effect implicit transfers to the poor through subsidized lending (see the discussion of Bill Clinton's "third way" in chapter 7). The Brazilian governments of the last decade have done all three. Putting an end to inflation taxation shifted the burden of taxation toward the middle classes and the rich. A series of conditional cash-transfer programs, which provide direct aid to families, has increased spending on antipoverty programs. Finally, the government has used its control of the Banco do Brasil and BNDES to transfer income by making loans to manufacturing firms that generate large numbers of jobs in politically crucial areas.

This mechanism of redistribution via the banking system has been studied in detail by Daniel Carvalho, who finds that firms eligible for loans from government-owned banks expand employment in regions where local politicians allied to the incumbent national government (the Social Democratic Party from 1994 to 2002, and the Workers Party since 2002) face a tough reelection fight. Importantly, his study finds no effects for firms that are ineligible for government bank loans or for firms that rely only on loans subsidized by the government but that are not directly provided by government-owned banks. As a result, employment expansion by firms in politically contested regions is associated with greater borrowing from government banks. In short, the evidence suggests that Brazil's post-1994 governments do not just encourage banks to lend to firms in order to encourage employment growth, they also use their power over banks to

---

[55] See "Brazilian Banks" (2012).

generate employment in order to increase their chances of winning local elections.[56]

The Two-Way Street of Banking and Politics

Through most of this book, we have focused on the effects of political pre-conditions on banking-system outcomes. The transition from autocracy to democracy in Brazil that began in the late 1980s is an important reminder that (as discussed in chapters 2 and 3) banking-system outcomes can also have dramatic unintended and unanticipated political consequences.

In Brazil, under the military dictatorship, inflation-tax banking was used, of necessity, as a tool of government—a fiscal policy option that was preferable to the alternatives of higher direct taxation on the wealthy or a smaller government. That choice set in motion an inflationary surge that undermined the legitimacy of the military dictatorship and set the stage for a transition to a democracy with a strong populist current, which has also—arguably for the first time—made substantial lending to the private sector one of the central purposes of Brazil's privately owned banks.

There is plenty of reason for optimism about the future of Brazilian banking. Brazil's recent financial-system stability assessment from the International Monetary Fund (2012a) is practically glowing. The IMF points to many positive aspects, including the high capital ratios of Brazil's banks, numerous improvements in the quality of bank regulation and supervision, evidence of significant competitiveness among Brazilian banks (despite the high level of concentration of the banking system), and the deepening of Brazil's capital markets.[57] Banking-system improvements have happened in the context of deep reforms to government and to fiscal institutions. Some researchers have argued that these are ushering in a new era in which

---

[56] Carvalho (forthcoming).

[57] With respect to competitiveness, Brazilian banks have long displayed very large spreads between loan and deposit interest rates. Researchers have investigated the extent to which these spreads are indicative of rents rather than compensation for risk. Some of the explanation for the high spreads is the high, nonremunerative reserve requirements faced by Brazilian banks. Although some researchers find evidence for above-normal profits in Brazilian banks, at least in their pricing of consumer banking products, others conclude that there is little evidence of cartel-like behavior. Furthermore, competition is clearly increasing over time. See the review in International Monetary Fund (2012a), especially 12 n. 2.

government policies will be able to focus on the long-term welfare of Brazil's citizens, not just making ends meet today.[58]

Another reason for optimism is that these improvements in banking-system and fiscal performance are occurring in a context of broad-based reforms, not only in the political system and fiscal policy, but also in trade policy, industry-privatization policy, and corporate governance. There is a substantial body of research showing that improvements in these areas lead to positive changes in domestic political systems by reducing opportunities for corruption.[59] In response to these policy changes, the growth in foreign direct investment in Brazil and the increase in the rate of initial public offerings of traded stock since the enactment of the Real Plan have been phenomenal. Finally, even the election to the presidency of left-wing populists, like Lula, did not undermine Brazil's economic reforms, as some had feared it might. Furthermore, in a December 2012 Supreme Court trial, many members of Lula's government were sentenced to jail terms for corruption—which many welcome as a sign of reduced tolerance of corruption by government officials.

The meteoric growth in initial public offerings is particularly encouraging because of what it says about the market's perception of the decline in the risk of expropriation of shareholders by the government. As chapter 2 explains, a high risk of expropriation from the government tends to favor concentrated ownership: majority shareholders have strong vested interests in rent seeking as a mechanism either to compensate them for the risk of expropriation or to reduce the risk of expropriation (for example, through bribery of government officials to circumvent expropriative taxes or regulations).[60] In Brazil over the past decade, however, companies have been using the Novo Mercado of the Bovespa (Brazil's stock exchange) to voluntarily adopt constraints on their corporate-governance practices (related to disclosures, stock voting rights, board membership, tag-along rights, and other corporate policies) that are specifically designed to reduce ownership concentration by increasing the protections offered to minority shareholders.[61] Adopting these voluntary improvements in corporate gov-

---

[58] Alston, Grove, and Wheelock (2013).

[59] See, for example, Khandelwal, Schott, and Wei (2012).

[60] For a formal model of the relationship between expropriation risk and the composition of share ownership, see Stulz (2005).

[61] Tag-along rights protect minority shareholders against tunneling by preventing dilution of their interests through the issuance of underpriced shares.

ernance has been shown to increase share trading, share value, and the likelihood that a company will raise equity in the market.[62] The fact that so many companies are finding it preferable to diversify their shareholder base is yet another strong indication of a reduction in government expropriation risk. Furthermore, these corporate policies are likely to improve private and public governance by reducing the extent of corruption.

All of this, however, does not guarantee a rosy future for Brazilian banking. Brazil's new institutional arrangements have not yet been sufficiently stress-tested by economic shocks. If Brazil were to experience a severe recession, say as the result of a real-estate bust that threatened the solvency of many borrowers and banks, would the government allow banks to fail, or would it come to their assistance? And if it assisted them, might it not return to a reliance on inflation taxation, given the continuing limitations on the ability to raise direct taxes?

The best cautionary tale about stressed banking systems in democracies with strong populist currents comes from the United States. Like contemporary Brazil, the United States in the 1990s used credit subsidies as a means of circumventing fiscal constraints that limited redistribution. In the United States, extrabudgetary "third way" policies that destabilized banks took the form of GSE mandates, CRA regulation, and too-big-to-fail support for large banks. In Brazil, despite the statutory limits on state governments' spending and bailouts of banks, the government has found alternative means to provide credit subsidies to targeted recipients, including lending by the remaining state-controlled banks, state bank acquisitions of troubled banks, and regulatory arm-twisting of large banks to assist troubled small ones. If the experience of the United States is any indication, managing banking crises in Brazil will be an ongoing process.

[62] Carvalho and Pennacchi (2012).

III

Going beyond Structural Narratives

14

||||||||||||||||||||||

Traveling to Other Places
Is Our Sample Representative?

The use of travelling is to regulate imagination by reality, and instead of thinking how things may be, to see them as they are.

Samuel Johnson (1773)

Science is built up with facts, as a house is with stones. But a collection of facts is no more a science than a heap of stones is a house.

Jules Henri Poincaré,
La science et l'hypothèse (1908)

Narratives and Identifying Causes

Economic analysis is all about determining causation. Economists want to understand the structure that connects observed facts. Structural models in economics seek to clearly identify the fundamental sources of shocks in the economy and explain how those shocks elicit the observed behavioral responses of individuals, corporations, governments, and bankers.

To see how useful structural thinking can be, consider the confusion that results from its absence. The 2007–09 U.S. subprime crisis provides an example. Reporters typically listed contributory causes, and some of the assembled lists were extraordinarily long. But some of the items on those lists were symptoms of the crisis, not causes, and others may have contributed to the crisis but were themselves the outcomes of other influences. To identify the underlying factors that caused the crisis, one must build a structural model that connects all the events in a way that convincingly disentangles their causal interconnections.

The dominant approach to identifying causal relationships in social science in general, and in studies of banking in particular, is the use of statistical techniques for imposing "identification restrictions" that guide causal inference. In essence, econometrics uses a priori views from economic and political theories about the likely channels of causation to help distinguish cause from effect in the analysis of correlations. We are enthusiastic advocates and practitioners of such statistical approaches to identifying causation.

At the same time, we believe that the country histories in this book illustrate the usefulness of an alternative, complementary approach, based on the study of the sequence of events in particular countries over long periods of time. Such narratives can be uniquely useful for identifying causal patterns, so long as they are more than a string of facts. As the epigraph from Poincaré so eloquently points out, assembling facts is essential, but not sufficient: to be informative, historical narratives must be connected to the logic of economics and politics. Our approach, therefore, is to develop "structural narratives," which combine the logic of economics and political bargaining with a careful examination of the specific historical events in individual countries. We believe that structural narratives can provide convincing evidence about the factors that were most important in shaping political, economic, and financial history.

Inevitably, this narrative approach is based upon the historical judgments of the author, which all readers—and subsequent authors of other studies—must judge for themselves. We say this not by way of apology but rather to emphasize that all causal inferences—whether in statistical analyses or in narrative history—depend on a priori judgments about channels of influence. Such judgments must be evaluated first on the basis of their internal logical coherence and second on the applicability of those stories to other cases. The best test of causal stories—whether derived from narrative or statistical analyses—is whether the implied patterns are applicable to other cases and data.

We do not regard our narratives as the final word, either about the histories of the countries that we have studied in this book or about the structure of the Game of Bank Bargains in general. We hope that other scholars will evaluate our interpretations, and those of others, not only with statistical analyses but also by comparison with detailed narratives for other countries or competing narratives for the five countries that we have analyzed. Indeed, we think it is high time to restore a balance to social science by emphasizing the role of narratives in causal inference and by insisting on a balance between statistical and narrative evidence.

The unique aspects of any country's history make it virtually impossible to capture the evolution of its banking system, and the political and economic history that surrounds it, by identifying a small set of attributes that are common to a broad range of countries (as a statistical panel study of countries over time would require). Narratives offer opportunities for causal inference in social science precisely because the factors that must be analyzed differ so much across countries and over time. Fitting the square peg of history into the round hole of statistical panel analyses is likely to obscure as much as it reveals about how broad differences in banking systems emerge across countries.

Structural narratives demonstrate the ways that political and economic institutions mitigate or magnify the influences of economic and political shocks on real-world outcomes. That is, structural narratives are key building blocks of informed statistical modeling. Familiarity with facts also can identify the shortcomings of ideas or frameworks that do not allow for the contingencies of place and time—a point we return to at length in the next chapter.

There are, however, some limits to the narrative approach. Most obviously, a case study is not necessarily representative. The collection of structural narratives in this book, even when viewed against a theoretical framework (in chapter 2) and a broad discussion of the modern world (in chapter 3), is inherently limited by the fact that it represents the experiences of only five countries. Detailed, interpretive histories take a great deal of time to research, to formulate, to write, and to read. A book like this one, therefore, simply could not have been written about all the countries in the world, or even most of them.

What one can do, however, is to generalize from these specific narrative histories by connecting some of their lessons to the experiences of other countries. We relate the evidence from cross-country statistical studies of the recent past to three lessons that emerge from our case studies: namely that, all other things being the same, democracies are more conducive to a broad distribution of bank credit than autocracies; that, all other things being the same, democracies with liberal institutions that make it difficult for bankers and populists to form coalitions are more conducive to both a broad distribution of bank credit and the absence of banking crises; and that government safety nets tend to destabilize banking systems, and such safety nets tend to arise not for reasons of economic efficiency but because they are outcomes of political bargains. These are not the only lessons that emerge from our narratives: they just happen to be the most obvious and important ones that can be tested against cross-country statistical studies.

We also briefly discuss the experiences of four countries that a skeptical reader might propose as counterexamples to the idea that democracy is more conducive to the development of stable and efficient banking systems than autocracies: China under Deng Xiaoping and his successors, Germany under Otto von Bismarck, Japan during the Meiji Restoration, and Chile under Augusto Pinochet. We show that three of these cases—China, Germany, and Japan—actually fit the theory we advance in chapter 2 quite well. The growth of Chile's banking system under Pinochet may indeed be an exception, although the evidence is far from clear cut. Chile managed to build a successful private banking system despite a lack of checks and balances to limit the power of a dictator. But it did so only in the wake of a bank privatization and bailout that was typical of what one expects to see when bankers operate under an authoritarian regime in which they are uncertain about their property rights. Indeed, Chile's bank privatization shortly after Pinochet came to power in the 1970s was remarkably similar to that of Mexico in the 1990s under the PRI (see chapter 12).

In short, when we do our level best to find evidence that is inconsistent with the general patterns that emerge from our structural narratives, the most we can do is point to a single case that may not cleanly fit the framework. We conclude that the experiences of the United Kingdom, the United States, Canada, Mexico, and Brazil analyzed in our detailed structural narratives are broadly representative of the basic patterns of banking development under democracy and autocracy.

Some Simple Cross-Country Statistical Evidence

In order to see whether our sample of five cases is broadly representative, let us start with some simple statistics. In chapter 1, we note that if abundant credit is defined as a ratio of private bank credit to GDP one standard deviation above the mean level over the period 1990–2010 (about 83 percent of GDP), and if a highly stable banking system is defined as one that has been crisis-free since 1970, then only six out of 117 countries —Australia, Canada, Hong Kong, Malta, New Zealand, and Singapore— meet the threshold for being both credit abundant and crisis free. Obviously, no single statistical measure can fully capture the differences across countries in credit abundance or banking-system stability. For example, the absence of banking crises could simply reflect a stable macroeconomic environment rather than a well-designed banking system. Nonetheless, as a rough gauge of cross-country differences, these measures are useful.

What do these "very successful six" countries have in common? Three of them—Hong Kong, Singapore, and Malta—are city-states or small islands rather than large countries. We hypothesize that it should be much easier to avoid banking bargains that are harmful to the general society (that is, bargains that lead to scarce credit or banking instability) in a society where lack of economic diversity makes for much simpler politics. What coalition might be formed among agrarian populists, small bankers, and politicians representing rural districts in a country that has virtually no agricultural sector, such as Hong Kong or Singapore? Indeed, in an entrepôt city-state, the interests of manufacturers, bankers, and politicians are naturally aligned: they must maintain a stable, efficient, open economy or risk becoming so poor and backward that they get swallowed up by a neighboring country. There is simply too much at stake for the economic and political elites, and too few other interest groups lobbying for alternative uses of the banking system, to divert the society from a path that leads to stable and abundant credit.[1]

The three other countries on the list of the "very successful six"— Australia, Canada, and New Zealand—share two features. First, they were all part of the British Empire. (Indeed, all six of these countries were at one time British colonies.) Second, they are among the world's most stable and long lived democracies. Political scientists often use the "polity score" (a metric of political competition and political institutions developed by Monty Marshall and Keith Jaggers) to measure the extent of

---

[1] If the list of the "very successful" countries had been assembled in 2012, Cyprus would have been included. It, too, is an island nation. Cyprus, however, is part of the eurozone, and so its monetary policy is not determined independently. Also, Cyprus, as a member of the European Union, could not limit the extent to which its banks held concentrated positions in the sovereign debts of other member countries (such as Greece). If Cyprus had remained independent of the European Union and the eurozone, then it might have remained on the list of "very successful" countries. In that sense, its departure from the list reinforces the view that political homogeneity (which Cyprus's connection to the eurozone and the European Union reversed) explains why so many of the "very successful" countries tend to be islands or city-states.

democracy and autocracy. We normalize their scale to run from 0 to 100 and follow conventions in the political-science literature that place the threshold for democracy at 80.[2] Although single quantitative measures of democracy are imperfect, they provide a useful means of capturing important differences among political systems, especially when one takes long-run averages of yearly scores. The polity scores for the period 1925–2010 for Australia, Canada, and New Zealand are all 100 (the maximum). The average polity score for that period worldwide is 52.6. Indeed, even if we include the city-states and small islands that are part of the "very successful six," we are struck that there is only one autocracy in the group, Singapore (with a polity score of 40 on average since independence from Britain).[3]

Australia, Canada, and New Zealand have something else in common: the structure and political histories of these three countries tended to mitigate the ability of populists and bankers to form coalitions that disadvantage everyone else. We have already discussed the roles of centralized economic policy making and an unelected senate in structuring the Game of Bank Bargains in Canada in chapter 9 and thus will not recapitulate that information here.

We are struck by the fact that New Zealand's political institutions, like those of Canada, developed under the threat of a majority (the Maori) that might have been hostile to the commercial aspirations of its British settlers. Thus, when the first representative political institutions were established in New Zealand in the 1850s, veto gates were created in the decision structure of the government that limited the power of the Maori, including an unelected upper house (which remained in existence until 1950) and a governor general with veto power over legislation.

Australia did not have an unelected upper house (its senate has been elected since its creation), but it became independent from the United Kingdom in stages: it was not until 1986 that it achieved full independence from the British courts and Parliament. Moreover, like Canada and New Zealand—and unlike the United States—Australia had a constitution that granted the national government centralized control over eco-

---

[2] Specifically, our scores are derived by adding 10 to the Marshall and Jaggers (2011) polity2 score and then multiplying by 5.

[3] Hong Kong and Malta do not receive polity scores from Marshall and Jaggers. Hong Kong has never been a fully separate, sovereign state. Malta's population is too small to warrant its inclusion in the polity dataset.

nomic and banking policy: populists could not form coalitions with bankers and then enact policies to their liking by winning successive victories in individual states, as happened in the United States throughout much of its history.

A skeptical reader might point out that we have set a very high threshold for identifying countries with abundant credit and stable banks. What happens if we set a standard for success that only requires countries to have been crisis-free since 1970 and have an average level of bank credit to GDP equal to the mean for all countries? The list of successes now expands to a list of the "successful thirteen" countries: the "very successful six" are joined by the Bahamas, Bahrain, Barbados, Belize, Macao, Mauritius, and South Africa. Six of the additions are small islands or city-states. With the exception of Macao, all of the countries on this expanded list were once British colonies or protectorates, and all of them achieved their independence peacefully.

South Africa is the additional large country on the list of the "successful thirteen." Like Canada and New Zealand, South Africa is a democracy that for most of its history gave English settlers power beyond their numbers. Indeed, the 1910 constitution of the Union of South Africa, as well as its subsequent revisions and enabling laws, went to great lengths to disenfranchise the country's numerically dominant African and Indian populations. The British in South Africa, ironically in cooperation with the Boers, whom they had compelled to be part of the Union by force, did not just create an unelected and malapportioned upper house (the way they did in Canada and New Zealand): they aggressively whittled away at the laws governing the franchise so that by 1956 "blacks" and "coloureds" had no political voice at all.

South Africa's 1997 constitution finally established full and equal suffrage for all South Africans, but because it was a brokered agreement between the apartheid government and the African National Congress, it contains a number of institutions designed to forestall attempts to redistribute income and wealth. First and foremost among these is a weak president who is not directly elected by the population but indirectly elected by the lower house of parliament. His right to veto legislation is then limited by a constitutional court. Second, the upper house of parliament, which must approve all legislation, is not elected but appointed by the provincial legislatures, with each province having the same number of representatives regardless of its population. Moreover, depending on the type of bill under consideration, the passage of legislation by the upper house may require a supermajority. In fact, under some circumstances, bills in the lower house must also be passed by supermajorities. In sum, although South Africa's political institutions were not crafted with bank regulation in mind, those institutions make it very hard for populist movements to form coalitions with bankers to enact bank regulatory policies that benefit them at the expense of everyone else.

If the "very successful six" and "successful thirteen" tend to be either city-states, small islands, or democracies with institutions that limit populist currents, then what do their mirror images look like? That is, what are the characteristics of the countries that are preternaturally crisis prone and that provide very low levels of private credit relative to their GDP?

If we invert the "very successful six" threshold and ask which countries have had at least two systemic banking crises since 1970, and also have had an average ratio of private credit to GDP at least one standard deviation below the mean since 1991, we find that there are two "very unsuccessful" countries: Chad and the Democratic Republic of the Congo. It would not take lengthy argumentation to show that these are among the least democratic countries in the world (their average polity scores since 1970 have been 30 and 26, respectively).

If we invert the criteria for the "successful thirteen" and ask which countries have had at least two banking crises and a ratio of private credit to GDP equal to or less than the mean since 1991, we obtain a list of the "unsuccessful sixteen" countries—most of which have been persistently autocratic, have had short experiments with democracy that ended in coups, or have only recently begun to experiment with democracy after long periods of autocratic rule. In addition to Chad and the Democratic Republic of the Congo, the "unsuccessful sixteen" include Argentina, Bolivia, Brazil, Cameroon, the Central African Republic, Colombia, Costa Rica, Ecuador, Kenya, Mexico, Nigeria, the Philippines, Turkey, and Uruguay. For the period since 1970, the average polity score for this group is only 58; it would be lower still if we took the average over a longer period. Of these countries, only three maintained average polity scores above 80 for the period 1970–2011: Costa Rica (100), Colombia (88), and Turkey (82). In sum, we are struck by how few exceptions there are to a general pattern: countries with stable banking systems that provide abundant credit tend to be stable democracies with institutions that limit the opportunities for bankers and populists to form rent-seeking coalitions; countries with unstable banking systems that provide low levels of credit tend to either be autocracies, democracies of very recent vintage, or democracies in which the institutions that limit rent seeking are weak.

Going beyond Simple Bivariate Relationships

An even more skeptical reader might point out that these patterns in the data do not necessarily imply a causal relationship. Such a reader might argue that stable and efficient banking might foster democracy rather than vice versa, or that some unobserved factor might be causing both democracy and a stable, efficient banking sector.

A number of researchers have exploited statistical techniques to address these questions. One approach is to employ instrumental variables. This is a statistical technique in which a third variable that cannot plausibly be interpreted as causing an outcome on its own (in our case, banking development), but which is related to the hypothesized cause of that outcome (in our case, the level of democracy), is used to control for the possibility that causality might be operating in both directions. A recent study that employs such an approach, by Philip Keefer, finds not only that democratic political institutions are robustly correlated with the growth of bank credit but also that democratic political institutions work by providing more secure private-property rights.[4]

A study by James Barth, Gerard Caprio, and Ross Levine employs instrumental-variables methods to explore the causal mechanisms that link democratic political institutions to high levels of credit and banking-system stability. They find that democratic political institutions are associated with greater ease in obtaining a bank charter and fewer restrictions on the operation of banks. They also find that the tight regulatory restrictions on banks created by autocratic political institutions are associated with less credit and less bank stability. This analysis is broadly consistent with a number of findings from our structural narratives. It suggests that countries' choices of regulatory policies, and the supervisory structures to implement them, are predictable outcomes of those countries' political

[4] Keefer (2008).

arrangements. Complex regulatory frameworks with greater regulatory discretion are more likely to arise in environments with greater corruption. Core political factors, including the extent of constraints on the executive branch of government and the degree of accountability of politicians, predict the degree of regulatory discretion, the extent to which governments regulate the activities of banks, the extent of entry barriers in banking, and the extent to which governments protect banks from private market monitoring and discipline. The implication is that complex, discretionary regulatory systems that limit entry and encourage bribery tend to be chosen in environments where politicians are less accountable to citizens.[5] Their results also suggest that regulatory and supervisory choices tend to be the outcomes of political bargains, not the results of the application of economic principles by wise and disinterested legislators seeking to achieve banking-system efficiency.

Researchers have also used statistical techniques to control for the possibility that some unobserved characteristic of countries jointly determines both democracy and banking development. They do so by exploiting variation within countries over time: basically, they ask whether changes in political institutions toward more democracy precede (rather than follow) changes in the amount of bank credit. This technique is employed by Michael Bordo and Peter Rousseau, who analyze 17 countries over the period 1880–1997. They find that several measures of the extent of democracy—proportional representative election systems, frequent elections, universal female suffrage, and a low propensity for revolutions or coups—are favorable preconditions for the expansion of banking credit. They also find that expanded banking credit precedes rather than follows higher economic growth.[6] A more recent study that exploits within-country variation, by Marc Quintyn and Geneviève Verdier, examines the entire world from 1960 to 2005 and shows that the ability of financial liberalizations to produce sustained bank-credit growth depends on a country's political institutions: regimes that are more democratic and more stable are much more conducive to sustaining credit growth than other regimes.[7] In short, however one looks at statistical data, the

---

[5] Barth, Caprio, and Levine (2006).

[6] Bordo and Rousseau (2006). See also Bordo and Rousseau (2012), which shows the robustness of these results to the inclusion of other factors.

[7] Quintyn and Verdier (2010).

results suggest that the causal narratives of our five case studies are broadly representative of the experiences of other countries.

Government Safety Nets for Banks

One of the other major lessons that emerges from our structural narratives is that government safety nets for banks, such as deposit insurance, actually tend to be destabilizing. Our narratives also suggest that these safety nets emerged not because they were economically more efficient but as the outcomes of political bargains. Indeed, the notion that deposit insurance, bailouts, and other government-provided support are essential for stabilizing banks is belied by Canada's experience: despite the highly cyclical nature of the Canadian economy and the absence of deposit insurance for most of its history, Canada has never experienced a significant banking insolvency crisis (and its last significant liquidity crisis was in 1839). This fact is particularly striking when one considers that, for most of that time, including the Great Depression, Canada operated without even a lender of last resort: the Bank of Canada was not founded until 1935.

As we show in chapter 6, nationwide deposit insurance was instituted in the United States in 1933 in spite of the widespread understanding of its adverse consequences. As then-candidate Franklin Roosevelt wrote in a 1932 letter to the *New York Sun,* deposit insurance "would lead to laxity in bank management and carelessness on the part of both banker and depositor. I believe that it would be an impossible drain on the Federal Treasury."[8] Protection of banks, however, in 1933 and since, serves an important political purpose: to reduce the cost of funding for the banks that enjoy its protection. That protection tends to be greatest in environments where banks have the power to demand it.[9]

Do these patterns extend to the experiences of other countries? Is deposit insurance a source of instability, and is it an outcome of a political bargain? There is a broad literature on deposit insurance around the world, much of which employs cross-country statistical comparisons. Its central conclusions are that the more generous the safety net, the more unstable the banking system, and that political influences have been cen-

---

[8] Quoted in Prins (2009), 139.

[9] Caprio and Klingebiel (1996); Demirgüç-Kunt and Detragiache (2002); Cull, Senbet, and Sorge (2005); Honohan and Klingebiel (2003); Barth, Caprio, and Levine (2006), chapter 4; Demirgüç-Kunt, Kane, and Laeven (2008); Beck and Laeven (2008).

tral to government decisions to expand safety nets. Several studies find that more generous safety nets predict more banking crises. Those studies also find that the destabilizing effects of deposit insurance are especially great in institutionally weak political environments.[10] Other studies of the mechanisms through which protection encourages risk taking show that deposit insurance makes the funding costs of banks less sensitive to the risks the banks undertake.[11]

The role of politics in governments' decisions to adopt deposit insurance is also clearly apparent. The literature shows that identifiable political circumstances substantially increase the probability of enacting deposit insurance. In 1980, only 20 countries guaranteed deposits; by 2003, 87 countries did so. A study of the factors that led to deposit-insurance adoption during this period by Asli Demirgüç-Kunt, Edward Kane, and Luc Laeven concludes that political pressures, both internal and external to the country, played an important role. The external pressures include advice from the World Bank and circumstances relating to candidacy for membership in the European Union. The study also captures internal political pressures through a variety of domestic political measures (polity score, the extent of corruption, the complexity of bureaucracy, constraints on the executive branch of government, and proxies for political competition and democratic accountability). The results of this study indicate that democracies that weakly constrain the authority and discretion of the executive branch of government are more likely to adopt deposit insurance. It also offers some evidence that corrupt countries are more likely, all else being equal, to adopt deposit insurance. Finally, the study finds that when deposit insurance is adopted in the wake of a financial crisis, governments tend to design their systems especially poorly, resulting in even greater problems of moral hazard.[12]

Yes, but What about China?

A preternaturally skeptical reader might now be tempted to hunt for individual cases that constitute exceptions to our framework. To that reader we say that individual exceptions to patterns do not constitute evidence

---

[10] Demirgüç-Kunt and Detragiache (2002); Cull, Senbet, and Sorge (2005).
[11] For example, Demirgüç-Kunt and Huizinga (2004).
[12] Demirgüç-Kunt, Kane, and Laeven (2008).

that a pattern does not exist. The fact that some people smoke like chimneys and live to be 100 does not falsify the theory that cigarettes cause cancer.

Nevertheless, we think that it is incumbent on us to give skepticism its due. After all, the discovery of enough exceptions suggests that something essential may be missing from a conceptual framework. Let us then start with a case that likely will be on the minds of many readers: China, in which the banking sector has grown large in recent decades, in a political context that is very far from democratic. We also look at three other cases in which banking systems expanded rapidly and remained stable—Japan during the Meiji Restoration (1868–1912), the German Empire (1871–1918), and Chile under Pinochet (1973–90)—and enquire about the nature of their political institutions.

According to our theory, autocracies can generate fast-growing and at least locally stable banking systems when the government is strong enough to centralize decision making, but not so strong that it can reduce the property rights of bankers, bank stockholders, and depositors with impunity. Japan during the Meiji Restoration and Germany under the Iron Chancellor are examples of these kinds of centralizing autocracies. If the groups in control of the government have untrammeled power, however, it will be extraordinarily difficult to create a private banking system, because no promise they make not to expropriate the banks will be credible. China is an example of this kind of authoritarian system, and as a result it does not actually have much of a private banking system at all: a system of state-owned banks dominates the credit markets. China's absence of a successful private banking system, therefore, fits our theory. Chile under Pinochet may be something of an exception, but that exceptionalism is not clear cut: the Pinochet government managed to build a robust private banking system only after a disastrous bank privatization that had many of the hallmarks of similar fiascos in other authoritarian regimes.

China

The Chinese government has privatized large swaths of the economy—particularly in agriculture, manufacturing, and mining—and these sectors have propelled the growth of the Chinese economy over the past three decades. China's large banks have not, however, been truly privatized;

they are all government-controlled and remain largely government-owned. Their primary mission is to provide credit to state-owned enterprises (SOEs). The loans provided by these banks often result in large losses. When banks' loan losses become very large, they are absorbed explicitly by the state through a bailout (the most recent of which was in 2000). Furthermore, because even the privately controlled banks in China are subject to substantial expropriation risk, their activities are quite limited. What would keep the government from forcing any banker to lend to some pet government enterprise, lend to some pet project run by a government crony, or place 50 percent of his deposit base into the central bank and earn zero percent interest? As we discuss below, those who invest in the Chinese banking system know going in that they are subject to arbitrary actions by the state and that they may be called upon to perform favors for the state or its SOEs. Those SOEs are favored by the state because they generate employment and political support for the Communist Party, but in doing so they rack up losses for the banks that provide them with credit.

Under the long dictatorship of Mao Zedong, normal banking functions did not exist in China. As in other communist countries, banking in China essentially amounted to an accounting system for tracking cash flows associated with central planning. It had nothing to do with attracting deposits, granting credit, clearing market transactions, or managing risk. Until the economy was liberalized after Mao's death in 1976, wages and prices were set by the government, lifetime employment was guaranteed, and production was monopolized by SOEs. The government was in effect the owner of all assets and output: it had unrivaled political power and economic control.

This government-owned economy had an obvious problem: for private individuals, the incentives to produce were weak, and the incentives to cheat the government were strong. Mao's successors came to recognize that the continuation of a government-run economy would make China increasingly irrelevant in the world. Unless they privatized the economy, China could ultimately become as militarily and diplomatically inconsequential as North Korea. Thus, starting in the mid-1980s and accelerating in the 1990s, a series of reforms allowed nearly all prices to be set by the market. Private enterprise was allowed, even encouraged. Many SOEs were wholly or partly privatized.

The decision to modernize China's financial sector to promote continuing economic growth coincided with Deng Xiaoping's famous "southern tour" in 1992, which solidified support for his reformist economic agenda. SOEs were privatized—with the exception of some key industries.[13] Privatization occurred piecemeal, with large initial stakes retained by the government or by government-controlled "legal persons" (a legal construct that includes government entities of various kinds and SOEs). Firms were permitted to use the stock exchanges that had been created in Shanghai and Shenzhen in the early 1990s, as well as the Hong Kong stock market, to raise funds in domestic and foreign equity markets.

The banking system created to accompany this economic liberalization was, however, completely state dominated. In addition to the central bank (the People's Bank of China), it initially consisted primarily of four giant government-owned banks—the Bank of China, the China Construction Bank, the Agricultural Bank of China, and the Industrial and Commercial Bank of China. Each of these banks was meant to specialize in financing particular sectors or types of transactions, but over time all four banks became more similar in their functions. Subsequently, other state-controlled banks and private banks were permitted to operate, but these were of very modest scale. By the end of 1994, the central bank had permitted nonstate banks to organize a total of only 130 branches, 98 subbranches, and 724 offices below the subbranch level, while the big four state-owned banks possessed 138,081 offices below the subbranch level.[14] As of 2003, the four biggest state-owned banks still accounted for approximately 55 percent of all the assets in the banking system. These state-owned banks continue to dominate the banking system, although new nonbank sources of credit have become important in recent years.

The state ownership of the largest banks in China is no accident: it allows the government to reward its friends and generate employment, which is crucial to the survival of the regime. The dominant source of economic growth, however, is the private sector, and private-sector investment drives the business cycle. But the ability of the private sector to invest depends crucially on its access to credit, and the amount of credit available varies over time in response to mandates from the People's Bank of China.

---

[13] Some shares in banks were sold, but they remain government controlled.
[14] Branstetter (2007), 31.

When inflation rises, the People's Bank restricts credit growth, rationing credit in favor of SOEs. It does so partly because of the political connections of their managers, but also because the employment provided by SOEs is so politically crucial. The workers in China's cities do not support the government because they believe in communism or the Chinese Communist Party; they support it because the Party gives them their jobs. Thus, when credit becomes scarce, the brunt of credit rationing is felt by the high-growth firms in the private sector with fewer political connections.[15]

Interest rates on banks' loans and deposits are set by the government. Interest-rate regulation has multiple functions. First, a high spread between loan and deposit interest rates provides a profit cushion to the big state-owned banks. This cushion is important because the loans from state-owned banks to SOEs produce large and continuous losses. Hundreds of billions of dollars' worth of loan losses were written off (absorbed by the government, and thus paid for by the treasury) in the early 2000s, and most analysts judge that state-owned banks have probably generated nonperforming loans of similar magnitudes in the decade since. These losses remain unrecognized: they are simply rolled over into new, "evergreened" loans.[16] Second, maintaining low interest rates on deposits limits pressure to appreciate the currency and thus helps to support export growth.[17] In short, China's banking system cannot be characterized as having succeeded in channeling large amounts of credit to private, competitive uses through good risk management.

China's banking sector is not, therefore, a success story of private banking development under authoritarianism. The ability of the banking system to sustain China's remarkable growth rates of the past three decades appears uncertain.[18] Inefficient directed lending, interest-rate controls, and periodic massive bailouts remain essential tools for sustaining the political regime. If the Chinese banking system were truly private and could set interest rates and allocate credit according to efficiency criteria, the result-

---

[15] Branstetter (2007); Brandt and Zhou (2007); Ayyagari, Demirgüç-Kunt, and Maksimovic (2010).

[16] Branstetter (2007); Brandt and Zhou (2007).

[17] Although capital inflows other than foreign direct investment and limited purchases of equity are prohibited, there are ways for foreigners to disguise capital inflows (Prasad and Wei [2007]), which they would be more encouraged to do if the government permitted interest rates to rise.

[18] Pei (2006); Calomiris (2007).

ing shrinkage of state-owned enterprises would pose a huge political risk to a regime that basically buys political quiescence with factory jobs. Many analysts recognize that continuing growth in China depends on freeing the banking system from state control, but it is hard to see precisely how China's political institutions will change to make such liberalization feasible.

Germany

What then of Germany? Did the growth of banking and heavy industry not coincide with the rule of Otto von Bismarck, who was a one-man cabinet to the German Kaiser? And was it not the case that Bismarck was a Prussian aristocrat who is primarily known for centralizing power in a unified German state?

There is no doubt that the German approach to universal banking was associated with rapid expansion of credit, particularly to industry. It was also a new model of banking. Perfected in the last quarter of the nineteenth century, it combined nationwide branch banking, lending, deposit taking, securities underwriting, and asset management under the same roof. It therefore gave the largest banks far more control over industrial firms than banks in the United States or England. Typically, a German bank began its relationship with an industrial firm by lending to it, often on a very short-term basis, with the loans financed by deposits. As the firm grew and its financing needs expanded, the same bank underwrote equity offerings for it. Those equity offerings could be placed in the bank's network of asset-management accounts. These practices concentrated voting power and control over industrial firms within the banking system, thereby facilitating stockholders' ability to discipline corporate management. Indeed, the cartelized nature of the German economy during this period is often traced, at least in part, to the influence of the large banks that sought to create an orderly market (that is, one without a lot of competition).

The German central bank controlled the supply of banknotes and maintained convertibility of the currency into gold. A network of savings banks and credit cooperatives—which together accounted for roughly 30 percent of financial-system assets by 1913—each developed its own private institutions for mutual monitoring and emergency assistance during times of financial turmoil, which were similar in some respects to the successful interbank arrangements observed in Canada and antebellum Indiana and

Ohio. Germany's banking system not only provided abundant and diverse sources of credit, but it was virtually crisis free from 1860 to 1930 (with the exception of the 1873 crisis, which occurred during the early phase of Germany's banking system's development).[19]

The question before us, then, is whether Germany during the late nineteenth century constitutes an exception to the patterns identified in our structural narratives. What was the constellation of political institutions that underpinned the German banking system?

The answer is that, despite its autocratic features, Germany actually had a number of representative institutions that limited the authority and discretion of its chancellor and Kaiser. Until its political unification in 1871, Germany was a politically fragmented and loosely connected group of sovereign states. Bringing these states together into a single federation, dominated by Prussia, involved both war—particularly the military defeats of Austria and France by Prussia in 1866 and 1871 respectively— and negotiation. In fact, the states retained their own local governance structures. Each constituent state had its own parliamentary system, and the German Empire itself had a bicameral legislature. The Reichsrat was an unelected upper house that represented the interests of the constituent states. The Reichstag (lower house) was popularly elected under rules of universal adult male suffrage. In order to become law, bills had to be passed by a majority in both the Reichsrat and the Reichstag.

None of this is to say that Germany's political institutions were unambiguously democratic. The Reichsrat had more power than the Reichstag. Neither house could initiate legislation: they could only block, amend, or pass it. The chancellor reported to the Kaiser, not to the legislature, and only the Kaiser could remove him from office. The German Empire was, however, a far cry from what Germany would become under Hitler in the 1930s. The German chancellor did not have unlimited authority and discretion. He was not Mao Zedong or Deng Xiaoping. He could not reduce property rights at will. Indeed, he could be removed from office—as Bismarck himself found out in 1890, when he was forced out by Kaiser Wilhelm II. Impor-

---

[19] For discussions of the operations of the German banks and their regulation, performance, and role in German economic development and industrialization, see Jeidels (1905); Riesser (1911); Whale (1930); Gerschenkron (1962); R. Tilly (1966, 1967, 1982, 1986, 1992, 2010); Eistert (1970); Calomiris (2000), chapter 4; Guinnane (2002); Fohlin (2011).

tantly, none of the chancellors that followed Bismarck—at least until Hitler —achieved the same kind of authority or continuity in power.

Bismarck needed Germany's financiers and industrialists as much as they needed him. Germany at the time of unification was backward and poor. To catch up economically and militarily with its rivals, the German government promoted economic policies designed to industrialize the country, among which was a program of chartering banks to finance that industrial base. Indeed, the government's promotion of Germany's universal banks was crucially linked to military and colonial ambitions.

When the German Empire was formed, it was far from clear that it would succeed as a territorial state: it was threatened by the growing Russian Empire in the east, the Austro-Hungarian Empire to its south, and France in the west. Given that the survival of the state depended on building the economic capacity to defeat those rivals, Bismarck needed to pull the nascent country's industrialists and financiers into a coalition. Many of them were not Prussian; they came from western or southern provinces that were in many respects outside of the chancellor's control.

In short, the rapid growth of the German banking system in the late nineteenth century is not an exception to the patterns we identify in our structural narratives. In the first place, the growth of the banking system was driven by the need to create the basis for a successful state. In the second place, Bismarck did not have untrammeled power; his authority was limited by an unelected upper house and a lower house that was elected on the basis of universal adult male suffrage. The German chancellor had greater authority than a U.S. president or a British prime minister; but he did not have a rubber-stamp congress as Mexico's Porfirio Díaz did at the end of his long reign, and he could not predetermine elections as in Brazil under the Old Republic.

Japan

How about Japan? Does it present an exception to the patterns we have identified? As of 1973, Japan was the only country outside Western Europe, the United States, or other countries of British colonial settlement to achieve a per capita income matching that of Western Europe.[20] The crucial early

---

[20] Maddison (2001) estimates Japan's 1973 per capita GDP at $11,439 (in units of constant 1990 purchasing power), compared to $11,534 for Western Europe and

period of rapid growth in Japan was the four decades prior to World War I, a period when Japan transformed itself into a world power through a conscious process of imitating Western institutions and promoting industrialization and export-led growth. From 1878 to 1914, Japan's GDP grew at an annual rate of about 4 percent, and exports grew at nearly twice that rate.[21] Japan, therefore, is a unique historical case of early non-European economic development.

As late as the 1860s, Japan was a relatively isolated agrarian economy with a low per capita income. Its backwardness was made readily apparent by the arrival in 1853 of a U.S. fleet under the command of Commodore Matthew Perry, who forcibly opened up Japan to foreign commerce under the threat of naval bombardment. Japanese elites, like other elites we have discussed, realized that they needed to modernize their economy or else become a province or colony of a competing state.

The underlying weaknesses of the Japanese economic system were clear: it closely resembled the European feudal system. The need to modernize this economy set off a decade-long struggle resulting in what is rather inaccurately referred to as the Meiji Restoration. The emperor was restored to power, but under a new system of government that came to resemble that of the West. It took several decades to work out an appropriate set of political institutions, culminating in the Meiji constitution of 1890. Japan's political system was one of limited contestability. The emperor was not a constitutional monarch, but he shared power with a bicameral legislature. The upper house of the legislature was composed of nobles and oligarchs, many of whom had military backgrounds; the lower house was directly elected, although property qualifications meant that only a very small slice of Japanese society (perhaps as small as 1 percent) was entitled to run for office. The lack of cohesion among the oligarchy that controlled the upper house gave rise to political parties that competed aggressively for seats in the lower house.[22]

During the three decades prior to World War I, the Meiji government actively promoted economic growth. Japan not only industrialized and de-

---

$16,172 on average for the United States, Canada, Australia, and New Zealand. Eastern Europe averaged $4,985, the former USSR averaged $6,058, Latin America averaged $4,531, Africa averaged $1,365, and Asia, excluding Japan, averaged $1,231.

[21] Patrick (1967), 242–43.

[22] Ramsayer and Rosenbluth (1998), chapters 2–4.

veloped a military capable of soundly defeating the Russians in the Russo-Japanese War of 1905, but it also became a major trading partner of the West, and an active borrower in London's capital markets.

As in Germany, the Meiji government understood that a modernized financial system was a key to its political and military ambitions.[23] The existing financial system of small, informal lenders was replaced with a modern financial system, consisting of government-chartered, limited-liability commercial banks and other financial institutions modeled on examples from the West. Japan originally imitated the U.S. national banking system, but, seeing it as problematic in several respects, the government soon switched to a system of banking charters more akin to the British system, including the chartering of a central bank operating under the gold standard. From 1888 to 1901, the number of banks and the amount of bank lending rose sixfold. This growth was associated with the codification and unification of bank charters under the Bank Act of 1890, which encouraged open competition in the banking system.

The Meiji banking system was a mix of extremely large banks that operated as the treasury arms of big industrial and commercial groups, known as Zaibatsu; special-purpose banks that were sponsored by the government; and more than 1,000 small banks that served local or regional markets. During the Meiji period, those small banks used their influence with one of the two major political parties, the Seiyukai, to block legislation promoted by the large banks to impose minimum capital requirements. The goal of that proposed legislation was to limit competition by forcing smaller banks to merge or close.[24]

Economic historians ascribe much of Japan's developmental success to its banking system. Not only was the banking system designed "in advance of the industrial demand for its loans and other financial services" by a government that sought to promote industrial growth and exports, but banks—particularly the larger ones—were chartered in order to play precisely that role, and they succeeded in doing so.[25] The special-purpose banks were used by the government to promote fixed investments in agri-

---

[23] Patrick (1967), 240.

[24] The larger banks finally got their way in 1927. Ramseyer and Rosenbluth (1998), chapter 8.

[25] Patrick (1967), 277. For quantitative analysis of the links between financial factors and growth in Japan from 1880 to 1913, see Rousseau (1999).

culture, industry, electric power, and transportation. The government itself played an active role in these banks: it guaranteed their dividends at 5 percent for the first ten years of their charters. The ministry of finance appointed their officers and directors. The government also provided financial assistance when troubles arose. For example, the Industrial Bank was bailed out in 1913 after it made government-mandated loans to gold-mining companies during the Russo-Japanese War that were not repaid.

What are we then to make of the case of Japan? When we strip down the Meiji system to the bare wood, we see an authoritarian political system dominated by powerful oligarchs with deep ties to the military, which adopted some of the trappings of Western representative government because those oligarchs could not agree with one another.[26] The architects of the Meiji constitution had quite consciously studied and borrowed from the political systems of the United States, England, Germany, and Spain. From Germany they adapted the form of the legislature and the rules governing it. The result was a political system that was a good deal less democratic than even the German version. But neither the Japanese emperor nor his prime minister had untrammeled power. Moreover, as in Germany, the parties in control of the government in Meiji Japan understood that they needed the country's industrialists and bankers as much as, if not more than, the industrialists and bankers needed them. They could not abrogate property rights at will if they wanted to survive as a state. Indeed, the government bailout of the Industrial Bank in 1913 signaled the government's awareness that its success depended on the survival of the banking system. That the Meiji political system gave rise to a growing banking system that was used to fund a crash course in economic modernization is hardly surprising.

Chile

Chile in the late twentieth century was a more extreme case of autocracy than either the German Empire or Meiji Japan. Under the brutal dictatorship of Augusto Pinochet from 1973 to 1990, it lacked even the symbolic institutions of representative government. Pinochet and his military government tortured and murdered their opponents, suspended the constitution, closed the congress, and banned political parties.

---

[26] Ramseyer and Rosenbluth (1998), chapters 2 and 3.

Chile's banking system experienced remarkable growth under Pinochet's regime. Bank credit relative to GDP grew eightfold from 1975 to 1990, from 5 percent of GDP to 41 percent, and then continued growing after Pinochet was forced from power, reaching 69 percent of GDP by 2010.[27] The successful liberalization of banking also was accompanied by the creation of an active stock market and the privatization of the pension system, which gave rise to the growth of a large system of private pension funds that were active purchasers in local debt and equity markets. That involvement has propelled impressive growth in Chile's capital markets: by 2000, Chile boasted one of the highest proportions of equity to GDP among emerging-market countries. Financial development of both banks and capital markets has accompanied and contributed to Chile's remarkable economic development: Chile's per capita real GDP nearly tripled from 1985 to 2011.[28]

Casual empiricism would therefore suggest that Chile under Pinochet is a clear exception to the patterns we have identified in this book, but when one looks more closely, the growth of the Chilean banking system does not look quite so exceptional. The Pinochet dictatorship brought to an end a nearly four-decade-long experiment in democracy and an almost equally long period of financial repression. From the 1930s to the mid-1970s, Chile had a small and tightly regulated financial system.[29] Under the presidency of Salvador Allende (in office 1970–73), that small banking system was easily nationalized: the government simply bought the shares of the few banks that existed, and it could buy them at low prices precisely because the financial sector had been repressed for so long.[30] The

---

[27] Data are from World Bank (2012).

[28] International Monetary Fund (2012b).

[29] Financial repression both before and during the Allende government was the result of five main policies. First, interest-rate ceilings on loans implied substantial negative real rates of interest to banks. Second, interest-rate ceilings on deposits limited savers' incentives to deposit funds into banks. Third, government-directed credit mandates targeted specific borrowers, forcing banks to make unprofitable loans to politically favored constituencies. Fourth, high cash-reserve requirements at the central bank forced banks to hold a substantial portion of their assets at the central bank in the form of a zero-interest loan. Finally, the very high rate of inflation maintained by the government amplified the economic costs of the interest ceilings, the reserve requirements, and the directed credit policies.

[30] One bank remained outside government control: the Banco do Chile, which remains Chile's largest bank.

Allende government not only nationalized Chile's banks, it also expropriated the mining industry and expanded a land reform that had been initiated under Allende's predecessors. Allende also expanded social-welfare programs and paid for them with an inflation tax. When the Allende government was overthrown, it was running a fiscal deficit of 14 percent of GDP, and inflation had reached an annualized rate of 1,000 percent.[31]

The Pinochet government reversed Allende's policies. It passed a dramatic fiscal reform in 1975, which eliminated its deficit by 1976. It cut tariffs and encouraged foreign direct investment. It also privatized many of the firms that had been nationalized by Allende. There were a number of remarkable features of these reforms, not the least of which was their rapidity.[32]

One thing that was not remarkable, however, was the process by which the Pinochet government reprivatized its banking system. In 1975, when the government auctioned off the banks, the government's stance toward a privately owned economy was far from clear. Some elements of the military preferred an economy that was government controlled or guided, because they were concerned that Chile's lack of comparative advantage in many lines of industry would undermine its national security. Those junta members continued to exert considerable influence until 1978, when Pinochet won a power struggle with General Gustavo Leigh of the air force, forcing him out of the government.[33]

Making the bank privatization even more problematic was the fact that the military government faced no sanction for breaking its promises, so no promise it made was deemed credible. In fact, in the midst of a crisis of the country's savings and loan institutions in June 1975, the government arbitrarily limited deposit withdrawals, forcing the rescheduling of their obligations. This precipitated an almost total collapse of Chile's S&Ls. The evidence strongly suggests that Chile's potential bankers were nervous about the fact that the government could reduce their property rights at will and had multiple mechanisms for doing so—including the manipulation of the deposit-reserve requirements imposed by the central

---

[31] De la Cuadra and Valdes (1992), 14.

[32] Details about the Chilean liberalization can be found in Díaz Alejandro (1985); Edwards and Edwards (1991); de la Cuadra and Valdes (1992); and Beim and Calomiris (2001), 122–26.

[33] Edwards (2010), 105, 108–9.

bank.[34] Not surprisingly, Chile's bankers offered low prices when the government auctioned off the banks, and even those prices were artificially inflated by the fact that the government allowed the bankers to borrow up to 90 percent of the purchase price of the banks from the same government entity that was auctioning them.[35] To further support investments in banks, no limit was placed on insider lending after banks were purchased.

The process of Chile's bank privatization was therefore remarkably similar to that in Mexico in 1991–92 under the PRI: the banks were purchased in leveraged buyouts that put little of the bankers' own capital at risk. Bankers thus had strong incentives to engage in massive insider lending and to take wild risks. Chile's bankers went on a lending spree. The comparison to the Mexican bank privatization of 1991–92 is also apt in that Chile's bankers, like Mexico's, were granted considerable regulatory forbearance. "[R]ules on collateral and secured loans were simple and many loans were not properly secured; rules on nonperforming loans and provisions for loan losses were below international standards; and rules on the assessment and classification of loan risks were implemented gradually . . . [T]he rules about connected lending were enforced poorly and banks were able to take advantage of many loopholes in the regulatory system."[36] As in Mexico, a very high proportion of the loans advanced by Chile's banks therefore went to related parties, which is to say to enterprises owned by bank directors or their relatives, and many of those loans were granted at lower rates of interest than were charged to unrelated parties.[37]

An additional parallel to the Mexican case is that the government followed a fixed-exchange-rate regime that overvalued the currency[38] and

---

[34] Barandiarán and Hernández (1999), 6; Martínez and Díaz (1996), 58.
[35] Barandiarán and Hernández (1999), 5.
[36] Barandiarán and Hernández (1999), 8.
[37] Barandiarán and Hernández (1999), 10.
[38] In countries with pegged exchange rates, government-protected banks with low or negative net worth face strong incentives to borrow in foreign currency because interest rates are typically lower, especially as the risk of a devaluation mounts. Moral hazard encourages this type of borrowing because the risk of capital loss from a currency devaluation, which is inherent in foreign currency-denominated borrowings, is borne by taxpayers. Devaluation can add substantially to the resolution costs of a banking crisis. This explains why the so-called twin crises of exchange-rate devaluation and banking collapse that were so common in emerging-market countries during the 1980s and 1990s tended to produce much larger cleanup costs than other crises.

then allowed the banks to fund themselves by borrowing abroad in dollars.[39] As in Mexico, the government ultimately had to devalue the currency, precipitating a collapse of many of the banks that had liabilities in dollars but assets denominated in local currency. The inability of many banks to service their liabilities forced the government to intervene and bail out both the creditors and debtors of the banks. As in Mexico, the prospect of bailouts encouraged moral hazard, so that government bailouts became an ongoing and escalating process. Between 1981 and 1986, the government intervened in 21 Chilean financial institutions, accounting for slightly over half of the assets of the banking system. Some of them were liquidated. Others had their balance sheets cleaned up at public expense and then were reprivatized.[40] When they were taken over, the liquidators found that roughly one-quarter of the banks' loans had been made to related parties. At the Banco de Santiago, related-party loans equaled 45 percent of the bank's portfolio.[41]

How the Pinochet government reestablished credibility so that the Chilean banking system ultimately emerged as the strongest in Latin America is a story that is still to be written. We hypothesize that by the mid-1980s, Pinochet did not have to convince the population that his dictatorship was not a threat to their property rights. Rather, the threat to property rights had come from the left-wing democratic government that he had overthrown. It was therefore possible for Pinochet to make a credible commitment to financial property rights, that is, to the security of bank shares and deposits.

What to our minds is particularly impressive is that the disaster of 1982–83 did not seem to damage the public view that the Pinochet dictatorship was committed to policies that would enhance, rather than reduce, property rights in finance. The government instituted improvements in its prudential regulatory system beginning in 1985.[42] Chilean reforms proved to be far more effective than those of many developed countries in creating a credible system of prudential regulation based on transparent accounting, substantial capital requirements, and limited safety

[39] In Mexico, the exchange rate followed a crawling peg rather than being a strictly fixed rate. Barandiarán and Hernández (1999), 9.

[40] Barandiarán and Hernández (1999), 20–44.

[41] Barandiarán and Hernández (1999), 45, 47.

[42] Ramirez and Rosende (1992).

net protection. Since 1983, Chile has therefore avoided the banking crises that plagued many other Latin American countries and many developed economies.

Conclusion

Our answer to the central question posed in chapter 1—why can't all countries construct banking systems capable of providing stable and abundant credit?—is that political conditions constrain what is possible. History, and the political institutions that arise from it, play an essential constructive role in banking but also limit what is feasible within each country's banking system.

A major theme of this book is that every country's banking system is the result of a Game of Bank Bargains, which determines the rules that define how banks are chartered, how they are regulated, and how they interact with the state. Those outcomes, in turn, determine how well the country will perform along two key dimensions: the degree of private access to credit and the propensity for banking crises.

Chartered banks are always the outcomes of political partnerships that include both the government and the coalition of citizens that wins control over shaping the banking system. The state depends on banks as a source of revenue, lending, and other financial assistance. States need banks, and banks cannot function without the active cooperation of the state to define their legal identity, preserve their contractual rights, and allow them to function under predictable rules that will attract depositors, stockholders, and borrowers.

In a consolidated, centralized autocracy, the government cannot constrain itself from expropriating banks, which means that private actors have very weak incentives to found banks that provide private credit at arm's length. As a result, highly centralized autocratic regimes, such as that of China, tend to produce banking systems that are state owned. When an autocrat cannot fully centralize power, it is possible for the autocrat to form a partnership with a group of financiers to establish a private banking system, but that banking system will not resemble the independent credit intermediaries found in finance textbooks. The banks exist to finance the government and the nonfinancial business interests of their directors. The Game of Bank Bargains is played by a small and exclusive group of government officials and businessmen who are often closely linked by a variety of personal and political ties.

Democracy generally achieves outcomes superior to those of autocracy, because a democratic government's ability to expropriate is limited by political and legal institutions. Although credit tends to be more readily available under democracy, expropriation of bank assets by the voting majority presents a new risk, and barriers to bank entry may still distort and limit credit availability. In democracies, the supply of bank credit available to private parties tends to be much greater than in autocracies, but democracies are not uniform in this respect or in the degree to which they suffer from instability of credit due to crises. The historical circumstances that shape the formation of the political institutions and coalitions that control banking outcomes are crucial in determining the extent to which democracies suffer scarce credit and banking crises.

15

IIIIIIIIIIIIIIIIIIIIIIIII

Reality Is a Plague on Many Houses

Our late experience has taught us that many of those fundamental principles, formerly believed infallible, are either not of the importance they
were imagined to be; or that we have not at all adverted to some other far
more important and far more powerful principles, which entirely overrule
those we had considered as omnipotent.

Edmund Burke,
"Speech on Conciliation with America" (1775)

Ignorance is preferable to error; and he is less remote from the truth who
believes nothing, than he who believes what is wrong.

Thomas Jefferson,
Notes on the State of Virginia (1781–82)

In chapter 2, we present a framework for thinking about the connections between different sets of political preconditions and the extent to
which banking systems achieve abundant and stable bank credit. We
show how banking systems arise from a process of political bargaining
that we call the Game of Bank Bargains. That game is one in which parties
with diverging interests come together to form coalitions that determine
what sorts of banks will be created and how they will function. The historical narratives in this book demonstrate the usefulness of those categories by showing how the logic of bargaining applies in and is connected to
the specific histories of several countries.

We do not regard the categorization of government and banking systems in figure 2.1 as an immutable framework for organizing the various ways that politics and banking are connected; reducing the world of
politics and banking to a small number of categories is simply a helpful
and imperfect means of organizing our thinking. Indeed, those categories
evolved as we wrote this book, and we expect that as we learn more in the
future, our categorizations will be refined further. As Burke and Jefferson
insist in the epigraphs to this chapter, scientific understanding follows a
perpetual learning process in which the discarding of flawed premises is as

essential as the accumulation of facts.[1] This applies as much to the modern world and its banking arrangements as to other observable phenomena.

We are not, therefore, attempting to sell a handy, timeless model to explain everything about the failures and successes of banks. We are, however, attempting to illustrate the power of a particular way of thinking about the connections between politics and banking for understanding how banking-system performance varies across time and countries. Our framework combines the knowledge of history with an understanding of the logic of bargaining. In addition to yielding insights about the world that we observe, this way of thinking also has important *negative* implications —that is, implications that call for revision of commonly held ideas or generalizations. Here we review some of the most important ones.

The House of Economic Theories of Banking Crises

Even a superficial acquaintance with the basic facts of banking history reveals an obvious problem with all the dominant theories of banking crises: they are *general* theories that conceive of banking crises as arising from aspects of banking that are common to all times and places. As we show in this book, banking crises are not a regular occurrence across time and countries, and therefore they cannot be a consequence of any general economic characteristics about banks. Rather, they are the consequence of general economic characteristics about banks coupled to the specific political circumstances in which banks operate.

General theories of banking crises posit three aspects of banking, some combination of which is presumed to cause crises: bank structure, interbank connections, and human nature. Bank structure refers to the maturity and liquidity mismatch between banks' relatively illiquid and long-

---

[1] In 1775, Burke was pleading for pacifism toward the American colonies in the British parliament. He revealed the flaws in the arguments in favor of a hard-line response, which he asserted was justified neither by principles nor by practical considerations. His concerns proved prescient when the British were defeated. In 1781, Jefferson was arguing against the acceptance of any of the three dominant hypotheses for explaining certain geological and paleontological observations about sea shells. In his view, science would progress better from honestly recognizing its ignorance (the absence of any plausible hypothesis) than from accepting the most reasonable of three far-fetched views.

lived loans and their relatively liquid and short-lived liabilities. Structural theories regard banking crises as the result of the inherent exposure of banks to "liquidity risk" arising from this mismatch.[2]

Theories involving interbank connections invoke the problem of externalities: each banker chooses his bank's holdings of liquid assets and his bank's leverage (the level of debt relative to equity capital) based on what is optimal for that bank alone. Bankers do not take into account the spillover effects (externalities) created by the fact that their bank is part of a system in which each bank is connected to other banks. In particular, a failure at one bank can precipitate problems at other banks. According to this class of crisis theories, the primary role of regulation is to "internalize" externalities by forcing banks to hold more cash assets and to maintain lower leverage ratios than they would choose to do voluntarily. The absence of sufficient regulation to internalize externalities, therefore, is the cause of banking crises.[3]

A third, and older, line of thought is the view that human nature is itself to blame for banking crises. According to this view—which is closely associated with the late professors Hyman Minsky and Charles Kindleberger —humans are myopic, and financial markets and banks oscillate between moments of excessive optimism and excessive fear (sometimes referred to as exuberance, followed by revulsion).[4] When optimism dominates, banks do not manage their risks adequately—they make too many risky loans, maintain insufficient cash assets, and become too highly leveraged—and bank failures result.

The problem with all three of these general theories is that they cannot explain why banking crises are not equally likely across all countries and all of recent history. Human nature is a constant. Banks' balance sheets, and the complex networks of interbank linkages, have existed for centu-

---

[2]The first formal theory was advanced by Diamond and Dybvig (1983), and there have been many variations produced since. The early theories of liquidity risk implausibly focused on exogenous consumption demands as the source of shocks. More recent work has seen liquidity shocks as emerging from problems associated with default risk. One particularly creative version of this more recent work is Dang, Gorton, and Holmstrom (2012).

[3]See, for example, Freixas, Parigi, and Rochet (2000).

[4]Minsky (1975); Kindleberger and Aliber (2011). The model of Dang, Gorton, and Holmstrom (2012) can generate similar repeating cycles in a setting governed by rational agents and asymmetric information.

ries. But banking crises have been remarkably absent in many eras and places despite the presence of all these potential causes.

According to these theories, Canada, for example, should have been prone to banking crises but in fact was not. It would take a heroic effort to demonstrate that Canadians are any less myopic than anyone else. Canadian bankers have to balance the maturities of their assets and liabilities, just like bankers in other countries. They have also participated in complex global interbank networks since the early nineteenth century. Yet Canadian banks, throughout their history, have, with two minor exceptions in 1837 and 1839, avoided systemic banking crises. Moreover, prudential regulation was a fairly recent introduction in Canada, as was the establishment of a central bank. According to the structural theory of banking crises, Canadian banks should therefore have faced a higher liquidity risk than banks in many other countries. According to the externalities theory and the myopia theory, the absence of activist prudential regulation in Canada during most of its history should have led to banking crises, but it did not.

It is not that the core ideas of these economic theories are "wrong": on the contrary, there is substantial evidence that the sources of risk they identify are real. The history of banking crises, including the subprime crisis in the United States, shows that the exposure to liquidity risk associated with banks' reliance on short-term debts to fund their operations can put financial institutions at risk if debt holders refuse to roll over those debts. Similarly, the subprime crisis showed that counterparty risks in complex financial systems can lead to the transmission of adverse shocks among financial institutions. Consistent with the Minsky-Kindleberger view, studies of the pricing of risky assets find that market perceptions of risk vary over time (although it is not clear whether this fluctuation reflects myopia or pricing "fundamentals").

The variation across countries and over time in banking instability does not show that theories of banking crises are irrelevant; rather, it shows that the three categories of general problems that they identify are not *sufficient conditions* for causing banking crises. The structure of banks entails liquidity risk, but banks can overcome that risk by acting prudently—specifically, by maintaining sufficient amounts of cash assets, by limiting their leverage, and by entering into arrangements of mutual liquidity-risk insurance with other banks (e.g., through a privately organized bank clearinghouse). Interbank linkages can create externalities within the banking system, but again, proper risk management and the creation of effective banking institutions can limit the associated risks. Bubbles in housing, stock markets, or risky debt instruments may arise for many reasons. That does not mean, however, that banking crises must follow. Whether they do is a function of choices made by bankers regarding how much cash to hold, how much equity they should raise, and how diversified they should be across different classes of loans and other assets.

The decisive influences determining whether the threats highlighted by these three theories will result in banking crises are *political*. If the government decides to establish generous safety nets protecting banks and does not accompany those safety nets with a politically credible commitment to prudential regulation, then banks will become less cautious in their management of liquidity risk, solvency risk, and counterparty risk. We cannot emphasize this point strongly enough: the extent of safety nets and prudential regulation are choices made by politicians, and in making those choices they are generally motivated by maximizing what is good for their own short-run political futures, not what is socially desirable in the long run.

Politics also gives rise to shocks that are generally not envisioned in economic approaches to bank risk. Wars, coups, and other stresses on government finances can produce political pressures on banks and expropriations of banks by governments. These may be of many forms and varying degrees of intensity: during the U.S. Civil War, banks voluntarily facilitated the North's war efforts by taking on a large amount of debt as a group, while during the Mexican Revolution banks were expropriated outright. Political coalitions might block the development of an adequate system of taxation, as occurred throughout most of Brazil's history, so that governments use the banks to levy an inflation tax. In so doing, they undermine the ability of banks to operate as credit intermediaries. Indeed, the very structure of the banking system, and therefore its susceptibility to adverse shocks, is an outcome of politics. For example, limits on branching in the United States until the late twentieth century prevented banks from being able to diversify their lending across regions and therefore made them more vulnerable to local economic shocks, such as swings in agricultural prices.

Leaving politics out of the theory of banking crises truly omits the prince from the play. Political outcomes of the Game of Bank Bargains shape the rules under which banks operate and determine the shocks to which they are subject. The dramatic political differences across times and places where banking crises are absent or frequent show that a political-economy approach to thinking about banking crises is essential to understanding when and where they are likely to occur.

The Houses of Stabilizing or Destabilizing Bank Concentration

A large theoretical and empirical literature examines a variety of bank attributes to determine their effects on profitability and stability. One hotly debated question is whether banking systems that are more concentrated —that is, which consist of a small number of large banks—are more or less profitable and more or less stable. There are numerous theories about the effects of concentration, and they do not all point in the same direction. On the one hand, concentration is sometimes held to enhance both profitability and stability because it allows banks to create valuable franchises, gives them market power, and allows them to diversify risk. On the other hand, concentration is sometimes held to work against profitability and stability because it can give rise to banks that governments believe are too big to fail (thus encouraging moral hazard) or because it can give rise to tolerance by investors of poorly managed banks. Some models suggest that greater profitability and instability can both result from greater concentration.[5]

The empirical literature has not identified a robust relationship between concentration and instability. One comprehensive cross-country study examines the experiences of 69 countries over the period 1980–97 and asks whether the likelihood of a systemic crisis is related to the degree of banking-system concentration. The authors find that crises are less likely in banking systems with higher concentration. They also find, however, that regulations that limit competition give rise to a greater risk of a banking crisis.[6]

---

[5] The literature is vast. See Boyd and De Nicoló (2005); Beck, Demirgüç-Kunt, and Levine (2006); Keeley (1990); Berger et al. (2004); Boyd and Runkle (1993); Boyd, De Nicoló, and Smith (2004); Matutes and Vives (2000); Hellman, Murdock, and Stiglitz (2000); O'Hara and Shaw (1990); Carletti and Hartmann (2003).

[6] Beck, Demirgüç-Kunt, and Levine (2006).

This result should not come as a surprise to readers of this book. Whether concentration is associated with banking stability or with instability depends on the *political context* within which concentration occurs. The U.S. banking system did not become more stable when it became more concentrated, owing to the political bargain that accompanied increasing concentration after 1990. That bargain gave big banks rents in the form of market power, too-big-to-fail protection, and lax prudential regulation in exchange for their commitments to share those rents with favored constituents. In England prior to the mid-nineteenth century, the Bank of England dominated the London market, and yet it had to pay for that privilege politically through policies that promoted moral hazard in the bills market. The result was a quasi-monopolized banking system that lurched from crisis to crisis. Scotland's banking system included three specially chartered banks and many other banks; it was more competitive and much more stable. In Canada, concentration and stability in banking have gone hand in hand since its creation as a sovereign nation, and they have done so because of the political bargain that avoided taxpayer-funded bank bailouts and prevented banks from taking advantage of their market power. A very different political bargain in Porfirian Mexico also resulted in both concentration and stability, but for a different reason: concentration of banking in the hands of the elite ensured a politically stable rent-sharing arrangement—while the regime lasted. Once the regime fell, however, the banking system collapsed.

The message of our country studies, therefore, is that concentration and stability are both outcomes of the political Game of Bank Bargains. One does not cause the other: both are caused by the political bargains that shape banking. Because there are many different political environments, there are many different types of banking bargains, and there is no consistent empirical relationship between concentration and stability.

The House of Ahistorical Reasoning

An overarching theme of this book is the recognition that useful propositions about banking generally are only true *contingently,* depending on historical context. That historical context changes as the result of influences outside of the banking system—most obviously, in the modern era, as the result of changes in the technology of war, communication, and transportation that gave rise to democratic nation-states. In Britain and the United States, the expansion of the franchise brought pressure on politicians to increase the number of bank charters so as to make credit more easily available. Somewhat less obviously, technological changes that were later adapted to banking, such as improvements in information technology, made it harder to sustain the monopoly privileges of unit bankers. Bankers could now gather information about potential borrowers even if they lived far away from the bank's office, and depositors could access their funds from ATM networks.

Few propositions about the intersection of politics and banking are reliable when applied to countries across the board, irrespective of historical context. Does centralization of political power improve banking-system performance? It may or may not, depending on the political context in which centralization occurs. In Canada, centralization of chartering authority was associated with greater competition. In the late-twentieth century United States, the centralization of chartering authority was part of a different political bargain for nationwide banks and GSEs—one that traded market power and government protection privileges for new mandates. Does legislation to reduce safety-net protection stabilize banking? In Chile in the mid-1980s it did, but in countries with different political circumstances, such limits have been abandoned during crises (for example, the 1991 FDIC Improvement Act's limits on bank protection in the United States were abandoned during the subprime crisis).

Researchers who do not take history seriously wind up reducing the study of complex banking systems to an analysis of correlations among various influences (such as democracy, concentrated banking, and insured deposits). This approach often fails to find connections because the influences being modeled are considered without taking context into account. And when such a modeling approach does find empirical correlations, the meaning can be misinterpreted because the correlations identified by the researcher reflect deeper, omitted influences on all the variables being measured.

Economists and others who study banking and hope to improve banking systems' performance must learn to think about banks, and the potential desirability of reform proposals, in the context of the political and technological environment in which banking outcomes are determined. Understanding why some banking systems can deliver stable and abundant credit, while others cannot, requires studying the political foundations on which banking systems are built in each country, and the nature of the coalitions that control the outcomes in each country's Game of Bank Bargains.[7]

Shifts over time in the nature of bank bargains within countries may reflect dramatic political changes. Most obviously, revolutions and other fundamental changes in the nature of government occurred in each of the countries we study. The Glorious Revolution of 1688 and the long resulting political struggle between Britain and France were fundamental shifters in the banking history of Britain. The competitive military pressures on Britain's relatively small population remained a central theme of its political history: they drove increases in suffrage, which initially promoted banking competition in the nineteenth century, and during the middle decades of the twentieth century reduced the importance of bank credit in the economy. The American Revolution made the chartering of banks possible, and the U.S. Constitution allocated the political power to determine how banks would be chartered and regulated in a manner that had lasting influence. Subsequent major events in U.S. history, such as the Civil War, also shaped the structure of the banking system. In Mexico and Brazil, banking crises arose primarily from political struggles. These crises produced dramatic changes in the structure of the banking system, including expropriations and hyperinflations. Such shocks crowded out the meager supply of private credit that the banking systems had been directing toward favored recipients and ushered in long periods of severe financial repression.

---

[7]Although it is beyond our scope to elaborate on these at length—this is a book intended to describe the world as it is, not to imagine it as it might be—we would point to several recent contributions to the theory of regulatory reform that take into account the political challenges of reform and that design regulations specifically to be robust to those challenges. These contributions emphasize that robust reforms of financial policies tend to rely on simplicity of regulatory rules (which enhances the ability of everyone to understand them and of regulators to enforce them), regulatory rules that are automatically and transparently enforceable (which minimize politically manipulated discretion), and government subsidies whose costs are transparent (which increase accountability). Contributors include Barth, Caprio, and Levine (2006, 2012); Demirgüç-Kunt, Detragiache, and Merrouche (forthcoming); Cihak, Demirgüç-Kunt, and Johnston (2012); Calomiris (2009, 2010a,b, 2011a); Calomiris and Herring (2012); Calomiris and Powell (2001); Calomiris, Heider, and Hoerova (2013); and Acharya, Adler, and Richardson (2011).

In addition to these dramatic political shifts, other, more gradual shifts often caused the dominant political coalition in charge of banking policy to be replaced by a new coalition. Whether such shifts occur, however, and whether they alter banking bargains, depends not only on shifts in demographics or sectoral growth opportunities but also on a country's political institutions.

Consider the similarities and differences between Canada and the United States during the nineteenth and early twentieth centuries. As western migration and transportation improvements empowered agrarian interests, both countries saw somewhat similar agrarian populist challenges to the banking status quo. Canada's political institutions, however, were designed to resist those challenges, and Canada's original banking structure remained virtually intact. In Canada, there was a conscious attempt to craft political institutions to reduce the likelihood of earth-moving political changes. Its political system was shaped not by the revolutionary founders of a new country but by the British, to reduce political risks that might threaten the finance, trade, and infrastructure expansion that were central to the British imperial strategy. Canada's 1840 Act of Union and Canada's Constitution of 1867 were designed to insulate its economic and financial systems from political risks, including the pressures of populist agrarian movements.

In the United States, however, the alliance between agrarian populists and unit bankers replaced the early special chartering arrangements of the pre-1830 period with free chartering but rejected nationwide branch banking and thereby maintained effective barriers to entry. Throughout their histories, the key difference between the U.S. and Canadian banking bargains was a U.S. constitutional structure that decentralized bank chartering authority and failed to insulate the financial system from populist politics. This institutional difference made it possible for populist movements to partner with bankers and government to fashion a banking system that suited their interests (including the national banking system, the Federal Reserve System, and the various innovations in government policy toward banks during the 1930s). In the late twentieth century, shifts in population from rural areas to cities, along with banking distress, technological change, and other influences that favored bank consolidation in the United States, produced a new winning coalition whose core was an unlikely partnership between newly emerging nationwide banks and activist groups.

History teaches us that although taxonomies and theories of politics and banking (like that in figure 2.1) are quite useful, the history of banking cannot be distilled into propositions about causal connections flowing purely from political coalitions to banking outcomes. Banking shapes politics, too. As we discuss in chapter 3, banking systems that serve the fiscal interests of the state have proved as important to the survival and expansion of nations as military and international trade strategies. Banking systems are not just an outcome of politics; they also shape the coalitions that bargain in the future rounds of the Game of Bank Bargains.

Banks not only shape the state through their influence on its financial and military capabilities; they also affect the bargaining power of the private parties that participate in the Game of Bank Bargains, in autocracies and democracies alike. A group that becomes part of a winning coalition gains wealth and political power, which reinforce its bargaining position going forward. Bank bargains can therefore become quite durable, such as those struck by Mexican elites under Porfirio Díaz. Canadian banks built nationwide franchises from an early date, then used their influence to defeat or absorb populist challengers. Entrenched unit bankers in the United States preserved their entry barriers for 150 years, despite the enormous economic and social costs of unit banking. Even in the face of unprecedented financial weakness in 1933, unit bankers were able to use their political influence to secure federal deposit insurance and other regulations that preserved their status and ended the bank consolidation movement that threatened them.

Political circumstances also influence financial innovation and entrepreneurship, which shape the development of financial instruments and services. Private and public entrepreneurial activities that guide financial innovations in both banking and state finances play important roles in determining the economic functions of banks and in shaping the outcomes of wars and the growth of empires.

Most obviously, the creation of chartered banks and bills of exchange—the hallmarks of early modern banking—were innovations that altered both the history of banking and the nature of the state. Scotland—where the freedom to determine banking locations and services was most pronounced in the eighteenth and early nineteenth centuries—was a hotbed of banking innovation, and the successes of Scotland's banking system—which combined banknotes, interest-bearing deposits, branch banking, lines of credit, and other features—not only contributed to England's desire to open up its banking system to competition beginning in the 1830s but also established precedents for modern banking throughout the world.

Individual actors also matter in shaping outcomes—and they matter because of their ability to identify opportunities for forming political coalitions and for implementing financial innovations. Consider Alexander Hamilton, who not only was instrumental in framing the U.S. Constitution but also crafted financial strategies for chartering banks and building institutions of public finance. He knew how to build political consensus: as secretary of the treasury, he was able to overcome opponents to the chartering of the Bank of the United States, who viewed his policies as unconstitutional and contrary to their interests. There are many other examples of political entrepreneurs whose ideas and ability to build coalitions have made a difference in banking history. Andrew Jackson successfully opposed the rechartering of the Second Bank of the United States, while Nicholas Biddle fumbled that political battle: many historians believe Biddle could have won if he had played his cards differently.[8] José Limantour, the financial wizard of Porfirian Mexico, provides another example. He figured out how to craft a stable coalition of regional power brokers and financiers to finance a state that had been unstable for decades; he also invented loan securitization to facilitate government liquidity support for Mexico's banks in the wake of the U.S. panic of 1907. Loan securitization has been widely imitated since then. In short, outcomes in the Game of Bank Bargains are not mechanically determined by the mathematics of coalitions: effective political entrepreneurs can both magnify historical tendencies and confound them.

Individuals in central positions of power at critical moments still make a difference for banking outcomes. In 1994, House Speaker Newt Gingrich crafted the Contract with America and led the Republican Party in its successful quest for control of the House of Representatives. The Republican Party in the 1990s and early 2000s was divided over the question of reforming housing finance, especially the GSEs. Some Congressional leaders favored reforms that would have reduced GSE risks. If Gingrich had sided with those reformers and made GSE reform a Republican political goal, that opposition might have blocked the expansion of GSE subsidies and

---

[8] Perkins (1987); Schweikart (1988).

other housing-finance policies in the late 1990s and early 2000s. Because Gingrich occupied a position of importance, however, the political value to the GSEs and their supporters of convincing him not to embrace reform was very high.

Even some of the failures of visionary political entrepreneurs are quite telling, as they help us to track the ebbs and flows of political power over time. William Jennings Bryan failed to win the presidency repeatedly around the turn of the twentieth century and was thus prevented from enacting his agrarian populist platform, which included price inflation, the preservation of unit banking, and federal deposit insurance. Bryan's tireless populist campaigning, however, eventually bore fruit in policies that were enacted with the prodding of Henry Steagall and others, and the acquiescence of Franklin Roosevelt, in the 1930s.

The House of Libertarian Utopianism

As we show in chapter 2, the extent to which banking systems are able to achieve the two key measures of success—abundant credit and the absence of banking crises—depends critically on their political environment. As we show in chapter 3, as a matter of history as well as logic, the aspirations of the modern state have required it to charter and make use of banks, and those banks have played key roles in the coevolution of the modern state and modern banking. That logic is illustrated at length by the country studies in this book. The notions that banking systems can arise spontaneously, or that they could function efficiently without active government involvement, are utopian fantasies.

Scotland's laissez-faire environment of the eighteenth and early nineteenth centuries came closest to the utopian banking ideal, but even there, banks relied on the laws and the physical protection of the state to function. Furthermore, the Scottish banking system's ability to avoid public-finance obligations, chartering limits, and other meddling reflected very special circumstances. The most important was that Scotland could operate with relatively little government involvement in its banking affairs precisely because English banking was the primary locus of bank rent sharing with the state. Without England's banking system, Scottish banks would have had to play a much greater role as public-financing devices and could not have been as insulated from politics as they were. After all, if Scotland had been a fully independent state it could not have shed its parliament in 1707—a crucial act of unilateral political disarmament that underlay its free-banking deal with the crown!

The narrow libertarian conception of the ideal state sees its roles as confined to providing defense and enforcing voluntary contracts under a clear rule of law. Under that conception, libertarian theorists argue that there is no role for the state in chartering or regulating banks. But that view is founded on an incomplete conception of the state. The state needs banks as a financing tool. States without banks cannot and have never existed. Indeed, ironically, it is precisely the most basic function of the state recognized by libertarian theorists—defense—that makes banks so important.

Throughout history, military and economic competition among states has been a driving force in bank chartering and regulation. The fact that organized violence is a key function of the state has been the single most important reason that states have needed to charter and control banks. The narrow conception of the state that omits an activist role for government in the shaping of banking errs in two fundamental ways. First, as a matter of history, it ignores the central and necessary role of government in creating effective banking systems. The world of Renaissance banking was one of perennial credit scarcity. Second, it ignores the ineluctable logic of how—for better or worse—governments must create and allocate power: any government choosing to forbear from using banks as a tool to gain military and economic advantages would soon be replaced by a stronger government that did. Like it or not, banking policy will always be a powerful tool of statecraft. To narrowly conceive of the state as only a courtroom in which laws are enforced is to ignore the political foundations of all laws and the military and economic foundations of the competition among political regimes.

The House of All-Powerful Autocrats

In our discussion of autocracy in chapter 2, we distinguish among autocracies according to the degree to which they centralize power. The notion of the all-powerful, autocratic "stationary bandit"—an individual with so much power that he can control everything without seeking anyone else's consent, and who can take as much as he wants from whomever he pleases—is a useful abstraction for political scientists and economists.

There are real-world approximations to this type of autocracy, such as Saddam Hussein's Iraq, in which a small group of people wielded nearly absolute control over the rest of the population; but even there the dictator had to rely on allies. Absolute centralization of power in a single autocrat has never existed.[9]

Our case studies of autocracies—Mexico and Brazil until as recently as the 1990s—show that in real-world autocracies, rulers always must seek out allies and reward their services. Those allies must be coaxed to devote their resources and their efforts to assist the autocrats. Banks in autocracies cannot be founded by decree alone: they must be able to attract capital and deposits, provided on the basis of an expectation of economic gain.

The banking systems formed from alliances between autocrats and others are not all the same. When an autocratic government achieves some degree of political centralization—as in Mexico during the reign of Porfirio Díaz—banks become linchpins in a complex network of industrialists, bankers, and government officials who form various kinds of explicit partnerships, including intermarriage. These kinds of political systems tend to restrict bank chartering to members of that elite network, and bank loans tend to be almost exclusively channeled to those parties. In these systems, bank lending is lower than is typically found in democracies, and the banking system can be fragile because it is subject to expropriation when the government experiences a serious fiscal shock (including, for example, a revolution, as happened in Mexico in 1911). Nevertheless, in a centralized autocracy compared to many other autocracies, lending is abundant, and the banking system is stable.

In contrast, when the national governments of autocracies are weak and power is decentralized, such complex networks—which require mutual monitoring of participants and enforcement of penalties against opportunistic behavior—are not viable. Brazil under the first years of the empire and during the Old Republic provides examples of such autocracies. Not only did they fail to establish robust national business networks, but they also found it difficult to extract tax revenues from regional elites who resisted central-government encroachment. Under these circumstances, the chartering rules for banks were among the few things that the national

[9] For a comparative discussion of how bargaining occurs in authoritarian regimes, see Haber (2006b).

government could control, and it was driven by necessity to use that chartering authority to extract inflation-tax revenues, despite the fact that turning the banking system into a mechanism for collecting the inflation tax resulted in a financial system so repressed that even members of the elite had difficulty getting bank loans.

The House of Populism

In our taxonomy of democracies in chapter 2, we draw out their differing implications for credit abundance and banking stability. Those theoretical perspectives, and the narrative histories of the countries we have studied, reveal an ironic fact about popular sovereignty: democracies that least constrain the political power of majority rule tend to disadvantage the majority. It is a rare populist government that chooses policies that are conducive to both abundant credit and banking stability. Indeed, the short-term pursuit of abundant credit may make the banking system unstable and reduce the supply of credit in the long run.

The populist notion that the absence of constraints on majority rule results in more power and greater opportunities for the common man is based on a misunderstanding of the way democracies function. The "agency" problem of democracy is that elected representatives have incentives that often conflict with the interests of the people they are supposed to represent. Representatives can sell their votes in many ways, and there is an active political market for deals that is often hard for voters to observe and even harder for them to control. We have laid bare some of the most important deals that gave rise to banking legislation and showed how special interests, party platforms, log rolling, and other features of the Game of Bank Bargains produce agreements among legislators that tend to serve special interests at the expense of the interests of the majority.

Given that reality, constraints on populism can be useful in limiting the ability of special interests to take wealth and political power from the majority. Supermajority voting rules, voting rules that give disproportionate power to small groups (such as the allocation of two senators per state in the United States), bicameral legislatures, independent judicial review of legislation, judiciaries that serve for life (and in Canada, an appointed upper house of the legislature), and similar checks and balances all limit the ability of the representatives of a majority of citizens to make decisions that affect the lives of all. By requiring agreement among many diverse parties, such "veto gates" reduce the ability of elected politicians to embrace policies that come at a cost to many members of society.

Canada's practice of appointing senators rather than electing them, along with the overrepresentation of smaller provinces in the senate, may strike many readers of this book as odd, if not completely wrong-headed. Nevertheless, these features of Canada's political institutions, as well as first-past-the-post elections for its lower house, have given rise to a banking system that is stable and provides prodigious amounts of credit to households and business enterprises. That banking system, in turn, has financed the growth of an economy that is remarkably large considering Canada's limited resource base. Indeed, the vast majority of Canada's territory cannot be cultivated: it is simply too cold to grow anything but trees farther than 100 miles north of the U.S. border. Seen in this light, one cannot help but wonder how much higher per capita incomes in the more resource-blessed United States would have been if the U.S. economy had not lurched from banking crisis to banking crisis across its history.

The House of Federalist Faith

Every American schoolchild learns that the U.S. Constitution is the greatest conception of government ever known (although they receive that opinion typically without having learned anything about other countries' constitutions). Part of the success of the U.S. Constitution is due to the fact that it divides the federal government into three equally powerful branches and then divides the legislative branch into a Senate and House of Representatives. Another feature of the U.S. system of government is the division of authority between the federal government and those of the states. Indeed, the United States is unusual in that the Constitution protects the policy autonomy of states, awarding them all powers not expressly granted in the Constitution to the federal government. These provisions of the U.S. Constitution are regarded as key protections against the amassing of power and unwise actions by the national government. This view finds considerable support in various studies of the "market-preserving" consequences of federalism.[10]

[10] Weingast (1995); Qian and Weingast (1997).

Our review of U.S. banking history shows that there is truth to this view, but only up to a point. Divisions of power under the U.S. federal structure have meant that for most of American history, the national government could not determine the size and structure of the banking system. Prior to the 1990s, states played the dominant role in chartering and regulating banking. Even after the national government asserted control over the supply of banknotes during the Civil War (and later allocated it to the Federal Reserve), states controlled the branching rules under which both national and state banks operated, and no banks (whether national or state-chartered) could operate in more than one state. This federalist banking structure did, in fact, limit the ability of any political bargain to control banking outcomes simply because no comprehensive nationwide political bargain was possible. It is also true that competition among the states worked in favor of eliminating the special chartering of banks in the early nineteenth century, just as it promoted the relaxation of suffrage restrictions and other barriers to political and economic competition at the state level.

The limits implied by federalism on the U.S. Game of Bank Bargains did not, however, result in a stable or efficient banking system. The fragmentation of the banking system created by state laws against branching prevented banks from competing or diversifying across regions and limited their size and scope of operations. The result was an unstable banking system that allocated credit inefficiently. More fundamentally, competition among states did not result in efficient bank chartering and regulation, even within the individual states. Local coalitions of agrarian populists and unit bankers were able to craft rules that suited their interests and were contrary to the interests of others. Competition among states did not result in efficient chartering rules because states had monopoly rights over the chartering of banks within their physical domains. It is true that bad chartering regimes could disadvantage a state, but it is also true that the relative disadvantage was limited by the fact that no state could decide to charter *nationwide* banks. Manufacturing interests and the general population suffered from limited access to credit and an unstable financial system.

The House of Partisan Finger Pointing

Politicians like to portray the shortcomings in the banking system, especially banking crises, as part of a morality play in which their political opponents, acting in concert with a small number of nefarious individuals, produce outcomes that harm the majority of citizens. This strategy resonates with voters, as evidenced by the strong sales of books about the 2007 U.S. subprime crisis that accused a handful of greedy bankers and dishonest politicians of causing the crisis.

These tales may win votes and sell books, but they are not accurate descriptions of the reality of the Game of Bank Bargains. In a democracy, successful political coalitions, by definition, cannot be narrow. For a set of regulations to become important and lasting determinants of the banking system, they must reflect broad and bipartisan support. Finger pointing that identifies the culprit on the other side of the aisle is not just self-serving: it ignores the basic logic of political arithmetic. To survive, a coalition must be broad enough to win electoral battles. That means that coalitions in favor of a particular regulatory outcome that is not actually in the public interest often combine unlikely partners: parties that may not share an ideology, class, occupation, or much of anything else. In fact, these unlikely partners may actively loathe one another—but that does not keep them from doing business when there is something to be gained from cooperation. Such unlikely partnerships are, ironically, more stable precisely because they bring together groups that do not share natural affinities, and thus they span a broader swath of the electorate. The bargains that they strike are therefore less subject to becoming overturned by elections that transfer control of the government from one political party to another.

Examples of such unlikely partnerships in democracies abound. In the United Kingdom in the early twentieth century, an alliance was formed between labor unions, who pressed for better working conditions for their rank and file and more political power for themselves, and politicians in the Liberal Party who were intent on maintaining the British Empire. The franchise was broadened, labor laws were reformed, and the empire endured for another four decades. The nineteenth-century United States provides another obvious example of a partnership between people with dissimilar backgrounds and economic interests: a coalition of populist farmers who distrusted elites of any variety made common cause with unit bankers against big banks. More recent U.S. history provides yet another example: in the 1990s, a coalition of urban activist groups espousing populist ideologies forged an alliance with too-big-to-fail banks and

GSEs that aligned the incentives of powerful members of both the Democratic and Republican parties. This coalition set in motion a process that undermined lending standards for all Americans and helped precipitate the subprime crisis of 2007.

Although all of these coalitions endured for many years, political and economic changes inevitably lead to changes in the partnerships that control banking outcomes. Unlikely partnerships do not last forever. Is it possible to foresee changes in the structure of partnerships? For example, what can one say about the likely persistence of the current political alliance between megabanks and activist groups in the United States? We are not in the forecasting business, and we do not think that the outcome is clear. What can be said with some certainty, however, is that if that partnership persists into the future, some recontracting will be required. The merger wave in U.S. banking during the 1980s and 1990s created strong partnering opportunities between big banks and activist groups, which took the form of CRA agreements. But the merger wave is over, and the banking crisis has deeply damaged popular support for both large-scale banking and risky mortgage lending. In the current U.S. environment, it is far from clear what sort of alliance will govern the Game of Bank Bargains in the future.[11]

There is a saying apparently coined by Whispering Saul, a financial wizard quoted in the *Atlantic* magazine in 1979: "If you sit in on a poker game, and you don't see a sucker at the table, get up. You're the sucker."[12] Following Saul's advice will likely save you a bundle of money and significant heartache. Unfortunately, in the Game of Bank Bargains, you cannot get up: you are effectively strapped to your chair. If you live in the United States, for example, unless you are willing to go into hiding off the grid somewhere in rural Hawaii or northwestern Idaho, you cannot avoid the risk of costly crisis-related credit-supply disruptions, job losses, and bailout costs, all of which have been part and parcel of the U.S. version of the Game of Bank Bargains for two centuries. As a member of the majority of

---

[11] One potential indicator of a change in the alliance between the megabanks and the activist groups has been the reduction in bank branches in low-income neighborhoods since the subprime crisis. Since 2008, 1,826 branches have closed, and 93 percent of those closings were in ZIP codes where the household income is below the national median. See Bass and Campbell (2013).

[12] Spooner (1979).

citizens—who generally have not been part of the winning coalitions in the U.S. Game of Bank Bargains—you are a source of income to the winning players. You are the sucker at the table, and you cannot leave.

In the Game of Bank Bargains, there does not necessarily have to be a sucker at the table. Government regulatory policies toward banks may be benign and designed to achieve competitiveness, broad access to credit, and long-run stability. In Canada, in Scotland during the eighteenth and early nineteenth centuries, and in Victorian Britain, the banking game had no obvious sucker.

More often, however, the coalitions controlling bank regulation channel rents to themselves. They see the scarcity or instability of credit that may result from those regulations as a necessary price for establishing a banking system able to extract and deliver rents. Sometimes such a coalition includes politicians and bankers who split the proceeds from an inflation tax, as occurred through much of Brazilian history. Sometimes it is made up of a group of politicians intent on consolidating their rule, who are allied to a network of financiers and industrialists, as occurred in Porfirian Mexico. In other times and places, winning coalitions include unlikely partnerships between populists and bankers, as occurred repeatedly in the United States.

Unlike citizens in an autocracy, citizens in a democracy may be able to shape the outcomes of the Game of Bank Bargains. To do so, however, they must achieve two daunting tasks. First, they must share an understanding of how the Game of Bank Bargains produces distortions, rents, and subsidies. Second, they must coordinate their actions to enact lasting reforms that may be contrary to the interest of the coalition in control of the regulation of banking. People have busy lives, as workers, parents, students, and homemakers. Financial affairs and politics are complicated. It takes a great deal of time and effort to figure out what is going on under the surface, and even more to organize a collective effort to achieve reform. For most people, mitigating the costs they bear as taxpayers probably isn't worth the effort—especially since their attempts will likely meet determined opposition from the well-organized coalition that benefits from the status quo ante.

One reason that it can be hard for common citizens to challenge the position of the coalition that controls banking system outcomes is that the dominant coalition sometimes compromises with opponents to defuse their efforts. The Game of Bank Bargains generally does not result in winner-take-all outcomes. The dominant coalition may be willing to make some concessions to challengers as a means of avoiding risky political confrontations. For example, the Bank of England was willing to discount bills with brokers on liberal terms in the early nineteenth century to reduce the calls for the chartering of competing banks. Similarly, in Canada during the twentieth century, finance companies that were engaged in mortgage lending were able to obtain limited deposit insurance as part of a deal that preserved the control of the dominant banks. Eventually, this resulted in the deal whereby smaller lenders were absorbed by the large banks. In Brazil, despite the financial repression wrought by the government's use of the banking system as a source of inflation-tax revenue, nonbanks (for example, *financieras*) were permitted to act in the shadow of the banking system to supply credit, and some depositors could circumvent or mitigate inflation taxation by using treasury-bill repurchase agreements or by purchasing inflation-indexed bonds. Not coincidentally, those who could exit the Brazilian financial system or launch successful opposition to inflation taxation were spared the costs of the inflation tax.

The House of Regulatory Reform

A famous economist and political scientist, Charles Lindblom, once advanced the idea that, in an ideal world, policy makers would best achieve desirable outcomes by combining the dexterous fingers of markets with the strong pushing thumbs of government.[13] Economists who are mindful of the potential value of government interventions often conclude their studies of banking systems with reflections on the policy implications of their findings—typically, formulating a list of ideas for improving banking regulation. Clearly, there is lots of room for improvement in banking around the world, including in the United States.

The problem is that while economists like to develop ideas about optimal government policies, including banking regulation, politicians are not in the business of implementing those ideas. In reality, banking policies reflect deeply entrenched political partnerships, which fashion banking bargains to make them difficult to undo.

---

[13] Lindblom (1977), 65.

One of our central messages is that societies do not choose their banking systems in any meaningful sense. Instead, they get the banking system that their political institutions and dominant coalitions permit. Thus, a reformer interested in expanding and stabilizing bank credit in an autocratic country run by an entrenched elite would be wasting her time lobbying for limits on deposit insurance or increases in capital requirements. Any meaningful reform would have to begin by pushing for a transition to democracy. As we show in chapter 2, without such a fundamental political change, an autocratic country is unlikely to be able to construct a banking system that can deliver abundant and stable credit. Needless to say, a call for a democracy will probably not be welcomed by the entrenched elite that is running the country.

The prospects for meaningful bank regulatory reform are more favorable in a democracy like that of the United States. A U.S. reform agenda that would end the subsidization of mortgage risk, end too-big-to-fail bailouts, create regulatory rules that would force banks to manage risk effectively and maintain adequate capital, and promote greater competition among large banks clearly would benefit the majority of citizens. It would reduce distortions in the allocation of credit, and it could bring an end to the succession of crises that has characterized the U.S. banking system. It is possible to identify specific technical measures that would be likely to achieve those changes, using as a guide the experiences of countries like Canada.

As we have emphasized, however, implementing reforms is not easy. It is challenging to assemble a winning coalition of like-minded people able to overcome the opposition of those that already control banking policy. Crises may mobilize constituencies for change, but powerful interests often succeed in using the crisis to strengthen their power. That was the result in 1913, when the Federal Reserve was founded to facilitate the operation of a fragmented banking system rather than to address the structural problems of unit banking. In the 1930s, instead of addressing the vulnerability of the banking system to agricultural income fluctuations and unit banking—the primary sources of bank failures in the preceding years—bank regulatory reforms further protected small, rural banks by instituting federal deposit insurance and new regulatory limits on bank consolidation. The regulatory reforms of 1989–91 wound down insolvent savings and loan associations and tinkered with regulatory capital requirements without actually constraining banks' and GSEs' abilities to undertake risk at public expense. In fact, banks made ample use of the new capital-requirements framework to build the hidden risks that revealed themselves in the 2007–09 subprime crisis. As of this writing, the reforms introduced in the wake of that crisis have done little to end the subsidization of housing risk, to prevent banks from continuing to abuse the same system of capital regulation to hide risks in the future, or to prevent too-big-to-fail bailouts. Indeed, Title 2 of the Dodd-Frank bill enshrined and institutionalized those bailouts while pretending to get rid of them.

Building Hamilton's House

What can well-intentioned, entrepreneurial reformers do to improve banking systems that are stuck in a bad political equilibrium (defined as one in which the deals struck in the Game of Bank Bargains are not conducive to abundant and stable credit)? One starting point for addressing the challenge of reform is a passage from Alexander Hamilton's 1795 *Report of the Secretary of the Treasury:* "To undo . . . requires more enterprise and vigor . . . than not to do. . . . This is particularly true where a number of wills is to concur. . . . It often happens that a majority of voices could not be had to a resolution to undo or reverse a thing once done, where there would not be a majority of voice to *do.* . . . This reasoning acquires tenfold force when applied to a complex Government like ours."[14]

Hamilton recognized here that any action undertaken by a complex system of representative government, like that of the United States, will be hard to reverse. The essence of the Hamiltonian formula for political entrepreneurship is finding the right moment to seek support for measures that might not be sufficiently favored in normal times, hoping that the complexity of the legislative process will prevent reversal once normal times return. According to this strategy, successful political entrepreneurs who can shape popular opinion at critical moments can make a long-term difference, for better or worse, because they can envision ways to engineer unlikely, hard-to-reverse actions during fleeting windows of opportunity.

[14] U.S. Senate (1828), 179.

The successful rejection of the destabilizing structure of banking and safety-net protection in the United Kingdom in the middle of the nineteenth century, discussed in chapter 5, is an example of a successful reform. A confluence of factors, including the demonstrated stability of the Scottish system, the demonstrated instability of the English system, and the open and deliberative parliamentary process and press coverage that exposed the flaws in the policies of the Bank of England together produced a shift in policy with lasting consequences. That story gives hope to proponents of reform within democracies.

As we show, however, the Bank of England was the initiator of reforms to some of those policies, partly because the political equilibrium that had given rise to its prior policies had already shifted. The reform of Bank of England discount policy in 1858 was not an example of the defeat of a dominant coalition but rather an outcome of prior shifts in the nature of the bargain among the state, the Bank of England, and the newly chartered English banks.

U.S. history contains examples of momentary actions that have had long-lived consequences, and one can argue that some of these changes were the results of an entrepreneurial political push. The windows of opportunity that gave rise to such actions often were crisis-related. Secretary Chase's goal to charter a system of national banks might never have been achievable without the pressing financing needs of the Civil War, which made requiring government bond backing for banknotes very appealing. The consequence was a national banking system that persisted for decades. As we show in chapter 6, however, innovative as that new system was, it did not threaten the existing coalition of agrarian populists and unit bankers; it mainly altered the distribution of rents by including the national government among the parties receiving their share.

Other entrepreneurial examples include the actions of bankers, such as A. P. Giannini and Hugh McColl, who took advantage of moments of banking distress—their windows of opportunity—to set important and lasting precedents that removed barriers to branching. Giannini was the early-twentieth-century visionary of branch banking. His initial attempts to expand the branching network of what would become the Bank of America were frustrated by unit bankers who lobbied California bank regulators to prevent the expansion. Giannini's opportunity finally came when agricultural distress led struggling unit bankers to reverse their opposition and solicit his acquisition of their banks.[15] Similarly, McColl, who ran North Carolina's NationsBank, used the banking distress of the 1980s to persuade regulators to relax prohibitions on branching to allow him to enter new areas in exchange for absorbing losses that otherwise would have required FDIC outlays.

Those entrepreneurs made a difference, but it would be overstating the case to say that the successes of Giannini and McColl mean that the efforts of private entrepreneurs can overcome the forces of political opposition. Rather, their successes reflected favorable shifts in underlying political coalitions: unit bankers facing the prospect of failure, and bank borrowers facing a possible collapse of bank credit, experienced a sudden change of heart, switching from opposing bank branching to supporting it. As in the case of the post-1857 British reforms, the successes of branch banking reflected political shifts that favored it, not the brute force of entrepreneurial will.

Perhaps the best examples of Hamilton's notion of political windows of opportunity were his chartering of the Bank of the United States in 1791 and the chartering of the Second Bank of the United States in 1816. But those actions also illustrate the importance of favorable exigent circumstances as well as the limits of political entrepreneurship. The chartering of the first Bank of the United States was greatly facilitated by the government's impecunious state of affairs. In 1811, the bank was not rechartered. The Second Bank of the United States, which was also chartered in reaction to a difficult state of affairs—the fiasco that was the War of 1812—did not survive its first rechartering battle in 1832. These events suggest that the costs of reversal that Hamilton was depending on may not be so high. If a sufficiently powerful political coalition stands to benefit greatly from undoing something, it is likely, sooner or later, to find a way.

Within a democracy, to sustain effective reforms in banking, more is needed than good ideas or brief windows of opportunity. What is crucial is *persistent popular support* for good ideas. That is easier said than accomplished. Self-interested groups with strong vested interests in forming powerful coalitions—a costly and time-consuming exercise—will distract and disinform the voting public, making it very hard for good ideas to

---

[15] See James and James (1954); Calomiris (2000), 65–67.

win the day. And even if they do prevail, self-interested coalitions will always be looking for an opportunity to reverse them.

That does not mean, however, that good ideas always lose. Sometimes long-neglected good ideas eventually win out as the result of fortuitous political circumstances that create lasting public support, based on the demonstrated consequences of ignoring them. The Thatcher revolution in Britain, discussed in chapter 5, is an obvious example: when bad policy choices produced sufficiently poor growth and high inflation, the electorate demanded a new approach and found many of the answers it was looking for.

Of course, the details of bank regulatory reform are more complicated than the ideas for reform brought by Thatcher, which included privatization of factories, liberalization of restrictions on competition in financial markets, and cuts in government spending. The consequences of bad policy choices in financial regulation are not immediately apparent (and sometimes do not emerge for many years). Not only is banking an inherently complicated subject, but it may be further complicated by dominant political coalitions precisely to make it difficult for the majority of voters to see what is going on. Consider the patchwork quilt of housing-finance subsidies in the United States, or the endless complexity of the Basel capital standards applied to banks.

Can the public rely on disinterested third parties (the media or academics) to sort out the validity of complex reform proposals? Such disinterested parties can be hard to identify.[16] When the stakes are high, experts can always be found to disagree with any position—both honestly and dishonestly. Indeed, honest mistakes in judgment by influential people, selectively promoted by vested interests, are just as dangerous as suborned dissembling. By all accounts, Carter Glass believed in the real-bills doctrine that underlay his antipathy for banks' involvement in securities markets and his willingness to make compromises on other issues (like deposit insurance) in order to limit bank involvement in securities trad-

---

[16] One interesting recent proposal, by Barth, Caprio, and Levine (2012), would establish a sentinel of independent experts to identify flaws in banking-system regulation and supervision and draw attention to threats to banking stability. We agree with the authors that this approach could offer—through mutual monitoring by its members —a means of establishing a credible and informed voice for improved regulation and supervision of banks.

ing. Similarly, Paul Volcker has demonstrated a career-long antipathy to commercial-bank involvement in securities trading. No one would say that either of these people advocated their positions dishonestly, and yet there are no living adherents of Glass's real-bills doctrine and few academics or other independent experts who support the Volcker Rule as a desirable regulatory reform.

What about the media? Could they lead a credible effort at regulatory reform? True experts on finance are rare in the media: if you are a financial wizard, being a reporter tends not to pay as much as being a banker. The result is that many reporters, even at top news outlets, deal with financial reform at a superficial level. Furthermore, reporters in all countries—including the United States—often have political loyalties that bias their reporting.[17] The lack of expertise and the biases of reporters make it hard for the public to rely on the media to disentangle complex arguments. For all these reasons, ideas for reform that can be conveyed in simple terms are the only ones that are likely to gain widespread popular understanding, much less support. Consequently it is harder to define and implement good policies in banking, where the issues are necessarily complicated.

Readers should not mistake our unvarnished appreciation for the realities and ironies of the political world, and the difficulties of bank regulatory reform, as cynicism or hopelessness. Despite its challenges, political entrepreneurship within a democracy can sometimes reshuffle the deck in the Game of Bank Bargains by getting participants in the game to revise their views of what best serves their interests, as Alexander Hamilton did in the 1780s and 1790s, and as Margaret Thatcher did in the 1980s. Those who wish to improve the world—including its banking system—must begin from a clear sense of how political power is allocated and identify gains for those that have the power to make beneficial changes happen. It does no good to assume, passively, that all alternative feasible political bargains must already have been considered and rejected. As George Bernard Shaw said, "The reasonable man adapts himself to the world; the unreasonable man persists in trying to adapt the world to himself. Therefore all progress depends on the unreasonable man."[18] Meaningful reform in a democracy depends on informed and stubborn unreasonableness.

---

[17] Hassett and Lott (2009).
[18] Shaw (1903), 238.

REFERENCES

Abrams, Burton, and Richard F. Settle. 1993. "Pressure-Group Influence and Institutional Change: Branch-Banking Legislation during the Great Depression." *Public Choice* 77: 687–705.

Acemoglu, Daron, and James A. Robinson. 2000. "Democratization or Repression?" *European Economic Review* 44: 683–93.

Acemoglu, Daron, Georgy Egorov, and Konstantin Sonin. 2012. "Dynamics and Stability of Constitutions, Coalitions, and Clubs." *American Economic Review* 102: 1446–76.

Acemoglu, Daron, Simon Johnson, and James A. Robinson. 2005. "The Rise of Europe: Atlantic Trade, Institutional Change and Economic Growth." *American Economic Review* 95: 546–79.

Acharya, Viral V., Barry Adler, and Matthew Richardson. 2011. "A Proposal to Resolve the Distress of Large and Complex Financial Institutions," New York University Stern School of Business Working Paper.

Acharya, Viral V., Matthew Richardson, Stijn van Nieuwerburgh, and Lawrence J. White. 2011. *Guaranteed to Fail: Fannie Mae, Freddie Mac, and the Debacle of Mortgage Finance*. Princeton: Princeton University Press.

Acworth, Angus W. 1925. *Financial Reconstruction in England, 1815–1822*. London: P. S. King & Son.

Advisory Commission on Regulatory Barriers to Affordable Housing. 1991. "Not in My Backyard: Removing Barriers to Affordable Housing." U.S. Department of Housing and Urban Development. July 8. www.huduser.org/Publications/pdf/NotInMyBackyard.pdf, accessed March 7, 2013.

Agarwal, Sumit, Efraim Benmelech, and Amit Seru. 2012. "Did the Community Reinvestment Act Lead to Risky Lending?" University of Chicago Booth School Working Paper.

Aguilar, Gustavo. 2003. "El sistema bancario en Sinaloa (1889–1926): Su influencia en el crecimiento economico." In *La banca regional en Mexico, 1879–1930*, ed. Mario Cerutti and Carlos Marichal, 47–100. Mexico City: Fondo de Cultura Económica.

Akerlof, George A., and Paul M. Romer. 1993. "Looting: The Economic Underworld of Bankruptcy for Profit." *Brookings Papers on Economic Activity* 24: 1–74.

Allen, Jason, and Walter Engert. 2007. "Efficiency and Competition in Canadian Banking." *Bank of Canada Review* (Summer): 33–45.

Alston, Lee J. 1983. "Farm Foreclosures in the United States during the Interwar Period." *Journal of Economic History* 43: 885–903.

———. 1984. "Farm Foreclosure Moratorium Legislation: A Lesson from the Past." *American Economic Review* 74 (3): 445–57.

Alston, Lee J., Wayne E. Grove, and David C. Wheelock. 1994. "Why Do Banks Fail? Evidence from the 1920s." *Explorations in Economic History* 31: 409–31.

Alston, Lee J., Marcus André Melo, Bernardo Mueller, and Carlos Pereira. 2013. "Beliefs, Leadership and Economic Development; Making the Critical Transition, Brazil 1964–2012." Mimeo.

Altunbas, Yener, Leonardo Gambacorta, and David Marqués-Ibañez. 2009. "Bank Risk and Monetary Policy." European Central Bank Working Paper 1075.

Anderson, Ronald, and Karin Jõeveer. 2012. "Bankers and Bank Investors: Reconsidering the Economies of Scale in Banking," Financial Markets Group Paper DP712 and Centre for Economic Policy Research Paper DP9146, September.

Andreades, Andreas. [1909] 1966. *History of the Bank of England, 1640 to 1903.* New York: Augustus Kelley.

Associated Press. 1999. "Fleet Paid Supporters to Attend Public Hearing." July 12. www.southcoasttoday.com/apps/pbcs.dll/article?AID=/19990711/NEWS/307119965&template=printart, accessed March 6, 2013.

———. 2005. "HUD Review: Fannie Mae Offices Misused." October 17, 2005. www.freerepublic.com/focus/f-news/1504347/posts, accessed November 6, 2012.

Atlas, John. 2010. *Seeds of Change: The Story of ACORN, America's Most Controversial Antipoverty Community Organizing Group.* Nashville, TN: Vanderbilt University Press.

Ayyagari, Meghana, Asli Demirgüç-Kunt, and Vojislav Maksimovic. 2010. "Formal Versus Informal Finance: Evidence from China." *Review of Financial Studies* 23: 3048–97.

Bae, Kee-Hong, Jun-Koo Kang, and Jin-Mo Kim. 2002. "Tunneling or Value Added? Evidence from Mergers by Korean Business Groups." *Journal of Finance* 57 (6): 2695–2740.

Baer, Werner, and Nader Nazmi. 2000. "Privatization and Restructuring of Banks in Brazil." *Quarterly Review of Economics and Finance* 40: 3–24.

Bagehot, Walter. [1873] 1962. *Lombard Street: A Description of the Money Market.* Rept. Homewood, IL: Richard D. Irwin.

Bair, Sheila. 2012. *Bull by the Horns: Fighting to Save Main Street from Wall Street and Wall Street from Itself.* New York: Free Press.

Baker, Philip. 1986. "Kuwait: The Taxation of International Commercial Transactions." *Arab Law Quarterly* 1: 141–57.

Banco do Brasil. 1875. *Relatorio do Banco do Brasil.* Rio de Janeiro: Banco do Brasil.

BancoVotorantim. 2013. "Investor Relations." www.bancovotorantim.com.br/web/

site/investidores/en/Conheca_o_banco/parceria.bb.html, accessed September 1, 2013.

Bank of Canada. Various dates. *Bank of Canada Review.*

———. Various dates. *Bank of Canada Statistical Review.*

Bank of England. Various dates. *Minutes of the Court of the Bank of England.*

Barandiarán, Edgardo, and Leonardo Hernández. 1999. "Origins and Resolution of a Banking Crisis: Chile 1982–86." Central Bank of Chile Working Paper 57.

Barman, Roderick. 1981. "Business and Government in Imperial Brazil: The Experience of Viscount Mauá." *Journal of Latin American Studies* 13: 239–64.

———. 1988. *Brazil: The Forging of a Nation, 1798–1852.* Stanford: Stanford University Press.

Barro, Robert, and Jong-Wha Lee. 2010. "A New Dataset of Educational Attainment in the World, 1950–2010." National Bureau of Economic Research Working Paper 15902. Data set available for download at www.barrolee.com/data/yrsch2.htm.

Barth, James R. 1991. *The Great Savings and Loan Debacle.* Washington, DC: American Enterprise Institute Press.

Barth, James R., and R. Dan Brumbaugh, eds. 1992. *The Reform of Federal Deposit Insurance: Disciplining the Government and Protecting Taxpayers.* New York: Harper Business.

Barth, James R., Philip Bartholomew, and Carol Labich. 1989. "Moral Hazard and the Thrift Crisis: An Analysis of 1988 Resolutions." In *Proceedings of the 25th Annual Conference on Bank Structure and Competition,* 344–84. Chicago: Federal Reserve Bank of Chicago.

Barth, James R., Gerard Caprio, and Ross Levine. 2006. *Rethinking Bank Regulation: Till Angels Govern.* New York: Cambridge University Press.

———. 2012. *Guardians of Finance: Making Regulators Work for Us.* Cambridge, MA: MIT Press.

Barzel, Yoram, and Edgar Kiser. 2002. "Taxation and Voting Rights in Medieval England and France." *Rationality and Society* 14: 473–507.

Bass, Frank, and Dakin Campbell. 2013. "Predator Targets Hit as Banks Shut Branches amid Profits." Bloomberg.com, May 2. www.bloomberg.com/news/2013-05-02/post-crash-branch-closings-hit-hardest-in-poor-u-s-areas.html.

Batíz V., Jose Antonio. 1985. "Trayectoria de la Banca en México hasta 1910." In *Banca y poder en México, 1800 1925,* ed. Leonor Ludlow and Carlos Marichal, 267–98. Mexico City: Grijalbo.

Bazdresch, Carlos, and Santiago Levy. 1991. "Populism and Economic Policy in Mexico, 1970–82." In *The Macroeconomics of Populism in Latin America,* ed. Rudiger Dornbusch and Sebastian Edwards, 223–62. Chicago: University of Chicago Press.

Beck, Thorsten, and Luc Laeven. 2008. "Deposit Insurance and Bank Failure Resolution: Cross Country Evidence." In *Deposit Insurance around the World: Issues of Design and Implementation,* ed. Asli Demirgüç-Kunt, Edward J. Kane, and Luc Laeven, 149–78. Cambridge, MA: MIT Press.

Beck, Thorsten, Juan Miguel Crivelli, and William Summerhill. 2005. "State Bank

Transformation in Brazil: Choices and Consequences." *Journal of Banking and Finance* 29: 2223–57.

Beck, Thorsten, Asli Demirgüç-Kunt, and Ross Levine. 2006. "Bank Concentration, Competition, and Crises: First Results." *Journal of Banking and Finance* 30: 1581–1603.

Beck, Thorsten, Ross Levine, and Alexey Levkov. 2010. "Big Bad Banks? The Winners and Losers from Bank Deregulation in the United States." *Journal of Finance* 65: 1637–67.

Beck, Thorsten, Ross Levine, and Norman Loayza. 2000. "Finance and the Sources of Growth." *Journal of Financial Economics* 58: 261–300.

Beck, Thorsten, Asli Demirgüç-Kunt, Luc Laeven, and Ross Levine. 2008. "Finance, Firm Size, and Growth." *Journal of Money, Credit and Banking* 40: 1379–1405.

Beim, David O. 2001. "Banco Itua Case Study." Mimeo.

Beim, David O., and Charles W. Calomiris. 2001. *Emerging Financial Markets.* New York: Irwin-McGraw Hill.

Bekaert, Geert, Marie Hoerova, and Marco Lo Duca. 2010. "Risk, Uncertainty, and Monetary Policy." National Bureau of Economic Research Working Paper 16397.

Benmelech, Efraim, and Tobias J. Moskowitz. 2010. "The Political Economy of Financial Regulation: Evidence from U.S. State Usury Laws in the 19th Century." *Journal of Finance* 65: 1029–73.

Benston, George. 1989. *The Separation of Commercial and Investment Banking: The Glass-Steagall Act Revisited and Reconsidered.* Norwell, MA: Kluwer Academic Press.

Berg, Aaron, and Stephen Haber. 2009. "Always Turkeys: Brazil's State-Owned Banks in Historical Perspective." Mimeo.

Berger, Allen N., Asli Demirgüç-Kunt, Ross Levine, and Joseph G. Haubrich. 2004. "Bank Concentration and Competition: An Evolution in the Making." *Journal of Money, Credit and Banking* 36: 627–48.

Bernstein, Asaf, Eric Hughson, and Marc D. Weidenmier. 2010. "Identifying the Effects of a Lender of Last Resort on Financial Markets: Lessons from the Founding of the Fed." *Journal of Financial Economics* 98: 40–53.

Bethell, Leslie. 1989. "The Independence of Brazil." In *Brazil: Empire and Republic, 1822–1930,* ed. Leslie Bethell, 3–44. New York: Cambridge University Press.

Bethell, Leslie, and José Murillo de Carvalho. 1989. "1822–1850." In *Brazil: Empire and Republic, 1822–1930,* ed. Leslie Bethell, 45–112. New York: Cambridge University Press.

Bevilaqua, Afonso S. 2002. "State Government Bailouts in Brazil." Inter-American Development Bank, Latin American Research Network Working Paper R-441.

Billings, Mark, and Forrest Capie. 2007. "Capital in British Banking, 1920–1970." *Business History* 49: 139–62.

———. 2011. "Financial Crisis, Contagion, and the British Banking System between the World Wars." *Business History* 53 (2): 193–215.

Binswanger, Hans P., and Mark R. Rosenzweig. 1986. "Behavioural and Material Determinants of Production Relations in Agriculture." *Journal of Development Studies* 22: 503–39.

Black, Sandra E., and Philip E. Strahan. 2001. "The Division of Spoils: Rent-Sharing and Discrimination in a Regulated Industry." *American Economic Review* 91: 814–31.

———. 2002. "Entrepreneurship and Bank Credit Availability." *Journal of Finance* 57: 2807–33.

Bodenhorn, Howard. 1990. "Entry, Rivalry, and Free Banking in Antebellum America." *Review of Economics and Statistics* 72: 682–86.

———. 1993. "The Business Cycle and Entry into Early American Banking." *Review of Economics and Statistics* 75: 531–35.

———. 2000. *A History of Banking in Antebellum America: Financial Markets and Economic Development in an Era of Nation-Building.* Cambridge: Cambridge University Press.

———. 2003. *State Banking in Early America: A New Economic History.* New York: Oxford University Press.

———. 2006. "Bank Chartering and Political Corruption in Antebellum New York: Free Banking as Reform." In *Corruption and Reform: Lessons from America's Economic History,* ed. Edward Glaeser and Claudia Goldin, 231–57. Chicago: University of Chicago Press.

———. 2007. "The Political Economy of Reform in Jacksonian New York." Mimeo.

———. 2011. "Federal and State Banking Policy in the Federalist Era and Beyond." In *Founding Choices: American Economic Policy in the 1790s,* ed. Douglas Irwin and Richard Sylla, 151–76. Chicago: University of Chicago Press.

Bordo, Michael D. 1985. "Some Historical Evidence (1870–1933) on the Impact and International Transmission of Financial Crises." *Revista di storia economica* 2: 41–78.

———. 2007. "The Crisis of 2007: The Same Old Story, Only the Players Have Changed." In *Globalization and Systemic Risk,* ed. Douglas D. Evanoff, David S. Hoelscher, and George G. Kaufman, 39–50. Singapore: World Scientific Publishing.

———. 2008. "Growing Up to Financial Stability." *Economics E-Journal* 2: 1–17.

Bordo, Michael D., and Christopher M. Meissner. 2012. "Does Inequality Lead to a Financial Crisis?" National Bureau of Economic Research Working Paper 17896.

Bordo, Michael D., and Angela Redish. 1987. "Why Did the Bank of Canada Emerge in 1935?" *Journal of Economic History* 47: 405–17.

Bordo, Michael D., and Peter L. Rousseau. 2006. "Legal-Political Factors and the Historical Evolution of the Finance-Growth Link." *European Review of Economic History* 10: 421–44.

———. 2012. "Historical Evidence on the Finance-Trade-Growth Nexus." *Journal of Banking and Finance* 36: 1236–43.

Bordo, Michael D., and David C. Wheelock. 2007. "Stock Market Booms and Monetary Policy in the Twentieth Century." *Federal Reserve Bank of St. Louis Review* 89: 91–122.

———. 2009. "When Do Stock Market Booms Occur?" In *The Origin and Development of Financial Markets and Institutions from the Seventeenth Century to the Present,* ed. Jeremy Atack and Larry Neal, 416–49. Cambridge: Cambridge University Press.

Bordo, Michael D., Angela Redish, and Hugh Rockoff. 2011. "Why Didn't Canada Have a Banking Crisis in 2008 (or in 1930, or 1907, or . . .)?" National Bureau of Economic Research Working Paper 17312.

Bordo, Michael D., Hugh Rockoff, and Angela Redish. 1994. "The U.S. Banking System from a Northern Exposure: Stability versus Efficiency." *Journal of Economic History* 54: 325–41.

Bornstein, Morris. 1954. "Banking Policy and Economic Development: A Brazilian Case Study." *Journal of Finance* 9: 312–13.

Bowen, H. V. 1995. "The Bank of England during the Long Eighteenth Century, 1694–1820." In *The Bank of England: Money, Power and Influence 1694–1994,* ed. Richard Roberts and David Kynaston, 1–18. Oxford: Oxford University Press.

Boyd, John H., and Gianni De Nicoló. 2005. "The Theory of Bank Risk-Taking and Competition Revisited." *Journal of Finance* 60: 1329–43.

Boyd, John H., and David E. Runkle. 1993. "Size and Performance of Banking Firms: Testing the Predictions of Theory." *Journal of Monetary Economics* 31: 47–67.

Boyd, John H., Gianni De Nicoló, and Bruce Smith. 2004. "Crises in Competitive versus Monopolistic Banking Systems." *Journal of Money, Credit and Banking* 36: 487–506.

Braggion, Fabio, Narly Dwarkasing, and Lyndon Moore. 2012. "From Competition to Cartel: Bank Mergers in the U.K. 1885 to 1925." Mimeo.

Brandt, Loren, and Xiaodong Zhu. 2007. "China's Banking Sector and Economic Growth." In *China's Financial Transition at a Crossroads,* ed. Charles W. Calomiris, 86–136. New York: Columbia University Press.

Branstetter, Lee. 2007. "China's Financial Markets: An Overview." In *China's Financial Transition at a Crossroads,* ed. Charles W. Calomiris, 23–78. New York: Columbia University Press.

"Brazil: Failure Demonstrates Pressure on Small Banks." 2012. *Euromoney.* October.

Brazil, Ministerio do Trabalho, Industria e Comércio. 1946. "Serviço de Estatistica da Previdência do Trabalho: Levantamento do custo de vida no Brasil." Available from IPEA website, www.ipeadata.gov.br, accessed December 27, 2012.

"Brazilian Banks: No More Free Lunch." 2012. *Economist.* October 20.

Breckenridge, Roeliff M. 1899a. "Bank Notes and Branch Banks." *Sound Currency* 6: 49–56.

———. 1899b. "Branch Banking and Discount Rates." *Sound Currency* 6: 1–14.

———. 1910. *The History of Banking in Canada.* Washington, DC: National Monetary Commission, 61st Congress, 2nd session, Senate Document 332.

Brewer, Elijah. 1995. "The Impact of Deposit Insurance on S&L Shareholders' Risk/Return Trade-Offs." *Journal of Financial Services Research* 9: 65–89.

Brewer, Elijah, and Julapa Jagtiani. 2013. "How Much Did Banks Pay to Become Too-Big-to-Fail and to Become Systemically Important?" *Journal of Financial Services Research* 43: 1–35.

Brewer, Elijah, and Thomas H. Mondschean. 1991. "An Empirical Test of the Incentive Effects of Deposit Insurance: The Case of Junk Bonds at Savings and

Loan Associations." Federal Reserve Bank of Chicago Working Paper WP-91-18.

———. 1992. "Ex Ante Risk and Ex Post Collapse of S&Ls in the 1980s." *Economic Perspectives,* Federal Reserve Bank of Chicago (July–August): 2–12.

Brown, Craig O., and Serdar Dinc. 2005. "The Politics of Bank Failures: Evidence from Emerging Markets." *Quarterly Journal of Economics* 120: 1413–44.

Broz, J. Lawrence, and Richard S. Grossman. 2004. "Paying for Privilege: The Political Economy of Bank of England Charters, 1694–1844." *Explorations in Economic History* 41: 48–72.

Brunt, Liam. 2006. "Rediscovering Risk: English Country Banks as Proto–Venture Capital Firms in the Industrial Revolution." *Journal of Economic History* 66: 74–102.

Bullock, Charles. 1895. "The Finances of the United States from 1775 to 1789." *Bulletin of the University of Wisconsin: Economic, Political Science, and History Series* 1: 117–273.

Bunce, Harold L., and Randall M. Scheessele. 1996. "The GSEs Funding of Affordable Loans." Washington, DC: Office of Policy Development and Research, U.S. Department of Housing and Urban Development, Housing Finance Working Paper HF-001.

Butler, David, and Gareth Butler. 1994. *British Political Facts 1900–1994.* 7th ed. London: Macmillan.

Butts, George. 1998. "Testimony of George Butts, President, ACORN Housing Corporation, in Support of the Proposed Acquisition by NationsBank of the Bank of America, July 9." www.federalreserve.gov/bankinforeg/publicmeetings/19980709 panel14.PDF, accessed November 14, 2012.

Calomiris, Charles W. 1988a. "Institutional Failure, Monetary Scarcity, and the Depreciation of the Continental." *Journal of Economic History* 48: 47–68.

———. 1988b. "Price and Exchange Rate Determination during the Greenback Suspension." *Oxford Economic Papers* 40: 719–50.

———. 1989. "Deposit Insurance: Lessons from the Record." *Economic Perspectives,* Federal Reserve Bank of Chicago (May–June): 10–30.

———. 1990. "Is Deposit Insurance Necessary? A Historical Perspective." *Journal of Economic History* 50: 283–95.

———. 1991. "The Motives of U.S. Debt-Management Policy, 1790–1880: Efficient Discrimination and Time Consistency." *Research in Economic History* 13: 67–105.

———. 1992a. "Greenbacks." In *New Palgrave Dictionary of Money and Finance,* ed. Peter Newman, Murray Wilgate, and John Eatwell, 2: 281–84. London: Macmillan.

———. 1992b. "Do Vulnerable Economies Need Deposit Insurance? Lessons from US Agriculture in the 1920s." In *If Texas Were Chile: A Primer on Bank Regulation,* ed. P. L. Brock, 237–349, 450–58. San Francisco: Sequoia Institute.

———. 1993a. "Greenback Resumption and Silver Risk: The Economics and Politics of Monetary Regime Change in the United States, 1862–1900." In *Monetary Regimes in Transition,* ed. Michael D. Bordo and Forrest Capie, 86–134. New York: Cambridge University Press.

Calomiris, Charles W. 1993b. "Financial Factors in the Great Depression." *Journal of Economic Perspectives* 7: 61–85.

———. 1995. "The Costs of Rejecting Universal Banking: American Finance in the German Mirror, 1870–1914." In *Coordination and Information: Historical Perspectives on the Organization of Enterprise,* ed. Naomi R. Lamoreaux and Daniel Raff, 257–322. Chicago: University of Chicago Press.

———. 2000. *U.S. Bank Deregulation in Historical Perspective.* Cambridge: Cambridge University Press.

———. 2001. "An Economist's Case for GSE Reform." In *Serving Two Masters, yet Out of Control: Fannie Mae and Freddie Mac,* ed. Peter Wallison. Washington, DC: AEI Press.

———. 2005. "Capital Flows, Financial Crises, and Public Policy." In *Globalization: What's New?,* ed. Michael M. Weinstein, 36–76. New York: Columbia University Press.

———. 2006. "Alan Greenspan's Legacy: An Early Look; The Regulatory Record of the Greenspan Fed." *American Economic Association Papers and Proceedings* 96: 170–73. A longer version of the paper is available online at www.aei .org/publications/filter.all,pubID.28191/pub_detail.asp.

———, ed. 2007. *China's Financial Transition at a Crossroads.* New York: Columbia University Press.

———. 2008. "Testimony to the Committee on Oversight and Government Reform of the U.S. House of Representatives." December 9. Available at wwwo.gsb .columbia.edu/faculty/ccalomiris/papers/CalomirisF&FTestimony2008.pdf.

———. 2009. "The Subprime Turmoil: What's Old, What's New, and What's Next." *Journal of Structured Finance* 15: 6–52.

———. 2010a. "Reassessing the Fed's Regulatory Role." *Cato Journal* 30: 311–22.

———. 2010b. "The Political Lessons of Depression-Era Banking Reform." *Oxford Review of Economic Policy* 26: 540–60.

———. 2011a. "Banking Crises and the Rules of the Game." In *Monetary and Banking History: Essays in Honour of Forrest Capie,* ed. Geoffrey Wood, Terence Mills, and Nicholas Crafts, 88–132. Abingdon, U.K.: Routledge.

———. 2011b. "The Mortgage Crisis: Some Inside Views." *Wall Street Journal.* October 27. http://online.wsj.com/article/SB10001424053111903927204576 574433454435452.html, accessed May 23, 2013.

———. 2013. "How to Promote Fed Independence: Perspectives from Political Economy and U.S. History." Mimeo. March.

Calomiris, Charles W., and Ian Domowitz. 1989. "Asset Substitution, Money Demand, and the Inflation Process in Brazil." *Journal of Money, Credit and Banking* 21: 78–89.

Calomiris, Charles W., and Gary Gorton. 1991. "The Origins of Banking Panics: Models, Facts, and Bank Regulation." In *Financial Markets and Financial Crises,* ed. R. Glenn Hubbard, 109–73. Chicago: University of Chicago Press.

Calomiris, Charles W., and Richard Herring. 2012. "Why and How to Design a Contingent Convertible Debt Requirement." In *Rocky Times: New Perspectives on Financial Stability,* ed. Y. Fuchita, R. Herring, and R. Litan, 117–62. Washington, DC: Brookings Institution Press.

Calomiris, Charles W., and Charles M. Kahn. 1991. "The Role of Demandable

Debt in Structuring Optimal Banking Arrangements." *American Economic Review* 81: 497–513.

———. 1996. "The Efficiency of Self-Regulated Payments Systems: Learning from the Suffolk System." *Journal of Money, Credit and Banking* 28: 766–97.

Calomiris, Charles W., and Joseph R. Mason. 2003a. "Fundamentals, Panics, and Bank Distress during the Depression." *American Economic Review* 93: 1615–46.

———. 2003b. "Consequences of U.S. Bank Distress during the Depression." *American Economic Review* 93: 937–47.

———. 2004. "Resolving the Puzzle of the Underissue of National Bank Notes." *Explorations in Economic History* 45: 327–55.

Calomiris, Charles W., and Thanavut Pornrojnangkool. 2009. "Relationship Banking and the Pricing of Financial Services." *Journal of Financial Services Research* 35: 189–224.

Calomiris, Charles W., and Andrew Powell. 2001. "Can Emerging Market Bank Regulators Establish Credible Discipline? The Case of Argentina, 1992–99." In *Prudential Supervision: What Works and What Doesn't*, ed. Frederic S. Mishkin, 147–96. Chicago: University of Chicago Press.

Calomiris, Charles W., and Carlos Ramirez. 2008. "The Political Economy of Bank Entry Restrictions: Theory and Evidence from the U.S. in the 1920s." Mimeo.

Calomiris, Charles W., and Larry Schweikart. 1991. "The Panic of 1857: Origins, Transmission, and Containment." *Journal of Economic History* 51: 807–34.

Calomiris, Charles W., and Eugene N. White. 1994. "The Origins of Federal Deposit Insurance." In *The Regulated Economy: A Historical Approach to Political Economy*, ed. Claudia Goldin and Gary Libecap, 145–88. Chicago: University of Chicago Press.

Calomiris, Charles W., and Berry Wilson. 2004. "Bank Capital and Portfolio Management: The 1930s 'Capital Crunch' and Scramble to Shed Risk." *Journal of Business* 77: 421–56.

Calomiris, Charles W., R. Eisenbeis, and R. Litan. 2012. "Financial Crisis in the US and Beyond." In *The World in Crisis: Insights from Six Shadow Financial Regulatory Committees*, ed. R. Litan, 1–60. Philadelphia: Wharton Financial Institutions Center.

Calomiris, Charles W., Florian Heider, and Marie Hoerova. 2013. "A Theory of Liquidity Requirements." Mimeo. June.

Calomiris, Charles W., R. Glenn Hubbard, and James Stock. 1986. "The Farm Debt Crisis and Public Policy." *Brookings Papers on Economic Activity* 2: 441–85.

Calomiris, Charles W., Daniela Klingebiel, and Luc Laeven. 2005. "Financial Crisis Policies and Resolution Mechanisms: A Taxonomy from Cross-Country Experience." In *Systemic Financial Crises: Containment and Resolution*. ed. Patrick Honohan and Luc Laeven, 25–75. New York: Cambridge University Press.

Cameron, Rondo. 1967a. "England, 1750–1844." In Rondo Cameron, with the collaboration of Olga Crisp, Hugh T. Patrick, and Richard Tilly, *Banking in the Early Stages of Industrialization: A Study in Comparative Economic History*, 15–59. New York: Oxford University Press.

———. 1967b. "Scotland, 1750–1845." In Rondo Cameron, with the collaboration of Olga Crisp, Hugh T. Patrick, and Richard Tilly, *Banking in the Early*

Stages of Industrialization: A Study in Comparative Economic History, 60–99. New York: Oxford University Press.

Cameron, Rondo, with the collaboration of Olga Crisp, Hugh T. Patrick, and Richard Tilly. 1967. *Banking in the Early Stages of Industrialization: A Study in Comparative Economic History.* New York: Oxford University Press.

Campbell, Sybil. 1928. "Usury and Annuities of the Eighteenth Century." *Law Quarterly Review* 176: 473–91.

Canada Department of Finance. 2003. "Power Financial Corporation Submission to Minister of Finance: Future Structure of the Canadian Financial Services Industry." www.fin.gc.ca/consultresp/mergersrespns_16-eng.asp.

Canadamortgage.com. n.d. "Government Housing and Mortgages in Canada." www.canadamortgage.com/articles/learning.cfm?DocID=37, accessed February 29, 2012.

Canadian Bankers Association. 2012. "Domestic Banks' Financial Results Fiscal Year End for the Years 2006–2011." www.cba.ca/contents/files/statistics/stat_banksann_db251_en.pdf, accessed August 6, 2013.

Cannan, Edwin, ed. 1925. *The Paper Pound of 1797–1821: The Bullion Report, 8th June 1810.* London: P. S. King & Son.

Canner, Glenn B., Wayne Passmore, and Brian J. Surette. 1996. "Distribution of Credit Risk among Providers of Mortgages to Lower-Income and Minority Homebuyers." *Federal Reserve Bulletin* 82: 1077–1102.

Cantor, Richard, and Frank Packer. 1994. "The Credit Rating Industry." *Federal Reserve Bank of New York Quarterly Review* 19 (2): 1–26.

Capie, Forrest. 2002. "The Emergence of the Bank of England as a Mature Central Bank." In *The Political Economy of British Historical Experience, 1688–1914.* Oxford: Oxford University Press.

———. 2009. "Financial Crises in England in the Nineteenth and Twentieth Centuries." Mimeo. June.

———. 2010. *The Bank of England: 1950s to 1979.* London: Cambridge University Press.

Capie, Forrest, and Mark Billings. 2001. "Profitability in English Banking in the Twentieth Century. *European Review of Economic History* 5: 367–401.

———. 2004. "Evidence on Competition in English Commercial Banking, 1920–1970." *Financial History Review* 11: 69–103.

Capie, Forrest, and Alan Webber. 1985. *A Monetary History of the United Kingdom, 1870–1982.* London: Allen & Unwin.

Caprio, Gerard, and Daniela Klingebiel. 1996. "Bank Insolvencies: Cross-Country Experience." World Bank Policy Research Working Paper 1620.

———. 2003. Banking Crises Database. Washington, DC: World Bank. www1.worldbank.org/finance/html/database_sfd.html.

Cárdenas, Enrique. 2000. "The Process of Accelerated Industrialization in Mexico, 1929–1982." In *An Economic History of Twentieth-Century Latin America,* vol. 3, *Industrialization and the State in Latin America: The Postwar Years,* ed. Enrique Cárdenas, José Antonio Ocampo, and Rosemary Thorp, 176–204. London: Palgrave.

Carletti, Elena, and Philipp Hartmann. 2003. "Competition and Stability: What's Special about Banking?" In *Monetary History, Exchange Rates and Financial*

Markets: Essays in Honor of Charles Goodhart, ed. Paul Mizen, 202–51. Cheltenham, U.K.: Edward Elgar.

Carmagnani, Marcello. 1994. *Estado y mercado: La economía pública del liberalismo mexicano, 1850–1911.* Mexico City: Colegio de México and Fondo de Cultura Económica.

Carnel, Richard Scott. 2001. "Federal Deposit Insurance and Federal Sponsorship of Fannie Mae and Freddie Mac: The Structure of the Subsidy." In *Serving Two Masters, yet Out of Control: Fannie Mae and Freddie Mac,* ed. Peter J. Wallison, 56–83. Washington, DC: AEI Press.

Carosso, Vincent P. 1970. *Investment Banking in America: A History.* Cambridge, MA: Harvard University Press.

Carr, Jack, Frank Mathewson, and Neil Quigley. 1994. *Ensuring Failure: Financial System Stability and Deposit Insurance in Canada.* Toronto: C. D. Howe Institute.

———. 1995. "Stability in the Absence of Deposit Insurance: The Canadian Banking System, 1890–1966." *Journal of Money, Credit and Banking* 27: 1137–58.

Carvalho, Antonio Gledson de, and George Pennacchi. 2012. "Can a Stock Exchange Improve Corporate Behavior? Evidence from Firms' Migration to Premium Listings in Brazil." *Journal of Corporate Finance* 18: 883–903.

Carvalho, Daniel R. Forthcoming. "The Real Effects of Government-Owned Banks: Evidence from an Emerging Market." *Journal of Finance.*

Caselli, Fausto Piola. 2013. "Papal Finance, 1348–1848." In *Handbook of Key Global Financial Markets, Institutions, and Infrastructure,* vol. 1, *Globalization of Finance: An Historical View,* ed. Gerard Caprio. 207–20. London: Elsevier.

Catão, Luis A. V. 1992. "A New Wholesale Price Index for Brazil during the Period 1870–1913." *Revista brasileira de economia* 46: 519–33.

Central Bank of Somalia. 2011. "The Central Bank of Somalia Act Law No. 130 of 22 April 2011." http://media.wix.com/ugd//beb93a_870b1ad62ece694a4f3ecc9041ff88b6.pdf, accessed May 6, 2013.

Cerutti, Mario. 1985. "El préstamo prebancario en el noreste de México: La actividad de los grandes comerciantes de Monterrey, 1855–1890." In *Banca y poder en México, 1800–1925,* ed. Leonor Ludlow and Carlos Marichal, 119–64. Mexico City: Grijalbo.

———. 2003. "Empresario y banca en el norte de Mexico, 1879–1910: La fundación del Banco Refaccionario de la Laguna." In *La banca regional en México, 1870–1930,* ed. Mario Cerutti and Carlos Marichal, 168–215. Mexico City: Fondo de Cultura Económica.

Cetorelli, Nicola, and Michele Gamberra. 2001. "Banking Market Structure, Financial Dependence, and Growth: International Evidence from Industry Data." *Journal of Finance* 56: 617–48.

Cetorelli, Nicola, and Philip Strahan. 2006. "Finance as a Barrier to Entry: Bank Competition and Industry Structure in Local U.S. Markets." *Journal of Finance* 61: 437–61.

Chapman, John M., and Ray B. Westerfield. 1942. *Branch Banking: Its Historical and Theoretical Position in America and Abroad.* New York: Harper and Brothers.

Checkland, Sydney G. 1975. *Scottish Banking: A History, 1695–1973.* Glasgow: Collins.

Chester, Norman. 1975. *The Nationalisation of British Industry 1945–51.* London: Her Majesty's Stationery Office.

Christie, Robert. 1866. *A History of the Late Province of Lower Canada: Parliamentary and Political, from the Commencement to the Close of Its Existence as a Separate Province.* Montreal: Richard Worthington.

Churchill, Winston S. 1998. *A History of the English-Speaking Peoples.* Abridged. London: Cassell.

Cihak, Martin, Asli Demirgüç-Kunt, and R. B. Johnston. 2012. "Good Regulation Needs to Fix the Broken Incentives." World Bank Working Paper.

Clague, Christopher, Philip Keefer, Stephen Knack, and Mancur Olson. 1999. "Contract-Intensive Money: Contract Enforcement, Property Rights, and Economic Performance." *Journal of Economic Growth* 4: 185–211.

Clapham, John. 1944. *The Bank of England: A History.* 2 vols. Cambridge: Cambridge University Press.

Clinton, William. 1999a. "Remarks by the President at the Democratic National Committee Labor Dinner at the Mayflower Hotel." July 22.

———. 1999b. "Statement by the President at the Signing of the Financial Modernization Bill." U.S. Treasury Department of Public Affairs. November 12.

Coerver, Don M., Suzanne B. Pasztor, and Robert M. Buffington. 2004. "Cantinflas," in *Mexico: An Encyclopedia of Contemporary Culture and History.* Santa Barbara: ABC-CLIO Inc, 57–61.

Coffman, D'Maris. 2013. "Fiscal Experimentation in Early Modern Europe: Excise Taxation and the Origins of Public Finance in Britain." Mimeo.

Coffman, D'Maris, Adrian Leord, and Larry Neal, eds. 2013. *Questioning Credible Commitment: New Perspectives on the Glorious Revolution and the Rise of Financial Capitalism.* Cambridge: Cambridge University Press.

Collins, Michael. 1995. *Banks and Industrial Finance in Britain, 1800–1939.* Cambridge: Cambridge University Press.

———. 2012. *Banking and Finance: Money and Banking in the UK: A History.* New York: Routledge.

Common Cause. 2008. "Ask Yourself Why . . . They Didn't See This Coming." September 24. www.commoncause.org/site/pp.asp?c=dkLNK1MQIwG&b=4542875, accessed August 5, 2013.

Conant, Charles Arthur. 1910. *The Banking System of Mexico.* Washington, DC: National Monetary Commission, 61st Congress, 2nd Session, Senate Document 493.

Condon, Bradly, and Tapen Sinha. 2003. *Drawing Lines in Sand and Snow: Border Security and North American Economic Integration.* Armonk, NY: M. E. Sharpe.

Congressional Budget Office. 1992. *The Economic Effects of the Savings & Loan Crisis.* Washington, DC: Congressional Budget Office.

Correa, Ricardo. 2008. "Bank Integration and Financial Constraints: Evidence from U.S. Firms." Board of Governors of the Federal Reserve System, International Finance Discussion Paper 925.

Coy, Peter. 2008. "Bill Clinton's Drive to Increase Homeownership Went Way Too Far." *Businessweek.* February 27.

Cragoe, Matthew. 2008. "The Great Reform Act and the Modernization of British Politics: The Impact of Conservative Associations, 1835–1841." *Journal of British Studies* 47: 581–603.

Crisp, Olga. 1967. "Russia, 1860–1914." In Rondo E. Cameron, with the collaboration of Olga Crisp, Hugh T. Patrick, and Richard Tilly, *Banking in the Early Stages of Industrialization*, 183–238. New York: Oxford University Press.

Cull, Robert, Stephen Haber, and Masami Imai. 2011. "Related Lending and Banking Development." *Journal of International Business Studies* 42: 406–26.

Cull, Robert, Lemma Senbet, and Marco Sorge. 2005. "Deposit Insurance and Financial Development." *Journal of Money, Credit and Banking* 37: 43–82.

Cunningham, William. 1907. *The Growth of English Industry and Commerce in Modern Times*. Cambridge: Cambridge University Press.

Curry, Timothy, and Lynn Shibut. 2000. "The Cost of the Savings and Loan Crisis: Truth and Consequences." *FDIC Banking Review* 13: 26–35.

Curtis, C. A. 1947. "Evolution of Canadian Banking." *Annals of the American Academy of Political and Social Science* 253: 115–24.

Dang, Tri Vi, Gary Gorton, and Bengt Holmström. 2012. "Ignorance, Debt and Financial Crises." Mimeo. February.

Davies Ward Phillips & Vineberg LLP. n.d. *Acquiring or Establishing a Canadian Bank: A Guide for Foreign Banks,* http://www.dwpr.com/en/Resources/Publications/2009/Aquiring-or-Establishing-a-Canadian-Bank-A-Guide-for-Foreign-Banks, accessed September 2, 2013.

Davis, Lance E., and Robert E. Gallman. 2001. *Evolving Financial Markets and International Capital Flows: Britain, the Americas, and Australia, 1865–1914.* Cambridge: Cambridge University Press.

Davis, Lance E., and Robert A. Huttenback. 1988. *Mammon and the Pursuit of Empire*. New York: Cambridge University Press.

DeHaven, Tad. 2009. "Three Decades of Politics and Failed Policies at HUD." Cato Institute Policy Analysis Paper 655.

Dehejia, Rajeev, and Adriana Lleras-Muney. 2007. "Financial Development and Pathways of Growth: State Branching and Deposit Insurance Laws in the United States, 1900–1940." *Journal of Law and Economics* 50: 239–72.

De la Cuadra, Sergio, and Salvador Valdes. 1992. "Myths and Facts about Financial Liberalization in Chile, 1974–1983." In *If Texas Were Chile: A Primer on Banking Reform,* ed. Philip Brock, 11–101. San Francisco: Institute for Contemporary Studies.

Del Angel-Mobarak, Gustavo. 2002. "Paradoxes of Financial Development: The Construction of the Mexican Banking System, 1941–1982." Ph.D. diss., Stanford University.

———. 2005. "La Banca Mexicana antes de 1982." In *Cuando el estado se hizo banquero: Consecuencias de la nacionalización bancaria en México,* ed. Gustavo del Ángel-Mobarak, Carlos Bazdresch, and Francisco Suárez Dávila. Mexico City: Fondo de Cultura Económica.

Del Angel-Mobarak, Gustavo, and César Martinelli Montoya. 2009. *La estatización de 1982 de la Banca en México: Un ensayo en economía política.* Mexico: Centro de Estudios Espinosa Yglesias.

Del Angel-Mobarak, Gustavo, Stephen Haber, and Aldo Musacchio. 2006. "Normas contables bancarias en México: Una guía de los cambios para legos diez años después de la crisis bancaria de 1995." *El trimestre económico* 73: 903–26.

Dell'Ariccia, Giovanni, Deniz Igan, and Luc A. Laeven. 2012. "Credit Booms and Lending Standards: Evidence from the Subprime Mortgage Market." *Journal of Money, Credit and Banking* 44: 367–84.

DeLong, J. Bradford. 1991. "Did J. P. Morgan's Men Add Value? An Economist's Perspective on Financial Capitalism." In *Inside the Business Enterprise: Historical Perspectives on the Use of Information,* ed. Peter Temin, 205–50. Chicago: University of Chicago Press.

de Luca, Giuseppe. 2013. "Milanese Finance, 1348–1700." In *Handbook of Key Global Financial Markets, Institutions, and Infrastructure,* vol. 1, *Globalization of Finance: An Historical View,* ed. Gerard Caprio, 185–96. London: Elsevier.

Demirgüç-Kunt, Asli, and Enrica Detragiache. 2002. "Does Deposit Insurance Increase Banking System Stability? An Empirical Investigation." *Journal of Monetary Economics* 49: 1373–1406.

Demirgüç-Kunt, Asli, and Harry Huizinga. 2004. "Market Discipline and Deposit Insurance." *Journal of Monetary Economics* 51: 375–99.

Demirgüç-Kunt, Asli, and Edward J. Kane. 2002. "Deposit Insurance around the Globe: Where Does It Work?" *Journal of Economic Perspectives* 16: 175–95.

Demirgüç-Kunt, Asli, Enrica Detragiache, and Ouarda Merrouche. Forthcoming. "Bank Capital: Lessons from the Financial Crisis." *Journal of Money, Credit and Banking.*

Demirgüç-Kunt, Asli, Edward J. Kane, and Luc Laeven. 2008. "Adoption and Design of Deposit Insurance." In *Deposit Insurance around the World: Issues of Design and Implementation,* ed. Asli Demirgüç-Kunt, Edward J. Kane, and Luc Laeven, 29–80. Cambridge, MA: MIT Press.

de Vries, Jan, and Ad van der Woude. 1997. *The First Modern Economy: Success, Failure, and Perseverance of the Dutch Economy, 1500–1815.* New York: Cambridge University Press.

Diamond, Douglas. 1984. "Financial Intermediation and Delegated Monitoring." *Review of Economic Studies* 51: 393–414.

Diamond, Douglas W., and Philip H. Dybvig. 1983. "Bank Runs, Deposit Insurance, and Liquidity." *Journal of Political Economy* 91: 401–19.

Diamond, Jared. 1997. *Guns, Germs, and Steel: The Fates of Human Societies.* New York: W. W. Norton.

Díaz Alejandro, Carlos F. 1985. "Goodbye Financial Repression, Hello Financial Crash." *Journal of Development Economics* 19: 1–24.

Dickson, Peter G. M. 1967. *The Financial Revolution in England: A Study in the Development of Public Credit, 1688–1756.* New York: Macmillan.

Drelichman, Mauricio. 2013. "Spanish Finance, 1348–1700." In *Handbook of Key Global Financial Markets, Institutions, and Infrastructure,* vol. 1, *Globalization of Finance: An Historical View,* ed. Gerard Caprio, 259–68. London: Elsevier.

Drelichman, Mauricio, and Hans-Joachim Voth. 2008. "Debt Sustainability in Historical Perspective: The Role of Fiscal Repression." *Journal of the European Economic Association* 6: 657–67.

———. 2010. "The Sustainable Debts of Philip II: A Reconstruction of Castile's Fiscal Position, 1560–1598." *Journal of Economic History* 70: 814–43.

———. 2011a. "Lending to the Borrower from Hell: Debt and Default in the Age of Philip II." *Economic Journal* 121: 1205–1227.

———. 2011b. "Serial Defaults, Serial Profits: Returns to Sovereign Lending in Habsburg Spain, 1566–1600." *Explorations in Economic History* 48: 1–19.

Duhigg, Charles. 2008. "At Freddie Mac, Chief Discarded Warning Signs." *New York Times.* August 5. www.nytimes.com/2008/08/05/business/05freddie.html?pagewanted=all&_r=0.

Dunne, Gerald. 1960. *Monetary Decisions of the Supreme Court.* New Brunswick, NJ: Rutgers University Press.

Dye, Alan. 1998. *Cuban Sugar in the Age of Mass Production: Technology and the Economics of the Sugar Central, 1899–1929.* Stanford: Stanford University Press.

Eckardt, H. M. P. 1913. "Canadian Banking." *Annals of the American Academy of Political and Social Science* 45: 158–70.

Economides, Nicholas, R. Glenn Hubbard, and Darius Palia. 1996. "The Political Economy of Branching Restrictions and Deposit Insurance: A Model of Monopolistic Competition among Small and Large Banks." *Journal of Law and Economics* 39: 667–704.

Economopoulos, Andrew, and Heather O'Neill. 1995. "Bank Entry during the Antebellum Period." *Journal of Money, Credit, and Banking* 27: 1071–85.

Edwards, Sebastian. 2010. *Left Behind: Latin America and the False Promise of Populism.* Chicago: University of Chicago Press.

Edwards, Sebastian, and Alejandra C. Edwards. 1991. *Monetarism and Liberalization: The Chilean Experiment.* Chicago: University of Chicago Press.

Eichengreen, Barry. 2008. *Globalizing Capital: A History of the International Monetary System.* Princeton: Princeton University Press.

Eistert, Ekkehard. 1970. *Die Beeinflussung des Wirrschaftswachstums in Deutschland von 1883 bis 1913 durch das Bankensystem.* Berlin: Duncker and Humblot.

Elizondo Mayer-Serra, Carlos. 2001. *La importancia de las reglas: Gobierno y empresario después de la nacionalización bancaria.* Mexico City: Fondo de Cultura Económica.

Ellul, Andrew, and Vijay Yerramilli. 2010. "Stronger Risk Controls, Lower Risk: Evidence from U.S. Bank Holding Companies." National Bureau of Economic Research Working Paper 16178.

Elmer, Peter J., and Steven A. Seelig. 1998. "The Rising Long-Term Trend of Single-Family Mortgage Foreclosure Rates." Federal Deposit Insurance Corporation Working Paper 98-2.

Engerman, Stanley L. 1970. "A Note on the Economic Consequences of the Second Bank of the United States." *Journal of Political Economy* 78: 725–28.

Engerman, Stanley L., and Kenneth L. Sokoloff. 1997. "Factor Endowments, Institutions, and Differential Paths of Growth among New World Economies: A View from Economic Historians of the United States." In *How Latin America Fell Behind: Essays on the Economic Histories of Brazil and Mexico, 1800–1914,* ed. Stephen Haber, 260–304. Stanford: Stanford University Press.

Engerman, Stanley L., and Kenneth L. Sokoloff, with contributions by Stephen Haber, Elisa Mariscal, and Eric Zolt. 2012. *Economic Development in the*

Americas since 1500: Endowments and Institutions. New York: Cambridge University Press.

English, William B. 1996. "Understanding the Costs of Sovereign Default: American State Debts in the 1840's." *American Economic Review* 86: 259–75.

Epstein, David, Sharyn O'Halloran, and Geraldine McAllister. 2010. "Delegation and the Regulation of Finance in the United States Since 1950." Mimeo.

Espinosa Rugarcía, Amparo, and Enrique Cárdenas Sánchez. 2011. *Privatización bancaria, crisis y rescate del sistema financiero.* Vol. 3. Mexico City: Centro de Estudios Espinosa Yglesias.

Evanoff, Douglas D., and Lewis M. Segal. 1996. "CRA and Fair Lending Regulations: Resulting Trends in Mortgage Lending." *Economic Perspectives,* Federal Reserve Bank of Chicago (November): 19–46.

———. 1997. "Strategic Responses to Bank Regulation: Evidence from HMDA Data." *Journal of Financial Services Research* 11: 69–93.

Evans, Eric J. 1983. *The Great Reform Act of 1832.* London: Methuen.

Fahlenbrach, Rüdiger, Robert Prilmeier, and René M. Stulz. 2012. "This Time Is the Same: Using Bank Performance in 1998 to Explain Bank Performance during the Recent Financial Crisis." *Journal of Finance* 67: 2139–2185.

Federal Deposit Insurance Corporation. n.d. "Historical Statistics on Banking." http://www2.fdic.gov/hsob/index.asp.

Federal Reserve Board. 1943. *Banking and Monetary Statistics.* Washington, DC: U.S. Government Printing Office.

———. 1971. *Banking and Monetary Statistics.* Washington, DC: U.S. Government Printing Office.

———. 1999a. "Public Meeting Regarding Fleet Financial Group Inc., and Bank-Boston Corporation. July 7, 1999." Transcript. www.federalreserve.gov/events/publicmeeting/19990707/, accessed October 30, 2012.

———. 1999b. "Order Approving Merger of Bank Holding Companies." September 7. www.federalreserve.gov/bankinforeg/publicmeetings/19990707_panel9.pdf, accessed March 6, 2013.

———. n.d. "Flow of Funds Database." www.federalreserve.gov/apps/fof/FOFTables.aspx, accessed August 1, 2013.

Feler, Leo. 2012. "State Bank Privatization and Local Economic Activity." Mimeo.

Ferguson, E. James. 1961. *The Power of the Purse: A History of American Public Finance, 1776–1790.* Chapel Hill: University of North Carolina Press.

Ferguson, Niall. 1998a. *The House of Rothschild: Money's Prophets, 1798–1848.* New York: Viking Penguin.

———. 1998b. *The House of Rothschild: The World's Banker, 1849–1998.* New York: Viking Penguin.

Fischer, Brodwyn. 2008. *A Poverty of Rights: Citizenship and Inequality in Twentieth-Century Rio de Janeiro.* Stanford: Stanford University Press.

Fishback, Price, and John Wallis. 2012. "What Was New about the New Deal?" NBER Working Paper 18271.

Fishback, Price V., Jonathan Rose, and Kenneth Snowden. 2013. *Well Worth Saving: How the New Deal Safeguarded Home Ownership.* Chicago: University of Chicago Press.

Fishback, Price, Kenneth Snowden, and Eugene N. White, eds. Forthcoming. *Housing and Mortgage Markets in Historical Perspective.* Chicago: Chicago University Press.

Fishbein, Allen J. 1992. "The Community Reinvestment Act after Fifteen Years: It Still Works, but Strengthened Federal Enforcement Is Needed." *Fordham Urban Law Journal* 20: 293–310.

———. 2003. "Filling the Half-Empty Glass: The Role of Community Advocacy in Redefining the Public Responsibilities of Government-Sponsored Housing Enterprises." In *Organizing Access to Capital: Advocacy and the Democratization of Financial Institutions,* ed. Gregory D. Squires, 102–18. Philadelphia: Temple University Press.

Fisman, Raymond, and Inessa Love. 2004. "Financial Development and Intersectoral Allocation: A New Approach." *Journal of Finance* 59: 2785–2807.

Flandreau, Marc. 2003. "Caveat Emptor: Coping with Sovereign Risk under the International Gold Standard." In *International Financial History in the Twentieth Century: System and Anarchy,* ed. M. Flandreau, C. L. Holtfrerich, and H. James, 17–50. New York: Cambridge University Press.

Flandreau, Marc, and Juan H. Flores. 2009. "Bonds and Brands: Foundations of Sovereign Debt Markets, 1820–1830." *Journal of Economic History* 69: 646–84.

Flandreau, Marc, and Stefano Ugolini. 2011. "Where It All Began: Lending of Last Resort and the Bank of England during the Overend-Gurney Panic of 1866." Norges Bank Working Paper 2011/03.

Flandreau, Marc, Christophe Galimard, Clemens Jobst, and Pilar Nogues-Marco. 2009. "The Bell Jar: Commercial Interest Rates between Two Revolutions, 1688–1789." In *The Origin and Development of Financial Markets and Institutions from the Seventeenth Century to the Present,* ed. Jeremy Atack and Larry Neal, 161–208. Cambridge: Cambridge University Press.

Flandreau, Marc, Juan H. Flores, Norbert Gaillard, and Sebastián Nieto-Parra. 2010. "The End of Gatekeeping: Underwriters and the Quality of Sovereign Bond Markets, 1815–2007." In *NBER International Seminar on Macroeconomics,* 53–92. Cambridge, MA: National Bureau of Economic Research.

———. 2013. "Global Financial Brands and the Underwriting of Foreign Government Debt since 1815." In *Handbook of Key Global Financial Markets, Institutions, and Infrastructure,* vol. 1, *Globalization of Finance: An Historical View,* ed. Gerard Caprio, 281–300. London: Elsevier.

Flannery, Mark J., and W. Scott Frame. 2006. "The Federal Home Loan Bank System: The "Other" Housing GSE." *Economic Review, Federal Reserve Bank of Atlanta* 3: 33–54.

Florida Minority Community Reinvestment Coalition. 2003. "The Anatomy of a CRA Agreement, Presented by Haydee Diaz." Greenlining Institute. November 14. www.fmcrc.org/reinvestment.html, accessed March 7, 2013.

Fohlin, Caroline. 2011. *Finance Capitalism and Germany's Rise to Industrial Power.* New York: Cambridge University Press.

Freedman, Charles. 1998. "The Canadian Banking System." Bank of Canada Technical Report 81.

Freixas, Xavier, Bruno M. Parigi, and Jean-Charles Rochet. 2000. "Systemic Risk,

Interbank Relations, and Liquidity Provision by the Central Bank." *Journal of Money, Credit and Banking* 32: 611–38.

Fry, Maxwell J. 1988. *Money, Interest, and Banking in Economic Development.* Baltimore: Johns Hopkins University Press.

Gamboa Ojeda, Leticia. 2003. "El Banco Oriental de Mexico y la formación de un sistema de banca, 1900–1911." In *La banca regional en México, 1870–1930,* ed. Mario Cerutti and Carlos Marichal, 101–33. Mexico City: Fondo de Cultura Económica.

Garber, Peter M. 2000. *Famous First Bubbles.* Cambridge, MA: MIT Press.

Gatell, Frank Otto. 1966. "Sober Second Thoughts on Van Buren, the Albany Regency, and the Wall Street Conspiracy." *Journal of American History* 53: 19–40.

Gayer, Arthur, Walt Rostow, and Anna Schwartz. 1975. *The Growth and Fluctuation of the British Economy, 1790–1850: An Historical, Statistical, and Theoretical Study of Britain's Economic Development.* Brighton: Harvester Press.

Gelderblom, Oscar, and Joost Jonker. 2011. "Public Finance and Economic Growth: The Case of Holland in the Seventeenth Century." *Journal of Economic History* 71: 1–39.

———. 2013. "Low Countries Finance, 1348–1700." In *Handbook of Key Global Financial Markets, Institutions, and Infrastructure,* vol. 1, *Globalization of Finance: An Historical View,* ed. Gerard Caprio, 175–84. London: Elsevier.

Gerschenkron, Alexander. 1962. *Economic Backwardness in Historical Perspective: A Book of Essays.* Cambridge, MA: Belknap Press.

Giedeman, Daniel C. 2005. "Branch Banking Restrictions and Finance Constraints in Early-Twentieth-Century America." *Journal of Economic History* 65: 129–51.

Gilbert, Alton. 1991. "Supervision of Undercapitalized Banks: Is There a Case for Change?" *Federal Reserve Bank of St. Louis Review* 73: 16–30.

———. 1994. "Federal Reserve Lending to Banks That Failed: Implications for the Bank Insurance Fund." *Federal Reserve Bank of St. Louis Review* 76: 3–18.

———. 1995. "Determinants of Federal Reserve Lending to Failed Banks." *Journal of Economics and Business* 47: 397–408.

Gilbert, Martin. 1991. *Churchill: A Life.* New York: Henry Holt.

———. 1997. *A History of the Twentieth Century,* vol. 1, *1900–1933.* New York: Avon.

Goldschmidt, Raymond W. 1933. *The Changing Structure of American Banking.* London: George Routledge & Sons.

Goldsmith, Raymond W. 1969. *Financial Structure and Development.* New Haven, CT: Yale University Press.

———. 1986. *Brasil, 1850–1984: Desenvolvimento financiero sob um século de inflação.* Rio de Janeiro: Banco Bamerindus do Brasil.

Golembe, Carter H. 1960. "The Deposit Insurance Legislation of 1933: An Examination of Its Antecedents and Its Purposes." *Political Science Quarterly* 75: 181–200.

Golembe, Carter H., and C. Warburton. 1958. "Insurance of Bank Obligations in Six States during the Period 1829–1866." Washington, DC: Federal Deposit Insurance Corporation.

Goodhart, Charles A. E. 1988. *The Evolution of Central Banks*. Cambridge MA: MIT Press.

Goodhart, Charles A. E., and Andrew D. Crockett. 1970. "The Importance of Money." *Bank of England Quarterly Bulletin* 10: 159–98.

Gorton, Gary S. 1989. "Public Policy and the Evolution of Banking Markets." In *Bank System Risk: Charting a New Course, Proceedings of a Conference on Bank Structure and Competition*, 233–52. Chicago: Federal Reserve Bank of Chicago.

———. 2010. *Slapped by the Invisible Hand: The Panic of 2007*. New York: Oxford University Press.

Gorton, Gary, and Andrew Metrick. 2011. "Securitized Banking and the Run on Repo." *Journal of Financial Economics* 104: 425–51.

Gouvin, Eric J. 2001. "The Political Economy of Canada's 'Widely Held' Rule for Large Banks." *Law & Policy in International Business* 32: 391–426.

Graham, Douglas H. 1982. "Mexican and Brazilian Economic Development: Legacies, Patterns, and Performance." In *Brazil and Mexico: Patterns of Late Development*, ed. Sylvia Hewlett and Richard Weinart, 2–55. Philadelphia: Institute for the Study of Human Issues.

Grant, A. T. K. 1937. *A Study of the Capital Market in Post-war Britain*. London: Macmillan.

Greenspan, Alan. 1988. "An Overview of Financial Restructuring." In *Proceedings of the 24ᵗʰ Annual Conference on Bank Structure and Competition*, 1–9. Chicago: Federal Reserve Bank of Chicago.

———. 1990. "Subsidies and Powers in Commercial Banking." In *Proceedings of the 26th Annual Conference on Bank Structure and Competition*, 1–8. Chicago: Federal Reserve Bank of Chicago.

———. 2000. "Letter to Congressman Richard Baker." May 19. Available at http://bodurtha.georgetown.edu/FreddieMac/articles/Greenspan%20Details%20His%20Concerns%20Over%20Fannie%20Mae,%20Freddie%20Mac.htm, accessed August 1, 2013.

———. 2005. "Regulatory Reform of the Government-Sponsored Enterprises." Testimony before the Committee on Banking, Housing and Urban Affairs, U.S. Senate, April 6, www.federalreserve.gov/boarddocs/testimony/2005/20050406/default.htm.

Grinath, Arthur, John J. Wallis, and Richard Sylla. 1997. "Debt, Default, and Revenue Structure: The American State Debt Crisis in the Early 1840s." National Bureau of Economic Research Historical Working Paper 97.

Grossman, Richard. 2010. *Unsettled Account: The Evolution of Commercial Banking in the Industrialized World since 1800*. Princeton: Princeton University Press.

Grubb, Farley. 2008. "The Continental Dollar: How Much Was Really Issued?" *Journal of Economic History* 68: 283–91.

Gruben, William C., and Robert McComb. 1997. "Liberalization, Privatization, and Crash: Mexico's Banking System in the 1990s." *Federal Reserve Bank of Dallas Economic Review* (First Quarter): 21–30.

Guinnane, Timothy W. 2002. "Delegated Monitors, Large and Small: Germany's Banking System, 1800–1914." *Journal of Economic Literature* 40: 73–124.

Guiso, Luigi, Paola Sapienza, and Luigi Zingales. 2004. "Does Local Financial Development Matter?" *Quarterly Journal of Economics* 119: 929–69.

Gunther, Jeffrey W., Robert B. Moore, and Genie D. Short. 1996. "Mexican Banks and the 1994 Peso Crisis: The Importance of Initial Conditions." *North American Journal of Economics and Finance* 7: 125–33.

Gurley, John G., and Edward S. Shaw. 1960. *Money in a Theory of Finance.* Washington, DC: Brookings Institution.

Gurley, John G., Hugh T. Patrick, and Edward S. Shaw. 1965. *Financial Structure of Korea.* Seoul: Bank of Korea.

Haber, Stephen. 1991. "Industrial Concentration and the Capital Markets: A Comparative Study of Brazil, Mexico, and the United States, 1830–1930." *Journal of Economic History* 51: 559–80.

———. 1997. "Financial Markets and Industrial Development: A Comparative Study of Government Regulation, Financial Innovation, and Industrial Structure in Brazil and Mexico, 1840–1930." In *How Latin America Fell Behind: Essays on the Economic Histories of Brazil and Mexico, 1800–1914,* ed. Stephen Haber, 146–78. Stanford: Stanford University Press.

———. 1998. "The Efficiency Consequences of Institutional Change: Financial Market Regulation and Industrial Productivity Growth in Brazil, 1866–1934." In *Latin America and the World Economy Since 1800,* ed. John H. Coatsworth and Alan M. Taylor, 275–322. Cambridge, MA: David Rockefeller Center for Latin American Studies/Harvard University Press.

———. 2003. "Banks, Financial Markets, and Industrial Development: Lessons from the Economic Histories of Brazil and Mexico." In *Macroeconomic Reform in Latin America: The Second Stage,* ed. José Antonio Gonzalez, Vittorio Corbo, Anne O. Krueger, and Aaron Tornell, 259–93. Chicago: University of Chicago Press.

———. 2005. "Mexico's Experiments with Bank Privatization and Liberalization, 1991–2003." *Journal of Banking and Finance* 29: 2325–53.

———. 2006a. "The Political Economy of Latin American Industrialization." In *The Cambridge Economic History of Latin America,* vol. 2, *The Long Twentieth Century,* ed. Victor Bulmer-Thomas, John Coatsworth, and Roberto Cortes Conde, 537–84. New York: Cambridge University Press.

———. 2006b. "Authoritarian Government." In *The Oxford Handbook of Political Economy,* ed. Barry Weingast and Donald Wittman, 693–707. New York: Oxford University Press.

———. 2008a. "Banking with and without Deposit Insurance: Mexico's Banking Experiments, 1884–2004." In *Deposit Insurance around the World: Issues of Design and Implementation,* ed. Asli Demirgüç-Kunt, Edward Kane, and Luc Laeven, 219–52. Cambridge, MA: MIT Press.

———. 2008b. "Political Institutions and Financial Development: Evidence from the Political Economy of Bank Regulation in the United States and Mexico." In *Political Institutions and Financial Development,* ed. Stephen Haber, Douglass C. North, and Barry R. Weingast, 10–59. Stanford: Stanford University Press.

———. 2012a. "Where Does Democracy Thrive? Climate, Technology, and the Evolution of Political and Economic Institutions." Mimeo.

———. 2012b. "Politics and Banking Systems." In Stanley Engerman and Kenneth L. Sokoloff, with contributions by Stephen Haber, Elisa Mariscal, and Eric Zolt, *Economic Development in the Americas since 1500: Endowments and Institutions*, 245–94. New York: Cambridge University Press.

Haber, Stephen, and Herbert S. Klein. 1997. "The Economic Consequences of Brazilian Independence." In *How Latin America Fell Behind: Essays on the Economic Histories of Brazil and Mexico, 1800–1914*, ed. Stephen Haber, 243–59. Stanford: Stanford University Press.

Haber, Stephen, and Aldo Musacchio. 2013. "These Are the Good Old Days: Foreign Entry and the Mexican Banking System." National Bureau of Economic Research Working Paper 18713.

Haber, Stephen, Douglas C. North, and Barry R. Weingast. 2008. "Political Institutions and Financial Development." In *Political Institutions and Financial Development*, ed. Stephen Haber, Douglass C. North, and Barry R. Weingast, 1–9. Stanford: Stanford University Press.

Haber, Stephen, Armando Razo, and Noel Maurer. 2003. *The Politics of Property Rights: Political Instability, Credible Commitments, and Economic Growth in Mexico, 1876–1929*. New York: Cambridge University Press.

Haber, Stephen, Herbert S. Klein, Noel Maurer, and Kevin J. Middlebrook. 2008. *Mexico since 1980*. New York: Cambridge University Press.

Habyarimana, James. 2010. "The Benefits of Banking Relationships: Evidence from Uganda's Banking Crisis." Mimeo.

Hagerty, James. 2012. *The Fateful History of Fannie Mae: New Deal Birth to Mortgage Crisis Fall*. Charleston, SC: History Press.

Halcrow, Harold. 1953. *Agricultural Policy of the United States*. New York: Prentice Hall.

Hammond, Bray. 1947. "Jackson, Biddle, and the Bank of the United States." *Journal of Economic History* 7: 1–23.

———. 1957. *Banks and Politics in America from the Revolution to the Civil War*. Princeton: Princeton University Press.

———. 1970. *Sovereignty and an Empty Purse: Banks and Politics in the Civil War*. Princeton: Princeton University Press.

Hanley, Anne G. 2005. *Native Capital: Financial Institutions and Economic Development in Sao Paulo, Brazil, 1850–1905*. Stanford: Stanford University Press.

Harris, Ron. 2000. *Industrializing English Law: Entrepreneurship and Business Organization, 1720–1844*. Cambridge: Cambridge University Press.

Hassett, Kevin A., and John R. Lott. 2009. "Is Newspaper Coverage of Economic Events Politically Biased? Analyzing the Impact of Partisan Control of the Presidency and Congress on Media Coverage, 1985 to 2004." Mimeo.

Haubrich, Joseph G. 1990. "Nonmonetary Effects of Financial Crises: Lessons from the Great Depression in Canada." *Journal of Monetary Economics* 25: 223–52.

Hawke, John D., Jr. 1988. "Paul A. Volcker and Domestic Bank Regulatory Policy." Presentation at the annual meeting of the American Economic Association. December 28.

Hawtrey, Ralph. 1932. *The Art of Central Banking*. London: Frank Cass.

———. 1938. *A Century of Bank Rate*. London: Longmans, Green.

Hayek, Friedrich A. 1939. "Introduction." In Henry Thornton, *An Inquiry into the Nature and Effects of the Paper Credit of Great Britain,* 11–64. London: Allen & Unwin.

———, ed. 1978. "Introduction." In Henry Thornton, *An Enquiry into the Nature and Effects of the Paper Credit of Great Britain.* Fairfield, NJ: Augustus M. Kelley.

Haynes, Hopton. 1700. "Brief Memoirs Relating to the Silver and Gold Coins of England, with an Account of the Corruption of the Hammer'd Monys and the Reform of the Late Grand Coynage at the Tower and the Free Country Mints." Lans. MS. DCCCI. British Museum.

Hellman, Thomas F., Kevin C. Murdock, and Joseph E. Stiglitz. 2000. "Liberalization, Moral Hazard in Banking, and Prudential Regulation." *American Economic Review* 90: 147–65.

Hernández-Murillo, Rubén, Andra C. Ghent, and Michael T. Owyang. 2012. "Did Affordable Housing Legislation Contribute to the Subprime Securities Boom?" Federal Reserve Bank of St. Louis Working Paper 2012-005.

Hoffman, Philip, Gilles Postel-Vinay, and Jean-Laurent Rosenthal. 2007. *Surviving Large Losses: Financial Crises, the Middle Class, and the Development of Capital Markets.* Cambridge, MA: Belknap Press.

Holloway, Thomas. 1980. *Immigrants on the Land: Coffee and Society in São Paulo, 1886–1934.* Chapel Hill: University of North Carolina Press.

Honohan, Patrick and Daniela Klingebiel. 2003. "The Fiscal Cost Implications of an Accommodating Approach to Banking Crises." *Journal of Banking and Finance* 27: 1539–1560.

Horvik, Tord, and Solveig Aas. 1981. "Demilitarization in Costa Rica: A Farewell to Arms." *Journal of Peace Research* 4: 333–51.

Horvitz, Paul. 1991. "The Causes of Texas Bank and Thrift Failures." In *If Texas Were Chile: A Primer on Bank Regulation,* ed. Phillip L. Brock, 131–60. San Francisco: Sequoia Institute.

Hughes, Jonathan R. T. 1960. *Fluctuations in Trade, Industry, and Finance: A Study of British Economic Development, 1850–1860.* Oxford: Oxford University Press.

Hughes, Joseph P., and Loretta Mester. 2013. "Who Said Large Banks Don't Experience Scale Economies? Evidence from a Risk-Return-Driven Cost Function." Federal Reserve Bank of Philadelphia Working Paper 13-13, April.

Hurst, James W. 1973. *A Legal History of Money in the United States, 1774–1970.* Lincoln: University of Nebraska Press.

Husock, Howard. 2000. "The Trillion-Dollar Bank Shakedown That Bodes Ill for Cities." *City Journal* (Winter). www.city-journal.org/html/10_1_the_trillion_dollar.html, accessed August 1, 2013.

———. 2008. "The Financial Crisis and the CRA." *City Journal* (October). www.city-journal.org/2008/eon1030hh.html, accessed August 1, 2013.

Hutchcroft, Paul D. 1998. *Booty Capitalism: The Politics of Banking in the Philippines.* Ithaca, NY: Cornell University Press.

Huybens, Elisabeth, Astrid Luce Jordan, and Sangeeta Pratap. 2005. "Financial Market Discipline in Early-Twentieth-Century Mexico." *Journal of Economic History* 65: 757–78.

Igan, Deniz, Prachi Mishra, and Thierry Tressel. 2012. "A Fistful of Dollars: Lobbying and the Financial Crisis." In *NBER Macroeconomics Annual 2011, Volume 26*, 195–230. Cambridge, MA: National Bureau of Economic Research.

Independent Bankers Association of America v. Smith, 534 F.2d 921. D.C. Circuit Court of the United States.

International Monetary Fund. n.d. *International Financial Statistics*. http://elibrary-data.imf.org/FindDataReports.aspx?d=33061&e=169393, accessed August 1, 2013.

———. 2012a. "Brazil: Financial System Stability Assessment." IMF Country Report 12/206.

———. 2012b. "World Economic Outlook Database, October 2012 Update." www .imf.org/external/pubs/ft/weo/2012/02/weodata/download.aspx, accessed March 25, 2013.

IPEA (Instituto de Pesquisa Econômica Aplicada, Brazil). n.d. www.ipeadata.gov .br.

Izquierdo, Rafael. 1995. *La política hacendaría del desarrollo estabilizador, 1958–1970*. Mexico City: Fondo de Cultura Económica.

Jaffee, Dwight. 2010. "Reforming the U.S. Mortgage Market through Private Market Incentives." Paper presented at conference "Past, Present and Future of the Government Sponsored Enterprises." Federal Reserve Bank of St. Louis. November 17.

Jaffee, Dwight, and John M. Quigley. 2007. "Housing Subsidies and Homeowners: What Role for Government-Sponsored Enterprises?" *Brookings-Wharton Papers on Urban Affairs* 103–49.

———. 2009. "Housing Policy, Mortgage Policy, and the Federal Housing Administration." Mimeo.

———. 2011. "The Future of the Government Sponsored Enterprises: The Role for Government in the US Mortgage Market." National Bureau of Economic Research Working Paper 17685.

James, Marquis, and Bessie R. James. 1954. *Biography of a Bank: The Story of Bank of America NT&SA*. New York: Harper & Bros.

Jayaratne, Jith, and Philip E. Strahan. 1996. "The Finance Growth Nexus: Evidence from Bank Branch Deregulation." *Quarterly Journal of Economics* 111: 639–68.

Jeidels, Otto. 1905. *Das Verhältnis der deutschen Grossbanken zur Industrie mit besonderer Berücksichtigung der Eisenindustrie*. Leipzig: Duncker & Humblot.

Jiménez, Gabriel, Steven Ongena, Jose-Luis Peydro, and Jesus Saurina. 2007. "Hazardous Times for Monetary Policy: What Do Twenty-Three Million Bank Loans Say about the Effects of Monetary Policy on Credit Risk-Taking?" Tilburg University Center Discussion Paper 2007-75.

Jobst, Clemens P., and Pilar Nogues-Marco. 2013. "European Commercial Finance, 1700–1815." In *Handbook of Key Global Financial Markets, Institutions, and Infrastructure*, vol. 1, *Globalization of Finance: An Historical View*, ed. Gerard Caprio, 95–108. London: Elsevier.

Johnson, Joseph F. 1910. *The Canadian Banking System*. Washington, DC: National Monetary Commission, 61st Congress, 2nd Session. Senate Document 583.

Johnson, Simon, and James Kwak. 2010. *13 Bankers: The Wall Street Takeover and the Next Financial Meltdown.* New York: Pantheon.

Johnson, Simon, Peter Boone, Alasdair Breach, and Eric Friedman. 2000a. "Corporate Governance in the Asian Financial Crisis." *Journal of Financial Economics* 58: 141–86.

Johnson, Simon, Rafael La Porta, Florencio López-de-Silanes, and Andrei Shleifer. 2000b. "Tunneling." *American Economic Review* 90: 22–27.

Jones, Eric. 1981. *The European Miracle: Environments, Economics, and Geopolitics in the History of Europe and Asia.* New York: Cambridge University Press.

Jones, Geoffrey. 1993. *British Multinational Banking, 1830–1990.* Oxford: Clarendon Press.

Jones, Matthew T., and Maurice Obstfeld. 2001. "Saving, Investment, and Gold: A Reassessment of Historical Current Account Data." In *Money, Capital Mobility, and Trade: Essays in Honor of Robert Mundell,* ed. Guillermo A. Calvo, Rudi Dornbusch, and Maurice Obstfeld, 303–64. Cambridge, MA: MIT Press.

Jordà, Óscar, Moritz Schularick, and Alan M. Taylor. 2011. "Financial Crises, Credit Booms, and External Imbalances: 140 Years of Lessons." *IMF Economic Review* 59: 340–78.

Jornal do commercio (Rio de Janeiro). Various dates.

Kaufman, Henry. 2011. Remarks at the Foreign Policy Association Statesman Dinner, December 6. Retrieved from www.fpa.org/ckfinder/userfiles/files/Statesman%20Dinner_Kaufman_2011.pdf.

Keefer, Philip. 2008. "Beyond Legal Origin and Checks and Balances: Political Credibility, Citizen Information, and Financial Sector Development." In *Political Institutions and Financial Development,* ed. Stephen Haber, Douglass C. North, and Barry R. Weingast, 125–55. Stanford: Stanford University Press.

Keeley, Michael C. 1990. "Deposit Insurance, Risk, and Market Power in Banking." *American Economic Review* 80: 1183–1200.

Keogh, Daire, and Kevin Whelan. 2001. *Acts of Union: The Causes, Contexts, and Consequences of the Act of Union.* Dublin: Four Courts Press.

Kerr, Andrew W. 1884. *History of Banking in Scotland.* Glasgow: David Bryce & Son.

Keyssar, Alexander. 2000. *The Right to Vote: The Contested History of Democracy in the United States.* New York: Basic Books.

Khandelwal, Amit K., Peter K. Schott, and Shang-Jin Wei. 2012. "Trade Liberalization and Embedded Institutional Reform: Evidence from Chinese Exporters." Mimeo. October.

Kiff, John. 2009. "Canadian Residential Mortgage Markets: Boring but Effective?" International Monetary Fund Working Paper 09/130.

Kindleberger, Charles P., and Robert Z. Aliber. 2011. *Manias, Panics, and Crashes: A History of Financial Crises.* New York: Palgrave Macmillan.

King, Robert G., and Ross Levine. 1993. "Finance and Growth: Schumpeter Might Be Right." *Quarterly Journal of Economics* 108: 717–37.

King, Wilfred T. C. 1936. *History of the London Discount Market.* London: George Routledge & Sons.

Klein, Herbert H., and Ben Vinson III. 2007. *African Slavery in Latin America and the Caribbean.* 2nd ed. New York: Oxford University Press.

Knight, Alan. 1986. *The Mexican Revolution: Porfirians, Liberals, and Peasants.* New York: Cambridge University Press.

Kroszner, Randall. 1999. "Is It Better to Forgive Than to Receive? Repudiation of the Gold Indexation Clause in Long-Term Debt During the Great Depression." Mimeo.

Kroszner, Randall, and Raghuram Rajan. 1994. "Is the Glass-Steagall Act Justified? A Study of the US Experience with Universal Banking before 1933." *American Economic Review* 84: 810–32.

Kroszner, Randall S., and Philip E. Strahan. 1999. "What Drives Deregulation? Economics and Politics of the Relaxation of Bank Branching Restrictions." *Quarterly Journal of Economics* 114: 1437–67.

Krueger, Anne O. 1974. "The Political Economy of the Rent-Seeking Society." *American Economic Review* 64: 291–303.

Krueger, Anne O., and Aaron Tornell. 1999. "The Role of Bank Restructuring in Recovering from Crises: Mexico, 1995–1998." National Bureau of Economic Research Working Paper 7042.

Krugman, Paul. 2008. "Fannie, Freddie and You." *New York Times.* July 14, 2008.

Kryzanowski, Lawrence, and Gordon S. Roberts. 1993. "Canadian Banking Solvency, 1922–1940." *Journal of Money, Credit and Banking* 25: 361–76.

Kulikoff, Allan. Forthcoming. "'Such Things Ought Not To Be': The American Revolution and the First National Great Depression." In *The World of the American Revolutionary Republic: Land, Labor, and the Conflict for a Continent,* ed. Andrew Shankman. New York: Routledge.

Kynaston, David. 1995. "The Bank of England and the Government." In *The Bank of England: Money, Power and Influence, 1694–1994,* ed. Richard Roberts and David Kynaston, 19–55. Oxford: Oxford University Press.

"Labour Party Conference: Ed Miliband's speech in full." 2011. *Daily Telegraph.* September 27. www.telegraph.co.uk/news/politics/ed-miliband/8791870/Labour-Party-Conference-Ed-Milibands-speech-in-full.html, accessed March 8, 2013.

Laeven, Luc. 2001. "Insider Lending and Bank Ownership: The Case of Russia." *Journal of Comparative Economics* 29: 207–29.

Laeven, Luc, and Fabian Valencia. 2010. "Resolution of Banking Crises: The Good, the Bad, and the Ugly." International Monetary Fund Working Paper 10/146.

———. 2012. "Systemic Banking Crises Database: An Update." International Monetary Fund Working Paper 12/163.

Lamoreaux, Naomi R. 1991. "Bank Mergers in Late Nineteenth Century New England: The Contingent Nature of Structural Change." *Journal of Economic History* 51: 537–57.

———. 1994. *Insider Lending: Banks, Personal Connections, and Economic Development in Industrial New England.* New York: Cambridge University Press.

Landes, David S. 1999. *The Wealth and Poverty of Nations: Why Some Are So Rich and Some So Poor.* New York: W. W. Norton.

———. 2000. *Revolution in Time: Clocks and the Making of the Modern World.* Cambridge, MA: Harvard University Press.

Lane, Carl. 1997. "For a 'Positive Profit': The Federal Investment in the First Bank of the United States, 1792–1802." *William and Mary Quarterly* 54: 601–12.

La Porta, Rafael, Florencio López-de-Silanes, and Guillermo Zamarripa. 2003. "Related Lending." *Quarterly Journal of Economics* 118: 231–68.

La Porta, Rafael, Florencio Lopez-de-Silanes, Andrei Shleifer, and Robert W. Vishny. 1997. "Legal Determinants of External Finance." *Journal of Finance* 52: 1131–50.

———. 1998. "Law and Finance." *Journal of Political Economy* 106: 1113–55.

Law, John. 1705. "Money and Trade Considered." In *Great Bubbles*, ed. Ross B. Emmett, 1:168–231. London: Pickering & Chatto.

Leach, H. Derrick. 1969. "Canadian Chartered Banks." *Financial Analysts Journal* 25: 133–40.

Lee, Soo Jin. 2010. "Performance Comparisons across Merger Cohorts: The US Banking Industry after Branching Deregulation." Working Paper, Columbia University.

Lees, Francis A., James M. Botts, and Rubens Penha Cysne. 1990. *Banking and Financial Deepening in Brazil*. New York: Palgrave Macmillan.

Leff, Nathaniel. 1997. "Economic Development in Brazil, 1822–1913." In *How Latin America Fell Behind: Essays on the Economic Histories of Brazil and Mexico, 1800–1914*, ed. Stephen Haber, 34–64. Stanford: Stanford University Press.

Levi, Darrel. 1987. *The Prados of São Paulo, Brazil: An Elite Family and Social Change, 1840–1930*. Athens: University of Georgia Press.

Levi, Margaret. 1997. *Consent, Dissent, and Patriotism*. New York: Cambridge University Press.

Levine, Ross, and Sara Zervos. 1998. "Stock Markets, Banks, and Economic Growth." *American Economic Review* 88: 537–58.

Lewis, Michael. 2010. *The Big Short: Inside the Doomsday Machine*. New York: W. W. Norton.

Libecap, Gary. 1998. "The Great Depression and the Regulating State: Federal Government Regulation of Agriculture, 1884–1970." In *The Defining Moment: The Great Depression and the American Economy in the Twentieth Century*, ed. Michael D. Bordo, Claudia Goldin, and Eugene N. White, 181–226. Chicago: University of Chicago Press.

Lichtblau, Eric. 2012. "Gingrich's Deep Ties to Fannie Mae and Freddie Mac." *New York Times*. February 3.

Lindblom, Charles. 1977. *Politics and Markets: The World's Political-Economic Systems*. New York: Basic Books.

Lindert, Peter H. 1994. "The Rise of Social Spending, 1880–1930." *Explorations in Economic History* 31: 1–37.

———. 2004. *Growing Public*, vol. 1, *The Story: Social Spending and Economic Growth since the Eighteenth Century*. Cambridge: Cambridge University Press.

Lindert, Peter H., and Jeffrey G. Williamson. Forthcoming. "American Incomes before and after the Revolution." *Journal of Economic History*.

Lipset, Seymour Martin. 1960. *Political Man: the Social Bases of Politics*. Garden City, NY: Anchor Books.

Lobo, Eulália Maria Lahmeyer. 1978. *História do Rio de Janeiro: Do capital comercial ao capital industrial e financeiro*. Rio de Janeiro: IBMEC.

Lockhart, James. 1972. *Men of Cajamarca: Social and Biographical Study of the First Conquerors of Peru*. Austin: University of Texas Press.

Lucinda, Cláudio. 2010. "Competition in the Brazilian Loan Market: An Empirical Analysis." *Estudos económicos* 40: 831–58.

Ludlow, Leonor. 1985. "La construction de un banco: El Banco Nacional de México, 1881–1884." In *Banca y poder en Mexico, 1800–1925*, ed. Leonor Ludlow and Carlos Marichal, 299–346. Mexico: Grijalbo.

———. 2003. "El Banco Mercantil de Veracruz, 1898–1906." In *La banca regional en México, 1870–1930*, ed. Mario Cerutti and Carlos Marichal, 134–67. Mexico: Fondo de Cultura Económica.

Luna Argudín, María. 2006. *El congreso y la política mexicana, 1857–1911*. Mexico: Colegio de México and Fondo de Cultura Económica.

Mackey, Michael W. 1999. "Report of Michael W. Mackey on the Comprehensive Evaluation of the Operations and Function of the Fund for the Protection of Bank Savings (FOBAPROA) and the Quality of Supervision of the FOBAPROA Program, 1995–1998." Unpublished report.

Maddison, Angus. 2001. *The World Economy: A Millennial Perspective*. Paris: Organisation for Economic Cooperation and Development.

Magaloni, Beatriz. 2006. *Voting for Autocracy: The Politics of Party Hegemony and its Demise in Mexico*. New York: Cambridge University Press.

Majewski, John. 2004. "Jeffersonian Political Economy and Pennsylvania's Financial Revolution from below, 1800–1820." Mimeo.

Marchant, Anyda. 1965. *Viscount Mauá and the Empire of Brazil: A Biography of Irineu Evangelista de Sousa, 1813–1889*. Berkeley: University of California Press.

Marichal, Carlos. 1985. "El nacimiento de la Banca Mexicana en el contexto latinoamericano: problemas de periodización." In *Banca y poder en México, 1800–1925*, ed. Leonor Ludlow and Carlos Marichal, 231–66. Mexico: Grijalbo.

———. 2002. "The Construction of Credibility: Financial Market Reform and the Renegotiation of Mexico's External Debt in the 1880s." In *The Mexican Economy, 1870–1930: Essays on the Economic History of Institutions, Revolution, and Growth*, ed. Jeff L. Bortz and Stephen Haber, 93–120. Stanford: Stanford University Press.

Markiewicz, Dana. 1993. *The Mexican Revolution and the Limits of Agrarian Reform, 1915–1946*, Boulder, CO: Lynne Rienner.

Marks, Bruce. 1998. "NACA, National Non-profit Activist Group, Testifies in Support of the NationsBank Merge with Bank of America." www.federalreserve.gov/bankinforeg/publicmeetings/19980709_Panel5.PDF, accessed May 23, 2013.

———. n.d. "Testimony of Bruce Marks, Chief Executive Officer, Neighborhood Assistance Corporation of America (NACA)." House Committee on Financial Services. http://archives.financialservices.house.gov/banking/91200mar.pdf, accessed October 29, 2012.

Marshall, Monty, and Keith Jaggers. 2011. "Polity IV Project: Political Regime Characteristics and Transitions, 1800–2011." Data set available at www.systemicpeace.org/inscr/inscr.htm.

Marsilio, Claudio. 2013. "Genoese Finance, 1348–1700." In *Handbook of Key Global Financial Markets, Institutions, and Infrastructure*, vol. 1, *Globalization of Finance: An Historical View*, ed. Gerard Caprio, 123–32. London: Elsevier.

Martin, Stephen, and David Parker. 1995. "Privatization and Economic Performance throughout the UK Business Cycle." *Managerial and Decision Economics* 16: 225–37.

Martínez, Javier, and Alvaro Díaz. 1996. *Chile: The Great Transformation*. Geneva: United Nations Institute for Social Development.

Martínez Peria, María Soledad, and Sergio L. Schmukler. 2001. "Do Depositors Punish Banks for Bad Behavior? Market Discipline, Deposit Insurance, and Banking Crisis." *Journal of Finance* 56: 1029–51.

Mason, Joseph R., and Joshua Rosner. 2007a. "How Resilient Are Mortgage Backed Securities to Collateralized Debt Obligation Market Disruptions?" Mimeo.

———. 2007b. "Where Did the Risk Go? How Misapplied Bond Ratings Cause Mortgage Backed Securities and Collateralized Debt Obligation Market Disruptions." Mimeo.

Matthews, Philip W. 1921. *The Bankers' Clearing House: What It Is and What It Does*. London: Sir I. Pitman.

Matutes, Carmen, and Xavier Vives. 2000. "Imperfect Competition, Risk Taking, and Regulation in Banking." *European Economic Review* 44: 1–34.

Maurer, Noel. 2002. *The Power and the Money: The Mexican Financial System, 1876–1932*. Stanford: Stanford University Press.

Maurer, Noel, and Andrei Gomberg. 2004. "When the State is Untrustworthy: Public Finance and Private Banking in Porfirian Mexico." *Journal of Economic History* 64: 1087–1107.

Maurer, Noel, and Stephen Haber. 2007. "Related Lending and Economic Performance: Evidence from Mexico." *Journal of Economic History* 67: 551–81.

May, Thomas E. 1896. *The Constitutional History of England since the Accession of George the Third: 1760–1860*. 3 vols. London: Longmans, Green.

Mayer, Christopher, Karen Pence, and Shane M. Sherlund. 2009. "The Rise in Mortgage Defaults." *Journal of Economic Perspectives* 23: 27–50.

McCarty, Nolan, Keith T. Poole, and Howard Rosenthal. 2006. *Polarized America: The Dance of Ideology and Unequal Riches*. Cambridge, MA: MIT Press.

———. 2013. *Political Bubbles: Financial Crises and the Failure of American Democracy*. Princeton: Princeton University Press.

McGrane, Reginald C. 1924. *The Panic of 1837: Some Financial Problems of the Jacksonian Era*. Chicago: University of Chicago Press.

McGroarty, Patrick. 2013. "Somali Banking Starts from Ground Up." *Wall Street Journal*. April 21. http://online.wsj.com/article/SB10001424127887324763404578433253051605678.html.

McInnis, Edgar. 1959. *Canada: A Political and Social History, Revised and Enlarged*. Toronto: Rinehart.

McIvor, R. Craig. 1958. *Canadian Monetary, Banking, and Fiscal Development*. Toronto: Macmillan Co. of Canada.

McKay, Collins. 2008. *The Duke of Queensberry and the Union of Scotland and England: James Douglas and the Act of Union of 1707*. London: Cambria Press.

McKinnon, Ronald I. 1973. *Money and Capital in Economic Development*. Washington, DC: Brookings Institution.

McLean, Bethany. 2005. "The Fall of Fannie Mae." *Fortune*. January 24.

———. 2012. "The Meltdown Explanation That Melts Away." Reuters, March 19. http://blogs.reuters.com/bethany-mclean/2012/03/19/the-meltdown-explanation-that-melts-away/.

McLean, Bethany, and Joe Nocera. 2010. *All the Devils Are Here: The Hidden History of the Financial Crisis*. Steamboat Springs, CO: Portfolio Publications.

McQuerry, Elizabeth. 1999. "The Banking Sector Rescue in Mexico." *Federal Reserve Bank of Atlanta Economic Review* 84 (3): 14–29.

Meltzer, Allan H. 2003. *A History of the Federal Reserve*, vol. 1, *1913–1951*. Chicago: University of Chicago Press.

Meltzer, Allan H., and Scott F. Richard. 1981. "A Rational Theory of the Size of Government." *Journal of Political Economy* 89: 914–27.

Merton, Robert C. 1977. "An Analytic Derivation of the Cost of Deposit Insurance and Loan Guarantees: An Application of Modern Option Pricing Theory." *Journal of Banking & Finance* 1: 3–11.

Mexico. INEGI (Instituto Nacional de Estadística Geografía e Informática). n.d. *Estadísticas históricas de México*. http://biblioteca.itam.mx/recursos/ehm.html, accessed March 18, 2013.

———. 2009. *Estadísticas históricas de México*. Mexico City: INEGI.

Mexico. Secretaria del Estado y del Despacho de Hacienda y Crédito Público y Comercio. 1913. *Anuario de estadística fiscal, 1912–13*. Mexico, D.F.: Imprenta del Gobierno.

Meyer Cosío, Rosa María. 1985. "Empresarios, crédito, y especulación." In *Banca y poder en México, 1800–1925*, ed. Leonor Ludlow and Carlos Marichal, 99–118. Mexico: Grijalbo.

Mian, Atif, Amir Sufi, and Francesco Trebbi. 2010a. "The Political Economy of the Subprime Mortgage Credit Expansion." National Bureau of Economic Research Working Paper 16107.

———. 2010b. "The Political Economy of the U.S. Mortgage Default Crisis." *American Economic Review* 100: 1967–98.

Minsky, Hyman P. 1975. *John Maynard Keynes*. New York: Columbia University Press.

Miron, J. 1986. "Financial Panics, the Seasonality of the Nominal Interest Rate, and the Founding of the Fed." *American Economic Review* 76: 125–40.

Mitchell, Wesley C. 1903. *A History of the Greenbacks: With Special Reference to the Economic Consequences of their Issue; 1862–65*. Chicago: University of Chicago Press.

Mitton, Todd. 2002. "A Cross-Firm Analysis of the Impact of Corporate Governance on the East Asian Financial Crisis." *Journal of Financial Economics* 64: 215–41.

Moggridge, Donald E. 1972. *British Monetary Policy, 1924–1931: The Norman Conquest of $4.86*. London: Cambridge University Press.

Mokyr, Joel. 1990. *The Lever of Riches: Technological Creativity and Economic Progress*. New York: Oxford University Press.

Moody's Investors Service. 2008. *Global Bank Rating Methodology: Transparent/Predictive/Consistent*. www.moodys.com/sites/products/TopicAttachments/ GBRM/Global_Bank_Rating_Methodology_Brochure.pdf, accessed August 1, 2013.

Moore, Barrington. 1966. *Social Origins of Dictatorship and Democracy: Lord and Peasant in the Making of the Modern World*. Boston: Beacon.

Morgan, Donald P., Bertrand Rime, and Philip E. Strahan. 2004. "Bank Integration and State Business Cycles." *Quarterly Journal of Economics* 119: 1555–84.

Morgan, Edmund S. 1975. *American Slavery, American Freedom: The Ordeal of Colonial Virginia*. New York: W. W. Norton.

Morgenson, Gretchen. 2011. "Slapped Wrists at WaMu." *New York Times*. December 17. www.nytimes.com/2011/12/18/business/in-a-wamu-settlement-with-the-fdic-slapped-wrists.html?ref=washingtonmutualinc.

Morgenson, Gretchen, and Joshua Rosner. 2011. *Reckless Endangerment: How Outsized Ambition, Greed, and Corruption Led to Economic Armageddon*. New York: Henry Holt.

Morris, Ian. 2011. *Why the West Rules—for Now: The Patterns of History, and What They Reveal about the Future*. New York: Farrar, Straus and Giroux.

Morton, Walter A. 1978. *British Finance, 1930–1940*. Madison: University of Wisconsin Press.

Moss, David, and Sarah Brennan. 2004. "Regulation and Reaction: The Other Side of Free Banking in Antebellum New York." Harvard Business School Working Paper 04-038.

Munn, Charles W. 1981. *The Scottish Provincial Banking Companies, 1747–1864*. Edinburgh: John Donald Publishers.

Munro, John H. 2013. "*Rentes* and the European Financial Revolution." In *Handbook of Key Global Financial Markets, Institutions, and Infrastructure*, vol. 1, *Globalization of Finance: An Historical View*, ed. Gerard Caprio, 235–45. London: Elsevier.

Murillo, José Antonio. 2002. "La banca en México: Privatización, crisis, y reordenamiento." Banco de México Working Paper.

———. 2005. "La banca después de la privatización: Auge, crisis y reordenamiento." In *Cuando el estado se hizo banquero: consecuencias de la nacionalización bancaria en México*, ed. Gustavo del Angel-Mobarak, Carlos Bazdresch, and Francisco Suárez Dávila, 247–304. Mexico City: Fondo de Cultura Económica.

Murphy, Anne L. 2009. *The Origins of English Financial Markets: Investment and Speculation before the South Sea Bubble*. Cambridge: Cambridge University Press.

Musacchio, Aldo. 2009a. "Drawing Links between Corporate Governance and Networks: Bankers in the Corporate Networks of Brazil, Mexico, and the United States circa 1910." *Entreprises et histoire* 54: 16–36.

———. 2009b. *Experiments in Financial Democracy: Corporate Governance and Financial Development in Brazil, 1882–1950*. Cambridge: Cambridge University Press.

NACA (Neighborhood Assistance Corporation of America). n.d. "Purchase Program." www.nacalynx.com/nacaWeb/purchase/purchaseProgram.aspx?language=, accessed October 29, 2012.

Nader, Ralph. 2001. "How Fannie and Freddie Influence the Political Process." In *Serving Two Masters, yet Out of Control: Fannie Mae and Freddie Mac,* ed. Peter J. Wallison, 110–19. Washington DC: AEI Press.

Nakane, Márcio, and Daniela Weintraub. 2005. "Bank Privatization and Productivity: Evidence for Brazil." *Journal of Banking and Finance* 29: 2259–89.

Nathan, Alli, and Edwin H. Neave. 1989. "Competition and Contestability in Canada's Financial System: Empirical Results." *The Canadian Journal of Economics/ Revue canadienne d'économique* 22: 576–94.

National Community Reinvestment Coalition 2007a. *CRA Manual.* www.communitywealth.org/_pdfs/tools/cdfis/tool-ncrc-cra-manual.pdf, accessed March 21, 2013.

———. 2007b. *CRA Commitments.* http://community-wealth.org/_pdfs/articles-publications/cdfis/report-silver-brown.pdf, accessed March 21, 2013.

Neal, Larry. 1990. *The Rise of Financial Capitalism: International Capital Markets in the Age of Reason.* New York: Cambridge University Press.

———. 1998. "The Financial Crisis of 1825 and the Restructuring of the British Financial System." *Review, Federal Reserve Bank of St. Louis.* 80: 53–76.

Neal, Larry, and Stephen Quinn. 2001. "Networks of Information, Markets, and Institutions in the Rise of London as a Financial Center, 1660–1720." *Financial History Review* 8: 7–26.

Neal, Larry, and Eugene N. White. 2012. "The Glass-Steagall Act in Historical Perspective." *Quarterly Review of Economics and Finance* 52: 104–13.

Negrin, José Luis. 2000. "Mecanismos para compartir información crediticia: Evidencia internacional y la experiencia mexicana." Dirección General de Investigación Económica, Banco de México, Working Paper no. 2000–05. Mexico City: Banco de México.

Ness, Walter P. 2000. "Reducing Government Bank Presence in the Brazilian Financial System: Why and How." *Quarterly Review of Economics and Finance* 40: 71–84.

Neufeld, Edward P. 2001. "Adjusting to Globalization: Challenges for the Canadian Banking System." In *The State of Economics in Canada: Festschrift in Honour of David Slater,* ed. Patrick Grady and Andrew Sharpe, 325–51. Ottawa: Center for the Study of Living Standards

Ng, Kenneth. 1988. "Free Banking Laws and Barriers to Entry in Banking, 1838–1860." *Journal of Economic History* 48: 877–89.

Nichols, Mark W., and Jill M. Hendrickson. 1997. "Profit Differentials between Canadian and U.S. Commercial Banks: The Role of Regulation." *Journal of Economic History* 57: 674–96.

North, Douglass C., and Barry R. Weingast. 1989. "Constitutions and Commitment: The Evolution of Institutions Governing Public Choice in 17th Century England." *Journal of Economic History* 49: 803–32.

Nourse, Edwin G., Joseph S. Davis, and John D. Black. 1937. *Three Years of the Agricultural Adjustment Administration.* Washington, DC: Brookings Institution.

Obstfeld, Maurice, and Alan M. Taylor. 2004. *Global Capital Markets: Integration, Crisis, and Growth.* Cambridge: Cambridge University Press.

O'Halloran, Sharyn, and Geraldine McAllister. 2012. "Delegation and the Regulation of Finance in the United States since 1950." Mimeo.

O'Hara, Maureen, and Wayne Shaw. 1990. "Deposit Insurance and Wealth Effects: The Value of Being 'Too Big to Fail.'" *Journal of Finance* 45: 1587–1600.

Olson, Mancur. 1965. *The Logic of Collective Action: Public Goods and the Theory of Groups.* Cambridge, MA: Harvard University Press.

Olveda, Jaime. 2003. "Bancos y banqueros en Guadalajara." In *La banca regional en México, 1870–1930,* ed. Mario Cerutti and Carlos Marichal, 291–320. Mexico City: Fondo de Cultura Económica.

Oñate, Abdiel. 1998. "La crisis de 1907–1908 y el sistema bancario mexicano." In *La banca en México, 1820–1920,* ed. Leonor Ludlow and Carlos Marichal, 181–200. Mexico City: Instituto Mora.

O'Rourke, Kevin H., and Jeffrey G. Williamson. 2000. *Globalization and History: The Evolution of a Nineteenth-Century Atlantic Economy.* Cambridge, MA: MIT Press.

Pak, Susie J. 2013. *Gentlemen Bankers: The World of J. P. Morgan.* Cambridge, MA: Harvard University Press.

Park, Haelim. 2012. "The Conservatism of British Banks in the Interwar Period Re-examined." Mimeo.

Patrick, Hugh T. 1967. "Japan, 1868–1914." In Rondo E. Cameron, with the collaboration of Olga Crisp, Hugh T. Patrick, and Richard Tilly, *Banking in the Early Stages of Industrialization,* 239–89. New York: Oxford University Press.

Patterson, Edward Lloyd Stewart. 1917. *Banking Principles and Practice.* New York: Alexander Hamilton Institute.

Pei, Minxin. 2006. *China's Trapped Transition: The Limits of Developmental Autocracy.* Cambridge, MA: Harvard University Press.

Peláez, Carlos Manuel. 1975. "The Establishment of Banking Institutions in a Backward Economy: Brazil, 1800–1851." *Business History Review* 49: 446–72.

Peláez, Carlos Manuel, and Wilson Suzigan. 1976. *Historia monetária do Brasil: Análise da política, comportamento e instituiçoes monetárias.* Brasília: Editora Universidade de Brasília.

Perkins, Edwin. 1987. "Lost Opportunities for Compromise in the Bank War: A Reassessment of Jackson's Veto Message." *Business History Review* 61: 531–50.

———. 1994. *American Public Finance and Financial Services, 1700–1815.* Columbus: Ohio State University Press.

Petersen, Mitchell, and Raghuram G. Rajan. 2002. "Does Distance Still Matter? The Information Revolution in Small Business Lending." *Journal of Finance* 57: 2533–70.

Pezzolo, Luciano. 2013. "Venetian Finance, 1400–1797." In *Handbook of Key Global Financial Markets, Institutions, and Infrastructure,* vol. 1, *Globalization of Finance: An Historical View,* ed. Gerard Caprio, 301–17. London: Elsevier.

Philippovich, Eugen von. 1911. *History of the Bank of England and Its Financial Services to the State.* Washington, DC: National Monetary Commission, 61st Congress, 2nd Session, Senate Document 591.

Phillips, John A., and Charles Wetherell. 1995. "The Great Reform Act of 1832 and the Political Modernization of England." *American Historical Review* 100: 411–36.

Pincus, Steve. 2009. *1688: The First Modern Revolution*. New Haven: Yale University Press.

Pinto, Edward J. 2011. "Government Housing Policies in the Lead-up to the Financial Crisis: A Forensic Study." American Enterprise Institute. www.aei.org/files/2011/02/05/Pinto-Government-Housing-Policies-in-the-Lead-up-to-the-Financial-Crisis-Word-2003–2.5.11.pdf, accessed March 21, 2013.

Pinto, Edward J., and Peter Wallison. 2011. "Why the Left is Losing the Argument over the Financial Crisis." *The American: The Online Magazine of the American Enterprise Institute*. December 27. www.american.com/archive/2011/december/why-the-left-is-losing-the-argument-over-the-financial-crisis, accessed August 1, 2013.

Plumb, John H. 1967. *The Growth of Political Stability in England: 1675–1725*. London: Macmillan.

Potash, Robert A. 1983. *Mexican Government and Industrial Development in the Early Republic: The Banco de Avio*. Amherst: University of Massachusetts Press.

Prasad, Eswar, and Shang-Jin Wei. 2007. "Understanding the Structure of Cross-Border Capital Flows: The Case of China." In *China's Financial Transition at a Crossroads*, ed. Charles W. Calomiris, 144–92. New York: Columbia University Press.

Pressnell, Leslie S. 1956. *Country Banking in the Industrial Revolution*. Oxford: Clarendon Press.

Prins, Nomi. 2009. *It Takes a Pillage: Behind the Bailouts, Bonuses, and Backroom Deals from Washington to Wall Street*. Hoboken, NJ: John Wiley and Sons.

Qian, Yingyi, and Barry R. Weingast. 1997. "Federalism as a Commitment to Preserving Market Incentives." *Journal of Economic Perspectives* 11: 83–92.

Quinn, Stephen. 1997. "Goldsmith-Banking: Mutual Acceptances and Inter-banker Clearing in Restoration London." *Explorations in Economic History* 34: 411–32.

———. 2008. "Securitization of Sovereign Debt: Corporations as a Sovereign Debt Restructuring Mechanism in Britain, 1694 to 1750." Mimeo.

———. 2013. "Dutch Bank Finance, 1600–1800." In *Handbook of Key Global Financial Markets, Institutions, and Infrastructure*, vol. 1, *Globalization of Finance: An Historical View*, 64–72, ed. Gerard Caprio. London: Elsevier.

Quinn, Stephen, and William Roberds. 2009. "An Economic Explanation of the Early Bank of Amsterdam, Debasement, Bills of Exchange, and the Emergence of the First Central Bank." In *The Origin and Development of Financial Markets and Institutions from the Seventeenth Century to the Present*, ed. Jeremy Atack and Larry Neal, 32–70. Cambridge: Cambridge University Press.

———. 2010. "How Amsterdam Got Fiat Money." Federal Reserve Bank of Atlanta Working Paper 2010-17.

Quintyn, Marc, and Geneviève Verdier. 2010. "'Mother, Can I Trust the Government?' Sustained Financial Deepening: A Political Institutions View." International Monetary Fund Working Paper 10/210.

Rajan, Raghuram G. 2010. *Fault Lines: How Hidden Fractures Still Threaten the World Economy*. Princeton: Princeton University Press.

Rajan, Raghuram, and Luigi Zingales. 1998. "Financial Dependence and Growth." *American Economic Review* 88: 559–86.

Rajan, Uday, Amit Seru, and Vikrant Vig. 2010. "Statistical Default Models and Incentives." *American Economic Review* 100: 506–10.

Ramirez, Carlos D. 1995. "Did J. P. Morgan's Men Add Liquidity? Corporate Investment, Cash Flow, and Financial Structure at the Turn of the Twentieth Century." *Journal of Finance* 50: 661–78.

———. 1999. "Did Glass-Steagall Increase the Cost of External Finance for Corporate Investment? Evidence from Bank and Insurance Company Affiliations." *Journal of Economic History* 59: 372–96.

———. 2002. "Did Banks' Security Affiliates Add Value? Evidence from the Commercial Banking Industry during the 1920s." *Journal of Money, Credit and Banking* 34: 393–411.

Ramirez, P., and F. Rosende. 1992. "Responding to Collapse: The Chilean Banking Legislation after 1983." In *If Texas Were Chile: A Primer on Banking Reform*, ed. Philip Brock, 193–216. San Francisco: Institute for Contemporary Studies.

Ramseyer, J. Mark, and Frances M. Rosenbluth. 1998. *The Politics of Oligarchy: Institutional Choice in Imperial Japan.* New York: Cambridge University Press.

Ratnovski, Lev, and Rocco Huang. 2009. "Why Are Canadian Banks More Resilient?" IMF Working Paper 09/152.

Razo, Armando. 2008. *Social Foundations of Limited Dictatorship: Networks and Private Protection during Mexico's Early Industrialization.* Stanford: Stanford University Press.

Redish, Angela. 1984. "Why Was Specie Scarce in Colonial Economies? An Analysis of the Canadian Currency, 1796–1830." *Journal of Economic History* 44: 713–28.

———. 2003. "The Mortgage Market in Upper Canada: Window on a Pioneer Economy." In *Finance, Intermediaries, and Economic Development*, ed. Stanley Engerman, Philip Hoffman, Jean-Laurent Rosenthal, and Kenneth Sokoloff, 111–31. Cambridge: Cambridge University Press.

Reid, Margaret. 1982. *The Secondary Banking Crisis, 1973–1975: Its Causes and Course.* London: Macmillan.

Reinhart, Carmen, and Kenneth Rogoff. 2009. *This Time Is Different: Eight Centuries of Financial Folly.* Princeton: Princeton University Press.

———. 2011. "From Financial Crash to Debt Crisis." *American Economic Review* 101: 1676–1706.

Reynolds, Clark W. 1970. *The Mexican Economy: Twentieth-Century Structure and Growth.* New Haven: Yale University Press.

Richards, R. D. 1958. *The Early History of Banking in England.* London: Frank Cass.

Richardson, Gary, and William Troost. 2006. "Monetary Intervention Mitigated Banking Panics during the Great Depression: Quasi-Experimental Evidence from the Federal Reserve District Border in Mississippi, 1929 to 1933." National Bureau of Economic Research Working Paper 12591.

Riefler, Winfield W. 1930. *Money Rates and Money Markets in the United States.* New York: Harper and Brothers.

Riesser, Jacob. 1911. *The Great German Banks and their Concentration, in Connection with the Economic Development of Germany.* Washington, DC: U.S. Government Printing Office.

Riguzzi, Paolo. 2002. "The Legal System, Institutional Change, and Financial Regulation in Mexico, 1870–1910: Mortgage Contracts and Long Term Credit." In *The Mexican Economy, 1870–1930,* ed. Jeffrey Bortz and Stephen Haber, 120–60. Stanford: Stanford University Press.

Riker, William H. 1982. *Liberalism against Populism: A Confrontation between the Theory of Democracy and the Theory of Social Choice.* San Francisco: W. H. Freeman.

Roberts, Richard O. 1958. "Bank of England Branch Discounting, 1826–59." *Economica* 25: 230–45.

Roberts, Richard, Brian Reading, and Leigh Skene. 2009. "Sovereign Rescues: How the Forgotten Financial Crisis of 1914 Compares with 2008–2009." London: Lombard Street Research.

Robinson, James A. 2006. "Debt Repudiation and Risk Premia: The North-Weingast Thesis Revisited." Mimeo.

Rockoff, Hugh. 1974. "The Free Banking Era: A Reexamination." *Journal of Money, Credit, and Banking* 6: 141–67.

———. 1984. *Drastic Measures: A History of Wage and Price Controls in the United States.* New York: Cambridge University Press.

———. 1985. "New Evidence on Free Banking in the United States." *American Economic Review* 75: 886–89.

———. 2000. "Banking and Finance, 1789–1914." In *The Cambridge Economic History of the United States,* ed. Stanley Engerman and Robert Gallman, 643–84. New York: Cambridge University Press.

Rodden, Jonathan A. 2006. *Hamilton's Paradox: The Promise and Peril of Fiscal Federalism.* New York: Cambridge University Press.

Rodríguez López, María Guadalupe. 2003. "Paz y bancos en Durango durante el Porfiriato." In *La banca regional en Mexico, 1870–1930,* ed. Mario Cerutti and Carlos Marichal, 254–90. Mexico City: Fondo de Cultura Económica.

Romer, Thomas, and Barry R. Weingast. 1991. "Political Foundations of the Thrift Debacle." In *Politics and Economics in the 1980s,* ed. Alberto Alesina and Geoffrey Carliner, 175–214. Chicago: University of Chicago Press.

Romero Ibarra, Maria Eugenia. 2003. "El banco del estado de Mexico, 1897–1914." In *La banca regional en Mexico, 1870–1930,* ed. Mario Cerutti and Carlos Marichal, 216–51. Mexico City: Fondo de Cultura Económica.

Rose, Jonathan, and Kenneth Snowden. 2012. "The New Deal and the Origins of the Modern American Real Estate Loan Contract in the Building and Loan Industry." Mimeo.

Rothbard, Murray N. 2012. *The Panic of 1819: Reactions and Politics.* La Vergne, TN: BN Publishing.

Rousseau, Peter L. 1999. "Finance, Investment, and Growth in Meiji-Era Japan." *Japan and the World Economy* 11: 185–98.

———. 2003. "Historical Perspectives on Financial Development and Economic Growth." *Federal Reserve Bank of St. Louis Review* 84: 81–105.

Rousseau, Peter, and Richard Sylla. 2003. "Financial Systems, Economic Growth, and Globalization." In *Globalization in Historical Perspective,* ed. Michael Bordo, Alan Taylor, and Jeffrey Williamson, 373–413. Chicago: University of Chicago Press.

———. 2004. "Emerging Financial Markets and Early U.S. Growth." *Explorations in Economic History* 42: 1–26.

Rousseau, Peter L., and Paul Wachtel. 1998. "Financial Intermediation and Economic Performance: Historical Evidence from Five Industrialized Countries." *Journal of Money, Credit, and Banking* 30: 657–78.

Santarosa, Veronica A. 2012. "Financing Long-Distance Trade without Banks: The Joint Liability Rule and Bills of Exchange in 18th-Century France." Mimeo.

Schlesinger, Jacob, and Michael Schroeder. 1999. "Law Requiring Banks to Aid Poor Is Being Attacked by Phil Gramm." *Wall Street Journal.* July 27.

Schularick, Moritz, and Alan M. Taylor. 2012. "Credit Booms Gone Bust: Monetary Policy, Leverage Cycles, and Financial Crises, 1870–2008." *American Economic Review* 102: 1029–61.

Schulz, John. 2008. *The Financial Crisis of Abolition.* New Haven: Yale University Press.

Schuster, Felix. 1923. *The Bank of England and the State.* London: Longmans, Green.

Schwartz, Anna Jacobson. 1947. "The Beginning of Competitive Banking in Philadelphia, 1782–1809." *Journal of Political Economy* 55: 417–31.

———. 1992. "The Misuse of the Fed's Discount Window." *Federal Reserve Bank of St. Louis Review* 74: 58–69.

Schweikart, Larry. 1987. *Banking in the American South from the Age of Jackson to Reconstruction.* Baton Rouge: Louisiana State University Press.

———. 1988. "Jacksonian Ideology, Currency Control, and 'Central Banking': A Reappraisal." *Historian* 51: 78–102.

Seiler, Robin. 2001. "Estimating the Value and Allocation of Federal Subsidies." In *Serving Two Masters, yet Out of Control: Fannie Mae and Freddie Mac,* ed. Peter J. Wallison, 8–39. Washington, DC: AEI Press.

Shaffer, Sherrill. 1993. "A Test of Competition in Canadian Banking." *Journal of Money, Credit and Banking* 25: 49–61.

Shaw, Edward S. 1973. *Financial Deepening in Economic Development.* New York: Oxford University Press.

Shaw, George Bernard. 1903. *Man and Superman.* New York: Brentano's.

Sheppard, David K. 1971. *The Growth and Role of UK Financial Institutions, 1880–1962.* London: Routledge.

Sherman, Jill. 2013. "Buyers of New Homes Boosted by 95% Mortgage Guarantee." *Times.* March 20. www.thetimes.co.uk/tto/business/budget2013/article 3717878.ece.

Smith, Bruce D. 1985a. "American Colonial Monetary Regimes: The Failure of the Quantity Theory and Some Evidence in Favour of an Alternate View." *Canadian Journal of Economics* 18: 531–65.

———. 1985b. "Some Colonial Evidence on Two Theories of Money: Maryland and the Carolinas." *Journal of Political Economy* 93: 1178–1211.

Smith, Peter H. 1991. "Mexico since 1946: Dynamics of an Authoritarian Regime." In *Mexico since Independence*, ed. Leslie Bethell, 321–96. New York: Cambridge University Press.

Sola, Lourdes, Christopher da Cunha Bueno Garman, and Moíses S. Marques. 2001. "Central Bank Reform and Overcoming the Moral Hazard Problem: The Case of Brazil." *Brazilian Journal of Political Economy* 21: 40–64.

Solt, Eric. 2009. "Standardizing the World Income Inequality Database." *Social Science Quarterly* 90: 231–42. Updated data set (version 3.1) available at http://myweb.uiowa.edu/fsolt/swiid/swiid.html.

Sorkin, Andrew R. 2009. *Too Big to Fail*. New York: Penguin Group.

Spooner, John D. 1979. "Smart People, Smart Money: Meet a Stockbroker's Round Table of Financial Sages." *Atlantic Monthly*. June.

Spruyt, Hendrik. 1994. *The Sovereign State and Its Competitors*. Princeton: Princeton University Press.

Stasavage, David. 2002. "Credible Commitment in Early Modern Europe: North and Weingast Revisited." *Journal of Law, Economics, and Organization* 18: 155–86.

———. 2003. *Public Debt and the Birth of the Democratic State: France and Great Britain, 1688–1789*. New York: Cambridge University Press.

———. 2007. "Partisan Politics and Public Debt: The Importance of the 'Whig Supremacy' for Britain's Financial Revolution." *European Review of Economic History* 11: 123–53.

Statistics Canada. 1983. *Historical Statistics of Canada*. 2nd ed. Toronto: Statistics Canada.

Stein, Stanley J. 1957. *The Brazilian Cotton Textile Manufacture: Textile Enterprise in an Underdeveloped Area*. Cambridge, MA: Harvard University Press.

———. 1958. *Vassouras: A Brazilian Coffee County*. Cambridge, MA: Harvard University Press.

Stevens, Donald Fithian. 1991. *Origins of Instability in Early Republican Mexico*. Durham, NC: Duke University Press.

Stigler, George. 1971. "The Theory of Economic Regulation." *Bell Journal of Economics and Management Science* 2: 3–18.

Stiglitz, Joseph E., Jonathan M. Orszag, and Peter R. Orszag. 2002. "Implications of the New Fannie Mae and Freddie Mac Risk-based Capital Standard." Fannie Mae Papers I. 2.

Strouse, Jean. 1999. *Morgan: American Financier*. New York: Random House.

Stulz, Rene M. 2005. "The Limits of Financial Globalization." *Journal of Finance* 60: 1595–1638.

Suárez Dávila, Francisco. 2010. *La reprivatización bancaria fracasada: Una tragedia nacional en tres actos*. Mexico: Centro de Estudios Espinosa Yglesias.

Summerhill, William R. 2003. *Order against Progress: Government, Foreign Investment, and Railroads in Brazil, 1854–1913*. Stanford: Stanford University Press.

———. 2008. "Credible Commitment and Sovereign Default Risk: Two Markets and Imperial Brazil." In *Political Institutions and Financial Development*, ed. Stephen Haber, Douglass North, and Barry Weingast, 226–58. Stanford: Stanford University Press.

Summerhill, William R. Forthcoming. *Inglorious Revolution: Political Institutions, Sovereign Debt, and Financial Underdevelopment in Imperial Brazil.* New Haven: Yale University Press.

Sussman, Nathan, and Yishay Yafeh. 2006. "Institutional Reform, Financial Development, and Sovereign Debt: Britain 1690–1790." *Journal of Economic History* 66: 906–35.

Swagel, Phillip. 2009. "The Financial Crisis: An Inside View." *Brookings Papers on Economic Activity* 40: 1–78.

Swanson, W. W. 1914. "Present Problems in Canadian Banking." *American Economic Review* 4: 304–14.

Sylla, Richard. 1975. *The American Capital Market, 1846–1914.* New York: Arno.

———. 2000. "Experimental Federalism: The Economics of American Government, 1789–1914." In *The Cambridge Economic History of the United States,* vol. 2, *The Long Nineteenth Century,* ed. S. L. Engerman and R. E. Gallman, 483–541, 924–30. Cambridge: Cambridge University Press.

———. 2008. "The Political Economy of Early U.S. Financial Development." In *Political Institutions and Financial Development,* ed. Stephen Haber, Douglass C. North, and Barry R. Weingast, 60–91. Stanford: Stanford University Press.

Sylla, Richard, and Peter L. Rousseau. 2003. "Financial Systems, Economic Growth, and Globalization." In *Globalization in Historical Perspective,* ed. M. D. Bordo, A. M. Taylor, and J. G. Williamson, 373–413. Chicago: University of Chicago Press.

———. 2005. "Emerging Financial Markets and Early US Growth." *Explorations in Economic History* 42: 1–26.

Sylla, Richard, John B. Legler, and John J. Wallis. 1987. "Banks and State Public Finance in the New Republic, 1790–1860." *Journal of Economic History* 47: 391–403.

Taylor, Alan M. 1998. "On the Costs of Inward-Looking Development: Price Distortions, Growth, and Divergence in Latin America." *Journal of Economic History* 58: 1–28.

Taylor, John B. 2009. *Getting Off Track: How Government Actions and Interventions Caused, Prolonged, and Worsened the Financial Crisis.* Stanford: Hoover Institution Press.

Temin, Peter. 1968. "The Economic Consequences of the Bank War." *Journal of Political Economy* 76: 257–74.

Temin, Peter, and Hans-Joachim Voth. 2013. *Prometheus Shackled: Goldsmith Banks and England's Financial Revolution after 1700.* New York: Oxford University Press.

Tenenbaum, Barbara A. 1986. *The Politics of Penury: Debts and Taxes in Mexico, 1821–1856.* Albuquerque: University of New Mexico Press.

Theimer, Sharon, and Pete Yost. 2009. "Did ACORN Get Too Big for Its Own Good?" Associated Press. www.msnbc.msn.com/id/32925682/ns/politics-more_politics/t/did-acorn-get-too-big-its-own-good/, accessed March 6, 2013.

Thomas, William. 1978. *The Finance of British Industry, 1918–1976.* London: Methuen.

Thorne, Roland G. 1986. *The History of Parliament*. London: Secker & Warburg.

Thornton, Henry. 1802. *An Enquiry into the Nature and Effects of the Paper Credit of Great Britain*. London: John Hatchard.

Tilly, Charles. 1975. "Reflections on the History of European State-Making." In *The Formation of National States in Western Europe*, ed. Charles Tilly and Gabriel Ardant, 3–84. Princeton: Princeton University Press.

———. 1990. *Coercion, Capital and European States: AD 990–1992*. Cambridge, MA: Blackwell.

Tilly, Richard H. 1966. *Financial Institutions and Industrialization in the Rhineland, 1815–1870*. Madison: University of Wisconsin Press.

———. 1967. "Germany." In Rondo E. Cameron, with the collaboration of Olga Crisp, Hugh T. Patrick, and Richard Tilly, *Banking in the Early Stages of Industrialization*, 151–82. New York: Oxford University Press.

———. 1982. "Mergers, External Growth, and Finance in the Development of Large Scale Enterprise in Germany, 1880–1913." *Journal of Economic History* 42: 629–58.

———. 1986. "Germany Banking, 1850–1914: Development Assistance for the Strong." *Journal of Economic History* 15: 113–52.

———. 1992. "An Overview of the Role of the Large German Banks up to 1914." In *Finance and Financiers in European History, 1880–1960*, ed. Youssef Cassis, 92–112. New York: Cambridge University Press.

———. 2010. "Banking Crises in Three Countries, 1800–1933: An Historical and Comparative Perspective." *Bulletin of the GHI* 46: 77–89.

Tiratsoo, Nick, and Jim Tomlinson. 1998. *The Conservatives and Industrial Efficiency, 1951–1964: Thirteen Wasted Years?* London: Routledge.

Tomlinson, Jim. 1994. "British Economic Policy since 1945." In *The Economic History of Britain since 1700*, ed. Roderick Floud and Deirdre McCloskey, 3: 255–83. Cambridge: Cambridge University Press.

Topik, Steven. 1980. "State Enterprise in a Liberal Regime: The Banco do Brasil, 1905–1930." *Journal of Interamerican Studies and World Affairs* 22: 4.

———. 1987. *The Political Economy of the Brazilian State, 1889–1930*. Austin: University of Texas Press.

Trevelyan, George M. 1922. *British History in the Nineteenth Century (1782–1901)*. London: Longmans, Green.

Triner, Gail D. 2000. *Banking and Economic Development: Brazil, 1889–1930*. New York: Palgrave.

Unal, Haluk, and Miguel Navarro. 1999. "The Technical Process of Bank Privatization in Mexico." *Journal of Financial Services Research* 16: 61–83.

Uniform Law Conference of Canada. n.d. "Harmonization of the Federal Bank Act Security and the Provincial Secured Transaction Regimes." Uniform Law Conference of Canada. www.ulcc.ca/en/cls/ppsa-bp1.html, accessed March 9, 2012.

United States Bureau of Economic Analysis. Various dates. *Banking and Monetary Statistics*. Washington, DC.

United States Bureau of the Census. 1975. *Historical Statistics of the United States, Colonial Times to 1970*. Washington, DC: U.S. Government Printing Office.

United States Department of the Treasury. 2008. *Blueprint for a Modernized Financial Regulatory Structure.* Washington, DC: Department of the Treasury.

United States General Accounting Office. 1996. *Financial Audit: Resolution Trust Corporation's 1995 and 1994 Financial Statements.* Washington, DC. July.

United States House of Representatives. 2008. Committee on Oversight and Government Reform, 110th Congress, 2nd Session. "Hearing: The Role of Fannie Mae and Freddie Mac in the Financial Crisis." Serial Number 110-180.

————. 2010. Committee on Oversight and Government Reform. 111th Congress, Staff Report. "Follow the Money: ACORN, SEIU and Their Political Allies." February 18.

United States Senate. 1828. *Reports of the Secretary of the Treasury of the United States Prepared in Obedience to the Act of the 10th May, 1800.* Washington, DC: Duff Green.

————. 1991. *Secondary Mortgage Markets and Redlining: Hearing before the Subcommittee on Consumer and Regulatory Affairs of the Committee on Banking, Housing, and Urban Affairs, United States Senate, One Hundred Second Congress, first session, February 28, 1991.* Washington, DC: U.S. Government Printing Office.

————. 2011. Committee on Homeland Security and Governmental Affairs, Permanent Subcommittee on Investigations. "Wall Street and the Financial Crisis: The Anatomy of a Financial Collapse." April 13.

Urdapilleta, Eduardo, and Constantinos Stephanou. 2009. "Banking in Brazil: Structure, Performance, Drivers, and Policy Implications." World Bank Policy Research Working Paper 4809.

Valadão, Marcos Aurélio Pereira, and Ivo T. Gico Jr. 2009. "The (Not So) Great Depression of the 21st Century and Its Impact on Brazil." Catholic University of Brasilia Working Paper No. 0002/09.

Velde, François. 2013. "John Law and His Experiment with France, 1715–1726." In *Handbook of Key Global Financial Markets, Institutions, and Infrastructure,* vol. 1, *Globalization of Finance: An Historical View,* ed. Gerard Caprio, 169–74. London: Elsevier.

Vittas, Dimitri, Patrick Frazer, and Thymi Metaxas-Vittas. 1988. *The Retail Banking Revolution: An International Perspective.* London: Lafferty.

Von Mettenheim, Kurt. 2006. "Still the Century of Government Savings Banks? The Caixa Econômica Federal." *Brazilian Journal of Political Economy* 26:39–57.

Vreeland, Edward B. 1910. *Interviews on the Banking and Currency Systems of Canada.* National Monetary Commission 61st Congress, 2nd Session, Senate Document 584.

Walker, David. 1986. *Kinship, Business, and Politics: The Martinez del Rio Family in Mexico, 1824–1867.* Austin: University of Texas Press.

Walker, Edmund. 1923. "Canadian Banking." *Annals of the American Academy of Political and Social Science* 107: 136–48.

Wallis, John J., Richard Sylla, and Arthur Grinath. 2004. "Sovereign Debt and Repudiation: The Emerging-Market Debt Crisis in the United States, 1839–1843." National Bureau of Economic Research Working Paper 10753.

Wallis, John J., Richard Sylla, and John B. Legler. 1994. "The Interaction of Taxation and Regulation in Nineteenth-Century U.S. Banking." In *The Regulated Economy: A Historical Approach to Political Economy,* ed. Claudia Goldin and Gary Libecap, 121–44. Chicago: University of Chicago Press.

Wallison, Peter J. 2001. *Serving Two Masters, yet Out of Control: Fannie Mae and Freddie Mac.* Washington, DC: AEI Press.

——. 2011. *Dissent from the Majority Report of the Financial Crisis Inquiry Commission.* Washington, DC: AEI Press.

Wallison, Peter J., and Charles Calomiris. 2009. "The Last Trillion-Dollar Commitment: The Destruction of Fannie Mae and Freddie Mac." *Journal of Structured Finance* 15: 71–80.

Wang, Ta-Chen. 2006. "Courts, Banks, and Credit Market in Early American Development." PhD diss., Stanford University.

Washington Times. 2009. "GOP Uses ACORN to Fight Redlining Law." October 12. www.washingtontimes.com/news/2009/oct/12/gop-uses-acorn-fight-bank-redlining-law/print/.

Weaver, S. Roy. 1913. "Canadian Banking Legislation." *Journal of Political Economy* 21: 136–42.

Weicher, John C. 2001. "Setting GSE Policy through Charters, Laws, and Regulations." In *Serving Two Masters, yet Out of Control: Fannie Mae and Freddie Mac,* ed. Peter J. Wallison, 120–38. Washington, DC: AEI Press.

Weingast, Barry R. 1995. "The Economic of Political Institutions: Market Preserving Federalism and Economic Development." *Journal of Law, Economics, and Organization* 11: 1–31.

——. 1997. "The Political Foundations of Democracy and the Rule of Law." *American Political Science Review* 91: 245–63.

Wettereau, James O. 1942. "The Branches of the First Bank of the United States." *Journal of Economic History* 2: 66–100.

Whale, P. Barrett. 1930. *Joint Stock Banking in Germany.* London: Macmillan.

Wheelock, David C. 2006. "What Happens to Banks When House Prices Fall? U.S. Regional Housing Busts of the 1980s and 1990s." *Federal Reserve Bank of St. Louis Review* 88: 413–29.

Wheelock, David C., and Paul Wilson. 2012. "Do Large Banks have Lower Costs? New Estimates of Returns to Scale for U.S. Banks." *Journal of Money, Credit, and Banking* 44: 171–99.

White, Eugene N. 1983. *The Regulation and Reform of the American Banking System, 1900–1929.* Princeton: Princeton University Press.

——. 1984a. "Voting for Costly Regulation: Evidence from the Banking Referenda in Illinois, 1924." *Southern Economic Journal* 51: 1084–98.

——. 1984b. "A Reinterpretation of the Banking Crisis of 1930." *Journal of Economic History* 44: 119–38.

——. 1985. "The Merger Movement in Banking, 1919–1933." *Journal of Economic History* 45: 285–91.

——. 1986. "Before the Glass–Steagall Act: An Analysis of the Investment Banking Activities of National Banks." *Explorations in Economic History* 23: 33–55.

——. 2011. "Implementing Bagehot's Rule in a World of Derivatives: The Banque de France as a Lender of Last Resort in the Nineteenth Century." In *Monetary and Banking History: Essays in Honour of Forrest Capie,* ed. Geoffrey Wood, Terence C. Mills, and Nicholas Crafts, 72–87. London: Routledge.

White, Eugene N. Forthcoming. "Lessons from the Great American Real Estate Boom and Bust of the 1920s." In *Housing and Mortgage Markets in Historical Perspective,* ed. Price Fishback, Kenneth Snowden, and Eugene N. White. Chicago: Chicago University Press.

White, Horace. 1902. "Branch Banking: Its Economies and Advantages." *Sound Currency* 9: 51–64.

White, Lawrence H. 1984. *Free Banking in Britain: Theory, Experience, and Debate, 1800–1845.* London: Cambridge University Press.

White, Lawrence J. 1991. *The S&L Debacle: Public Policy Lessons for Bank and Thrift Regulation.* Oxford: Oxford University Press.

———. 1992. "The Community Reinvestment Act: Good Intentions Headed in the Wrong Direction." *Fordham Urban Law Journal* 20: 281–92.

Wicker, Elmus. 1985. "Colonial Monetary Standards Contrasted: Evidence from the Seven Years' War." *Journal of Economic History* 45: 869–84.

Wilcox, James A. 2009. "Underwriting, Mortgage Lending, and House Prices, 1996–2008." *Business Economics* 44: 189–200.

Williamson, Steven. 1989. "Bank Failures, Financial Restrictions, and Aggregate Fluctuations: Canada and the United States, 1870–1913." *Federal Reserve Bank of Minneapolis Quarterly Review* (Summer): 20–40.

Willit, Virgil. 1930. *Selected Articles on Chain, Group and Branch Banking.* New York: H. W. Wilson.

Winton, J. R. 1982. *Lloyds Bank 1918–1969.* Oxford: Oxford University Press.

Wood, Gordon S. 1991. *The Radicalism of the American Revolution.* New York: Alfred A. Knopf.

World Bank. 2012. "Financial Structure Dataset." September 2012 update. http://go.worldbank.org/X23UD9QUX0.

Wright, Gavin. 1986. *Old South, New South: Revolutions in the Southern Economy since the Civil War.* New York: Basic Books.

Wurgler, Jeffrey. 2000. "Financial Markets and the Allocation of Capital." *Journal of Financial Economics* 58: 187–214.

Ziegler, Dieter. 1990. *Central Bank, Peripheral Industry: The Bank of England and the Provinces, 1826–1913.* Leicester: Leicester University Press.

INDEX

Page numbers for entries occurring in figures are followed by an *f* and those for entries in notes, by an *n*.